Money Talks

Bob Rosefsky's Complete Program for Financial Success

Money Talks

Bob Rosefsky's Complete Program for Financial Success

Robert S. Rosefsky

175 YEARS OF PUBLISHING

1807 1982

John Wiley & Sons, Inc.

New York
Chichester
Brisbane
Toronto
Singapore

STAFF CREDITS

Designer: Laura C. Ierardi
Cartoons: Anne Green
Illustrations: John Balbalis with assistance
 of the Wiley Illustration Department
Editor: Dr. Leonard B. Kruk
Supervising Editor: Eugene Patti
Photo Editor: Elyse Rieder

Library of Congress Cataloging in Publication Data:

Rosefsky, Robert S.
  Money talks.

  Includes index.
  1. Finance, Personal. I. Title.

HG179.R647 1982   332.024   82-8561
ISBN 0-471-87330-6   AACR2
Printed in the United States of America

10 9 8 7 6 5 4 3 2

To my wife, Linda Sue, and to my children, Debbie, Michelle, Adam and Joshua. Greater riches no person could ever have.

Preface

I've been offering people advice on money for more than 20 years; first as a lawyer and a banker, then as an author, teacher, broadcaster, columnist, and private consultant. For about the first 15 of those years, nothing changed very drastically. Interest rates moved up and down only very slightly; new investment opportunities were rare; new laws and regulations were infrequent.

But in recent years changes have started taking place with shocking rapidity. Interest rates have gyrated like an out-of-control roller coaster. New investments have come at us like an artillery barrage: NOW accounts, IRAs, All-Savers, money market funds, repurchase agreements, variable certificates, and more. New tax laws, new credit legislation, new investment regulations have poured out of Washington like a waterfall. And new concepts have popped up in news headlines and casual conversations: T-bill rates, creative financing, tax deferred retirement plans, and so on.

Confusion reigns supreme! So how do you cope?

This book is designed to give you a firm grip on understanding and handling your money matters. It is written in down-to-earth language to help you get around so much of the mumbo jumbo spoken by lawyers, insurance people, stockbrokers, and the like. It is structured so that you can get a grasp on the *basic patterns* of money management; though specific items, such as interest rates and tax forms, may change from time to time, knowing the *basic patterns* will allow you to adjust to changing circumstances.

Here are some other unique features of the book:

□ A chapter that tells, in the form of a story, how the economy works and how it affects your day-to-day well being. You'll find the adventures of the Log People, the Fish People, and the Berry People amusing as well as instructive.

□ *Consumer Beware* stories at the end of each chapter alert you to problems and pitfalls that you may never have anticipated.

□ *Personal Action Checklists* at the end of each chapter guide you in doing the calculations and evaluations you will have to make to reach sound and profitable conclusions in handling your own financial matters.

In this rapidly changing and confusing world, you cannot afford to ignore your own continuing financial education. There are too many opportunities to overlook (cutting your taxes, investing successfully, beating inflation). There are too many pitfalls to overlook (con games, dangerous contracts, misleading and deceptive salespersons). This book can be your passport to financial security, to self-confidence in money matters, and to peace of mind.

**Robert S. Rosefsky,
Los Angeles, California**

Contents

Money Talks

Bob Rosefsky's Complete Program for Financial Success

Part One | Basic Concerns

1 | The Economy: How It Works and What It Means to You

There are many factors at work in the world that can influence your financial well-being: your work, your budget, your investments, your future security. The more you know about these factors, the better you can cope with them. To ignore them can be dangerous. This chapter explains, in story fashion, the bearing these factors have on your life. In reading it, you'll gain an understanding of such things as:

□ Why some individuals (or companies, or nations) achieve greater financial success than others.

□ What makes prices go up and down.

□ How unexpected forces (such as the weather, international incidents, etc.) can affect your personal situation.

□ How modern technology can provide you with career advancement and a better life.

□ How the actions (or inactions) of the government can affect the economic health of the nation, of your employer, and of your family.

Forces That Shape Our Lives

You're looking for a job and you've had two interesting offers. One is from a firm that manufactures a fancy and expensive sports car. Both the company and the car have an exciting and glamorous image, the working environment is very attractive, and the initial pay is very appealing.

The other offer is from a firm that manufactures a hand-held video camera/recorder. The product has been a smashing success since it was introduced: lightweight, inexpensive, and virtually foolproof in operation, it has promise of all but wiping out the traditional home movie market and of taking a major share of the home video cassette/recorder market. But the company itself lacks the "pizazz" of the sports car firm, the working environment seems rather dull, and the starting pay isn't as good as at the car company. Which do you choose?

Rather than jump at the offer that seems more attractive on the surface, you decide to do some research into the matter. You learn that the sports car manufacturer has very stiff competition from both American and foreign automakers. Further, there was a governmental ban on foreign sports car imports, but that ban has just been lifted and the international competition will become even more threatening. And to top matters off, your research indicates that if business in general slows down—which it seems to be on the verge of doing—fancy sports cars are one of the first products that people will stop buying. And if people stop buying a product that you're involved in making, you could be out of a job.

The picture is quite different with respect to the hand-held video camera/recorder. The company has a huge lead on all of its competitors. Its research department is on the verge of introducing new technology that will bring the price of the product down, thereby making it available to millions more consumers. Moreover, the product offers such wide access to low-cost entertainment and educational material that sales would virtually defy any national recession.

Now you reevaluate the job choices: the higher starting pay and the glamour of the sports car company don't seem quite as important when you consider the future growth opportunities. Indeed, you might conclude, there is very limited future potential with the sports car company. The video company, on the other hand, though stodgy and lower paying at the outset, may well offer a vastly more rewarding future career to you.

This brief example of choosing between two jobs illustrates some of the economic forces that can shape your future. And as your career is shaped, so is your financial, emotional, and social well-being. These same forces, and others, can also affect the possible success of any investment program you might embark upon. Similarly, your ability to afford such items as a house, a college education for your children, and a comfortable retirement can be definitely influenced by these economic factors.

In short, our financial affairs (and our personal affairs as they are affected by our financial affairs) do not operate in a vacuum. Every day there are elements, some subtle, some direct, which can make our lives better or worse. Some of these elements cannot be avoided, but many of them can be either avoided or countered if we understand them and know what kind of actions to take.

Let's now explore basic workings of the economic forces and influences that can have a bearing on our lives. This is not intended to be a scientific enquiry into economics, but rather a background and a foundation to aid you in putting to best use the specific information you'll learn throughout the balance of this book. Not only will this background information help you to arrive at the best specific financial decisions, but it should also give you an understanding of many of the perplexing and frustrating phenomena you hear about in the news every day. Understanding these phenomena, rather than hiding from them or being misled by them, can allow you to function better at work and at home in both the short and long term.

A Serious Game

Imagine a football game: two teams of large and garishly costumed gladiators about to bash heads in front of thousands of screaming spectators. Instead of dividing the game into four quarters of 15 minutes each, let's look at it from a totally different perspective. The game represents certain *forces* at work on the playing field. The effectiveness of those forces will be largely controlled by certain *influences* that are brought to bear. The final effect of these forces and the influences acting upon them will be that one team wins and one team loses.

☐ *Forces.* The forces at work on the playing field include the brute physical power of the players themselves, plus their individual and collective desire to win.

☐ *Influences.* Many different things can give shape and direction to the basic forces. The *training* and *equipment* available to the players can influence the efficiency with which they use their brute power. The *motivation* imparted by the coach and the *cheering* of the crowd can strongly influence their individual and collective desire to win. And the weather—an uncontrollable influence—can override all of the other factors.

☐ *Effects.* The forces clash, shaped and directed as they are by the various influences, and one team emerges the winner, the other the loser.

The economy is similar to this make-believe football game. There are forces at work. There are certain factors that influence the forces. And there are various results that occur depending on which forces have been influenced in what way. The effects, or results, can have a bearing on how you live your life. Further, the same forces and influences can be present in the economy of your *family* as well as in the economy of your city, state, or nation.

Forces

The basic forces involved in an economic entity are these:

☐ *Work power.* This is the basic capacity of the population to work and produce.

☐ *Human nature.* comparable to a football team's desire to win (or lack thereof), any given population—be it a family, a company, or government—has certain innate needs and desires: to survive, to compete, to protect or expand its territory. Aspects of human nature in the economic sense can be expressed as expectations, greed, desire for power, and concern for the welfare of the citizens that make up the population.

Influences

The influences that can give shape and direction to the basic forces in an economic entity are many and varied. Some of the main influences are listed below, briefly and in no particular order. Compare them to the influences that shape the forces at work in the football game. Later in this chapter we'll take a closer look at these influences.

Information Education is to an economic population what training is to a football team. And after the basic training, the quality of continuing education will further shape the team's success. In the economic population, continuing education consists of an ongoing awareness of facts and trends obtainable through scrutiny of the news media and specialized publications pertaining to one's pursuits.

Government Policies Government policies and philosophies have a tremendous bearing on the forces at work in an economic population. Governmental influences include how the government will tax the people, how the government will spend money, and what relationships the government has with other governments.

Management and Labor Within a given company or industry, the quality of management is akin to the quality of coaching on a football team. And the degree to which the workers cooperate with management is comparable to the team spirit or lack thereof on the football team. This can also be viewed as one aspect affecting productivity.

Technology (Research and Development) Whether it's you examining job opportunities, as illustrated at the start of this chapter, or a company exploring new and better ways to make its products, the importance of the influence of technology cannot be overlooked.

Nature A frozen or muddy football field can render the most powerful team harmless. A drought, a flood, an excessively cold winter can cripple the financial well-being of an otherwise healthy family, industry, or region.

Natural Resources A family may have a naturally gifted musician, artist, football player, or entertainer who can enrich the whole family's lives, both personally and financially. Likewise, a company may have a file drawer full of exotic and potentially profitable patents. Similarly, a nation may have untapped reserves of petroleum or minerals. Having natural resources is one thing; putting them to productive and profitable use is another.

Marketing Some people are better salespersons than others. The skills with which a product or service is packaged, advertised, and sold will have a bearing on the economic strength of a given entity.

Capital Investment If an economic entity seems attractive enough to outsiders, the outsiders might be willing to invest in that entity. Such investments, put to proper use, can further enhance the well-being of the entity. An entity that is unattractive to outsiders can suffer accordingly.

The Law of Supply and Demand This is one of the most basic laws of economics, and of the world in general. It can exert a profound influence on your attempts to succeed economically. If you grow watermelons and the harvest is too bountiful, you may bring more melons to the market than people are willing to buy. You may then have to drop your price to avoid taking home unsold watermelons, and you could end up a big loser. If the harvest is just right but the weather is cold when you come to the market with your melons, people may not be interested in buying the thirst-quenching fruit at all, and again you may end up a loser. In the former case, the supply exceeded the usual demand. In the latter case, the supply was customary, but the demand was low. On the other hand, if your harvest is just right and the demand is high because the weather is hot and dry, you could reap a tremendous profit on your melons.

Luck This is, to be sure, a very unscientific aspect of the science of economics. But it is ever-present in virtually every one of the other influences. Whether good or bad, it's unpredictable and unavoidable. The ability to take advantage of good luck and avoid the ravages of bad luck can make a distinct difference between success and failure in an economic endeavor.

As noted, these influences are not stated in any particular order. In many cases they overlap, intertwine, and influence each other. But whether taken individually, in combination, or as an aggregate, they do shape and give direction to the human forces that constitute an economic population.

Effects and Results

The forces go to work and are influenced one way or another by the various factors mentioned above. Here's a brief rundown of some of the potential effects that we'll explore in the course of this chapter:

☐ Inflation or deflation (rising or falling prices and wages).
☐ Employment or unemployment (good jobs or lack thereof).
☐ Growth of an economy, or recession.
☐ Survival of an economic entity or termination of the entity.
☐ An attractive investment climate or an unattractive one.
☐ Surpluses or deficits (having money in the bank or being excessively in debt).

Many of these effects and results can become influences in their own right. The football team suffers a loss and the score against them is so lopsided that the players are humiliated. This effect—humiliation—lowers their morale to such a point that they lose their next game, which they had been heavily favored to win. The effect has become a cause in its own right. Or a company develops a highly touted product only to have the public ignore it because of a poorly designed advertising campaign. Not only does the company lose money because of the high costs of introducing the new product, but some of the top managers leave in protest over the marketing program, and the company suffers even further as a result. The effect—poor sales—has become an influence in its own right on the future of the company.

Fish, Berries, and Logs

To get a better idea of how these forces and influences interact in an economic population, let's examine the history of three fictional primitive tribes: The Fish People, the Berry People, and the Log People. Any similarities between the economic concerns of these ancient folk and your own family's, your employer's, or your nation's are not coincidental.

Where It All Began

The Fish People lived at the water's edge. They had learned to make spears, and they harvested a bounty from the sea. Their work was not physically demanding, but it required patience, cunning, and long hours. As long as they were willing to work, there were fish to be caught. An endless supply of fish seemed assured, and their leader, Mug, told them that they could indeed become rich through hard work and through the expansion of their fishing grounds along the shoreline and out to sea. What fish they didn't need for their own purposes they would trade with the Berry People for berries and with the Log People for logs. Men, women, and children all worked. They saw no limit to the amount of fish they could catch and thereby no limit to the amount of berries and logs they could acquire from their neighbors. Their energies and their expectations were high. They desired to expand and to become ever wealthier.

A few miles inland, on a plateau blessed by constant sunshine and fresh ocean breezes, lived the Berry People. The plateau was covered with thousands of wild berry bushes of all kinds—black, huckle, rasp, straw, and goose. These sweet delicious berries were always in demand by the Log People and the Fish People. Nature blessed the Berry People: The berries grew in abundance with little need for care. The only work that the Berry People had to do was to pick their crop. What they didn't keep for themselves, they packaged to deliver to the neighboring tribes in return for their products. With the sun, the rain, and the soil doing most of their work for them, the Berry People tended to be lazy and greedy. Their leader, Wump, assured them that everything was going their way, and while they should appreciate their good furtune, they should also take advantage of it and live the good life. Wump saw no need to plan for the future. The future, it appeared, would take care of itself.

Beyond the plateau the land rose into wooded hills. This was the domain of the Log People. They had devised tools to cut down the plentiful trees that surrounded them, and they traded the logs to their neighbors for fish and berries. The neighbors found the logs necessary for building fires, creating shelters, and fashioning additional tools for their own uses. Work for the Log People was very demanding physically. Cutting the trees down and chopping them into pieces with their primitive tools was bone-wearying. It had become custom among the Log People for only the men to work since their physical prowess was greater than that of the women. The women tended to the home and to the needs of their men, who returned exhausted from their work at day's end. They were content with their modest lot and aspired to neither wealth nor power. Their leader, Theodore, had told them, "This is the way it has always been with us, and this is the way it probably always will be."

By mutual agreement, the three tribes had decided that for trading purposes one fish equal in length to Mug's forearm would be equal to one basket of berries the size of Wump's head, which in turn would be equal to one log the length of Theodore's leg. Thus, if the Fish People wanted to acquire ten logs, they would have to deliver ten appropriately sized fish to the Log People. And so on.

The three tribes lived in relative harmony, trading among themselves as their needs and desires dictated, and otherwise leaving each other alone. The following, in no particular order of importance, are some of the occurrences that shaped the lives and welfare of these tribes. As you read, bear in mind the economic influences that were outlined earlier.

The Empty Forest

As long as the Log People had ever known, the big trees had always been there. Many years before, when all the tribes were much smaller, all of their needs had been filled by chopping down just two or three trees a year. But in recent years the tribes had all expanded considerably and were demanding much more wood than they had formerly needed. The Berry People were building ever more elaborate log huts, the Fish People needed logs to make rafts, and all three tribes were making ever more furniture, tools, fences, and fires for heat and for cooking.

Whereas the big trees used to be just a few minutes' walk from the Log People's village, the choppers now had to walk farther to get to the available trees.

Theodore had done too little calculating, and he had done it too late. Never having been faced before with the problem of not having trees readily available close at hand, the thought of planting new trees had never dawned on him. And when he finally did realize that new plantings were needed, he was dismayed to discover that it took many years for the seedlings to grow into mature trees. Meantime, it was now taking the choppers three hours to get to the mature trees and six hours to drag the logs back to the village. The amount of time to create a single log had multiplied many times over what it had been before. This meant that it was costing the Log People dearly to acquire one fish or one basket of berries. Mankind was suffering its first energy crisis.

Though blessed with a natural resource that could be renewed, the Log People had failed to do so, and they were suffering accordingly. Further, by failing to anticipate an ever-increasing cost of acquiring the natural resource, their problems were compounded. Eventually, Theodore would invent the wheel, which would make possible the creation of a wagon. This would sharply cut down the time and energy needed to get to and retrieve the logs. But in the meantime, waiting for their new plantings to mature, the Log People settled into an era of economic distress.

All Dried Up

As far as the Berry People ever knew, it always rained when it was supposed to. How shocking it must have been to them, then, when one year it did not rain. The first known drought in the history of the Berry People was devastating. Many of the berry bushes produced no fruit at all; some bushes withered and died; and the berries that did grow were puny and withered. The Log People and the Fish People would no longer accept one basket of berries in equal trade for a fish or a log because the berries were of such poor quality. They insisted on two baskets for one fish or one log, and the Berry People found themselves with no choice. Until they could remedy the problems caused by the drought, they would have to do with fewer fish and fewer logs. The unpredictable forces of nature had seriously undercut the life of the Berry People, and Wump, their leader, vowed to do something about it.

Wump searched the surrounding countryside and finally discovered what he felt would be the solution to their problem: an underground spring of fresh water. He told his people that if the drought continued, their only salvation would be to carry buckets to the spring and bring water back for the bushes. Indeed, the drought continued into the next season, but the Berry People had grown so lazy throughout the fat years that they were unwilling to work hard carrying water to save themselves. Many of them refused to accept Wump's warnings about the ultimate consequences if they failed to work hard, believing that the rains would come the next day, or the next, or the next. But the rains didn't come and the Berry People were on the edge of extinction.

Fearing the worst, Wump retired to his private quarters to concentrate all of his thought powers on how to save his people. It came to him in a flash! The head of the underground spring was at a point of land higher than the Berry People's plateau. Why not, Wump reasoned, fashion a trench leading from the spring to our plateau. "We could then direct the water to flow through the trench and onto our parched berry bushes."

He announced his plan to the people, telling them that it would take a lot of hard work to dig the trench, but that once it was completed abundant water would flow to their bushes. Faced with the ultimate crisis, the

Berry People agreed to do the necessary work. Within a few weeks, the trench had been dug and properly lined, and the water began to flow. Soon the bushes would be blooming again, and they'd be back to one basket of berries for each fish or each log. Prosperity was just around the corner.

Wump had researched the problem and had developed a means of coping with it. Wump's technology—the first irrigation canal—had overcome the adverse forces of nature, as well as the weak spirit of his people. Wump also knew that they should never again take for granted that the rains would fall. Planning for the future was something that had to be done, for, Wump admitted to himself in his private moments, it *was* possible for the spring to dry up someday.

The Disappearing Fish

The trees were always there for the Log People, the rain always fell for the Berry People, and the fish always swam close to the shore settlement of the Fish People—until one strange day when the fish disappeared. Disbelief quickly spread throughout the village, and each man, woman, and child had to run into the water to see for himself. It was a fact. The fish were gone. In panic, they ran up the shore and down the shore and put rafts out to sea. Far from their village the fish still swam, but why did they no longer swim near the village, where it was so convenient to catch them? Mug stood knee-deep in the water in front of the village and tried to reason the answer. It came through his nose. There was a strange and offensive odor to the water. Mug sniffed, and sniffed again until the odor could be identified. It was the odor of human waste.

Mug realized immediately why the fish had disappeared. For as long as he could remember, the Fish People had disposed of their waste in the water near the village, relying on the tides to carry it out to sea. But little by little over the years, the saturation of the water had become so dense that the tides could no longer wash the water clean. Simply enough, the fish were repelled by the polluted water and sought other grounds.

Mug disclosed his findings to the village council and told them that unless drastic action was taken immediately, their hopes and dreams would quickly fade. It would be necessary, he suggested, for the waste to be carried to some distant inland point and buried. He realized that this would drain the work power of the people, but only by doing so would the water eventually cleanse itself and allow the fish to return. The Fish People were motivated to realize their expectations. So they commenced an energetic program of waste disposal.

In just a few months the water had cleansed itself and the fish had returned. Even though it was more costly to the Fish People in terms of their time to remove the waste from the village, they were willing to do the necessary work.

They had realized that their well-being could be affected by polluting their environment and they were willing to pay the price to correct the problem. That price had been reasonable enough. Had the price been much higher, Mug worried, the people might have objected to paying it and the village could have been split into factions moving up the coast and down the coast, thus destroying the entity of the Fish People.

The First Price Wars

It had taken many years for the Log People to recover from their first energy crisis. To insure that it would not happen again, they planted as many trees as they possibly could as close to their village as space allowed. But during the time it took for these new plantings to become mature trees, the Fish People and Berry People had taken their own steps to avoid being caught in a shortage of logs from the Log People. The Fish People had started to collect driftwood and found that it was very suitable for repairing their huts. The Berry People found that dead bushes made excellent fuel for their fires—better, in fact, than the Log People's logs. The Fish People and the Berry People began an active trade between each other in driftwood and dead berry bushes. That was the situation when the Log People's new trees came to maturity. Not only did they have more logs available than the other tribes needed, but there was now an added factor: competition. Berry bushes burned better and driftwood was more decorative. The supply of logs was too great and the demand too little. The Log People were again facing poverty. They literally had logs to burn.

Faced with stiff competition from their neighbors and being on the losing side of the law of supply and demand, the Log People had no choice but to cut the price of their logs if they were to survive. Instead of trading one log for one fish or one basket of berries, they traded two logs. In effect, the cost to the Log People of one fish or one basket of berries had doubled. Since berries and fish were still relatively scarce—at least compared with the supply of logs—the Log People saw no end to their dilemma. If by some chance the fish crop doubled or the berry crop doubled, the Log People could return to their one-for-one trading basis. But for the time being they had too many logs available to buy too few fish or berries. This dilemma—otherwise referred to as "too much money chasing too few goods"— has come to be known as one of the basic causes of a phenomenon called inflation. Another historical first for the Log People!

The Value of Good Hard Work

The horror of the drought stayed in the minds of the Berry People for many years. Adding to this the constant reminder that the underground spring could someday dry up, Wump succeeded in creating a force of energetic workers out of what had been lazy playboys and playgirls.

Wump organized the workers into efficient squadrons. One squadron tended the underground spring and continually looked for new sources of water. Another squadron tended to the irrigation canal to make sure it had no leaks or diversions. Another squadron dug catch basins to store excess water, and yet another tended to the pruning and fertilizing of the berry bushes. The Berry People knew that their crop would grow only on that particular plateau. They had no desire to plant in other areas, but they realized that by improving the specific yield on the plateau berry bushes they could become more wealthy.

Wump urged the workers on to exert themselves, and he congratulated them lavishly for jobs well done. The workers appreciated Wump's concern for their welfare, and they cooperated with his plans to the best of their ability.

The fruits of their labors were soon evident: some of the bushes grew twice as many good berries as they had in the past; and still others grew fewer berries, but they were much larger, much sweeter, and much more desirable. Because of this cooperation between Wump, the manager, and the workers, the Berry People had become more efficient. They were turning out more goods and better goods for a given amount of labor. Building upon his earlier technological advance (the irrigation canal), Wump had succeeded in increasing the productivity of the population.

Smoking a Fish

After the Fish People had implemented their waste disposal program, they eventually found that there were more fish than ever in the waters off their village. Now they faced a curious dilemma: they could catch more fish than they could trade to the other tribes. Still keenly motivated by their desire for wealth and expansion, they deliberated on what to do with this excess of natural resource. At the heart of the problem was the fact that there was no way to keep a fish after it had been out of the water for a day or so. It simply rotted and had to be thrown away.

If only there was some way that fish could be kept for an indefinite period. The village council met in Mug's hut to deliberate on the matter. They threw some fish over the fire for that evening's meal and commenced their discussions. Someone suggested that a freezer be invented, but Mug noted that they did not as yet have a place to plug it into. Other ideas flowed freely, with discussion and debate ensuing. The proceedings became so intense that the council forgot about the fish that were on the dying fire. Many hours later, still not having reached a conclusion, hunger got the best of them. They were dismayed to find that the fish had been too thoroughly cooked. The juices were dried out and the meat smelled of the wood smoke.

Thus they all had to go to bed without any supper that evening. But, on a hunch, Mug did not throw away the overcooked fish. He put them into a box to see what might happen to them in the next few days.

Three days later, Mug sniffed at the box of overcooked fish. To his amazement, they did not smell rotten. He picked off a piece of flesh and tasted it. It was dry and smoky tasting, but curiously appealing. Mug said nothing of his discovery and three days later tried it again. It still tasted good. Then Mug announced the great breakthrough to a general meeting of the Fish People.

Purely by accident, technology had created a new product: smoked fish. Experiments began with different kinds of fish and different kinds of woods to find the combination that would extend the usefulness of smoked fish for the longest possible time. In the ensuing weeks the techniques were refined and perfected.

The Log People and the Berry People were at first skeptical of this new edible item, but on tasting it and testing it they found it satisfying. The popularity of the smoked fish spread rapidly among the tribes. In addition to providing a new taste sensation, it also solved two other important problems that the tribes faced. One problem was that the people could never travel more than one day from their village, because they couldn't carry a supply of fish that would last them that long. If they could carry a supply of fish that would last them many days, they could explore realms far beyond their villages and expand their universe accordingly.

The other problem was that there were occasional shortfalls in the amount of fish needed to satisfy their daily appetites. By laying in a supply of smoked fish, they could get through those brief shortages comfortably. Needless to say, all of these factors meant more sales for the Fish People. Here, technology (albeit accidental) as applied to the natural resources of the Fish People allowed them to gain some control over the law of supply and demand. No matter how high or unexpected the demand, they could meet it with either fresh or smoked fish. And if demand should drop, they could either smoke the fish or leave it in the water until needed. And by insuring themselves of a market for one form of fish or another during all seasons, the Fish People were able to keep their village budget on an even keel.

Bad News, Good News

Meanwhile, back in the Log People's village, Theodore and his advisors were trying to figure out a way to avoid the problem of an oversupply of logs. They reviewed the factors that had caused the problem in the first place. Their major mistake, they discerned, was that they had relied on false or incomplete information in deciding how many new trees to plant. It had all happened so long ago that they couldn't remember precisely, but they felt that they had either been told, or had let themselves believe, that there was a market for as many trees as they could produce. Thus, the overplanting. Now, in retrospect, they realized how detrimental that information had been.

Theodore explained that they must, from that time on, seek out proper and correct information upon which to base their planting decisions. "Let's determine," he urged his people, "just how many logs we can really sell at a fair price, and we'll plant accordingly." This was no easy task, for they all well knew that it took many years between the planting and the cutting of the trees. Theodore assigned people to ferret out the facts: How large will the populations of the tribes be when today's plantings mature? What kind of demand will they have for logs at that time? What kind of competition can be expected at that time from driftwood and dead bushes? Are there other kinds of trees that can be planted that will be more salable? Can farming techniques be developed to make the trees grow taller and faster while still retaining the quality of the wood, if not improving it?

Theodore sent his people out to study these intricate questions. They worked hard at their tasks and returned a year later with their recommendations. Theodore acknowledged that specific answers were elusive, but he felt much more confident in guiding his people with this researched information than he had with the suppositions, guesses, and impulsive thinking that had guided them in the past. He took the conclusions to each of the clusters in the village who tended their own groves. He gave them lessons in how to plant, how much to plant, and how properly to tend the growing trees.

It took a full generation for all of this effort to pay off, but the rewards were worth the wait. The Log People had utilized education, market research, and the proper dissemination of information to stabilize and strengthen their economic well-being.

A Crushing Blow

Many years had passed since Wump had stirred the Berry People to new heights of productivity. Things were going perhaps a bit too well for the Berry People, and the old ways of laziness and greed had begun to seep back into the population. Wump was much older now, and his influence on the people was not as direct. His apparent successor, Terwilliger, was intrigued by tales of the good old days when the Berry People had to do little work and were richly rewarded by nature.

In his zeal, Terwilliger cast about for ways that the Berry People could do less work, at less expense, and nevertheless earn more fish and logs. He hit upon an idea that was greeted with unanimous approval by his followers. They would double the size of the berry baskets. Despite the cost and time involved in making the new larger baskets, they were confident that the investment would be well worth it. By using the double-size baskets, they would save considerably on their packing costs, on replacing baskets, and on overall handling. In short: less work, less expense, and more net income.

Terwilliger was delirious with the prospects for his new plan, and his enthusiasm spread rapidly. So confident was everyone in Terwilliger's ideas that nobody bothered to question him. Terwilliger sent messengers out to the Log People's village and the Fish People's village to inform them of the forthcoming event: "New, bigger, better berry baskets for all!" He posted signs on hundreds of trees to extol the virtues of the new baskets and promised discounts for advance orders of the new product.

Terwilliger was even able to obtain a personal audience with Mug of the Fish People and Theodore of the Log People to tell them of the new advanced product. Both Mug and Theodore responded politely saying

that it sounded very interesting and they'd certainly be willing to give the new baskets a try. Terwilliger interpreted their remarks as an enthusiastic endorsement of the new baskets, and he returned to the Berry village with orders to put the entire current crop into the new baskets at once. He was so sure that the demand would be great that he risked putting the entire crop on the market all at once.

The pickers picked their fingers to the bone to fulfill Terwilliger's orders. Thousands and thousands of double-size baskets were laid out on the delivery wagons. Terwilliger himself escorted the first wagon to the Fish People village and presented the first basket to Mug. Mug was flattered by the gift and poured the double basket of berries into a large bowl for his family to taste. Then, to everyone's shock, they discovered that the berries on the bottom of the basket had been crushed by the weight of the berries on the top of the basket. Fully one-third of all the berries in the basket were damaged, and Mug expressed his feeling that he had been cheated by this new means of packaging. "You told me I'd be getting two baskets' worth of berries in one, and in fact I only have a little more than one basket's worth of usable berries! You led me to believe that I was getting fair value for my two fish! I've been cheated!"

Stunned and embarrassed, Terwilliger apologized. He admitted that they had never tested to see whether or not the double-size baskets would create any crushing problems. They had just assumed that if a single-size basket did not resulted in crushing, neither would a double-size basket.

But it was too late for Terwilliger and the Berry People. Bad word of mouth quickly spread from Mug to the entire village and then to the Log People's village. Terwilliger had put the entire current crop on the line and now found it difficult even to give it away. The bulk of the crop rotted in the double baskets and the Berry People were flung into all but instant poverty. Their underlying force—greed—had been thrown back in their faces by dreadful marketing procedures. Despite the quality of the product, the lack of research, poor packaging, and misleading advertising had resulted in a disaster for the people in the Berry village.

Help Wanted

One aspect of the smoked fish development brought unexpectedly good results: loaded with a multi-day supply of fish, all of the tribes were able to venture out of their villages into previously unexplored areas. They found numerous other tribes specializing in their own products. To the north there were tribes that produced wheat, chickens, and apples. To the south there were tribes that produced barley, bananas, and a strange bubbling fermented beverage that the natives called "beer." None of these tribes had ever seen a fish—either fresh or smoked. The Fish People were anxious to take advantage of this vast new market for their product. But they had some serious problems. All of the available population was already working overtime to supply fish to the Berry and Log tribes. And the leadership of the Fish People had long ago determined that no one but the Fish People should work the teeming waters by the village. How then could they catch more fish to sell to these outlying tribes?

First, the leaders had to agree that the basic tradition of the Fish People should be changed and that outsiders should be allowed to work in their village. Second, they had to create a reason for outsiders to *want* to work in the fishing village. Passing the law to allow outsiders to work was relatively easy. But how could they induce the members of the other tribes to want to work there? They decided to allow any such outsiders a share of profits generated by the sale of fish to the outlying tribes, in addition to a basic wage for their labor. The women of the Log People, who hitherto had not been accustomed to working, found this an attractive proposition. By this time much of the log cutting had become easier due to improved tools, and the women were freer to explore other opportunities for themselves. They welcomed the chance to be productive in their own right and were further satisfied that their village would benefit from the added wealth that they would bring home. Even some of the more energetic Berry People found the offer intriguing, and thus the first export business was created.

Governmental policy, coupled with the creation of an incentive to invest (in this case time rather than money), was responsible for bringing a new era of prosperity to the three tribes.

Making Munny

The discovery of the outlying tribes and the commencement of trading with them brought great changes to the Fish, Berry, and Log People. Steps were taken to improve the efficiency of their internal trading. As the populations of the three tribes had grown, it was becoming ever more cumbersome to handle fish, berries, and logs each time a transaction occurred. The leaders of the tribes agreed to create small tokens, made of stones, that would represent either a fish, a basket of berries, or a log. Thus, instead of trading the goods themselves, they could trade the tokens that represented the goods. Each token was referred to, in their primitive language, as a "Munny." Now, if a Fish Person sold a large quantity of fish, he could take Munnies in exchange, rather than load himself up with berries and logs that he might not need at that time. Later, if that Fish Person wanted to acquire a basket of berries, he could trade a Munny for it rather than having to carry a fish clear across town.

Before long, the more entrepreneurial members of the tribes began to accumulate large quantities of Munnies, and to protect themselves against thieves they asked the leaders of the tribes to oversee the creation of a bank that would hold their Munnies for them.

In addition to their Munny tokens, the three tribes had many other things in common. They were physically close to each other; they had many similar traditions and beliefs due to their centuries of living near and trading with each other; and they felt a common need to help defend each other against any outside attacks. Eventually, they decided to formalize their communal interests by creating a pact that was to bind them together in an alliance called the United Tribes. Meanwhile, and in similar fashion, the tribes in the north had joined together as the Wheat/Apples/Chicken Alliance. And the southerly producers of barley, bananas, and beer had joined together as the 3-B Federation. Each of these two other groups had created their own tokens representing their products, and the Alliance tokens, the 3-B tokens, and the Munny tokens were freely interchanged as the groups traded actively among each other. For many years all the peoples of these nations regarded one Alliance token as being equal to one Munny token which was equal to one 3-B token. And for all those years the amount of trade among the nations was equal. Each bought and sold the same amount from each other year in and year out.

The Building Binge

Then some unusual things began to happen in the United Tribes, which until now had been the biggest and most powerful of the nations. The government of the United Tribes decided to build a series of magnificent roads connecting each of the three villages. Many citizens objected because the project promised to be very expensive and there was serious doubt that such magnificent roads were in fact needed. Further, it was noted, the government didn't have any Munny with which to build such roads. The government countered the arguments by saying, "We are here to decide what is best for our people. If we don't need the roads today, we'll certainly need them in the future as our population grows. Further, with roads like the ones we have in mind, we will be the envy of the Alliance and the 3-B Federation. Our national pride is at stake. And there's no problem about Munny. We will simply borrow it from our citizens. If they lend us ten Munnies for one year, we will repay them with eleven Munnies at the end of the year. That will get us all the Munny we need."

But, critics asked the government, how will the citizens be repaid? "Again, easy," the government replied. "Since each and every citizen of the United Tribes will benefit from these magnificent new roads, we will require each and every citizen to pay one Munny per year until all the loans have been repaid to our investors. We will call this a 'tax.' "

The program got underway, and the government announced its plans to borrow Munnies from the citizens. The opportunity to earn one extra Munny per year for each ten invested was too good for most citizens to resist. They rushed to the bank to take out their unused Munny to lend it to the government. This shocked the bank managers deeply. "We can't survive under such competitive pressure from the government," they claimed. "And if we don't survive you'll have no place to store your Munny." The bankers were told by the government that that matter would be attended to at some other time.

The magnificent roads were barely completed when the government, proud of itself, announced plans to build lovely gardens and rest stops along the roadways. Again, they would borrow and again they would tax the citizens to pay for the improvements.

Some of the citizens began to complain that they could never use the magnificent roadways because they didn't have enough of their own Munny to buy a wagon. Heeding their plight, the government assisted these people in the purchase of wagons, again borrowing and again taxing the citizens to pay for these expenses.

There seemed to be no end in sight to the government's spending. And the more they spent, the more they borrowed, and the deeper in debt they went. The citizens—taxpayers—finally rebelled. "We've had enough! We're paying a lot of Munny in taxes and we're not getting benefits in return! Something has to change and it has to change quickly!"

This incident describes what is known as *fiscal policy*. Fiscal policy has to do with how a government decides to spend money and how it will raise the money it does spend—normally through taxation. If a government's income from taxation and outgo through expenses are equal, it is said that the government has a balanced budget, just like a family's or a business's. If a government takes in more money than it spends, it is said to have a surplus; if it spends more than it takes in, it is said to have a deficit. The fiscal policy of a government as determined by its population and by its leaders can thus have many influences on the well-being of the people.

The other unusual development in the United Tribes was the insatiable craving for beer, available only through the 3-B Federation.

The Beer Bust

For a long time, the trade between the United Tribes and the 3-B Federation was equal. But for inexplicable reasons, the United Tribes thirst for beer began to increase at a rapid pace. The United Tribes citizens were hooked on beer. Despite the warnings of the government, the citizens continued to consume beer in ever greater quantities.

The rulers of the 3-B Federation saw a unique opportunity. "First," they said, "the United Tribes will consume all the beer we can produce, and seemingly at whatever price we decide to charge. Second, one day we're liable to run out of the pure mountain spring water we use to make our beer. And by the time that day comes, either the United Tribes or the Alliance may have discovered their own pure mountain spring water and we'll be bankrupt. We ought to charge all we can for our product now while we have it to sell. We can stash away all the surplus tokens we make and use it for the day when our own supply of water runs out."

So it was that the 3-B Federation quadrupled the price of beer to the United Tribes. The citizens of the United Tribes were, to say the least, shocked. But they insisted on having their beer. The government told them that there was not enough Munny floating about to pay for the beer.

But the citizens were not to be denied their beverage. Rather than risk being thrown out of office, the leaders of the government agreed to create new pieces of Munny. "But you can't do that," critics argued. "A piece of Munny can be created only when there is a fish, a basket of berries, or a log available to back it up. You can't carve more Munnies than there are fish or berries or logs!"

"Oh no? Watch us!" replied the government. And they proceeded to create vast stockpiles of additional Munnies, which they made available to the citizens of the United Tribes by allowing the bank to lend more Munnies to individuals.

This enabled the United Tribes to buy all the beer they wanted with reckless abandon. The citizens of the 3-B Federation, meanwhile, were being flooded with Munnies. They in turn used the Munnies to buy chickens and wheat and apples from the Alliance. But the Alliance grew cautious about accepting so many Munnies. "It used to be," they said, "that one Munny was equal to one fish or one log or one basket of berries. But there are so many Munnies floating about these days that we are not sure exactly what they are worth. Perhaps they're worth only half a fish or a log or a basket of berries. If that's the case, then we're going to double the price in Munnies for our wheat, chicken and apples."

Very soon thereafter the beer-guzzling citizens of the United Tribes found that products they purchased from the Alliance cost twice what they used to. They were at an impasse: either continue paying double the price for their wheat, chickens, and apples, or give up beer, or revamp their own internal policies to improve their economic strength in the three-nation marketplace.

The foregoing incident reflects what is known as governmental *monetary policy*. Monetary policy is that part of a government's program that regulates the amount of money flowing throughout the economy. As the case of the beer bust illustrates, creating too much money can cause economic disruptions; creating too little money can prevent an economy from growing. Perhaps the greatest economic debates of the last century have been with regard to monetary policy. There is no sure-fire, long-lasting formula that is guaranteed to work. But the farther away a government is from the "right" formula, the more effect it can have on the financial well-being of its citizens.

Here and Now

The adventures and misadventures of these primitive peoples are meant to illustrate some of the most basic economic influences that we live with on a day-to-day basis. All of these various influences intertwine, overlap, and bounce back and forth on each other. Let's now put these phenomena into a more modern perspective by examining again, in no particular order, some incidents in recent American and world history that illustrate the workings of the various influences and the results that they can cause.

Productivity

Productivity in a very broad sense is a measurement of efficiency: how much work can be generated by a given individual or a group of individuals, considering the cost of paying for raw materials, labor, capital, and overhead? Here are some examples:

You work in a factory that makes farnolas. At your work station, you are capable of turning out ten farnolas an hour. You think you could do better than that, but the inspector who comes around to examine your work every so often is a very unfriendly person and you get aggravated each time he appears. You know that this slows down your output, but you can't seem to help it.

One day you find yourself troubled with a stiff neck. In the ensuing days it seems to get worse and worse, and you find that it's so uncomfortable that you're able to turn out only nine farnolas an hour. Your productivity has thus dropped 10 percent.

A co-worker points out that there is an air conditioning vent aimed directly at your neck. It has been blowing a very gentle stream of cool air toward you and, you realize, that is the cause of the stiff neck. You redirect the air flow and within a day your stiff neck has disappeared. Your output quickly returns to ten farnolas an hour. By a very simple and inexpensive change, your productivity has been increased.

The owner of the farnola factory discovers that the inspector has been antagonizing many of the workers. He replaces the inspector with a much more friendly person, thus removing that hourly aggravation. You are now able to turn out eleven farnolas an hour with no trouble at all. The same holds true for all the other workers who had been subject to the scrutiny of the former inspector. By a simple change in manpower, the owner of the factory has been able to increase overall productivity at no additional cost. This can mean greater profits for the owner and any stockholders of the company. And if workers are paid on an incentive basis, it can also mean increases in their pay.

On the other hand, say that the manufacture of farnolas creates a very fine dust in the factory. One of the workers complains of discomfort from the dust. A health inspector is called in to examine the problem. Shortly thereafter the government issues an order to the factory owner that all workers must be protected from the dust. This is despite the fact that there has been only one complaint in the entire history of the factory. The owner equips all workers with simple and inexpensive masks to wear during working hours. This will enable him to satisfy the government and continue his production at minimal cost.

But the original complainant still complains: The masks aren't enough. The government inspector returns and orders the factory owner to install an elaborate and costly air filtration system to protect the workers. The factory owner complains bitterly, but the government official tells him that the filtration system will help improve the productivity of his workers: "They won't be sick from the dust in the air." "But," the owner counters, "we've never had a problem with illness or lack of productivity because of the dust." Neither of them is certain what the effects of the expensive filtration system will actually be, but the owner does know one thing: the system would be so costly to install that he could no longer operate his factory at a profit. The gains in productivity would have to be so dramatic to offset the cost of the filtration system that the owner is certain it can't be done.

High productivity in one part of a work environment can be offset by low productivity in another area. For example, all of the farnola makers are doing a superb job. Their morale is high and their energy boundless. They get their average hourly output up to fifteen farnolas and the management is thrilled. Meanwhile, down in the shipping department things are chaotic. The foreman is lazy and ineffective, and the workers are surly and uncooperative. Many orders are filled incorrectly, many are mailed to the wrong address, and some are lost altogether. On top of all these problems, the rate of filling orders is very slow and a serious backlog develops. Customers who have ordered farnolas from the factory are very distressed. They ask for refunds, cancel their dealings with the company, and spread the word about the company throughout the community. Thus, in spite of the excellent productivity at the manufacturing level, the net result is negative because of the poor productivity at the shipping level.

There are many factors that can increase or decrease productivity—be it that of an individual, a company, or an entire industry. Relationships between management and the workers is one of the most obvious factors. Cooperation, or lack thereof, between the two can have a decided and immediate effect on the output of individuals and the company as a whole.

Cooperation isn't just backslapping and encouraging words. Management also must create an efficient working environment, cost considered, that will allow the workers to proceed at the best and most efficient rate. The environment includes such elements as temperature control, lighting, sound control, general cleanliness, and the availability (and condition) of extra amenities such as dining areas, toilets, recreational facilities, and other matters that can improve employee morale.

Examine the various aspects of productivity in your home, your work environment, and your school situation. Where and how can matters be improved? Is the cost of making those improvements justifiable? Be your own efficiency expert. It could mean extra money in your pocket.

Government

The stories of the primitive tribes have already illustrated how government fiscal and monetary policies can affect the economic status of individuals and entire nations. (See "The Building Binge" and "The Beer Bust.") The interrelationship of fiscal and monetary policies can create additional phenomena in an economic environment. Witness the United States in the late 1970s and early 1980s. After many years of heavy spending, the government found itself deeply in debt. The government paid for its spending by taxing the citizens to a point where they began to scream and by borrowing. The government's borrowing needs became so great that it began to pay whatever interest rate it had to in order to get the funds it needed.

As the government paid ever higher interest rates when it borrowed, individuals and businesses found that they could get a better return on their investments by lending money to the government than they could by lending money to banks and savings associations. They began to drain their money out of the banks and savings associations to lend it to the government. Then the financial institutions began to scream: "The government is limiting the interest rates that we can pay to investors, but the government goes ahead and pays whatever interest rates it cares to. If this trend continues, then individuals and businesses won't be able to borrow money from us to buy or produce cars, houses, television sets, and so on. Our whole economic system will grind to a halt."

In 1978 the government took the first step to allow banks and savings associations to compete more equally with the government. They allowed these institutions to offer savings certificates, which would pay investors approximately the same interest rate as the government paid when it borrowed. But what seemed to be a solution only caused more problems. If the banks and savings associations paid more interest to investors, they would also have to charge higher interest to borrowers. Indeed, interest rates on all kinds of loans immediately began to soar to record high levels. These higher interest costs made the price of everything go up: houses, cars, food, fuel. As prices soared, workers demanded higher wages to keep up with the rising cost of living. If the farnola factory had to pay its workers more, it would then have to charge more for the product it made. Thus, higher prices caused higher wages, which in turn caused still higher prices, which in turn would cause still higher wages. This is a classic example of what is known as the wage–price spiral, more commonly referred to as inflation.

In 1980 the government instituted the Depository Institution Deregulation Committee (DIDC), whose task was to remove government regulation from the financial industry. In 1981 the Reagan administration persuaded Congress to legislate restraint on government spending and also to pass sweeping tax-cut laws. The hoped-for net effect of these major governmental changes would be to return much of our nation's money to the individuals who earned it in the first place. It may take many years before the ultimate effect of these new governmental directions is known. For better or worse, they will have sweeping impact on the financial welfare of millions of people.

International Matters

Our government's policy with respect to other nations can also have an important bearing on our own individual well-being. For example, our long-standing policy of allowing free trade between the United States and Japan was largely responsible for the influx of Japanese-made autos into the United States. At first, back in the 1960s, it was a mere trickle of curious little cars that had limited appeal to a population more interested in horsepower and fancy trimmings. But within a decade the trickle had become a flood, until almost one out of every four cars sold in the United States was manufactured in another country—a heavy percentage in Japan. Japan's ability to export cars to the United States created tens of thousands of jobs for Japanese workers and destroyed the jobs of tens of thousands of American workers. It helped create a boom for the Japanese economy, allowing the Japanese to buy many more dollars with a given amount of Yen. Compare that with the relative values of the berries, logs, and fish that our primitive tribes used.

It's been said that the presence of so many Japanese autos in the United States isn't all bad. It started the trend toward smaller cars with better gas mileage, which in turn resulted in our cutting back on fuel consumption by roughly 8 percent between 1978 and 1981, and made the energy crisis appear to be far less ominous than it had seemed earlier.

In 1981 the American and Japanese governments worked out an agreement that would limit the number of Japanese cars to be exported into the United States. This, in theory, would give a boost to the American automobile makers. But it's certain that the Japanese will not necessarily curtail the number of cars they manufacture. They'll simply sell them somewhere else. Suppose they begin an export campaign to China, whose economy is expected to surge during the 1980s. Some years from now, the American manufacturers may want to sell automobiles to China and they may well find that the Chinese market has already been cornered by the Japanese. Millions of American-made cars that could have been sold to China thus might not be.

This oversimplified example illustrates the complexity of international commerce. Prediction of specific results is impossible, but your own awareness of the existence of these ever-shifting ebbs and flows can assist you in being a more judicious consumer.

Technology

The irrigation canal that the Berry People built and the fish smoking technique that the Fish People developed were examples of technological development that improved conditions for the respective populations. Advancing technology, based on research and development, plays an extraordinary role in our economy. Technological advancement directly relates to productivity in most cases. And lack of technological advancement can mean stagnation.

Probably the most stunning example of technological advancement has been in the area of electronics. The cost of doing calculations today is a tiny fraction of what it was just a few years ago. Consider the effect on your checking account, for example. Every day millions of checks are processed throughout the American banking system. This massive flow of paper would slow down drastically—and our overall economy with it— if we didn't have the sophisticated computers we have today. You may pay a few dollars a month in service charges for your checking account. Lacking the electronic marvels that process all the checks, your monthly costs for those same services rendered by individual human beings might be $20, $30, $40 a month or even more. There's no way to calculate actual figures, but the productivity of that industry has increased almost infinitely as a result of electronic advancements. The same is true for virtually every major industry that processes information—insurance, stock brokerage, government, education, manufacturing, retailing, and so on.

On the other hand, one very important industry that has been accused of technological lag is the home building industry. It has been asserted that many components of a house could be assembled in a factory, to be bolted in place on the homesite. This type of assembly-line approach could reduce the cost of housing considerably. Yet manufactured housing, as this is called, is very slow in arriving.

What technological advances have affected you in your home life and work life in recent years? Are they for better or for worse? How might advancing technology affect your job in the foreseeable future?

Information

Information in the general sense is gathered both from education (basic and advanced) and from what we learn through the media (print and broadcast, general and specialized). To the extent that we do or don't take advantage of the information available to us, we can improve our lots considerably, or not at all.

Sometimes the creation and implementation of information can work apparent miracles. In the late 1950s, the Russians put the first man into orbit around the Earth. Americans were caught flat-footed—we were years away from being able to duplicate that feat. We seemed to lack both the sense of purpose and the skilled people needed to carry out such a mission. When John F. Kennedy was inaugurated president in 1961, he urged the nation to move forward to put a man on the moon by the end of that decade. The nation was stirred by his encouragement and commitment to that project, but it seemed an impossibility. Given the necessary support by the government, however (and here again we see the interweaving of various intangible influences), our educational facilities immediately began supplying skilled technicians who, indeed, succeeded in putting more than one man on the moon by the end of the decade. It will be up to future historians to determine whether the effort was worthwhile, but the space program illustrates that, given information (as well as government support), seemingly impossible goals can become realities.

The creation and flow of information will have a major impact on the United States economy during the 1980s and 1990s and onward as the undeveloped nations of the world learn, grow, and become consumers of products that we will manufacture for sale to them. Roughly three-quarters of the earth's population is still considered undeveloped. In those nations 60 to 90 percent of the population still works at agriculture to create enough food to feed the population. (In the United States, only about 2 percent of the population feeds the other 98 percent.) As the citizens of these undeveloped nations learn more about agriculture and health, they will become more self-sufficient and secure. As they learn basic trades and skills, they will become better able to support themselves and their families. As they continue to improve their lot—largely through education and training—they will have money to spend on such things as tools, medicines, books, and teachers. This in turn will beget more information, greater skills, and more income. Sooner than later, these billions of people will be buying things that we've long since been accustomed to buying: tennis shoes and blue jeans, tape recorders and tennis rackets, furniture and television sets, movie tickets, and so on and on. For many generations to come, these billions of people will look to the existing industrial nations to provide most of these goods—and our economies will boom. Eventually, those nations will be self-sufficient in most of those goods, and whole new trends of international economy will emerge. But for the next 20 to 50 years, information will be the seeds planted abroad that will bear fruit back home.

Capital Investment

Even with all the skills, enthusiasm, and technology that an individual or business can muster, money is still needed to make things happen. Every large business—even a General Motors, an IBM, an Exxon, or the like—started as a small business. And small businesses grew because they were able to attract money: capital investors. A company whose management, product, and profitability are attractive to investors will be able to raise more capital to improve and enlarge itself. And working for such a company can, simply put, mean career advancement for you.

Not all capital investment comes from outsiders. Specific businesses must also have reason to believe that they can invest their own money internally and reap rewards accordingly. Here again we see the intertwining of various economic influences: the government can create incentives for a business to invest in its own future. For many years, the United States government has offered a variety of tax credits to businesses that invest in new technology and equipment. By making such investments a business can reduce its taxes while at the same time improving its ability to create and sell its products and services and thus earn even greater profits and create more jobs in the future.

Marketing

Everybody is selling something. When you apply for a job, you are selling yourself. The "package" that you present to the employer can determine whether you get the job. In addition to looking at your resume and application, the employer will observe how you dress, how you speak, how you move about. He may or may not be impressed by your level of enthusiasm, your knowledge of his company and industry, and your overall personality. Applying for a job is, in short, a marketing effort that you make on your own behalf. The better you market yourself, the better chance you'll have for your own individual success.

Similarly, the employer must make efforts to market his own product. Those efforts include knowing the marketplace; learning what the competition is and will be doing; designing a package that will appeal to the public; informing the public of the benefits of the product (advertising); and establishing a price structure for the product that the public will accept.

As we noted in the case of the farnola factory, a good product can be stymied by, for example, a sloppy shipping department. Likewise, a good product or service can fail because of improper marketing. Witness the double basket for berries that was discussed earlier in this chapter.

Just as your employer must continually seek newer and better ways to market his products or services, so must you if you are to achieve your fullest potential. How can you better market yourself today in your work situation? And how can you assist your employer in better marketing the products or services that he creates?

Nature and Natural Resources

In the late 1960s, It was determined that there were vast reserves of oil off the northern shore of Alaska. But having such valuable natural resources is one thing; getting them out on a cost-effective basis is quite something else. Nature itself was one of the major obstacles in retrieving the northshore oil. The frozen wasteland of that part of the world posed monumental problems to the oil companies. After having surmounted the problems of getting the oil out of the ground, it then had to be transported to where it could be put to use. This involved the creation of a mammoth pipeline—one of the greatest engineering challenges in the history of mankind.

Even though the pipeline was to run across virtually uninhabited territory, there was concern expressed for the environment. What if the pipeline burst and spewed oil across the tundra? Would it affect plant life? Animal life? Many people said, "So what! We need the oil and we need it fast." But those concerned with the environment filed lawsuits to assure that all necessary precautions were taken to prevent any damage. This delayed the construction of the pipeline by many years and increased the cost of the pipeline by hundreds of millions of dollars.

During this time of delay, the MidEast oil-producing nations suddenly quadrupled the cost of oil to its customers around the world, the major one being the United States. This threw the economy of the entire world into a turmoil that has lasted for many years and whose effects may still be felt by the end of the century.

One can only speculate: What would have happened if the Alaska pipeline had been built as originally projected without the many years' delay caused by environmental concern? Could there have been enough oil flowing out of Alaska early enough to forestall the effects of the OPEC price increases? And, if so, what shape would our economy have taken throughout the otherwise turbulent 1970s had there been no "energy crisis"?

The question cannot be answered, but the circumstances that allow it to be asked should highlight for you the critical role that natural resources and nature can play in our economic system. Many of these forces are beyond anyone's control. Floods, droughts, and hurricanes will do what they will, and we can take only protective precautions. Having valuable natural resources does not necessarily insure that the population will benefit therefrom. Great Britain has often been referred to as "an island of coal surrounded by fish." In addition to those resources, Great Britain also has considerable oil reserves in the North Sea. Yet in spite of this natural wealth, the economy of Great Britain has suffered for decades. Without the wealth the nation might have collapsed altogether, but having the wealth has not prevented it from suffering social and economic decay.

Japan offers an interesting contrast to Britain. Both are small, densely populated islands not far from the mainland. Yet Great Britain, with all of its natural resources, has had a failing economy, while Japan, which has a dearth of natural resources, has been booming. Japan has to import virtually all of its steel and petroleum, and yet it has become the world's major maker of automobiles. It could be concluded that Britain's social and political systems have not allowed it to take full advantage of its natural resources while Japan's systems have allowed for relative prosperity despite the lack of essential natural resources.

Having the natural wealth is important, but putting it to the highest and best use for the benefit of the citizens requires more than simply good fortune.

The Results

It has not been the intent here to give you textbook definitions of such things as inflation, recession, deficits, surpluses, and other economic phenomena. Rather, it is hoped that the foregoing discussion will help you understand the influences at work in the world, in our nation, and in your own individual environment, as all these things can affect you as an individual. Further study on your own will be necessary if you wish to have a greater understanding of the more sophisticated and academic aspects of these economic phenomena. In the meantime, it is hoped that the trials and tribulations of the Fish People, the Log People, and the Berry People—and all the ramifications thereof—will give you a workable understanding of why prices go up and down, why wages go up and down, why job opportunities come and go, why taxes must be raised (and sometimes lowered), and why our government sometimes intervenes in our own daily lives—for better or worse.

Further, it is hoped that this basic introduction into the forces that shape our economic well-being will assist you in understanding and putting to practical use the lessons you'll learn throughout the balance of this course—becoming a smart shopper, a wise investor, a sensible homeowner or tenant, and an overall efficient manager of your financial affairs.

Personal Action Checklist
How Do You React?

As this chapter has illustrated, a great many matters—both close-at-hand and remote—can have an effect on your personal financial well-being. An awareness of those matters should alert you to defensive or corrective actions that you might take to protect yourself. Consider the following list of incidents that may have had a bearing on you in the past year. Think deeply about the not-so-obvious effects. What reactions did you have, or could you have had, either to fend off harmful effects or take advantage of good effects?

Incident	Effects on you, directly or indirectly	Your reactions —actual or possible
☐ Strikes (local, regional, or national)	_____	_____
☐ Weather conditions	_____	_____
☐ Business conditions for your employer	_____	_____
☐ Business conditions in your city, in the nation	_____	_____
☐ Your own health	_____	_____
☐ Health of your family	_____	_____
☐ Changes in tax laws	_____	_____
☐ Changes in working conditions	_____	_____
☐ International incidents	_____	_____
☐ Your acquiring more education	_____	_____

Consumer Beware
Knowledge is the Best Investment

The world is full of opportunities. It's also full of pitfalls. It takes knowledge to distinguish between them.

J.L. first sought advice in January of 1980, stating very directly: "I'm an economic dummy. I really have no idea why things happen in the world of money. I've found it easier just to trust people, rather than read or study a lot of economic mumbo-jumbo. Right now I have my life savings—more than $20,000—in a savings certificate at my bank. Lately a salesman has been after me to invest all that money in silver. He says that inflation will eat up everything I earn on the bank account, but silver will make me rich. What should I do?"

At the time, silver was selling at a then historic high price of $50 an ounce. It had, indeed, been soaring in price—along with gold—and the phenomenon had created quite a stir in the financial community.

J.L. was told: "Silver is extremely speculative. You'd be taking an extraordinary risk by putting all your life savings into it. While it's true that inflation may erode some of the future buying power of your money in the savings plan, your money *will still be there* when you need it or want it. The price of silver, on the other hand, is subject to all kinds of possible pressures, whims, manipulations, and unpredictable influences. You could profit. But you could also lose a bundle. If you can't afford the risk, don't take it."

Shortly thereafter a massive scandal erupted in the silver market. Two Texas billionaire brothers had attempted to "corner," or control, the world silver supply. Their attempts failed, and the price of silver rapidly plunged to about $12 an ounce.

J.L. sought advice again in April of 1980. Tearful, voice quaking: "I should have listened to you instead of to the salesman. I trusted him because he told me what I wanted to hear. I put the whole sum into silver, and I'm all but wiped out. I should have known better. Now my life, my future, are in ruins. Is there anything I can do?"

What would you have told J.L.?

2 | Work and Income

If your work is pleasant, challenging, and financially rewarding, you will feel fulfilled and satisfied. But if your work is none of the above, everything in your life can turn sour. Nobody ever said it would be easy to find the right combination of elements for your working hours, but the goal is worth striving for. Along the way there will have to be compromises with respect to money, opportunities for advancement, working environment, getting along with your bosses and co-workers, and so on. Seeking the right balance among those compromises is a challenge in itself. This chapter will discuss the more important aspects of work and income and will help you to evaluate many of the decisions you'll have to make, such as:

☐ Based on your aptitudes and attitudes, what type of work would be most rewarding to you?
☐ What is a given job really worth: putting a dollar sign on the basic wage, the fringe benefits, and the future potential?
☐ What are the best methods you can use to acquire the jobs that are right for you?
☐ What actions can you take if your legal or financial rights as an employee are infringed upon?

The Role of Work in Your Life

Work is perhaps the single most powerful force in shaping your life. It is your work that creates the vast bulk of all your income. It is that income, put to proper use, that allows you to be self-sufficient. It provides you with the necessities of life as well as whatever luxuries may be within your reach. Income that isn't needed for current uses can be invested for your future welfare.

Work is a form of training ground. The job you do today gives you experience. That experience should enable you to accept future work tasks that will be more challenging, more rewarding, and more promising of greater benefits.

And work can—for better or worse—play an important role in many of the nonfinancial aspects of your life. The type of work you do can clearly shape a great deal of your social life, leading you into friendships and activities that generate from the working environment.

Your work can also influence the uses you make of leisure time—not only weekends and vacations during your working years, but also that vast expanse of leisure time that befalls you when you retire. Some of you may engage in leisure-time activities and involvements directly related to your work activity. Others may charge off in the opposite direction, seeking activities as remote from work as possible. And still others, because of their psychological involvement with their work, may be unable to find any leisure activities that offer any ongoing sense of pleasure or reward. For this group, leisure time can be frustrating and retirement bleak: "It takes me the first half of my vacation to unwind from work and during the second half I'm gearing myself up to go back to work. I didn't really relax at all." Or, "I worked so hard all my life that I never generated any outside activities. Now here I am with all the time in the world, and nothing to do with it."

As a well-planned working career progresses, it should create increasing leisure time along with increasing dollars to spend in that leisure time. If you are to cope with, and make the most of, this powerful force that shapes so much of your life, it's necessary to look at work in a broader perspective than simply a means of filling the hours from nine to five. You must look at not only what you might be doing today, tomorrow, or next week, but where your aspirations and abilities can lead you. You must examine the many ways by which you can prove yourself so that you can maximize the rewards and pleasures available to you through work. Finally, you must consider how you can most efficiently use the fruits of your labor—your income—to satisfy current and future needs and desires.

Factors in Choosing Your Work

You have an extraordinary range of opportunity available to you in choosing your work. In every part of the country, there is access to community colleges and state universities that offer relatively low-cost educational opportunities that can lead to virtually any type of career. The economy of our nation is dynamic and expanding in a multitude of directions, thus offering new types of work opportunity and ever-increasing chances for advancement within a chosen field of endeavor.

The vastness and diversity of the United States make possible a range of work activities unparalleled by any other nation: We farm lobsters in New England, peanuts in Georgia, timber in Washington. From "Silicon Valley" in California, through the breadbasket of the Midwest, and on to Wall Street, we lead the world in the production of such things as microelectronics, edible grains, and investment opportunities. We are at the forefront of many new technologies and sciences which will in turn create challenging new opportunities: genetic engineering, laser technology, satellite communications, space exploration, weapons and defense systems, and much more. Even our leisure activities generate tens of billions of dollars per year worth of jobs for our citizens, ranging from neighborhood health clubs to professional sports teams to our worldwide exporting of movies and television programs.

In short, your ability to achieve your fullest potential in your work has very few limitations. Achieving full potential is often interpreted as "success"—a term that generally implies making a lot of money. That's not necessarily an accurate description of achieving full potential. Indeed, there are many people who work so hard and so long to make a lot of money that they never find themselves with the *time* available in which to enjoy the *money* they've made. They may consider themselves failures.

There are important criteria other than money. Consider such rewards as a sense of self-satisfaction; the pride and pleasure that one can feel from being creative, from being innovative, from being part of a winning team; a sense of personal growth and development that enhances your social, family, and community life. These matters are often referred to as aspects of "psychic income"—you can't spend them, but they can be invaluable. Everyone must determine his or her own proper balance of the various rewarding aspects of work: money, leisure time, advancement, personal pleasures derived from the work environment, camaraderie, and pride in one's own achievements or the achievements of the team you're working with. That sense of balance is not easily achieved. Many people work years or decades before sensing that they have achieved the right balance. Many people never find it. Many people give up prematurely because they feel it's beyond their grasp. And many others never strive to achieve it at all. There is no easy formula or rule of thumb that can guide you toward achieving the balance that is right for you. It's an ongoing quest, subject to change as your own individual needs and desires change. Your own ability to achieve the right sense of balance will depend on your own desire to do so and on a number of other factors, which we'll now examine.

Attitudes and Aspirations

Your choice of work, and your pursuit of success, will be shaped, not only by your own attitudes and aspirations, but by those of others as well. Evaluate for yourself the extent to which each of the following influences might affect your choice of work and career goals:

☐ Your own individual, self-formulated ideas of what you want to achieve for yourself.

☐ The degree to which you mold your own ideas of success based on what you perceive in other people. For example: "My friend Pat seems to have everything going just right. If I could achieve the same things that Pat has achieved, I'd be very satisfied."

☐ The degree to which you are directly influenced by others in your choice of work. For example: A teacher may sense that you have certain aptitudes, and without your being aware of it may motivate you to seek a career that you might not have otherwise considered. Or a parent or other well-meaning relative may either gently nudge or emphatically push you in one career direction or another, perhaps for their own sense of self-satisfaction more than for yours.

□ The extent to which you are influenced by traditional social values. Will you be satisfied with adopting the type of life that our general society has typically offered: "a good job, a nice family, living in a pleasant neighborhood and becoming part of the community?" Do you aspire to more than that? Or do you rebel against those values?

□ The extent to which a change in your immediate family circumstances can reshape your attitudes. For example, on the one hand, "I had great dreams for myself, but now I must make them secondary to the demands of my family." Or, on the other hand, "I had great dreams for myself, and now with the help and support and encouragement of my family, I can begin to achieve those goals."

□ The extent to which you are encouraged or discouraged by the support, or lack thereof, of your employer. Can you profit from the support you receive from your employer? Can you overcome the lack of support from your employer?

□ The extent to which you view your current work as merely a "job" or, rather, one step on the ladder of a long-range career.

How do you really feel about all of these elements? Are you satisfied? Can you distinguish between the positive influences and the negative influences as they affect your own attitude? Can you take advantage of the good influences? And can you walk away from the bad influence?

Education

It's generally acknowledged that education is the major foundation upon which a successful career is built. As Table 2-1 illustrates, the more education a person receives, the greater the income they'll receive throughout their work career and throughout their life.

Table 2-1

Income and Education

Education Attained	Total Income, Age 18 to 64
Elementary school, Less than 8 years	$ 404,085
Elementary School, 8 years	$ 491,000
High School, 1 to 3 years	$ 552,200
High School, 4 years	$ 677,801
College, 1 to 3 years	$ 772,763
College, 4 or more years	$1,054,543

Projections based on 1980 per capita income, interpolated from 1977 study. Amounts shown indicate *relative* differences between respective groups, based on 1980 income levels. Rise in personal income in future years not taken into account.

These figures are only relative since future inflation and income-tax implications cannot be predicted. As a relative comparison, however, they clearly indicate that the college graduate will earn roughly 50 percent more than the high school graduate over the indicated spans. However, as attractive as the college graduate's lifetime earnings seem to be relative to the high school graduate, the cost of obtaining that education casts some serious questions on the matter for a great many individuals. Table 2-2 illustrates the rising trends in obtaining a college education.

Table 2-2   **Rising College Costs**

If you were to start a four year college career in	. . . Your cost for four years (room, board, tuition) would be about . . . .
1983	$23,110
1984	24,200
1985	25,690
1986	27,270
1987	28,940
1988	30,710
1989	33,000
1990	35,420

These amounts represent costs at an average state (public) university. For private universities the amounts would be roughly double. *Source:* Oakland Financial Group.

A dilemma of considerable magnitude arises: The parents of an 18-year-old high school graduate tell their child that they have scrimped and saved to help provide higher education for the child. They tell the child, "We've managed to put together $30,000 and it's yours to educate yourself as you see fit. If you need more than that to achieve your educational aims, you'll have to pay for it on your own. If, though, you decide that you don't want to acquire any further education, we'll invest that $30,000 for you and turn the whole sum—investment plus earnings—over to you in 30 years. Then you can do with it as you wish."

They are generous parents indeed. What would you do if that choice were presented to you? Or if you were the parent of a high school graduate and you'd been able to get your hands on that much money, how would you attempt to influence your child in making a decision?

Which would be better: education, with a presumably more enriching life and career? Or, plain and simple, the money?

Assume that the parents were able to invest the $30,000 safely, for a 30-year term at a 10 percent interest rate, tax exempt, compounding annually. (As this is written, such investment opportunities are available.) With the earnings being reinvested each year (that is, compounded), the initial $30,000 will have more than tripled during the twelfth year. By the twentieth year, the fund will exceed $200,000, and with continued compounding, the investment fund will exceed *half a million dollars* by the end of the thirtieth year! At that time the high school graduate will be 48 years old and his investment will, at the continuing 10 percent rate, provide him with an annual income of over $50,000! That's over and above any income he generates from work. Or if the investment and compounding continue, the total fund will exceed $1 million by the time the high school graduate reaches age 55; and by age 65—normal retirement age—there will be more than $2.5 million available to provide a reasonably comfortable retirement, even considering inflation.

Even if the invested money were to earn a lower interest rate and be taxed, it could still provide a million dollar nestegg by the time the individual was nearing retirement.

On the other hand, let's assume that the student does spend the $30,000 on a college education. It's not unreasonable to assume that he will earn, say $5000 more per year because of his education. If he prudently invests that $5000, it will take him less than six years to accumulate a $30,000 nestegg—the same that was spent on college. Not only can he invest that nestegg and have it grow almost as rapidly as in the prior example; he will also have $5000 or more extra spending money each year from that time on.

As with overall career satisfaction, discussed earlier, the answer to this dilemma does not lie simply in dollars. Earnings aside, the value of a college education becomes a relative and very personal matter for each individual to evaluate.

College offers more than simply career training opportunities. Students have access to educational opportunities beyond those strictly required for career matters, and the broader one's background, the better equipped one may be to take advantage of future opportunities, both for personal enrichment and for career advancement. Also available are the opportunities to interact with people from different backgrounds, different cultures, different attitudes—a life experience difficult to duplicate in an on-the-job situation.

The debate over the value of *college* may never be resolved, but there can be very little argument as to the point that *education*—college, on-the-job training, or self-education—plays an integral role in career advancement and achieving one's fullest potential. Learning job skills, in whatever fashion, can provide entree into the job market, where further skills can be learned and further advancement obtained. Sharpening existing skills can also help provide more rapid advancement. Moreover, acquiring outside skills that aren't necessarily related to current employment can broaden one's entire career horizon and income potential.

In short: Educational facilities *alone* do not necessarily equip a person for a bigger or better or more rewarding career. It's *what one does* with the educational facilities available that will make all the difference.

Aptitudes

Aptitude, in the career sense, generally means what you're best suited for. But what one is best suited for may not necessarily be the thing one enjoys most or from which one can generate the level of income commensurate with the desired lifestyle. For example, a young man worked in his father's clothing store after school hours and during vacations. During those years, his father innocently, but persuasively, convinced the young man that he should take over the clothing store when he graduated from college. Because of the extensive on-the-job training, the young man had an aptitude for retailing; security and income seemed assured by following that course. But the young man never really liked retailing; and he always resented—though never questioned overtly—his father's persuasions; and while the income and security were comfortable enough, he swiftly felt stifled, unproductive, discontented. By common methods of measurement, his aptitude was for retailing. But for him it was the wrong career.

What, then, is aptitude? It's a very precarious balance of a number of personal elements, some of which can be measured, some of which defy measurement. Few and fortunate are those who have a good grasp of all the various elements, for they might enjoy fulfilling careers in every sense of the word. Most of us have to compromise on one or more points, but that doesn't mean a rich and active career can't be attained. Guidance counseling can be of some help in aiding us to sort out these various elements, and it would be recommended if a clear focus isn't available at any point. The elements, in brief, are these:

- □ What do you enjoy doing?
- □ What do you do well? (This is not the same as the above element. Many of us do things well but don't necessarily enjoy doing them. And many of us enjoy doing certain things that regretably we don't do that well. The difference should be noted.)
- □ What can you do that will generate a desirable level of income, security, and future potential income and security?
- □ To what extent, if any, are you seeking to satisfy, or must you satisfy, the expectations of others? Many people, such as the young retailer noted earlier, embark on careers not necessarily because that's what they would have chosen on their own, but because others—parents, spouses, in-laws—expected it of them.

Personal Experience

Your own personal experiences, both at work and in your private life, can affect your career choice and the success you might achieve in a chosen career. Any prior work experience you may have had, whether paid or volunteer, can indicate whether or not you like a particular type of work, whether you are good at it, and whether the general field interests you. Furthermore, any prior work experience that you have performed well can lead to personal references that you can put to use later in seeking more permanent employment.

Other personal experiences—at work, in leisure activities, in social or civic involvements—can help you determine if you enjoy working with people or if you're more of a loner; if you tend to be a leader or a follower; if you're content being confined to a specific location for extended periods of time, or if you feel a strong need to be out and around in different locations; if your span of concentration on menial tasks is long or short; if you accept criticism constructively or if you rebel against it; if you're a fast learner or a slow learner; if you're aggressive or shy with others; if your ambitions are greater or less than your peers; if your energies can be sustained for long periods, or if they come and go in spurts; and if you are basically a patient person or an impatient person.

Examine your personality traits as they have been evidenced by your experiences. Which will be helpful in your work and which will be detrimental? Which might be enhanced, which might be corrected, and which might worsen? Overall, which kind of work opportunities will most happily blend with these traits to provide you with maximum satisfaction without having to go through painful compromises?

The Changing Composition of the Work Force

Patterns of work life in America are changing. In the years to come, very few individuals will be left untouched by some of these continuing changes. To be aware of the emerging trends that can affect your career is to be prepared to cope and to adjust. Let's briefly examine some of these trends.

Age and Sex

The percentage of males participating in the work force is diminishing while the percentage of females is sharply increasing. As Table 2-3 illustrates, the participation rates for men of all ages was 82.4 percent in 1960, and it is projected to decline to 76.7 percent by 1990. For females of all ages, the participation rate was 37.1 percent in 1960 and is expected to climb to 51.4 percent by 1990.

Men are entering the work force later in life than in past years due to longer schooling, and they are leaving the work force sooner because of earlier retirement programs. Improvements in disability and health-care benefits in recent years have also enabled men to leave the labor market when health problems have arisen; in past years the limited availability of such benefits tended to keep men tied to their jobs longer.

Further, a drastic drop in the birth rate—from 23.7 births per thousand population per year in 1960 to 16.2 births per thousand population per year in 1980—has resulted in more women being able to work uninterrupted by childbearing. Expanded day-care facilities and increased tax benefits for child-care expenses have also motivated many more women to enter the work force.

These factors, plus rapid gains by women in achieving equal educational and job opportunities, are resulting in dramatic shifts in the roles assigned to men and women. Role separation is being replaced by role sharing within the marriage structure for vast numbers of married couples. In addition, the increase in the number of working wives provides

Table 2-3 | **Labor Force Participation Rates 1960–1990**

Sex	Age	Participation Rates (Percent)*	
		1960	Projected 1990
Male	16-19	58.6	62.6
	20-24	88.9	82.7
	25-34	96.4	93.7
	35-44	96.4	94.0
	45-54	94.3	89.3
	55-64	85.2	69.2
	65+	32.2	16.2
	TOTAL	82.4	76.7
Female	16-19	39.1	54.9
	20-24	46.1	74.7
	25-34	35.8	66.0
	35-44	43.1	63.4
	45-54	49.3	59.9
	55-64	36.7	42.2
	65+	10.5	7.2
	TOTAL	37.1	51.4

*Proportion of each age in labor force.
Source: U.S. Bureau of Labor Statistics, Special Labor Force Reports, 1977

some protection to a married couple in the event of a layoff—compared to previous situations when the family unit depended predominantly on the man's income.

In the years ahead the competition will continue to heighten between males and females for comparable jobs and comparable pay. The number of two-income families (currently slightly more than 50 percent of all married couples) will continue to increase. What had been traditionally "male jobs" and "female jobs" will begin to intermix and with rare exceptions sexual distinctions in the work force will all but disappear. How will these shifting demographic trends work to your advantage? To your disadvantage?

Geographical

Major shifts in the nation's population have also been dramatic and will continue for many years ahead. The mass migration from the "snow belt" to the "sun belt" began shortly after World War II. Since that time, cities in the southerly half of the nation have tended to boom while many metropolitan areas in the northerly half of the nation have actually dwindled in population. But the trend is not necessarily permanent. The population explosion in the nation's southwest quadrant has begun to severely drain that arid area's water resources. Also, since most of that region depends on hydroelectric sources for most of its energy needs, the cost of household and industrial energy has begun to rise at an alarming rate—and is likely to continue to do so. Many migrants to the sunny Southwest, when faced with air conditioning bills in their modest dwellings of $200 to $300 per month are likely to pack up and return to the snow belt, there to take their chances with the winter heating bills.

Many Northern communities, debilitated by population losses over the past decades, are beginning to show signs of a rebirth. Inner-city land, vacant or in disuse, is being converted into new industrial parks and residential complexes. These attractive new facilities, designed to lure jobs and incomes back into the decaying cities, might not reverse the trend to the sun belt, but they could definitely slow it down by the late 1980s or early 1990s. Finally, as improved energy sources—nuclear, solar, and as yet undeveloped means—become more commonplace by the end of the century, shifting population trends will become even more unpredictable.

In considering your work opportunities, you can't afford to ignore the implications of population shifts. Your location can affect your employer's ability to attract the kinds of workers he needs to enable the company to prosper. Lacking that ability, the company—and your career—could flounder. It isn't just the old cities that may find themselves having difficulty attracting population. Many sun belt cities have grown so rapidly that housing costs have skyrocketed, making it difficult for employers to import workers who can afford the housing in the area. They're faced, in effect, with a form of Catch-22: "Things got so bad here because they were so good."

Many of your parents and grandparents may have immigrated to the United States from Europe, Asia, Latin America, or Africa. They may have arrived here with little or no choice as to where they would live or what kind of work they could do. You do have those choices, and to the extent that you study the alternatives available to you, you can assist yourself in creating a career that will offer you the fullest potential in the surroundings of your choice.

Financial Rewards

The line of least resistance in choosing one's work is to go for the job that offers the best pay. Of all the factors that might affect your choice of work, perhaps none is as persuasive as money. But, as the vignette at the start of chapter 1 indicated, that can be a mistake. As you may recall, the choice there was between higher income today but little advancement opportunity in the future, or less pay today with much more rewarding future potential. You must, of course, scrutinize the promised potential with great care. There's a critical difference between a well-researched analysis of a company's future possibilities and succumbing to fast-talking exaggerations of a personnel interviewer. If a company seems overly anxious to hire you at a lower than ordinary starting wage, but with overblown promises of future advancement and salary raises, you should be cautious and undertake judicious research before accepting such an offer.

Beyond the base earnings that you may be offered, it's essential that you carefully evaluate the full range of fringe benefits that may be available. In a 1981 survey by the U.S. Chamber of Commerce, the average value of fringe benefits for the American worker was put at approximately $5600 per year. Here is a rundown of the major fringe benefits you should know about. The Personal Action Checklist at the end of this chapter will allow you to evaluate and compare fringe-benefit packages at various places of employment.

Pension Plans

When a company offers a pension plan to its employees, the employer puts aside a certain sum of money for the benefit of eligible employees every year. In accordance with what is known as the "vesting plan," you must work for the company for a given number of years before those benefits are locked up on your behalf. Normally, you don't receive the money in the pension plan until you retire. Pension plan benefits vary considerably from one company to another. (See chapter 22 for a more detailed discussion of pensions and vesting.)

Profit-sharing Plans

These are similar to pension plans. A certain percentage of the company's annual profits are divided up among employees, and you're entitled to your share in accordance with the vesting plan. Commonly, your vested interest will not be paid out until you quit or retire. A particularly attractive aspect of pension and profit-sharing plans is that you don't have to pay income taxes on your employer's contributions during the years in which that money is credited to your pension or profit-sharing account.

Health-insurance Plans

Health-insurance plans are among the most common type of fringe benefits offered to employees. Because the employer purchases this insurance on a group basis—covering many employees under a single contract—it's far less expensive protection than what you'd have to pay to buy it individually. Health-insurance protection through your employer may be minimal—covering little more than a certain percentage of your doctor and hospital bills—or it may be very extensive, including virtually all medical costs you incur, plus such additional items as a share of dental bills, prescription costs, psychiatric care, and physical examinations.

Life Insurance

Life insurance is not as common a benefit as health insurance, but it is growing. As with group insurance, the employer is able to purchase the coverage for many employees at a lower cost than you could obtain on your own. Group life insurance might be a flat fixed sum or might vary in relation to your earnings at the company.

Educational Programs

Many employers will pay all, or a part of, the cost of courses and seminars that either it recommends or you wish to take in the furtherance of your career. That education is an asset you can take with you wherever you go.

Paid Vacations, Holidays, and Sick Leave

While this may not be as important as some of the above fringe benefits, the availability of paid time off should obviously be compared in evaluating employment opportunities. How much paid time off is available to you as a starting employee, and how much does that paid time off increase over the years?

Sick pay benefits, coupled with disability payments in the event of an extended absence from work, can be much more important than paid vacations. Determine how much regular pay you'd receive in the event of absence due to sickness or accident, and find out how long it would continue. When the sick pay benefits run out, does the employer offer any kind of long-term disability program that would pay you all or a portion of your income?

Investment Programs

Many companies offer employees the opportunity to buy stock in the company at a lower price than they would have to pay through normal channels. Some companies also offer savings programs in which the company will make contributions in a fixed proportion to what the employee himself puts in.

Miscellaneous

There is no limit as to the types of fringe benefits employers can offer. Depending on the company, you might find particular advantage in the dining facilities available to employees, recreation and entertainment facilities on or off the premises, the availability of parking, the scheduling of retirement and financial planning seminars, maternity benefits, and access to counseling for drug abuse, alcohol abuse, and family problems.

In addition to evaluating the fringe benefits *before* you commence employment, you must also evaluate those benefits you've acquired at the time you're considering *leaving* a job. If you leave before your pension rights are fully vested, you could be giving up tens of thousands of dollars that would ultimately be yours if you remained with the company for just a few more months or years. You may be giving up a medical-insurance program that won't be available to you at a new place of employment. You may be giving up a substantial amount of life-insurance protection that might be quite costly to obtain on your own.

In some cases, you can maintain the health- or life-insurance programs on your own if you leave the company by making the premium payments yourself. This will afford you at least some measure of protection if your new employer doesn't offer such plans. It may also be possible for you to transport your vested pension benefits from an old employer to a new one. Under the Employee Retirement Income Security Act of 1974, the portability of vested pension rights is permitted if the new employer is willing to accept these benefits into his plan. But you must see to it that these arrangements are made on your behalf. If you don't do it for yourself, it's doubtful that the employer will do it for you.

What Jobs Are Available?

Obviously, one important factor that will affect your work choice is the availability of jobs in your chosen field in your community at the time you're seeking employment. If you live in Lincoln, Nebraska, and you're anticipating a career in marine biology, you're going to have to think about moving. The same goes for the would-be lumberjack growing up in Miami, Florida, the aspiring movie star whose home is Duluth, Minnesota, and so on. As the completion of your education and the commencement of work get closer, you should begin a careful analysis of desired job opportunities in your home community. It would be wise to explore such opportunities in neighboring communities as well. And if you're inclined to depart the homestead altogether, there's no limit to your potential. The placement office at your school will give you guidance. If your career interests lie in a different city or state, you should contact the respective state department of employment to learn what career opportunities exist in that new residence.

By way of a very broad national projection, the U.S. Department of Labor has prepared employment estimates in a variety of job descriptions. Table 2-4 is an excerpt of the Labor Department study. It's important to note that these figures are only projections subject to considerable possible change from unforeseen economic shifts and other trends that could reshape various occupational groupings. The figures are also based on a total national count; there's no attempt to break down job figures on a local basis. Thus, these figures should be used only as a very broad and general guideline.

The Job Quest

Seeking a job—that will lead to a career—is a matter of selling. If a prospective employer is to buy your services on terms you are seeking, he or she must be convinced that your services will be able to generate a profit once you have acquired the necessary training, if any specialized instruction is called for.

Any successful sales person knows that advance preparation is essential if a sale is to be concluded on favorable terms. In the selling process that we call seeking employment, advance preparation is most critical. Your "sales kit" consists of a number of different elements.

□ Your résumé is the history of your past experience in school and at work. it should accurately and succinctly inform your prospective employer of all the various forms of training you've had that would be

Table 2-4 | **Job Openings in the 1980s**

Occupation	Estimated Employment 1978	Projected Requirement 1990	Percent Change 1978-1990	Annual Average Openings 1978-1990
Accountants	985,000	1,275,000	29.4	61,000
Airplane mechanics	132,000	145,000	10.1	3,500
Airplane pilots	76,000	110,000	43.9	3,800
Architects	54,000	77,000	42.6	4,000
Automobile mechanics	860,000	1,060,000	22.7	37,000
Bank officers	330,000	510,000	54.5	28,000
Bookkeeping workers	1,830,000	2,045,000	11.8	96,000
Building custodians	2,251,000	2,704,000	20.1	176,000
Business-machine repairers	63,000	98,000	56.0	4,200
Buyers	115,000	142,000	23.5	7,400
Carpenters	1,253,000	1,390,000	10.9	58,000
Chemists	143,000	178,000	24.0	6,100
Computer operating personnel	666,000	665,000	−.2	12,500
Computer programmers	247,000	320,000	29.6	9,200
Computer service technicians	63,000	121,000	92.5	5,400
Computer systems analysts	182,000	250,000	37.4	7,900
Construction laborers	860,000	970,000	12.8	49,000
Cooks and chefs	1,186,000	1,564,000	31.9	86,000
Cosmetologists	542,000	624,000	15.1	28,500
Dental hygienists	35,000	65,000	85.7	6,000
Dentists	120,000	155,000	29.2	5,500
Drafters	296,000	367,000	24.0	11,000
Economists	130,000	183,000	39.2	7,800
Electricians (construction)	290,000	350,000	20.7	12,900
Engineering and science technicians	600,000	760,000	25.1	23,400
Engineers	1,136,000	1,441,000	26.8	46,000
Firefighters	220,000	270,000	21.0	7,500
Health service administrators	180,000	282,000	57.1	18,000
Industrial machinery repairers	655,000	1,085,000	66.0	58,000
Lawyers	487,000	609,000	25.0	37,000
Librarians	142,000	160,000	12.7	8,000
Life scientists	215,000	280,000	28.4	11,200
Lithographers	28,000	45,000	61.1	2,300
Machine tool operators	542,000	609,000	12.4	19,600
Machinists	484,000	566,000	17.0	21,000
Musicians	127,000	177,000	39.4	8,900
Newspaper reporters	45,000	53,000	19.6	2,400
Nurses, registered	1,060,000	1,570,000	49.9	85,000

Table 2-4 | **Job Openings in the 1980s** *(Continued)*

Occupation	Estimated Employment 1978	Projected Requirement 1990	Percent Change 1978-1990	Annual Average Openings 1978-1990
Nurses, licensed practical	518,000	840,000	62.2	60,000
Office machine operators	160,000	202,000	26.2	9,700
Painters	484,000	550,000	13.6	26,000
Pharmacists	135,000	185,000	37.0	7,800
Physical therapists	30,000	45,000	50.0	2,700
Physicians and osteopathic physicians	405,000	560,000	38.1	19,000
Photographers	93,000	107,000	15.0	3,800
Plumbers and pipefitters	428,000	513,000	19.9	20,000
Police officers	450,000	550,000	22.7	16,500
Public relations workers	131,000	163,000	24.4	7,500
Purchasing agents	185,000	267,000	44.3	13,400
Psychologists	130,000	171,000	32.1	6,700
Receptionists	588,000	752,000	27.9	4,000
Retail trade sales workers	2,851,000	3,785,000	32.8	226,000
Secretaries and stenographers	3,684,000	5,357,000	45.4	305,000
Social workers	385,000	475,000	24.2	22,000
Teachers: kindergarten and elementary	1,322,000	1,652,000	24.9	86,000
Teachers: secondary	1,087,000	861,000	−20.8	7,200
Teachers: college and university	673,000	611,000	−9.2	11,000
Truck drivers: local	1,720,000	2,040,000	18.4	64,000
Truck drivers: long distance	584,000	689,000	18.0	21,500
Typists	1,044,000	1,246,000	19.4	59,000
Veterinarians	33,500	45,000	35.6	1,700

appropriate to the employment, as well as personal and social activities that would establish your broader profile as an individual. The value of an employee lies not just in getting a specific task accomplished. The employer wants the tasks accomplished by individuals who will get along well with their fellow workers, who will exhibit a constructive and productive attitude, and who will be, in general, well-rounded members of the community.

☐ Your references. Written references from anyone you've been involved with in terms of work or responsibility are important. This would include, not just full-time work situations, but part-time and charitable work and involvement with civic, religious, or social organizations. The thicker your file of references, the more easily you'll be able to establish your reputation for trustworthiness, integrity, and industriousness. Lack of references may not necessarily mean that you won't get a job. But an accumulation of honest references from responsible individuals can enhance your opportunities for current employment and future advancement.

☐ Your presentation. Résumés and references may depict the experience you've had, but they don't necessarily tell a prospective employer what you can do with this experience. This is perhaps the most critical aspect of your "sales pitch": what can you do for the employer that other applicants for the job might not? Applicants normally have an opportunity to make their presentation during the job interview.

Prior to that interview, the aggressive job seeker will have taken the time to learn as much as possible about the prospective employer—products, services, strengths, weaknesses. There are a number of sources that you can investigate to build your information. Check the local newspaper for stories about and advertising by the firm. The local Chamber of Commerce and Better Business Bureau might have more detailed information. The firm might publish information about itself that can be helpful, and if you can speak with current employees of the firm you might be able to generate even greater insight.

If the firm is publicly held—that is, its stock is traded on one of the exchanges—stockbrokers will be able to acquire more specific financial information, particularly any recent prospectus that the company has issued in conjunction with an issuance of stock, as well as annual earnings reports that the company is expected to make available to its stockholders. Stock brokerage firms can also put you in touch with reports by financial analysts that may go into even greater depth regarding the company, its past, present, and projected future. Much of this information you'd probably want anyway just to determine whether the company is one with which you want a lasting involvement; and much of it will enhance your presentation when you go to your job interview. It involves a reasonable amount of homework that could pay off handsomely.

Experience: An Invaluable Teacher

Job seekers are often disappointed that they can't find exactly what they're looking for. You may be distressed in thinking that you have to settle for second best, or third or fourth best. But in reality, such a decision need not be detrimental to your long-term career goals. In fact, choosing other occupational activities could enhance your ultimate career.

Experience is an invaluable teacher. Even though a given work activity may not directly coincide with your chosen career goals, you can learn from it. You can learn added skills that may be of value in the future. You can learn about people, about corporate intrigue and the workings of the hierarchy; you can learn about the kind of energy it takes to improve yourself and how its lack can set a person back. The experiences of learning, observing, and always doing your best at whatever task is assigned will be to your ultimate credit.

For many people, career goals may not come into clear focus until they have gone through a variety of work experiences. Over a period of perhaps many years, certain work activities that seem pleasurable and profitable may evolve from the varied background one has gone through. Job hopping in search of instant gratification is certainly not recommended. But reasonable job experimentation with an eye toward choosing a permanent (or even semi-permanent) career could be effective.

Changing Careers

A 1977 study by the U.S. Department of Labor based on census surveys indicates that nearly one-third of all American workers may be changing their careers over a given five-year period. Changing *careers;* not just jobs. A job change implies going from one employer to another, but doing the same work. A career change is much more drastic: altering virtually the total mode of one's work, whether with the same employer or with a new one, or on one's own.

Although there are no valid statistics concerning the success quotient in career changes (did the change bring the money, the happiness, the challenge, the contentment you were seeking?), it would seem to be an infectious phenomenon that will attract increasingly larger numbers of people.

Children have been reared from their earliest days to think in terms of "what do you want to be when you grow up?" They are seldom asked, "How many different things would you like to be when you grow up?" Many individuals choose a career at an early age with the assumption that it will be their one and only career—that they will learn, grow, and flourish in that endeavor. Little if any thought is ever given to the possibility that the chosen career may be limited in its overall satisfactions. Many people are poorly prepared for the day that often arrives when they find their careers have reached a dead end. They acquired neither the skills nor the outside interests nor the sense of flexibility that could assist them in a career change. Many may recognize the need or value of making such a change but may be reluctant to move for fear of giving up the security of what they have already accomplished. They may thus resign themselves to continuing an unsatisfying career without ever knowing the consequences of a change.

Many others, though, will have acquired other skills, other interests, and a sense of flexibility that could broaden their perspective and allow them easily to adapt to a new career situation.

You may never have the slightest notion about changing your career until you encounter one of the various factors that can motivate you to begin to seek a change. Figure 2-1 illustrates the typical flow patterns of

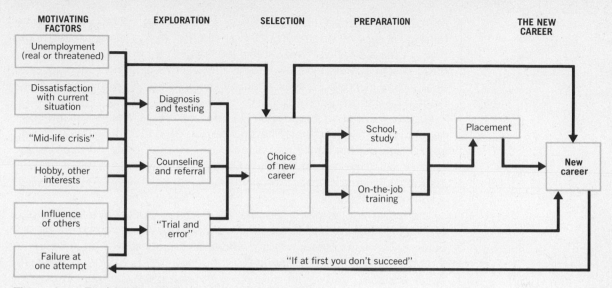

Figure 2–1 Typical flow patterns in a career change
Source. Adapted from a study by the Rand Corporation, "Mid-life Career Redirections, 1975."

a career-change experience. Look at the far left column, "Motivating factors." Any one of those factors, or others not included in this chart, may prompt you to begin exploration, which can include diagnosis and testing as well as counseling and referral. Many will opt for the "trial and error" aspect of exploration, which can be costly, time consuming, and frustrating.

Donald and Mickey

Let's briefly trace the career-change patterns of Donald and Mickey. Donald started as a salesman in a large chain of shoestores, and within a few years had become assistant manager of one of the chain's most important stores. But the owner's son, who was about to graduate from college, had expressed a desire to be the manager of Donald's store, and Donald began to fear that he might find himself suddenly unemployed. He had long enjoyed his hobby of assembling electronic kits, and he wondered if there might not be some better career opportunities for him in that field.

The motivating factors—suspected unemployment and an enjoyable hobby—led Donald to do some exploring. He had his aptitude in electronics tested and made careful inquiry in his community about job opportunities that would put his skills and interests to best use. After due exploration he made his selection. He would train himself to work on the development of new game cartridges for the popular video games that were capturing the nation's imagination, attention, and money. He took some appropriate courses in electronics at a local community college and did some apprentice work for a company that was manufacturing the game cartridges. He was able to do this in the evening while maintaining his flow of income from the shoestore. In the few months it took him to prepare for his new career, the game cartridge company developed a successful new device, and they hired Donald to develop variations on it. His new career began with great promise. And, as it is said, Donald hit the ground running.

Mickey was not so successful. He had been relatively happy and successful as a musician—playing in a combo at local nightclubs. The life suited him, but his family was appalled. They nagged at him constantly to seek out a more respectable profession—to work in a bank, to sell insurance, to be a stockbroker: something that would enable him to wear a suit and tie to work.

The family nagging was the main motivating force in Mickey's career change. He just wanted to get it over and done with and get them off his back. So he didn't bother with any diagnosis or counseling. He just looked through the want ads for the first opportunity he could find in a "white collar position," and within a week he was involved in a training course for life-insurance sales. "I'll try it," he said, "and if I don't like it, I'll start all over again." To be sure, his first few weeks in the new career were disastrous. He liked neither the work, the people he dealt with, the hours, nor the need to sell life insurance to unwilling, unsuspecting, and often unfriendly prospects. Mickey then took the "if at first you don't succeed" route back to the beginning, where the failure at his first attempt motivated him to seek some professional counseling. The counselor told him that he'd do best as a musician, and that his family would just have to learn to live with it. With newfound confidence in himself, Mickey went back to his old job with the combo and lived happily ever after.

Your Work and Income: Protection and Regulation

Your financial and legal rights as an employee are regulated and protected by a variety of federal and state laws. It's important that you be aware of how these laws can affect your work and income. Following is a brief summary of the most important such laws.

Your Paycheck

The Internal Revenue Service requires that your employer withhold a certain amount from your pay to be applied toward your income-tax obligations for the year. Additional amounts will be withheld to be applied toward your Social Security taxes and other state and local income taxes. It's then the employer's responsibility to forward these amounts to the appropriate taxing authorities.

The amount that is withheld from your pay should approximate as closely as possible your actual income-tax obligation for the year. The majority of workers have more withheld than is actually necessary to pay their taxes. The result is that they get a refund for the amount that has been overpaid when they file their federal tax return the following year. The average refund check is in excess of $600. These workers are, in effect, paying about $50 a month into an account with the government, upon which they earn no interest at all. The government has the use of their money all year without paying anything for the privilege.

W-4 Form

The amount that is withheld from your pay is based upon your total pay before any deductions, or "gross earnings," adjusted by the number of *allowances* you claim on the W-4 form you filed with your employer when you began work. The more allowances you claim on your W-4 form, the less will be withheld from your pay, and thus the higher your take-home amount. You are entitled to claim as many allowances as are reasonable, as long as the total amount withheld during the year approximates your true tax obligation. You can claim allowances for yourself and for members of your family; this number is usually the same number as the exemptions you claim on your federal tax return. You can also claim additional special allowances if, for example, you itemize your income tax deductions and if you are entitled to certain income-tax credits. A worksheet accompanies the W-4 form that explains in detail how these special allowances work.

Many workers have gotten into the habit of receiving their annual refund check. It's like an extra bonus to them; some view it as a form of forced savings. But the fact remains that they are earning no interest on that money. W-4 forms can be amended simply and quickly by paying a visit to your personnel office. You can amend your W-4 form to reflect the proper number of allowances so that your take-home pay will be increased and you'll receive no refund check. Amending your W-4 form to the correct amount needed to pay your taxes can enable you to have more money to spend or invest as you see fit throughout the year, rather than allowing the government to spend or invest it as it sees fit without rewarding you accordingly.

W-2 Form

By the end of January of each year you should receive a set of W-2 forms from your employer. These forms reflect the total amount you were paid for the prior year and the total amounts that were withheld for federal and state taxes and for Social Security. The information on the W-2 form will assist you in completing your annual 1040 or 1040A form, and a copy of the W-2 should be attached to your federal and state returns. One copy should be kept for your own records. The W-2 form enables the Internal Revenue Service to verify your total pay and the amount that was withheld.

1040 ES Form

If you receive income that is not subject to withholding and you expect that your federal tax obligation will be more than $100 for the year, you are expected to pay an estimated tax quarterly during the year. The federal form 1040 ES contains a worksheet that will assist you in estimating your total tax obligation from income not subject to withholding. You are expected to pay one-fourth of the total estimated tax each quarter, accompanied by the appropriate 1040 ES papers. Your state may also require you to file a similar form for state estimated taxes. Income that is not subject to withholding can include such items as money received from independent contract work, tips, and investment income.

Workers' Compensation

If you suffer injuries in conjunction with your employment, you are entitled to certain benefits under the Workers' Compensation Law of your state. These laws differ from state to state, but all states do have such laws. You may be entitled to benefits even if the injury occurred as the result of your own fault. But if you injured yourself deliberately, or if you were drunk or under the influence of drugs, you might not be entitled to benefits.

Workers' Compensation benefits can include both medical expenses and reimbursement for lost income. Both types of benefits have limitations depending on the state program.

In general, if you accept Workers' Compensation benefits from your employer, you might not be able to bring a lawsuit against him for loss or damages you may have suffered. If a situation arises in which it appears that the Workers' Compensation benefits and other medical insurance will not adequately compensate you, it would be advisable to consult an attorney at the earliest possible time. Each state has Workers' Compensation review boards that will evaluate claims and pass judgments accordingly.

It's not prudent to wait until after an injury has occurred to find out what Workers' Compensation benefits might be available to you. Check now with your employer to determine the extent of possible coverage.

Unemployment Insurance

If you are discharged from a job that is covered by unemployment insurance, you are entitled to a weekly check to tide you over until you find satisfactory employment with another company. The unemployment-insurance program is administered separately by each state. Unemployment insurance funds are generally paid in by employers, with some additional subsidy from the federal government.

If you are discharged, you should immediately file a claim with your nearest state unemployment office. You will have to appear in person each week to claim your check. You will be expected to be ready, willing, and able to accept any suitable full-time job that becomes available to you. If the employment office offers you such a job and you refuse to take it, you could lose your unemployment benefits.

If you are discharged from a full-time job, you can take on a part-time job and still receive *partial* unemployment benefits. If, after discharge, you receive Workers' Compensation income, severance pay, or a pension from the former employer, you may be ineligible for unemployment-insurance benefits. If your claim for benefits is turned down, you are entitled to file an appeal with the unemployment-insurance office.

If you leave a job voluntarily, you will not likely be eligible for any unemployment benefits. The following dilemma can occur: Michelle worked at a job that was covered by unemployment insurance. But the company was having hard times, and Michelle feared that her job was in jeopardy. She quit the job in order to have time to seek another more secure job. One week later she learned that had she remained on the job, she indeed would have been discharged because of a mass layoff in the company. It took her two months to find another suitable job. During that two months she did not receive a penny of unemployment insurance because she had quit voluntarily. Had she remained on the job for one more week and been discharged, she could have been entitled to unemployment insurance for almost two full months.

Many workers wrongly view unemployment insurance as a form of welfare. It is not that at all. It is insurance. If you had a fire in your home, you certainly wouldn't refuse the payments from the insurance company. If you were ill, you certainly wouldn't refuse payments from the health-insurance company. Unemployment insurance is the same type of thing: Premiums are paid for your protection, and the benefits should not be turned down because of pride or lack of knowledge of the situation.

Employee Retirement Income Security Act (ERISA)

Also known as the Pension Reform Law of 1974, this complex law establishes a variety of protections for your rights under any pension or profit-sharing plan that your employer may offer. A more detailed discussion of ERISA is contained in chapter 22. One of the most important requirements of ERISA is that all employees covered by such plans be provided with a description of their benefits under the plans at least once a year. A great deal of your financial welfare—particularly for the future—may depend on your expected benefits under a pension or profit-sharing plan. The description you receive should not be treated lightly. Read it carefully, and if any part of it is not clear, seek clarification from your personnel office.

The Individual Retirement Account (IRA) was also created as part of ERISA. Effective in 1982, all employees—even if they are covered by a pension or profit-sharing plan at work—will be eligible for the IRA program. It offers excellent benefits and a tax-sheltered means of helping to provide for your own comfortable retirement. See chapter 22 for further details.

Your Right to Work, and Discrimination

The Constitution of the United States does *not* contain any guarantees of your right to work. Historically, employment in the United States has been based on the concept of the employers being willing to hire workers when they see fit and firing workers when they no longer want to keep them. But in recent years a number of federal and state laws have been passed to protect workers from discriminatory hiring and firing practices. These laws don't necessarily guarantee that you'll get a job or that you won't be fired. If you are denied a job or fired from a job in violation of these laws, you still have to pursue your own rights through the appropriate state or federal agencies. But at least some protection now exists where little used to.

Here's a rundown on these major federal laws. Most states have adopted parallel laws and have established agencies to administer them. If you have specific questions or problems, contact the nearest office of the U.S. Department of Labor or your state Department of Labor for assistance.

The Federal Fair Labor Standards Act

This law protects minors from being employed in "oppressive" jobs. This can include jobs that are hazardous or detrimental to the health and well-being of minors. Laws adopted by individual states may further protect minors. In most states, minors under 14 are not allowed to take jobs, and work permits are required for minors until they reach a prescribed age, depending on state law. These laws also limit the number of hours and times of day during which minors can work.

The Age Discrimination in Employment Act (1967)

This applies to workers between the ages of 40 and 65. It is a violation of the law for covered employers to refuse to hire or wrongfully discharge individuals in that age bracket because of age alone. Other discriminatory practices are also barred except where good cause is shown.

The Fair Employment Practices Law

Also known as the Civil Rights Act of 1964, this law, as amended through the years, provides perhaps the broadest antidiscriminatory measures. Under that law, "It is unlawful for an employer to fail or refuse to hire or to discharge any individual, or otherwise to discriminate against any individual with respect to compensation, terms, conditions or privileges of employment because of such individual's race, color, religion, sex or national origin." Sections of the law apply such prohibitions to employment agencies and labor unions as well as employers.

There are some exceptions under this law. For example, religious groups are not required to hire members of other religions. A Japanese restaurant has the right to hire a Japanese chef without fear of violating the law. An employer cannot be required to hire a worker of one sex when a job reasonably requires that a member of the other sex is more appropriate—such as a restroom attendant. Furthermore, distinctions in pay and in other employment matters can be allowed if the company has a good faith seniority system, a system by which pay and promotions are based on merit or quantity or quality of production, or a system that distinguishes among employees who work in different locations.

The Equal Employment Opportunity Commission (EEOC), created as a part of this law, has power to begin actions in court to correct or eliminate violations of the law. Parallel state or local agencies may, however, provide a complainant with more efficient means of resolving a problem.

Wage and Hour Laws

The federal wage and hours laws derive from the Fair Labor Standards Act and basically apply to people whose work is in any way involved with interstate or foreign commerce. If your work doesn't fall into that category, you'll likely be protected by your state Wage and Hour law as administered by your state labor department. These laws generally set a maximum number of hours you can be required to work each week and, further, establish a minimum wage to which you are entitled. These limits have been subject to change in recent years. Check what current regulations are in your job.

Health and Safety Regulations

State and local building and industry codes require building owners and employers to be responsible for the safety conditions within work areas covered by the laws.

The Federal Occupational Safety and Health Act sets standards to protect the health and safety of workers in their working environment. If an unsafe condition exists as specified by the act, an employee can complain to the Federal Department of Labor, which in turn can require the employer to correct the condition.

As a general rule, if you as an employee complain about an employer, under OSHA or the other federal employment laws, it is illegal for the employer to retaliate against you for your having made a complaint.

Union Matters

Tens of millions of workers are members of labor unions. Labor unions negotiate wages and other benefits for members and can act on behalf of members if unfair employment practices occur.

The National Labor Relations Act of 1935 and the Labor–Management Relations Act of 1947 (also known as the Taft–Hartley Law) govern relations between management and labor with respect to unions. Under the National Labor Relations Act employers are prohibited from:

☐ Unreasonably interfering with employees who are attempting to organize a union or bargain collectively.

☐ Discriminating against workers by imposing hiring conditions that discourage union membership.

☐ Interfering with a labor union in its formation or administration.

☐ Refusing to bargain collectively with appropriately elected representatives of the employees.

☐ Discriminating against any worker because he has complained against the employer under the law.

The Labor–Management Relations Act generally prohibits employees and unions from:

☐ Forcing workers into joining a union.

☐ Refusing to bargain collectively with an employer once the employer has received proper certification of the union's status as the employee's bargaining agent.

☐ Becoming involved in illegal work stoppages.

☐ Requiring an employer to pay for work that was not performed.

☐ Charging excessive initiation fees or union dues to employees belonging to the union.

The Federal National Labor Relations Board (NLRB) is the agency that oversees these laws relating to unions and management.

Garnishment

If you do not pay your legal debts, your creditors can sue you and obtain a judgment against you. That judgment may entitle them to "garnish" your wages. In other words, your employer could be legally required to send a portion of your wages to the judgment creditors.

Under the Federal Consumer Credit Protection Act (1968), also known as The Truth in Lending Law, there are limits to how much of your pay can be garnished by a creditor. Most states have similar laws. Check to determine local regulations.

Aside from the financial aspects of a garnishment, such an event can be extremely embarrassing to the garnished employee. Federal law prohibits an employer from discharging an employee just because his wages have been garnished. If, however, an employee's credit performance becomes so improper that the employer is overloaded with garnishment claims, the employer could make a good case for dismissing the employee.

Employment Policies and Contracts

The terms and conditions of many workers' employment are covered by contracts, either directly between employer and employee or between employer and union. These contracts should spell out all pertinent matters relating to employment, including pay, raises, fringe benefits, vacation privileges, sick-pay provisions, and causes for rightful termination. If your employment is covered by such a contract, it is your duty to acquaint yourself with all of these various provisions and to act accordingly. When the term of the contract expires, either you or your union representative will have to renegotiate all of the appropriate terms. Such renegotiation should commence many months before the actual termination date to avoid possible failure to agree on new terms, which could result in your termination.

Most workers are not covered by contracts but by the ongoing employment policies of the employer. Except where state or federal law prevails, many of these policies can be changed at the sole discretion of the employer. Such changes could occur with respect to fringe-benefit programs, sick-pay benefits, hours and place of employment, and pay-raise schedules. To the extent possible, you should protect yourself by obtaining the current policies in written form and by obtaining whatever promises you can that the employer will give you ample advance notice of any intended changes in the policies.

Success Is What You Make It

Your success, your achievements, your advancements in your work and career will depend on more than just fulfilling your basic duties as an employee. Your awareness of and participation in your employer's striving for improvement can enhance your value to the employer. Your initiative, your creativity, and your willingness to cooperate can all help move you up the ladder toward higher pay, greater recognition, and career advancement. Your current job may not be what you have in mind for a lifetime career, but every good experience can build your knowledge, and every good performance can result in a positive reference that will help you achieve the ultimate potential you are seeking for yourself.

Viewed positively and patiently, your work can provide you with an ongoing sense of challenge and achievement. Viewed negatively and impatiently, your work and your personal life can end up in a rut. The choice is yours.

Personal Action Checklist
What Is Your Real Income?

Real money income consists of both wages and fringe benefits. Wages are visible every time you get your paycheck, but fringe benefits are difficult to evaluate. Following is a list of common fringe benefits. Note the ones you now enjoy. If your employer didn't make them available to you, estimate how much it would cost you to obtain them on your own. Tally the total value of all your current fringe benefits. Compare the value of that package with what may be available from another employer you may be thinking of transferring to.

Benefit	Value, or Cost of Obtaining Benefit on Your Own (Per Year)
☐ Health insurance	$_____
☐ Disability insurance	_____
☐ Life insurance	_____
☐ Pension contributions	_____
☐ Profit-sharing contributions	_____
☐ Investment-fund contributions	_____
☐ Automobile	_____
☐ Uniform allowance	_____
☐ Educational programs, seminars	_____
☐ Dental insurance	_____
☐ Legal insurance	_____
☐ Club membership	_____
☐ Use of athletic, other facilities	_____
☐ Scholarship program for your children	_____
☐ Retirement counseling	_____
☐ Personal financial counseling	_____
☐ Medical, psychological counseling	_____
☐ Other_____	_____
_____	_____
_____	_____

Consumer Beware
Career "Opportunities" Can Prove Costly

"NOW . . . LEARN AT HOME IN YOUR SPARE TIME . . . START AN EXCITING NEW CAREER AS A BRAIN SURGEON/GENETIC ENGINEER/MOVIE STAR/ASTRONAUT/ U.S. SENATOR/NOVELIST!!! . . . . etc."

The ads appear everywhere—inside matchbook covers, on bulletin boards, in newspapers and magazines. Most of the so-called career opportunity ads are more mundane than those noted above, but the appeal is just as compelling: get out of your rut and start making BIG money.

Great care should be taken before embarking on a mail-order education that promises you more than you can reasonably expect. Abuses in the field of mail-order education include:

□ Excessively high costs.

□ Promises of future high-paying jobs, which in fact can't be delivered.

□ Restrictive contracts that make it difficult to get a refund if you're not satisfied.

If you do aspire to learning new skills, or embarking on a new career, take these steps first:

Find out whether appropriate training is available through local high school extension courses, community colleges, or universities. If so, you might be able to receive better training, at a far lower cost, than you could through mail order. Many such programs are scheduled so as not to conflict with your regular work routine.

Talk to local employers to determine whether, in fact, there are job openings in the field you're considering. Learn also whether they offer on-the-job training for such careers. It might be possible to get paid while you learn.

If you do think that mail-order education is the way you want to go, investigate the school very carefully before you sign any contracts. Check with the Better Business Bureau and consumer protection agencies in both your own city and the city in which the school is based. By whom is the school accredited? Get the names of former students and determine their extent of satisfaction with the course. Show the course curriculum to local teachers and employers in that field and get their impressions. Above all, before you sign a contract, be certain you know the total cost involved (including finance charges) and what your rights are regarding cancelation and refunds.

Part Two | Getting What You Need

3 | Creating a Workable Plan: Goal-Setting and Budgeting

Many people—perhaps too many—spend all of their income with little thought for the future. When the future arrives, as it inevitably does, they find themselves ill-prepared to cope with it. They might not be able to buy the house they had yearned for, or educate their children, or look forward to a secure retirement. On the other hand, there are those people who can enjoy the present, yet still know that their future desires will be met. They are the ones who have set goals and who have embarked on a well-disciplined plan to meet those goals. This chapter will explore the ways and means you can set and reach the goals that are right for you, including:

☐ How you can sort out the high-priority goals and the low-priority goals you may have for yourself.
☐ How to identify the specific sources of money which, if properly funded over the years, will allow you to meet your goals.
☐ How to use some simple tools that can tell you whether your goal achievement program is proceeding on target.
☐ How you can adjust your current spending program to help assure that you can meet your ultimate future goals.

Setting Goals

To cope with your personal finances efficiently and to manage your money most productively, you must have a plan. This plan should set forth as clearly as possible your goals, current and future, and the steps you'll take to meet those goals. Further, for the plan to be truly functional, it must be reexamined periodically and revised when necessary. Personal circumstances change over the years, and as they do, so will many of our needs, desires, and long-range aspirations.

The essential element of any personal financial plan include: How should I distribute income to best accomplish current and future needs and desires? How much will I spend today and how much will I put away for the future?

To answer the above questions, let's look at the matter in terms of goals or objectives—specific uses to which your dollars will be put. Let's further break down your spendable money into two broad categories:

Today Dollars and Tomorrow Dollars. Today Dollars are those applied toward meeting current and continuing needs and goals. Tomorrow Dollars are those that, while available today, aren't spent for current needs but are put away in one form or another for future use.

Tomorrow Dollars can be accumulated directly; we put aside a portion of our spendable Today Dollars into savings plans and other forms of investment. Or Tomorrow Dollars may be accumulated indirectly; deductions are made from our paychecks for pension plans, profit-sharing plans, and Social Security. Also, some of our spent Today Dollars may come back to us in the future; a portion of our mortgage payments on our homes will theoretically come back to us when we later sell or refinance the home; and a portion of our ordinary life-insurance premiums may be available to us in the future should we wish to cash in or convert our policies.

Sorting Out Goals

An efficient financial plan demands that we maintain a focus as clear as possible on our specific goals. Obviously, it will be much easier to focus on the more immediate goals than it will on the longer term ones. Many long-term goals may not really have taken complete shape yet and some will arise that we may not have fully anticipated. Not only do we have to attach numbers to our goals (how much will we need for what purpose, and when will we need it), but we also must assign *priorities* to our goals: which are more important, and which must we strive more deliberately to accomplish?

There are two main sorting processes. The first is to determine current and continuing goals on the one hand and the future goals (near term and far term) on the other. The other sorting process concerns the priorities of our goals. Some goals will naturally demand a higher priority than others, although it's up to each individual and family to make such determinations.

Let's look at an example of the difference between "Must" and "Maybe" goals with regard to one family's future aspirations. Howard and Hedda have an eight-year-old child and it is their fervent desire that the child receive a college education on graduation from high school some ten years hence. When that day arrives, Howard and Hedda don't want to say, "We're sorry but you can't go to college just now. We don't have enough money."

They know that they must have either the money or the ability to borrow or generate the money for their child's college education at a specific future point. For them this is a Must goal. If they have not reached their goal at the appointed time, the results would be most unsatisfactory.

On the other hand, Howard and Hedda have also dreamed of taking a trip to Europe. They'd like to do it within about five years if they could, but it's not that critical. If circumstances dictate that they're never able to take the trip, they'll be disappointed but it wouldn't be all that devastating. This aspiration falls into the Maybe goal category: if they don't ever achieve it, not that much has been lost in the trying.

Although each individual and family sets its own goals based on desires and needs, there is one particular goal that has a Must quality for most everybody: having enough money to live on when work ceases—that is, on retirement.

If, on reaching that time, we find we don't have adequate funds, we can't go back 10, 20, or 30 years and accumulate the necessary nest egg that will provide us with the retirement lifestyle we were hoping for. We must have the needed funds at that appointed time. It's all too easy at the age of 20 or 30 or even 40 to ignore the importance of this Must goal—it's too far off to warrant thinking about. But sound financial planning, even at a very young age, requires that this Must goal be kept in mind and planned for at the earliest possible time.

Common sense suggests that the prudent person create a well-disciplined plan that will allow him to reach the Must destination at the appointed time. This generally entails putting away future dollars in such a form as to give the highest degree of assurance that we'll have the needed money at the right time. The techniques that offer the highest level of assurance for this program are "fixed income investing" techniques.

Once a well-disciplined program is underway to meet the Must goals, the prudent individual might begin planning for the Maybe goals, using more speculative techniques, such as the stock market, to achieve them. These various investment techniques are discussed in later chapters, along with other matters relating to our spending programs.

Changes and Trade-offs

It would indeed be attractive if, at any age, we could program all of our financial needs and desires into a computer and let the machine create and maintain a plan that would help us achieve our various goals. But, alas, technology cannot yet take into account the shifting patterns of human activity. As we grow and mature, old goals are accomplished or abandoned, and new ones arise, perhaps unexpectedly. These shifts, whether drastic or imperceptible, will require a revision of our financial plan. Further, as we pass old goals and strive toward new ones, we may have to make certain trade-offs—adjustments in priority to allow us to accomplish something that may not have been there yesterday.

In short, a workable financial plan is only as valid as its revisions. In addition to developing the disciplines of saving wisely and spending prudently, one must also develop the habit of periodically reviewing and, where needed, revising the overall plan that will most clearly satisfy the sought-after lifestyle. For the family it may be a yearly meeting at which everyone sits down to discuss, analyze, evaluate, and make plans for the future regarding family finances. For the individual it may be an annual meeting with a banker, accountant, lawyer, or other adviser to do the same. An important part of such a review is to go step by step through each expense and each item of future needs and ask yourself: "Am I doing it right; am I getting bogged down in unproductive spending habits; will I arrive at my appointed destination on time with the right amount of dollars in my pocket?"

A Goal Worksheet— Current Needs

Table 3-1 is designed as a worksheet. It lists all the common immediate and continuing goals that we must be constantly achieving and contains spaces for inserting the amounts you are currently spending (or setting aside) to meet these goals, as well as projected amounts that you will be spending one and two years from now. The exercise of filling out the worksheet serves several purposes: it can help to provide a clearer picture of your actual current financial situation; it will aid you in anticipating future goals as your needs may change; and it can help you determine what expenses might be modified to supply more spendable dollars in another area.

Table 3-1   **Goal Worksheet—Current and Ongoing Expenses**

	Current Estimated Monthly Expenses	Estimated Monthly Expenses One Year from Now	Estimated Monthly Expenses Two Years from Now
1. Food and beverage	_____	_____	_____
2. Shelter	_____	_____	_____
3. Clothing and other textile needs	_____	_____	_____
4. Protection against risk (insurance)	_____	_____	_____
5. Entertainment	_____	_____	_____
6. Education	_____	_____	_____
7. Medical and health-care costs	_____	_____	_____
8. Transportation	_____	_____	_____
9. Little "rainy day" fund	_____	_____	_____
10. Cost of credit	_____	_____	_____
11. Travel and recreation	_____	_____	_____
12. Personal business matters	_____	_____	_____
13. Children's allowances	_____	_____	_____
14. Miscellaneous personal expenses	_____	_____	_____
15. "Luxuries"	_____	_____	_____
16. Charity and religious expenses	_____	_____	_____
17. Income taxes	_____	_____	_____

Each of the items contained in the worksheet is discussed in more detail. For your own purposes, you might want to break down any of these items into its more specific components.

As you calculate each monthly expense, whether current or anticipated, include within the expense any debt repayment that may be a part of the total expense. In other words, any payments on an automobile loan would apply toward your overall transportation expense. Try also, to the best of your ability, to separate from debt payments that portion attributable toward interest, and include those interest items under the category "cost of credit." It's important to get a clear-cut picture of what all of your credit is actually costing you, and it may come as quite a surprise.

1. *Food and beverage.* This would include food and beverages consumed at home and at restaurants. Don't overlook alcoholic beverages, lunch money, snack money, and the tips you might leave when dining or drinking out.

2. *Shelter.* Your overall shelter costs should be broken down into various components, which include the following:

Basic expense: rent or mortgage payment. If you are an owner, remember that a portion of your mortgage payment applies to the reduction of your debt. This portion, referred to as principal, will theoretically be recovered at some future time when you sell or refinance the property. But because that future time is probably unknown at present, the total mortgage payment should be considered as a current expense.

Property taxes. In most communities, property owners are billed twice each year for property taxes. The tax bill may include separate allocations to the city, the county, the school district, and any other jurisdictions with the right to tax local properties. In addition to this overall property tax cost, homeowners must include separate taxes for any special assessments. Special assessments are levied when, for example, a sewer line is installed, sidewalks are put in, streets are widened, and so on.

Property insurance. Commonly, property insurance includes forms of protection in addition to the basic coverage of your dwelling and its contents, such as public liability coverage and medical payments coverage for costs incurred by people who may be injured on your premises, plus specially scheduled protection for loss or theft of valuable property.

Utilities. In an ever-increasingly energy conscious world, the cost of utilities (electricity, heat, water) is no longer taken for granted. Indeed, those costs have mounted considerably and have imposed a harsh burden on many people. In evaluating current and future utility costs, it would be wise also to evaluate how those costs can be reduced by various energy-saving techniques. Ample literature on this is generally available from utility company offices and home improvement supply dealers and at your local library or bookstore. It might be worth investing in a periodic inspection of the various mechanical elements in your home—heating system, air conditioning, plumbing, wiring—to determine whether there is any energy waste involved, and correcting it. Any machine can lose its efficiency as it grows older, and an inefficient heating plant or air conditioning unit could be costing you needlessly.

Telephones are another form of utility. A simple evaluation of your telephone service could result in substantial cost savings—if you're paying for more telephones than you realistically need or for "fancy" equipment, you might be able to eliminate those extras and realize extra dollars in your pocket instead. If your local calls are measured on a time basis, how much a month could you save by reducing each conversation by simply a minute or two? If you make frequent long-distance calls, are you taking full advantage of the nighttime and weekend discounts available?

Maintenance and repairs. Typically, this will be an accumulation of small amounts but in the annual aggregate can become a substantial sum. Further, there is always the possibility of minor disasters, some of which are preventable through an alert maintenance system; others are totally unpredictable. A program of preventive maintenance can be decidedly less costly than one of after-the-fact maintenance.

Renovation and improvements. We may renovate and improve our dwellings cosmetically or functionally. Cosmetic improvements would include redecorating, painting, landscaping. Functional improvements might entail new kitchen equipment, adding or expanding rooms, installing a pool, converting a storage area into usable living space, and so on. Much of this renovation and improvement activity is appropriate and worth the expense, and much of the expense can be recaptured on a later sale of the property. But caution must be noted with regard to certain improvements that can be excessive. Because modernization costs can be extensive, the homeowner embarking upon such projects must bear in mind the ability to recapture those expenses on subsequent resale and might best consult a local real estate firm first to determine the potential value of the improvements.

Appliances, and reserves for replacements. Under the general category of shelter, there are a number of expensive items many of us take for granted: television sets, kitchen appliances, water heaters, and the like. All of these items have a limited lifetime and will have to be replaced. Many people choose to wait until the end is at hand, and then there often ensues a scramble to find money in the budget for this. A more prudent course might be to establish a "Reserve for Replacements," a fund that would build a little month by month and alleviate much of the pain accompanying replacement costs.

3. *Clothing and other textile needs.* Clothing expenses tend to be based on two predominant factors: need (function) and style (frivolity). No guidelines are suggested other than prudence, and the caution that all too many budgets are thrown into disarray because of excessive purchases of clothing and accessories.

Other textile needs include sheets, towels, blankets. Although these may be relatively minor budget items, shopping with an eye toward durability and washability can keep replacements at a minimum.

4. *Protection against personal risk.* This category includes your program, for individual or family, of protecting your cash flow against the risks of illness, accident, and the unexpected premature death of the breadwinners. Health insurance, disability income insurance, and life insurance are discussed in more detail in later chapters. But as current and continuing expenses, actual out-of-pocket costs must be carefully calculated and allocated in your overall budget/goal program. Much of this protection may be available to you in the form of fringe benefits at work, and you may not actually incur out-of-pocket expenses. To the extent that you do, however, you must include them in your expense listings. Regarding ordinary life insurance that you have purchased privately, a portion of what you pay in will be available at some later time should you cash in the policy. Insofar as the premium payments now represent an out-of-pocket expense, you should consider them as such and utilize the conversion values in your future planning.

5. *Entertainment.* Much of the money we spend on entertainment tends to be spent impulsively. This is natural; when we get the urge to escape, we don't always stop to examine how the expenses might affect our normal budgetary program. The frequent result: a severe budget "leak."

Take the time to make a detailed listing of all entertainment expenses so that you can determine where excesses might lie.

Among your overall entertainment costs you might include the following: admissions to movies, theaters, musical events; cable television subscription costs; admissions to sporting events; costs of sporting equipment and fees or memberships at sports facilities; books and periodicals (for other than educational purposes); dining and drinking out, if you haven't already included them in "food and beverages"; at home parties and get-togethers; special events, including not just the cost of tickets, food, and drink, but also special clothing and accessories purchased for that event that might seldom be used again.

6. *Educational expenses.* This should include any expenses for private school tuition, religious education tuition, adult education expenses, and all reading materials related to such schooling or used apart from normal schooling activities. Include also the expenses of tutors, as well as fees and expenses for school clubs, uniforms, equipment, and printed materials.

7. *Medical and health-care costs.* Over and above any premiums you may pay for health insurance, include here any costs you incur that are not reimbursable by any insurance program. In addition to doctor visits, include prescriptions, dental expenses, eye glasses, ambulatory devices (e.g., crutches), hearing aids, therapeutic equipment, and the costs of any other special treatments or devices needed.

8. *Transportation.* This should include the cost of both privately owned vehicles and public transit—and don't overlook the cost of motorcycles and bicycles, their maintenance, repairs, and parts.

Chapter 6 discusses transportation costs in greater detail.

9. *Little rainy day funds.* We should distinguish "little rainy day" funds to be used in your immediate and continuing budget program from "big rainy day" funds for your long-range budget program. The little rainy day fund is a handy source of money—perhaps kept in a savings account—that can be used to equalize some of the inevitable fluctuations that occur in a month-to-month spending program. It should be added to regularly and tapped as little as possible. The more it can grow, the better off your big rainy day fund will be, should major future needs arise.

10. *Cost of credit.* Apart from interest that you may be paying on your home mortgage, which is included in the shelter category, you should distinguish what costs you are incurring for all your other credit uses. This would include revolving charge accounts at department stores, interest on loans at banks, credit unions, and consumer finance companies; interest on credit card lines, interest on overdraft checking lines, interest on personal loans payable to other individuals, interest on second mortgages you may have taken out on your home, and interest on insurance premiums (which may be charged to you if you are paying monthly or quarterly instead of annually). The cost of credit is too easily buried in your overall payments, and not enough attention is paid to this cost, which can add from 10 to 30 percent of the goods and services you're purchasing, depending on the sources of credit. Only by determining a clear picture of the actual dollar cost of your credit will you be able to decide whether you are using credit excessively. The use of credit is discussed in more detail in later chapters.

11. *Travel and recreation expenses.* This should be considered as a category separate from your normal transportation and entertainment expenses. Primarily it refers to vacations, travel to visit family, attend out-of-town weddings, and other functions. The cost of children's activities, such as summer camp, should also be included. Expenses in this category include transportation, lodging, meals, entertainment, tips, shopping (souvenirs, etc.), car rental fees, babysitting fees, special clothing and equipment, and any costs involved in maintaining your dwelling while you are away.

12. *Personal business.* Into this category fall all those expenses you incur in keeping your personal and family matters under control: legal fees, accounting fees, income tax preparation charges, investment advisory expenses, safety deposit box rentals, checking account costs, and the purchase of necessary equipment and supplies related to these matters (a calculator, stationery, filing equipment, etc.).

13. *Children's allowances.* This is a minor item perhaps, but it is important in setting the tone of a family's financial status. Factors to be considered in establishing allowances are: the degree of control over spending habits that parents wish to exert, the amount of allowance received by your children's peers (peer group pressure can be stronger than you might think), the amount that the children themselves contribute to family needs (housework, odd jobs). Although allowances themselves may be of low to medium priority, the establishment of discipline and control regarding the children's own financial status is of the highest priority. The size and conditions under which an allowance is given can have a considerable effect on a child's ability to establish a sense of self-sufficiency and self-worth. The matter should not be regarded lightly, even when children are at an early age.

14. *Miscellaneous personal expenses.* This is something of a catch-all, but it can't be ignored. Experience has shown that individuals and families with financial problems will have an excessively large and unspecified "miscellaneous" category in their expense program. If all the miscellaneous expenses are carefully noted, it's much easier to bring a runaway budget under control.

Among myriad other common miscellaneous expenses, you should include: money for snacks; cosmetic expenses (haircuts, beauty parlor costs, and all related accessories, salves, etc.); gifts purchased for others or for yourself; pet supplies and veterinarian fees; tobacco costs; various toys and trinkets purchased for your children or yourself; equipment and supplies for hobbies. Another miscellaneous expense is gambling, whether for state lottery tickets or for other forms of betting.

15. *"Luxuries."* This is an optional category designed for those who genuinely have a goal of acquiring certain luxuries as a part of their immediate and continuing expense program. What are such luxuries? It all depends on the individual—obviously, what one might consider a luxury, another might view as an ordinary acquisition. Luxuries must be designated in terms of priority with regard to all your other expenses. What else might you be willing to give up in order to acquire them?

16. *Charity and religious expenses.* This would include membership in religious organizations and contributions to them, as well as other ongoing charitable contributions made during the year, such as the local United Fund, Red Cross, medical-oriented charities (heart fund, cancer association, muscular dystrophy fund), and so on.

17. *Income taxes.* Most of us never see the money we pay to the government (federal, state, and local where applicable)—it's simply deducted from our paychecks. If we have instructed our employers to withhold the proper amount, the annual withholding sum will cover our total tax obligation. If we have underwithheld, we will have a tax bill to pay each April. If we have overwithheld, we have a refund coming. Your employer will ask you to complete a W-4 form in which you list your exemptions and dependents. That form controls how much will be withheld from your regular salary. Some people may prefer to over-withhold, looking forward to a "bonus" when their tax refund comes each year. In a sense, this is a form of enforced saving, except that you don't get any interest on your money.

If you are self-employed, you will have to make quarterly payments of your estimated income tax due, as well as of your self-employment tax (the parallel to Social Security for the employed). Because those estimated tax payments are due only four times each year, it might be overly tempting not to worry about them until they fall due. But coming up with one-fourth of your annual income tax bill at those appointed times might be difficult if you have not embarked on a well-disciplined program to set aside the money for meeting those payments. One method would involve setting aside the necessary amount each week in a separate "untouchable" fund so that you don't have to throw your budget out of joint each quarter (see Table 3-2).

Coordinating Current Goals with Future Goals

Once you've established what the spending patterns are in meeting immediate and continuing goals, you'll next have to assign priority to those goals. But first you must get the broad picture of your future goals, both near and long term. If, after making all the appropriate adjustments in your immediate goal program you can find excess dollars available, you must then choose whether to apply those dollars to other immediate goals or to perhaps more important longer term goals.

"Discretionary income"—the excess dollars available once your basic needs are met—now enters the picture. How will you spend those excess dollars? They could be spent on frivolities that might be quickly forgotten. Or they could be allocated to future needs, to provide pleasures whose values may be much more treasured.

The ability to meet your long-term goals will be largely shaped by the demands of your immediate goals. Only you can determine what each of those sets of goals will be. You are unique. A budgetary program should serve as a discipline in meeting the goals that you individually have set. Often, individuals and families will adopt "rule of thumb" budget

Table 3-2 | **Annual Budget for Four Person Families**

Item	Lower Budget (under $15,000) Percent of Total Expenses	Intermediate Budget ($15,000–30,000) Percent of Total Expenses	Higher Budget (over $30,000) Percent of Total Expenses
Food	31.0	24.6	20.9
Housing	19.1	22.4	23.0
Transportation	7.9	9.0	7.9
Clothing	6.9	6.0	5.9
Personal care	2.5	2.1	2.0
Medical care	9.3	5.7	4.0
Miscellaneous family consumption	4.3	4.9	5.6
Other items	4.2	4.3	4.9
Personal income taxes	8.2	14.8	20.9
Social Security and disability	6.2	6.1	4.7

NOTE: Totals may not add to 100 percent because of rounding.
Source: U.S. Department of Labor, latest data available.

programs to keep their spending habits in line. Such programs may work to an extent, but if they haven't been created with the individual's own particular needs in mind, the ultimate result can be a high level of dissatisfaction.

Shaping Future Goals

Table 3-3 lists some of the more common major goals that most individuals and families anticipate. These goals are not listed in any order of priority; this is for you to determine. If you can complete the columns

Table 3-3 | **Major Future Goals**

	How Much Will Be Needed?	When Will It Be Needed?	Amount per Year
Education	_____	_____	_____
Housing (new shelter)	_____	_____	_____
Retirement	_____	_____	_____
"Stake" for your children	_____	_____	_____
"Stake" for yourself	_____	_____	_____
Care of elderly or disabled	_____	_____	_____
"One shot" expenses	_____	_____	_____
"Big rainy day"	_____	_____	_____

accompanying the goals, even in rough fashion (since many may be several years away for you), you'll begin to get a better idea about what priorities you want to attach to them.

How can one anticipate these major future needs without knowing the effects of inflation? Not only are these effects uncertain, but those of a continuing increase in personal income are also not known. Historically, with a few exceptions, the rate of personal income in the United States has exceeded the rate of inflation. It would not be totally safe to say that this trend will continue, though studies indicate it should. Thus, for purposes of completing this worksheet, it might be best to assume your future needs based on current dollar values, and then adjust the worksheet each year or two to reflect changes that have occurred. If expenses and income continue to increase at approximately the same rate, then the portion of your budget set aside for future goals should show a similar increase. In other words, if you're earning $18,000 a year and are able to put aside 5 percent of that after all expenses have been met ($900), and some years from now your earnings are $25,000 and you're still able to put aside 5 percent after all expenses have been met ($1250), your annual savings/investments will be growing at a rate to help you meet the higher priced goal when it arrives at that future time.

Let's now take a closer look at each of the suggested items in the future goal list.

Education. This refers to higher education for children, and, in the light of current trends, it can be a most foreboding goal. Educational costs are increasing rapidly in both public and private school sectors. College education is a goal that traditionally must be met at a fairly fixed point. Though it is possible, most young individuals would not want to delay their college training by more than a year or two because of a shortcoming in the financial area.

Preparations to meet this goal must begin at the earliest possible time. These preparations can include a savings/investment program; acquiring an awareness of loan, grant, and scholarship programs; and communications between parents and child regarding the child's own contribution to the financial needs, such as through work.

Housing (new shelter). The individual or family currently owning a home and anticipating buying a bigger and better one in the future have an advantage over those currently renting: they will be building some equity in their existing home that can be applied toward the purchase of a new one. Current renters must accumulate a large enough down payment to enable them to obtain their first home. That home, once acquired, can become a growing asset that will assist them in meeting other goals later in life. Later chapters on housing provide assistance in working out the arithmetic of buying versus renting and focus on this particular priority and how it can be accomplished.

Retirement. With rare exceptions, this is the most predominant "Must" goal for everyone. You don't have a chance to do it over if you reach a point when work ceases and there's not enough to live on. Whatever your aims, it's not too early to begin focusing on this important goal. The chapter on financial planning for retirement contains more guidelines to help you achieve that focus.

Stake for your children. Many families have a goal of acquiring enough money to provide their children with a stake to help them get started in life. The stake might be used to help them buy a home, to get them started in business or professional practice, or just to provide a cushion to assist them in coping with the world's vagaries. If this is one of your goals, you must give it priority in line with other goals.

Stake for yourself. As discussed in chapter 2, career changing is becoming a more prevalent phenomenon in our society. Many of these changes involve going into business for oneself, and very often a substantial stake is needed. Unfortunately, the concept of going to work for oneself does not always loom clearly on the horizon and so it's difficult to put a priority on such a goal. Consider it accordingly, and keep it in mind each time you renew and revise this list of goals and priorities.

Care of elderly or disabled. This should perhaps be called a "need" rather than a "goal," since we all hope that those near and dear to us will be able to maintain themselves throughout their lifetime. But it doesn't always work out that way. Parents and other close relatives may, through circumstances beyond anyone's control, become dependent on us for a measure of support. If this likelihood can be anticipated, it can be planned for and better coped with.

"One-shot" expenses. These might be "Must" goals, or they could be "Maybe" goals. They can include such items as a "once in a lifetime" trip, a large wedding for one's child, a major purchase of jewelry or luxury items, or a generous gift to a charity or other institution. These are voluntary goals, and their priority may be high or low, depending on you. The higher the priority, the earlier the planning must be done.

Big rainy day. In the discussion of current and continuing goals and needs we mentioned the "little rainy day" fund. The big rainy day fund is directed more to major unanticipated expenses that any individual or family might confront—uninsured medical expenses and recuperative costs; extended periods of lay-off from work; emergency needs of other family members for various purposes; uninsured losses, and so on. Generally, this is an item of fairly high priority. Proper insurance programs can minimize much of the risk and there's always the possibility that the fund will never be needed and that it can, at some point, be allocated into other goal requirements.

The Sources from Which Future Goals Can Be Accomplished

In addition to keeping a careful watch on your goals and their shifting priorities, it's also important to maintain a careful vigil on the sources of money that will allow you to accomplish these goals. They, too, might be subject to change over the years, and it's obviously important to be able to adjust goals and priorities in line with adjustments in the sources of money.

Income from Work

This, obviously, is the primary source from which your current and continuing goals will be met. To the extent that you don't use all your current income in meeting your current goals, the remainder will be put aside to meet future goals.

Savings/ Investments

This is actually a double source, consisting of the income you earn in your savings and investment plans and the principal that you ultimately might use to meet various goals. Depending on the manner of placement of these funds, you may have a reliable or an unreliable source of dollars. Prudence can assure your future; speculation can demolish it. Be well aware of possible consequences before you make any decisions in this extremely important area.

Equities

Homeowners are building a source of future funds as they reduce their mortgage debt. Owners of ordinary life-insurance policies likewise are building a source of future funds. Both forms of equity—your share of ownership—can amount to substantial sums. If they are tapped too early, by refinancing your home or prematurely cashing in your life-insurance policies, the ability to meet future goals may be seriously impaired. Know what these values are and what they can amount to in the future. Later chapters on housing and life insurance will assist you in determining those future values.

Borrowing

Borrowing can provide a most convenient way of meeting goals. Certainly with regard to housing, transportation, and such other major items as college tuition, borrowing allows you to accomplish what otherwise may take many years of accumulating. But borrowing is little more than a means of accelerating the use of future income, with an added cost factor of 10 to 30 percent, depending on the credit source used. It should also be well noted that funds that are borrowed and have to be repaid in the future will probably affect the budget flow when the funds are being repaid. Prudent borrowing can enhance your current, continuing lifestyle; imprudent borrowing can devastate your future lifestyle.

Enforced Savings— Pensions, Social Security, Profit-sharing Plans

These represent a form of what would otherwise be current income, shifted to future accessibility. To many people, these forms of enforced savings represent all, or a substantial part, of the sources for meeting long-range goals, particularly retirement. But a danger exists in overestimating the total of these sources. Many people may find their reliance on these sources has been in error—there simply isn't as much as expected. Even though access to these sources may be many years off, it's vital that a reasonably close estimate of what will be available is maintained on a continuing basis.

Inheritances, Gifts, and Other Windfalls

For most of us this category may be a complete imponderable. But if you have any reasonable assurance that inheritances or gifts will be coming your way, it would be wise to try to determine the amount involved; this can have a considerable effect on your other ongoing financial plans. Whenever an inheritance can be anticipated, be sure you understand the impact of the tax laws on it. Federal taxes can take a substantial bite out of inherited property if it is sold at a gain. It's the net amount, not the gross amount, that you should assimilate into your budget.

The Financial Statement—a Planning Tool

Can you imagine buying an automobile with no dashboard indicators on it? No speedometer, no gas gauge, no mileage indicator, no oil, brake, or battery warning lights? And to top it off, the hood is sealed shut, requiring two days in the shop every time you want to check your oil, battery, and other innards.

It might be okay for an occasional spin down to the supermarket, but to take it out on the highway would be risky, to say the least.

In much the same sense, any individual, family, or business needs a proper set of financial indicators plus easy access to the inner workings, so that periodic tune-ups can be done quickly and simply.

A thoughtfully prepared and *regularly updated* financial statement is a neat and invaluable package of gauges, meters, and warning lights. It can tell you how fast you're going, how your fuel is holding out, how much fuel you'll need in the future, how smooth your ride is.

Financial statements provide a picture, at any given time, of the exact financial condition of the person or business involved. But it's important to remember that these financial statements reflect the condition only on the given day. The value of a single statement is limited. The true value comes in comparing it with past statements, so that changes in growth and strong and weak points can be spotted and evaluated.

The financial statement consists of three major elements: assets, liabilities, and net worth.

Assets

Assets are the sum total of everything you own, plus everything owed to you. The value of assets is figured as of the date of the statement. Because the value of many assets can and does change, it's essential to evaluate them anew each time a statement is prepared, if it's to be accurate.

Included among your assets are your house, cars, personal property, bank accounts, cash value of life insurance, stocks, and other securities. Also included are money or property due you as a result of a pending inheritance, personal debts owed to you, property settlements, and so on.

Liabilities

Liabilities are debts—everything you owe. As with assets, these are figured as of the date of the statement, and values must be updated accordingly to insure the accuracy of your statement.

Included among liabilities will be the mortgage on your home, amounts owed on personal loans, amounts owed on contracts, and other personal debts. A detailed financial statement will break down financial liabilities into long term and short term. This can aid an analysis of your condition by distinguishing which debts will fall due within, say, one year and which will fall due at some more distant point.

Net Worth

Your net worth is the difference between assets and liabilities. it should be on the plus side. You arrive at net worth by subtracting liabilities from assets. The business executive regards it this way: if he wanted to close up shop altogether, he would sell off all assets and use the money to pay off all liabilities. What's left would be his net worth.

Here's a simple example of how net worth is calculated on one particular item. Joe has a car valued at $6000. However, he still owes the bank $2000. Therefore, his net worth in this asset is $4000. The asset (car, $6000) minus the liabilities (debt to bank, $2000) equals net worth, $4000.

Other Components

Simple personal financial statements will also include a brief summary of your annual earnings and living expenses, as well as schedules of your life insurance holdings, your investments, and your property, both real and personal.

From time to time you might be required to provide personal financial information to obtain credit or other services. In such instances, you'll probably have to sign a statement that says, in essence, that the information you have given is accurate; that you have given the information with the intent that the other party can act in reliance on it; that you have not withheld any pertinent information; and that you agree to notify the other party of any adverse changes in your circumstances. In providing this information and then signing the statement, you are legally binding yourself to the accuracy of the information given. If you give false or incomplete information, and the other party acts on it, you may be putting yourself in jeopardy. An insurance policy can conceivably be voided, a loan can be declared in default, a debt can be refused discharge in bankruptcy proceedings. Although such happenings may be rare, they can occur and the proper way to avoid them is to be certain that the information on any kind of financial statement is accurate. Figure 3-1 illustrates a typical financial statement provided by financial institutions (usually at no cost). After you have filled it out, consider the uses to which it can be put.

The Uses of the Financial Statement

As a Safety Valve

An ongoing program of updated financial statements can help you spot troubles before they get out of hand. A financial mess can be lurking beneath the surface for years before it begins to hurt. For example, you may be involved in a gradual buildup toward becoming overly extended with debts. By tracing your indebtedness over the years via your financial statement, the signals might become evident early enough to warn you to correct the situation. Or your nest egg may not be growing as rapidly as it should be, and this can be spotted by comparing a series of annual financial statements. It's all a matter of "keeping track" and the financial statement program can be a most important tool for this.

For Keeping the Reins on Your Credit

Good credit, wisely used, can be of immense value. Knowing well in advance your borrowing needs and your borrowing capabilities helps assure the wise use of credit. Through your financial statements, you can maintain a close vigil on your current debts, your depreciating assets (items that need replacement in the future, such as a car), and your anticipated future income (your ability to afford tomorrow's obligations). Of course, you realize without looking at some figures that you'll need a new car two years from now. But considering what other things you might have to borrow for between now and then, how will that car loan fit into your overall plans at that time? The financial statement gives you the current data that can help you cope with the future.

To Help Protect You Against Loss

If you keep your financial statements up to date—at least yearly—you'll be forcing yourself to keep accurate current valuations on all your property. The value of any property is subject to change, and only by knowing true current values can you be sure of obtaining the necessary insurance to protect you against loss.

In Maintaining a Sensible Life-Insurance Program

Sound planning dictates that provision be made to maintain comforts in the event of the premature death of a breadwinner. Life insurance is the most common means of providing for this. A life-insurance program should be planned in conjunction with the availability of other assets that can be cashed in to provide for needs. The financial statement provides a reliable current indicator of available assets that can be converted readily into cash without undue sacrifice should the necessity arise. This can help you tailor your life-insurance program to your specific needs rather than guessing what that program should consist of.

To Help Establish a Worry-free Estate Plan

Your progressive financial statements provide the best possible at-a-glance gauge of how much and what type of estate planning you need. Prudent estate planning requires a regular checkup of your net worth: which assets and liabilities are increasing and decreasing? At what rate? Until what time? Which assets and liabilities can be shifted out of the estate to obtain maximum tax benefits and assure a proper distribution

PERSONAL FINANCIAL STATEMENT

Santa Monica Bank

As of _____ 19 _____

SMB

Purpose of Loan: _____

Source of Repayment: _____

Name in Full	Soc. Sec. No.	Age	☐ Married ☐ Unmar. ☐ Sep.	No. of Dep.
Residence Address (No., Street, City, State, Zip Code)	Phone No. (Inc. Area Code)	Yrs. at Address	☐ Rent ☐ Own	

Previous Addresses If at above address less than 5 years (No. and Street, City, State, Zip Code)

Employer	Position	No. Yrs.	Address (No. and Street)	City	Phone & Ext.

If You Are Married, You May Apply for a Separate Account.

Complete this part only if: 1. Your spouse will also be contractually liable for the account, OR 2. You are relying on alimony, child support or maintenance as income, OR 3. You want us to consider your spouse's income or other community property for the purpose of this application for credit.

Name and Address of Spouse or Former Spouse	Soc. Sec. No.	Age	Area Code-Bus. Phone ( )
Name and Address of Spouse's or Former Spouse's Employer	Position	How Long Yrs.____ Mos.____	Mo. Earnings $

ASSETS			DOLLARS		LIABILITIES			DOLLARS
CASH	Santa Monica Bank	Office		NOTES PAYABLE TO BANKS	Santa Monica Bank	Office		
	Other Banks				Other (Itemize)			
STOCKS AND BONDS	Listed (Schedule A)							
	Unlisted (Schedule A)							
ACCOUNTS AND NOTES RECEIVABLE	Relatives, Friends and Business			OTHER NOTES AND ACCOUNTS PAYABLE	Real Estate Loans (Schedule B)			
					Contracts payable (Itemize)			
LIFE INSURANCE	Cash Surrender Value				Loans on Cash Surrender Value			
REAL ESTATE	Improved (Schedule B)							
	Unimproved (Schedule B)			OTHER LIABILITIES				
	Trust Deeds and Mortgages (Schedule C)							
OTHER PERSONAL PROPERTY	Automobile							
	Other (Itemize)			NET WORTH	TOTAL LIABILITIES (TOTAL ASSETS MINUS TOTAL LIABILITIES)			
	TOTAL ASSETS				TOTAL			

ANNUAL INCOME	(Refer to Federal Income Tax Returns for Previous Year)	ANNUAL EXPENDITURES	(Refer to Federal Income Tax Returns for Previous Year)
Salary or Wages		Real Estate Loan Payments	
Dividends and Interest		Payments on Contracts and other Notes	
Rentals (Gross)		Property Taxes and Assessments	
Business or Professional Income (Net)		Federal and State Income Taxes	
Other Income		Insurance Premiums	
(You do not have to list income from alimony, child support or maintenance unless you want the Bank to consider it for the purpose of this application for credit.)		Estimated Living Expenses	
		Other	
TOTAL INCOME		**TOTAL EXPENDITURES**	

INSURANCE:

LESS — TOTAL EXPENDITURES

NET CASH INCOME

Insurance on Buildings $ _____   Accident/Health Insurance $ _____

Automobiles: Coll. $_____   Ded. $_____   Comp. $_____

Life Insurance Co. Name _____   Amount_____

Beneficiary of Life Insurance _____

N-123 (Rev. 5-77)   (PLEASE READ IMPORTANT STATEMENT ON REVERSE BEFORE SIGNING)

Figure 3–1   New financial statement

SCHEDULE A: LISTED AND UNLISTED STOCKS AND BONDS OWNED

No. of Shares or Par Value	Description	Issued in name of (as joint tenants, community or separate property)	Cost	Market Value
Listed:				
			Total Listed	
Unlisted:				
			Total Unlisted	

Are any of the above Securities pledged to secure a debt? (If yes describe)

SCHEDULE B: REAL ESTATE

Address (Also Give Brief Phys. Descrip.)	* Title in Name of:	Purch. Date	Cost	Market Value	Trust Deed, Mortgage or Other Liens			
					Unpaid Balance	Rate	Monthly Payment	Held By
		TOTAL						

Is any of above Real Estate subject to declaration of homestead?　Yes　No

*Indicate how title is held in above real properties by following abbreviations:
J/T - Joint Tenancy; T/C - Tenancy in Common;
S/P - Separate Property; C/P - Community Property

Are you leasing any Real or Personal Property?　Yes　No　　If yes, give details as to terms of leases

SCHEDULE C: TRUST DEEDS AND MORTGAGES OWNED

Name of Payer	Street Address, & Type of Improvements	Unpaid Bal.	Terms	1st or 2nd Lien	Market Value of Prop.
	TOTAL		X X X	X X X X	

GENERAL INFORMATION

Have you ever failed in business or compromised debts with your creditors?　Yes　No　　If yes, give details

Are any of your assets pledged, or in any other manner unavailable for paying debts?　Yes　No　　If unavailable or pledged, give details

Are there any suits, judgments, executions or attachments against you pending?　Yes　No　　If yes, give details　　DO YOU HAVE A WILL?　YES　NO

Are any of your assets held in Joint Tenancy, Tenancy in Common or Community Property?　Yes　No
If yes, give details

Are you contingently liable for any Endorsements or Guarantees?　Yes　No
If yes, give details

For the purpose of procuring and establishing credit from time to time with you, each of the undersigned furnish this statement as being true and accurate.

The undersigned agree to and will notify you immediately in writing of any material change in the financial condition of the undersigned and in the absence of such notice or of a new and full written statement, this may be considered as a continuing statement and substantially correct; and it is hereby expressly agreed that upon application for further credit, this statement shall have the same force and effect as if delivered as an original statement of the financial condition of the undersigned at the time such further credit is requested. In consideration of the granting of such credit the undersigned and each of them agree that if the undersigned or any or either of them, or any endorser or guarantor of the obligations of the undersigned or any or either of them at any time fail or become insolvent or commit an act of bankruptcy, or if any deposit account of the undersigned or any or either of them with you, or any other property of the undersigned or any or either of them held by you be attempted to be obtained or held by writ of execution, garnishment, attachment, or other legal process, or if any of the representations made above prove to be untrue or if the undersigned or any or either of them fail to notify you of any material change as above agreed, or if any such material change occurs, then and in either case all obligations of the undersigned or any or either of them held by you shall immediately become due and payable without demand or notice. All sums at any time in any deposit account shall be subject to Bank's right to set-off for liabilities owed to the Bank by any of the undersigned, to the fullest extent permissible by applicable law, and upon any other personal property of the undersigned or any or either of them in your possession, from time to time, to secure all obligations of the undersigned and each of them, either as borrower or guarantor, held by you, and further agree that all obligations or any part thereof, of the undersigned or any or either of them held by you, both matured and unmatured, may at any time be charged against the balance of any deposit account of the undersigned or any or either of them with you, without notice to the undersigned, unless required by applicable law.

I hereby certify that I have carefully read the above statement, including the reverse side, and it is a complete, true and correct statement of the undersigned to the best of my knowledge and belief.

Applicant's Signature　　　　　Date　　　　　Co-applicant's Signature — If this is to be a joint account.　　　Date

Your spouse's signature is not required if this is to be your separate account. If you want us to consider your spouse's income or credit history in making our credit decision, your spouse's authorization is needed.

Spouse's Signature — To authorize verification of income or credit history ONLY.　　　Date to survivors? Which assets have actual earnings or income potential and to what extent? A concise inventory and evaluation of these factors can be gained from your financial statements.

In Helping to Plan Your Long-range Budget

The financial statement, regularly updated, is a simple device to keep your current and future goals in clear focus and to provide an ongoing measurement of the sources from which those goals will be met.

As an Aid in Borrowing

On those occasions when a financial statement is required as a condition to getting a loan, you'll expedite matters considerably if you are prepared with a current statement as well as those of recent years. It will speed up application processing and will serve as evidence of your financial good housekeeping.

Some Thoughts on Spending Habits

It's the object of this chapter and this book to help guide you in establishing financial habits that will allow you to accomplish your individual goals. But all too often we are waylaid from those ultimate goals by strange and often inexplicable outside circumstances. We live in an age of instant gratification, constantly bombarded by commercial messages urging us to acquire products that will provide happiness and satisfaction in almost every phase of our day-to-day life.

Spending habits born out of impulse, gullibility, or low sales resistance can be extremely counterproductive to one's financial welfare. To some degree, we are all subject to impulsive spending, but the more aware we can become of this susceptibility, the more readily we'll be able to control it.

Spending habits may have been unconsciously dictated to us by our observations of our parents and we should evaluate what spending habits are inherited and determine their good and bad points. Peer group pressure—"keeping up with the Joneses"—can also influence our spending habits, and succumbing to it can be costly and unsatisfying.

Spending habits can be a powerful force in shaping your overall financial well-being, which in turn can have a considerable effect on your social, psychological, and personal well-being. To the extent that spending habits control you, you'll have a much more difficult time achieving your own personal potential; when *you* control these habits, you will indeed be the master of your fate.

Personal Action Checklist
Taking the "Dollar Diet"

Do you have too much month left at the end of the money? When budgets fail to balance, it's generally because too many dollars have dribbled away in unnoticed fashion. Big items—utility costs, rent, mortgage payment, car payment, etc.—are fairly easy to trace. But the variety of "miscellaneous" expenses are too easily gone and forgotten. This results in the "Miscellaneous Bulge," and a good cure may be the Dollar Diet. Using this page, or a separate notebook, keep track of every nickel, dime, quarter and dollar that you spend for the next month. At the end of that time you should be able to identify the spending habits that are causing the problem, and corrective action can be instituted. Sample items usually found in the Miscellaneous Bulge include the following. Keep track of them.

Miscellaneous Budget Items	List Your Expenses and Dates Thereof for One Full Month			
☐ Cigarettes	___	___	___	___
☐ Gum, candy, other sweets	___	___	___	___
☐ Magazines, newspapers	___	___	___	___
☐ Liquor, beer, wine—both for at-home use and out	___	___	___	___
☐ Gasoline, other car care	___	___	___	___
☐ Movies, other entertainment tickets	___	___	___	___
☐ Records, tapes (music, video)	___	___	___	___
☐ Beauty, barber, cosmetics costs	___	___	___	___
☐ Carfare, taxis	___	___	___	___
☐ Restaurants	___	___	___	___
☐ Minor clothing items	___	___	___	___
☐ Laundry, dry cleaning	___	___	___	___
☐ Gifts, greeting cards	___	___	___	___
☐ Adornments for person or home	___	___	___	___

Consumer Beware
Goals Should Satisfy Yourself, Not Others

Linda and Gary faced a dilemma common to many young married couples. Many never resolve it satisfactorily, often because they don't know how to cope with the influences that bear upon them. There is no easy solution, but perhaps their story can help you resolve similar problems that you might face.

"We both have good jobs with a lot of potential. Right now money is tight, but we're confident that we can afford to buy a home in the near future. We've been scouting around, and we've found a funky old cottage about 20 miles out of town right on the lake. It's run down and would need a lot of work, but the price is right, and we love the location. Even with improvements, it would still be funky, but it's 'our thing.' Not permanently, of course, but at least for five, maybe ten years.

"That's where the problem arises. Our folks, and a lot of our friends, have been hounding us to buy a place in a certain neighborhood that's the 'in' place for up-and-coming career couples. It supposedly has class and prestige, and everyone tells us we can mingle with the 'right people,' make good business and social contacts, and so on.

"But to us it's stuffy and phony. However, we can't deny that it does offer those contact opportunities and whatever advantages may come from living in the 'right' neighborhood. It would cost a lot more than our funky bungalow, and we'd really be strapped to make the monthly payments. But, then, our friends and family say, 'You'll reap a bigger profit when you sell the "right" place, compared with what you might gain when you sell the bungalow.' And no doubt they're right.

"When we boil it all down, it's the two of us against a lot of them. We know we're young and naive. We respect the experience of others. But we've come to feel guilty—if we buy the bungalow we're being self-indulgent and foolish. If we buy into the 'right' area, we're being sensible and mature—supposedly. Just who are we supposed to be trying to please anyway?"

The ending, at least for Linda and Gary, was a happy one. They bought the bungalow, fixed it up, and eventually their friends and family admitted that they had done the right thing.

As Linda later put it: "The final decision came down to this—do we strive toward goals that we ourselves have set, or do we live our lives as others want us to? Well-meaning though the others may have been, we have to express our own independence and live our own lives. Fortunately, we made the right choice. Other couples in the same boat might have done better to listen to the others. To each his own—as long as you know what your own is."

4 | The Smart Shopper

You can be better off by $1,000 a year, maybe even more! That's how much you, as a Smart Shopper, can save in your routine shopping for food, pharmaceuticals, clothing, and the like. Not all the techniques outlined in this chapter will work for all people. But if you don't try them, you'll never know. Smart Shopper techniques that you'll learn about in this chapter include:

☐ How to recognize your built-in bad shopping habits and replace them with good, money-saving habits.
☐ How to cut 10 percent, 20 percent, and even more from your food and pharmaceutical expenses.
☐ How to look good without spending excessively at the clothing store.
☐ How to get the best values for your money when shopping for furniture, appliances, and other big-ticket items.

The Bad Habits

Every day we are bombarded with hundreds if not thousands of advertising messages: on television, radio, billboards, newspapers, magazines, and in our mail. Millions of dollars are spent every day on market research and advertising to create the most effective pursuasions. Advertising can be a very good thing insofar as it can educate us as to the choices we have for various products and services in the marketplace. But advertising must also be approached with caution: Aside from those relatively infrequent instances when advertising may be misleading (see chapter 5), advertising can create buying habits that can prove costly. It can motivate us to buy on impulse, spending dollars that we might have otherwise put to better use. It can induce us to stick with one specific product when other comparable products might be less costly and equally satisfying. It can prompt us to pay more money for a product that promises certain benefits, when comparable products offer the same benefits at a lower cost.

Advertising isn't all to blame. No ad ever reached out and twisted anyone's arm to buy a particular product. We also must blame our own tendencies to be impulsive and unwilling to take a few extra moments during each shopping decision to pick the product that can satisfy our needs at the best possible price.

If you have any doubts about the general tendency toward poor shopping habits by the average American, conduct a simple experiment *after* you've read this chapter: Be a supermarket spy. Push a cart so as not to raise suspicion and follow other shoppers up and down the aisles of the supermarket. Notice how they succumb to impulse, brand favoritism, and lack of doing adequate comparisons. After a short time, you'll be tempted to tap your fellow shopper on the shoulder and suggest, "You know, you really could save money by buying X instead of Y, and I'm sure you'll be just as happy with it." If you're not emboldened enough to do that, you'll at least feel confident that *you* know how to save as much as 20 percent on the bulk of your shopping—and for a family that spends an average of $100 a week on such items, or over $5000 a year, that's a savings of about $1000 per year.

Let's now examine some of the specific Smart Shopper techniques, particularly those that can be employed at the supermarket, where the majority of our normal shopping budget is spent. (All price comparisons referred to in the following material are based on regular prices, not on specials or discounts.)

The Good Habits: Food

Unit Pricing

A 14-oz. bottle of Heinz ketchup at 66¢ is a lot cheaper than a 44-oz. bottle at $1.45. Correct? Yes and no. The smaller bottle is cheaper than the big bottle, but the ketchup inside, *per ounce,* is much more expensive in the smaller bottle. The ketchup in the small bottle is 4.71¢ per ounce (66 divided by 14 equals 4.71). The ketchup in the big bottle is 3.29¢ per ounce (1.45 divided by 44 equals 3.29). In other words, the exact same product—Heinz ketchup—is 1.42¢ per ounce cheaper when bought in a big bottle compared to a small bottle (4.71 minus 3.29 equals 1.42). Put another way, an ounce of ketchup from the big bottle is 30 percent cheaper than an ounce of ketchup from the small bottle.

This is what's known as unit pricing: calculating the price of a product by the unit (ounce, pound, etc.) rather than by the container it comes in. Here are some other examples.

An 8-oz. box of Crispy Sunshine Saltine Crackers was 73¢ and a 16-oz. box of the exact same product was 89¢. That means that the crackers in the small box are 9.1¢ per ounce and the crackers in the big box are 5.6¢ per ounce—a difference of 3.5¢ per ounce, or a 38 percent savings if you bought the crackers in the big box.

Crest toothpaste: a 1.4-oz. tube at 59¢ comes to 42.1¢ per ounce. An 8.2-oz. tube at $1.76 comes to 21.4¢ per ounce—a difference of 20.7¢ per ounce or a savings of almost 50 percent if you buy the big tube.

A substantial number of commonly purchased products—food, cosmetics, pharmaceuticals, and the like—are packaged in a variety of different-size containers. With few exceptions, very attractive savings can be realized by buying the larger size containers. And also, with very few exceptions, the products in the larger containers can remain every bit as fresh if properly stored. Many shoppers, in an effort to keep their weekly expenses down, will choose the smaller containers without giving the matter a second thought. This can be a costly mistake. The foregoing examples and the table that follows give abundant evidence of the savings that can be realized by taking advantage of unit pricing.

In states without unit pricing laws very few stores offer price tags that show the cost per unit of a given item. It's up to the shopper to do his or her calculations to determine where the best buys are. As the examples indicate, you simply divide the price of the product by the number of ounces in the container to get the cost per ounce of the product. It would certainly pay to take a pocket calculator with you on a few trips to the market and figure the prices on products you commonly buy. After a few times, you'll become accustomed to the differences and the calculator won't be necessary any longer. It takes only a little practice for the unit pricing technique to become second nature. The Personal Action Checklist (PAC) at the end of this chapter provides you with a good starting point: Calculate the different costs per ounce of the commonly purchased products listed at the market you generally shop at. What kind of savings can be realized by buying the larger quantity containers as compared with the smaller containers? Are there instances in which the larger size is not the better buy?

Table 4-1 illustrates a number of other unit pricing comparisons. Prices noted will obviously be different at different times and at different places, but the prices used were regular prices and not sale prices.

Brand Label versus Generic Label

A 10-oz. jar of Welch's grape jelly: 85¢. A 10-oz. jar of a grape jelly with the market's own label: 65¢—a savings of 20¢, or 23.5 percent. Unless you or your children are true connoisseurs of grape jelly, the difference in taste may be insignificant—especially after you've covered it with a layer of peanut butter and sandwiched the whole gooey mass between two slabs of bread. But even if there is a distinguishable difference in taste, is it worth the sacrifice for the 23.5 percent savings?

Brand name products are those regional or national items whose names are known to us through advertising and general familiarity. Generic products are those which are privately labeled for specific stores or chains of stores. In many cases, the quality of generic products is equal to their brand name counterparts. Indeed, many are made by the same manufacturers and to the same specifications. Some generic products may not have the same quality as their brand name counterparts, but the difference may be so slight as to justify buying them for the savings that can be realized. At the very least, a trial of the generic products is certainly warranted. If you're dissatisfied, you're always free to go back to the brand label. But if you're satisfied with the generic label, you can reap substantial savings.

Table 4-1 | **Unit Pricing Comparison**

Product	Size	Cost per Package	Cost per Ounce	Savings per Ounce in Larger Package
Kellogg's cornflakes	8 oz.	$ .64	8.0 ¢	
	18 oz.	1.30	7.2 ¢	10%
Wesson cooking oil	16 oz.	$ .91	5.7 ¢	
	48 oz.	2.29	4.7 ¢	17.5%
Mortons salt	8 oz.			
	(2 4-oz. shakers)	$ .49	6.1 ¢	
				82%
	26 oz.	.29	1.1 ¢	
Best Foods real	8 oz.	$ .59	7.4 ¢	
mayonnaise	32 oz.	1.53	4.8 ¢	35%
Mott's applesauce	8 oz.	$ .37	4.6 ¢	
	35 oz.	1.08	3.1 ¢	33%
Del Monte sweet peas	8.5 oz.	$ .36	4.2 ¢	
	17 oz.	.49	2.9 ¢	31%
Hawaiian Punch				
(6 8-oz. cans)	48 oz.	$1.99	4.1 ¢	56%
Single can	46 oz.	.83	1.8 ¢	
Skippy peanut butter	6 oz.	$ .89	14.83¢	
	40 oz.	4.89	12.25¢	17%
Del Monte sweet	8 oz.	$ .95	11.9 ¢	
pickles	22 oz.	1.84	8.4 ¢	29%
Listermint mouthwash	6 oz.	$ .99	16.5 ¢	
	32 oz.	2.79	8.7 ¢	47%
Ore-Ida frozen french	12 oz.	$ .69	5.75¢	
fries	40 oz.	1.69	4.23¢	26%
Dole crushed	8¼ oz.	$ .40	4.8 ¢	
pineapple	20 oz.	.75	3.8 ¢	21%
Nescafe instant coffee	2 oz.	$1.29	64.5 ¢	
	10 oz.	4.09	40.9 ¢	37%
Parke-Davis hydrogen	4 oz.	$ .76	19 ¢	
peroxide	16 oz.	1.49	9.3 ¢	51%
Phillips milk of	4 oz.	$1.09	27.3 ¢	
magnesia	26 oz.	3.19	12.3 ¢	55%

Pharmaceuticals and Prescriptions

Generic products also offer considerable savings in the drugstore. Table 4-2 compares some common supermarket items, plus drugstore items that can be purchased without a prescription. (The survey was conducted at a major drugstore chain outlet, and the pharmacist on duty gave assurance that the generic products were comparable to the brand name products.) Many prescription items are also available in generic fashion and considerable savings can be realized on these as well. If

Table 4-2 | **Brand Name vs. Generic Label**

Product	Size of Package	Cost of Package	Cost per Ounce	Savings
Vaseline	15 oz.	$ 3.59	23.9 ¢	
Generic equivalent	16 oz.	1.89	11.8 ¢	51%
Triaminic cough				
syrup	4 oz.	$ 2.39	59.8 ¢	
Generic equivalent	4 oz.	1.29	32.3 ¢	46%
Mylanta antacid	12 oz.	$ 2.29	19.1 ¢	
Generic equivalent	12 oz.	1.69	14.1 ¢	26%
Naturite vitamin C	100 tab.	$ 2.98	2.98¢ (per 100 tab.)	
Generic equivalent	100 tab.	2.19	2.19¢ (per 100 tab.)	27%
Whiteworth rubbing				
alcohol	16 oz.	$ 1.54	9.6 ¢	
Generic equivalent	16 oz.	.65	4.1 ¢	57%
Curity cotton balls	260 (count)	$ 1.29	.5 (per ball)	
Generic equivalent	300 (count)	.99	.3 (per ball)	40%
Bayer aspirin	100 tab.	$ 1.77	1.77¢ (per tab.)	
Generic equivalent	100 tab.	.69	.69¢ (per tab.)	61%
All detergent	20 lb.	$11.25	$5.62 (per lb.)	
Generic equivalent	20 lb.	7.49	3.75 (per lb.)	33%
Planters mixed nuts	12 oz.	$ 3.19	26.6 ¢	
Generic equivalent	12 oz.	2.19	18.3 ¢	31%
Sunmaid raisins	15 oz.	$ 1.59	10.6 ¢	
Generic equivalent	15 oz.	1.29	8.6 ¢	19%
Log Cabin syrup	36 oz.	$ 2.33	6.5 ¢	
Generic equivalent	31 oz.	1.19	3.8 ¢	42%
Lipton instant tea	3 oz.	$ 2.64	88¢	
Generic equivalent	3 oz.	1.59	53¢	40%
Gala napkins	140 (count)	$ .85	.6 ¢ (per napkin)	
Generic equivalent	140 (count)	.63	.45¢ (per napkin)	25%
Heinz ketchup	32 oz.	$ 1.23	3.84¢	
Generic equivalent	32 oz.	.99	3.09¢	19%
Listerine mouthwash	32 oz.	$ 2.89	9.03¢	
Generic equivalent	32 oz.	1.59	4.97¢	45%

your doctor gives you a brand name prescription, ask him whether there is a generic equivalent that would satisfy him. Very often the doctor will be satisfied with the generic equivalent and will prescribe it for you instead of the brand name. But you must ask. If you don't ask the doctor at the time he writes the prescription, ask the pharmacist at the time you order the prescription. If he knows of a generic equivalent, he may call the doctor himself and ask the doctor's approval to substitute the generic prescription for the brand name prescription.

Combining Unit Pricing with Generics

Generic labeled products come in a variety of sizes just as the brand name products do. Let's take another look at the grape jelly. A 10-oz. jar of the Welch's brand name product was 85¢, or 8.5¢ per ounce. A 48-oz. jar of the Welch's was $2.21, or 4.58¢ per ounce.

The store label jelly was 65¢ for the 10-oz. jar, or 6.5¢ per ounce. The store also offered a 48-oz. jar with its own label on it for $1.79, or 3.72¢ per ounce.

The cost of one ounce of grape jelly, therefore, ranged from 8.5¢ per ounce for the small Welch's to 3.72¢ per ounce for the 48-oz. store label jar. That's a difference of 4.78¢ per ounce, or a savings of 56 percent!

This example illustrates the total savings that can be realized by combining unit pricing with the generic label shopping. These combined savings can be realized on scores of items at the market and in the drugstore, with little or no compromise in the taste or quality or nutritional value of the products.

Bulk Buying

Many stores will offer substantial discounts—10 to 20 percent—if you buy by the case. Indeed, in many cities there is a growing phenomenon of "warehouse"-type supermarkets which specialize in by-the-case merchandising, at much lower prices than at regular markets. In addition to the discounts you can obtain, buying in bulk quantity protects you against inflationary price increases on those products. If you buy a year's supply of, say, paper towels, you've insulated yourself against a price increase in paper towels for a year. That might be as much as an additional 10 percent. Further, by buying enough staples in bulk quantity, you might be able to cut down on the number of trips you might make to the market.

Most common non-food products have a virtually infinite shelf life—you can keep them in storage almost forever without there being any deterioration in their quality. Most canned, boxed, and bottled foodstuffs have shelf lives that can stretch for years. Here's a sampling of common products that can be stored for long times. If your market doesn't advertise bulk savings, ask the manager. You might be surprised at the bargains you can obtain.

☐ Paper products, such as napkins, towels, toilet tissue.

☐ Soap product, including detergents.

☐ Storage products, such as wax paper, aluminum foil, plastic bags for both food and garbage disposal.

☐ Pharmaceuticals, such as toothpaste, powders, rubbing alcohol, bandages, shaving creams, razors and razor blades, colognes and lotions, deodorants, shampoos, makeup, and so on.

☐ "Instant" powdered items: coffee, tea, juice products.

☐ Spices: salt, pepper, etc.

☐ Dehydrated products: milk, eggs, etc.

□ Food items in cans, bottles, and jars can have a shelf life of at least one year. Check with your store manager for specifics on each item.

□ Frozen foods: individual taste, plus the cost and availability of a freezer, may dictate how much bulk food you'd want to buy for frozen storage. Most food items, when frozen, will eventually undergo some deterioration. The U.S. Department of Agriculture recommends the following limits for these common products. Check with your store manager for details on other products.

beef and lamb roasts and steaks	8 to 12 months
veal and pork roasts	4 to 8 months
chops and cutlets	3 to 6 months
ground beef, veal or lamb and stew meats	3 to 4 months
chicken and turkey	12 months
duck and goose	6 months
fresh fish	6 to 9 months
fruits and vegetables (most)	8 to 12 months

Storage

To take advantage of the savings that can be gained through bulk shopping, you must, of course, provide proper storage facilities. A cool, dark, dry place is best for virtually all items. There's hardly a house or apartment that can't clear away a few cubic feet of space to store bulk-purchased items. If you really feel cramped for space, see the later discussion on "rummaging," by which you can gain not only added space but tax savings as well.

Convenience Foods

The experiment: Compare Aunt Jemima Frozen French Toast with French toast made from scratch. A 9-oz. box of the Aunt Jemima product contained six pieces of premade frozen French toast, at a cost of 83¢. We allocated 83¢ of raw product: milk, bread, eggs, and butter. Two teams: the fresh and the frozen. At the starting bell the fresh team began mixing the batter, dunking the bread, and placing it on the griddle. At the same time the frozen maker started inserting the frozen pieces into the toaster, two pieces at a time. We wanted to determine not only the quantity that could be made for the same amount of money but the time it took to make it.

The results: The fresh team made 12 full-sized pieces of French toast in the same time (give or take a minute) that it took for the toaster to defrost and heat six pieces of frozen product. The fresh product looked, smelled, and tasted delicious. The frozen pieces had no aroma and looked and tasted a bit like cardboard. The only drawback to the fresh side was that more clean-up had to be done, but that was well worth doing in view of the fact that there was twice as much finished product, and it was vastly more satisfying.

This was not what might be called the most scientifically controlled experiment ever conducted but it serves to illustrate very important points: Convenience can be expensive, not altogether satisfying, and not even time saving!

The extent to which you may choose to use convenience foods is a very individual matter depending on taste, your willingness to exert some of your own energy, the season of the year, and the whim of the moment. The only rule of thumb that can be proposed is to compare the "inconvenient" do-it-yourself way with the convenience-food way and determine whether the savings are worth it to you. In many instances the savings will be considerable. Examples: A 12-oz. packet of frozen Ore-Ida french fries was 69¢, or 5.8¢ per ounce. A sack of fresh potatoes was $1.89 for 10 lb., or about 1.2¢ per ounce—the frozen costing almost five times as much as the fresh per ounce. If peeling and slicing your own potatoes is not a hardship, why not take advantage of the extensive savings and enjoy the freshness as well?

As noted, the season can make a difference. A summertime purchase of fresh strawberries was 79¢ for 12 oz. The same amount of frozen strawberries cost exactly the same. Given the choice, which would you prefer? Obviously, during eight or nine months of the year fresh strawberries won't be available, so the frozen style is all you have to choose from. But when fresh products are available, compare their cost with the frozen variety, and compare the satisfaction you get from each.

Frozen vegetables may come with a conveniently packed pat of butter in the container, and the cost may be only a penny or two more than similar frozen vegetables without a pat of butter. The convenience element is that the packers have saved you the trouble of putting your own butter onto the vegetables. But that little pat of butter, at a penny or two, will actually be costing you about $5 a pound. The same goes for things like presugared cereals and a variety of other seasoned foods. If you're willing to pay the price to have the manufacturer do your buttering, your sugaring, and your seasoning for you, that's your choice. The extra pennies or nickels you spend on these products may seem invisible to you at the time you spend them, but they do mount up.

The Smart Shopper will get into the habit of using unit pricing, comparing brands with generic labels, buying bulk quantities when the best deals are available, and avoiding costly convenience foods. In addition, here are some other ways that the Smart Shopper will save money:

Coupons and Specials

Cents-off coupons are offered by both manufacturers and stores. Coupon offerings are abundant in your daily newspaper, particularly in the Wednesday and Thursday editions. Coupons may also be found in magazines, in your mail, on the market shelves, and on the products themselves. The main purpose of coupons is to motivate you to try a new product. You can determine for yourself whether the experiment is worth it. But if you don't use coupons on products that you *regularly* buy, you're throwing money away. The Smart Shopper will take perhaps an hour per week to scour the newspaper and magazine ads looking for coupons offering discounts on all products he or she commonly buys. Appropriate coupons will be clipped, sorted, and taken on the next trip to the market. The savings can be many dollars per week—an hour well spent.

The Wednesday and Thursday daily newspapers also contain the special offerings from your local markets for the coming week. These specials can be particularly attractive to the bulk buyer and may even justify driving a few extra miles to take advantage of them. If you shop during the latter part of the week, you are most likely to find the broadest selection of specially advertised items. Considering the cost of getting from one market to another, it may not pay you to buy a quart of milk here, a pound of apples there, a loaf of bread somewhere else. But if you prepare a careful shopping list containing all of your weekly needs, a careful study of the advertised specials can lead you to specific savings that might justify some extra travel.

Miscellaneous Money Savers
Shopping While Hungry

Don't. If you shop while you're hungry, you're more likely to load up your basket with nonessentials, snack foods, impulse items, and so on. Shop only after you've had a filling meal so you'll be less susceptible to wasting your shopping dollars on such items.

Shopping with a List

Carefully plan your needs in advance and write them down on a list. Stick to the list if you want to keep your budget in line. Once you've developed a habit of shopping from a list, your shopping trips will be that much more efficient in both time and money saved.

Snack Foods

Avoid them. They tend to be very costly and the nutritional value you get for your money is questionable. The following case history best illustrates this warning:

"I came home from work early one afternoon and found my children and a few of their neighborhood friends sitting around our kitchen table eating DingDongs. DingDongs are chocolate covered pastries enveloping a blob of white substance that to me looks like shaving cream, tastes like wet kleenex, and seems to have the nutritional value of soap bubbles. As I stood there and watched an entire box of DingDongs disappear before my eyes, I realized that our household went through $5 worth of DingDongs and similar snack foods per week. That's more than $250 per year! I immediately ordered an end to all DingDongs in our house. My children looked at me aghast. I didn't want to interfere with their after-school snacking, so I told my young teenaged daughters that rather than spend money on DingDongs, they could make cookies and cakes from scratch on their own. The prospect thrilled them and the next day they began their baking adventures. This not only satisfied them, but delighted them, for three or four days. Then the task of cleaning up after themselves began to get too much for them. The baking tapered off and so did the snacking. Not only did our food budget go down noticeably, but I'm sure I detected a drop in our dental bills as well."

Bend a Little

In general, supermarkets stock their highest profit margin items on the eye-level shelves. The better bargains for you—in terms of unit price and generic availability—will tend to be on the lower shelves. A little bit of bending will save you a lot of money.

Extra Bargains

Many markets will discount bread, pastries, and produce after it has been on display for a day or so. If the market doesn't advertise these items, ask your manager what he has available. If you're going to consume these products in the very near future, they can be every bit as satisfying as the fresher product, and at a distinct savings to you. Many markets also have a "thrift" shelf where slightly damaged nonconsummable items are placed. These can represent substantial savings; it's worth at least a look to see whether there are any products there that you'd otherwise buy at full price.

Know Your Local Market

Habit often finds us shopping at the same market most of the time. That's not necessarily a bad thing, but it's wise to get to know the other markets that are conveniently close to you. You might find that they offer a better price on most of the products you commonly buy. You won't know until you've spent a few shopping trips at most of them. Also, get to know the individual managers at each of the markets. Public relations is important in the supermarket (and drugstore) business. The managers are there to try to please the public, and the better they know you, the more likely they are to offer you that extra special little item: a better choice in the produce department or the meat department, a whispered tip that a certain item you're buying will be going on sale the next day, an offer to sell you an overstocked item at a discount.

The Good Habits: Clothing and Accessories

". . . That looks absolutely smashing on you. Wear it anywhere and you'll have the opposite sex enthralled."

". . . Your taste is excellent. I can tell that you're a real fashion leader."

". . . That's what absolutely everybody is wearing today. If you want to be with it, you'll buy it now before we run out of stock."

". . . As long as you're buying the slacks, you ought to get some nice things to go with it. Here's a nice matching sweater."

Vanity, thy name is clothing shopper. Young or old, male or female, few of us are immune to the flattering persuasions of the clothing salesperson. But Smart Shopper *is* immune. Smart Shopper keeps a firm grip on his or her common sense, never letting it succumb to moods, to ego, to fads, or to impulse. Smart Shopper has carefully studied his or her practical needs for clothing and accessories and is willing to take the time to shop for those items that offer the best value (appearance considered) for the money.

Personal appearance is, needless to say, very personal. Clothing is the most costly and the most visible element of your overall personal appearance. Only you can decide how you want to look or how you should look. There's little argument that the well-dressed and well-groomed person can enjoy certain advantages over the poorly groomed or slovenly dressed person. To that extent, appropriately attractive clothing and accessories can be considered an investment in one's social and business well-being.

On the other hand, excessive spending on clothing will not necessarily produce commensurate results. The overly dressed person can be looked upon by his or her peers as extravagant, excessive, or even in poor taste. Given your own individual circumstances—at school, at work, in social activities—you must find the balance that's right for you. And that balance must include both the desired appearance *and* the cost of creating that appearance. It's not the province of this book to suggest how you should look, but the following material can help you with the budget-balancing tricks of affording the look you do want to have.

Ego and Impulse

The brief quotes at the beginning of this section are samples of just a few of the tricks of the clothing trade. But long before we enter the clothing stores, our brains and our egos have been preconditioned. With the possible exception of the automobile, no product that we commonly buy is more lavishly and glamorously advertised than clothing. The advertising lets us believe that we can look like models in *Vogue* or *Gentleman's Quarterly,* and the salesperson confirms it.

Nothing can cripple a budget more quickly and more devastatingly than our vanity and our impulsive natures. You can't fit designer jeans on a nondesigner body. But we spend ourselves silly trying. True, many otherwise aggressive salespersons will sometimes be honest enough to tell you that a particular outfit makes you look like a hippopotamus. But that's the exception. The rule is that they are there to sell clothing, and they know well that nothing sells clothing more rapidly than flattery. Arm yourself accordingly: Don't act on impulse; shop around for comparable items before you make a decision.

Embellish the Simple

You can stretch your clothing dollars farther by sticking to basically simple outfits and embellishing them with attractive accessories—as opposed to buying more decorative and more costly basic units. For example, a common men's outfit—navy blue blazer and gray slacks—can take on a variety of appearances depending on the accessories. Shirt and tie, open-neck shirt, turtleneck shirt—all give the basic unit a totally different look. Similar combinations are possible with basic women's outfits. A variety of simple accessories can offer much more diversity for the money in a wardrobe than can a variety of basic outfits.

Where the Good Buys Are

Check the advertising carefully in your local newspapers and go where the good buys are. Don't be embarrassed to shop at discount stores or through catalogues (Sears, Wards, etc.). You could save considerably through such outlets, particularly on such items as underclothing, pajamas, socks, stockings and the like.

Factory outlets can be an excellent source for buying stylish clothing at considerable discounts. Such outlets commonly buy overstocks from other stores and overruns from clothing manufacturers. You won't find the personalized attention that you do in specialty shops or boutiques, and you may not be able to open a charge account, but the savings may be well worth giving up those costly frills.

Thrift shops and "next-to-new" stores offer exceptional bargains if you're willing to spend the time rummaging around. And no one will know where you bought it if you don't tell.

Department stores and specialty shops often have special sales for their charge account customers. If what they have to offer meets your clothing needs at the time, good bargains can be had.

Miscellaneous Money Savers

A Sense of Timing

Use the calendar to your advantage. Buying clothing and accessories off season can represent substantial savings. Buy winter clothes in the spring and summer (when they are usually on sale); buy summer clothes in the fall and winter. You won't have an abundant choice of fashions or styles, but you can pick up bargains that will be well worth your shopping trip.

Seasonal sales are common with most large clothing and department stores. Major sales are usually after Christmas and after Easter. Shop early for the best selection.

Consider Seconds

Seconds (or irregulars) are items of clothing with minor flaws in them. The price of a second can be well below the price of an otherwise identical item. And the flaw itself may be so minor that no one would really notice it; or you could simply pass it off as a minor snag. With a lot of casual clothing, a minor flaw is not uncommon anyway. Factory outlets and discount stores are good sources of seconds.

Cleanability and Durability

How readily soiled will a particular garment get, and what will be required to clean it? Is it handwashable or must it be drycleaned? The care labels on the garments will indicate the recommended cleaning techniques. The durability and cleanability—or lack thereof—represent an important element of your overall clothing investment. The cost of cleaning your clothing or replacing worn clothing is also directly related to your personal habits and the care you take to protect and preserve your clothing.

Beware of Counterfeits

It has become very fashionable to wear clothing and carry accessories that have other people's names and initials on them. Presumably this is a sign of affluence, prestige, good taste, or an inability to resist a fad. There seem to be no other reasons why one person would want to wear the clothing that carries the initials of another person. But people do, and they are willing to pay heavily for the privilege. This fact has not been overlooked by manufacturers who are happy to create counterfeit versions of the designer-initialed items, but those versions may be woefully inferior to the genuine articles. So beware: If you find yourself obsessed with an opportunity to buy "genuine" Pucci-Gucci at a price that seems too good to be true, don't be disappointed if it falls into shreds after the first or second wearing. The counterfeit designer-clothing industry has reached multimillion dollar proportions. You're most likely to get stung buying such articles at swap meets, from street vendors, or from stores that seem to open one week and close the next.

Know Store Policies

If you buy a garment and take it home, will you be able to return it if it doesn't suit you? Will the store refund your cash, or will they simply allow you a credit against other purchases? Or will they refuse to take it back altogether? If the store does allow return privileges, how long does that privilege last? Many sales items might be purchased on an as-is basis, thereby preventing you from getting any kind of refund or exchange privilege. You must know this before you buy if you want to avoid disappointment. In any case you can safely assume that if you want to return any items, you must bring in your sales receipt in order to get credit or refund.

Buying for Children

As a general rule most children will outgrow most clothing before it has had a chance to deteriorate. Except for one or two "dress" outfits, it can be false economy to buy top-of-the-line clothing for children. Look to the same factory outlets, discount stores, and special sales for the best bargains on children's clothing.

Rummaging

In the earlier discussion on buying in bulk, we noted that you might be hard-pressed for space to store those products. You can kill two birds with one stone by having an annual rummaging through your closets and dressers to get rid of excess, unusable, or unneeded clothing and other personal items. If you don't know a worthy hand-me-down recipient, you can donate your used clothing to any one of a number of thrift shops or charities in your community. If you itemize your income-tax deductions, you can claim a deduction for the donated clothing. Itemize everything specifically and make sure you get a signed receipt for the clothing from the thrift shop. You create added storage space, you save a few tax dollars, and you provide inexpensive clothing for someone in need—a good project all the way around.

The Good Habits: Major Home Furnishings

Your overall budget can be drastically affected by your need—or lack thereof—of major home furnishings: furniture, carpeting, appliances. Your budgetary capacity to buy furnishings may, in turn, influence the type of dwelling you choose to live in: large versus small, furnished versus unfurnished, shared versus alone. And, in weighing your housing/furnishing considerations, you must also take into account the following:

☐ How long will you be living in the given dwelling? If you're settling in for the foreseeable future, a bigger investment in furnishings is more easily justified. If you'll be living in the particular dwelling for only a year or so, it might not make sense to burden yourself with major expenses for furnishings. Realistically determine whether your job, your marital status, or the growth of your family will dictate a likely move in the near future.

☐ Are there youngsters (or pets) on the scene? Children (and dogs and cats) can wreak havoc on furnishings. A jelly spot on a sofa, a urine stain on a carpet, plus assorted tears, smudges, scratches, and other blemishes have to be expected when little ones are about. The family with young children and active pets must evaluate how their furnishings will withstand the onslaught. If you buy "fancy" and expensive furnishings while the children are very young, you may be faced with expensive cleaning and repair costs, or the furnishings could look a shambles by the time the children are grown and more responsible. It might make more sense to buy more modest furnishings while the children are young, then dispose of them later in favor of the more elaborate items.

☐ Will your tastes change? Major furnishings—particularly furniture and carpeting—are available in a wide variety of styles, ranging from conservative to what some people would call outlandish. Tastes do change, make no mistake about it. Will your selections today still please you one year, five years, ten years from now? There's no way of knowing for certain, of course, but it can be foolhardy to be overindulgent in choosing highly personalized furnishings, with respect to either design or color.

For example: Today you might be very excited about strong pastel colors in your upholstery and carpeting, accented by chrome and glass tables and accessories. It might indeed look beautiful. But say you weary of it within a few years. Or say your marriage terminates and King Solomon's wisdom can't help you and your ex divide up the furnishings. Or you move to a new location where the furniture absolutely clashes with your new surroundings. The market for used furniture is rather sparse, and the more highly personalized the individual items, the fewer buyers there may be for them. You may then look back on your original choice as money wasted, money that could tally many hundreds, if not thousands, of dollars.

You might be better off choosing a more conservative design and color range for the major items and accenting those pieces with relatively inexpensive accessories—throw pillows, lamp shades, area rugs, and the like. Those can be changed easily and inexpensively and can give your premises a very different look at a much lower cost than a whole new truck full of furnishings.

□ What is the focal point of your social life? Will you be doing a lot of entertaining at home, for either personal or business purposes? Or do you prefer to go out a lot for your social life? It may not be possible to afford both fine home furnishings and a lavish outside entertainment budget. Many people don't realize this until after they've invested heavily in furnishings and then find themselves in a budgetary crisis. Examine your preferences before you make your furnishing decisions. If you'll be spending a major portion of your social life at home, you can more easily justify more expense for the furnishings. If you'll be doing business entertaining at home, the expense may even prove to be a worthwhile investment. On the other hand, however, if you're not a homebody, you should structure your budget more to suit your "going out" needs and less to satisfy the at-home needs.

This book isn't intended to influence your taste, your sense of comfort, or your desire for convenience in home furnishings. Those are matters that you must determine for yourself. But the following guidelines may be helpful in getting you the best value for the home furnishing dollars you do decide to spend.

Furniture

Shop with great care! There can be vast differences in quality—both construction and upholstery—and you can't tell quality just by looking at the furniture. Shop at a number of stores before you make any decision and at each store ask the salesperson to go over the following points with you.

□ *Wood furniture* (tables, cabinets, dressers, etc.). How are the parts joined together? Is the piece all wood or does it utilize less expensive fiber board in unseen places? Does it stand firm and solid? Do moving parts (doors, drawers) fit and operate properly? What is the quality of the hardware (hinges, knobs, etc.) and how is it attached to the wood? What is the quality of the finish and any decorative elements? Bear in mind that for tables, a synthetic surface (such as formica) can wear more durably than wood.

☐ *Upholstered furniture* (sofas, chairs, matching pillows and cushions). Pay attention to the construction elements as with the wood furniture noted above. How is the fabric anchored to the piece? Do the patterns and colors match properly? How durable is the fabric? What are the sun- and soil-resistance factors of the fabric? What is the stuffing made of and how long will it hold its shape? How does it sit? Test it for firmness, comfort, clothing against fabric. The more carefully you shop, the more readily you'll see that better quality costs more. Only you can decide whether the better quality is affordable and worth the price for you.

☐ *Bargain items*. If you're handy with a paintbrush, you might find that unfinished wood furniture offers you better value for your money. Secondhand furniture in good condition and "seconds" (new furniture with minor flaws) can also be feasible alternatives in furnishing your dwelling.

☐ *Guarantees*. What protection do you have if something goes wrong: a leg comes unglued, fabric comes detached from the frame, cabinet door hinges fall off? Better furniture dealers will usually guarantee to fix or replace defects not due to normal wear and tear. Determine how long such a guarantee will last. "Cash and carry" stores may offer little or no guarantee; you may be totally on your own if something goes wrong. To erase any possible doubts, ask about the guarantee before you decide on your purchase, and then have it put in writing.

☐ *Delivery and setup charges*. Some furniture dealers will deliver and set up your furniture at no additional charge. (The cost of doing so is no doubt built into the price of the furniture.) Other dealers may charge. Still other dealers, such as the warehouse and factory outlets, may not offer delivery service at all. Depending on where you live and how easy the access is to the rooms into which the furniture will be placed, delivery and setup charges can add considerably to your overall cost. Shop these charges as carefully as you do the furnishings themselves. Naturally, if you have access to a truck and some strong-armed helpers, you can save considerably by arranging for your own delivery and setup.

☐ *Shopping tips*. Don't guess on color or size. If you guess wrong, you could end up with an expensive purchase that doesn't suit you. If you are buying pieces to go into an already partially furnished room, take color samples of the carpet, wallpaper, paint, and/or drapes with you to furniture stores. If that's not convenient, ask the furniture dealer whether he can give you a color swatch of the pieces you are interested in to take home and match against the existing room. Take careful measurements before you shop. Draw your room to scale on graph paper and test out different arrangements. Most large stationery stores sell plastic cut-out templates showing various sizes and types of furniture. This can be a handy tool to help you determine what pieces of what size can go where in any given room. If you are considering buying "movable" furniture—convertible sofas, reclining chairs, expanding tables—make sure you measure properly for both the basic and expanded versions of each piece.

☐ *Take your time.* Acting on impulse can be dangerous, as it is with any kind of shopping. Visit many stores looking for those whose reputation and inventory suit your budget. Scour the ads for sales: home furnishings are very sale-prone, and the best buys are available to those who are patient and willing to hunt.

Bedding (Springs, Mattresses)

The general consensus of consumer testers is that quality pays in bedding. A well-constructed box spring and mattress can last 20 years, perhaps even longer, without deterioration in support or comfort. An off-brand product may cost 20 to 30 percent less than a major brand, but it may last only half as long. Evaluate the choice accordingly. Major manufacturers and dealers often offer sales on bedspring and mattress items that are similarly constructed but do not have matching covers. Since you see the mismatched covers only when you take off the sheets, there's no reason not to take advantage of these special buys when available.

Carpeting and Other Flooring

The possibilities—and the price ranges—are limitless. Area rugs, bare polished wood, linoleum, vinyl tile, brick, fake brick, stone, fake stone, ceramic tile, adobe tile, and carpeting ranging from synthetic grass to luxuriously thick wool represent but a sampling of the possible types of flooring that you can obtain.

Personal taste, budget, durability and cleanability must all be taken into account when choosing flooring. Of particular concern in making a decision on flooring is the length of time you'll be in the premises. Most types of flooring, once installed, can't be taken with you from place to place. The obvious exception is area rugs. Carpeting, of course, can be removed, but it's usually difficult to install it in a new dwelling: wear patterns from the original dwelling will be quite evident and perhaps very unsatisfactory. Further, the cost of lifting, moving, recutting, and reinstalling old carpeting in a new dwelling can come close to the cost of brand new carpeting.

All carpeting and other flooring materials should be shopped for as carefully as furniture. Review all the tips and precautions stated above with respect to furniture. In addition, note that medium shades tend to be the best with respect to not showing soil and dirt; that patterned and multicolored carpeting tends not to show wear patterns as readily as solid-color carpeting; and that different types of carpet fabric have distinctly different levels of soil resistance and cleanability. Check all of these items with the salesperson as you shop. In addition to pricing the carpeting, determine the cost of padding and installation. And check the reputation of the dealer with the Better Business Bureau for reliability and willingness to adjust complaints.

Appliances

What you *need,* what you would *like,* and what you can *afford* are all up to you. Before you make buying decisions, bear in mind the following:

Installation   Will the items (particularly such things as dishwashers, disposals, trash compactors) fit into your existing space? Or will extensive work have to be done to accommodate them? If so, how much will that added work cost? Will any special installation be necessary for any given appliance? An electric clothes dryer may require special wiring. A gas clothes dryer will require a gas line. Both will require a venting outlet. Will you need special drain capacity for a dishwasher or disposal? Is your existing wiring suitable to carry window air-conditioning units? Central air conditioning? A refrigerator with a built-in ice cube maker will require a water line to the site. A gas water heater must be properly vented, as must a kitchen exhaust fan. Determine these special requirements from the dealer, and get cost estimates of the special requirements before you make your buying decision.

Service and Warranties   On major items (clothes washers and dryers, dishwashers, freezers, refrigerators, and room air conditioners) a one-year warranty for parts and labor is common. Additionally, the sealed systems in such units may have warranties for as long as five years. Examine the written warranty before you make a buying decision. Don't be content with just the salesperson's representations. Determine whether the dealer offers warranty service or it must be obtained from another source. Determine the reliability of the service source. A check with the local Better Business Bureau is advisable.

With smaller units (television sets, food processors, radios and phonographs, video recorders) much shorter warranties are common. With most television sets, the warranty for labor is 90 days, but some may be as long as one year. The warranty on the picture tube and other parts will commonly be one to two years. The source of service is again very important. Will the dealer or a nearby service center be able to correct warranty problems? Or will servicing involve time, money, and inconvenience for you?

For example, a comparison of two similar brand name food processors revealed the following: Though the warranties were identical, one brand had to be sent to a distant state for any warranty servicing, whereas the other could be repaired locally. Should a breakdown have occurred in the first unit, the cost of packing and shipping it, plus the return postage that was required under the warranty, represented more than 10 percent of the original purchase price of the unit. The latter unit could be serviced simply by delivering it to the original dealer, who in turn would arrange to have it sent to and picked up from the local service center.

With most such appliances, you can obtain a service contract to take care of problems once the original warranty has expired. Such service contracts may be worthwhile with more temperamental items that have short initial warranties, such as color television sets; but products such as refrigerators and freezers are constructed to last decades, and any major defects will usually show up during the initial warranty period. For products such as these, extended service contracts may not be worth the money. For items between the durability of a refrigerator or freezer and of the more defect-prone color television set, you could almost flip a coin as to the value of an extended service contract. The cost of an extended service contract for an automatic clothes washer or dryer or a dishwasher or room air conditioner may be less than the cost of one service call. If you're the type that's subject to having mechanical things break down all around you, you might feel more comfortable with the service contract. If you have a knack for being able to lubricate moving parts and the like, you might find a service contract an unnecessary expense.

Periodic servicing of some major appliances is definitely worthwhile if for no other reason than preventive maintenance. Furnaces and central air conditioning units should be checked and lubricated periodically, filters should be changed, and the entire systems should be checked for leaks. An annual checkup prior to the heating and cooling seasons, respectively, can be far less expensive, not to mention less inconvenient, than repairing a major breakdown.

Better to Rent?

At the start of this section we noted that individuals planning on a short stay in a given dwelling should exercise restraint before making major investments in furnishings. Rental of many furnishings could be a good alternative. In most cities there are furniture and appliance rental outlets that can provide a wide variety of style and designs. With many such outlets, a major portion of the rental you pay can be applied toward a purchase should you decide to keep a given item. Exchanges are often permitted as well; should you tire of a particular color, style, or design, you can exchange it for a different one with perhaps a slight adjustment in price. One of the main advantages of renting is that when you do move, you don't have to pay to move the furnishings with you. The rental outlet will come and pick them up and you're free to go without having to worry about a costly moving bill.

Paying for It

If you haven't yet established credit or if you've had credit problems, you'll likely be attracted to furnishing stores which offer ''easy credit terms . . . no down payments . . . past credit history no problem. . . .'' What appears in the advertising to be "easy credit" may indeed be costly. If a merchant or a lender is taking a risk on you, you will be charged accordingly.

Home furnishings represent major budget items and credit is commonly used to obtain them. Follow the guidelines set forth in chapter 14, Credit and Borrowing, and shop for the best terms available. Consider what financing terms a dealer might offer and compare those terms with banks and savings and loans in your area. For buyers with no credit or with credit problems, it might be far cheaper to obtain a co-signer for credit purchases rather than get involved with high-interest-rate lenders that ply their wares at the "easy credit" emporiums.

Information Sources

Consumer Reports magazine is the best single source for learning about and comparing home furnishing items. Visit your local library and review the issues for the last year or two, or go back as far as you have to to find valid comparisons of the item you're planning on buying. Kiplinger's *Changing Times* magazine is another excellent source, though its ratings are not usually as extensive as those in *Consumer Reports.*

With most appliances you can obtain specification sheets from the manufacturer or dealer. These give you abundant information about each product and you should read and compare different brands before you make your decision. Your best source of information is yourself: the more time you're willing to take to compare, to study, and to shop, the better equipped you'll be to make the right buying decision.

Personal Action Checklist
Unit Pricing: Prove It to Yourself

See for yourself what savings can be realized by taking advantage of unit pricing. While you're at it, compare brand name products with private label or generic products. Following are commonly purchased items at markets and drugstores. Add in any other items you often buy. Take a pocket calculator with you to make the exercise simpler.

| | Brand Name | | Private Label | |
| | Price per Ounce | | Price per Ounce | |
Item	Smallest Container	Largest Container	Smallest Container	Largest Container
☐ Mustard	___	___	___	___
☐ Ketchup	___	___	___	___
☐ Mayonnaise	___	___	___	___
☐ Grape jelly	___	___	___	___
☐ Peanut butter	___	___	___	___
☐ Vegetable oil	___	___	___	___
☐ White vinegar	___	___	___	___
☐ Tomato juice	___	___	___	___
☐ Cornflakes	___	___	___	___
☐ Milk	___	___	___	___
☐ Cottage cheese	___	___	___	___
☐ Sliced cheeses	___	___	___	___
☐ Crackers (saltines)	___	___	___	___
☐ Canned peas	___	___	___	___
☐ Canned pears	___	___	___	___
☐ Gelatin	___	___	___	___
☐ Sugar	___	___	___	___
☐ Flour	___	___	___	___
☐ Salt	___	___	___	___
☐ Aspirin	___	___	___	___
☐ Cotton balls	___	___	___	___
☐ Witch Hazel	___	___	___	___
☐ Milk of magnesia	___	___	___	___
☐ Antacid tablets	___	___	___	___
☐ Toothpaste	___	___	___	___
☐ Vitamin E	___	___	___	___
☐ Disposable diapers	___	___	___	___
☐ Other ___	___	___	___	___
___	___	___	___	___
___	___	___	___	___
___	___	___	___	___

Consumer Beware
Beating the High Price of Water

Would you pay four dollars for a gallon of ordinary water?

Of course not, you say, but you may have already done so many times.

Example: the local supermarket offers a six-pack of canned iced tea for $2.29. Six cans of 12 ounces each totals 72 ounces. At $2.29 (not including any sales taxes), that works out to 3.18¢ per ounce. There are 128 ounces in a gallon, so at 3.18¢ per ounce you are effectively paying $4.07 per gallon for canned iced tea. But all you are really getting is ordinary water, with a few cents worth of tea, or tea flavoring, added to it.

Likewise with a variety of juice products, which come either in cans or in concentrate form. How many quarts of Hawaiian Punch can you make from a jar of the concentrated product? Compare the cost of doing so with buying regular canned Hawaiian Punch. What other products offer you the same choice? If you've been buying the canned instead of the concentrate, how much extra have you been paying to buy water and haul it home from the market?

Paying $4.00 per gallon for ordinary water is, obviously, absurd. It's bad enough to pay $1.50 or so for a gallon of gasoline—but at least that product is capable of propelling a 4000-pound vehicle 20 to 30 miles at speeds in excess of 50 miles per hour. What will the water do by comparison?

It won't do to say that nobody is foolish enough to spend $4.00 for a gallon of water. The product wouldn't be on the market shelves if nobody bought it.

Calculate how much money you might have paid in the last year to buy water at the supermarket. From now on, be a Smart Shopper. Buy the concentrates and use your own tap water. Think of what can be saved, in both money and energy.

5 | Frauds and Swindles and How to Avoid Them

"There's a sucker born every minute," said P. T. Barnum decades ago. And the statement is as true today as it was in his time. Despite all of the consumer-education material available today, there is still an abundance of shady, misleading, and illegal business going on in every community every day. There are schemes that can relieve the unwary and the greedy from a few dollars, or from many thousands of dollars. And more often than not, the swindlers get away with their schemes and skip from one city to the next, laughing at their victims all the way. Chances are good that someday you may be a victim of consumer fraud. But you'll have a strong defense against that possibility if you heed the techniques in this chapter:

☐ Spotting and avoiding the deals that sound too good to be true; that promise something for nothing; that promise instant wealth, health, or success.
☐ Knowing whom to inform if you discover a fraudulent scheme in the works.
☐ Knowing where you can get help if you find yourself the apparent victim of a swindle.

Barnum Was Right

There are no reliable statistics on the extent of consumer fraud in America today. Neither victims nor swindlers tend to report very much about their transactions. But the Council of Better Business Bureaus has estimated that in one area alone—home improvements—more than $1 billion a year is taken in by swindlers!

Why are there so many victims, and why isn't something more being done about it? No one is immune from the wiles of the con man or the shady business operator. Young and old, rich and poor, all succumb to one scheme or another at one time or another. Because most business activities are indeed legitimate, we tend to trust people. We believe what we're told. We believe what we read in advertisements. And despite the ever-constant rule of *caveat emptor*—buyer beware—we are not wary enough. If we are led to believe that we are getting something that sounds too good to be true, or something for nothing, we tend to believe it. And we part with our money without even asking questions. Sometimes it's nothing more than our own greed that does us in. Sometimes we are simply gullible—believing all sorts of preposterous statements. And sometimes a salesperson wins our confidence so totally that we act as if we're hypnotized when we write out our checks.

Consumer fraud will never go away. Indeed it may never even diminish. It's not a violent crime. And in many instances it's not even that serious in terms of an individual's financial loss. Thus the citizens of our various cities and states may not be willing to pay the taxes needed to hire adequate police enforcement bureaus to deal with the problem. Further, according to a presidential crime commission study, over 90 percent of the victims of consumer fraud never do anything about it. The majority of the victims are not even *aware* of the fact that they've been defrauded until it's far too late to do anything about it. Those that may be aware of having been defrauded are reluctant to report it to the police, either out of embarrassment or out of belief that the police won't do anything about it. And that's often the case—not because the police don't want to, but because their available manpower is allocated toward more serious matters. Thus, with few exceptions, promoters and swindlers run free throughout our society, taking advantage of our weaknesses, our greed, our gullibility, and our basically trusting nature.

This chapter will explore some of the more common types of consumer fraud. Every type of fraud has endless variations, so don't for a moment think that the schemes described here are the only ones that you might fall victim to. In any kind of transaction you must be aware of certain *basic patterns,* which can indicate that you might be involved in a fraudulent setup. The basic patterns appear in the following situations:

☐ You're led to believe that you're getting something for nothing or are offered a deal that sounds too good to be true. There is no such thing as "something for nothing" and any deal that sounds too good to be true is usually neither good nor true.

☐ A salesperson (or even a stranger) tries to sell you something with such vigor or with such cleverness that you find yourself on the verge of spending money for something that you might otherwise have ignored. In such cases you must immediately ask yourself, "If this thing he's selling is so good and so beneficial, then why is he willing to sell it to me? Could it be that he'll get more benefit out of it by selling it to me than I can by buying it from him?"

☐ The advertising or the salesperson tells you that you can obtain something that is not otherwise available through normal channels. This may be a miracle cure for some ailment, a chance to get rich quick, or a chance to become famous. These offerings will do nothing but deplete your bank account.

One final warning before we embark on tales of the wild and wooly world of consumer fraud: While most advertising media (newspapers, magazines, radio, television) attempt to police the advertising that they present to the public, there are definitely flaws in the system. Some policing efforts are not adequate, and misleading advertising can slip past the censor's scrutiny. Further, misleading advertising that appears in an otherwise legitimate medium takes on an aura of legitimacy. "It must be so if it appeared in the daily paper. If it weren't legitimate, the newspaper wouldn't run it." Being constantly alert is no guarantee that you'll never get stung. But *lack* of constant alertness will almost guarantee that you *will* get stung.

Bait and Switch

This is probably the oldest game of all. The bait, very simply, is an extremely attractive enticement to lure you into a store in a buying frame of mind. The switch occurs when you are in the store ready, willing and able to buy. The clever salesperson diverts you from the bait item and switches you to another item that offers him a higher profit. The switch can happen in many ways, and even otherwise legitimate merchants often find themselves slipping into this form of deception.

For instance, you're sitting up with insomnia watching the late late show on television, and here comes good old Gideon Gotcha "out here in automobile land ready to sell you folks some real zing-doozies of some beautiful cars of all makes and models. Here's a 1980 Cadillac with only 1600 miles on it, in perfect condition, with brand new radial-ply-biased-steel-double-whitewall-hand-autographed tires, and a built-in Hammond organ in the back seat! And how much would you expect to pay for this beautiful car? About $15,000? Maybe at some other place, but not at Gideon Gotcha's! Would you believe only $3995!"

Right then you rush down to Gideon Gotcha's where, of course, you find that the lot is closed for the night. You camp on the doorstep until morning and when Gideon comes in to open up the shop, you hand him an envelope full of cash and tell him you want to buy the $3995 Cadillac you saw on television just a few hours ago.

"Oh, I'm really sorry," says Gideon, "but we sold it during the night. I got a call at my house from an old customer out in the country who insisted on having that very car, and he sent a courier at 4:00 A.M. with the cash. But now that you're here, maybe I can interest you in a brand new Caddie whose classic beauty will withstand the years better than the Mona Lisa. And since you came down so early in the morning, I could make a special deal for you . . ."

Or you see an ad in the newspaper for a wholesale meat firm offering an entire side of beef, cut and trimmed to your specifications, for only 79¢ a pound. A fantastic deal! You rush to the place and the butcher is happy to show you the particular side of beef that they had advertised.

"Of course," he points out, "it's got some funny green spots here and there, but maybe we can cut them out. Anyway, if you boil the meat for

15 or 20 minutes, it should kill any contamination that may have gone deeper. Now, if you don't like that particular side, we've got some regular sides over here in the cooler for $3.99 a pound."

Bait and switch tactics are outlawed by the Federal Trade Commission as well as by many state and local laws. But they still occur in abundance, and your best protection against getting involved is your own careful scrutiny of the advertising, your willingness to shop around for similar products, and your ability to resist the temptation in the first place.

Distinction should be made between bait and switch on the one hand and "loss leaders" on the other. A loss leader is a product offered by a merchant at a lower-than-normal price to entice you into the store where, it's hoped, you'll buy other merchandise as well as the loss leader. Supermarkets and discount stores use loss leaders all the time, and there's nothing wrong with this practice if you are getting the goods as represented and not a cheap replacement.

Where loss-leader advertising is employed, legitimate merchants will note in their advertising any catches in their offering, such as a limited supply, or will make clear that the offer is good only at certain stores or at certain hours. The Federal Trade Commission says that if a loss leader or other kind of promotional product is offered, the merchant is expected to have a sufficient amount on hand to meet what he reasonably expects to be the demand. Many merchants, realizing the value of pleasing their customers, will offer rainchecks if they run out of the supply of a loss leader. It might be worth inquiring of the merchant whether rainchecks will be given out should you get to the store and find that the loss-leader items are sold out.

If you detect a bait and switch operation in action in your community, alert the newspaper (or radio or TV station) where the advertising was placed. You may also want to notify the local Better Business Bureau and the police department. Very likely, nothing much will be done to the merchant who employed these tactics, but he'll be warned, and he may even promise not to do it again. Until next time.

Mail-order Madness

In terms of both dollar volume and number of incidents, the U.S. Mail probably is the single biggest carrier of fraudulent activity. Although many billions of dollars worth of perfectly satisfactory goods are sold through the mail each year, the level of abuse also runs very high. Mail-order swindlers owe their success, not just to the greed and gullibility of victims, but also to the fact that the fraud inspection division of the U.S. Post Office is woefully understaffed. A false or misleading advertisement can cover the country for many months before the postal inspectors are able to gather enough evidence to put a stop to it. In the meantime, the promoters will have made their fortune and disappeared, only to reappear shortly thereafter using a different name and selling a slightly different product. And the chase begins again, with the promoters always the winners.

For purposes of this discussion, mail-order can consist of either an advertisement seen in print or broadcast form, or an advertisement that comes to you in the mail. Either way you are dealing with unknown people, probably in a different city; and if something goes wrong, you're not as capable of getting it corrected as simply as if you were dealing with a local merchant. Many mail-order problems, as opposed to fraud, are simply the result of the wrong product being shipped or a defective product being shipped. If you're dealing with legitimate mail-order purveyors, those problems should be fairly easily correctable.

But if you find yourself in the hands of a mail-order swindler, it is safe to assume that there's virtually no chance of your ever getting satisfaction or your money back.

Following is a brief sampling of mail-order swindles, based on actual experience: To determine how cleverly the promoters toy with the minds and bank accounts of potential victims, I became an intentional victim of a number of offerings. The results should speak for themselves.

Vanity Rackets

The price of an ego trip can be high indeed. The vanity rackets prey on the common desire in so many people to be recognized. Ads offer to publish your book, your song, your poem, even your baby's picture in a directory sent to television producers.

Anyone who has ever tried to have a song or a book published through normal channels knows how frustrating it can be: rejection slips pour in, and it seems as though there's no way ever to achieve success. How wondrous it is, then, when you see an ad by a publisher soliciting your work. "Authors wanted." "Songwriters wanted." Technically the ads may not be illegal—they promise nothing specifically, but the high hopes of the victim-to-be lead him to believe that fame and fortune are just around the corner.

In the legitimate publishing world, most books and songs are created by established artists under contract to the publisher. In those rare instances when a publisher will acquire your work, he will pay you for the rights to publish.

In the vanity publishing world, the publishers will publish virtually anything, provided you pay them enough money. They may actually deliver printed copies of your book manuscript or produce recordings of your song, but the veiled promises of fame and fortune will never materialize. You will have paid a high price to have your ego massaged.

Do vanity publishers really seek quality? Or will they publish anything that comes in attached to a big enough check? To seek an answer to this question, I wrote an intentionally atrocious song and sent it off to three different vanity music publishers. If they were looking for any kind of quality, they would have rejected my lyrics instantly. They were as follows:

ETHEL IS MY ONLY LOVE

(sing slowly)

Oh oh oh oh Ethel
Ethel Ethel will you be my blessing
Cuz when I look at you and sigh,
It makes me feel high. Oh me oh my.
It seems like only yesterday that we were in high school together.
I can't believe how old we are now, forever.
Oh oh oh oh Ethel
I feel just lousy without you
You are my only love—not Rita anymore.
Seriously, I mean it.
Oh oh Ethel. Yeah yeah yeah.

This drivel was accepted, not once, not twice, but all three times by the vanity publishers. A sampling of some of the literature they sent me:

Dear Mr. Rosefsky:
We have good news for you! Your song has been rated #5 on our top 30 evaluation chart. We sincerely believe that your song poem, with the proper servicing, has the potential for a hit song. We have already contacted nearby publishers, and the response to it was positive. Publishers acceptance seems assured. If you have as much faith in your song as we have, you will want to take advantage of our offer.

Each of the three acceptances requested that I send in approximately $80 to $90 for "servicing" of the song. I inquired what might follow that initial servicing and was told that the next step would be to pay them $200 to $300 for complete scoring or orchestration. Following that, the sky was the limit. I could pay for as many records to be pressed as I wished to, and they would distribute them and I would receive royalties. Legitimate music publishers assured me that the normal channels of distribution were so clogged with the outpouring from legitimate producers that a product from a vanity publisher stood virtually no chance of even having the envelope opened, let alone being played on a radio station or distributed to record stores.

Tabloid newspapers found in supermarkets are perhaps the primary source of potentially fraudulent advertising. It was in one of those publications that I found a small classified ad offering $300 for my baby's picture. On inquiring, I learned that if the baby picture was acceptable, it would be published in a magazine that was distributed to movie and television producers who might be looking for child talent. I sent in a picture of my 30-year-old cousin, Herbie, who at the time weighed well in excess of 200 pounds. The photo was taken in the midst of an attack of indigestion. The movie magazine accepted the picture for publication provided I send them $12.95. Responsible people in the motion picture and television industries assured me that they had never heard of the magazine nor would they ever hire talent through such a publication. Yet it's likely that many thousands of checks for $12.95 each were sent to this publication by parents eager to have their children achieve fame and fortune.

Get-Rich-Quick Schemes

How far wrong can you go? You send away $10 or $15 for a book that promises to make you rich almost overnight. And if you don't like it, they promise to send you your money back. These types of ads abound because it's difficult to prove them illegal. You will indeed receive a book. Judging from all those I've seen, it will be a cheaply produced paperback, worth perhaps 50¢, which will attempt to motivate you to think great thoughts, and then instruct you in the ways of becoming rich: Write a similar book of your own, take out full-page ads in newspapers and magazines, and let people send *you* money. You'll also get your name on dozens of other mailing lists, one of which is likely to hit you for big money in the future.

Other types of get-rich-quick schemes are nothing more than blatant chain letters. On inquiring into such ads, you'll receive a letter instructing you to send $30 to a name at the top of an enclosed list. You're then to duplicate this letter five times and put your own name at the bottom of the list. Within weeks, the promoters promise, thousands of people all over the country will be sending you $30. Chain letters, under whatever guise, are illegal: They violate federal postal laws and most state postal laws. They proliferate faster than postal authorities can eliminate them. Not only do such schemes never produce money for you, but they could involve you in a federal lawsuit.

Work-at-home Schemes

These are more modest versions of the get-rich-quick promotions. They don't promise instant riches, merely a way to supplement your income by working at home in your spare time. They appeal to people who can least afford to lose money—the elderly, the invalid, the poor. Some of these schemes are nothing more than chain letters as described above. Other formats include:

Addressing Envelopes   You send $20 or so to the promoter and receive a kit instructing you how to address envelopes. You might even receive a sampling of blank envelopes to practice on. You also receive instructions as to how to approach local businesses to sell them your services as an envelope addresser. If you're clever enough and energetic enough, you may be able to acquire some business in this manner. But the fact is you are competing with the business's existing secretarial staff and with professional mailing houses that can turn out thousands of addressed envelopes in the time it would take you to do a few dozen.

Handicraft Kits   For your $10 or $20 you'll receive a kit of materials with instructions on how to turn them into baby booties, key chains, and the like. The promise is that once you've made the finished product, the company will buy it back from you in finished form at a profit to you. You make the seemingly simple product, send it back to the company, only to be told that it's not up to their standards. They're very sorry, they'll say, but perhaps you'd like to try again by ordering another kit.

The postal fraud authorities and the Council of Better Business Bureaus agree: They have never seen a work-at-home scheme that worked, except for the promoters.

Quackery

Lose weight . . . cure baldness . . . look younger . . . live longer . . . straighten kinky hair . . . curl straight hair . . . increase your bust line . . . grow taller . . . improve your sex life.

Shades of Snake Oil Sam, who sold caramel-flavored alcohol to the gullible from his travelling sideshow wagon.

Example: The ad told me that I could grow taller. Cost: $15 with a money-back guarantee if I wasn't satisfied. How far wrong could I go? For my money I received a single sheet of paper with a program of exercises entitled "Erecto-Dynamics." I was instructed to do these simple calisthenics for at least 20 minutes every day for a full year. But most important to the growing taller program was that I should stand up straighter. As for the money-back guarantee, it was contingent upon my having my height verified by a doctor before the start of the year program and at the end. Needless to say, the expense of having a doctor verify my height would be more than the money I'd get back from the promoter.

This type of mail-order business particularly concerns the postal fraud authorities, for, as they point out, not only can you lose money, but your health can be endangered by some of the devices sold. In some cases, people will fail to seek proper medical attention, relying instead on the pufferies of Snake Oil Sam's greatgrandchildren. If your condition can't be helped by a doctor, a physical therapist, or a program of exercise under the guidance of a coach, you certainly won't be helped by these mail-order offerings.

Frauds on the Street

When you respond to an advertisement, you have at least a few moments to think about the wisdom of doing so. But when you're confronted by a stranger on the street, the surprise element alone can often be enough to embroil you in a money-losing proposition.

The Pigeon Drop

This classic old scheme has dozens of variations. In a typical operation, an elderly person will be approached by a stranger in a shopping center or on a street corner. The stranger will chat with the victim for a few minutes to win his or her friendship and confidence. Then the stranger will announce that he or she has just found a wallet on a nearby bench, and the wallet contains a lot of money but no identification.

The stranger will suggest that the law of "finders keepers" prevails in such cases and will offer to split the finding with the newfound friend, the victim. At this point the victim is so taken in by the con man's friendship and generosity that the victim will do almost anything the con man advises. The con man will then quickly suggest that before they split the loot, they should double-check the legality with a lawyer, and that the victim, in order to show good faith, should put up an equal amount of cash and let the lawyer hold it while a decision is made as to who is entitled to the money.

At this point it sounds totally ludicrous that the victims would put up the cash, but they do time and time again—and it's often thousands of dollars that are involved. As soon as the victim delivers the cash, the whole package is left with the con man's "lawyer," who promptly disappears. The victim's money? Gone in a flash. Why elderly people? They tend to be more easily won over by the confidence game, they're more likely to have a substantial amount of cash in a savings account, and they're less likely to give chase. But no one is excluded from the potentials of the pigeon drop.

Here's one common variation on the scheme: Again, the victim is approached by a stranger who wins the victim's friendship in a few moments of conversation. The con man then suggests that they get involved in a friendly game of poker. At this point an accomplice will usually join the con man. The trio retires to a comfortable place and the game begins. The victim has soon won a substantial amount of money from the con man. The con man then suggests that the tables might turn and he, the con man, might become a winner. In such a case, the con man asks, how does he know the victim has cash to pay any losses? The victim is thus cajoled into producing a substantial amount of cash, and the con man suggests that his money and the victim's money be held by the third party to assure that winnings will be paid to the true winner. At this point the third party might disappear with the package of money or might switch the package with one containing slices of newspaper, depending on their exit arrangements. In either case, the victim will never see his money again.

Phony Goods

This type of swindle occurs mostly during the Christmas season, but it can pop up at any time, in any place. The scheme is decisive in its swiftness and simplicity. You're approached by a stranger on the street offering to sell you anything from watches to jewelry to perfume to a color TV set "still in the carton." The price is too good to be true, a real steal. It won't be until you get the item home, or until after the salesman has disappeared, that you find that the watch has no innards, the perfume is kerosene, the jewelry is cut glass, and the color TV set still in the carton is nothing more than a wooden box. Similar shenanigans can take place at flea markets and swap meets.

If you do fall prey to such a scheme, you can be certain that you will not be able to get your money back. If you are able to find the seller, he'll deny ever having seen you, and it's unlikely that the police will bother to assist you in what they would consider a relatively petty matter.

Frauds in the Home

You don't always have to go out seeking con men. Sometimes they'll come to you, either knocking on your door or calling on the telephone. As with street schemes, the element of surprise works in favor of the con man. He's prepared to sell you something, and you're totally unprepared for his pitch. And since he's coming to you rather than you going to his place of business, you have no way of knowing if you can ever find him again if things go wrong.

The Bank Examiner Swindle

You receive a call or a visit from someone who represents himself to be a bank examiner, a bank officer, or some type of governmental official looking into a problem at your bank. You might be told, for example, that the bank suspects one of the tellers of embezzling money. You're asked if you would cooperate with the authorities, go to the bank, withdraw a substantial sum of cash, give it to the so-called official, who will then redeposit it immediately into your account. They assert that in so doing, they can tell whether or not the accused teller is guilty of embezzlement. If you fall for such a swindle, you will never see your money again. Banking and law enforcement officials state most emphatically that representatives of banks or governmental agencies *never* call on the public in matters of this type, nor would they ever suggest that money be withdrawn from an account. If you are approached by anyone suggesting that you do so, contact the police immediately.

A close cousin of the bank examiner scheme is the Social Security inspector scheme. The so-called inspector will come to your house to inquire whether or not you have enough money to live on. He wants to help you in case you don't. He may request that he see the money you have. If you've got some put away in the cookie jar and give it to him for even a moment to count, say goodbye to it. He'll either use his nimble fingers to switch your money for a phony packetful or he'll simply run out the door and be gone.

In any of these cases, don't be fooled by seemingly official-looking credentials. They are easily forged and you wouldn't know what the real ones looked like in the first place.

Dump-and-run Tactics

A truck pulls into your driveway and the driver offers to spread a layer of slick new blacktop coating on your driveway for a modest sum of money—perhaps only $50 to $100. He'll tell you that he's just done the same for the supermarket parking lot a few blocks away and he had a little of the goop left over, so he wanted to pass on a good deal to the local neighbors. If you fall for such a trick, he'll indeed put the black goop on your driveway, where it will look nice and slick—until the next rain, when it will wash off onto your lawn where it will remain throughout the following seasons. You'll have paid an excessive sum of money for a few dollars worth of oil. And it will be a costly nuisance to get it out of your lawn. Bulk fertilizer is another commodity used in the dump-and-run scam.

A fast-moving dump-and-run operator can clear $1000 in an easy working day and he's on to the next neighborhood; $5000 in a week and he's on to the next town. These facts alone should serve as clear warning.

Home Improvements

Our homes are our castles. They're also among the favorite targets for swindlers. Not only are the stakes quite large in home improvement frauds, but the confusion and legal consequences can be devastating. Note the similar patterns that emerge in the following three case histories—stories that might almost be amusing if, in fact, they were not true.

The Squirrels

An elderly widow lived alone in a large three-story house surrounded by old overhanging oak trees. Though she was financially secure, the loneliness of her days left her an easy mark for the man who could win her confidence.

The home improvement salesman at the door was well trained—he had a briefcase full of everything, from siding to patios to kitchen remodeling plans. He quickly won the widow's confidence, and as she chatted eagerly with the pleasant enough salesman, he quickly learned how he could separate her from a lot of money. She told him about the antique furniture she had stored in her attic, and that she was worried about the squirrels that lived in the overhanging trees. They were able to find ways to creep into the attic and gnaw on the furniture. She feared that the furniture would be damaged beyond repair by these invading squirrels.

From that point on, the salesman's job was easy. Whether the furniture had any real value was immaterial. The sentimental value was enough to get the poor woman in a tizzy over its welfare. Perhaps she had not thought that a few dollars' worth of window screening could have blocked up the holes that the squirrels used to get into the attic. Or perhaps some chemical repellent could have kept the squirrels at bay. Such a suggestion, however, would have brought the salesman nothing for the time he spent listening to the lady's tale of woe.

"I've got just the thing for you," the salesman said, watching the woman's face light up in appreciation. "I can install some *squirrel deflectors* on your roof and that will solve the problem!"

He explained the plan in detail and drew up a contract, which she signed on the spot. Sometime later the squirrel deflectors were installed:

at random places on the old roof were placed sheets of shiny aluminum, each a few feet wide and about one foot high. The theory, according to the salesman, was that the squirrels who were about to jump from the trees onto the roof would be blinded by the sun glinting off the deflectors, so they wouldn't be able to land on the roof and instead would fall to the ground below. The salesman did not provide the woman with instructions on how to avoid injury from the falling squirrels. She seemed happy enough to know that the squirrels wouldn't make it to the roof. Nor was she concerned that the squirrels might be so venturesome as to try their leaps on cloudy days or at night, when the sun wasn't shining.

The only person blinded by the deflectors was the woman herself—the contract she signed cost her $1500. Further, the deflectors had been installed in such a shabby manner that her roof began to leak profusely. She then had to call a roofing contractor, who repaired the holes at a cost of a few hundred dollars more. Even as she related the whole epic to the roofing contractor, who in turn related it to me, there was doubt about whether or not she realized she had been victimized.

The Furnace

The man was sitting on his front porch enjoying a summer weekend afternoon. An eager and honest-looking young lad came trudging down the street laden with a variety of tools. Covered as he was from top to bottom with soot, it was obvious that the lad had been hard at work doing something. He approached the man on the porch and offered to clean out his furnace so it would be spic and span when the winter heating season arrived. The man was more struck by the energy and enthusiasm of the young lad than he was by the need to have his furnace cleaned out. But the price seemed right so he gave the lad the go-ahead. An hour or so later, the lad emerged from the cellar with baskets of soot. He invited the homeowner to investigate the job, but the homeowner felt confident that the job had been done properly so he paid the lad, who left with a bright thank you.

A few hours later a well-dressed man approached and addressed the victim. He explained that he was in charge of a crew of young men who were cleaning out furnaces in the neighborhood and he wanted to take a look at the furnace to make sure the boy had done the job properly. The homeowner gladly showed the man into the basement, where the furnace was inspected and approved.

The following day a third member of the team came to call. He said that he was a "furnace inspector," and he flashed a badge to verify the claim. He explained that he was checking up on the supervisor who in turn was keeping tabs on the fleet of boys. This natural progression of events seemed not to raise any doubts in the homeowner's mind and he permitted the "furnace inspector" to go into the basement. A few minutes later the "furnace inspector" came out sadly shaking his head and jotting something in a notebook.

"I'm afraid," the inspector told the homeowner, "that I have to condemn your furnace. There's a crack in part of the structure which could allow poisonous gasses to get into your house during the heating season."

The homeowner felt his jaw drop. Everything had seemed quite legitimate. The furnace had been properly cleaned, properly inspected, and now, apparently, it was being properly condemned. The inspector took him into the basement and with the aid of a flashlight showed him what appeared to be a hairline fracture in some part of the furnace. The barrage of warnings—fumes leaking . . . chance of fire . . . and so on—were all the homeowner needed to hear.

The "furnace inspector" surmised that to be completely on the safe side, the furnace should be replaced, since repairs were not an assurance of safety.

The next day the second man on the team reappeared, telling the homeowner that he had just heard that his furnace had been condemned. It just so happened that he represented a furnace installation company and he offered his help. Within an hour the homeowner had signed a $2000 contract for the installation of a new furnace.

It wasn't until the old furnace had been removed, the new one installed, and a substantial amount of money paid on the contract that the homeowner learned that the old furnace was not in fact defective and that he had paid more than twice the fair price for the new furnace. At that point, his contract had been sold to a finance company and he had virtually no legal means of getting out of his obligation to pay. (If merchandise is faulty or defective, Federal Trade Commission regulations permit the buyer to withhold payment to the third party, that is, the lender.)

The Model Home

The quick-talking salesman knocked at the door and told the gullible young couple that their house had been chosen as part of an advertising program. They would receive a "free" aluminum siding job on the house. All they had to do was tell their friends and neighbors and any passersby who had done this magnificent work. Thereby, the home improvement company would receive many referrals and everybody would be happy. The young couple couldn't sign the contract fast enough.

The work was done, and a month later, to the couple's amazement, they received a bill from a finance company for the first installment on a very expensive contract. Then—too late—they read the contract in detail. It stated quite clearly that they were obliging themselves to pay for the entire siding installation, but that they would receive a discount for every referral they made that resulted in another installation for the company. If they made enough referrals that resulted in enough contracts, then presumably their own job would have cost them nothing.

Is this a fraud or not? The contract was explicit but the young couple failed to read it or understand it. It could be said that this was a fair business deal and if the couple didn't understand the terms, they should legally bear the consequences. However, after the end of the second month, the siding began to peel and their "model home" began to look a shambles. They called the improvement company to repair the shoddy work, but the company's phone had been disconnected and they were nowhere to be found. The finance company that had purchased their contract was demanding payment. The couple had to hire a lawyer at considerable cost to attempt to void the allegedly fraudulent contract. They were successful, but they were still out of pocket many hundreds of dollars and had to repair the house at their own expense.

In addition to the "too good to be true" and "something for nothing" appeals of the home improvement pitchman, there are some other aspects of the sales presentation that should cause you to be wary.

Warning Signals

The "Perfect" Guarantee   The materials and their installation might be accompanied by an "unconditional lifetime money-back" guarantee. The guarantee is only as good as its written statements and only as good as the ability of the guarantor to perform. If there is to be a guarantee, it should be spelled out in explicit detail and you should understand exactly what is and is not guaranteed. Even though the guarantee might appear to be iron-clad, how about the ability of the firm to honor it? If they're not in business a month or a year after your job is completed, the best guarantee in the world is meaningless.

Big Savings   There may be representations that the work will save you many hundreds of dollars over what it would cost through other contractors. You can never know this for sure unless you have properly drawn plans and specifications and obtained bids from reputable local contractors. Until you have done that, the salesperson's words are nothing more than puffery.

"Will Last Forever"   The salesman may make representations that the materials, such as aluminum siding, are "maintenance free forever." No substance yet discovered by science and affordable to the average homeowner is maintenance free forever.

"Sign up Now or Never"   The salesman will be very anxious to get you to sign a contract right away. He knows that if you don't, and if you have time to think about the deal, he may lose you. This is where the pressure will begin. He may try to convince you that getting other prices will be a waste of your time; that his price is certainly the lowest; and that if you don't sign right now, his low price won't be available later. This "now or never" kind of pressure may sound convincing. Note well: when you're dealing with legitimate contractors, there's no job that can't be contracted for a day or so later as well as it can at that moment. If you feel that by not signing right away you're losing out on something special, you had best begin preparing yourself for the worst.

Credentials   A reputable home improvement contractor's past history will speak for itself. You can visit his place of business and you can talk to customers who have used his services. The shady home improvement promoter will make a big fuss about his credentials. He may have become a member of the Chamber of Commerce and the Better Business Bureau in your community and he may well have established a bank account and lines of credit with local suppliers. But all of these credentials don't necessarily mean that he can get the job done properly or that you're getting good value for your money. It can indeed be difficult to spot the credential-laden con man from the honest businessman, since such credentials apply equally to both. It's necessary for you to look behind the credentials and try to spot the other warning signals.

Brand Names   Another ploy used to gain respectability involves the use of major brand names by the promoters. There have been hundreds of cases in recent years involving improvement swindlers using the names of national firms to convince customers that they themselves are legitimate. The impression given is that the promoter is in direct alliance with the manufacturer, with the implication being that such national firms certainly wouldn't condone anything but the highest quality workmanship with regard to their products, and thus the salesman must be of the highest repute.

In fact, anyone can go out and buy most of these name brand products. Many homeowners have been bilked, believing that the contractor will use such brand name products, only to find when the job is done that inferior brands have been used.

How to Avoid the Rackets

Unless you are absolutely certain of a contractor's reputation and integrity, you must follow these steps if you want to avoid being swindled on a major home improvement project:

1. Do not sign any home improvement contracts unless you have prepared or received firm, clear, detailed plans and specifications.
2. Do not sign any home improvement contracts until you have received comparable bids from local reputable contractors based on those plans and specifications.
3. Do not sign any home improvement contracts until you have had the documents checked by an attorney.
4. Do not sign any home improvement contracts until you have discussed with your banker the overall financing of the project.

If you want the job done right and you want to get the most for your money, there are no shortcuts around these steps. It might seem like a lot of work, but when you consider that you may be spending thousands of dollars and risking damage to your house should you hire unqualified people, it should be worth the effort.

Investment Schemes

"Here's the deal, with a rock solid guarantee: You give me your money— $1000 . . . $5000 . . . $10,000 . . . whatever—and if at any time you're unsatisfied with what I'm doing with it, just let me know and I'll immediately return the unused portion thereof."

Who would fall for an offer like that? You'd be surprised. When it comes to the area of investments—making your money grow—greed and gullibility reach their peak and the opportunities for fraudulent activities are infinite. The fast-buck artists promise instant fortunes and huge tax savings in stocks, commodities, gold, silver, gemstones, land, and virtually anything else that might capture a victim's attention. You might be solicited through the mail or through advertising, but one of the most common and insidious media used by investment promoters is the telephone.

The Boiler Room

In a typical boiler room operation, a fleet of fast-talking hard-driving salespersons will telephone would-be victims all across the country, offering their latest and greatest miracle for getting wealthy. How will they have gotten your name? Very likely from mailing lists: If you subscribe to any financial periodicals or if you have bought any money-related products such as books or other investment offerings, your name will be on those lists and will be sold by the list owner to all comers.

Following is a replica—with little exaggeration—of what you're likely to hear if you receive a telephone call from a boiler room operation:

"Good morning, Mr. Rosefsky, this is J. Fairly Nicely of Mammoth Investments on Wall Street. If you can give me just three minutes of your time, I'd like to tell you about a way that you can double your money within six months. Would you be interested in hearing about that? . . . Mammoth has been authorized to sell a private placement of stock in Amalgamated International—you've heard of them, of course—they've just discovered one of the world's largest linoleum deposits, and mining of the linoleum is expected to start next week. I'm authorized to offer you 500 shares at $10 per share, but the offer is good only for the next hour. Now get this: We know for a fact that the big brokerage firm—Merrill-Lynch-Hutton-Shearson-Bache-Webber—is going to the market with a public offering six months from now and we have just confirmed that the offering price will be $20 per share. You'll double your money in six months, but you've got to buy now. Could you hold on just a moment, my other phone is ringing . . . (You now hear him supposedly talking on another phone.) . . . Yes, Mr. Rockefeller, we still have some shares left in the linoleum venture. How many would you like? . . . Yes, Mr. Rockefeller . . . 200 shares at $10 apiece . . . that'll be fine, I'll have the paperwork in the mail before the end of the day. Now Mr. Rosefsky, as I was saying, I just sold 200 shares, so I can offer you only 300, but if you really want the 500, maybe I can arrange for it. . . . You seem hesitant; is there any reason why you wouldn't want to double your money in six months?"

Yes, people do run to their check books and send money to J. Fairly Nicely and his ilk without hesitation or fear. And that's probably the last they'll ever see of it. But that's not the last they'll hear of J. Fairly Nicely, for he'll sell their name to other boiler room operations and some other day, in some other way, they'll be offered a partnership in a veal farm, a future interest in a grove of tarantula trees, or syndication rights on a herd of prize winning naugahydes.

The pitchman's spiel is so frenetic that it doesn't give the victim time to think about anything other than doubling his money. If the would-be victim did stop to think, the first thought that might cross his mind would be: "If this deal is so good, how come you're selling it to me? Why don't you just keep it all yourself?" If that question is asked of the pitchman, the answer will be: "I've hocked my house, my wife, my kids, and my gold fillings to raise every penny I could to buy into this. And with every penny I make on my commissions, I'm buying more. I can't buy enough of it. In six months I'll retire on my fortune. I can't buy it all, but I'm buying all I can." He may even sound all choked up at this point.

Your best defense against the wiles of the boiler room operator is to take advantage of a technical device built into your telephone. Alexander Graham Bell, in his great wisdom, saw fit to include this item for the benefit of those being pestered by boiler room operators. It's called the hang-up button. It works like a charm.

Ponzis and Pyramids

Charles Ponzi was a hustler who plied his skills in Boston during the 1920s. He so popularized an ancient scheme that it has carried his name ever since—the Ponzi scheme. It was simple, straightforward, and attracted victims like a magnet. It worked like this:

Ponzi told victims, "You give me $100 today and in 30 days I'll give you back $120." Thirty days later he did just that. His own initial investment of $20 paid off, since he now had avid believers who would do exactly what he said. "Want to try it again for another 30 days?" The first wave of investors took the plunge again. Ponzi had no trouble soliciting a second wave of investors and he used their money to pay off the first wave. Then he would solicit a third wave and use their money to pay off the second wave, and so on, until one day Ponzi simply took the money and ran.

A Ponzi scheme, then, is in essence a plan whereby new investors are constantly solicited and their money is used to pay off older investors. Keeping the investors happy keeps the money pouring in, but at some time the promoter will skip.

Closely related to the Ponzi scheme is the pyramid scheme, which is the basis for chain letters. The pyramid scheme also involves using new investors to pay off old ones. The promoters who start pyramid schemes can make money, but at the risk of jail sentences, for the schemes are illegal and in many states a criminal offense.

A pyramid involves giving money to someone whose name is at the top of a list, then erasing that name and inserting your own name at the bottom of the list. You then give the list to as many people as there are names on the list. As your name hits the top of the list, you'll supposedly collect money from everyone who is involved in the pyramid. Example: a list of 10 names will be sent to 10 people. Each of them will send it to 10 people, so now there are 100 people involved. Each of the 100 will send the list to 10 people, so now there are 1000 involved. If this is carried out to the tenth level, you will note that 10 billion people will be involved in the pyramid. That's more than double the population of the entire earth. And that is where the pyramids eventually collapse: They simply run out of people who are willing to participate and the victims find that their names never move up the list beyond one or two notches.

The Ponzi and pyramid concepts are at work in most types of investment schemes. If the boiler room operator selling shares in the linoleum mine wants to keep his investors happy and spreading the good word, he may pay them a token dividend a few weeks after they invest. This not only reassures them that the promised wealth is on its way but it also gives them a false sense of security and inhibits them from alerting the authorities to the scheme. Naturally, in such an event, the money to pay the dividend to the initial investors comes from the second wave of investors. And so it goes.

Land Frauds

Will Rogers once said, "Land is the best investment there is cuz they ain't going to print no more of it." Tens of thousands of people have taken that remark seriously and have lost uncounted hundreds of millions of dollars on land swindles. They may not have realized that Will Rogers was a comedian. A lot of his remarks were said in jest, and this statement may have been one of his biggest jokes.

Rogers statement, amplified by land salespersons, implies that we all ought to rush out and buy land before there is no more left to buy. A prudent purchase of land for investment or future building purposes takes time and careful study and does involve some risk. (See Chapter 18 for a more detailed discussion.) But a rush to buy land—as urged by the salesperson—means impulse, and impulse means a high probability of mistakes. If you don't buy this week, this month, or this year, there's going to be plenty still available next year or next decade. Yes, the price might be going up, but so does the price of everything. So does your income. The price can also go down. It happens every day.

Are we running out of land? The state of Colorado contains just over 100,000 square miles, or roughly 64 million acres. It's estimated that by the year 2000 there will be roughly 320 million people living in the United States. You could put the entire population of the United States in the year 2000 within the boundaries of the state of Colorado at a density ratio of only 5 people per acre. That's like giving the average-sized family three-quarters of an acre (a parcel roughly 100 by 300 feet) and plots a little less than half that size for singles. Colorado would then have a population density of 3200 people per square mile. This compares with 75,000 per square mile in Manhattan today, 16,000 people per square mile in Chicago, 12,000 people per square mile in Detroit, and 7000 people per square mile in Los Angeles.

Land fraud schemes flourished in the 1970s and then slowed down as the impact of a newly created federal agency—the Office of Interstate Land Sales Regulation—began to be felt. Unscrupulous salesmen sold unwitting victims worthless swampland in Florida and barren desert in Arizona under the guise of "future retirement communities," "vacation rancheros," and just plain double-your-money-in-a-hurry investment opportunities.

But swindlers are not to be outdone by the creation of a mere federal agency. They simply went into hiding, to emerge again in another guise. In the field of time-sharing resorts, many of the same patterns have emerged that were prevalent with the land sales: high pressure "opportunity meetings," "if you don't buy now, the price will go up tomorrow" tactics, and the like. While many time-sharing opportunities may be valid, there will also be many situations in which the facilities don't exist or in which the promoters will take the money and run. (Chapter 7 contains more details on time sharing.)

All That Glitters . . .

Early indications are that gold, silver, and precious gems will be the subject of many fraudulent schemes throughout the 1980s. Examples will include:

☐ Counterfeit coins passed off as real.

☐ Bars of lead covered with gold or silver paint passed off as real bullion.

☐ Junk or low-grade gemstones, or plastic, passed off as precious gems.

☐ Contracts for future delivery of any of the above, which are never fulfilled.

Despite all the promises and guarantees offered by salespeople, a would-be investor in precious metals or gems faces serious risk unless he obtains an independent appraisal of the items before parting with his cash. Chapter 19 contains more detailed information on the proper evaluation of these precious items.

What to Do About It

The sad fact is that if you do become a victim of a fraudulent scheme, there's little chance you'll get your money back unless you're willing to spend a lot of time and a lot more money on legal fees. And even if you are willing to spend money on legal fees, you can't sue someone you can't find: the con man knows to disappear quickly and totally.

Even though the chances of getting your money back may be slim, you still should take action if you believe you've been defrauded. If nothing else, your action may help put a stop to certain fraudulent practices, thus benefitting your fellow citizens. And if they do the same, their actions will benefit you. Here are the main sources of possible help:

Federal Trade Commission

This is a governmental agency charged with many areas of responsibility including deceptive business practices. The FTC is based in Washington and has regional branches in Atlanta, Boston, Chicago, Cleveland, Dallas, Kansas City, Los Angeles, New Orleans, New York, San Francisco, and Seattle. FTC officials emphasize, however, that they are not in a position to represent individual consumers.

Information regarding possible deceptive practices can come to the attention of the FTC in a number of ways. Complaints from individual consumers are probably the predominant way. In addition, newspaper clippings and complaints from other businessmen also supply information.

The FTC does not have the staff or the funds to investigate every complaint that comes to its attention. When there is enough frequency of a certain type of complaint against a given company, the investigative staff may look into it. If, after due investigation, the FTC has reason to believe that a deceptive practice has occurred, the agency will call this to the attention of the alleged offender and attempt to work out what is called a "consent order." A consent order is a rather curious document in which the alleged offender promises not to do what he has been accused of doing, but does not admit that he was guilty of doing it. In other words, in effect, he's not guilty but he promises he won't do it again. If he does violate the consent order, serious punishment can follow. If the offender does not feel he has done anything wrong and does not want to sign a consent order, the matter must proceed to the law courts.

From the time that consumer complaints start trickling in until the time a consent order or court determination is obtained, many months can elapse. If an out-and-out fraudulent activity has been underway, the perpetrator may have long since vanished by the time the consent order is issued.

Why doesn't the FTC alert the public when first receiving complaints? Wouldn't this help tip off the public at the earliest stages of the game? While such warning bulletins might be of some value to some people, there are dangers inherent in such a course. Many innocent parties could suffer if announcements were made by the FTC on the basis of a mere suspicion of a violation of the law. It is possible for a jealous or angry competitor to set up a malicious campaign against a perfectly innocent businessman. Investigation is necessary before any allegations of law-breaking can be justified. Further, if the FTC were to tip its hand too early, doing so might harm the agency's ability to obtain justice later on in the courts. Thus, there is a need for some degree of secrecy until the basic investigative work has been completed and a complaint is issued.

The Federal Trade Commission does not have immediate injunctive powers: It cannot come swooping down on an alleged deceptive business practice and order it to cease and desist on the spot. The agency must go through the consent order ritual which, as noted, can take months.

If the FTC is limited in its powers, it is even more limited by a closed-mouth public. This federal agency can function only if it gets the input from the public. Lacking that input, it has nothing to go on. While it may serve little purpose in your own situation to alert the FTC to a deceptive business practice, doing so could aid the agency on the broader scale of bringing such practices to an end.

The Postal Service

Contact the Mail Fraud Division of the U.S. Postal Service if you suspect that the U.S. mails have been used to perpetrate a fraud. As with the FTC, the postal service is limited in the available money and manpower to track down every complaint, but it does what it can. The more complaints there are on a given matter, the better chance the Postal Service has of obtaining a satisfactory conclusion.

State and Local Governmental Agencies

All 50 states have some form of consumer-protection office. Frequently it's associated with the Attorney General's office. Many large cities also have consumer-protection agencies. As with the aforementioned federal agencies, lack of money and manpower deter these agencies from being able to assist you in getting satisfaction in a fraudulent situation, but they should be contacted anyway, immediately, and with all pertinent details. If there seems to be any hope at all of apprehending the promoters, your local police or sheriff's office should also be contacted.

In addition to governmental agencies, there are a number of nongovernmental sources of possible assistance.

Your Local Newspapers and Broadcast Services

Newspapers, radio stations, and television stations throughout the nation have been doing an ever-expanding job of surveillance and reporting on consumer fraud. These columns and reports are provided at considerable expense by the media as a public service. Very often they're able to resolve matters right on the spot.

Better Business Bureaus

Better Business Bureaus can be helpful before the fact: a call to your local BBB prior to entering into a transaction might disclose whether or not the person you're dealing with has a record of complaints with the bureau. BBB personnel might also be able to give you general guidelines as to types of suspect business endeavors. The BBB might also be able to provide arbitration services to help you iron out a dispute you have with a local business. If you're dealing with a business located in another city, you would be well served to contact the Better Business Bureau in that city to determine whether the firm has a clean record. Understand that if a business has a clean record with the BBB, it does not necessarily mean that all is on the up and up. The clever con man will know how to keep his BBB record clear and will also time his activities cleverly enough so that he can be out of town before the complaints begin hitting the BBB office.

Financial Institutions

Banks, savings and loan associations, credit unions, and consumer finance companies are all actively involved on a day-to-day basis with the flow of IOUs generated from all kinds of business activities. If a deceptive practice is under way, an alert to these institutions could help bring an end to the activity. Such institutions might be involved in buying fraudulently induced IOUs, and tens of thousands of dollars' worth of paper can be generated before anyone is aware that a fraud is in the works. The sooner the institutions know of it, the sooner they can stop buying the IOUs, and that can be the death knell for the fraudulent endeavor.

Your financial institution can also be of help to you if you consult them regarding your own financial situation before you get involved in signing any contracts. The astute loan officer might spot trouble in a situation that you might not otherwise be aware of.

Small Claims Court

Your local Small Claims Court can be of assistance in settling a claim of fraudulent or improper business practices, *if* you can locate the party who has wronged you. Small Claims Courts differ from place to place, but in general you do not need a lawyer to represent you. If the amount of money involved in a claim exceeds a certain limit (perhaps $750 or $1000, depending on the court), the Small Claims Court will not hear your case. Contact your local court to determine their rules and procedures.

A Tasty Recipe

Take one heaping enticement of "get rich quick!" or "earn big money fast!" or "something for nothing!"

Add one flickering reaction of "how far wrong can I go?" or "what have I got to lose?"

Fold in one prevailing attitude of "it can't happen to me!"

Simmer well.

This is the recipe upon which the wild and wooly world of consumer fraud is based. No one is immune. Your common sense is your best defense against getting involved and losing money. If you are to be a successful consumer and manager of your finances, heed the following cautions:

1. Analyze your needs and desires before you make a commitment to buy anything.

2. Obtain a basic knowledge of the product you're seeking to buy.

3. Compare the product you're interested in with that offered by other manufacturers and retailers.

4. Study carefully the guarantee behind the product, as well as the reputation of the manufacturer and retailer.

5. Realistically analyze your financial ability to obtain the item and shop carefully for financing arrangements.

6. Take prompt and appropriate action in the event that the product or service does not live up to your expectations, or up to the representations made by the seller.

Personal Action Checklist
Fraud-Avoidance Techniques

This is a two-part exercise. First, ask yourself the following questions—and jot down reasonable answers—before you enter into any dealing with persons whose reputations are uncertain or unknown. Having read this chapter and answered the questions honestly, your choice should be clear.

Second, obtain and write down for future reference the local telephone numbers of the indicated consumer-protection sources.

1. If I'm not satisfied with the product or service I get from this person, what assurance do I have that I'll be able to get my money back?
2. Does this deal sound too good to be true, or like I'm going to be getting something for nothing?
3. Am I being pressured to sign up right away, or to buy right away, lest I lose the chance forever?
4. If the secret method (or investment technique, etc.) is so good, why is the salesperson selling it to me? Could it be that he or she will make more money by selling it to me than I can make by buying it?
5. Have I checked with the appropriate consumer-protection sources to learn what I can about this company?
6. Do I really need the product or service that's being sold? And can I get it through other sources without any worry about satisfaction?

Telephone Numbers:
Better Business Bureau
City, State Consumer Protection Agency
Small Claims Court
Consumer journalists (radio, TV, newspaper)
Federal Trade Commission (nearest office)

Consumer Beware
Learning to Say "No"
Can Save $$$$$$$$$

While many fine products are sold door-to-door, there are also many flimflams conducted in that mode. Getting rid of a pesky door-to-door salesperson is not quite as easy as getting rid of a telephone solicitor (hanging up is swift, simple, and foolproof). But an old friend, best known as Sybil the Intrepid, had a way of saying "no" with such style and flair that anyone can benefit from her tactics.

Here, for example, is how Sybil the Intrepid once handled a door-to-door vacuum cleaner salesperson:

Sybil: Oh, I've heard about your product, and I understand it's simply marvelous. I'm so glad you stopped by. And just at the right time. My carpets are a mess.

Salesperson (rising enthusiastically to the unexpected welcome): I'd be happy to come in and give you a demonstration . . . no obligation of course.

Sybil: That would be wonderful! The only problem is, I'll have to see your identity card before I can let you into the house. Security, you know.

Salesperson: No problem. Here's my card from the company.

Sybil: No, that's not what I had in mind. You know what I mean—your *identity* card.

Salesperson (now becoming slightly flustered and confused): Well . . . here's my driver's license . . . my voter registration card . . . my Visa card . . . my library card. . . .

Sybil (remaining as calm and pleasant as can be): No, no . . . those aren't what I mean. I mean your *identity* card. You know, your card that verifies you aren't a member of the Communist Party.

Salesperson (now almost apoplectic): But I've never heard of such a thing. I don't have such a card.

Sybil (with a straight face that would make your hair curl): There there now . . . that's perfectly all right. You just come back any time with your proper identity card, and I'd love to have you come in then and show me your wonderful vacuum cleaner. Bye now. (The door closes ever so gently.)

True story. Sybil was a master at saying "no" . . . a trick that too many of us learn too late. This is not meant as an affront to people who earn a legitimate living selling door-to-door, but rather as a defense for those who are apt to part with good money when they confront the occasional bad apple who makes a not-so-legitimate living selling door-to-door.

6 | Transportation

"Urban sprawl" is a very accurate way of describing today's typical American city, whether large or small. We have a lot of space to use, and we've used it. In the process, we've put a lot of distance between our homes, our places of work, our shopping centers, our recreational facilities. "Getting there" used to be no problem in the days—pre-1973—when cars, gasoline, and mass transit were relatively inexpensive. But today the cost of moving about is a serious matter and must be taken into account in anyone's financial planning. This chapter will help you solve the common problems you face in trying to keep your transportation expenses in line:

☐ Should you buy a car, and if so, what kind is right for you?
☐ How do you deal with car dealers?
☐ What kind of financing arrangement is best for you?
☐ How much car insurance should you have, and how much will it cost?
☐ What is your car warranty worth?
☐ What are your alternatives to buying a car?

Getting from Point A to Point B—What Are Your Choices?

The average cost of owning, financing, operating, and insuring an automobile is now about 30¢ for each mile driven, and rising. This means:

☐ If you drive a mile or two to pick up a loaf of bread at the supermarket, the cost of getting to the market and back will be higher than the cost of the bread itself.
☐ If you drive around the block a few times looking for a parking space, you could spend as much money as you would have if you had parked in a paid lot.
☐ That inexpensive treat of not so many years ago—the weekend drive in the country—can now cost you $20, $30, $40.
☐ If you drive a 20-mile roundtrip commute to work, it's costing you $30 per *week* to get to your job and back.

In short, getting from point A to point B—particularly by automobile—is an expensive proposition. If you were driving before October 1973—when a gallon of gas was less than 50¢ and a well-equipped medium-sized car could be purchased for about $4000—today's high costs are still difficult to comprehend. If you didn't start driving until after October 1973, you won't remember how much driving used to be taken for granted.

That fateful date—October 1973—was when the oil exporting countries began the doubling, tripling, and quadrupling of oil prices. Not only did that cause the price of gas at the pump to begin a crazy upward spiral, but it also did the same to the cost of manufacturing cars. The cost of delivering the raw materials (steel, rubber, glass, etc.) to the manufacturing site increased proportionately, as did the cost of delivering the finished car to the dealership. And as manufacturing and delivery costs skyrocketed, so did the cost of the cars themselves, as did the financing costs for both the dealer and the buyer.

Yet, while the auto becomes more and more of a luxury, decades of conditioning have patterned much of our lives around it: getting to work, shopping, school, recreation all depend largely on the availability of a car. In many cities, mass transit provides a less costly (and often less convenient) alternative. To the more adventuresome, motorcycles and mopeds provide a less costly (and less safe) alternative. To the energetic, bicycling, walking, and jogging may be the best alternatives of all.

The cost of driving cannot be taken for granted any longer. For most, it's a major budget item, and an increase or decrease in your driving can have a definite bearing on the rest of your budget. If you are choosing a dwelling or seeking a job, the cost of commuting must definitely be calculated. As noted above, a 20-mile daily roundtrip commute can cost $30 a week—$120 per month. That $120 per month in commuting costs is the same you'd pay on $10,000 worth of mortgage at current rates. In other words, if you didn't have to drive to and from work, that $120 per month could be paying off a $10,000 higher mortgage.

Your overall ability to make ends meet and manage your money prudently requires that you keep your driving to a minimum and that you utilize all means of less expensive transportation whenever possible (carpooling, mass transit).

The Costs

The 30¢ per mile figure noted above is, of course, an approximation. It's based on a small-sized car being driven 15,000 miles per year and kept for four years. Because so much depends on individual circumstances, it's very difficult to peg an exact figure for the cost of a car, but the 30¢ price can be used as a fairly reliable average guideline. It takes into account the following:

☐ The depreciation (difference between the purchase price and what it might be worth when you later sell it or trade it in).

☐ Operating and maintenance costs (including tune-ups, oil, tires, lubrication, and average necessary repairs).

□ Interest (presuming that the car is financed for an average of three years).

□ Taxes and fees (including sales tax, property taxes, registration, titling fee, license costs, necessary inspections).

□ Insurance (public liability, collision, comprehensive).

□ Gasoline (the amount of which can vary considerably depending on your driving habits and your maintenance of the automobile).

The following factors will affect the cost per mile of driving your car:

Equipment   The cost, the weight, and the usage of optional equipment can have a distinct bearing on your overall operating costs. Example: An air-conditioning unit is one of the more expensive optional extras that can be installed in a car. The cost can exceed $700. In addition, the cost of registration, insurance, and interest will increase accordingly. And further, the use of the air conditioning can decrease your gas mileage by as much as 12 percent (see Table 6-1).

Maintenance   Proper regular tune-ups can improve your gas milage by almost 13 percent (see Table 6-1). Proper tire inflation and rotation can also improve gas milage as well as the overall ridability of the car. And a periodic "trouble-shooting" checkup by a reliable garage can help prevent costly problems before they occur.

Insurance   The number of cars on your auto policy, the number of drivers, and the safety record of the drivers can have a major effect on your car insurance costs. The later section on car insurance explores these matters in greater detail.

Driving Habits   Hot-rodding, drag racing, excessive speeding, and jackrabbit starting can diminish your gas mileage and also create more wear

Table 6-1 | **How Speed, Air Conditioning and Tune-ups Can Affect Gas Milage**

	Speed				
Miles per gallon	30 mph	40 mph	50 mph	60 mph	70 mph
With air conditioner on	18.14	17.51	16.42	15.0	13.17
With air conditioner off	20.05	19.71	18.29	16.23	14.18
MPG Increase with air conditioner off	10.5%	12.6%	11.4%	8.33%	7.7%
Before tune-up	19.3	18.89	17.29	15.67	13.32
After tune-up	21.33	21.33	18.94	17.40	15.36
MPG increase after tune-up	10.5%	12.9%	9.54%	11.04%	15.3%

Source: U.S. Department of Transportation.

and tear on the basic mechanical aspects of the car. It may seem like fun, but it's going to cost you.

Knowledge   Knowing how to buy right, finance right, and insure right can definitely save you money. The more you know about the care and maintenance of your car, and the more of it that you can do yourself, the more money you'll save. A car care book or a short course in basic car maintenance can be an investment that pays for itself many times over each year.

Buying a Car

Individual tastes, habits, needs, and budgets being as different as they are, there is no fast rule of thumb which describes the "best" buy for anyone's dollars. And with an almost infinite variety of cars to choose from—differing in age, condition, size, equipment, and cost—even general guidelines are difficult to set forth. The following considerations, however, weighed carefully as you shop, can help you find the vehicle that's right for your needs and for your budget.

Needs Versus Desires

You must clearly distinguish between your automotive *needs* and your automotive *desires*. The difference between the two can cost you thousands of dollars with little to show for that money but some chrome, vinyl, and extra things that can go wrong in the car. For generations, American car buyers have been conditioned into believing that the automobile is a reflection of an individual's power, prestige, sex appeal, and success. If you can afford to succumb to that kind of hypnosis, feel free. The other side of the coin—never advertised by automotive manufacturers—is that when people find themselves in a financial jam, very often it's because they're paying far more for their car than their budget realistically can allow them to. If you're willing to sacrifice in other areas (housing, clothing, food, future savings, recreation) for the sake of a more luxurious car, that's your choice. Just be aware of the potential consequences.

In examining your automotive needs, be honest with yourself. How big a car do you really need? Some people can easily justify a bigger car, such as the salesman who may drive 50,000 or 100,000 miles a year. To him, the comfort is worth the price, and the price is largely tax deductible anyway. Some people justify size in terms of safety. Indeed, there have been studies showing that larger cars provide greater safety for the occupants than do some smaller cars. But as the trend to ever smaller cars continues and the number of bigger cars with which small ones can collide diminishes, the safety factor, while not to be totally ignored, may not be as critical as it was years ago.

Still other people will attempt to justify buying a larger car for those rare occasions when they think they might need one: Hauling extra passengers, cargo, luggage, pets, and so on. But if the majority of your driving will find only one or two occupants in the car, consider that it could be far cheaper for you to rent a larger car or a truck on those few occasions when the need arises, compared with investing now in a larger car that will rarely be fully utilized.

Your needs must also take into account the optional extras available with most cars. Do you live in a climate where air conditioning is essential many days of the year? Or is it a luxury that you might use only a few days of the year? Will you make use of the expensive factory-installed radio/tape deck? Factory-installed versions are much more costly than comparable equipment sold at automotive stores. If you really will make use of that equipment, consider buying the car without it and installing your own at a savings of perhaps $100 to $200.

Do you really *need* such frills as power windows, power antenna, power door locks, and the like? They really do not get you from point A to point B any more efficiently than would a car without them, but they'll cost hundreds of extra dollars. And each of these items is yet another thing that can break down and need servicing.

Fancy trim packages, which can also cost hundreds of dollars, serve absolutely no functional purpose except to massage the owner's ego. Such items include racing stripes, fancy wheel covers, vinyl roof, luxury upholstery, and interior folderol.

A full package of optional extras on a standard car can cost upward of $3000. It's worth repeating that for every dollar spent on extras, you'll spend more money on the financing, the insurance, and the registration for the car, plus extra gas that you'll burn hauling it all around. Optional extras are not a one-time expense: they'll be with you every month for as long as you own the car.

New Versus Used

A used car in good mechanical condition can provide you with decent transportation for many years and many tens of thousands of miles—at a much lower cost than a similar new model. Note the qualification: "In good mechanical condition." A prerequisite to buying a used car is a thorough analysis by a responsible mechanic. The buyer of a used car has no way of knowing what accidents or operating problems the car had in the past. The seller—whether dealer or private—may not be inclined to divulge all that is known about the car's history. Indeed, if the car has had more than one prior owner, the current owner himself may not have any idea about the car's history. The cost of a thorough inspection can be a very inexpensive way of finding out whether you're getting a good or a bad deal. The bad deal will end up costing you many times what the inspection will cost.

If you buy a used car from a private individual, you'll take it on an as-is basis, unless the seller agrees to some sort of private warranty. If he does, have him put it in writing. If you buy a used car from a dealer, the typical warranty runs for only 30 days and even with that, the buyer may have to absorb part of any repair costs. That warranty should also be expressed in writing.

Shopping Criteria

Since this textbook is devoted to money handling and not car handling, we'll leave the details of road testing and comfort testing up to the individual reader. Herewith, some of the financial considerations to be borne in mind when shopping for a new car.

After you've decided what pleases you with respect to size, color, equipment and handling, refer to the Personal Action Checklist at the end of this chapter for a guide to what you'll get for your money. The Checklist contains space for three comparisons. If you compare more than three cars, simply use extra paper to fill in the comparisons. In addition to the base price, list each optional extra and the cost thereof separately. This will cause you to stop and think twice about the value of those extras and will also give you a better comparison of the total product that you're getting for your money.

Very likely the dealer will quote you a price that's different from the total sticker price. That price will take into account the value of any car you are trading in. Haggling over the price of a new car is still one of the great old American traditions. The dealers almost expect that you'll haggle, and if you don't, you could be spending hundreds of dollars more than you have to.

When the dealer does give you a firm price, make certain that he puts it in writing, signs it, and states a date until which time that price will be good. You can't expect a dealer to give you a price and stick to it for more than a very few days. And you don't want to come back into the dealership a few hours, or a day or two, after you've been given the price, only to be told that the quote was good just at that moment if you had signed a contract right away.

Don't guess: be precise with each dealer's offerings with respect to warranty, extended service contracts, insurance (if the dealer will offer it), and financing terms.

To the extent possible, check the dealer's reputation in the community for service and adjustment of complaints. With respect to service, determine whether he offers pick-up and drop-off when the car is brought in for work, and whether or not the dealer has loan cars available, and at what price, should you have to leave your own car there for an extended period.

Games Dealers Play

The automobile business is extremely competitive. Competitiveness breeds anxiety, and that in turn may cause car salespeople and dealerships to now and then bend the ethics of good business practices in order to win a sale. Some of these practices are illustrated in the following tale. Try to spot the pitfalls as they occur.

You're planning to buy a car, and you've set your heart on a Rammer-Jammer XJKB. You've priced it at two dealerships, who are within a few dollars of each other: about $4000 in cash will be required over your old trade-in. You want to try one more dealership, which advertises heavily that they will "meet or beat any deal in town."

You and your spouse take a drive to that dealership one evening after dinner. A pleasant young chap takes you under his wing and suggests that you test drive the model you've been admiring. While you're driving around, you're very impressed with the seeming honesty and candor of this nice fellow and you're particularly intrigued when he suggests that the trade-in value of your old car might be $1000 more than what other dealers have quoted you! He explains that this dealer's inventory of used cars is very low and he's offering better deals on trade-ins to build up his inventory. What's more, the salesman confides, he thinks the boss has been overcharging too many customers, and he, as a bright honest young man, doesn't like people to get a raw deal. Thus, he tells you, he's going to take it upon himself to see that you get the best possible deal available, and the boss won't know the difference.

Back at the showroom, he takes you into his little office to do some calculating. After a few moments, he looks up at you with a smile. "If I can get the boss to agree on a deal that would take $3000 plus your trade-in, would you sign the contract tonight?"

$3000! You were almost willing to pay $4000 for exactly the same car at a different showroom. Of course you'd be willing to take a deal for $3000 if the boss will go along with it. The well-trained salesman spots your enthusiasm and proceeds.

"Look," he says, "the boss doesn't like me to approach him with proposed deals unless they're sure that the customer will take the deal. He doesn't like to waste his time haggling back and forth. If he knows he has a firm deal right at the outset, that means he's saving time and he'll give you a better price. Let me do this: let me fill out the contract showing a $3000 trade difference and you give me a good faith check for $50. That way, he knows he's got a firm deal *if* he signs the contract and you're not obligated for anything. If he doesn't go for the deal, he won't sign the contract and you're not obligated for anything. If he doesn't go for it, I'll give you back the contract and your check and you can rip them both up. What have you got to lose?"

You've got nothing to lose, or so you think. You're sitting there planning on how you can spend the $1000 you've just saved and itching to get behind the wheel of the new car that's just a signature away. You review what the salesman has just said. He's right. If the owner doesn't sign the contract, there's no deal.

"Okay," you say, "fill out the contract and I'll sign it."

He leaves the room with the signed contract and the check, and you and your spouse sit and snicker over the tremendous deal you're getting.

"I was ready to pay $4000, and we're stealing it for $3000," you say. (There's a little bit of larceny in all of us.)

You sit and wait for ten, then 20 minutes. You're getting impatient because you want that contract to come back signed by the owner so you can hop in your new Rammer-Jammer and be off, before they realize how you've taken them.

Just as you're about out of patience, the young man sticks his head in the door, smiles at you, and says, "I think everything is going to be okay. I'm going to take the car around to the service department and get it ready for you so you can take it home tonight if you want."

Your motor starts racing and you lean back to wait some more. Another ten minutes pass and an older man enters the room. He tells you he is the assistant boss. Very understandingly, he tells you that he appreciates how anxious you are to get into that new car. But, sadly, there seems to have been a snag. The pleasant young man that you were so fond of, it seems, has been doing a lousy job for the dealer. He makes mistakes on his estimates and he's trying to cut the prices lower than the dealer can afford. Very likely, the young man isn't long for this kind of business. As a matter of fact, the assistant boss continues, it seems as though the young man was off by $1000 on your deal. He vastly overestimated the value of your trade-in. "We'd love to have you in this car, because I know you want to be in it," the assistant boss says, "but we've just got to talk about a $4000 trade difference, not $3000." The bubble has burst.

"In the first place," the assistant boss goes on, "we didn't even give your trade car a test drive. Let me have the keys to it so our service manager can check it out and give you a fair trade-in price." Bewildered, you hand over your keys and he disappears with them.

You're confused and dejected. You know you want to get back the contract and your check, and though some suspicions are beginning to grow in your mind, there's still a glimmer of hope that you can correct this foul-up and still get the deal that you had already set your heart on. You and your spouse debate the matter in the privacy of the closing room and tentatively agree that if you can strike a deal somewhere between $3500 and $4000, maybe you'd still go for it since it would be better than any of the other quotes you'd been given.

The assistant boss reappears momentarily with your contract, which he hands over to you, and you tear it up. "Where's my $50 check?" you ask. He looks a little bewildered and guesses that it must still be in the boss's office. "Don't worry about it," he says, "I'll get it for you in just a few minutes. Now about your deal," he begins. "We've given your trade-in a good look and it needs a lot of work and new tires. A good deal for us would be $4300 plus your trade-in, but since you've been here so long and have been so patient, and since you were misled by the young fellow, we can bend some and let you have the new Rammer-Jammer for $4100."

You've been there over an hour already and the grind is beginning to wear you down. You finally concede, "$3900, not a penny more," knowing that he's winning. You're starting to wonder when you're going to get your $50 check back and what they are doing with your old car. You finally tell him that you think you had best go home and talk about the matter before making a decision, and you demand your check and your car keys. He promises that he will try to locate them right away and he leaves the room. You're getting tense now, but you still feel that you can get the deal for $3900, which is still a $100 better than the next best deal. You discuss it with your spouse and decide that since you've been here this long you might as well hang around a little longer and hope the deal can be wrapped up for $3900.

A few minutes later, salesman number three comes in. This is the boss and he's high pressure all the way. The hour is getting later and you're getting more and more tired. The boss now is pushing hard to close you at $4050, which, as he says, "I'm losing money on."

Then comes the clincher. You again demand your check and your keys and he comes back from a quick search to inform you sadly that the cashier has left for the night and the check has been locked up in the register. "Don't worry, it's perfectly safe there. If we don't close the deal tonight, you can come back and pick it up in the morning."

Furthermore, the used car appraiser has also left for the night and thinking that your old car had been accepted as a trade-in, he parked it in the lot and locked up the keys in his office. "Don't worry," says the boss, "we can give you a ride home tonight and pick you up in the morning to get your old car. I assure you, there's absolutely no problem. Now about this deal . . ."

The final thrust: "Look folks, I know how late it's getting, and I want to get out of here as badly as you do. Let me ask you this—if I give you the deal for $4000, will you take it, then we'll all go out and have a drink?" Resignation has finally set in and you agree to the deal. After all, it's still as good as the best deal you had any other place. Wearily, you reach for your pen.

Interwoven throughout this intrigue are four types of sales tactics (Did you recognize them?) which have brought a poor reputation to a small segment of the automobile sales industry. They are:

The Highball

In this trick, the salesman quotes a much higher trade-in value on your old car than is reasonable. Indeed, it sounded too good to be true, which causes the first strong opening pull on your purse strings. The opposite of the highball is the lowball, wherein the salesman looks at the sticker price on the new car and suggests a too-good-to-be-true discount from that price. The obvious tactic here is to lead you to believe that you're going to get a better deal than you thought possible, all the quicker to get you into the showroom where the heavy pressure can be applied.

The "T.O." Or "Takeover" Operation

This is a ploy involving a succession of salesmen ranging from low pressure up to high pressure. The first one's job is to soften you and win your confidence. Subsequent salesmen increase the pressure until the closer takes over. The process is designed to wear down your resistance gradually. The first salesman's job was accomplished when he got you to sit down in the closing office, not just in a mood to buy, but with a raging desire to buy, albeit at a price that would later turn out to be impossible. The success of the takeover operation depends on the next phenomenon:

The Bugged Closing Room

Unless you were an electronics whiz, you would probably not be able to determine whether or not a room was bugged. This indeed is a devious trick not generally employed by a legitimate dealer, but you never know what you're up against. By listening in on your conversations, the salesmen know just where your soft spots are and how far they can take you. If they determine that you are really thick skinned and have strong sales resistance, they can always fall back on the following:

The "Disappearing Check" Trick or the "Keys Are Locked up for the Night" Gambit

This is the last straw. By claiming to have "misplaced" something of value, such as a check or car keys, they are, in effect, nailing you to the wall until your resistance finally breaks. The best way to avoid being trapped in this manner is not to write any checks and to stand by as they test your trade-in car so you can retain the keys until the deal is either made or not made.

If you spot any of the above tactics in operation in your car shopping, you can be relatively sure that you're in for a high-pressure pitch that might lead you to signing a contract you otherwise wouldn't sign. Even though, in the above case, you thought you got away with the same deal you could have had elsewhere, that isn't necessarily so. Had you gone back to the other dealers for a follow-up bargaining session, you might have gotten a still better deal. Awareness of these tricks and a willingness to walk away from shady tactics when you spot them are necessary weapons when shopping for a car. The dealer sells hundreds of cars each month. You buy only one every few years. He knows a lot more about the tricks of bargaining and striking a deal than you do. He's entitled to a fair profit for whatever work he's involved in, just as you are, but that doesn't give him the right to take advantage of you—all of which leads back to the most important point: know whom you are dealing with. There's no substitute for a reputation of integrity.

Your Old Car: Selling It Yourself Versus Trading It In

It's difficult to determine whether you can do better by selling your own used car or by using it as a trade-in on a new purchase. First, check the used-car price directory and used-car lots to see what cars similar to yours are selling for (see Figure 6-1). The directory is available at all

1981 Chevrolet Model	F.O.B.	Average Wholesale	Average Retail
V8 Malibu			
Sport Coupe 2 door	$7572	$6200	$7640
Sport Sedan 4 door	7688	6200	7640
V8 Malibu Classic			
Sport Coupe 2 door	7902	6400	7860
Land Coupe 2 door	8166	6500	7970
Sedan 4 door	8035	6400	7860
V8 Wagons			
Malibu 4 door 2S	7865	6375	7835
Classic 4 door 2S	8142	6550	8025
Classic Estate	8413	6725	8220

NOTE: F.O.B. refers to original suggested retail price of the car, including standard equipment. Optional extras, destination charges, preparation charges, taxes and licensing fees not included. Average wholesale and retail prices are for clean reconditioned cars ready for sale. See separate listings in directory for increases/decreases in price due to equipment, condition, and mileage.

Figure 6–1   Abbreviated listing from typical used car price directory (as of Summer 1981).

dealerships and at most banks. Bear in mind that the prices on cars at lots are the asking prices, not necessarily the selling prices. If you can find a buyer who's ready, willing, and able to pay your price, it may be wise to make a deal. But before you can determine the wisdom of such a deal, you must go to various dealers to determine the different price that you'd be expected to pay with and without a trade-in.

If you can't find a ready, willing, and able buyer quickly, you might be in for more headache than the project is worth. You'll have to advertise the car for sale, and you'll have to be available when interested buyers want to come around to take it for a test drive. Not only could that be inconvenient; you could feel quite uncomfortable having a stranger take your car for a half-hour or so test spin.

Sales tax is another important factor to take into account. Customarily, when you offer an old car as a trade-in, you pay a sales tax on the difference between the selling price and the trade-in value. If you pay all cash for a car, you pay a sales tax on the total amount. Assuming a 6 percent sales tax rate, the tax on a $10,000 cash purchase would be $600. If you offer a trade-in valued at $4000, your cash difference is $6000 with a resulting sales tax of $360. In short, you save $240 by going the trade-in route. That alone might offset any better deal you could get by selling the car on your own. Check in your locality to determine current regulations on this matter.

How Much Haggling Room Do You Have?

Again, no rule of thumb, but here are some broad guidelines. Your haggling room will depend on the value of your trade-in, whether or not you're financing through the dealer (see Financing below), and how anxious the dealer is to move his current inventory. Very generally speaking, dealers work on a markup of about 20 percent. Thus, depending on the foregoing conditions, it might not be unreasonable to expect a discount of 5 to 10 percent off the sticker price. To get much more than 10 percent is going to take some hard bargaining, but if you don't ask for it, they're not going to volunteer it. *Consumer Reports* magazine publishes annual price listing of new model cars which can serve as a more specific guideline to your bargaining powers. Consult these lists before you go shopping.

When Is the Best Time to Buy?

Though some change in traditional patterns has been creeping into the industry, late summer and early fall still tend to be the times when dealers are clearing out their old inventory to make room for the new model cars shipped from the factories. While there may be a smaller assortment of cars to choose from at this time of year, there's a strong chance that you will get a better price than you might have earlier in the model year.

This is also a time when dealers tend to sell their demonstrator models—cars that have been driven by employees of the dealership. Demos can be very good bargains. They tend to be well-equipped and well taken care of, and many dealerships will offer them with full warranty, even though they have been driven for a few thousand miles or more.

Financing: Direct Versus Through the Dealer

Assuming you have the necessary trade-in or down payment and acceptable credit, most dealers can arrange financing for you right on the spot. You can also make your own financing arrangements through your bank (and in many instances, your car insurance company). Which is better?

It can be very convenient to have the dealer arrange for the financing. It saves you time, but it can cost you extra money. Determine the Annual Percentage Rate (APR) that the dealer will charge you for the financing. (See chapter 14 for a more detailed discussion of interest rates and installment loans.) Compare the dealer's APR with that offered by other lenders. The APR is the apples versus apples way of comparing interest rates. Have any APR quote put in writing and signed by the salesperson. If the dealer is charging more for the financing he's arranging for you, then obviously it wouldn't pay to deal with him, unless there are other extenuating circumstances, such as the fact that you don't want to extend your credit any further at your regular bank.

Virtually all dealers will receive a rebate from the lender; it can be as much as a few hundred dollars, depending on the amount of financing involved. Thus, dealers are anxious to arrange financing for you. If you play the game advantageously, you'll let the dealer believe that you're going to do the financing through him before you make a commitment to purchase the car. This is liable to result in a lower price for the car, since the dealer will anticipate additional profit through the financing. He may, if he suspects your wise buymanship tactics, give you two prices for the car—one if you finance with them; one if you don't. Act accordingly.

One important advantage—in addition to saving on interest—in dealing with your own bank is that you are dealing with people who know you and who can be accommodating to you should problems arise. If the dealer arranges the financing for you, it may be with a bank or finance company you've never dealt with; it might even be with an out-of-town institution. In such a case, if you run into problems with lateness or other financial distress, the institution is liable to regard you as little more than a number in their computer and any accommodation may be hard to come by.

Wherever you arrange your financing, it's essential that you do not allow the loan to last longer than you expect to own the car. If you expect to trade every three years, you shouldn't finance for more than three years. (See the section on Credit Abuses in chapter 14 on how this timing of your loans can be important to you.)

Buying Versus Leasing

Leasing has become very popular in the last few years. It tends to be more advantageous for business than for individual purposes, but you might want to entertain the possibility of leasing.

If you do explore leasing, first be aware that the credit requirements for a lease tend to be much more stringent than for outright financing. This is because you are putting very little down payment into the deal and because leases tend to involve more expensive automobiles. With a lease, as noted, there's a fairly small down payment and monthly payments are lower than they normally would be on a straight financing. At the end of the lease term, you will have the right to buy the car at a pre-agreed-upon price, or you can simply turn the car back over to the dealer and walk away, assuming the car is in acceptable condition. For example, on a three-year lease, the residual value at the end of the lease might be approximately 50 percent of the original purchase price. Thus, on a $10,000 car, the residual value might be $5000. This is the price at which you can then buy the car. If it happens to be worth more than that on the open market, you can turn around and sell it and reap a profit. If it happens to be less than that on the open market, you have to make up the difference to the dealer. Customarily, at the end of a lease, the customer will either renew at a lower monthly rental or will start a new lease with a new car.

Tax pros and cons: If you buy a car outright and finance it, the interest you pay on the loan is tax deductible to you no matter what use you make of the car. If you lease a car as an individual, the only portion of the lease payments that you can legitimately deduct on your taxes is that usage of the car directly related to business purposes—and that does *not* include commuting to and from work. If you lease a car for business purposes, all of the lease payment can be deductible. Further, a lease doesn't tie up as much down payment money. If you have the money available, you can invest it rather than put it toward a car. The earnings can offset some of your lease expense. A visit with an accountant would be worthwhile to sort out the specific tax advantages and disadvantages in leasing, depending on your intended use of the car.

Warranties

Historically, the common warranty on new cars has been for 12 months or 12,000 miles, whichever comes first. In other words, if you drive 12,000 miles during the first 11 months of ownership of the car, the warranty expires after you've reached the 12,000th mile. Or if you've only driven 10,000 miles after one year of ownership, the warranty will have expired after the end of the first full year. Check with dealers when you shop to find out if additional warranties are included in the purchase of a new car.

Most manufacturers also offer an extended service plan for one year or more on new car purchases. The cost of these extended service plans will vary depending on the make and model of the car. Some have deductibles—minumum amounts which you must pay yourself; and most provide a fixed price for a rental car should you need one while yours is being serviced under the extended plan. The typical extended service contract will cover the engine, drive train, and transmission and may also cover parts of the electrical system, the braking system, the front suspension, the air conditioning, and the steering. In 1979, Consumers Union, a product-testing organization, studied a variety of extended service plans and suggested that they generally weren't worth the money. But changes in the plans and increasing repair prices since that date may justify such an expense. At least you'll have peace of mind in knowing that you're protected against major repair bills. On the other hand, the more you know about the proper operation and maintenance of your car, the less need you'll feel to have an extended service contract.

Automobile Insurance

An adequate package of automobile insurance protects you against the hazards inherent in owning and using an automobile: damage to the machine itself, and damage that it may cause others for which you might be responsible. Each state has imposed a requirement that motorists must maintain a minimum level of financial responsibility in the event that they are involved in an automobile accident. Most commonly, this minimum responsibility is met by obtaining an automobile insurance policy, which includes the all-important public liability protection.

The typical automobile insurance policy packages many different types of insurance altogether. These types of coverage are:

Public Liability for Bodily Injury This is the single most important financial aspect of your automotive insurance policy, and possibly of your entire personal insurance program. Should your car injure or kill other people, this aspect of coverage will defend you against claims and will pay any claims for which you're found to be legally responsible. Coverage is generally broken down into two phases: one for injury to a single individual involved in an accident and a second phase for all individuals involved. The limits of coverage are usually expressed as follows: $10,000/$20,000. This coverage would protect you for up to $10,000 worth of claim from any single individual and for up to $20,000 for all parties injured in the accident. The amount of protection you choose is up to you. You may have to comply with a minimum required by your state, which may be as low as $10,000/$20,000 (more commonly expressed as 10/20). Of, if you are prudent and aware of the potential circumstances, you may choose much higher limits, perhaps as high as $100,000/$300,000, or even higher if it's available. The difference in cost between the minumal coverage and the more extensive coverage is only a few dollars per month—an investment that many would have a hard time turning down.

Public Liability for Property Damage   If your automobile causes damage to the property of others, this aspect of coverage will defend you against claims and will pay claims for which you are found to be legally responsible. The limit of coverage is usually expressed as a number following the limits for bodily injury liability. For example, overall public liability limits of 25/50/10 would mean that your property damage liability limits are $10,000 (following the bodily injury limits of $25,000 and $50,000). In this case, if you caused injury to the property of others, you would be protected for up to $10,000 of such damage.

Property damage liability covers damage to the property of *others*— not to your own property. It can include damage to the automobiles of others when involved in an accident or damage caused to buildings if a driver hits one. Property damage coverage will usually not be less than $5000 and a ceiling of $50,000 should be adequate in most situations. It's difficult to conceive of an auto accident causing much more physical damage to property than that, although it is possible if you crash into a new Rolls-Royce or career through the lobby of a modern retail building.

Your public liability protection for bodily injury and property damage will cover you in your own car or if you're driving someone else's car, as well as covering other persons who drive your car with your permission. It also provides legal defense for claims made against you.

Medical Payments   If you, or members of your household or guests who are driving in your car, are injured while driving (or even if struck while walking), the medical payments provision will reimburse all reasonable actual medical expenses arising out of the accident up to the limits of the policy. Generally, these payments will be made regardless of who was at fault. The minimum may be as low as $500, but much greater coverage than that can be obtained at a reasonable added annual cost. As with the public liability portions of the coverage, the prudent motorist would do well to consider taking much higher than minimal limits on the medical payments provisions, for the added extra cost is small indeed compared with the immediate protection obtained.

Uninsured Motorists   Regretfully, not everyone who drives an automobile is insured, or is adequately insured. You might be caused serious harm by a motorist with little or no insurance protection. You could be out of pocket tens of thousands of dollars in medical expenses and lost income, and the party at fault may have little or no money with which to reimburse you for the damage he or she has caused. (Generally, property damage is not covered.) Although the courts may find the person legally responsible for making payments to you, he or she may not be financially responsible and you may never be able to recover. Uninsured motorist protection is designed to take care of this problem, providing you with reimbursement for your losses through your own insurance company.

Unfortunately, we don't have a choice as to who might cause us harm in an automobile. It could be a perfectly adequately insured individual, or it could be the uninsured individual, or a hit-and-run driver whom we will never see again. This form of protection is quite inexpensive and the motorist is assuming an unnecessary risk by not having it.

Comprehensive Insurance   This is a broad form of protection for loss caused other than by collision. It includes damage to your car due to fire, loss due to theft, glass breakage, riots, windstorm, hail, and other types of miscellaneous damage. Limited protection on contents is also available. Deductibles are common in such policies. If the deductible is, for example, $50, then the motorist will have to pay the first $50 worth of any such loss, and the insurance company will pay for damages over the deductible amount. You should check your policy to determine whether you are protected against theft if you leave your car unattended and/or unlocked. Some policies will not protect the motorist under these circumstances.

Collision Insurance   This coverage protects you against damage done to your own car should you be in a collision with another car or an object such as a telephone pole or a building. Collision insurance also usually carries a deductible amount. If car A and car B collide and the accident was the fault of the driver of car A, his property liability insurance will pay for the damage to the owner of car B, and car A's owner's collision insurance will pay for the damage to car A. Compared with the other forms of automobile insurance, collision protection tends to be fairly expensive. If you're driving a car more than five or six years old, the cost of the collision protection might be so high as to discourage you from obtaining that protection in view of the limited recovery you can expect on an older car. Weigh the cost and the protection accordingly.

How Much Will It Cost?

The cost of automobile insurance can vary considerably depending on the age, safety record, and occupation of the owner, and purposes for which the car is used. It's common knowledge that younger drivers have to pay a higher rate for their automotive insurance, primarily because those drivers have a generally bad statistical record when it comes to accidents and claims. Some companies will offer discounts for drivers with safe records and for younger persons who have taken certain driver education courses. Other discounts may be available where more than one car is insured and where compact cars are involved. In shopping around for the best automobile insurance protection package, all available discounts should be inquired about from each agent.

The amount of the various deductibles can also have a bearing on the total premium cost. As with deductibles in other forms of personal insurance, you are assuming a higher risk in exchange for paying a lower premium. The premium saved is an actual savings, whereas the higher risk may never occur.

A Word About "No-fault" Auto Insurance

If you've ever witnessed the typical fender-bender, you've seen both drivers leap out of their cars and commence bleeping at each other in a furious rage. Even though both drivers may be totally insured, and neither may end up out of pocket as a result of the accident, it's a matter of pride, if nothing else, that each establish blamelessness. Each will want the other's insurance company to pay for the damages, and each may be concerned that if his insurance company has to pay, premiums may be increased as a result of the accident. This, in fact, may be true in certain cases.

Where extensive injuries or damages are involved, the question of who is at fault can become critical to the rights of all the parties. If the solution is not clear cut, and if the damages are extensive enough, each party may find itself involved in a lawsuit to determine who is at fault. The question of fault will ultimately determine which insurance company has to pay for what damages. In addition to actual physical damages to property or to a person, injured parties might also claim that they endured "pain and suffering," knowing that the courts may award damages to parties who have so suffered in many cases. It may be difficult to understand why a dollar value can be placed on physical pain and mental anguish, but the concept has been embedded in our legal system for close to two centuries.

For many years, the hassles over who was responsible for automobile accidents and who suffered how much damage, either physical or mental, had created extraordinary congestion in our courts and added extravagant costs to the settlement of claims. It was not unusual for a lawsuit involving an automobile accident to take three or four years to be heard by the courts in some states, and the addition of medical costs, legal expenses, and related fees boosted the asking price on many claims to levels that tested the imagination.

The result was that injured parties might have to wait years before they received their settlement. In the meantime, insurance companies that were having to pay out very high settlements had to pass the cost along to their insureds, which meant ever-increasing automobile insurance premiums for the general public.

All parties involved in these lawsuits agreed that something had to be done to correct the situation. The best available solution, at least to date, has been the advent of what's known as "no-fault" auto insurance. Many states have adopted such plans, and there has been talk in Washington for a number of years regarding a federally mandated no-fault form of automobile insurance for the entire nation.

Under the typical no-fault legislation, insured parties are paid for certain losses and medical expenses (including lost income) regardless of who is at fault in the accident. These expenses are limited by state law.

Although many states have reported good experience with no-fault, the public at large has still not noticed any improvement in the cost of its automobile insurance. There are a number of reasons for this. One is that the costs of repairing automobiles, along with the costs of repairing people's bodies, has continued to skyrocket in spite of the existence of no-fault legislation. Because premiums have to be kept in line with the payments that the insurance company anticipates it will have to make to claimants, the cost of premiums has accordingly continued its climb.

Another possible reason for the lack of overall success with the no-fault program has been the so-called threshold concept. If an innocent party is injured by another, the sums he or she may be paid under a no-fault plan may not nearly fully compensate for the actual damages suffered. The no-fault concept can eliminate bickering between the parties on relatively minor amounts of money, yet it would be contrary to our legal rights to prevent an innocent party from seeking full compensation for actual damages incurred. The threshold concept suggests that if your actual immediate medical expenses are nominal, then the ultimate losses you might suffer from being out of work, or pain and suffering, would likely be minimal or nonexistent. If your actual medical expenses are high, it's more likely that you will truly have suffered related losses.

Although the law differs from state to state, the threshold concept generally allows for further lawsuits if the actual medical expenses have exceeded a certain level or threshold. Let's say that the threshold is $2500. If your immediate medical expenses do not exceed that amount, you may not be allowed to pursue further claims. If your actual expenses do exceed it, you may be able to proceed with your other claims. Critics of the system have suggested that doctors and patients will conspire together to create a medical expense history high enough to satisfy the minimum threshold, thus allowing the injured party to pursue a higher suit.

Automobile Clubs

Another form of worthwhile insurance can be obtained through automobile clubs. For a modest annual fee these clubs provide towing insurance, which will get your car to a service station at no out-of-pocket cost to you should it break down on the road. Auto club insurance can also provide you with bail in the event of arrest; travel services are an added plus included with the price of the annual premium.

Car Pooling

Comfort and convenience aside, it can definitely pay to become involved in a car pool. Whether it's to work, to pick up and deliver children at school, or even a supermarket car pool, there can be considerable savings in the cost of operating your automobile. Table 6-2, based on a 1980 U.S. Department of Transportation study, gives some examples of the annual savings that can be realized by continuous participation in a car pool.

Rent-a-Car

Renting cars is an ever-growing business. Aside from the commonplace airport and hotel car rental agencies used in conjunction with business travel and tourism, car renting is increasingly popular with residents of highly populated urban centers where ownership and parking of automobiles is costly and inconvenient. There are a number of major national rental firms with computerized reservation services and garage facilities well located in most major cities. These include Hertz, Avis, National, Dollar, Budget, and Thrifty. There are hundreds of smaller regional or local firms which, because they don't have the high advertising and rental overheads, can offer much lower prices on rentals. Another recently popular concept is "rent-a-wreck," which offers drivable vehicles at a low

Table 6-2 | **Annual Car-pool Savings**

Roundtrip Commute (Miles)	Type of Car	Cost of Driving Alone	Cost of Shared Driving Carpool	
			2 Persons	4 Persons
20	subcompact	$ 726	$ 398	$ 217
20	standard	1062	582	316
40	subcompact	1262	718	398
40	standard	1857	1053	582
80	subcompact	2194	1250	718
80	standard	3251	1844	1053

price, if you don't mind that they may be covered with dents, dings, rips, and tears. If appearance is no object, this might be a most inexpensive way to rent a car. But if long-distance travel is in your plans, you may prefer a larger agency where better mechanical service is assured.

Whatever your rental needs, it definitely pays to shop around for the best deal. Many rental firms regularly offer discounts at special times of the week, month, or year. Discounts are also available through magazine ads and through a corporate account that your company may have with one of the major rental firms.

Rental plans can vary considerably. Most popular are those which charge a fixed amount per day plus a fixed amount per mile driven; alternatively, you may pay a fixed amount per day with a set number of miles included as part of that charge. In both cases the customer pays for gasoline used. If you can reasonably determine the number of miles you expect to drive the car, you can easily figure which of these two plans would be cheaper for you.

The major rental firms also offer the capability of picking up a car in one city and leaving it in another. Depending on the cities involved, there may or may not be a drop-off charge. Determine in advance exactly what drop-off charges would be connected with inter-city usage.

Car rental firms will also offer you two different types of insurance: collision and medical. If you do *not* have their collision insurance, you will be responsible for the deductible in the event of any damage to the car. The deductible can be $250 or more. If you buy the collision insurance at a cost of a few dollars per day, you will not be responsible for any deductible. Is it worth it? Chances are you may be covered for part of the deductible on your private auto policy anyway. In that event, you're buying duplicate coverage. But if an accident does occur with the rental car, you could spend a considerable amount of time filling out forms and answering questions if you didn't purchase their insurance. Many users buy the collision insurance just to avoid that kind of nuisance, figuring that it's easily worth the few dollars should an accident occur.

With respect to the medical policy, determine whether the plan will pay for injuries if you are otherwise covered by your own auto policy or health insurance plan. If the car renter's insurance will not pay you if you are otherwise covered, then it doesn't make sense to acquire the car renter's insurance. If you don't feel adequately covered by your own policies, then the car renter's insurance is a relatively inexpensive way to give yourself short-term protection.

A Look Ahead

America's dependence on the automobile will be with us for many years to come, but little by little the picture is changing, with electronics the wave of the future. Already, tens of thousands of workers are able to do their work at home via computer terminals which can relay all necessary information between the worker's home and the central place of business (or central computer). This number will grow to hundreds of thousands in a few years, and eventually to millions. Most of the people affected by this revolution will be those who deal in information and services: stock brokers, insurance employees, bookkeepers, accountants, and so on. They will simply find it not necessary to "go to work" in the traditional sense. By working at home, or at some nearby neighborhood facility to which they can walk, they'll eliminate the need for an automobile.

Similarly, as chapter 7 notes, many other common functions which now depend on the automobile will be taken over by electronics. We'll do our banking through a computerized hook-up to our telephone/television complex. We'll be able to order our goods from the supermarket by means of the same device, and the market will send one truck to deliver what 50 or 100 cars used to have to go and pick up. Large-screen TV sets in the home will replace driving to the movies. Two-way video telephones will replace countless business meetings, commutes, and conferences.

In short, the electronics revolution can be a step in the right direction toward solving the energy crisis. These changes—which are inevitable—will allow you (or require you) to change many of your habits and ways of thinking, ways that affect your financial welfare and your work/leisure cycle. Each individual will have to determine for himself or herself whether resistance to change hurts more than acceptance of change.

Personal Action Checklist
Car Shopping Comparison

Use this checklist to help yourself compare offerings from various dealers. Remember, the price of a car itself is not the only factor that determines how good a deal is.

	Dealer A	Dealer B	Dealer C
☐ Base price of car	_____	_____	_____
☐ Cost of optional extras items (list items separately) _____	_____	_____	_____
	_____	_____	_____
	_____	_____	_____
	_____	_____	_____
	_____	_____	_____
☐ Dealer prep, delivery charges	_____	_____	_____
☐ Total sticker price	_____	_____	_____
☐ Trade allowance on your old car	_____	_____	_____
☐ Trade difference: new car cost less trade-in	_____	_____	_____
☐ Sales tax and license cost	_____	_____	_____
☐ How long will this offer be good?	_____	_____	_____
☐ Financing: What APR is offered?	_____	_____	_____
☐ Insurance: If offered, terms and cost	_____	_____	_____
☐ Reputation for fair dealing	_____	_____	_____
☐ Reputation for service and adjustment of complaints	_____	_____	_____
☐ Convenience in getting to and from when service is needed	_____	_____	_____
☐ If buying a used car:			
physical condition	_____	_____	_____
mechanical condition	_____	_____	_____
extent of warranty	_____	_____	_____
☐ Treatment by salesperson	_____	_____	_____

Consumer Beware
Service Station Sharpies Commit Highway Robbery

Most service station operators are honorable and reliable businessmen. Sad, then, that a small scattering of sharpies smudge the reputation of an otherwise honest industry.

Long-distance travelers are particularly vulnerable to these tactics— far from home, in strange territory, they stop for gas and find themselves facing such money-gouging abuses as:

☐ Tire "honking." While you're not looking, a swift kick at your tire, with a boot that has a sharp nail point embedded in the toe, gives you a sudden flat and a sales pitch to buy a costly new tire.

☐ Slashing. A few quick slices with a well-hidden razor blade can destroy a fan belt or a radiator hose in an instant.

☐ The "white smoke trick." The attendant sprays a few drops of a chemical on your hot engine, and a cloud of white smoke erupts. It's actually harmless, but you're then susceptible to a pitch for costly engine repairs—which, of course, aren't needed in the first place.

☐ Bubbling battery. Drop a few grains of Alka-Seltzer, or the like, into a battery and watch it bubble over. The unwary will find themselves paying for a new battery before they have time to say "plop, plop, fizz, fizz."

☐ Shocking shocks. A few dribbles of oil under one's shock absorbers are enough to convince many drivers that the absorbers are shot and need replacement. The same can hold true for the transmission and so on.

The common ploy following any of these tactics is a stern and concerned statement by the attendant to the effect that "you ought not drive more than a few hundred feet with your car in this condition . . . ."

The best protection against such events is to know the operation of your car; have it properly serviced before you set off on a long trip; never leave the car while it's being serviced; keep your eye on the attendant at all times. If you really do suspect a problem, take it to another station for a second opinion. Better still, you might want to take it to a dealer who sells your make of car.

7 | Leisure and Recreation

"All work and no play makes Jack a dull boy . . . and Jill a dull girl." How true those words can be. And how easy it is for our workaday routine to get the best of us, so that we spend the bulk of our leisure time—evenings, weekends, vacations—doing little more than sitting and staring at a television set. Sometimes it doesn't even matter if the set is turned on.

Our work week is growing shorter—from about 50 hours at the start of this century to about 35 hours currently. Less work time means more leisure time. And more leisure time gives every individual a choice: vegetate or "re-create." This chapter is intended to stimulate you to plan how you can combine your spendable dollars and your spendable leisure time in the most rewarding way. You'll learn how to:

☐ Seek out vacation and holiday activities that you can affordably enjoy.
☐ Make use of the professional services of a travel agent.
☐ Evaluate the opportunities to buy, rent, or share vacation facilities.
☐ Shop for the best values in at-home electronic leisure equipment.
☐ Make yourself aware of no-cost or low-cost personal enrichment activities that can enhance your life.

"Re-creation"

How much of your disposable income should you devote to recreation and leisure? That's a very personal decision that each individual and family must make for themselves. Some people will go overboard on their leisure expenses, leaving them in a budgetary bind. Some people will consciously choose to curtail other types of expenses—living in a more modest dwelling, driving a more modest car—in order to enjoy their leisure freely. And still others will forgo their leisure activities so that they can live in the more elaborate dwelling and drive the more elaborate car. To each his own. No one can dictate the proper balance for someone else. If you're overspending on leisure, you can either make adjustments or suffer the consequences. The same holds true if you are not partaking of any meaningful leisure activities. This chapter will help you think about the balance that you'd like to achieve and may motivate you to take action. We will explore two broad basic areas of leisure, and the important financial considerations relating to them. Those areas are: vacation and travel, and recreation at home.

Vacation and Travel

From the weekend camping trip to the elaborate cruise or European junket, you want to be certain that everything goes just right. It's a shame to waste money, but it's even more disappointing to have wasted time. You can always go out and make more money, but you can never go out and make more time. Careful planning is essential if you want to make the most of your time and money.

Using a Travel Agent

Throughout this book we'll be discussing the importance of using professional help to best protect your financial interests: the real estate agent in buying and selling a home, the accountant in working on your taxes, the lawyer for a variety of purposes, and so on. The proper professional to assist you with your vacation and travel plans is a travel agent.

A well-trained and experienced travel agent has many tools at his or her disposal to assist you in getting the most out of your vacation dollars. Among these tools are:

☐ *The Official Airline Guide* (OAG), which gives updated flight information on virtually every commercial flight in the United States, as well as many international flights. Included in the OAG are arrival and departure times, fare structures, type of equipment flown on each route, and meals and other services offered on the flight. The OAG is an excellent device for getting an overview of all the different ways you can get from point A to point B and back again. (But as Table 7-1 points out, some further checking may be in order to verify and update OAG information.)

☐ Directories of hotels, resorts, car rental agencies, and cruises are available at most major travel agencies. These directories provide abundant detailed information on costs, facilities, reservation requirements, and often the quality of the various services and facilities. The directories also contain maps of the communities in question, showing locations of hotels, amusements, and air, bus, and train terminals.

☐ Brochures are in abundance at every travel agency. These are publications by airlines, resorts, states, nations, and tour-packaging companies. They provide an excellent means for familiarizing yourself with various travel opportunities, price ranges, available dates, and other useful information.

☐ All of the above information is supplemented by the travel agent's own personal experiences and the experiences of his or her colleagues at the agency. Travel agents will travel extensively to examine resort facilities, convention facilities, and other matters of concern to their clientele. They can provide worthwhile recommendations on hotels, restaurants, sightseeing, and basic do's and don'ts in given cities or resort areas. A well-equipped travel agency will also have up-to-date travel books for customer browsing.

☐ The age of electronics has indeed arrived at the travel agency. Many agencies today are equipped with computers that can instantly show the agent the availability and times of flights, data on hotel rooms, rental car prices, and even weather reports in most cities of destination. The computer acts as an instant update of all the other material at the agent's disposal.

A travel agent can give you advice and guidelines on choosing a vacation that will satisfy your interests and budget. The agent, furthermore, can make all necessary reservations for travel and accommodation. The more advance time you give the agent to work on your plans, the wider choice you'll have of flights, hotel rooms, rental cars, and the like. Visiting a travel agent at the last minute will likely prove frustrating, but even in such cases the agent can probably do more for you than you could on your own.

What does a travel agent cost? The travel agent will not charge you for his or her services except, perhaps, for long-distance phone calls and other out-of-pocket expenses made on your behalf. The travel agent is paid on a commission basis by the airlines, hotels, cruise operators, and tour packagers that he books for you. In some cases, a travel agent may actually be able to save you money. He may be aware of a group package tour whose itinerary virtually matches the travel you are planning. By making arrangements for you to take part in the group tour, you could cut your travel costs considerably. If the agent doesn't volunteer such information, ask him if he knows of any such possibilities.

Choosing a travel agent is like choosing any other kind of professional advisor. Personal recommendations are always worth seeking out. The neatness and efficiency of the travel agent's office can also often be a giveaway to the quality of his work, or lack thereof. The agent should be a member of the American Society of Travel Agents (ASTA) and should have credentials from the International Air Transport Association (IATA).

A Wealth of Information

In addition to the printed material a travel agent can offer you, there is an abundance of literature on travel that you should take advantage of at the earliest possible planning stages. Whether you're traveling on your own or with a guided tour group, the more you can learn about your places of destination, the more choice you'll have as to what you'll want to see and do. Visit your local bookstore and choose from among the following worthwhile publications:

☐ The three "Fs": Temple Fielding, Eugene Fodor, and Arthur Frommer. These three noted travel authors and their respective organizations publish a wide variety of books covering major travel destinations throughout the United States and around the world.

☐ The Mobil *Travel Guides* cover various segments of the United States and are very detailed with respect to hotels, motels, and sightseeing facilities. They also contain discount coupons at various amusements and attractions.

☐ Sunset Guides publishes an extensive series of travel books covering the Western part of the United States, Canada, and Mexico.

☐ Michelin guides provide excellent information on many major European cities and countries.

☐ Magazines also abound. *Travel and Leisure,* published by American Express Company monthly, contains in-depth articles on a wide variety of travel destinations. So-called city magazines—published in and about major American cities such as Los Angeles, New York, Chicago, and many more—offer up-to-date travel, sightseeing, and dining possibilities in those cities. Write to the Chamber of Commerce of the cities you plan to visit and ask them how you can obtain these city magazines and any other tourist information they may have available.

Public libraries will have many of these publications available but not always on the most up-to-date basis. Particularly with the books noted, it might be better to spend the money to get the most recent edition rather than rely on out-dated information that might be in the older library books.

Air Fares

Until the late 1970s, the cost of airplane travel was very tightly regulated by the federal government. With very few exceptions, the cost of flying from one city to another would be the same no matter which airline you flew, no matter what time you flew, no matter how often you flew. With their fares thus fixed by the government, there was very little the airlines could do to compete for passengers other than to promise more attentive service, more tasty meals, or more frequent departures.

The government began to allow deregulation of the airlines in the late 1970s, and it's a trend that seems certain to continue through the 1980s. Taking away the regulations means increasing the competition with respect to fares, and the result has been a veritable maze of new fare structures for the air traveler. Depending on which airline you're dealing with, you're likely to find different classes of service (first class, coach class, economy class). You'll find different fare structures for each of the different classes (regular fare, "supersaver" fare, family fare, and fares that offer free stopovers in extra cities). You'll find that these different fare structures for the different classes of service will further differ depending on the time of year, the time of week, and the time of day you travel. Finally, you'll find that many of these fare structures will have restrictions as to when they are available. You may have to reserve your seats so many days in advance; you may have to purchase your tickets so many days in advance; you may have to stay a certain length of time in a given destination.

It's all a rather maddening process. If you use a travel agent to book your air passage, be certain that the agent does check every possible alternative available to you. If you're doing your own booking and want to have the full choice of fares and departures, you will have to call every airline that flies from your city to the city of destination to check (and double-check) all of their possible fare structures and departure times. If you think that's a waste of time, examine Table 7-1, which illustrates the spectrum of fares available between Los Angeles and Phoenix as a short flight example and Los Angeles and New York as a cross-country flight example.

As the table illustrates, the hour or so you spend with a travel agent or on the telephone yourself can result in considerable savings. If you don't take the time to inquire what the best air fares are, you may simply be sold the highest priced ticket and never know the difference. It's said that if there are 200 people on a flight from city A to city B chances are that all 200 of them have paid a different price for their ticket. You can pay the high price or the low price. You all get there at the same time. The choice is up to you.

Seasonal Bargains

Perhaps the best way to stretch your travel dollar farthest is to take advantage of the seasonal bargains in many major resort areas. You may not have the best possible weather, but the low prices may more than make up for the climatic situation. Off-season hotel prices in many major resort and tourist areas can be as little as one-half to one-third the high-season price. Samples include resorts in Las Vegas, Arizona, and Florida, where summertime prices are a fraction of wintertime hotel rates.

Table 7-1

Sampling of Airline Fares

On One Given Day, The Following Fares Were Available from Various Airlines

Los Angeles/Phoenix, Round Trip

☐ Economy, both flights on a Saturday or Sunday	$ 78
☐ Economy, any day, off hours	78
☐ Economy, both flights Monday through Friday	118
☐ Economy, any day, peak hours	128
☐ Coach, any day	138
☐ First class, any day	280

Los Angeles/New York, Round Trip

☐ Excursion fare (stay over one Saturday, stay not more than 60 days, and pay at least two weeks in advance)	
—day coach, one airline	$450
—day coach, another airline	480
—night coach, both above airlines	390
☐ Regular coach fare, travel good for one year	600
☐ First class fare, travel good for one year	750

Similarly, England and Europe in the winter can be much cheaper than during the hot and crowded summer months. If the weather is of secondary concern to you and you primarily want to see the sights and partake of the tourist opportunities, ask your travel agent to explain the off-season fare alternatives that are available. You could see more of the world for less money than you may have imagined.

Near-home Vacations

If air, bus, or train fares threaten to use up too much of your vacation budget, consider the travel opportunities within an easy day's drive of your own home. How many New Yorkers have never been to Boston or Washington, or vice versa? How many San Franciscans have never been to Los Angeles, and vice versa? And so it goes throughout the nation. Close-to-home opportunities for fun, adventure, and enrichment are abundant no matter where you live. Not to take advantage of these opportunities is to deny yourself re-creation.

Package Tours and Resorts

If you're not inclined to hassle over travel details, there are thousands of "package trips" available to you. Whether you're traveling within the United States or abroad, a package trip offers an almost-all-inclusive price for your vacation, which includes travel, accommodations, sightseeing, the services of a guide where appropriate, and some meals and extras. Package tours are available through resorts, airlines, travel tour companies (such as American Express), and major travel agencies. Sometimes, but not necessarily always, package tours can save you money. It's always wise to compare what the same travel would cost if you bought each separate component (air, hotel, rental car, etc.) separately. The experienced traveler probably will prefer to create his or her own package. The novice might appreciate the convenience and possible cost savings of the package.

If you are considering a package tour, whether to a resort or to another continent, study and evaluate the brochure that details what you get for your money. Pay attention to the following:

☐ Most packages are advertised as costing "from" a certain amount of dollars. That little word *from* is vitally important. It describes the *lowest* possible price for the package, and that price might include lesser hotel rooms and restaurants. If you would prefer better accommodations or meals, you might, on carefully examining the brochure, find that your true price is considerably more than the minimum price. You also might find, on inquiring about booking, that the minimum accommodations are sold out and the only ones available are the higher priced ones. This can be very disappointing because you will have already set your desires, only to find out that you can't achieve them without paying substantially more money. The earlier packages are booked, the better chance you'll have of getting the minimum price, if that's what you prefer.

□ Many of the advertised "extras" may not represent a true travel bargain, but on the surface they seem appealing. A "free welcoming cocktail" or a "free bottle of champagne" in your room may sound alluring but it's worth only a few dollars at most. The more important things to evaluate in terms of cost are the basic room accommodations and meals, if any.

□ If meals are included as a part of the package, determine what kind of menu and what kind of choices will be available to you. The basic package price might include minimal food service with anything extra being at an added cost. You can avoid disappointment by finding this out in advance.

□ If recreational facilities are included as part of the package, such as tennis or golf privileges, determine whether those facilities are available at any time you want them, or only at certain fixed times, which may be inconvenient for you.

□ If the package includes transportation, when will the flights leave? Night flights can knock your body clock awry and render you incapable of enjoying your destinations.

□ How much free time will you have, particularly on a multi-city guided tour? There are always horror stories coming out of some tour groups, indicating that the travelers were herded around like sheep. After a few days of that, you might not know whether you're in Athens, Greece or Athens, Georgia. To protect yourself, make sure you examine the day-to-day itinerary, which should be included in the travel brochure published by the package company. Too little free time can leave you exhausted; too much free time can mean that you'll be out spending money on your own, and that can leave you broke. Look for the happy balance with your travel agent as your guide.

Do-it-yourself Tours and Vacations

The more adventuresome or more experienced traveler probably will prefer to make his or her own arrangements. This means more time spent in the detailed planning stages, but more free time during the trip itself to do what you wish, rather than to do what the tour guide says it's time to do. Careful research is the key to arranging a successful do-it-yourself trip to other cities or even to a resort. Refer to the list of books and magazines mentioned earlier in this chapter to start your homework.

One of the chores that the do-it-yourselfer will have to face that the package traveler needn't be concerned about is: How do you get around once you've arrived at your destination? If it's to be by rental car, make your reservations well in advance. Popular tourist cities and resort areas often have a slim choice of cars, particularly during busier seasons. (Review the discussion on rental cars in chapter 6 for further advice on getting good value for your money.)

For inter-city travel, particularly on a foreign trip, rail and bus travel passes may be available. These passes offer unlimited travel within a certain area and for a specific length of time. They can represent a considerable savings over booking individual travel from city to city. Keep in mind that some of these passes for European travel must be purchased in the United States.

When booking do-it-yourself travel, it's essential that you get all of your reservations confirmed in writing from the hotels, car rental agencies, and any other facilities you'll be using. Make certain that those confirmations spell out exactly what you are getting for your money: the type of room, the price of the room, the arrival and departure dates, and the type and price of the car you may be reserving. Take these written confirmations with you. If you get into an argument with a desk clerk over the facilities you've ordered, your written confirmation will go a long way toward assuring that you will get what you have bargained for. Also, if you pay any deposit in advance, be certain to get a receipt for that deposit; and make sure when you make final payment for your stay that you are given the proper credit for that deposit.

Cruises

Cruises have often been thought of as an indulgence only for the wealthy. But when you consider that for one all-inclusive price you receive your room, your meals, entertainment, all facilities of the ship, and transportation from port to port, the price of a cruise may not be much different than a stay of comparable length at a resort or a moderately budget-wise trip abroad. If, that is, you plan far enough in advance.

Cruises, like tour packages, are advertised on a "from" basis. The price quoted in the advertising is the minimum price. For that price you will get the least desirable stateroom on the ship. It will probably be on the lowest deck, inside (as opposed to an outside room with a porthole), and at the far end of the ship (either fore or aft) where the motion of the boat will be more noticeable than in the center. But aside from the stateroom, all passengers have equal use of all facilities on the ship at all times. The food is the same, the entertainment is the same, the access to all facilities is the same. Experienced cruisers know that these minimum staterooms can't be all that bad: they are the first ones to be sold out on virtually every cruise. If a minimum stateroom isn't available to you, the price of better staterooms escalates rapidly. Since life on a cruise ship is spent predominantly in the public rooms and on shore, and the stateroom is used for little else than to sleep and change clothes in, the booking of a minimum stateroom should not prove a hardship to most travelers.

The all-inclusive price means just that: elaborate meals, snacks, and midnight buffet; nightly professional entertainment and dancing to live bands; daily movies; plus lectures and lessons on a wide variety of subjects. Not included are alcoholic beverages, laundry, tips, and on-shore expenses. All of these expenses are, of course, up to the individual. With respect to tipping though, the cruise lines generally recommend a tipping formula, which most passengers customarily observe. The formula suggests tips ranging from $1 to $3 per person per day for your room steward and your dining room waiter. Additional tips for deck stewards, maitre d' and wine stewards are warranted as services received from them. The traveler is the final judge on whether or not to tip and how much.

With respect to on-shore expenses, travelers should be cautious of acquiring things (jewelry, perfume, watches, and the like) which they could obtain at home for a similar price. When shopping in foreign ports, it's always important to ask: "If I'm not satisfied with this when I get it home, how can I get the matter corrected?" It's one thing to visit a local jewelry store where you bought a watch that stopped working. It can be quite something else to try to get a watch fixed if you bought it in a tiny shop in some exotic Caribbean island.

In planning a cruise, your travel agent can provide you with schedules of all ships leaving from accessible ports. Many cruise bookings also offer substantial air fare discounts to get you from your home town to the port city. The travel agent or the cruise line can provide you with deck plans of ships you may be interested in. Study the deck plans carefully. Notice where the minimum-rate rooms are and where higher-rate rooms are. Choose that which will give you adequate comfort, cost considered.

Trip Insurance

Whether you're going on a cruise, a package trip, or a do-it-yourself trip, it may be possible for you to buy insurance that will provide a refund if you or a member of your family becomes ill and thus unable to travel. Such insurance may also provide that if a close member of your family who was not planning on taking the trip becomes ill, with the result that you have to cancel your trip to be with that relative, then you can also get a refund. Ask your travel agent for details on this trip insurance. The more members of your family planning the trip, the more sense such insurance makes. It's not inexpensive, but if you have to forfeit a substantial deposit in the event of illness, it may be worthwhile.

Home-Exchange Programs

If you're the trusting type, a home-exchange program can offer you the best of both worlds: the chance to live in a distant city at very little expense. The idea behind a home exchange is that you swap residences with a family in another city—either in the United States or abroad. In addition to eliminating hotel bills, you also have kitchen facilities at your disposal so that you can save considerably on food costs. In some cases it is even possible to swap the use of each other's automobile.

Ask your travel agent for the names and addresses of various home-exchange programs. Sponsors of these programs usually charge a modest fee for either putting you in touch with other persons interested in swapping or providing you with a subscription to a swapping listing. When you've found a good match—that is, someone who lives in a place where you'd like to visit and who wants to come to where you live—you should correspond in detail with them to make certain that you both know enough about the home and facilities to satisfy each other. To the extent possible, get personal references on the other individuals so that you can feel a sense of trust, since they will be living in your home. But the fact that you are living in each other's homes does help keep the level of trust elevated. You needn't own a house to get involved in an exchange; apartments and condominiums can be just as acceptable as a single-family home.

Pocket Money

Travelers checks are the best way to carry money with you on a vacation. Personal checks and credit cards might not be accepted at restaurants, shops, and hotels (though most such facilities in most tourist areas do accept common credit cards). Cash is convenient, but if lost, it's gone forever. For a very modest cost, travelers checks offer a virtually universally acceptability and protection against loss. If travelers checks are lost, the issuing company can arrange for an immediate refund.

Travelers checks are available at most major banks and through some travel agencies. They are issued by such companies as American Express, Bank of America, Citicorp, Visa, and Mastercard. The cost of travelers checks is about $1 per $100 worth of checks. Many banks and savings and loan associations will make travelers checks available to their customers at no charge.

Foreign Money

If you are traveling to another country, you'll have to convert at least some dollars into the currency of that country. You'll likely be able to charge hotel bills and restaurant bills on most major credit cards, but you'll need local currency for such things as taxis, minor purchases, tips, and the like. Unless you've established a bank account in the foreign country, it will be extremely difficult for you to cash a personal check. Travelers checks are, again, the best way to carry money. Cash your travelers checks at local banks. You'll obtain a much better rate of exchange than you will at hotels, shops, or restaurants. Another alternative is to buy foreign-denominated travelers checks before you leave the United States. You can buy travelers checks issued in pounds, French francs, German marks, and Japanese yen at major banks' international departments or through American Express facilities. In so doing, you pay the exchange rate at the time you obtain the travelers checks rather than at the time you cash them in the foreign country.

Precautions Before You Leave Home

Before you leave home on a vacation, secure your financial interests and peace of mind by taking a few simple precautions. If you don't have a trustworthy person to stay at your home while you're away, make certain that all valuables are out of harm's way. Either put them in a safety deposit box at your bank or leave them with someone you trust. Be certain to stop all mail and newspaper deliveries by contacting the Post Office and newspaper circulation office. For less than $10 you can buy time clocks that turn your lights on and off at various times of the day and night to make it appear that someone is living in the home. Ask neighbors to keep an eye out for any strange persons around your home. If you leave your car in the driveway, it will accumulate dust and tip off a would-be burglar that the home is empty. Leave a car key with a neighbor or friend and ask him or her to move the car around every few days and to keep it dusted off. Check with your property insurance agent to determine what coverage, if any, you have for valuables you plan to take with you. What additional coverage might be advisable? Alert your local police that you will be away; very often they will keep an extra eye on the property for you. Consider hiring a private patrol service to provide surveillance on your home while you're away. Check with your local telephone company to see whether they have a call-forwarding service that will inform callers how you can be reached if you do, in fact, wish to be reached.

Make arrangements for all payments falling due during your absence to be made. If that's not feasible, explain to your creditors that you will be gone for a while and ask them if they can waive any late charges or make other accommodations in your absence. If you neglect to take care of such matters, you risk having late payments show on various accounts, which could be detrimental to your credit rating. If you have an investment program with a stockbroker, determine what action, if any, you might want the broker to take in your absence, depending on the ebbs and flows of the stock market. If that's not practical, leave word with the broker as to how you can be reached if the need arises. If you have any savings certificates or other securities maturing during the time you'll be absent, make arrangements with the bank or broker accordingly. The better you take care of such details before you leave, the better time you'll be able to have.

Know Your Rights

If you are traveling on a common carrier—particularly an airplane—make certain you know in advance what your rights are in the event you get bumped from your flight or in the event your luggage is lost or damaged. Bumping means that you have had your reservation canceled; there's no room for you on the plane. The Federal Aviation Administration requires that airlines make payments to passengers who are bumped. Determine what the current regulations are at the time you make your flight reservations. There are limitations on how much an airline is responsible for in the event of lost or damaged luggage. Determine current regulations in that matter as well. (As a matter of general precaution, never pack valuables in luggage that is to be checked. Rather than risk the anguish of even a temporary loss, carry those valuables with you onto the plane.)

Buying Big-ticket Vacation Items

It's a curious facet of human nature: most people are not in their "right mind" when they are planning a vacation or when they are actually on the vacation. During the planning stages, there's an aura of excited anticipation that surrounds the family, and common sense does not always penetrate that aura. That's the time when one is likely to say, with a burst of wild enthusiasm, "Let's go for broke and *buy* that camper we've always been talking about, or that speed boat we've always been talking about!" Or while on the vacation itself, a similar loss of reality can occur, in response to which one might say, "It's foolish to spend money *renting* a place here—let's *buy* a place!"

Then, in the rosy glow of a vacation mentality, you find that you've plunked down a few thousand dollars and signed a whopping contract for the balance of payments on the new motor home, speedboat, or vacation home.

Remember, before you write that check or sign that contract, that you've read these paragraphs and consider the following:

☐ On a minimal purchase of any of those items—say $20,000—the interest alone that you will pay on your debt will be in the neighborhood of $2000 to $3000 per year. That amount, in itself, can pay for one or more very nice vacations. Is it worth it?

☐ For the first year or two, or maybe even three, you'll get great enjoyment out of your purchase. But human nature being what it is, we tend to want to change the scene every few years for our vacations. Three years from now will you still want to go traveling in your van, or boating in your boat, or spending your vacation in a place that by now may have become boring to you? Your thoughts at the time you made the purchase may be, "We'll love it forever!" But a few years later you may wish you'd never taken the plunge. The time to think of that is *before* you take the plunge.

If you're contemplating a big-ticket vacation expenditure—such as a van, a boat, or your own home or condo—the best precaution is to proceed on a test basis. Rent for a year or two and see if it's really your style. The rental will probably cost you less than the interest alone on a purchase, and if you don't like it, you're able to walk away with no obligation trailing behind you. Contrary to what many salespersons may tell you, it's *not* always that easy to unload an unwanted camper, boat, or home in a distant resort area.

Time Sharing— Easy Solution?

Time sharing is a recent phenomenon. Simply stated, time sharing means that you buy the right to use a specific apartment, condominium, or resort facility for one or two or more specific weeks during the year. Part of the time-sharing concept is that you can exchange your specific location for one of many others each year. If you weary of your condo in Waikiki after a few years, you can swap it for a villa in Switzerland or a resort in Miami or a castle in Spain.

It all sounds very attractive. Indeed, the concept is plausible and some people have found great satisfaction in it. But the time-sharing phenomenon is also rife with misrepresentation and outright fraud. Many people have purchased time-sharing interests in resorts that were never built. Many find that the facilities are vastly inferior to the way in which the salesperson represented them. Many find that the so-called guaranteed cost is not guaranteed at all—that increasing assessments on owners boost the cost much higher than was anticipated. And, to make matters worse, many find that the exchange privileges are not as represented or are not available at all.

Time-sharing sales pitches are very high pressure. (See the discussion of land sales in chapter 5.) The most prudent approach to a time-share sales offering is to visit the place in person to be certain that it is as it is represented to be. Study your contract carefully to determine what your exchange privileges, if any, might be, and what added costs you might have to incur in the future. If you're not certain what the contract states in these matters, hire an attorney to review it for you. It may be many years before there is adequate governmental regulation of the abuse-ridden time-sharing industry. In the meantime, all due caution is worthwhile.

Recreation at Home

Major vacation travel may occur only once every few years, and only a few weekends may be devoted to camping, traveling, or sightseeing. But every day, day in and day out, there are excess hours of leisure time to fill at home, or within your community. Following are some considerations—financial and otherwise—on some of those predominant modes of filling your leisure time at home.

Electronics

It wasn't so long ago—in the late 1940s—that television was an infant. For a few hours a day, on one or two channels, you had your choice of watching pie-in-the-face comedians, grunt-and-groan wrestlers, slap-dash roller derby, and a smattering of news. It was all done in black-and-white on very small and very expensive screens.

In the space of just a single generation, television became the most pervasive and most influential medium for entertainment, news, and information in the history of mankind. And it's all in living color, on big screens that cost less than the early sets did a few decades ago.

Now, though, in the 1980s, we'll start looking back on television as we knew it as a quaint antique compared to the newly emerging electronic phenomena that will become one of our predominant leisure-time fillers.

Electronics offers ever-increasing sophistication and capability at ever-decreasing costs. By the end of this decade, virtually every home in America will have one or more of the following: cable television offering dozens of channels; dish antennas capable of receiving scores, if not hundreds, of television channels from satellites hovering in space; video player/recorders; wide screen television sets—five feet or more across; home computer terminals capable of interacting with the television for educational purposes, for work purposes, and for game playing.

And commonplace by the year 2000 will be video/computerized facilities that will print newspapers and magazines on recyclable plastic sheets right in our living rooms; that will allow us to work at home and interact with our home offices; that will serve as mail-order catalogues and banking facilities; and that will permit us access to virtually everything that's ever been filmed or printed via giant computers reached through satellite connections.

In short, we're at the early stages of the electronics revolution and the emergence of new techniques and equipment will shape our leisure lives to a great extent.

With so many electric marvels due in the future, it can be frustrating to deliberate here and now what investments should be made in electronic leisure equipment. "Should I buy something today only to have it become obsolete next month by a more advanced model?" The point is well taken. But whatever you do invest in today you can still enjoy for many years, while planning the next investment in more advanced equipment. Let's examine some of the specific items that may be tempting you currently.

Video Player/ Recorders

Probably the most popular of the new electronic wonders are the video player/recorders. There are two basic types: cassette and disc. The cassette players can record, whereas the disc players can play only prerecorded material that the user buys or rents. Let's take a closer look at the pertinent details, all of which are, of course, subject to rapid change as technology advances.

Cassette Players   As noted, these can be used to record anything that is broadcast through your television set—including incoming cable and pay TV signals. There are two cassette systems: Beta and VHS. Each system uses a slightly different technology and tape. The two systems are not compatible; you cannot play or record a Beta tape on a VHS machine and vice versa.

When cassette player/recorders were first introduced in the early 1970s, they were priced at about $2000 and they had very little flexibility. Currently, you can obtain top-quality equipment in either Beta or VHS for well under $1000 and the machines are equipped with internal computers that allow you to set them to turn on, record, and turn off many days in advance. Other common features in both systems include fast forward, slow motion, and freeze-frame capability.

Prerecorded tapes, including movies, sporting events, and instructional material, can be purchased or rented. Many video shops in larger cities offer membership plans for tape rentals. By paying an annual fee, the daily rental rate for cassette tapes can be as low as $3 to $4. Compare that with the cost of taking the family to a movie theater. Blank recording tapes with a capacity of upwards of six hours can be purchased for $10 to $15.

In shopping for a cassette player/recorder, bear in mind the following criteria: will you really benefit from the costly optional extras included in many sets, or will you be better off with a lower cost, no-frills set? What type of warranty comes with the set? Parts? Labor? If service is needed, can it be done locally or must the set be sent away to a service bureau? Competition is very keen with these products, so it will pay to shop around and seek discounts at local dealers.

Disc Players   Just as there are two types of noncompatible cassette players, there are two types of noncompatible disc players. One uses a tiny laser beam to scan the grooves on the disc; the other uses a stylus, or needle, just as a regular phonograph does. Because of their inability to record, disc players are less appealing for general in-home use. They are, though, less costly than the cassette machines. Both players and prerecorded discs are 20 to 30 percent less than the cassette machines and tapes.

In addition to stores that sell and rent prerecorded material, many public libraries are now offering prerecorded discs and cassettes to their local communities.

Computers, Games and Teletext

Technology is advancing so rapidly with these devices that it's difficult to predict what will be available to the public next month, let alone next year. The basic component is the typewriter-sized home computer which can be attached to a television set, a printing machine, and/or your telephone. The cost of these units ranges from a few hundred dollars to thousands of dollars depending on their capabilities.

Popular uses of the at-home computer include budgeting and financial planning, instructional programming, and a wide variety of games. Many more sophisticated uses are available to the small businessman and the professional person, including billing, inventory control, and a host of other bookkeeping and calculating functions. If you acquire a home computer for business use, you can take advantage of tax deductions by way of depreciation and the investment tax credit for the purchase of business-related equipment.

Teletext, which has been largely experimental until now, will become widespread within the next few years. Teletext is capable of providing a veritable encyclopedia of printed information on your television screen. You might, for example, be able to get access to up-to-date stock market information, weather conditions, local schedules for amusements and sporting events, and the full range of everything you might read in the classified advertising section of your newspaper. By interacting with a computer and the telephone lines, teletext can provide two-way capabilities. For example, you'd like to send some flowers to your parents on their anniversary. Your teletext can display florists in your neighborhood, and what kind of bouquets they have available at varying prices. You'll be able to access a picture of the respective bouquets, and then, using a hand-held remote control device, you can instruct the teletext to order the flowers of your choice, have them sent to your parents wherever they may be, and have the cost deducted directly from your bank account or charged to your credit card. The florist will receive the order through his or her teletext device and your bank will be electronically notified of the transaction as well.

Shopping for a home computer and the accompanying programs and games will take a lot of careful homework. How much use will you really make of the equipment? Can you justify the cost of doing the projected work on the computer or can you get it done as simply and more inexpensively using more traditional methods? Rapid change is expected in the home-computer market, so you must decide whether you will be buying something that will too quickly become obsolete or that will serve justifiable purposes for at least three to five years. And as with the video player/recorders, you must determine the extent of warranty as well as availability and cost of service for computer units. Finally, beware of what has befallen many home-computer buyers: after the novelty wears off, it is relegated to the expensive toy status, gathering dust in a forgotten corner of your family room.

Large-screen Television

Many observers of the electronics industry predict that there is a great boom coming in the sale of large-screen television sets. Currently there are two basic types of large-screen sets whose image ranges from three feet to six feet, diagonally measured. There are one-piece self-contained units; and there are two-piece units with separate projection equipment and a screen that must be set at a specific distance and angle from the projector. The one-piece units tend to be more expensive, more furniture-like, and less obtrusive. The two-piece units tend to offer a more vivid picture at a lower cost, but the two-piece arrangement may be disruptive to one's furniture layout.

Large-screen television sets range between $2000 and $4000, but technological advancement is expected to bring the price down over the coming years. Eventually, utilizing fiberoptics, large-screen television sets may be hung on a wall like a picture. In the meantime, the existing large-screen sets are strictly a luxury purchase. They definitely can enhance the pleasure you get out of watching television; if you can justify the added cost of that extra pleasure, you may want to begin shopping around for a large-screen TV.

Personal Enrichment

A great deal of your leisure time can be put to rewarding and productive use without spending much money. Look into the activities that may be available at your local library, college, church or synagogue, or community center, often at no charge. You're likely to find a delightful assortment of concerts, art exhibits, theatrical presentations, and lectures.

Carefully examine the continuing-education catalogues of your local community college or university. It's not all dry academic matter. Such programs are usually liberally sprinkled with a variety of courses and seminars that can amuse, entertain, and stimulate as well as educate. These programs are generally offered on weekends and evenings so that you can take advantage of them without interfering with your work.

Volunteer work—through religious and civic organizations—can be a very rewarding use of your leisure time. Volunteers are eagerly sought, and by helping others you can help yourself.

Sports, Hobbies, and Out-on-the-town

Whether it's an individual activity such as jogging, or a group activity such as joining a softball team, sports and athletics are among the most popular modes of spending leisure time—and generally have minimal cost. There are, though, some areas where financial considerations should be taken into account.

Health Spas and Athletic Clubs (Tennis, Golf, Racquetball, etc.) Membership in such facilities can be very expensive, and you must determine whether the cost will be justifiable for you. You may be subjected to a rigorous sales pitch designed to convince you that you'll spend every waking nonworking hour on the premises becoming a better person. And in all likelihood, you will be expected to sign a long-term contract committing you to monthly payments for your membership. If it's at all possible, take a trial membership to see whether this particular facility is really right for you. Will you use it as much as the salesperson tells you? And will the benefits to you be as delightful as the sales brochure suggests? Determine how long the facility has been in business and talk with current members to ascertain their level of satisfaction. Be aware that many such facilities run into financial problems. This can result in a sharp increase in cost to members; or in the worst case (not that uncommon), the facility simply closes down and disappears along with the money you've paid in.

Individual Sports and Hobbies Many of these activities—such as skiing, sailing, scuba diving, photography—can involve considerable investment on your part. If you are already committed to such activities, you know well what it is costing you. If you are contemplating embarking on any such activities, calculate in advance the cost of getting set up. Then, as with the health spas and athletic clubs, give it a trial run first to see if it's really right for you. Once you've spent many hundreds of dollars, if not more, on gear and equipment, if you then find that it's not your cup of tea, you might be hard pressed to sell all that used equipment.

Professional Sports If you're a "sports nut" and you live in a major league city, (for baseball, football, hockey, basketball, soccer), you know how expensive it can be to satisfy your cravings. If you're a frequent devotee of any of these sports, consider buying and sharing season's tickets with other fans. The total cost to you over the full season might be considerably less for the same number of admissions as if you were buying tickets individually for each event. Also, inquire periodically at the respective ticket offices to determine when discount plans and group plans may be available. Your employer or union may also offer discount packages to sporting events.

A Night on the Town   Dining out and attending movies or concerts are a regular item on many people's leisure-time schedule. That's all well and good, but bear in mind that the expenses for such activities are often not inconsiderable, and they are also the expenses that tend to get forgotten about in budget calculations. Since we often do such things on impulse, and since part of the activity itself finds us under the influence of external substances, it can become all too easy to ignore what the particular activity is costing. When you say, "Sure let's have another bottle of wine" enough times in a month, you could unwittingly be impairing your ability to buy necessities the following month. And since a very high percentage of dining out activity is paid for by credit card instead of hard cash out of pocket, the temptation to spend more than what is reasonable is easily succumbed to. Further, if the credit card bill isn't paid in full by the end of the month, you'll start building up interest costs, which can end up increasing the price of that meal or that bottle of wine by 20 percent, 50 percent, or even 100 percent if you wait long enough to get the bill paid.

Out-on-the-town expenses should be budgeted in advance and whenever possible paid for by cash or check. Nobody is telling you not to have a good time. You just must be careful of having too good a time right now at the expense of not being able to afford a good time some months hence.

The Ultimate Leisure

The poet William Wordsworth wrote these lines:

The world is too much with us
late and soon, getting and spending,
we lay waste our powers.
Little we see in nature that is ours.
We have given our hearts away, a sordid boon.

Wordsworth, a nature lover himself, was bemoaning the fact that we get so caught up in the day-to-day business of life that we neglect to take advantage of the beauties and pleasures that nature has provided us. We have, as he says, given our hearts away—sold out to the daily tumult of our regular work routine—and while that may have its own rewards, we may be missing out on other things more valuable. A more modern (and anonymous) philosopher put it more succinctly on a popular poster: "Don't run so fast that you can't smell the flowers."

Personal Action Checklist
Vacation Planner

No worksheet can help you determine how much pleasure you'll have on a vacation. But this Planner can aid you in calculating and comparing the costs of various leisure holidays. Estimate each item carefully. A travel agent can be of great help, at no additional cost to you. Bon Voyage!

Travel expense item	Estimated cost		
	Vacation #1	Vacation #2	Vacation #3
Getting there			
☐ Airplane	_____	_____	_____
☐ Bus	_____	_____	_____
☐ Train	_____	_____	_____
☐ Car	_____	_____	_____
☐ Meals, lodging en route	_____	_____	_____
Getting about			
☐ Rental car	_____	_____	_____
☐ Busses, tours, excursions	_____	_____	_____
Room and board			
☐ Hotel, motel (are any meals included?)	_____	_____	_____
☐ Meals (not included in hotel price)	_____	_____	_____
☐ Snacks, drinks	_____	_____	_____
Activities			
☐ Equipment usage and rental (boats, skis, lifts, horses, etc.)	_____	_____	_____
☐ Amusements (movies, amusement parks, concerts, plays, etc.)	_____	_____	_____
Miscellaneous	_____	_____	_____
Total estimated expense	_____	_____	_____
Amount of money available to pay for vacation	_____	_____	_____
Amount to be financed (loans, credit cards, etc.)	_____	_____	_____
Interest cost on amount financed (assuming you pay it all off in 12 monthly installments)	_____	_____	_____

Consumer Beware
The Troubles with
Time Sharing

Time sharing is a relatively new concept for vacationing. For a fixed amount of money, you obtain the right to use a resort facility for one or two weeks per year. But many emerging abuses in the time-sharing industry illustrate the old adage, The Big Print Giveth, The Small Print Taketh Away. Examples:

What the big print in the ad says, or what the salesperson tells you	What the small print in the contract says
Time share interests start at only $1000 down, for one week per year.	At that minimum price, if it's a ski resort, your week will be in July. If it's a condo in the Caribbean, your time is hurricane season. In-season rates start at $5000.
Low monthly payments, never to exceed $100 . . .	. . . except for miscellaneous assessments for repairs, added taxes, promotion, advertising, and such sundry items as the managers may from time to time determine they need or want.
If during any year you don't wish to use your facilities, you can swap the use for any of our 126 other resort facilities throughout the world.	Of course, since you bought the cheapest unit in the package, you can swap only for a one-week stay at the Thrifty Motel in Pittsburgh during January. Or you can have a lovely villa in Tasmania, but you have to get there at your own expense.
If you don't sign up for this fabulous deal within 60 minutes, you may have forever passed up the chance of a lifetime . . .	. . . unless you come back tomorrow, or next week, or next month, when the same deal will be available.

Time-sharing sales tactics are traditionally high pressure, and the contracts control your rights, not what the salesman tells you. Resist impulse. Study the offering carefully before you sign. Better still, visit the resort first to make sure it's really there and really has the facilities that it's represented to have.

Part Three | A Roof over Your Head

8 | Buying a Home

Where to live? House, apartment, condominium? Central city, suburban, or somewhere in between? How much of your available budget should be devoted to housing, at the possible expense of other needs or desires? Scrimp now for the sake of something better in the future? Or spend now and not worry about the future?

There are no easy answers to these questions. Each individual or family must decide what will best suit their own specific needs and desires, taking into account the applicable financial, geographical, architectural, and personal factors involved. This chapter will help you evaluate those important factors, and will also help you resolve these other common problems:

☐ How to find a dwelling in the right price range.
☐ How to make the best use of real estate agents.
☐ How to handle the contracts and other documents involved in a housing transaction.
☐ How to get ready for the "closing" when you buy a house or condominium.
☐ How to know your legal rights as a home buyer.

The Dilemma

Financial Factors

A house (or condominium) is the single largest purchase that most individuals will ever make and they generally have to live with it longer than most other purchases. A mortgage loan is the biggest debt most people will ever incur, and monthly payments (including utility costs and maintenance obligations) will represent a major portion of most budgets.

If you have the down payment available to allow you to purchase a home and if you can meet the monthly payments without unduly crippling your budget, owning a home can offer very attractive financial benefits. The interest you pay on your mortgage, as well as the property taxes, will provide substantial deductions on your income-tax return. This can result in a substantially lower federal income tax, and the money saved on taxes can be applied toward your housing costs. Through these tax breaks, the government, in effect, subsidizes homeownership.

Homeownership also offers the possibility of attractive profits. Home values have been rapidly accelerating in most parts of the country, and the trend seems likely to continue. Not only are the profit potentials attractive, but tax laws favor those who sell their homes at a profit. When a home is sold at a profit, it is possible to postpone the payment of capital gains taxes for an indefinite period. And for home sellers over 55 years of age, a substantial portion of their profit can be excluded from taxes altogether. These aspects of taxation on the sale of a home will be discussed in more detail in chapter 12.

Geographical Factors

You cannot afford to overlook the cost involved in getting to and from work, shopping, schools, and other places, whether by private automobile or by mass transit.

Consider, for example: You are choosing between dwelling A and dwelling B. The two dwellings are otherwise equal except that dwelling A is close to work, shopping, and so on, whereas dwelling B is further removed. Dwelling A will cost you $100 per month more than dwelling B for the basic overhead. It would seem on the surface, then, that dwelling B is the better choice. But if you calculate carefully, you find that in order to live in dwelling B, you'll be spending $120 per month extra in travel costs, plus an extra 20 hours of time each month in getting to and fro. All things considered then, dwelling A would appear to be the cheaper in the long run.

The condition of the general neighborhood must also be considered. Is it in a state of decline or likely to be so? Is it stable? Is it showing signs of improvement? These matters not only can affect your comfort and state of mind, but, particularly where ownership is concerned, they can have an important bearing on the future value of your house when you decide to sell. Two otherwise equal dwellings could have considerably different price tags because of the condition of the neighborhood. It might seem tempting to save money by choosing the dwelling that's in the declining neighborhood, but in the long run that might prove to have been an imprudent decision.

Architectural Factors

When making a housing decision you should consider the architectural aspects: design, layout, size, and physical condition of the premises. Design is largely a matter of taste, but communities generally dictate that certain designs command a higher price. All other elements of a given choice of dwellings being equal (layout, size, and physical condition), a choice of the more costly design can be a ticklish matter. Do the esthetics of the design offer a level of satisfaction that will be rewarding and that will continue into the foreseeable future? Does the more costly design add a measure of prestige to your status, which may be desirable? Or, on the other hand, is the design merely cosmetic, offering nothing more tangible than a diminished checking account?

Layout and size are very practical considerations that the individual or family must weigh in regard to specific needs, both current and future.

Will the layout be comfortable and functional? Will the size be correct for the future as well as the present? If you have a family, will the dwelling accommodate added members should they occur; will the size be more than is needed in the future when children move out on their own?

The physical condition of the premises is one of the most important aspects to be considered in choosing a dwelling. Most of us can tell if walls need painting, or if doors and windows close properly, or if roof shingles are falling off. But the prudent dwelling shopper could find it valuable to invest in a professional service that can evaluate all of the physical aspects of the premises. In larger cities, there are firms that specialize in home inspection; in smaller cities, one might hire a building contractor who can render the service. The service should include a close examination of the structural elements of the building, the mechanical elements (plumbing, electrical wiring, built-in appliances), and the likely need for repair or replacement of any of the building's components. If one is renting, such extensive inspection may not be necessary. But a thorough check of the premises is still called for if one is to avoid aggravations and hassles with a landlord.

Personal Factors

Personal considerations must be balanced with all of the other above factors. Often, we can be subtly motivated into making a housing decision based not on what we ourselves prefer, but on what we think others might prefer for us—friends and family urging us to live in a particular area because that's the "in" area, and so on. We must suit our own lifestyle rather than the whims of others.

Some people may be just plain apartment dwellers and nothing may ever change that. Others may abhor apartment living and would never be satisfied with one regardless of how much money they may save in the process. Some people may hate the thought of commuting long distances or of traveling on public transit. Others may find it to their liking.

Some people may have a green thumb and an urge to own their own "turf," and a house is the only thing that will satisfy them. Growing potted plants in an apartment just isn't the same for them.

Some people may prefer the privacy that a house offers, while an apartment or condominium may be desirable to those who feel more comfortable with other families close at hand.

If an individual or family hasn't yet settled into a fixed living pattern, an apartment may be more appropriate because of the flexibility it offers. When a lease is up, you can simply move on.

Some people enjoy the pleasures of their own dwelling—whether house, condominium, apartment—while others are constantly on the go, enjoying other pleasures—skiing, hunting, fishing, traveling. The former might prefer to invest more of their funds in their housing because they'll make greater use of it. The latter might prefer more modest housing since a larger portion of their spendable dollars goes to outside pleasures.

The person with a knack for patching, painting, fixing up, and taking care of things might feel more comfortable in his or her own home, whereas the person with ten thumbs is likely to feel put upon if faced with taking care of the myriad items that need attention in a home. To such a person, the apartment or condominium might be preferable, particularly if the landlord or condominium developer is responsible for most of the maintenance on the premises.

Future personal plans must also be considered. Some may desire to live more modestly than they can otherwise afford, looking forward to bigger and better things in the future. Others, perhaps feeling that their future is secure, may prefer to spend to their upward limits for their current housing needs.

If one is to arrive at a decision best suited to current and future needs, as well as current and future budgets, all these factors must be taken into account.

The Personal Action Checklist at the end of the chapter contains various factors that must be considered in making a decision on a dwelling.

Types of Housing

Houses

Inflation, particularly rising labor and material costs, has pushed the cost of the average new single-family home skyward. Along with the sharply escalating costs of building a home come comparable expenses for financing it. Interest rates on mortgages, which had been in the 5 to 6 percent range through the 1950s and well into the 1960s, shot to upwards of 14 to 17 percent by the early 1980s. Higher prices and higher interest rates mean larger down payments and larger monthly payments, and a great many people found the house of their dreams priced out of their reach.

Although it is possible to rent a house, outright ownership is the more common means of acquiring this type of dwelling. The usual mode of purchasing involves a cash down payment that might represent as little as 5 percent of the purchase price, up to a more common range of 20 to 30 percent. The balance of the purchase price is paid over an extended period of time, frequently running as long as 20 to 30 years. The buyer's promise to repay the remaining balance is secured by signing an IOU commonly referred to as a mortgage. (In some states this is referred to as a "trust deed.")

During times of high home buying costs and high interest rates, many would-be home buyers find themselves priced out of the market. But there are some innovative techniques which could allow you to buy a house in spite of the high costs.

Shared Housing   Two or more individuals or families can chip in to buy a house. They will split the down payment and the monthly payments in accordance with whatever agreement they reach among themselves.

Indeed, many builders throughout the country have embarked on construction of houses designed for sharing. Typically, these houses will have private bedroom suites for each owner, and common living room, dining room, and kitchen areas which the owners share. Shared housing is comparable to having a "roommate" in a rental situation, with the important difference being that you own your share of the dwelling and can reap the financial benefits therefrom.

Land Leasing   In this situation, the buyer buys only the house and leases the land upon which the house sits for a long term (upwards of 50 years). Ownership of the land is retained by the former owner/seller. The new buyer will pay an agreed-upon monthly rental to the seller for the land lease and will arrange his own mortgage financing for the purchase of the house. The advantage to the buyer in this arrangement is that the purchase price is lower than it would be had he purchased the land as well as the house.

Both shared housing and land leasing can have legal intricacies, and the advice of a lawyer is essential before entering into either type of arrangement.

Condominiums and Cooperatives

Condominiums and cooperatives are a relatively new form of dwelling ownership. They are somewhat similar, and are often confused, but their differences should be well understood. Both refer to multiple housing complexes, and in each case an individual resident has a form of ownership. In a *cooperative,* each resident owns what's called an undivided percentage of the total building. In a condominium, the resident owns only his or her own specific dwelling unit.

Here's how they both work. Picture what you would call an apartment house, five stories high, with four apartments on each floor. All of the apartments are of equal size and value. On a cooperative basis, each of the 20 residents would own an undivided one-twentieth of the total building. In effect, it's like 20 partners owning the whole project, each having an equal vote. The cooperative owners enter into an agreement that sets forth what type of vote is necessary to take various actions. For example, it may require a simple majority vote—11 out of the 20—to commit the group to improvements or repairs of a certain value. It might take a three-quarters vote, or 15 out of the 20, to commit all of the members to major expenses. And it may take a unanimous vote to reach an agreement to sell the project. Each cooperative group determines its own rules and regulations.

Each member, or family, that belongs to the cooperative will have an individual lease agreement with the cooperative for the premises they occupy. If not an actual lease, there will be some form of agreement in the cooperative documents permitting a particular member of the cooperative to occupy a particular apartment within the building. This mas-

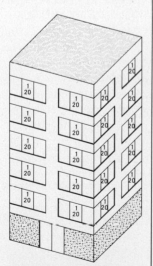

Co-op Owner owns undivided 1/20 of whole building, with right to live in one specific unit

ter agreement among all the cooperative members will also spell out such matters as the right to sublease one's apartment to nonmembers of the cooperative; the right to sell one's interest in the cooperative to outsiders; the rights of members to sell, or bequeath interest in the cooperative to members or nonmembers of their family. Not unlikely, any members of the cooperative who wish to dispose of their interest in one way or another may first be required to offer it back to the other members of the cooperative, perhaps at a pre-agreed-on price, or based on a pre-agreed-on formula for setting a price.

The business affairs of the cooperative may be run by a volunteer member of the group or by a hired professional, depending on the size and complexity of the building management. The cooperative as principal owner, and its members indirectly, will be responsible for all the building occupancy costs, including property taxes, property insurance, utilities, and maintenance. In all likelihood, the cooperative will have borrowed money—a mortgage—to make the property purchase (or construction) in the first place. Each of the individual members will have signed on the mortgage to individually insure payment.

In a *condominium* each of the 20 occupants, individuals or families, own their own separate and distinct unit. As in a cooperative, all of the individual owners enter into agreement with all of the others regarding basic management of the property, maintenance of the common areas, and rights of the individual owners to sublease and sell to parties of their own choosing. Each owner is responsible for individual property taxes and property insurance, and, as with a cooperative, is additionally responsible for taxes and insurance as they apply to the common areas of the building.

Condominiums and cooperatives can come into being in one of two ways: An existing building can be converted into condominium or cooperative ownership, or a new structure may be developed and sold to occupants on a condominium or cooperative basis. In the former case, the owner of an existing apartment house will negotiate with the tenants for them to "buy" their apartments either jointly (cooperatively) or individually (as condominium owners).

In the latter case, a developer will begin construction of a building and instead of renting each individual unit to tenants, will sell each individual unit to the owners. This is particularly common with condominiums, and is not without problems. As a new condominium project is being developed, there is a dual form of ownership. The developer owns all of the unsold units, and each buyer owns his or her separate unit. As each occupant buys into a new condominium development, he or she will sign a contract with the developer that sets forth the rights of the developer and of the individual owners until such time as an agreed-on percentage of all units are sold, at which time the condominium owners' association will take over the developer's position to determine management and

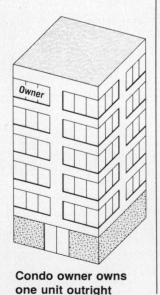

**Condo owner owns
one unit outright**

occupancy policies. But the developer, to protect his own interests, will likely reserve many rights to himself that would otherwise be relegated to the association.

For example, the owner may reserve the right to rent units that have not yet been sold, at whatever price the owner deems fit. He would do so, obviously, to create income while waiting for the units to be sold. This could create a serious conflict, for part of the building consists of owner-occupied units and part of the building consists of rental units, which tend to be more transient. The owners may resent the tenants, particularly if the tenants are paying a considerably lower sum for the privilege of occupancy than the owners. But if the developer's lawyer has drawn a tight contract, the individual unit owners will have very little they can say or do about the situation.

A number of other serious problems can occur in new condominium developments. Many of these problems have occurred in such abundance in various parts of the country that state laws have been created to control the advertising and sales of condominiums.

☐ The developer may reserve ownership of the recreational facilities, for which he charges a use fee to the occupants. Unless the contract states otherwise, the developer may reserve the right to increase those fees to whatever level he sees fit. Thus, what may have been represented in the sales brochure as a fixed monthly expense can increase considerably shortly after an individual owner takes occupancy.

☐ The developer may scrimp on construction, knowing that once each individual unit is sold it will be up to the individual owner to take care of individual maintenance of the unit. If he was to remain a landlord, and therefore responsible for ongoing maintenance, he more likely would use better quality materials and labor in the construction process. But since he is going to walk away from it as soon as the condominium contract is signed, he may try to save money on construction and let the owners worry about taking care of the problems that will inevitably arise.

☐ An owner may complete and sell a portion of a project and then run into financial difficulty. If things get bad enough and the developer defaults, the construction lenders might find themselves with the project in their hands, and the individual owners who have already bought units may find themselves having to pay off such loans, as well as taxes and insurance for the entire project, including those units that have yet to be sold.

In a house, owners are free to do as they please as long as they don't break any laws or create any nuisances. They can sell when they like, to whom they like, at the price the market will bear. But in condominiums and cooperatives many of the rights of the owners are subject to their contract with the condominium or cooperative association, and also possibly with the original developer, who has retained certain rights in the complex. Owners may be required to offer their units back to the association before they can sell them on the open market, and their rights to sublease may be severely limited. Although many have regarded condominiums as the best of both worlds—the convenience of apartment living with the advantages of home ownership—these contractual agreements often prove that this is not the case.

Mobile Homes

A generation ago, mobile homes had a poor image. The parks were often sloppily kept by the managers, banks were reluctant to lend money on mobile home purchases, and the units themselves were often subject to severe depreciation over the years. Today, however, mobile homes have a vastly new and better image. Many parks are well located, efficiently laid out, handsomely landscaped, and comparable in many respects to permanent home subdivisions. Lenders have opened the door to mobile home financing, and builders are constantly improving their construction techniques.

Mass production construction methods allow manufacturers to offer a mobile home buyer a better value in terms of square footage than a buyer of a permanent home of equal size may be able to obtain. Further, mass purchasing of furniture and appliances allows dealers to offer fully furnished units at very attractive prices.

A mobile home dwelling customarily involves a combination of ownership and rental. The unit itself is purchased from a dealer and is often financed on a long-term installment loan basis. Such financing can be more costly than conventional mortgage financing, but the conventional long-term mortgages aren't that frequently available for mobile home purchases. The unit is then shipped to the owner's destination, usually at the owner's expense, where it is moored on its pad and hooked up to the available water, gas, and electricity. The owner pays a rental for the pad to the park management and is responsible for individual insurance and utility costs. In some instances, of course, a mobile home purchaser may have the unit installed on property which he or she already owns, and thus avoid the rental fee.

Though mobile homes may really not be as mobile as they were a generation ago, an owner does have some limited degree of flexibility in moving the dwelling from one site to another. The farther the distance, the higher the cost, so long-range moves may not be feasible. If there's a slight possibility that a mobile home may be moved to a different location, the would-be buyer must understand explicitly what costs he or she may be confronting. Such costs may offset the initial lower price of the mobile home when compared with a permanent home.

Because mobile homes are not of the same permanent construction as regular houses, an owner must be alert to the possibility of a depreciation in value, compared with the more customary increase in value that permanent homes enjoy. In shopping for a new mobile home, one should compare the prices of similar *used* mobile homes to get an idea about the likely future of the current purchase. In making a final decision, this depreciation should be carefully evaluated.

It's also important to consider the rental arrangements for the site upon which a mobile home is placed. Commonly, such sites are rented on a month-to-month basis. If the owner of the park decides to sell the entire property, that could mean eviction on short notice for the site renters, requiring a costly move of the mobile home. It may be advantageous to try to negotiate a long-term ground lease for a mobile home so as to eliminate, or minimize, the possibility of having to move on short notice.

Multiple Units

Other forms of dwellings are represented by multiple-unit buildings and townhouses (or, as they're called in some parts of the country, row-houses). The multiple-unit housing is most commonly the *duplex,* where two dwelling units occupy the same building, either side by side, or one above the other. Some structures may even house three units (a *triplex*) or four dwelling units (a *fourplex*). Beyond four, the buildings would more normally be referred to as apartment houses, although there is no precise legal definition of an apartment house. One may buy a duplex, or a triplex, or a fourplex with the intention of living in one of the units and renting out the others. This can prove to be an attractive situation if the style of living is suitable to you, for the rental income can offset your own dwelling costs, and even provide some attractive tax shelter. (A more detailed discussion of the tax-shelter benefits of rental real estate is provided in chapter 18.) It's also possible for the occupants of a multiple-housing complex to own their units on a condominium basis, or as a cooperative.

Townhouses, or *rowhouses,* are a series of connected dwelling units sharing common walls. These walls allow economy in construction, and the higher density of units on a given piece of property can also result in cost efficiencies. Townhouses, which may be owned individually, as a condominium or a cooperative, or which may be rented, offer a combination of house and apartment living that is attractive to many. They can provide more space than an apartment, at a lower price than a comparably sized single family home. If the walls between the adjoining units are well insulated, a homelike privacy can be maintained.

How to Buy a Dwelling at the Right Price

Buying a dwelling—and whether it's a co-op, a condo or a house, we'll use the all-encompassing term *house* for simplicity purposes—will be the largest and most complicated transaction you'll probably ever enter into. It's worth doing it right even if it means spending a lot of time and energy in the process.

The two critical elements in buying a house are:

1. Determining how much you can comfortably afford to pay (down payment and monthly payments); and

2. Finding the right house, at that affordable price, in a neighborhood that will suit you. A real estate agent can be of considerable value in this respect.

There are many considerations that have a bearing on these elements. They include:

☐ Your personal needs;

☐ Finding comparable values;

☐ Evaluating the age of the dwelling and the advantages or disadvantages therein;

☐ Warranties that may be available;

☐ Financing terms;

☐ Utility costs;

☐ Financing costs;

☐ Resale potential.

Your Price Range

You must take into account both the amount of down payment available and the monthly payments that can be afforded. The higher your down payment, the lower your monthly payments, and vice versa. As a starting exercise—before you even begin to look at houses—visit one or more local home financing institutions (banks, savings and loan associations, savings banks, mortgage brokers) and determine what *they* think you can afford. Their guidelines, even though they may be vague, will at least give you a starting point. Bear in mind that the home financing industry is expected to be going through a state of constant change throughout the 1980s as interest rates fluctuate up and down, and as new types of home financing plans become available. There is no valid rule of thumb that will hold true for any extended period of time. You'll have to take financing conditions as they are at the time you're ready to buy a house. It is reasonable to assume, however, that monthly housing costs for most families will be in excess of 40 percent of their after-tax income. For many families, it may take two incomes to allow them to buy a house. (For more details on financing, see chapter 9.)

Using a Real Estate Agent

In addition to scouring the classified ads in your local newspaper and visiting open houses at every opportunity, you should consider the value in finding a good real estate agent to help you in your housing quest. Many people think of using a real estate agent only when they sell a house. But there are many advantages to using a real estate agent when you are buying.

Most agents belong to an association of local real estate professionals called the "multiple listing service." This service publishes a directory, usually weekly, of all houses in the area that are for sale. The listings contain extensive information on each house, including its physical features and its costs. By using the listings, a real estate agent has access to the vast majority of all houses on the market. The listings provide considerably more information than you can glean from the classified ads. By using the listings, a real estate agent can help you locate the right house in the right neighborhood at a considerable savings to you of your time and energy.

A good agent is a skilled negotiator and should be able to help you bargain for the best possible price. And good agents are in constant touch with the financial markets so that they can help you obtain the financing that you'll need. Further, the services of a real estate agent cost the buyer nothing: the agent's commission is paid by the seller.

It's not easy to find a good real estate agent to represent you as a buyer. Many agents are leery, and perhaps rightfully so, of would-be buyers who are really just "lookers." They can't afford to spend much of their time unless they know that a would-be buyer is really serious. If an agent feels that a buyer really is serious, and that the buyer will, in fact, work with the agent all the way, then the agent is more likely to work hard on the buyer's behalf. It is not customary for there to be a contract between the real estate agent and the buyer; the agent acts on good faith between the parties.

If you do find an agent who is willing to work for you, be sure that he or she is willing to show you properties that are listed by firms other than his own. You want to be sure that you are getting a good look at all available properties in the community.

Looking for the Anxious Seller

The anxious seller is the person from whom you are most likely to get a good buy and accordingly is worth seeking out. A real estate agent can be of considerable help in locating anxious sellers. The listings referred to earlier often contain information that can help identify anxious sellers.

Here are the most typical types of anxious sellers:

☐ The house has been on the market for a particularly long time. The seller realizes that each month that goes by is costing him an extra month's worth of payments. The sooner he can unload this house, the quicker he can stop that drain on his funds.

☐ The house is already vacant. The seller has moved into a new dwelling and is making payments on both. Nothing can make a seller more anxious to sell than making monthly payments on two dwellings.

☐ There has been a major change in the family such as divorce or death. In either instance, the owner may be more anxious than usual to wrap up the sale of the property, if for no other reason than to relieve himself of the legal complications that go with such situations.

Drive a Hard Bargain

It's traditional that a seller will ask one price, the buyer will offer a lower price, and they will ultimately settle for something in between. Unless the demand for houses vastly exceeds the supply, this type of bargaining is almost taken for granted when buying a house. It may seem distasteful to you to bargain over the price, but be well forewarned that when *you* sell a house, buyers will haggle with *you* over the price. The real estate agents representing the buyer and the seller will generally convey the offers and counter-offers back and forth, so that you don't actually have to come face to face with the seller on this matter. All the more reason to consider using a real estate agent when you buy: the agent is better able to handle this delicate phase of the purchase than you might be.

Let's now examine some of the other considerations that can have a bearing on your purchase of a house.

Personal Needs

A good price on a too-small house today may prove to be a regretable decision if, in a few years, you have to either enlarge the house or tolerate the inconvenience of inadequate space. Similarly, if a house later proves to be too large for your needs, you may look back at the original purchase as having been more costly than necessary. Although changes in household size aren't always predictable, the possibilities must be considered, particularly when you're putting out many thousands of dollars for a down payment and signing an IOU for many more thousands.

Comparable Values

Assuming you've located an area in which you want to live, and taking into full account the costs of commuting to work, shopping, schools, and other facilities, you should try to determine if a specific house you're interested in is priced in a range comparable to others in the vicinity. Your real estate agent can help you by examining the records of recent sales in the area. All other things (size, quality, location) being equal, comparable houses should sell for comparable prices. You may be fortunate in finding a seller who is disposing of property on a distressed basis. That is, personal circumstances are requiring him or her to sell at less than what otherwise might be obtained. Such circumstances could be a job transfer, a drastic change in family situation, or the need for cash. Likewise, you may find someone who is asking the maximum they think the traffic will bear and unless you, the buyer, do some checking, you may succumb to their asking price, when in fact you could have perhaps obtained a better buy if you were armed with knowledge of comparable sales in the neighborhood.

Age of the Dwelling

Be careful not to compare apples with oranges. This is particularly true concerning houses that otherwise are equal in size and quality, but differ in age. The age of a house can have a distinct bearing on the value you may or may not be getting for your money. Aside from elements of decor, you have to evaluate the physical deterioration that may have occurred regarding either the old or the new house. In certain neighborhoods the old saying "They don't build them like they used to" may be perfectly true. Certain older homes may have been built with better quality materials and greater craftsmanship than more recent homes. However, the reverse can be true. It will take a detailed inspection by a qualified contractor to reveal to you the current condition and need for maintenance and replacement of such things as foundation, sidewalls, roof, heating system, plumbing, wiring, and specific appliances.

One advantage that may often be found in older homes is an older mortgage that carries a lower rate of interest. There can be an obvious benefit in assuming an older mortgage: not only may the interest rate be lower than the current going rate in your community, but the older mortgage will build up your equity at a faster rate. The older a mortgage gets, the greater portion of each monthly payment goes to principal and the less to interest.

For example, on a 30-year mortgage with 9 percent interest, you'll reduce the principal amount owing by 10.6 percent during the first 10 years, and by an additional 25.9 percent during the second 10 years. Assume that you had a $30,000 mortgage at 9 percent interest, set to run for 30 years. During the first 20 years, you will have reduced your debt from $30,000 to $19,050. You will have paid off, in other words, $10,950 of the total amount due. But that $10,950 reduction in your debt is not spread evenly over those first 20 years. During the first 10 years, the debt is reduced by $3180; during the second 10 years, the debt is reduced by $7770. Thus, if you step into a seasoned mortgage as opposed to a brand new mortgage, and you stayed for 10 years before moving on, a substantially larger portion of the payments you've made will come back to you when you sell.

Possibly offsetting this advantage will be the fact that with the older mortgage you may have to make a larger down payment, and thus tie up that much more of your money. A large down payment may also require a proportionately larger down payment from a buyer when you later sell the house. This could possibly prove to be a detriment. Careful analysis is called for.

Warranties

Unless warranties are specifically spelled out in a contract and agreed to by the parties, they might not be enforceable. Customarily, brand new homes are sold with a one-year warranty by the builder. (It is not customary for used homes to have warranties, but in recent years many real estate brokerage firms have been offering limited warranties to buyers of used homes.) New home warranties will generally cover the premises with respect to cracks, leaks, and breakdowns of mechanical equipment. In addition to such warranties, the buyer and seller might agree to specific clauses that should be included in the contract of sale. A seller may warrant, for example, that the roof is in excellent condition, and that if it leaks within the first 12 months, it will be repaired at his own expense. This is an agreement between these two parties, and if properly drawn and executed would bind the seller to perform his promise if, in fact, the roof does leak. A seller may offer such warranties as an inducement to a buyer; or a buyer may request such warranties from the seller as part of the overall bargain. It's strictly a matter to be negotiated between the parties. There is no legal requirement that a seller offer such warranties, and lacking anything in writing, the buyer has little protection.

Another form of warranty that may accrue to the buyer's benefit is the warranty on specific mechanical equipment. For example, a water heater may be installed with a seven-year guarantee. During the seven-year period, the house changes hands. The remaining guarantee on the water heater could accrue to the benefit of the new buyer. The same might be true of any other mechanical equipment.

In the purchase of a new house, the buyer should take care to determine whether or not mechanical equipment warranties are included in the builder's overall warranty and, if they are not, exactly what one's protection may be. For example, the warranty on a water heater may begin as of the date of installation. The unit may actually have been installed one year prior to the sale of the house to the ultimate buyer. Thus, one full year of the warranty may have already elapsed before the buyer even begins to use the appliance.

Any warranty—be it on a house, an appliance, or any other product or service—is only as good as its specific legal statements, and it's only as good as the ability of the warrantor to perform.

A salesperson may state that a warranty covers every conceivable thing that goes wrong with the house (or other product or service), but if the specific wording of the warranty itself does not so state, you might not be protected if a variety of things actually do go wrong. The salesperson's statements may not be enforceable and the actual wording of the agreement would control.

Or the warranty may actually state in full legal terminology that everything conceivable is covered. But such a warranty may be valueless if the person or firm who stands behind it cannot be expected to fulfill the terms of the agreement. If, say, a homebuilder is in severe financial distress, he may offer an unlimited warranty to attract customers, hoping to improve his business. If the unlimited warranty is in fact a successful sales tool, he may honor the terms of the warranty. But if the warranty doesn't sell enough homes, he may not be around to honor the warranties on those homes he has sold. The ultimate precaution, therefore, is to take steps to determine the financial solvency of the firm making the promise to perform on the warranty. If it's a well-known national manufacturer, you may not care to go to that trouble. But if it's a local firm or individual, it may be worth a few dollars to run a credit investigation through your local credit bureau. This can avoid the problem of having to come up with a lot of cash out of pocket to make your own repairs or replacments should a warranty not be honored by the person who made it.

Financing Terms

"How much down and how much a month?" Those are the predominant questions asked when considering any kind of financing—an appliance, a car, a house. It's not always as simple as that, though. To get the best value for your money in a housing buy, the amount of the down payment has to be compatible with the amount you actually have available, or have access to, without interfering with your other predictable financial needs. It's essential to bear in mind that once money has been used for a down payment on a house, that money cannot be retrieved unless you either refinance or sell the house, and both transactions can be costly and time consuming, if in fact they're feasible at all. If you have other possible needs projected for the amount of money you've saved up and are contemplating using as a down payment, you must carefully evaluate the effect of placing that money in the house. Other such needs could include emergency medical purposes, future tuition for your children's education, and plain old rainy day funds.

The monthly payments must similarly be compatible with your current and projected ability to meet them. In this respect, it's essential that you or your attorney closely examine the terms of a proposed mortgage. You must determine whether or not the payments will be constant, and for how long. In the last decade or two many mortgage lenders, caught off guard by sharply increasing interest rates, have built in clauses that can allow them to increase interest rates on mortgages at preestablished points. For example, mortgage payments may be set based on a 30-year payout, but the lender may have reserved the right to increase the rate of interest after the first 10 years of the mortgage have elapsed. These escalation privileges are discussed in more detail under the section on financing. In making your initial buying decision, these factors must be taken into account.

Utility Costs

Heating and electrical costs have risen drastically in most parts of the country in recent years. A generation ago, a home buyer may have paid little attention to utility costs, for they were a relatively small portion of the total out-of-pocket expenses involved in home ownership. Not so any longer. Energy conservation is not just a patriotic slogan; it's an economic necessity and must be considered carefully during the home-buying decision-making process. If you're buying a used home, it's necessary to determine the utility costs that the former owners incurred. Obviously, not all families will utilize the available energy in the same way, but that's at least a beginning guideline to help you determine the costs you'll be facing. If you're buying a new home, this task is more difficult. But if the same builder has erected comparable homes in the immediate vicinity, you might attempt to visit the owners of those homes and inquire about their utility expenditures. A visit to the local utility companies might also be helpful in getting these preliminary estimates. Also, a physical examination of the insulation in the house can be important. If there's adequate insulation, you'll be realizing a better bargain. If insulation is inadequate, you should evaluate the cost of bringing it up to standard compared with the cost of additional fuel you'll use because of its lack. Your local utility company and local building contractors can assist you in these considerations.

Furnishing Costs

Beyond the cost of the house itself, the cost of the money with which to finance the house, and the cost of utilities, you must also consider the cost of furnishing the house to suit your desires. If the decor is not satisfactory, how much will it cost to repaint, repaper, and otherwise change it? Other items that can run into considerable expense include carpeting, draperies, and cabinetry. You'll also want to determine how much of your existing furniture can be used in the new dwelling, and how much additional furniture you may need to complete the interior satisfactorily. Two houses, with all other things being equal, can differ considerably with regard to the furnishings that may be included or may have to be added. Evaluating these elements is part of your initial buying decision. Where will the money come from to provide the necessary furnishings and changes in decor? Do you have the cash available? Will you finance these purchases over the customary three- to five-year term of a home-improvement installment loan? Can you add the cost of these purchases to your overall cost of the home and include them in the mortgage? Whichever step you take, or whichever combination of steps, how will it affect the balance of your regular budget?

The bulk of the money you spend on furnishings cannot be recaptured. Used furniture has very little resale value. Changes in decor, including carpeting and draperies, may enhance the value of the property on a subsequent resale, but if they are too deteriorated or out of style, they could detract from the price. In other words, before you commit dollars to furnishing expenses on the new home, you must carefully evaluate the effect of such expenses on your overall budget.

Resale Potential

When buying a house, it may seem foolish to exercise your brain in guesstimating what you might be able to sell it for five or ten or 15 years in the future. Granted, there's no way to assuredly predict what any property in any community might bring even a year or two after purchase. But it may be foolish to ignore the question altogether. Some neighborhoods will evidence signs of slow and gradual deterioration, while others will seem to have a fairly assured future of increase in property values. There may be subtle changes underway in the neighborhood characteristics. This can have a decreasing effect on the value of property. If you envision the possibility of reselling the home within a relatively short period of time—say, four to seven years—your real estate agent should be able to help you estimate the possibility of increase or decrease in value. If you'll be in the home for longer than that, you'd probably do best to put your thoughts into the hunch category and hope for the best.

Once you've made all the necessary evaluations, you're ready to visit your attorney and discuss the terms of the sale.

Making the Purchase

You've found a house that is desirable and affordable. You've made an offer on it and the seller has accepted. What happens next? Commonly, the seller's real estate agent will prepare a brief memorandum of agreement setting forth the basic terms of the deal. Both parties will sign this memorandum and the buyer may be asked to pay some "earnest money" to bind the deal. The memorandum will control the situation until a more formal purchase contract is entered into.

The Purchase Contract

The purchase contract is a very important aspect of a real estate transaction. It sets forth the names of the parties involved, describes the property, dictates the terms and conditions of the sale, stipulates the kind of deed that the seller will deliver to the buyer, and states where and when the closing is to take place. Generally, a purchase contract will be prepared by the seller's representative, either a real estate agent or an attorney. One of the primary rules in the world of financial and legal transactions is that if the other party's representative has prepared a contract for your signature, you can and should assume that the contract will be structured to favor the other party. Only by having your own representative review the document can you be assured of the fullest protection of your own interests.

The Parties to the Contract

The names and addresses of the buyers and the sellers are set forth in the contract. Customarily, a married couple will acquire a house in joint names, or what is referred to as "tenants by the entirety." Although complications concerning the names of the parties may be rare, they nevertheless can occur. For example, the house may originally have been in the name of Mr. and Mrs. Jones. Since they bought the house, though, they have become divorced. By the terms of the divorce settlement, Mrs. Jones still retained a one-half interest in the house, even though she is no longer Mrs. Jones. In order for Mr. Jones to properly and legally sell the house, he would have to get his ex-wife's signature on the contract and deed. Lacking her signature, the contract may not be valid. If Mrs. Jones is unwilling to go along with the deal, the buyers could end up in a muddle. They'd probably be able to get back any money they had paid in, but they could have sacrificed considerable time in the process. Similar situations could result if one of the spouses had died.

What if the buyers sign a contract and before the actual closing decide that they don't want to buy the house? Perhaps a job transfer has been cancelled. Perhaps they've found another couple who wish to buy the house at a price higher than what they are paying for it? If the contract permits a "right of assignment," then the buyers can transfer their interest in the contract to another party.

For example, the Smiths, having been told of a job transfer, contract to buy the Jones' house for $80,000. Shortly thereafter the job transfer is cancelled, and the Smiths no longer have any need or desire to buy the Jones' house. But in the meantime they have met the Whites, who would be willing to pay $85,000 for the Jones' house. The Smiths, under the right of assignment clause, can assign their rights in the contract to the Whites and the Smiths could profit by $5000 as a result. In effect, then, the names of the buying parties would be changed in the contract. The Smiths would have to notify the Joneses that they were assigning their rights to the Whites. Unless the Joneses had reserved the right to approve of any such assignments, the Whites would then legally stand in the shoes of the Smiths as contractual buyers of the property.

Description of the Property

The purchase contract should contain the full legal description of the property—not just the street address. The proper legal description should be either a surveyor's description or a subdivision description. The surveyor's description generally indicates the boundaries, their length, and the angle measurements between the boundary lines, all relating to a particular starting point. The subdivision description may refer to a specific parcel within a larger subdivision, whose map has been filed under local legal requirements by the original developer of the property. Such a description might refer to a lot as "lot #17 of the XYZ subdivision, which is registered in the County Recorder's book of maps #576, at page 148."

It is almost always taken for granted that the property one buys does exactly match its technical legal description. And, indeed, in the vast majority of cases that is true. But it can happen that there is a discrepancy between the technical description and the apparent boundary lines of the property. You may think that a tree, or a fence, is actually within the boundaries of your property, when in fact the tree may have been planted or the fence built improperly many years ago on your neighbor's land. When this is discovered, an unfriendly battle known as a boundary-line dispute usually begins. Ultimately, prudence dictates that care be taken to determine that the property you are buying is the property that is technically described in the purchase contract.

Title

Your title to a piece of property represents the rights you have regarding that property. There may be certain restrictions as to how you can use any given piece of property; and your use of the property may be subject to the rights of other people. The purchase contract will commonly state that you are receiving "title free and clear of all liens and encumbrances, except as otherwise noted." What does this mean? It means that you are receiving the property without any restrictions and subject to no other rights of other people, unless such other restrictions or rights are specifically spelled out. If your contract says that you are receiving the right to use the property "free and clear," when in fact you are not, you may have the right to get out of the contract. Your lawyer or your title insurance company will search the appropriate records to determine whether, in fact, any other such rights or restrictions do exist. If you take title to property without being aware of other persons' rights or restrictions on you, you could find yourself in a difficult position when it comes to financing the property or later selling the property. It could also mean lawsuits to resolve whether or not the rights and restrictions are in fact valid. Restrictions on your use of the property and rights that others may have to use your property are referred to as "blots" on the title. The most common forms of blots are easements, liens, and restrictive covenants.

Easements   Many years ago the owner of a piece of property may have given a neighbor the right to lead cattle across the property to a watering hole. The neighbor may have paid for this right, and in return received a document setting forth that right. Later, when the owner of the property sold to another buyer, the neighbor's right to cross the property was included as a part of the deal. Thus, the new buyer acquired the property subject to the neighbor's right to use it. Unless and until the owners of the respective adjoining properties agree to terminate this right, making whatever payments and exchanging whatever documents are necessary, that right would continue down through all subsequent owners of the property.

This is a form of easement, and it exists today in many forms. It's not uncommon for a utility company to have easements across residential property for the purpose of installing utility lines and underground piping. These rights may have been reserved, but not yet exercised by the utility company. The fact that they have not yet exercised their rights does not mean that their easement has expired. Easements may have been created many years or many decades before, yet they will continue to run with the property until they are terminated by mutual agreement.

Liens   Laws on the subject of liens differ from state to state. A lien on the property comes into being when the owner of the property has a debt that has not been paid, and the creditor takes legal action to collect the debt. If the legal action is successful, the creditor may wind up with the right to force the owner to sell his or her property (real estate and personal) in order to satisfy the debt.

For example, John had borrowed $10,000 from Mary, and could not repay it when the debt became due. Mary began legal action, but John still refused to pay. Mary won a judgment against John that technically gave her the right to force a sale of John's house to satisfy the debt. Mary, in effect, had a lien on John's house. The lien was properly recorded according to state law. Anyone then buying John's house would own it subject to Mary's right to force a sale in order to satisfy John's debt to her.

Other liens can arise out of a property owner's failure to pay taxes, in which case the government will have a lien. Or if a property owner has failed to pay contractors or workers who have performed work on the property, what's known as a "mechanics lien" can arise.

Note that a debt alone does not give rise to a lien. The creditor must pursue the legal requirements set forth in the state in order to "perfect" the lien. Not until the lien is legally perfected does the creditor have any claim on the property. Because there are often many months between the signing of a purchase contract and the final closing of a real estate transaction, a lawsuit could occur in the meantime and result in a lien coming into being prior to the actual date of closing. Thus, it's common for a title search to occur both on the signing of the purchase contract and again just before the closing to make certain that no liens have arisen in the interim. A proper purchase contract should disclose the existence of any actual liens. If the contract does not disclose actual liens, the seller is promising to sell something that he can not in fact deliver: a "free and clear" title. In such a case the buyer should have the right to bow out of the contract and recoup any monies he had paid in. He might possibly also be entitled to damages suffered as a result of entering into the contract.

Restrictive Covenants   Restrictive covenants may prevent you from doing certain things on your property. For example, a restrictive covenant may state that you may not build a house of less than a certain value. Such a covenant, or promise, may have originated with the subdivider of the property who wanted to insure that the subdivision was developed with homes of at least a minimum quality. He would do so to protect the financial interests of all those persons buying his lots, for they would want to know that their investment in a house would not be tarnished by the construction of buildings of lesser values. Not long ago it was common to see restrictive covenants that would prevent an owner of property from selling to persons of certain races or religions. Such restrictive covenants are now illegal, but they still appear in various property documents, simply because lawyers have not bothered to delete them from the documents.

In condominium situations there may be restrictive covenants concerning the sale of the property. The owner of the condominium may be restricted from selling on the open market until he or she has first offered the property to other members of the condominium owners' association, or to the association as a whole.

Title Insurance   Even though all of the proper record books have been searched and no blots against your title have appeared, that doesn't prevent someone from making a claim against your property. Any such claim may be invalid, but it can be a costly nuisance for you to prove that it's invalid. Or in very rare cases, such an outside claim against your title may prove to be valid, and you could stand to lose a substantial sum of money, if not the property itself.

To prevent such problems and losses, homeowners acquire an insurance policy known as title insurance. This insurance policy protects both the homeowner and the mortgage lender against such claims. A title insurance policy does not establish the *value* of your property. It sets forth the maximum amount of monetary damages that you can expect to recover if a claim is made against your title.

The Deed   The deed is the legal document by which the title to the property passes from the seller to the buyer. It's the actual symbol of ownership. The purchase contract should spell out when you will get it.

The contract should also stipulate that the deed will be transferred at the time of closing. If the contract does not call for the deed to be delivered at the closing, you should receive an explanation before consenting to sign the contract.

There are different kinds of deeds, and they convey different interests in a piece of property. The highest and most complete form of deed is called a "full warranty deed." In such a deed, the seller warrants that he has clear title to the property (subject to any stated exceptions), that he is conveying the title to you, and that he will protect you against any outside claims made against the property.

The lowest form of deed is called a "quit claim deed." By this document the seller conveys to you whatever interest he or she may have in the property, with no further assurance as to title. By virtue of a quit claim deed the seller is saying, in effect, "I hereby quit, or give over to you, the buyer, any claim I may have to this property." If in fact the seller has full and complete title to the property, this is what is conveyed to the buyer. If in fact he has no claim whatever to the property, that too is what he is conveying to the buyer. In other words, a seller could convey to a buyer via a quit claim deed "all of my right, title, and interest in the Grand Canyon." The seller has no interest whatsoever in the Grand Canyon, but it's still a valid deed. He is simply giving over any rights that he may have, and it's up to the buyer to determine that those rights are worthless.

Once a buyer takes title to a property, he can convey only the title that he has received. You can't convey more than you actually own. If you receive a quit claim deed to a piece of property, and later want to sell it, you can't give anything more than a quit claim deed—unless it's been otherwise legally established that you do, in fact, have free and clear title.

The buyer should demand the highest form of deed that the seller is capable of delivering. If your purchase contract calls for you to receive a certain type of deed, and at the closing the seller does not deliver the type of deed he has committed himself to deliver, you technically might be able to void the deal or bargain for better terms.

There's a type of property transaction that is known as a "land contract." In this type of transaction, the right to use the property transfers to the buyer, but the buyer does not obtain a deed until certain contractual terms have been complied with. This might take many years. This type of transaction is discussed in greater detail in chapter 9.

Manner of Payment

The purchase contract will set forth the manner in which the buyer pays the seller for the property. See chapter 9 for a more detailed discussion of where the buyer obtains the money with which to pay the seller.

If a buyer is planning to obtain his own financing for the purchase, he should make certain that a "financing contingency" clause is inserted in the contract. This clause will state, in effect, that if the buyer is not able to obtain financing at an agreeable rate of interest by the date of the closing, then the buyer can back out of the deal with little or no penalty.

Closing Date

The purchase contract should set forth the date and the place of the closing. The closing is the official event at which the transfer of deeds, checks, and IOUs takes place. When a closing date is fixed, both parties must perform by that date or risk forfeiture. Of course, the parties can subsequently agree to amend the date of closing. This is often done, particularly in cases where financing arrangements have been delayed or where personal circumstances unavoidably alter the plans of either or both of the parties.

In some states the signed contracts and other documents are held by a third party pending completion of all the buyer's and seller's obligations. This is known as "escrow" and it is commonly performed by a title insurance company, an attorney, an escrow company, or the escrow department of a bank. The party holding the papers in escrow (the escrow agent) will have been instructed by both buyer and seller not to release the papers for the ultimate closing until all of the various obligations of buyer and seller have been performed as agreed. In cases where an escrow agent is used, the "close of escrow" is the same as the closing date referred to above.

The parties will usually agree to have the closing date (close of escrow) from one to three months after the signing of the purchase contract, though any other agreement is possible if the parties are willing.

Seller's Obligations

As part of the negotiations, the seller may agree to perform certain services or work on the property. For example: The seller agrees to have the house painted for the buyer's benefit. If the seller fails to perform as agreed, what recourse does the buyer have? It all depends on how carefully the seller's obligation was worded in the original purchase contract. The buyer may have no recourse. But if the buyer was careful enough and fussy enough to protect himself to the fullest, the seller's obligations would have been spelled out in detail, including the nature of the paint to be used, the number of coats to be put on, and specific damages should the seller not perform in accordance with the contract.

Default and Recourse

What if either of the parties fails to perform in accordance with the agreement? What are the rights of the other party? Much depends on the nature of the default, and how serious it is in relation to the overall transaction.

For example, if the seller has agreed to paint the house at his own expense and has done so substantially but has omitted some minor touch-up, this type of default would probably not destroy the entire transaction. In such a case, the parties could likely negotiate a quick and simple settlement. But more serious defaults—by either party—can create serious questions as to the rights of the parties. The broadest remedy to either party is to bring a lawsuit against the other for "specific performance." A judgment of specific performance would require the defaulting party to perform in accordance with the specific terms of the original contract.

Perhaps a simpler way of resolving disputes and defaults is for the buyer and seller to agree to arbitration proceedings in the event that one of them does not perform as promised. Arbitration could provide a quicker and less expensive means of resolving disputes than would lawsuits.

The Closing

Depending on what the parties have agreed to, the closing may take place at the offices of the mortgage lender, at one of the attorney's offices, at the title insurance office, or at the offices where the recording of the documents will take place. The signed deed, in accordance with the purchase contract, will be delivered to the buyer, and the appropriate monies or IOU's delivered to the seller. Also, the appropriate "adjustments" will be made, and payment passed accordingly.

Adjustments and Closing Costs

The adjustments are a prorating of any expenses that will have been incurred on the property by the seller. For example, property taxes on the house total $800 per year, payable in installments on January 1 and July 1. The closing between the buyer and the seller takes place on April 1. The seller will have previously paid a $400 property tax installment on January 1. This covers the first six months of the year. Thus, the buyer will have to reimburse the seller for $200 worth of property taxes, representing the period from April 1 to July 1, during which the buyer will have occupancy of the property.

By the time of the closing, the buyer should have also made arrangements with his insurance agent to have the property insurance in effect in his own name. He should also arrange with the local utility companies—gas, electricity, water—to have the meters changed over to his name effective as of the date of the closing. Even though the new buyer may not take occupancy until sometime after the closing, he will be responsible for these costs from the time of closing onward.

Other substantial sums of money can change hands at the closing. The closing is the appropriate time for the seller to pay any real estate commissions to the agent who represented him. The lawyers for the two parties involved and the title insurance company will also receive payments due to them. Perhaps the single biggest closing cost will be the fee that the borrower has to pay to the lender who made home financing arrangements. Under a federal law, the Real Estate Settlement Procedures Act (RESPA), a lender is required to give advance notice to a borrower of the closing costs, or a reasonable estimate thereof. The specifics of this law will be discussed in more detail in chapter 9.

With all of these payments changing hands at the closing, it's wise for the buyer to determine in advance how much cash will be required of him so that all payments can be made without embarrassment.

Recording

Individual state laws govern the recording requirements for the appropriate documents. The recording of the mortgage agreement is the responsibility of the lender, and the recording of the deed is the responsibility of the buyer. Recording these documents in the fashion required by state law puts the world on notice that the lender has a mortgage lien on the property and that the owner has ownership of the property. The buyer's attorney or title insurance company will theoretically have searched the title to the property up to the time of closing. But if the search was concluded days, or even hours, prior to the closing, it is possible for a lien to have snuck in against the property. Although this happens rarely, it can cause tremendous problems. Thus, the ultimate precaution is to have a search conducted at the time of closing to be certain that no liens have attached themselves to the property prior to the actual moment of transfer.

Where Does the Money Come From?

The material in this chapter has provided guidelines to finding a house and the steps one must take to legally obtain ownership of it. The following chapter will discuss a matter equally important to the hunting for and contracting for a house: Paying for it.

Personal Action Checklist
Homebuyers Guidelines

The following evaluations can be helpful in your quest to buy a home or condominium. Seek the aid of a real estate agent in doing this analysis.

Factors	Home #1	Home #2	Home #3
☐ Condition of neighborhood (present, and future trend)	_____	_____	_____
☐ Approximate miles driven per month to			
work	_____	_____	_____
schools	_____	_____	_____
routine shopping	_____	_____	_____
other	_____	_____	_____
☐ Transportation costs per month	_____	_____	_____
☐ Physical condition of building, including	_____	_____	_____
walls, foundation	_____	_____	_____
roof	_____	_____	_____
plumbing	_____	_____	_____
wiring	_____	_____	_____
heating, air conditioning	_____	_____	_____
landscaping	_____	_____	_____
appliances	_____	_____	_____
insulation			
☐ Estimated refurbishing costs, interior and exterior	_____	_____	_____
☐ Asking price	_____	_____	_____
☐ Down payment	_____	_____	_____
☐ Terms offered by seller	_____	_____	_____
☐ Price seller will probably accept	_____	_____	_____
☐ Monthly mortgage payments, including interest, assuming seller accepts your offer	_____	_____	_____
☐ Property taxes	_____	_____	_____
☐ Estimated utility costs	_____	_____	_____
☐ General maintenance and upkeep	_____	_____	_____
☐ Closing costs	_____	_____	_____

Consumer Beware
Check, and Double-check, Statements by Sellers

A home seller, or his real estate agent, might be tempted to stretch the truth when discussing certain features of a house or condo. If you're a buyer, the following precautions might be helpful in clarifying matters that would otherwise not be spelled out in the contract.

If the seller, or his real estate agent, says . . .	You should . . .
"Our utility bills are amazingly low . . . this home is really energy efficient."	Ask to see the last year's worth of actual bills. If seller doesn't have them, check with the utility companies. Understand, though, that different families will consume different amounts of energy.
"That water stain on the ceiling is from an old leak. We had it patched up watertight years ago."	Get a garden hose, and, with the owner's permission of course, simulate a heavy rain on the roof. You'll find out soon enough whether the leak is still there.
"The basement is dry as a bone, winter and summer."	Check with a flashlight for watermarks around the basement wall. Better still, hire a contractor, who'll know better what to look for, and what it means.
"Oh, we're just a quick 5/10/20 minutes from the school/freeway/airport . . . etc."	If time spent traveling is important to you, drive these routes yourself, at various times of day, to find out just what is involved.
"You'll just love the neighbors."	Go knock on the doors. Find out for yourself. They won't be there forever, but they can make a difference.

If conditions are found which you agree the seller is to correct, make certain that such corrections are clearly spelled out in the contract. And then make certain that the corrections are completed before the deal is consummated.

9 | Financing a Home

The great American dream has long been to own one's own home. But in recent years the complications of financing a home purchase have prevented vast numbers of people from realizing that dream. Is the dream now beyond reach? Not necessarily. This chapter will acquaint you with methods of home financing and will equip you with the knowledge you'll need to pursue your own dreams of owning a home. Among the techniques you'll learn about are:

☐ How to distinguish between, and evaluate, different types of home financing plans.
☐ Where you can shop for home financing.
☐ What home financing terms are negotiable.
☐ How to structure a financing package that will best match your housing budget.
☐ How to take advantage of the new concept of "creative financing" (and how to avoid the pitfalls that exist therein).

A Whole New Ballgame

A revolution in the way homes are financed began in the early 1980s. A brief historical perspective is in order: Until the advent of the 1980s, the cost of borrowing money—interest—rarely changed very much from year to year. Banks and other lenders were happy to lend money to home buyers for 30 years at a fixed interest rate. In other words, the interest rate that the borrower would pay would remain the same throughout the entire life of the mortgage. Thus, the buyer of a home could rest easy knowing that his single biggest monthly expense—his mortgage payment—would remain constant as long as he owned his house. This encouraged building and buying of homes; and home building became one of America's most important industries.

Look back, for example, to 1965. A bank or savings and loan association was then paying 4 percent interest on savings accounts to its depositors. The institution would then make a 30-year mortgage loan to a borrower at a 6 percent fixed interest rate. The difference between what the lender was paying his depositors (4 percent) and what he was receiving from his borrowers (6 percent) was the margin on which he would operate and hopefully realize a profit. He was committed to receive the 6 percent over a 30-year period, and he assumed, at that time, based on prevailing conditions and anticipated conditions, that he would continue to pay out the 4 percent over an indefinite period of time.

As chapter 1 recounts, cheap money started to come to an end in the 1970s. In 1975, the same lender mentioned above looked at his 6 percent mortgage loan, now 10 years old, and realized he was now paying not 4 percent to his depositors, but upwards of 7 percent on many of the deposit accounts. In other words, he was paying out as much as, if not more than, he was taking in. By the early 1980s, the gap had widened to a point where the financial health of many lenders was in jeopardy. Further, the cost of borrowing money had risen so dramatically, that many would-be home buyers could no longer afford to partake in that "great American dream."

It became quite apparent that in order to maintain the health of America's home-building and -lending industries, as well as to insure the ability of the American public to buy homes, new modes of financing had to be created.

Lenders and government regulators agreed that fixed-interest-rate mortgages had to be replaced with something else if the concept of reasonably priced homeownership was to be assured in the United States.

By the early 1980s, a new form of home financing had begun to emerge: "variable" or "adjustable" rate mortgages. In this type of home financing, the interest rate that the buyer/borrower pays fluctuates up and down over the life of the mortgage, depending on overall trends in interest rates. Some of these loans may have a limit as to how high or low the interest rate can go; others may not have limits. Also, the lender may adjust the interest rate without changing the monthly payment: the payment could remain the same, but the remaining life of the loan would be extended. The specific details of variable-rate mortgages will differ from place to place and from time to time. It is anticipated that by the late 1980s, variable-rate mortgages will have become the predominant form of home financing and fixed-rate mortgages will be largely a thing of the past.

Your dilemma right now is this: You are reading this book and perhaps planning on buying a house during this period of changeover. In your community, this very day, you might have an abundant choice from local lenders between fixed-rate mortgages and variable-rate mortgages. If you choose a fixed-rate mortgage, you will know exactly what your costs will be for as long as the agreement lasts. If you choose a variable-rate mortgage, it's impossible to know what your costs will be beyond a few months from now.

The revolution in home financing has also brought about another category often referred to as "creative financing." Creative financing generally involves the buyer and seller working out financing arrangements between themselves, sometimes with the participation of an institutional lender. The variety of creative financing arrangements is virtually unlimited. This chapter will explain the basic varieties, but, ultimately, any creative-financing deal is left to the ingenuity of the buyer, the seller, and the real estate agents and lawyers who represent them.

This confusing array of ways to finance a home purchase is likely to last for many years. The best way for you to cope with the confusion is to educate yourself so that you can accurately determine which alternative is best for you. This chapter will help you gain that knowledge. Since the variable and creative methods of financing are basically offshoots of the fixed-interest-mortgage concept, the main thrust of this chapter will be on the fixed-interest type of mortgage.

Your First Step

If you're planning on financing a home purchase, you should, after reading this chapter, begin to shop for available financing plans *before* you start looking for houses. Talk to various lenders in your community and get an idea as to the kinds of financing that may be available to you: how much down payment will be required, how much in monthly payments will be required, what other terms and conditions will the lender impose? This exercise will give you general guidelines as to the type of housing you can afford, and will make it easier for you to do your house shopping in the appropriate price range.

Further, if you can get a tentative commitment from a lender as to a financing arrangement, you'll be more confident in your actual house hunting, knowing that you can likely conclude a deal that falls within your price range. Also, knowing in advance what kind of financing you can realistically obtain can enable you to bargain better with a seller. If a seller is convinced that you are prepared to confirm a deal, and that you won't have to wait around for many weeks to find out whether you can get the financing, he may be willing to drop the price in order to save that waiting time. You have a lot to gain and nothing to lose from such a tactic.

How Home Financing Works

Say you're interested in buying a house that costs $80,000. You've saved up $10,000 of your own money, but that's all you have. How can you buy the house?

You can borrow the other $70,000. You can go to a bank, a savings and loan association, or any other lender that offers home financing and make arrangements to borrow the needed amount. If your application for the loan is approved and the loan is made, you will sign a document promising to repay the full amount to the lender over a period of time, plus an agreed-upon amount of interest. This document is commonly called a mortgage. (In some states—notably California—the document is referred to as a "trust deed" or "deed of trust." There are some minor technical differences between a mortgage and a trust deed, but the basic concept is the same.) This mortgage will also be referred to as a "purchase money mortgage," and a "first mortgage." With a purchase money mortgage, as in this case, you borrow the money to purchase the property. The designation of the mortgage as "first" means that the lender stands first in line to take back your property in the event you default in your obligation to make the payments.

Or there may already be a mortgage on the property that you might be able to "assume." Say that there is a mortgage on the property for $70,000. You could become the owner of the property by paying the seller your $10,000 in cash and then stepping into his shoes as the person responsible for making the payments on the existing mortgage. In effect, you assume his debt. You take it over. What if the existing mortgage on the property is only $65,000? After paying the seller your $10,000 in cash, you'll still be shy of the total purchase price by $5000. In such a case, the seller may be willing to take your IOU for the $5000. Your IOU would be known as a second mortgage. The terms of payment would be whatever you and the seller agreed to, and the seller, holding your second mortgage, would stand second in line behind the holder of the first mortgage to get paid off in the event that you defaulted on your obligations.

A mortgage contains two very important legal considerations. First, you are legally committing yourself to make the payments to the lender as agreed. Second, you are giving the lender the right to take steps to take back the property from you if you fail to make the payments. In other words, you have given the lender a security interest in the property as collateral for the loan.

If a borrower fails to make payments as agreed, the lender can begin a legal action known as a foreclosure proceeding. Foreclosure proceedings differ somewhat from state to state, but basically they allow the lender to cause the property to be sold at public auction. The lender recovers whatever money is owed to him out of the proceeds of the auction sale. The first mortgage holder gets first crack at the auction proceeds. If there is any money left over after the first mortgage holder is paid off, that can go to a second mortgage holder, and so on. For example: William owes $60,000 on a first mortgage and $10,000 on a second mortgage. William defaults and the property is foreclosed. The property is sold at auction, and after foreclosure expenses are taken out, $65,000 remains. The first mortgage lender will recapture his entire $60,000. The remainder, $5000, goes to the second mortgage holder. This means, obviously, that the second mortgage holder has suffered a $5000 loss on the transaction.

These basic elements of a mortgage are the same whether the mortgage has a fixed interest rate or a variable interest rate.

How Interest Is Figured

There are three elements of cost in a mortgage:

☐ The interest, which is the "rent" you pay for the use of the lender's money;

☐ The acquisition fees;

☐ The insurance costs.

In the standard fixed-interest-rate mortgage, your interest cost is calculated on the unpaid amount of the debt, or principal balance, at each given monthly point. Here's an example:

On a $70,000 mortgage, set to run for 30 years at a 12 percent interest rate, the monthly payments for interest and principal would total $720. During the first month of the mortgage loan, the debt that the borrower owes is the full $70,000. Since 12 percent of $70,000 is $8400, that would be the total interest for the full year if the debt did not change.

But we're interested now only in the first month, which is the first one-twelfth of the year. One-twelfth of the full year's interest is $700 (one-twelfth of $8400 equals $700). Therefore, $700 is the amount of interest due for the first full month of the mortgage. Thus, in that first month, the total payment of $720 is broken down as follows: $700 for interest, and the remaining $20 applied toward the debt.

Going into the second month, the debt due has been reduced by $20, from the original $70,000 to $69,980. During the second month of the mortgage the interest is calculated on this new debt of $69,980. One-twelfth of 12 percent of that amount equals $699.80. That's the amount of interest due during the second month. In the second month, therefore, your total payment of $720 is broken down as follows: $699.80 for interest, and $20.20 to reduce the debt.

The debt has now been reduced by an additional $20.20, leaving a full balance owing of $69,959.80 going into the third month. In the third month, the interest due is one-twelfth of 12 percent of $69,959.80, or $699.60. The payment for the third month is broken down as follows: $699.60 for interest and $20.40 to reduce the debt. A breakdown of the first three payments would thus be as follows:

	Interest	Principal	Debt remaining
First month	$700.00	$20.00	$69,980.00
Second month	699.80	20.20	69.959.80
Third month	699.60	20.40	69,939.40

That's the basic formula on which fixed-mortgage interest is figured. Succeeding months interest will be based upon the current balance remaining after the debt reduction in the previous month. As each month goes by and the amount of the debt shrinks, the amount of interest paid for subsequent months gets smaller and smaller. As the interest portion of your total monthly payment decreases, the principal portion obviously then increases. As you can see from this example, and from Table 9-1, the payments during the early years of a mortgage are mostly interest. It's not until many years into the mortgage that the interest and principal portions of each monthly payment equal each other. In the last few years of a mortgage, the principal portion is substantially greater than the interest portion.

Table 9-1 | **Typical Mortgage-Reduction Schedule ($60,000 Mortgage, 12 Percent Fixed Annual Interest Rate, 30-Year Term. Monthly Payments = $617.40. Annual Payments = $7410.00 [rounded]).**

Years Elapsed	Percent of Original Balance Remaining	Balance Due ($)	Approximate Portion of Annual Payments Applied to:	
			Principal	Interest
1	99.6	59,760	238	7,172
2	99.2	59,520	239	7,171
3	98.8	59,280	240	7,170
4	98.3	58,980	300	7,110
5	97.7	58,620	360	7,050
6	97.0	58,200	418	6,992
7	96.3	57,780	420	6,990
8	95.4	57,240	538	6,872
9	94.5	56,700	540	6,870
10	93.4	56,040	660	6,750
11	92.2	55,320	720	6,690
12	90.9	54,540	780	6,630
13	89.4	53,640	900	6,510
14	87.6	52,560	1,080	6,330
15	85.7	51,420	1,140	6,270
16	83.5	50,100	1,320	6,090
17	81.1	48,660	1,440	5,970
18	78.3	46,980	1,680	5,730
19	75.2	45,120	1,860	5,550
20	71.7	43,020	2,100	5,310
21	67.7	40.620	2,400	5,010
22	63.3	37,980	2,640	4,770
23	58.3	34,980	3,000	4,410
24	52.6	31,560	3,420	3,990
25	46.2	27,720	3,840	3,570
26	39.1	23,460	4,260	3,150
27	31.0	18,600	4,860	2,550
28	21.9	13,140	5,460	1,950
29	11.6	6,960	6,180	1,230
30	0	0	6,960	450

NOTE: Apparent discrepancies in some years due to rounding.

What about variable-interest-rate mortgages? If, in the mortgage discussed in the previous example, the interest rate were raised to 13 percent early in the life of the mortgage, the monthly payment could be boosted by as much as $50. But most typical variable-rate mortgages give the borrower the option of either paying the higher monthly payment, or keeping the original payment as it was. If the latter course is chosen, that will have the effect of extending the life of the mortgage beyond its original term. And since most people remain with a given mortgage for

only about ten to 12 years (before they sell the home and move elsewhere), most borrowers on variable-rate mortgages will prefer to keep
their original payment as it was. Consider this factor if you are deliber-
ating between a fixed-rate and a variable-rate mortgage.

Acquisition Costs

Although the interest that you pay on your mortgage is, as noted, the
rent you're paying for the use of the lender's money, you will also likely
have to pay certain fees to reimburse the lender for his costs in putting
the mortgage on his books. Practices vary in this regard from place to
place and from time to time, but it's not uncommon for the lender to
expect you to reimburse him for the legal expenses involved in preparing
the papers, for the credit bureau costs involved in checking your credit
history to determine your credit worthiness to take on the loan, for out-
of-pocket expenses for appraisals on the property, and for the cost of
the title search that the lender conducts for his own benefit.

In addition to the above fees you might be asked to pay "points" to
the lender. The "points" are a one-time added fee that the lender is
imposing on you to improve the yield on his investment. Generally, a
point equals one percent of the amount of the mortgage. Thus, two points
on a $70,000 mortgage would total $1400. All of these added costs—
the fees and the points—should be explained to you at the time you
make application for the mortgage. The manner of payment of these
expenses may be dictated by the lender, or they may be negotiated
between the lender and the borrower. They may be expected to be paid
in one lump sum at the time the loan is made, or they may be spread
over all or a portion of the life of the loan. The effect of the former will be
to reduce your available cash on hand; that of the latter will be to increase
your monthly payments slightly for a period of years.

One other type of expense that you might encounter is a mortgage
brokerage fee. If, for example, you were unable to obtain normal mortgage financing on your own, perhaps because of an inadequate down
payment or some problems with your credit history, you may turn to a
mortgage broker to find a loan for you through sources other than your
local banks and savings and loan associations. He might arrange for the
loan through private sources or through out-of-town institutions. He'll receive a fee for this service, which should have been negotiated in advance of retaining him. You may have the choice of paying his fee in
cash at the time he obtains a firm commitment for you, or you may be
able to add the fee to the amount of the mortgage and pay for it over
the life of the loan. Although private mortgage brokering is an upstanding
and legitimate business, abuses have been known to occur. Alleged
mortgage brokers may demand a fee in advance in order to work on
your case. They may deliver a mortgage whose terms are unacceptable
to you (the interest rate may be too high) or, if worse comes to worst,
they have been known to disappear into the night with your advance fee

in their pocket. Prudence would dictate that no fees be paid until a firm commitment is obtained, and even at that point you should check personally with the lender to determine that the mortgage commitment is in fact firm and reliable.

Insurance Costs

The lender may require you to obtain certain insurance to protect the lender's interest primarily, and to protect your own interest secondarily. Title insurance, as discussed in chapter 8, is almost universally expected by the lender, the cost of which will be born by the borrower. The lender will also expect the borrower to carry adequate fire insurance on the premises so that the lender will be protected in the event of such catastrophe. The lender may also urge the borrower to obtain life insurance, so that the mortgage debt can be paid off by the insurance proceeds in the event the borrower dies. And default insurance may be involved: this kind of insurance guarantees that payments will be made for a set period of time in the event the borrower defaults. FHA and VA insurance include this kind of protection for the lender. In addition, many private firms in recent years have begun offering mortgage default insurance, which, if carried by the borrower, will usually be at the borrower's own expense.

Escrow, or Reserve, Accounts

In some mortgage arrangements, the borrower may be required to pay an added monthly sum, which will be used to pay property insurance premiums and property taxes as they fall due. This is commonly known as an escrow account or a reserve account. Example: Your property taxes are $900 per year and your property insurance is $300 per year—a total of $1200 per year. With an escrow account, you will pay an additional $100 per month ($1200 per year) over and above the basic monthly payment covering interest and principal. The lender will hold this money for you and will pay your property taxes and insurance premiums out of that fund as those bills come due. Some lenders may require an escrow account; some may offer it as an option; some may not offer it at all. In some states, the lender will pay interest on the funds he holds for your benefit; in some states no interest will be paid. Budget-conscious homeowners often find that an escrow account can be a simple way of leveling out their total annual budget program. It can be easier and more convenient to pay out a fixed monthly amount rather than have to meet large insurance and property tax bills when they come due. Escrow accounts are normally analyzed by the lender once a year to determine how much will be needed in the account for the following year, and the lender will notify the borrower of any adjustments in the monthly payment.

Other Important Clauses

Mortgages can contain other important clauses that can affect your legal rights as well as your monthly payments. If you consent to such clauses on the signing of a new mortgage, or by assuming an existing mortgage, you have given the lender the right to exercise those privileges, and you should assume that he will take advantage of those rights.

Variable-rate Clauses   As noted earlier, variable-rate clauses can take many different forms and can differ from place to place and from time to time. The lender may be limited as to how often he can change the rate and there may be a maximum level to which the rate can be raised. With an institutional lender (bank, savings and loan association) the state or federal government may impose those limits. With private lenders—individuals and unregulated lenders—the limits may be more extreme.

The Balloon Clause, or Call Privilege   This type of clause allows the lender to demand that the entire loan be paid off at a set time. Example: We earlier referred to a $70,000 mortgage set to run for 30 years at 12 percent interest rate. The monthly payments were $720. Assume that the lender inserted a call privilege in that mortgage at the end of the fifth year. At that time the full balance owing would be about $69,900, almost as much as it was originally. If the lender exercises the call privilege, the borrower would have to pay the entire balance off at that time. The lender might be willing to refinance the remaining balance then, but at a higher interest rate. In short, a balloon clause, or call privilege, can have the same affect as a variable-rate clause. It can permit the lender to alter the interest rate at a given future time.

Assumption Clauses   An assumption clause in a mortgage means that the owner of a house can sell the house to another party and that new buyer can assume the existing debt. The new buyer, in other words, steps into the shoes of the former owner and become liable for the remaining balance on the debt, as well as all other terms and conditions of the mortgage. Assumption privileges are subject to the right of approval of the lender. The lender might, for example, refuse to allow a person with a known bad credit history to assume an existing mortgage. If you are contemplating buying a house that has an assumable mortgage, you should determine in advance whether or not you will be permitted to assume the mortgage. If you are entering into a new mortgage, the existence or absence of an assumption clause can have an effect on your ability to sell the house later.

Prepayment Clauses   You might come into a sum of money and wish to make advance payments on your mortgage, either wholly or partially. Do you have the right to do so, and if so, will it cost you anything? Some mortgages contain prepayment privilege clauses that allow you to make such advance payments on your debt without suffering any penalty. On the other hand, some mortgages have prepayment penalty clauses stating that you must pay a penalty if you do prepay early.

Open-end Clauses   These are rare but might be negotiated if requested. A typical open-end clause permits the borrower to borrow back up to the original amount of the mortgage at the same original interest rate, perhaps without paying any costs or fees in the process.

Shopping for Financing— Where to Go, What to Look For

If you're buying a house with an existing mortgage that you plan to assume, you're more or less locked into the terms of that mortgage. That doesn't mean that you can't discuss revision of any of the terms with the lender. It might be worth your while to do so to help tailor a different payment program that would be better suited to your own financial circumstances.

If you're buying a house and seeking your own original financing, the following shopping list, tables, and the Personal Action Checklist at the end of this chapter can help you to work out a deal that's best suited to your circumstances.

Where to Shop

The major sources of home financing are savings and loan associations and mutual savings banks (the latter appearing predominantly in the Northeastern states). Many commercial banks also offer home financing plans, as do some credit unions and insurance companies. There are also private mortgage brokers in most communities who act as middlemen in finding mortgage loans for home buyers. They will usually obtain the needed funds through institutional or private investors. Mortgage brokers will charge a fee for their services, and, as mentioned above, before entering into any commitment with a private mortgage broker, the terms of such an arrangement should be explicitly understood.

Kinds of Loans

The differences between fixed-interest and variable-interest loans has already been discussed. There's another broad distinction that should be considered, for it can have an effect on the amount of down payment you'll be required to make. This distinction is between insured loans and noninsured loans.

Lenders don't really want to foreclose on properties if the borrower defaults. Foreclosure is a messy, costly, and aggravating proceeding. A lender would much rather have some form of guarantee that all or a portion of the payments will be made as agreed. And, indeed, lenders *can* obtain insurance that will offer those guarantees. There are two main sources of this insurance: the U.S. government, and private insurance companies.

The U.S. government offers two types of insurance plans. One is offered through the Federal Housing Administration (FHA); the other is through the Veterans' Administration (VA). FHA will insure certain mortgage loans if both the buyer of the property and the property itself meet certain governmental requirements. The VA will also guarantee certain loans made to eligible armed services veterans, again providing that all qualifications are met. Because the government is guaranteeing repayment of these FHA and VA loans—at least in part—the lender is willing to take a greater risk with such loans than he would be were there no guarantee. In short, the lender is willing to make these loans to borrowers with smaller down payments. If you can meet either the FHA or VA restrictions, you might be able to obtain home financing with a smaller down payment than you may have suspected. Check with local lenders for current requirements.

Lenders can also obtain insurance through private companies. As with the FHA and VA loans, the private insurance plan means a lower risk for the lender, and he will therefore approve insured loans with a lower down payment than he would a noninsured loan. Borrowers might have to pay a slightly higher monthly payment as a result of their loans being insured, but the cost can be well worth it if it allows them to purchase a house with a relatively small down payment.

One relatively new type of insured loan is the FHA-245, also known as the "graduated payment plan." This type of loan is geared toward younger couples who might not otherwise be able to meet the high monthly payment requirements currently called for. In the graduated payment plan, the monthly payments for the first few years of the loan are lower than they would be under a regular plan. As the years go by, and as the borrower's income presumably increases, the payments increase accordingly.

Noninsured loans, whether of a fixed-interest or a variable-interest rate variety, generally require a down payment of roughly 20 percent of the purchase price of the property.

Acquisition Costs

What "points" and other fees will you have to pay in order to get the financing you're seeking? Under the Federal Real Estate Settlements Procedures Act (RESPA), lenders are required to give you a copy of a government booklet, "Settlement Costs," not later than three days after you have made your loan application. The information in this booklet is very important to you. It describes your rights under the federal law and contains helpful advice on completing your property transaction. The law also requires that the lender give you a good-faith estimate of all settlement costs (or closing costs, as they're often called) that will be charged. You should also determine whether the closing costs are to be paid in cash at the time of the transaction or whether those costs can be added into the mortgage and spread out over the life of the mortgage.

Interest Rates

What will be the original interest rate, and what fluctuations might it be subject to in the future? Table 9-2 is a handy guide to helping you find the monthly payment for any size mortgage at various interest rates and terms of repayment. Table 9-3 illustrates how different interest rates can affect your actual costs on a mortgage—and those cost differentials can be tremendous, as the table illustrates.

Table 9-2 | **Monthly Mortgage Payment Finder (Fixed Rate) (per $1,000)**

Annual Fixed Interest Rate (%)	Length of Mortgage			
	15 Years	20 Years	25 Years	30 Years
10	10.75	9.66	9.09	8.78
$10\frac{1}{2}$	11.06	9.99	9.45	9.15
11	11.37	10.33	9.81	9.53
$11\frac{1}{2}$	11.69	10.67	10.17	9.91
12	12.01	11.02	10.54	10.29
$12\frac{1}{2}$	12.33	11.37	10.91	10.68
13	12.66	11.72	11.28	11.07
$13\frac{1}{2}$	12.99	12.08	11.66	11.46
14	13.32	12.44	12.04	11.85
$14\frac{1}{2}$	13.66	12.80	12.43	12.25
15	14.00	13.17	12.81	12.65

Example: What would the monthly payment be (interest and principal) on a $50,000 mortgage for 25 years at 13 percent interest? Find the factor where the 13 percent line meets the 25-year line. That factor is 11.28. Multiply 11.28 by 50. The result is 564. The monthly payment, then, would be $564.

Table 9-3 | **How Interest Rates Affect Cost: $60,000 Mortgage for 30 Years**

Fixed Rate (%)	Monthly Payment	Total Amount Paid Out After			
		5 Years	10 Years	20 Years	30 Years*
10	526.80	31,608	63,216	126,432	189,648
$10\frac{1}{2}$	549.00	32,940	65,880	131,760	197,640
11	571.80	34,308	68,616	137,232	205,848
$11\frac{1}{2}$	594.60	35,676	71,352	142,704	214,056
12	617.40	37,044	74,088	148,176	222,264
$12\frac{1}{2}$	640.80	38,448	76,896	153,792	230,688
13	664.20	39,852	79,704	159,408	239,112
$13\frac{1}{2}$	687.60	41,256	82,512	165,024	247,536
14	711.00	42,660	85,320	170,640	255,960
$14\frac{1}{2}$	735.00	44,100	88,200	176,400	264,600
15	759.00	45,540	91,080	182,160	273,240

Example: What would be the difference in cost to you on a $60,000 mortgage between an interest rate of 13 percent and an interest rate of $13\frac{1}{2}$ percent? On the 13 percent loan, your monthly payments would be $664.20, and after 10 years you would have made payments totaling $79,704. On the $13\frac{1}{2}$ percent loan, your monthly payments would be $687.60, and after 10 years you would have made payments totaling $82,512. The $13\frac{1}{2}$ percent loan would have cost you $2808 more than the 13 percent loan over the first 10 years. To compare mortgages of any other amounts, use Table 9-2 to figure the monthly payments, and multiply those payments by the number of months in question.

*To find the total interest paid over the full 30-year life of the loan, subtract the original amount borrowed ($60,000) from each of the figures.

How Much Down Payment Is Required?

The amount of the down payment required, and the amount that you may have available for down payment, may not jibe. If you have more than enough, you're in good shape, but then you'll have to decide *how much* of your available funds you want to use as a down payment.* If you have less than the required amount, how will you raise the difference? If one lender requires a higher down payment than another, his interest rate may be lower or his other terms may be more favorable. These must be compared.

Table 9-4 illustrates how different-sized down payments can affect your total mortgage expense over a period of years. There is no easy solution to the dilemma as to how much of a down payment one should make. It must be resolved based on your own personal circumstances as they are now and as you expect them to be.

How Long Should the Mortgage Run?

The longer the mortgage, the lower the monthly payment. But that means a higher interest expense over the long term. However, it's unlikely that you'll stay with that mortgage for more than ten or 12 years, for the average American changes houses and moves on within that time. Table 9-5 illustrates the different cost factors involved for mortgages of varying terms.

Other Services from Lender

It's difficult to evaluate, but you should try to determine what additional kinds of financial services might be available to you from respective

Table 9-4

How Down Payment Affects Your Costs (Purchase Price $80,000, 30-Year Mortgage, 12 Percent Fixed Annual Rate)

Down Payment		Amount of Mortgage	Monthly Payment	Total Payments After		
% of Cost	Dollars			10 Years	20 Years	30 Years
5	4,000	76,000	782.04	93,844	187,689	281,534
10	8,000	72,000	740.88	88,905	177,811	266,716
15	12,000	68,000	699.72	83,966	167,932	251,899
20	16,000	64,000	658.56	79,027	158,054	237,081
25	20,000	60,000	617.40	74,088	148,176	222,264
30	24,000	56,000	576.24	69,148	138,297	207,446

Example: What will be the difference in cost to you if you make a 10 percent down payment versus a 20 percent down payment on an $80,000 purchase, assuming a fixed annual interest rate of 12 percent? With the 10 percent down payment, your monthly payment will be $740.88, and after 20 years you will have made payments totaling $177,811. With the 20 percent down payment you will have a monthly payment of $658.56, and after 20 years you will have made payments totaling $158,054, a difference of $19,757. (But by making the smaller down payment, you could have had $8000 extra money to invest or spend.)

*Bear in mind that available money that is not used for down payment can be invested and earning more money for you.

Table 9-5   How the Length of Mortgage Affects Your Costs (12 Percent Fixed Rate)

Original Amount of Mortgage	Number of Years to Run (Full Term)	Monthly Payment		Amount Paid After					
				5 Years	10 Years	15 Years	20 Years	25 Years	30 Years
60,000	15	720.60	Int.	33,456	58,872	69,708			
			Prin.	9,780	27,600	60,000			
			Total	43,236	86,472	129,708			
60,000	20	661.20	Int.	34,692	65,364	88,716	98,688		
			Prin.	4,980	13,980	30,300	60,000		
			Total	39,672	79,344	119,016	158,688		
60,000	25	632.40	Int.	35,364	68,568	97,872	120,156	129,720	
			Prin.	2,580	7,320	15,960	31,620	60,000	
			Total	37,944	75,888	113,832	151,776	189,720	
60,000	30	617.40	Int.	35,664	70,128	102,552	131,196	152,940	162,264
			Prin.	1,380	3,960	8,580	16,980	32,280	60,000
			Total	37,044	74,088	111,132	148,176	185,220	222,264
80,000	15	960.80	Int.	44,608	78,496	92,944			
			Prin.	13,040	36,800	80,000			
			Total	57,648	115,296	172,944			
80,000	20	881.60	Int.	46,256	87,152	118,288	131,584		
			Prin.	6,640	18,640	40,400	80,000		
			Total	52,896	105,792	158,688	211,584		
80,000	25	843.20	Int.	47,152	91,424	130,496	160,208	172,960	
			Prin.	3,440	9,760	21,280	42,160	80,000	
			Total	50,592	101,184	151,776	202,368	252,960	
80,000	30	823.20	Int.	47,552	93,504	136,736	174,928	203,920	216,532
			Prin.	1,840	5,280	11,440	22,640	43,040	80,000
			Total	49,392	98,784	148,176	197,568	246,960	296,532

Example: Compare a 25-year term and a 30-year term on an $80,000 mortgage at a 12 percent fixed interest rate. With the 25-year term, you will have made total payment during the first 15 years of $151,776, compared with a lesser amount—$148,176—during the first 15 years of the 30-year term. The difference in total payments between the two is $3,600. However, during that first 15 years you will have reduced your total debt by $21,280 on the 25-year plan, and only by $11,440 on the 30-year plan, a difference of $9840. In other words, if you sold the house after 15 years, you'd get $9840 more cash from the 25-year plan than from the 30-year plan. But you would have paid out $3600 in extra payments with the 25-year plan. Subtract that from the extra gain on the sale, and you have a net advantage of $6240 as a result of using the 25-year plan mainly because you've reduced your debt at a faster rate, and in doing so you reduced the interest accordingly.

lenders. Some may offer nothing more than friendly and helpful advice. Don't underestimate the value of this service. Advice can come in handy and may be the deciding factor in your choice of lender for your home financing.

Applying for Home Financing

After you've done your shopping for rates, terms, and other clauses, you will decide which institution or broker you want to make formal application to. Before you make your final application, it would be wise to spend a few dollars to examine your credit file at your local credit bureau to make sure that everything is in order. Erroneous information can find its way into your credit file, and you have rights under the Federal Fair Credit Reporting Law to have false information corrected. See chapter 13 for more details on your rights under this law. The lender will do a credit check on you, and if false information has not been corrected in your file it will cause delays in processing your application.

In addition to obtaining detailed financial information on you—including your income and your debts—the lender will also reserve the right to appraise the property you are buying. A title search will also be called for to assure the lender that he can be properly secured if a loan is made. Depending on the lender, these processing steps can take from a few days to a few weeks and might entail some fees that you will be expected to pay whether the loan is approved or not. You should determine in advance just how long the processing will take and what cost, if any, you will have to assume. Also, as noted earlier, the lender is required to give you a copy of the federal booklet "Settlement Costs," either in person at the time of your application or, if not then, no later than three days after the date of the application.

If your application is approved, you should obtain a copy of the lender's commitment, in writing, so that there is no mistake about the terms of the arrangement. It's very likely that any commitment will extend for only a limited time at the given interest rate. If the purchase transaction is not completed within that specified time, the lender could back out of the commitment, at least at the quoted interest rate. If you suspect that the transaction will not be completed within the time of the lender's commitment, you should move quickly to attempt to get it extended.

It could happen that a lender will approve your application, but with the contingency that you provide a co-signer; or the loan may be approved for a lesser amount than you had requested. In the event a co-signer is required, the lender is asking you to find someone else who will sign the IOU with you. This shouldn't be taken as an insult. It may merely mean that the lender doesn't feel comfortable with your age, the amount of job experience you've had, or your credit history. After payments on the loan have been made for perhaps one or two years, it's perfectly acceptable to request that the co-signer be removed from the obligation. If, at that time, the lender feels that you have been performing well on the obligation, he may well consent to remove the co-signer's obligation. Discuss this possibility in advance with the lender.

If the loan is approved for a lesser amount than you had requested, you will either have to increase the size of your down payment or negotiate a second mortgage with the seller. That possibility brings us to the realm of "creative financing" which, as discussed earlier in this chapter, has become a commonplace way of obtaining home financing.

Creative Financing

Creative financing covers any type of financing arrangement that a buyer and seller might negotiate privately, with or without the participation of outside lenders or investors. In short, creative financing describes the ways in which deals can be made when normal financing programs aren't feasible or available. Creative financing has made possible many otherwise impossible home purchases. But creative financing deals can involve legal intricacies, and nobody, neither buyer nor seller, should undertake a creative financing arrangement without the assistance of a lawyer.

Following are some basic types of creative financing arrangements, both established and emerging.

The Land Contract

The land contract is the granddaddy of creative financing plans. It's been around for a long time, having been used mainly by buyers who could not otherwise qualify for conventional home financing. Example: Sam, the seller, is asking $80,000 for his house. Bob, the buyer, would like to buy the house, but he has no money at all for a down payment. Bob knows there's no point at all in even asking a lender for financing, for with no down payment he'll be turned down cold. Sam isn't interested anyway in selling the house without a down payment, for he fears that a buyer who pays nothing down can walk away from the house at any time, leaving it in shambles. But when Bob offers Sam $90,000, Sam's ears perk up. Bob offers to pay $90,000, with no money down, and the full amount payable in equal monthly payments over a period of ten years at a 12 percent interest rate. Sam agrees and they enter into a land contract. The land contract states Bob's obligations to pay Sam, and further states that Sam will not deliver the deed to the property until Bob has made payments for at least five years. Everybody is happy and no outside lenders were involved.

The terms of a land contract can be virtually anything that the parties are willing to agree to, provided the state laws of usury (the maximum interest allowable) are not violated. During the first five years of this particular deal, Sam is technically still the owner of the property. His lawyer has advised him that if Bob defaults in the payments, Sam can move him out much more rapidly than he could if a deed had changed hands and Bob's obligation was that of a mortgagor.

Sam, as technical owner of the property, might even still have his own mortgage on the property. He will, of course, continue to make payments on his own mortgage. If he has negotiated well with Bob, he'll be receiving more from Bob than he will owe on his mortgage—thus he can realize some profit in the meantime.

The Wrap-around

The wrap-around mortgage is a relatively new variation on the land contract. Example: Sam, the seller, is asking $80,000 for his house. He would like to get $30,000 in cash as a down payment, and a buyer can then assume Sam's existing first mortgage of $50,000, which carries a very attractive 7 percent interest rate. The current going interest rate in Sam's community is 12 percent for first mortgages. Bob, the buyer, would like to buy Sam's house and is willing to pay the $80,000 purchase price. But Bob has only $5000 available for a down payment.

One solution is for Sam to take Bob's IOU for $25,000. This would be known as "carrying back" a second mortgage. If they agree upon terms, Bob would become the owner of the property and would make payments directly to the holder of the first mortgage; he would also make separate payments to Sam on the second mortgage.

But suppose they find that the holder of the first mortgage does not want to let a new buyer assume the mortgage. They'd like to get that old 7 percent loan off the books. Bob and Sam could then create what is known as a wrap-around mortgage or an all-inclusive mortgage. Bob would make payments directly to Sam to cover the amount due on both the first mortgage and the second mortgage. Sam in turn would continue making the payments on the first mortgage to the original lender. It's the combining of the first and second mortgage payments that result in the concept of the wrap-around.

Both the land contract and the wrap-around can pose very serious problems to a buyer who is not protected legally in the fullest capacity. In both cases, the original lender still has a mortgage on the property. If Sam, the seller, neglects to make his payments to the original lender, the house could be thrown into foreclosure, even though Bob, the buyer, has been dutifully making his payments to Sam. In short, in such a case, Sam has defrauded Bob, but Sam might be long gone before Bob realizes that there's any problem.

The Sleeping Second

If a buyer is anxious enough to find a seller, he might use a sleeping second as his creative financing tool. Example: Sam tried to sell his house for $100,000 but there were no takers. He dropped the price to $95,000, then to $90,000, then to $85,000, and finally to $80,000. Bob, the buyer, expresses some interest at the $80,000 price, but he wants some icing on the cake. The first mortgage on the property is $50,000, which Bob would assume. Bob then proposes a sleeping second. Bob will make a cash down payment of $10,000 and will give Sam a second mortgage for the remaining $20,000 due, but with the understanding that *no payments will be due* on the second for a period of, say, three years. At the end of three years, the second mortgage will become due and payable plus any interest that Sam and Bob may have agreed upon. Sam is happy because he gets his price. Bob is happy because he has utilized the sleeping second to keep his monthly payments low. He figures that after three years he'll be able to comfortably refinance the existing first and the sleeping second into a new mortgage.

Buying Down

This type of creative financing may be more commonly used in new housing, especially if a builder is having trouble selling his homes at the desired price. Example: Sam has built a new house which he hopes to sell for $80,000. However, current mortgage rates in his community are 15 percent, and that high interest rate is scaring away potential buyers. Every month that goes by with the house unsold costs Sam money. So, to make the house more attractive to a buyer, Sam arranges with a local mortgage lender to create financing which will be at the rate of only 12 percent interest for the first two years of the loan. After two years the interest will go back up to the 15 percent level. Sam will actually pay the lender the difference between the 12 percent and the 15 percent on the amount financed, but he figures it's cheaper to do that than to sit with the house unsold for many more months. Now Sam can offer the house to a buyer at a 12 percent interest rate, albeit only for two years. But they may be enough of an enticement to lure Bob, the buyer, into a deal.

Shared Appreciation Mortgage

A lender—either institutional or individual—agrees to offer home financing to Bob, the buyer, at substantially under the current going rate. Say the rate currently is 12 percent. The lender in this case offers to make a mortgage loan at, say, 8 percent. In return, the lender will receive a percentage of any profit that the owner realizes on a later sale of the house. Example: Bob buys a house for $80,000 and obtains a shared appreciation mortgage at an 8 percent interest rate. Bob will be obliged to give 30 percent of any profit to the lender upon the sale of the house. Some years later, Bob sells the house for $130,000—a $50,000 profit. The lender will receive 30 percent of that amount, or $15,000, as his share in the appreciation of the house.

Shared Appreciation Down Payment

This is similar to the shared appreciation mortgage, except that an investor will chip in part of the buyer's down payment with the promise that he, the investor, will receive a share of the profit on a later sale. Example: Bob needs $20,000 for a down payment to buy Sam's house. Sam is unwilling to take back a second mortgage, and Bob does not want to refinance a new first mortgage through a local lender. Bob finds an investor willing to make a shared appreciation down payment. The investor chips in $10,000 to match Bob's available $10,000, and gets, in return, a promise of a percentage of any profit that Bob may realize on a later sale.

Both the shared appreciation mortgage and the shared appreciation down payment carry risks for the lender/investor. Professional lenders and investors will have evaluated those risks carefully and will see to it that they are properly protected legally. A buyer entering into such an arrangement should also be certain that he or she has been properly protected in all of the legal documents, which can be very complicated.

Sources of Creative Financing

In most larger communities, major real estate brokerage firms have been developing their skills in putting together creative financing packages. Likewise, mortgage brokers have had experience in developing these plans. Both buyers and sellers should discuss the full range of creative financing possibilities with a real estate agent, and all such feasible possibilities should be kept in mind as an alternative to conventional institutional financing. But this one main warning bears repeating: Creative financing can be very complex, and neither buyer nor seller should enter into such a plan without competent legal advice.

Personal Action Checklist
Financing Comparisons

It's expected that most home financing plans will be based on a variable interest rate—a rate that can be adjusted upward or downward from time to time. Since it's impossible to know what future rate fluctuations will be, there's no way a borrower can accurately predict his or her actual mortgage costs over a long period of time. The dilemma is further compounded by the fact that different lenders use different formulas to vary the rate, thus making a comparison between lenders very difficult. The following checklist is not designed as an accurate cost comparison chart; rather, it's to help you ask the right questions in evaluating variable-rate financing plans. The more you know about how the plans work, the more judicious your decision can be.

	Plan A	Plan B	Plan C
□ What is the starting interest rate?	_____	_____	_____
□ How often can the rate be changed?	_____	_____	_____
□ How much can the rate be raised at any given interval?	_____	_____	_____
□ How much can the rate be raised over the life of the loan?	_____	_____	_____
□ How much can the rate be lowered at any given interval?	_____	_____	_____
□ How much can the rate be lowered over the life of the loan?	_____	_____	_____
□ By what outside index are the rate changes to be measured? (Consumer Price Index? Cost of funds? Prime rate?)	_____	_____	_____
□ Is there a prepayment penalty? If so, how much?	_____	_____	_____
□ If the rate is increased at any given interval, do you, the borrower, have the option of keeping the monthly payment the same (in which case the final maturity of the loan will be extended)?	_____	_____	_____
□ If answer to above question is yes, what limits are there, if any, to the option?	_____	_____	_____

Consumer Beware
Perils of Creative Financing

Quark wanted to buy Neutrino's house. The asking price was $120,000, with $20,000 to be paid down, and the buyer, Quark, to obtain his own financing for the remaining $100,000. But Quark couldn't afford conventional financing, so he convinced Neutrino to "carry back" an IOU for the $100,000. Quark agreed to pay Neutrino interest at a rate 2 percent higher than the going rate at local banks, which at that time was 14 percent.

Neutrino had an old existing mortgage with a balance of $90,000, at an interest rate of 9 percent. The deal between Quark and Neutrino was a "land contract": the title to the property was to remain in Neutrino's name for three years; Neutrino would continue to make payments on the original mortgage; and after three years Quark was to get his own financing and pay off whatever was then owed to Neutrino. The bank that held the original mortgage was never notified that Quark now had a vested interest in the property, by way of the land contract.

Neutrino turned nasty. Though he received Quark's payments regularly and promptly, he stopped making payments on the old mortgage to the bank. Quark never knew of this, for the delinquency notices were sent directly to Neutrino's office.

It wasn't until the bank started foreclosure proceedings and sent an appraiser to look at the house that Quark learned he was being victimized.

Neutrino had skipped town with Quark's $20,000 cash down payment, content to let that be his profit on the deal. Quark was left with having to pay off all back payments (duplicating all those he had already made), plus late charges, to prevent the house from being sold out from under him. And when the original three years had elapsed, Neutrino reappeared and refused to deliver the deed to Quark unless Quark paid him the remaining $10,000 that was owed him.

When Quark asked about the double payments and late charges he had had to make to avoid the foreclosure, Neutrino simply replied, "So sue me!"

Better to have a lawyer construct a creative financing deal properly from the outset, when the cost will be relatively small, rather than have to pay heavily later when the mess is piled so high that it smells.

10 | Housing Costs and Regulations

The cost of maintaining a dwelling does not end with writing your monthly mortgage or rent check. Home or condo owners in particular will feel a constant drain on their budget from such expenses as property taxes, property insurance, utilities, and maintenance. All of these items must be properly anticipated if you are to keep your financial affairs on an even keel.

In addition to costs, your dwelling situation can be affected by local rules and regulations that must be complied with.

This chapter is designed to assist you in planning sensibly to meet your overall dwelling costs and to alert you to the legal rights and responsibilities that pertain to dwellings. You'll learn how to:

☐ Choose the right type and right amount of property insurance.
☐ Take action to cut your property taxes if they are wrongfully too high.
☐ Get control of your utility and maintenance costs.
☐ Protect yourself and your property if neighbors or landlords violate housing rules and regulations.

Property Insurance

As with automobile insurance, discussed in chapter 6, property insurance provides two forms of protection. First, the insurance will provide reimbursement for loss or damage to the physical premises and the contents and furnishings. Second, the insurance will protect you in the event that harm comes to other people or to the property of other people. This latter form of protection is known as public liability insurance. As an owner or tenant of property, you can be responsible to others if they are harmed as a result of your negligence in maintaining the property. The law does not require you to maintain public liability insurance on your house or apartment, as it does on automobiles in most states. But the law will require you to pay damages should a court find that you were in fact responsible for injuries suffered by another. A lack of proper insurance on either the physical premises or for public liability can prove financially catastrophic.

In general, homeowners insurance will reimburse you in the amount needed to replace or repair lost or damaged property, based on its value at the time of loss. Some kinds of property tend to increase in replacement cost—such as a house or jewelry. Other types of property tend to decrease in value—such as furniture and carpeting. These changes in value are known as appreciation and depreciation. In spite of the fluctuations in replacement costs, it should be relatively easy to determine what those costs would be from year to year.

For those who rent, there is a special type of policy called the tenant's policy. It provides protection against loss or damage to furnishings and personal items as well as public liability protection.

The cost of your homeowners or tenants insurance will depend on a number of factors: the company you deal with; the risk rating of your property; and the amount of protection you seek.

The Company You Deal With

As with all other forms of insurance, property insurance is competitive. Rates for similar coverage can differ from company to company. The cheapest protection is not necessarily the best. You must try to gauge the extent of service you'll get from the company, their response to claims, and the possibility of increased premiums when claims have been submitted.

The Risk Ratings of the Property

Each property insured will be rated by the insurance companies according to relative risk factors. These factors can include location of the building and proximity to fire departments and fire hydrants; construction of the building (for example, brick as opposed to wood frame); proximity to other buildings; and fire and crime statistics in the neighborhood in which the building is located. Check with your agent to determine what precautions you might take to keep your property insurance premiums as low as possible. Such precautions might include the installation of fire extinguishers and fire retardant materials, the cleanliness of attics and basements (piles of combustible rubbish or souvenirs do not please insurance raters), security devices such as smoke detectors and burglar alarms, as well as the locking mechanisms used throughout the premises.

The Amount of Coverage You Desire

If you have a mortgage on your house, the lender will require that you carry at least enough fire insurance to protect his interest in the event the building is destroyed. That may be all the fire insurance you care to have—you'll take your chances, come what may. On the other hand, you may insure your property against virtually any hazard conceivable with the possible exceptions of earthquake, land slides, and tidal waves. (Floods may not be insurable in some areas; but check with your local agent regarding the federal flood insurance program that may provide protection for you against that hazard.) The amount and extent of coverage can affect your insurance costs considerably for obvious reasons. Prudent individuals will carry enough insurance to see to it that their routine is not materially disrupted by most foreseeable hazards. They are likely to be willing to take certain chances that some hazards won't occur, or if they do, they can get by without reimbursement for particular losses.

The Types of Policies and Coverage

Homeowners insurance comes in three primary forms: the basic form, or "Homeowners 1"; the broad form, or "Homeowners 2" (the tenants form is similar to the Homeowners 2 and is known as the Homeowners 4); and the comprehensive form known as "Homeowners 5." A special form, "Homeowners 3," combimes the broad form (HO2) coverage on personal property with the comprehensive form (HO5) coverage on the dwelling itself.

The Basic Form (HO1)

With HO1 your premise is protected against the most common risks. These risks include:

- ☐ Fire
- ☐ Lightning
- ☐ Windstorm
- ☐ Hail
- ☐ Explosions
- ☐ Riots
- ☐ Aircraft
- ☐ Vehicles
- ☐ Smoke damage
- ☐ Vandalism and malicious mischief
- ☐ Theft (except for certain exempt items, among which are credit cards)
- ☐ Breakage of glass in the building
- ☐ Loss suffered to personal property that you removed from endangered premises (e.g., the building next door to you is on fire and you flee into the night clutching some private possessions that are later lost or damaged—they are covered under your basic form policy).

The Broad Form (HO2)

The broad form (HO2) and the tenants form (HO4) provide protection against additional risks at a nominal extra cost. These additional risks include:

- ☐ Falling objects
- ☐ Collapse of the building
- ☐ Damage to the building due to the weight of ice or snow
- ☐ Certain damage caused by escape of steam and water from a boiler, radiator, or similar device
- ☐ Certain accidents involving electrical equipment, such as an overloaded circuit that blows out an appliance

The Comprehensive Form (HO5)

The comprehensive form is sometimes referred to as an "all risk" policy. But the comprehensive form will generally exclude certain risks from coverage, such as earthquake, tidal wave, sewer backups and seepage, landslides, floods, war, and nuclear radiation. See each specific policy to determine what exceptions do exist on the comprehensive form. Even though flood may be excluded from coverage, the federal government has acted to make flood insurance more easily available to homeowners in flood-prone areas. Your agent can give you details on this coverage and its cost. The added cost of the comprehensive protection may not be worth it to many homeowners, but each must examine his or her own circumstance to determine what kind of protection is best for the dollars available.

Protecting Other Property

The basic insurance applies to loss or damage occurring to the building itself. In addition, the typical homeowners policy also provides extended coverage for other forms of property. For example, such auxiliary buildings as garages and storage sheds will customarily be covered for 10 percent of the full value on the main building. In other words, if the main building is covered for $80,000, the auxiliary buildings will be covered for a total of $8,000. Your personal property within the home will be covered for 50 percent of the coverage on the house itself. Personal property that you take with you while away from home, with the possible exception of jewelry and securities, will be protected for 10 percent of the primary value. In the comprehensive and special plans, the protection for personal property away from home may be as much as 100 percent of primary value on the house itself.

If your home or apartment suffers damage and you are required to live elsewhere while the damage is repaired, the typical homeowners and tenants policies will provide you with additional living expenses—usually 10 percent on the basic HO1 policy and 20 percent on the broad and comprehensive policies—with the percentages calculated on the total primary value. In addition, your trees, plants, and shrubs will be covered for up to 5 percent of the primary value in the event they are damaged.

Public Liability

Homeowners policies will also contain public liability protection. Commonly, the homeowners policy will have up to $25,000 liability protection per occurrence, $500 in medical expenses payable to others, and $250 in property damages. For example: A guest in your house slips on a banana peel that you have negligently left lying in the hallway. The guest is unable to walk and an ambulance is summoned. X-rays reveal that he has fractured his hip and has also broken his wristwatch in the fall. The homeowners policy will provide up to $500 in medical expenses, which would probably have been required in such a case. They will reimburse the injured party for up to $250 in property damages, which would likely cover the expense of replacing the watch. The injured party then learns that he will be unable to work for a number of months and makes a claim against your homeowners policy. The public liability provision would pay him up to $25,000 in damages—loss of income—as a result of the accident, assuming that all facts proved that you were legally liable.

Public liability protection can be a bit more complicated for apartment tenants and condominium owners than it is for the owner or tenant of a single-family house. This is because a person may be injured in the common premises of a building, as opposed to your own single-family unit. Example: You reside in a multiple dwelling (either apartment or condominium). A guest coming to visit you trips and breaks a leg in one of the common areas of the building such as the parking lot, a hallway, or a stairway. The landlord or the condominium owner's association may have been negligent in causing the accident, but that does not prevent the injured party from suing you directly for damages, as well as suing the landlord or the association. If, in fact, the landlord or the owners' association does not have adequate public liability insurance to pay for such damages, the insured party could seek additional damages from you. Thus, a resident of a multiple dwelling should see to it that either the landlord or the condominium owners' association has adequate public liability insurance to protect all interested parties in the event of a claim for damages under such circumstances. If you as the resident of a multiple dwelling don't feel that the landlord or association does have adequate public liability insurance, you should protect yourself by having adequate public liability protection in your own policy.

The limits on these items of public liability can be increased considerably by paying an added premium. Vastly higher limits for public liability can be obtained at a fairly modest increase in premium, and the prudent homeowner might do well to consider obtaining a much higher level of protection than the basic policy offers.

Valuables

Valuable personal property may *not* be adequately covered for theft or loss under your homeowners or tenants policies. Valuable personal property can include such items as jewelry, paintings, sculptures, china, silver, cameras, projectors, collections (stamps, coins, medallions), golf clubs, furs, securities, cash, and credit cards. In order to be fully covered for loss of these items—whether at home or away—you may have to obtain a separate "personal floater." The cost of this added insurance can be considerable. You should seek the assistance of your agent in determining exactly what personal property is covered under your homeowners policy and under what circumstances you may wish additional protection for your valuables.

The Deductible

The amount of your premium will vary in relation to the deductible that you choose. The deductible is the amount you pay out of pocket for any losses before the insurance company becomes responsible. Some policies have a no-deductible clause, which means that the insurance company is responsible for the first dollar onward. A $50 deductible means that in any given occurrence, you must pay the first $50 worth of expense before the insurance company becomes responsible. Deductibles may be obtained for as much as $250 or $500. In choosing the higher deductibles you are exposing yourself to more potential risk in return for a lower premium. The premium will not be lowered as much as the risk will be enlarged. For example, the difference in premium cost between a $50 deductible and a $250 deductible may be only $20 or $30 but you're exposing yourself to $200 more potential risk. However, the premium expense is an actual out-of-pocket cost that you can save, whereas the added risk is only a possible expense that you may never incur. If you prefer to take your chances with the larger risks, then the higher deductible would be more economical for you.

The Co-insurance Clause

This can be extremely important. The co-insurance clause states generally that if you wish to receive full replacement value for any damage to the premises, you must insure the premises for at least 80 percent of its replacement cost. For example, a house has a current replacement cost (not counting the land and foundation) of $80,000. That means that at current going prices, it would cost $80,000 to duplicate the house, in its depreciated condition, on the existing foundation. (The land and the foundation are not included in figuring costs for insurance coverage because theoretically they can not be destroyed.) But the owner has insured the building for only $56,000, which is $8,000 shy of the 80 percent level of $64,000. The owner has a fire in the house that results in an actual loss of $16,000. But because he has not insured up to the 80 percent co-insurance level, the company will only pay him $14,000 instead of the full $16,000. Why? Because the owner's coverage was only seven-eighths what it should have been under the co-insurance clause ($56,000 is seven-eighths of $64,000). Thus, the owner will receive only seven-eighths of the actual damages ($14,000 is seven-eighths of $16,000). If the owner had insured the property for the full 80 percent co-insurance value, or $64,000, he would have recovered the full $16,000 on the loss. The difference in premium between the full 80 percent value and the lesser value would have been so relatively small that the owner could be accused of being woefully imprudent for not obtaining the balance of the 80 percent coverage.

Keeping up with Change

The prudent homeowner or tenant will make a careful inventory of all furnishings, appliances, and personal property and evaluate current market or replacement costs of those items in order to determine whether he or she is adequately covered by a basic homeowners policy. The owner or renter will also be aware of the effects of inflation in most areas of the country; the value of housing is steadily increasing and, in order to maintain the proper level of insurance protection, continual upward adjustments must be made. Many policies offer clauses that automatically increase the amount of coverage in line with inflation, for as the replacement value of the house increases, so must the amount of coverage if the owner is to be adequately protected. Policies may also be available which will pay you the full amount needed to rebuild your home no matter what the cost.

If a homeowner or tenant acquires new property, such as personal items, or disposes of old items that have been insured, the owner must notify the insurance company so that the new acquisitions can be properly covered and the old dispositions properly deleted. When the insurance company is notified, they will issue an endorsement amending the policy, which should be checked for accuracy and then attached to the policy itself.

Filing a Claim

In the event you do suffer a loss or damage, notify your insurance agent immediately. Even if you don't think that the loss is covered by insurance, you should still discuss the matter with your agent. It may, in fact, be covered. Depending on the extent of damage, the agent may require that you obtain estimates for the proper repair or replacement of damaged items. If a burglary or theft has occurred, it may be necessary to obtain copies of the police report. If someone is hurt on your property, you should also report this immediately to your agent, as a public liability claim may arise. Under the public liability provisions of your homeowners policy, the insurance company is obliged to provide legal defense for you against such claims as well as to pay any claims that are found to be valid. Delay in reporting to your agent could jeopardize your rights under your homeowners policy.

Property Taxes

Property taxes (also called real estate taxes) provide the money that allows your local government to operate. Owners of all non-exempt kinds of property are required to pay these taxes, in return for which the city provides services. A portion of the property taxes may also be allocated to the county and state jurisdictions within which the city is located to enable them to provide their respective services.

How are property taxes calculated? The residents of each city, at least in theory, determine the amount and type of services they wish. In order to meet the expenses of these services, the city must generate income from taxation. The city officials determine what types of property will carry what share of the overall tax burden. The city, through its assessor's office, undergoes a program by which each property in the city is evaluated. Representatives of the assessor's office visit each property in the city periodically to determine the actual value of each parcel. When the current value of every property is known, the *assessment rate* is applied.

For example, a given city may determine that residential property will be assessed at 20 percent of market value, while commercial property will be assessed at 25 percent, and industrial property at 30 percent. (Business and industrial areas frequently contribute a heavier share of tax dollars because they are using the property for income-producing purposes.) Thus, a house with a market value of $60,000 may be assessed at $12,000. In theory, all properties of the same type with equal market values are assessed equally.

Once the assessment rates are established, the city officials look at the outgo side of their budget and determine how much money is needed on the income side. They then determine the *tax rate*. Based on their budgetary needs, they may determine that the tax rate for a given year will be $100 for each $1000 of assessed valuation. Thus, the house with the $60,000 current value, which has an assessment of $12,000 (20 percent of the current market value according to the formula) will pay taxes of $1200 for the year.

The tax *rate* is adjusted annually to keep the city's income and expenses as close to equal as possible. Periodically, depending on local law and custom, all properties in the city, or a selection of properties in the city, may be reassessed to make sure that they are in line with the prevailing assessment program.

Commonly, homeowners are billed for their property taxes in two installments six months apart. If the homeowner has a mortgage escrow account, the tax bills will be sent to the mortgage lender, who will then pay the taxes. They will be paid out of this account to which the owner has made payments each month in addition to interest and principal.

Tenants are also indirectly paying a share of the tax because a portion of their rent is applied by the landlord to his tax bill on the property.

If a property owner defaults in the payment of his property taxes, the city can take steps to force the property to be sold at public auction to satisfy the unpaid taxes due.

Protesting Your Assessment

Local laws provide measures by which property owners can protest the assessment on their property and, if successful, reduce the assessment and thereby the taxes. Tenants, who have an indirect stake in the taxation on the property they occupy, can also take steps to have the assessment reduced. They can act as a group, in conjunction with the landlord, in the same way that individual property owners can.

Although each local assessor's office attempts to value equal properties equally, errors can occur. Equal properties are those comparable in size, location, and date and quality of construction. Example: Your house and your next-door neighbor's house are as identical as two houses can be. They were built at the same time by the same builder, and they are identical in size and room layout. Both houses have been maintained equally, and except for different decor, they are virtual twins. With one exception: your house is assessed for $15,000 while your neighbor's house is assessed for only $12,000. His annual tax bill, therefore, is roughly 20 percent lower than yours.

If an error exists concerning property that you own or occupy, nobody will take steps to correct that error other than yourself. An improper assessment can mean hundreds of dollars lost each year, year in and year out, so it behooves any property owner to examine the local assessment rolls every few years to determine that the property is, in fact, being properly assessed.

The steps are relatively simple. In most communities you may not even require the assistance of a lawyer unless you exhaust the normal appeals system and find it necessary to go to court. Visit your local assessor's office and, with their assistance, locate your property on the assessment rolls. It's usually listed by a code number or by the name of owner and street address. Compare as best you can the assessment on your property with the assessment on comparable properties in the immediately adjoining area. If the assessment on your property seems to be higher than that of your neighbor's, you might well have a chance of getting your assessment reduced.

Proceedings will differ from one city to another, but the common first step is to file a protest with the assessor's office. Since you will be expected to explain why you feel that your property is improperly assessed, your protest should note other comparable properties in the immediate area and their respective assessments.

If, after reviewing your protest, the assessor agrees with you, the assessment can be lowered. If the assessor does not agree with you, then you will probably be able to appeal his ruling to a higher board. If that fails, you may have to go to court with the help of a lawyer and a real estate agent who can provide expert testimony on your behalf as to the fair level of assessments in the neighborhood.

In most communities there is a limited period of time each year during which a protest can be filed. If you fail to file within that time, the assessment will stand as it is for the year. If you are successful in lowering your assessment, the reduction will not likely be retroactive to prior years. But the revised assessment should remain in effect for the current year and subsequent years unless and until a reassessment of the entire community takes place.

Utilities

The owner of a house will make arrangements with the local utility companies for them to provide gas, electricity, and telephone service. The individual owner will be responsible for paying for the utilities used. Utility bills, particularly for heating, can vary considerably throughout the seasons. Some utility companies offer budget payment programs in which the estimated annual total cost is broken down into relatively even payments, allowing the homeowner to maintain a program that does not disrupt other budget elements.

Not enough mention can be made of the importance of energy conservation. In addition to keeping your energy usage at a minimum—commensurate with your personal comfort needs—many states as well as the federal government offer attractive tax credits for energy saving improvements to your property. Explore these possiblities with your local utility companies.

Maintenance and Repairs

Human nature being what it is, we often don't get around to doing preventive maintenance for a house—such as seasonal lubrication and servicing of a heating plant—until we hear the creaks and rattles and one thing or another is about to self-destruct. Unexpected maintenance costs can be a severe jolt to any budget.

To the homeowner, a periodic inspection is an inexpensive insurance policy, alerting you to potential dangers and expenses. In addition to paying for current ongoing maintenance costs, the wise homeowner will set aside a reserve for replacements—a fund that will allow him or her to take care of these costs without having to interfere with borrowing lines, savings account, or ongoing regular budget.

Laws Regarding Housing

There are a number of laws that can affect the rights and obligations of both property owners and tenants. These laws will differ from state to state and from city to city, and you should make inquiry in your own locality as to any laws that might affect you.

Zoning

Cities commonly require the right to specify that certain areas may have only certain kinds of uses permitted on them. The city map will be divided into zones according to the uses allowed in those zones. The broad categories in zoning regulations are residential, commercial, industrial and agricultural. Within each category there may be subcategories. For example, within a residential category there may be zones for single-family housing only and zones in which multiple housing is permitted. Each specific zone may carry within it certain regulations applicable to that zone. In a commercial zone, for example, there may be a requirement that so many off-street parking places are available for each thousand square feet of building space.

Generally, zoning regulations are like a pyramid: higher uses are permitted in any of the lower use zones, but lower use of zones may not be permitted in the zones above them. Figure 10-1 provides an illustration: in most cities, the highest use is for single-family homes, often designated as R (for residential) -1. In areas zoned R-1, therefore, only single-family homes will be permitted. The next zone down may be designated R-2.

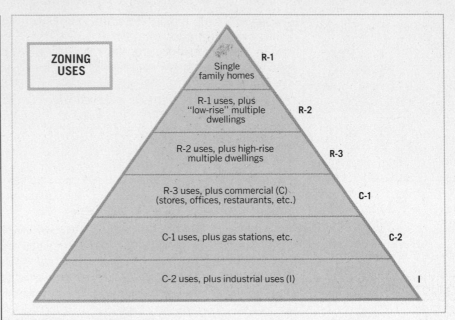

Figure 10–1   Zoning uses.

These zones would permit R-1 uses (single-family homes) plus "low-rise" multiple dwellings. The next zone down might be called R-3, and it would permit all R-2 uses, plus high-rise multiple dwellings.

Zoning ordinances may be changed from time to time as the city officials deem proper. You may be living in a single-family zone that is adjoined by an agricultural zone. Farmer Jones, who occupies a large section of the agricultural zone, is approached by a residential home builder to sell the land to him. At the same time, he's approached by a commercial shopping center developer who also wishes to buy the land. The homebuilder and the shopping center developer would both have to seek a change in the zoning from agricultural use to either residential or commercial use. You, as a resident in the adjoining single-family zone, could have a considerable stake in the outcome of this struggle. Conceivably, the development of an attractive housing subdivision could enhance the value of your property while a shabby development could cause a decrease in value. Similarly, a high-quality shopping center development could be to your advantage, whereas a low-quality shopping center could be unattractive to you and a detriment to your property value.

Zoning laws can restrict you or protect you in an effort to maintain the quality of your neighborhood. For example: you wish to set up a beauty parlor in your home. You hang a simple sign on your front porch and accept clientele. If your home is in a zone that prevents businesses from being operated in the home, any neighbors who object to this activity could have your business stopped because it is in violation of the zoning ordinances. Likewise, you could do the same if a neighbor similarly violates the zoning ordinances.

Residents of any municipality should make themselves aware of current zoning regulations and be on the alert for the possibility of any change in the immediate vicinity that could affect the value of their residence. Zoning hearings are usually open to the public, and customarily there are appeals that can be taken from unfavorable zoning rulings. If many people are affected by the possiblity of a zoning ordinance change, they can group together and hire an attorney to represent all of their joint interests.

Nuisances

Your next-door neighbor keeps a rooster that crows at dawn each morning, or plays a stereo at high volume each night into the wee hours, or burns strange or noxious chemicals at odd hours, or permits dangerous conditions to exist. These items, and scores of others like them, fall into the general category known as nuisances. If you're located in a multi-unit building, such as an apartment house or a condominium, you may be able to get some assistance from a sympathetic landlord or from the condominium owners' association. If you're a homeowner, you may have to resort to the local police, or to your own attorney, to get some satisfaction. Nuisance laws exist in almost every city, but enforcing them can involve feats of diplomacy that the local magistrates may be incapable of carrying out to your satisfaction. Some nuisances will fall under the jurisdiction of other laws. For example, opening a business in premises where businesses are not permitted could be in violation of zoning laws. Matters relating to health and safety could fall under the multiple-housing unit laws or health and safety codes of the city. If a nuisance exists within your immediate vicinity, it might be better for you to explore the possibility that laws other than nuisance laws control the situation.

Eminent Domain

The law of eminent domain permits a local government—perhaps city, county, or state—to acquire private property where it can prove that the need exists for the public welfare. The process is generally known as "condemnation," and it occurs where new highways and bridges are to be constructed, where urban-renewal programs take place, and where other public uses are called for. Owners of property threatened by condemnation are entitled to fair payment for their property. Procedures vary as to how property owners are compensated. Often there will be a hearing at which property owners present their claims for fair compensation. If an owner isn't satisfied with the offer, he or she may appeal, and if the appeal does not satisfy, the person may take the matter into the courts. The aid of a lawyer and a competent real estate appraiser is necessary in any condemnation situation.

The law of Eminent Domain can also affect your property indirectly, without actually taking any portion of it. For example, a new highway nearby may create noise and pollution problems for your house. None of your property has actually been taken, but the value of the property may suffer as a result. You may be entitled to some claim for damages as a result.

Anyone who is either buying or already owns property, whether residential, commercial, or industrial, should be aware of any possible eminent domain that could take place within proximity of your property. Knowledge of an impending condemnation might discourage you from buying certain property, and that knowledge can also permit you to take early action to best protect your interests if a condemnation threatens currently owned property.

Rent Control and Condominium Conversion Regulations

If you live in a multiple-dwelling unit, rent control ordinances and condominium conversion regulations can have a very important effect on your rights. These laws will be discussed in more detail in the following chapter, on renting.

Personal Action Checklist
Insurance Inventory

Whether you're a renter or an owner, it's important that your valuable personal possessions be adequately insured against damage or loss. Insurance coverage is generally advisable if the damage or loss of personal property would cause you financial distress. (Insuring items of sentimental value may be an unwise expense.) Too little coverage, or too much coverage, can be costly to you. This checklist will help you determine the right amount of coverage.

☐ How much coverage does your current owners (or renters) policy provide for loss or damage to personal property?

☐ What contingencies are there that could affect your recovery in the case of a loss? For example, must there be overt evidence of attempted burglary in the case of a disappearance? Is there a deductible?

☐ To what extent is your property (including cash and jewelry) protected if you suffer a loss while away from your home?

☐ If you suffer a loss, will you be reimbursed for the current replacement cost or for the depreciated value of the property?

☐ Do you have valuables listed on a separate schedule with the insurance company?

☐ How much does this separate scheduling cost? What added protection does it provide?

☐ With your insurance agent's help if necessary, complete the following inventory:

Items*	Current Protection	Replacement Cost	Depreciated Value	Most Recent Appraisal
Jewelry	_____	_____	_____	_____
Collections (coins, stamps, etc.)	_____	_____	_____	_____
Art	_____	_____	_____	_____
Chinaware	_____	_____	_____	_____
Silverware	_____	_____	_____	_____

Continued on next page

Items*	Current Protection	Replacement Cost	Depreciated Value	Most Recent Appraisal
Cash, securities kept at home	_____	_____	_____	_____
Musical instruments	_____	_____	_____	_____
Electronic items (TV, stereo, video recorder)	_____	_____	_____	_____
Sports equipment (skis, scuba gear, golf clubs)	_____	_____	_____	_____
Furniture and furnishings	_____	_____	_____	_____

*Do you have a color photo of each valuable item?

Consumer Beware
Mortgage Insurance
Can Be Confusing

There's one kind of insurance related to homeownership that really doesn't insure the property itself. Rather, it insures that your mortgage payments will be made in the event of the death or disability of the primary bread-winner in the family. Technically, it's a form of life or disability insurance and could really be considered a part of the subjects discussed in chapters 20 and 21.

But because it relates to homeownership, and because it is often sold by affiliates of banks and savings associations that provided the home financing in the first place, let's examine the pros and cons briefly here.

Since your overall mortgage debt is the largest you'll likely ever face, and since your monthly mortgage payments represent one of your major monthly obligations, it can be prudent to protect yourself against a ca-tastrophe that could affect your ability to meet your home loan debt.

Life insurance on your mortgage is generally of the "decreasing term" variety. The amount of protection decreases monthly as the amount of your debt decreases. Depending on your age and family circumstances, you might want to explore a level term or ordinary life policy instead of the decreasing term. You might be able to obtain better long-term pro-tection without greatly increasing the cost.

In the event of the death of the breadwinner, proceeds of mortgage life insurance are commonly paid directly to the lender. This may not be best for you. It might be preferable to obtain a policy that would pay the proceeds to your named beneficiary (spouse, children) to do with as they please. Rather than have the mortgage paid off, they might prefer to continue making payments or to sell the house with the original mortgage intact. If the interest rate on the mortgage is lower than the current rate, it could prove costly later if the survivors had need to refinance the prop-erty.

Disability policies make your monthly payments for you if you are un-able to work due to illness or accident. Many will have a 30- or 60-day "waiting period" before payments will commence. Compare the terms and costs of such policies, bearing in mind other sources of income that might be available to help you make your payments during a spell of disability. Your own insurance agent might be able to provide better coverage at lower cost than can the lender.

11 | Renting

Tens of millions of Americans rent their dwellings. Many do so because they've not been able to accumulate enough money to purchase a house or condominium. Others do so because they simply prefer the freedom and flexibility that comes with renting. Whether you're making a choice between renting and buying, or whether you have no choice in the matter, the rental of a dwelling entails many important legal and financial considerations. This chapter will make you aware of those considerations and will help you resolve common problems that come with renting. They include:

- ☐ What factors you should evaluate in deciding whether to rent or to buy.
- ☐ How to understand the terms of a lease, and how to negotiate a rental arrangement that's best for you.
- ☐ How you might be able to obtain the right to buy the place you've been renting, or want to rent.
- ☐ What to do if your rights as a tenant are violated.

If you are a renter, you are paying another person—the owner of property or the landlord—a fee for the privilege of living in his property. You may rent a person's house, or you may rent in a multiple-unit dwelling such as a duplex, a condominium complex, or an apartment house. Mobile home rentals are also not uncommon.

A renter will occupy a dwelling in one of two ways: on a month-to-month basis, or on a fixed-term basis. On a month-to-month basis, both the landlord and the tenant have the right to terminate the arrangement upon giving 30 days' notice to the other party. Commonly, the landlord will expect the tenant to comply with certain rules and regulations which will often be spelled out in a written agreement. On a fixed-term basis, the landlord and tenant will agree in a written document that the tenant has the right to occupy the premises for a specific amount of time, such as one or two years. The agreement between the two parties is referred to as a lease.

Pros and Cons of Renting

Many people, particularly in larger cities, are died-in-the-wool renters. They simply prefer the apartment mode of living—being close to other people, free of the cares that often go with ownership. To them, rental is a way of life, and the thought of buying a home may never enter their minds.

Many other people have no choice: They do not have the money available to make a down payment on a home, and thus they must be renters. This latter group is further broken down into two categories: those who prefer to spend their money on other things rather than accumulate it for a down payment, and thus will likely remain permanent renters; and those who desire to eventually become owners, and who will structure their budget so as to accumulate the necessary down payment. As they struggle to accumulate those funds, they often ponder the dilemma: Is it worth it to own a home, or should we just be content as renters?

There is no simple answer to the dilemma. Homeownership has long been considered one of the great American dreams. In decades gone by, that dream was reasonably attainable by a large segment of the population. But in the 1980s, with housing costs as high as they are and with so many other temptations upon which to spend one's money, that great American dream may be fading.

Traditionally, homeownership has long been considered a wise step financially. Over the long run, that probably remains true. But ownership is not necessarily the right answer for everybody.

To help you make a decision best suited to your own individual needs and desires and abilities, let's now examine the pros and cons of renting.

Flexibility

One of the primary advantages of renting—whether it's a house or an apartment—is the flexibility available. When a lease expires, the tenant is free to move on (or renew, assuming he or she and the landlord agree on renewal terms). There's no need to worry about selling, and no danger of getting caught with making payments on two dwellings, such as where sale is not completed by a homeowner prior to the time of moving out. The flexibility is even greater where furnished units are rented, for the chores of physically moving are considerably minimized. Largely for this reason, renting is often preferable for younger persons who have not yet settled into their chosen lifestyle or career, and who may not yet know what ultimate size their family will be. The same is true for older persons at or near retirement who may wish to be able to come and go as they please without the concerns of ownership.

No Money Tied Up

With very few exceptions, ownership requires a substantial sum of money to be tied up in the property. When one buys a house or condominium, it's necessary to make a substantial down payment. Further, as you make your monthly mortgage payments, a portion of which goes to reduce your mortgage debt, those additional sums are effectively tied up in the property. Money that's tied up in property ownership is money you do not have direct access to, and it's money that could otherwise be earning income for you if it were invested. Until you sell or refinance the property—either of which could be time consuming and costly—you cannot get at your money. In a rental situation, there's no need to tie up any large sums of money. A rental deposit, usually not in excess of two month's rent, will frequently be called for, but this is not a large enough sum to create any noticeable disadvantage.

Income-tax Implications

Ownership provides certain income-tax advantages that are not available to renters. Tax laws allow owners to take deductions for the interest they pay on their mortgage and the property taxes they pay. This can mean a substantial savings in taxes. Further, if you sell your home and realize a profit, that profit is subject to favorable tax laws. (See chapter 12 for a more detailed discussion.)

These tax advantages have often been the deciding factor for many people to purchase a home rather than to rent. But a closer look at the situation reveals that in many cases the advantages may not necessarily be as attractive as they seem on the surface.

For example: The Alpers have saved up $20,000 to use as a down payment for the purchase of a house. Considering the interest they pay on their mortgage and their property taxes, and their particular tax bracket, the ownership of the home results in an income tax savings of $2000 per year. Had the Alpers *not* bought a home, but instead invested the $20,000 at 12 percent interest, they would have earned $2400 per year—before income-tax considerations. In this particular case, careful arithmetic indicates that they may not be better off financially on a year-to-year basis as a result of buying instead of using their available funds for investment and renting their dwelling.

When analyzing specific financial advantages in owning versus renting, this income-tax factor should be carefully calculated based on your own tax situation. The numbers will differ from person to person, from deal to deal, and from year to year. The more costly the house and the higher the interest rate, the more favorable the tax advantage can be to an owner. But it's not an automatic bonanza. Many years ago, when the standard deduction was much smaller than it is today, the tax advantage of ownership was much more obvious. But in recent years the standard deduction has grown to such a relatively high percentage of income that careful arithmetic is necessary before final decisions are made.

No Chance of Profit (Or Risk of Loss)

One of the attractions of ownership is the chance that one may profit on a later resale. The tenant, of course, has no such chance for profit, but he or she also faces no risk of loss.

Indeed, the lure of profit often bears fruit. But profit is often the direct result of inflation, and although you may profit on the sale of your existing home, you'll soon realize that you have to live somewhere else, and the cost of acquiring new housing will have likely risen in step with the price of your old housing. Thus, your profit can be easily absorbed by the simple change from one dwelling to another.

Profit can also be reduced by two other factors: real estate commissions and income taxes. In all likelihood you will have used a real estate agent to help you sell your house, and a commission of 6 or 7 percent of the selling price goes to the agent. Further, if you sell your house at a profit, that profit is subject to federal income taxes. (If you sell your house at a loss, that loss is not deductible on your income-tax return.) See chapter 12 for further details.

No Protection Against Inflation

Neither owning nor renting can insure you of protection against inflation. For a month-to-month tenant, the rental can be increased on 30 days' notice. For a tenant on a lease, the rental can be increased upon a renewal of the lease (subject to any rent control ordinances that may exist in the community). The homeowner can expect increasing expenses for property taxes, property insurance, maintenance, repairs, and utilities. And if the homeowner is making payments on a variable-rate mortgage, his basic monthly payments can be subject to increases as well. The homeowner with a fixed-interest-rate mortgage has much greater protection against inflation because his monthly payments for interest and principal will remain constant for as long as he remains owner of the property.

Overall, homeowners do have a better chance to protect themselves from inflation, because as prices rise over the years, so will the value of their home. The only problem with this, as noted earlier, is that the prices of all other homes will have risen comparably so any profit you realize on the sale may be illusory when you purchase another house.

This particular advantge to homeownership is based on the assumption that housing values will continue to rise. But that phenomenon is by no means guaranteed. Housing markets are definitely subject to up and down fluctuations from time to time and from place to place. If your timing is unfortunate enough to find you buying when the market is high and wanting to sell when the market is low, this inflation-proofing advantage of homeownership may not exist. Indeed, you might have been better off renting.

No Building Equity

"Why rent and collect worthless rent receipts when we can own and be building a hefty equity in our home?" Fact or myth? Although it's true that rent receipts have no tangible value, the other side of the question can be misleading. The average stay in a dwelling by a typical American family is from seven to ten years, and during those early years of the common 30-year mortgage, the reduction of mortgage debt is very small indeed.

Equity is the difference between what your house is worth and what is owed on it. Part of each mortgage payment you make reduces your debt, and theoretically, when you later sell your property, you recapture that sum, plus any appreciation in the value of your house.

The chapter on financing discusses in more detail how interest is figured on mortgages. For the moment, note that during the first seven years of a 12 percent 30-year morgage, the reduction of debt on the mortgage is only about 5 percent of the total original mortgage.

For example, during the first seven years of a $70,000 mortgage that is set to run for 30 years at a 12 percent interest rate, that portion of your mortgage payments allocated to reducing the debt totals 5 percent of the total original mortgage, or $3500. In other words, after seven years of making payments on such a mortgage, you will have reduced your mortgage indebtedness from $70,000 to $66,500.

Added Expenses

If you're a tenant, the cost of certain repairs may be borne by the landlord, depending on the terms of the lease. If you're an owner, you'll usually have to bear most of these costs yourself, except in certain condominium or cooperative situations. As a tenant, you're probably limited in the number of alterations and modifications you can make to the premises. Again, the lease will control. Unless you're willing, on terminating your lease, to correct any personal modifications that you might have installed, you will be very limited in what you can do in a rental unit. As an owner, you're free to do as you please—paint the walls purple and pink if you like—as long as you're aware of the implications of such modifications when it comes time to sell the house or condominium. You run the risk of over-personalizing your premises and scaring away would-be buyers. You can also run the risk of overimproving the premises and thus pricing the dwelling out of the market for comparable units within that neighborhood. But bearing those factors in mind, the freedom of modifying your dwelling is vastly greater in an ownership situation than with a rental.

To Buy or to Rent— A Case History

Let's examine a situation in which a family is debating between buying and renting. This example does not presume to answer the dilemma. It's merely intended to serve as a guide, a framework, to help you know what arithmetic you should consider in trying to find the right answer for your own personal situation.

The Browns have found a condominium, and they have the opportunity of either buying or renting it. The purchase price is $80,000; the monthly rental would be $900, which would include all utilities, maintenance, and association dues.

If they buy, they have $10,000 in cash to use as a down payment, and the property has an existing $70,000 mortgage with an annual interest rate of 12 percent. The mortgage can be assumed. Monthly payments on interest and principal total $720. Property taxes are $120 per month, property insurance is $40 per month, and utilities and maintenance total $100 per month. Thus, if they buy, their total monthly cash outlay would be $980.

The Browns estimate that based on their current tax bracket, ownership will result in tax savings to them of $2000 in the first year, or $166 per month. (For example, if the Browns are in the 25 percent tax bracket and they have $8000 worth of deductible expenses for mortgage interest, and real estate taxes, over and above the standard deductions, they would save roughly $2000—25 percent of $8000—on their income-tax bill for the year. See the chapter on income taxes for a more detailed explanation.)

On the other hand, if they decide not to buy but to rent and they invest their $10,000 at 12 percent return, they will take in $1200 during the first year (before income taxes), or $100 per month. After taxes, they estimate that that $100 per month would shrink to $76 per month. Thus as Table 11-1 shows, they are looking at a difference of $10 per month net savings should they buy instead of rent. This alone might convince them to buy, particularly if they felt that they'd be living in the condominium for a period of years and had an opportunity to reap a profit upon a later sale.

But the Browns know their own circumstances very well: they suspect that within a year Mr. Brown's job might require them to move to a different city. They've also examined the local housing market and have found that prices are flat and seem likely to remain so for at least many months. Looking one year ahead, they realize that if they have to sell the condominium and find themselves without a buyer for just one month after they've been transferred, they will be out of pocket over $900. That would more than wipe out the monthly savings they'd have realized during that year by being owners instead of renters.

The Browns, it appears, are almost at a "toss the coin" situation. Table 11-1 illustrates the arithmetic of the Browns' dilemma. As the Browns' case illustrates, resolving the matter can depend basically on personal circumstances. How long might they stay in a given dwelling? How wisely might they invest their funds if they decide to rent instead of buy? Which way will the housing market turn? The case of the Browns is not intended to convince you to become a renter or a buyer, but merely to show you the arithmetic and the crystal-ball gazing that you must do in order to reach a conclusion best suited to your own circumstances. The table illustrates the actual cash flow differences in the choices the Browns have.

Table 11-1 | **The Browns: Renting Versus Owning**

Monthly Costs			
As Owners		As Renters	
Mortgage	$720	Base rent (including utilities)	$900
Property tax	120	Net earning on invested $10,000	76
Property insur.	40		$824
Utilities and maintenance	100		
	980		
Tax savings	166		
Net cost	$814		

Shopping for Rentals

Many of the same considerations apply to looking for a dwelling to rent as to looking for a dwelling to buy. How close will it be to your place of work, to shopping, to schools, to entertainment? What is the condition of the building and of the neighborhood? How large is the premises and will it suit your foreseeable needs for the time you'll be living there?

There are additional matters to be considered if you are looking for an apartment. You should talk to other tenants in the building and try to determine the level of service and care provided by the landlord. Are reasonable requests by tenants taken care of promptly and courteously? Is the building well maintained, both esthetically and mechanically? What has been the history of rent increases? Are there any local rent-control ordinances that apply to the building?

The renters' checklist at the end of this chapter will help you in your quest for an apartment.

Depending on your community, the classified ads in your local newspaper may be all you need to direct you to available apartments. In larger communities, you might find it desirable to seek the services of a rental agent. It's not uncommon for a rental agent to charge the tenant a fee for finding an apartment. Before you contract with a rental agent, determine what fees, if any, will be expected from you and get personal references from other individuals who have used that rental agent.

When you buy a house, you can reasonably expect that a real estate agent who is working for you will escort you from one house to another. But don't expect the same kind of service from a rental agent. In all likelihood, you will be given the address and instructions on how to view the apartment, and you'll be on your own to take care of yourself.

Depending on the supply of apartments in your community, and on the demand for them, you might find it necessary to leave a deposit with a landlord immediately if you find a place you like. If the demand is high and the supply low, a landlord will rent to the first interested party who puts up the necessary deposit. On the other hand, if the demand is low, the landlord might be willing to "hold" a given apartment for you for a day or two, perhaps even longer. In such a case it would be to your advantage to get that promise in writing from the landlord.

When you examine an apartment, determine whether the landlord expects you to rent on a month-to-month basis or to sign a lease. Examine the premises carefully and determine that everything is in proper working order (appliances, plumbing, electrical outlets). If you have children or pets, or expect to have them, make sure these will be acceptable to the landlord. And in addition to finding out what the monthly rental will be, find out what kind of deposits the landlord expects.

The Lease and Its Key Clauses

Renting a dwelling—be it a house, a mobile home, or an apartment—involves numerous rights and obligations between the landlord and the tenant. Those rights and obligations may be spelled out in a full-fledged contract called a lease. A lease is not of the same financial magnitude as the mortgage that corresponds to the purchase of a house, but it can entail many thousands of dollars that you will be paying, and you want to make sure you're getting what you bargained for.

The lease, basically, entitles you to occupy certain premises for a certain period of time at an agreed-on price. Here are some of the key clauses that could well affect the nature and cost of your occupancy.

Expenses

The lease should set forth exactly who is responsible for what expenses in connection with the property. If the landlord is responsible for all utilities and all real estate taxes, the lease should so state. If the tenant is responsible for individual utilities, will the tenant be separately metered so that the true utility costs can be exactly measured? If the tenant is paying based on a certain percentage of the total building occupancy and is not separately metered, will the tenant be getting a fair shake, or will he or she be paying more than actual utility usage? If the tenant is responsible for paying a portion of the property taxes, over and above the landlord's own payments, will that obligation be based on the proportionate rental of the individual unit to the total rental role of the whole building? Or will the tax obligation be based on an arbitrary percentage? These details should be explicit in the written agreement.

Repairs

Who will be responsible for *making* which repairs? And perhaps more important, who will be responsible for *paying* for the repairs that are made? The landlord may be responsible for seeing to it that repairs are made, but some repairs may be done at the tenant's expense, others at the landlord's. Generally, the landlord is responsible for repairing structural defects and for keeping the central heating unit in proper working order. The tenants may be responsible for attending to their own repairs on minor items within the premises, including but not limited to plumbing leaks and defective appliances. If you have examined the premises before you sign a lease, you should be able to determine what possible repair bills you might be facing during your occupancy. If you, or the contractor you hire to assist you in your evaluation, determine that you would be more than normally vulnerable to repair costs, you might want to renegotiate the repair clause of your lease with the landlord before you sign.

Quiet Enjoyment

Quiet enjoyment is a legal term that assures you of the right to privacy and quiet in your occupancy of the premises. If the landlord fails to deliver quiet enjoyment—that is, fails to keep the adjoining neighbors from playing air hockey next to your bedroom wall at four o'clock in the morning— you will have the right to either withhold your rent payment or get assistance in the courts in upholding your rights.

Extra Fees

Does your monthly rental include all of the features of your occupancy, or will added costs be hidden in the small print on the back page of the lease, such as parking fees, use of recreational facilities, and assessments for improvements in the common areas? All rental costs and fees should be clearly understood prior to the signing of any lease.

Renewal Options

Will you have a right to renew your lease on the expiration of the original term? Not all leases contain this privilege, and it may be one worth bargaining for. Without a renewal option, the landlord can ask whatever the market will bear when the original lease term expires. If the tenant is not willing to pay what the landlord is asking, the landlord has the right to have the tenant move out. A renewal option is for the protection of the tenant: he or she has the right either to stay on at the agreed-on rental or to move out. It's reasonable to expect that the rental rate on a renewal will be higher than on the original term, so the landlord can be protected against rising costs. Even at a higher rent, though, the renewal option does offer the tenant flexibility and choice, things often worth paying for.

Some leases may contain an automatic renewal clause. When such a clause exists, the lease may automatically renew for another term (identical to the original term) unless the tenant gives written notice to the landlord that he or she does not wish to have the lease renewed. If you are involved in such a lease and you fail to give the proper notice, you could become responsible for lease payments for an additional term. For example, if the original term was for one year and the automatic renew clause goes into effect, you could become responsible for an additional year's rent.

Sublease Privileges

You may be subleasing *from* another party, or you may wish to sublease *to* another party. If you are subleasing from the original tenant, you will be subject to the terms of his or her lease. Prior to subleasing from another party, you might want to determine whether in fact that party has the right to sublease to you, and if the landlord has given his consent, if such consent is called for in the original lease. If you sublease from another party, and that party does not have the legal right to sublease to you, the landlord technically could evict you, and perhaps the main tenant as well, for the lease would have been violated.

On the other hand, if you wish to have the right to sublease to other parties while you are the main tenant, you had best make certain that the lease contains this privilege. In the sublease clause, the landlord may or may not reserve the right to approve of any sublessee, generally for reasons of credit worthiness. Unless the landlord consents, the fact that you subleased to another party will not relieve you of your obligation to pay the rent.

A sublease privilege is one that favors the tenant. It gives the tenant the flexibility of being able to move out before the lease has expired and to defray obligations by allowing another party to live in the apartment or house. If you do sublease to another party, you must make certain in advance that the party is credit worthy and reliable. It would pay to obtain a credit history on the party to whom you're subleasing to determine these relative factors.

Security Deposits

There are three possible types of security deposits that you might be required to pay: deposits to insure the payment of the rent, cleaning deposits, and breakage deposits. The rental deposit is usually designated to cover the last month's rent of the lease. This gives the landlord some protection in the event that you move out early. The fact that you do move out early does not necessarily relieve you of your remaining obligations under the lease. Technically, if you move out after 18 months of a 24-month lease, you'll be liable for the remaining 6 months. The landlord will apply the one month's deposit that you have paid toward that six months' obligation and will be able to commence legal proceedings to collect the remaining five months' worth of rent from you.

An additional clause that can be to the tenant's benefit would be one stating that the landlord must make a reasonable attempt to rent vacated space, and if he is able to rent the premises during the term of your vacancy, that all or a portion of the rent that he collects from another tenant occupying your premises will apply toward your obligation. For example, you vacate your premises six months early. Your monthly rental is $300. The landlord has received a $300 security deposit from you that he applies to your remaining obligation, which leaves you owing the landlord $1500. The landlord is successful in renting the apartment for $200 a month for the six-month period. The $1200 that he thus takes in should apply toward your $1500 obligation, leaving you with a debt of $300.

Cleaning and breakage deposits may or may not be refundable, depending on the agreement between the tenant and the landlord. If the premises does need cleaning, the landlord can be expected to apply the cleaning deposit to that task and the tenant will not receive any of his or her deposit back. If damage or breakage has occurred, the damage deposit will be applied to making the necessary repairs, but the tenant's obligation may not be limited to the amount of the breakage deposit. If the breakage or damage exceeds the amount of the deposit, and the lease stipulates that the damages aren't limited to that amount, the landlord can pursue the tenant for the excess needed to make the appropriate repairs.

For the fullest protection of the tenant, both parties should closely examine all aspects of the premises before the tenant takes occupancy to determine the condition of cleanliness and what damages exist at the time the tenant takes occupancy. For example, there may be a crack in a wall that would normally be covered by a piece of furniture or a wall hanging. If it's there when the tenant takes occupancy, the fact should be noted on the lease document so that no one can claim that you as the tenant caused the damage during the period of your occupancy. The tenant and the landlord may trust each other implicitly, but the tenant has to remember that when he or she moves out there may be a different landlord who will not remember that the crack was there at the time the tenant moved in. Color photos of the premises can be particularly helpful in this regard.

Improvements

The tenant of an apartment or a house may wish to make certain improvements on the premises during the term of occupancy. Normally, if improvements are easily removable, such as carpeting, they would remain the property of the tenant. Some improvements, however, may not be quite so portable. For example, a tenant may install built-in bookcases, or a wet bar. Unless the tenant and the landlord have agreed in advance, improvements of this sort might be claimed by the landlord as his property. If any improvements are to be made in the premises, the landlord and the tenant should agree, before the improvements are made, who will have the benefit on the termination of the lease.

Amending the Lease

Even though a lease is a binding legal contract, it can be amended at any time on mutual agreement of the landlord and tenant. (The same holds true in a purchase contract for a house or condominium.) If the parties do agree to any amendments in the contract, changes can be accomplished. Proper consideration (payment) is made between the parties, and the amendment is properly signed by both parties. Any of the above clauses could thus be inserted into a lease agreement even after the agreement has originally been signed and occupancy has been taken. Whether or not to make any amendments on the lease is a matter of bargaining, and if one party is giving up certain rights, he or she will naturally want to receive certain other rights in exchange. Before any rights or obligations are exchanged, legal advice should be sought on the specific consequences of such actions.

Insurance

The landlord must insure himself with respect to damage to the building, such as by fire. But you, as tenant, will be responsible for insuring your own possessions. See chapter 10 for a discussion of tenant's insurance. If the building is extensively damaged by a fire or other catastrophe, you may not be able to occupy your apartment. In arranging for your own tenants insurance, determine whether you will be provided with any form of reimbursement for added living expenses you may incur for temporary quarters until your building is again available to you.

Month-to-Month Tenancy

Not all tenants have a written lease. Many people occupy dwellings on a "month-to-month" basis, without the benefit of any written documents. This, in effect, is a one-month lease, which allows the landlord to alter the terms by giving one month's notice and allows the tenant to vacate by giving one month's notice. Laws may differ from state to state on precisely what the rights of the parties are on a month-to-month lease. Generally, a landlord wishing to raise rents or a tenant wishing to move out must give at least one month's notice from the start of any month of their respective intentions to do so. For example, if a tenant wishes to vacate on March 1, he or she should give proper notice to the landlord not later than the preceding February 1. If this is done, the rental obligation will cease after February, as will the right to occupy the apartment. If, though, notice isn't given until, say, February 10, the landlord might technically be able to hold the person on as a tenant and expect the rental due for the month of March.

Combinations of Leasing and Buying

There can be situations in which an individual becomes a tenant and then an owner. He or she may have a lease with an option to buy, or one with a first refusal to buy. Arrangements of this sort may be particularly favorable to occupants who are not certain of their future. For example, a job transfer moves a family to a new city. They're not sure if the job will work out or if they'll want to stay in that new city. Because of their uncertainty, they don't want to commit themselves to purchasing a house, but they do want to live in a nice dwelling. At the end of the year, if they've decided to stay, they don't want to have to trouble themselves with moving again from a rental unit to a house that they may then decide to purchase. They might therefore look to lease a house or condominium for a one-year period, with the right, after the year, to buy that house or condominium should they so desire.

A Lease with an Option to Buy

A lease with an option to purchase puts the parties in this status: as tenants they have the right to occupy the premises for the stated time and for the stated rental. At any time during their tenancy, they have the right to notify the owner of their intent to purchase the property at a previously agreed-on price. During the period of tenancy, the owner cannot sell the property to any other party, unless the tenants agree to release their option to buy.

Here's an example. The Greens lease a house at $600 per month with an option to buy the house for $60,000. They may exercise their right to buy at any time during their tenancy, but at least 30 days before the end of the lease. If they wish to exercise their option, they give the owner the proper notice and enter into a sales agreement. If they fail to give the proper notice within the allotted time, their option will expire and they will no longer have the right to purchase at the agreed-on price.

By entering into a lease with an option to buy, the owner of the premises is taking his property off the market for at least the term of the lease. He has no assurance that the tenant will in fact buy the property from him, and he may be forgoing an opportunity to lease or sell the property to others at a better rental or purchase price. Thus, the owner of the property can well be expected to charge a premium for the lease, and perhaps for the purchase as well. In other words, although the property might normally rent for $500 per month, he may charge $600 per month. Also, the property might normally have a market value of $57,000, and he may put an asking price of $60,000 on it.

Market conditions existing at that time will also have a bearing on the pricing. If there are more houses on the market than there are willing buyers, the owner may be happy to enter into such a lease/purchase arrangement. If, though, there are more buyers than houses available, the reverse could be true and a heavy premium might have to be paid.

Depending on individual circumstances, a lease with an option to buy can be a very desirable arrangement for certain individuals. In exchange for the extra rental or purchase price that may have to be paid, a considerable measure of flexibility can be obtained. The arrangement can also eliminate the need for making a second move, the cost of which may well offset the extra price being paid on the lease or purchase.

A Lease with a Right of First Refusal

A lease with a right of first refusal to purchase is another alternative that should be considered by persons falling into the above circumstances. Under a lease with a right of first refusal to purchase, the tenant does not have an outright guarantee that he can purchase the property at a preestablished price. The tenant and the owner will agree on an ultimate purchase price, but the owner will still be free to offer the property for sale to others during the term of the tenancy, subject, however, to the right of the tenant to meet or beat any bona fide offer that the owner may acquire. Here's how such an arrangement might work. The tenant and the owner agree on a $600 per month rental, and a $60,000 purchase price after one year. The tenant is not obliged to purchase at all, but may do so at that price if the property is still available at that time. During the period of the tenancy, the landlord has the right to offer the property for sale to anyone at all. Another would-be buyer offers $62,000. The tenant then has the express right to meet or beat that $62,000 offer within a period of, say, ten days after he's been notified by the landlord of the offer. If the tenant wishes to meet the offer, he can become the owner. If the tenant does not wish to meet the offer, he must give up the property.

In the case of a lease with a first refusal to purchase, the landlord is not taking the property off the market, as he does under a lease with an option to purchase. Thus, the landlord might be less inclined to charge a premium price for either the rental or the purchase. The tenant under such an arrangement, however, does run the risk of not being able to buy the property at the desired price. The trade-off—a possibly lower rent and purchase price versus a possible inability to buy the property—has to be carefully evaluated. Leasing with a right of first refusal can be an attractive alternative to leasing with an option to purchase, and either of these may be more desirable than an outright lease or an outright purchase, unless the family is so certain of its plans that it doesn't need the flexibility offered by these alternatives.

Rent Laws

Virtually every city has ordinances pertaining to health and safety measures in multiple-residence dwellings. These ordinances require landlords to maintain proper levels of sanitation, structural soundness, adequacy of plumbing and wiring, and precautions against fire. Such ordinances may vary considerably from city to city. If a tenant feels that his rights have been violated with respect to these health and safety ordinances, he should notify the landlord. If a violation of an ordinance is not corrected, the appropriate city offices should be notified. Rent-control laws and condominium-conversion laws have come into being in great profusion in recent years. These laws are designed to protect the interests of tenants, and you should become aware of any such laws that exist in your community.

Rent Control

Rent-control laws, in general, impose limits on the amount of rent increases that a landlord can impose on a tenant. A brief summary of the major aspects of the rent-control law of the city of Los Angeles will give you an idea of how a typical law works to protect the tenants.

In Los Angeles, the rent-control ordinance covers virtually all multiple-dwelling rental units, but it does exclude so-called luxury units: apartments which were renting for more than $750 at the time the ordinace went into effect in 1978. For those luxury units, landlords are free to increase rents as they wish, subject to the law of supply and demand in the marketplace.

For all rental units covered by the law, landlords are permitted to increase the rent only once each year. The maximum that the rent can be increased per year is 7 percent. Thus, if an apartment was renting for $400 per month during the past year, the landlord can only increase the rent by 7 percent of that amount, or $28, for the current year.

There are some exceptions to this limitation. If a tenant voluntarily moves out of an apartment, the landlord can set the rent for a new tenant at whatever level he wishes. If a $400-a-month apartment is vacated, the landlord can charge a new tenant $500 per month—or more, if he can find tenants willing to pay the price. A landlord is also permitted to increase the rent over and above the 7 percent limit if he provides certain additional services to the tenant, such as additional garage space, an air conditioning unit, and various improvements to the premises.

Perhaps as important as the limitation on rental increases is the provision in the Los Angeles ordinance that a landlord cannot evict a tenant without good cause, such as failure to pay rent or violation of the rules and regulations of the building. In effect, a tenant who pays the rent and obeys the regulations can remain in the apartment indefinitely on a month-to-month basis and is protected against rent increases within the stated limits.

Needless to say, landlords do not like such rent-control ordinances and point to such restrictions as reason for their cutting back on services to the tenants.

Condominium-Conversion Laws

Leonard, the landlord, owns a ten-unit apartment house, which he wants to sell for $300,000. But the economy is weak and he has a hard time finding anyone who wishes to make the investment. Leonard then has a clever idea. Instead of looking for a single buyer for the whole building, why not convert the building into condominiums and sell each unit separately for $40,000 each. It may take some additional paperwork, but he will probably be able to dispose of the building faster and at a much better price: $400,000 instead of $300,000.

This is an example of what is known as condominium conversion: apartments being converted into individual condominiums. More than a trend, it has become a phenomenon, particularly in larger cities. People who had been tenants in a particular apartment for many years suddenly found themselves being given the choice of moving out when their lease was up or buying the apartment that they had previously rented. This worked a hardship on many tenants. If they could not come up with the necessary down payment, they had to move out and find new quarters. On the other hand, many other tenants found it an attractive situation. If they could strike a good deal with the landlord/seller, they could convert their nondeductible rent payments into substantially tax-deductible mortgage payments. Further, they would own their unit and hopefully be able to sell it at a profit sometime in the future.

Condominium-conversion laws were passed to protect the former type of tenant: the ones who found themselves dispossessed of their living quarters, often because of greedy and inconsiderate landlords.

Condominium-conversion ordinances typically will require at least a majority approval of existing tenants before a landlord can convert the property into condominiums. The ordinance may also require approval of the city, which may not be easy to obtain depending on the supply and demand of existing rental units in the city.

Example: The city of Santa Monica, California, has an extremely restrictive condominium-conversion ordinance. It's actually a part of that city's rent-control law. The population of Santa Monica is 80 percent renters, and the renters have been successful in gaining political control of the city and passing these laws. It is not uncommon in that city for all of the renters of an apartment building *and* the landlord to request the city to permit the building to be converted into condominiums, only to have the city refuse to allow that to happen. Thus, while condominium-conversion ordinances can protect some individual tenants, it can also, as in this case, work to stifle the desires of other renters to become owners of their units.

If you are a tenant, you may someday have to face the possibility of having your apartment converted into a condominium. If that time arrives, you should consider the alternatives: What advantages would there be to you to become an owner and what advantages to remain a tenant, even if it means having to move. The chapters in this book on buying and financing a house can give you guidelines to help you make a prudent decision.

Personal Action Checklist
A Guide for Renters

If you're comparing rental dwellings, this checklist will help you determine the respective advantages and disadvantages of various sites. The cheapest rent doesn't necessarily mean the best dwelling. If you choose one place and find you're unhappy with it, bear in mind the cost, energy and aggravation involved in finding another place and making the move.

	Dwelling A	Dwelling B	Dwelling C
☐ Monthly rent	_____	_____	_____
☐ Month-to-month, or lease? If lease, for how long?	_____	_____	_____
☐ If lease, do you have options to renew? At what rental?	_____	_____	_____
☐ Total amount of deposits required (security, cleaning)?	_____	_____	_____
☐ Will deposits earn interest? Rate?	_____	_____	_____
☐ Estimated miles traveled per month to work, school, routine shopping.	_____	_____	_____
☐ Estimated travel cost per month?	_____	_____	_____
☐ Is there a resident manager to handle problems?	_____	_____	_____
☐ Other tenants' opinions of building management?	_____	_____	_____
☐ General condition of building, grounds, your specific unit?	_____	_____	_____
☐ Are pets allowed?	_____	_____	_____
☐ Is the building governed by any local rent-control ordinance? If so, what is the extent of your protection?	_____	_____	_____
☐ Extra amenities available: pool, rec room, parking, laundry, storage area.	_____	_____	_____
☐ Security provisions: doorman, access to entryway, lighting?	_____	_____	_____

Consumer Beware
Look Before You Lease

Renting an apartment (or house) on a month-to-month basis does not constitute a particularly heavy commitment on your part. If things don't work out, you can leave on giving 30 days' notice in the proper fashion.

But signing a lease for a year or two can involve thousands of dollars, and if things don't work out you could be caught in a costly hassle or have to endure considerable inconvenience. To avoid those problems, take these precautions before you sign a lease:

☐ Determine whether there are objectionable noises from adjoining apartments. There may be little you can do to silence a tuba-playing neighbor once you've moved in. It might be a sign to look elsewhere.

☐ Check with other tenants in the building to learn how the landlord adjusts complaints, makes needed repairs, and otherwise fulfills his obligations under the lease.

☐ A rapidly growing phenomenon is the rental of condos. You rent a single unit which is owned by an individual, rather than by a landlord who owns the whole building. In many such cases the owner of the unit has bought it as an investment and is renting it out until he or she can later sell it at a profit. The owner may reside in another city or may simply not be concerned with the ongoing welfare of his tenants. In situations like this, overall management of the building is diluted, and there can be considerable difficulty in maintaining tenant satisfaction. A committee of absentee owners simply cannot maintain the same level of efficiency as can an on-premises landlord or management company. If you're faced with these possibilities, be forewarned accordingly.

☐ Learn the landlord's policies with respect to returning security deposits. If he's reputed to be slow, nit-picky or argumentative, be prepared to exert your legal rights to insure getting back whatever you're entitled to within the proper time limits set forth in your state's (or city's) laws.

12 | Selling Your Home

Perhaps the only transaction more complicated than buying a home is selling a home. Indeed, many people often find themselves doing both simultaneously. When selling a home—or even when vacating a leased dwelling—there are so many personal details to attend to that many of the important financial aspects of the matter are overlooked. This can be a costly error. This chapter will point out these important financial aspects and will prepare you to deal with them. They include:

☐ Setting the proper price and terms for the sale of your home.

☐ Getting your money's worth from your real estate agent.

☐ Investing the necessary time and money to bring the best possible offers from would-be buyers of your home.

☐ How to take advantage of tax laws that apply when you sell your home, and when you move.

☐ How to get out of a leased dwelling in the proper fashion.

Selling your home—be it a house, a condominium, or a cooperative—could be a very leisurely activity or a very hectic one. It's leisurely if you have all the time in the world; if you have not made a commitment to move into another dwelling until you've sold your existing one; if you're not under pressure to commence a new job in a different location. These situations are the exceptions rather than the rule. Most often selling a home is hectic: You've already committed to a new dwelling, either by choice or because of a change in job, and you feel that you must sell your home by a certain date or risk having to make payments on two dwellings.

Time can be a costly pressure. Under the crush of a deadline, you are likely to accept a lower price than the house might otherwise bring. And you're liable to make other mistakes—financial or legal—that you could later regret. It's easy to say that you should allow yourself ample time to sell your house. But it's not always that easy, particularly when a job transfer occurs.

If a job transfer causes you to move, your first step should be toward your personnel office to find out what assistance your employer will offer you with respect to the sale of your home and your moving expenses. Many employers will provide financial and legal assistance in such cases. But you may have to ask for it. If you're changing jobs to go with a new employer and a move is necessitated, determine what assistance the new employer will offer with respect to the relocation. Beyond assistance from your employer, your best helper in the often complex and frantic selling of a home is yourself.

What's Your Home Worth?

Your home is worth just what a willing buyer is prepared to pay for it. Not one penny more.

In recent years, throughout most of the country, housing prices have escalated rapidly. This has led to an often irrational and inaccurate rumor mill about what houses are worth. If you fall into this dangerous trap, you could do yourself serious financial harm.

Here's an example: The Flemings, who live across the street from you, have just put their house on the market. You plan to do the same in a few months, so the Flemings' success is of keen interest to you. Their house is almost identical to yours, and you know that they paid $40,000 for it back in the 1970s. That's about the same price you paid for yours. You understand that the Flemings are asking $140,000 for their house! If their house is worth that, could yours be worth any less? Yes! It could be worth much less. Because the Flemings house may not be worth anywhere near $140,000. The fact that they're asking that price doesn't mean at all that they'll get it. They might, in fact, be happy to accept $100,000 or even less. You may never actually find out what price they did sell it for, for they may be embarrassed to admit that they took far less than the price they were originally asking. In the meantime, if you make the mistake of getting caught up in the greed-motivated mystique of housing prices and as a result you overprice your house, you could be sitting for many months with no interested buyers even making an offer. Those months can cost you plenty.

Say it costs you $500 per month to maintain your existing house— mortgage payments, property insurance, and property taxes. You haven't been able to sell your house by the time you've had to move into your new dwelling. Every month that goes by after that date will cost you $500. In six months time you will have thrown $3,000 down the drain. Money isn't the only factor. There will also be anxiety, security problems, concern over vandalism, and other problems associated with being an absentee owner. Who will keep the landscaping looking trim in the summer? Who will shovel the snow in the winter? It might well have been wiser for you to have asked a lower price in the first place and sold the house quickly rather than have subjected yourself to the added cost and aggravation of owning two houses at once. See the discussion on the anxious seller in chapter 8.

Setting the Price

For the above reasons, setting a realistic price for your home is the first and most important order of business. A realistic price is a factor of many things, some of which are not easy to calculate. Factors to consider are the condition of the home itself, the condition of the neighborhood, how anxious you are to sell, how much "paper" you're willing to carry, whether or not your existing mortgage is assumable, and the availability of new financing at the time you are selling.

Condition of the House

Are you trying to sell what real estate people call a "move-in gem" or a "fixer-upper"? You must put yourself in the shoes of would-be buyers and see the house as they see it. Is it visually appealing, is it structurally safe, is it mechanically sound? The more positive the answers to these questions, the higher the price you can ask and get.

Condition of the Neighborhood

Is the general neighborhood in a state of improvement or decline? There's not much you can do about it if it's in a state of decline except to be ready to accept a lower price than you otherwise might have hoped for. You have to anticipate that a prudent buyer will recognize the trend of the general neighborhood and structure his offer to you accordingly. What about the immediate vicinity of your home? If your surrounding neighbors' houses are eyesores, that can have a negative effect on the value of your home. It might be worth a diplomatic chat with any such neighbors to urge them to correct the eyesores. It might even be worth your chipping in to help them do so in order to help you get a better price on your house.

How Much "Paper" Are You Willing to Carry?

If a potential buyer does not have as much cash down payment as you're asking, you may well have to consider taking his IOU (in the form of a second mortgage) in order to get your asking price. This will be discussed in more detail later in the chapter, but it must be considered as an element of setting your price in the first place.

How Anxious Are You to Sell?

In this respect price and time work hand in hand. The more time you have, the higher price you can afford to ask, with the knowledge that you can always lower the asking price as your ultimate deadline gets closer. When time is of the essence, you can't afford the luxury of overreaching on your price. The more critical the time factor, the closer to the actual market your pricing must be.

Is Your Existing Mortgage Assumable?

An assumable mortgage, particularly one whose interest rate is lower than the current market rate, can be one of the most attractive features of the deal you are offering. You can't afford to guess whether or not the mortgage is assumable. The assumability of any mortgage will depend on the credit-worthiness of the party who wishes to assume the mortgage. Further, the lender may have reserved the right to alter the interest rate if the mortgage is assumed. You should determine with as much certainty as possible what the terms and conditions would be to have a buyer assume your mortgage.

Is Financing Available?

It could be to your advantage to visit with local mortgage lenders to determine what kind of financing they would offer on the sale of your house. Not only can this help you set a realistic price, but it can also help facilitate a sale to a buyer who is seeking new financing.

Seeking Comparables

After taking into account all of the above factors, perhaps your best guide to determining a proper price is to seek comparable sales in the past few months. Try to find houses similar to yours that have recently sold and determine the selling price. Your best source of information on this point will probably be local real estate brokers. Any firsthand information you can gather on your own from friends and neighbors will also be helpful. But be certain that you determine the actual *selling* price of any comparable properties, not the *asking* price. As noted earlier, there can be a big difference between the two.

Condominium and Cooperative Restrictions

If you are selling a condominium or your interest in a cooperative building, you may be restricted in your ability to sell. Any such restrictions would be contained in the condominium or cooperative master agreement. You may, for example, be required to offer your unit back to the other owners at a fixed price, or at a price to be agreed upon, before you can offer it to the public at large. Examine the master agreement closely with the help of a lawyer if necessary to determine what restrictions, if any, you must comply with.

Using a Real Estate Agent

Does it pay to use a real estate agent to sell your house, or should you try to sell it on your own and save the commission costs? Real estate commissions on the sale of a house average about 6 percent. On a $100,000 sale, the commission would be $6,000.

If time and money are no object to you as a seller, you might want to try, for a limited time, to sell it on your own. But sooner or later, except in rare cases, time and money will be of concern to you. If you've made arrangements to move into another dwelling and you haven't sold your old home before you take occupancy of the new one, you'll be faced with the double-payment problem mentioned earlier. It only takes a few months of these double payments to quickly equalize what the real estate commission might have been.

If you try to sell your home on your own, give yourself a time limit: If you haven't received any acceptable offers within that time limit, it might be best to turn to real estate professionals for assistance.

What can a real estate agent do for you as a seller?

Market and Pricing   A good agent knows the condition of the market in your general neighborhood and can help you set a realistic price in accordance with the pricing criteria mentioned earlier.

Financing A good agent will be familiar with financing capabilities in your community at the time you are interested in selling. He or she will have regular contact with mortgage lenders and will know what kind of down payments, interest rates, and other conditions apply currently. He or she should also be able to assist a potential buyer in obtaining financing.

Advertising Are you prepared to write—and pay for—effective advertising that will lure buyers to your home? Those are among the duties of the real estate agent, and you can test their effectiveness in creating good advertising by scouring the classified ads in search of advertising that you find particularly appealing.

Showing Your Home A real estate agent should be ready, willing, and able to show your home to prospective buyers at any time. You might not be able to do this because of your work commitments. Further, the agent should be able to separate casual lookers from serious buyers and save you time accordingly.

Sales Force Not only will the individual agent be working for you, but so will all of the other members of the sales force of the firm. Thus you multiply the number of potential sources of buyers.

Multiple Listing Service In most communities most real estate firms belong to the multiple listing service, which publishes a directory of all houses for sale through real estate agents in the community. If your home is listed in the multiple listing directory, virtually every agent in town will be capable of acting as a salesperson for you. If a firm other than the one with whom you've contracted brings in a buyer, the commission will be split between the firms, with your own agent getting a specified share of the commission.

Negotiating As you'll note from the earlier chapter on buying a house (chapter 8), a buyer who is working with a real estate agent has a skilled negotiator at his side. The same goes for a seller who is working with an agent. You may be skilled at whatever you do, but you may not be skilled at the fine art of negotiating a price on the sale of a house. In this respect alone, a good agent can prove worthwhile.

Objectivity It's only natural for homeowners to become sentimentally, if not emotionally, involved in their home. The decor, the furniture layout, the traffic patterns—all of these are your own creation and are important to you. But to a would-be buyer, it may all look like a hodgepodge. It's much easier for a real estate agent to take an unbiased view of the property and convince a buyer that everything can be altered to suit the buyer's own tastes and desires. You can't be your own best salesperson if you would take offense at a potential buyer's turning up his or her nose at your own creations. The real estate agent can overcome this problem, and can help earn his or her commission in the process.

Finding a Good Agent

As in acquiring any other kind of professional help, it's important that you determine the reputation and integrity of any particular real estate agent, as well as the firm that she or he works for. Gather personal references from other people who have used the services of that individual or firm. How were they to deal with on a personal level and on a professional level? How would former clients rate their performance with respect to the creativity and the placement of advertising; their availability to show houses; their negotiating skills; their access to financial markets; their willingness to stick to their guns even if a particular property doesn't seem to attract potential buyers? You should also check with the local county Board of Realtors to learn whether the individual and firm are in good standing. Check also with the State Board of Licensing that controls real estate brokers and sales agents to determine that their license requirements have been met and maintained.

As you interview potential real estate agents, you will discuss the price that they feel they can obtain for your house. When you do, beware of a practice known as "high-balling." An agent, overanxious to get the listing, may lead you to believe that he or she can deliver a buyer at a much higher price than you might have expected. You could thus be lured into signing a long-term exclusive agreement with an agent whose actual performance may be far less than what you would have wanted. The real estate industry has a code of ethics designed to protect the public, but as in any industry, abuses will occur. And once you've signed a listing contract with a real estate firm, you have little recourse if they don't live up to your expectations.

The Listing Contract

Normally, a real estate agent will require you to sign an exclusive listing contract that will bind you to his or her firm for as long as the contract states. Six months is a normal minimum term in many communities. In addition to the length of time the agreement is to run, the contract will set forth your asking price. But there is no assurance whatsoever that the agent will be able to deliver a buyer willing to pay that price. Thus, the asking price stated in the listing contract is not binding on anyone. It's merely a target toward which the agent will be shooting.

In a standard listing contract, you, the seller, will be responsible for paying a commission to the agent if the agent brings in a buyer ready, willing, and able to pay your asking price. If such a buyer is brought in, and you have changed your mind and don't want to sell to that buyer, you will still be responsible for paying the commission to the agent. If another firm other than the one you're dealing with brings in the ultimate buyer, your own agent will still get a portion of the commission.

Negotiating the Commission

Generally, the real estate agent will state what commission he or she expects to receive, but it can be worth your while to negotiate for a lower commission. Nothing ventured, nothing gained. If it appears that the house will be easy to sell—because of its condition, the location, the asking price, or other factors—the agent might be willing to accept a lower commission. On the other hand, if it appears that the house will be difficult to sell, the agent may seek a higher than customary commission. Whatever commission is decided upon, it will be due and payable upon the final closing of the transaction. If a listing contract expires without the agent having brought in a buyer, you are then free to contract with any other agent or to renegotiate an extension of the contract with the original agent.

Preparing Your Home for Sale

If you want to sell your home as quickly as possible and at the best possible price, it may be worth spending some money and energy putting the house in the best possible condition to attract and convince buyers. Some of these expenses can be deducted from any profit you realize, thus cutting your tax liability. Consider the following:

The Exterior

The exterior appearance of the house and grounds is vitally important. Many potential buyers will cruise around the area, and their first impression of the outside will stick in their minds. Even a house that is elegant inside can scare away buyers if the outside looks shabby. Make sure your lawn is kept in proper trim and that hedges, bushes, and other foliage are properly cared for. Depending on the time of year, you might want to plant seasonal flowers to give the property a better appearance. Be sure your gutters and downspouts are all properly placed. A few gallons of paint to touch up exterior trim can be very important. Homeowners often neglect to notice some of the signs of wear and tear on their houses because they have become accustomed to them. Ask some friends over to give you their honest opinion of what might need improvement to aid sales potential. Get rid of all debris or unsightly matter around the house. Winter in northern climates adds a visual problem to any house. Be certain that snow is shoveled off the drives and walkways and that icicles are removed from overhangs. If winter days tend to be gray and dull in your area, talk to an electrician about some exterior lighting, which can improve the visual qualities of the exteriors, particularly in the late afternoon hours when many prospects are likely to call.

If there are any signs that indicate that you aren't keeping the outside of the house in good shape, a prospective buyer may well suspect that there are problems lurking inside as well.

Step Inside

A would-be buyer entering your home should get the impression that it is bright and cheery, light and airy. To give a bright and cheerful impression during the daylight hours, raise the shades and open the blinds and curtains. If there is a room, such as a den or study, that you want to have appear particularly cozy, the reverse might be true. Try various combinations of natural and artificial light to achieve the best effect for each room.

The Kitchen

The kitchen may be the most important room to many would-be buyers. Do what you have to do to make it sparkle. Stock a supply of kitchen deodorant: We often fail to notice odors in our kitchens because we're accustomed to them, but they could be displeasing to a prospect. Freshen the air as well as the physical aspects of the room.

Touching Up

Any buyer examining a house will be constantly thinking, "How much will we have to spend to put the place in the kind of shape we want it to be in?" Your real estate agent can help you determine where touching up might improve the salability of the house. For example, some rooms could benefit from a painting, particularly if they are currently painted with a very strong color. Light neutral colors will tend to please more buyers. Items such as dirt smudges on the woodwork or torn window screens can leave a decidedly negative impression on buyers, but they can be very simple to correct.

Closets and Storage Space

If your closets, basement, and attic are cluttered, that will discourage buyers. Before you commence showing your house, scour these areas thoroughly. Get rid of everything you don't need. Give whatever you can to charities—you can get a handsome income-tax deduction by doing so—and throw away anything you can't give away. Otherwise, you'll just end up having to pay to have it moved to your new location. To keep your closets looking as spacious as possible, remove all nonessentials and nonseasonal clothing.

Mechanicals

Assume that any serious buyer will sooner or later check to see that everything in the house is in proper working order. To minimize troubles in this regard, make sure that everything does work properly: electrical circuits, light switches, plugs, doorbells, plumbing, windows, furnace, air conditioning, and so on. Call a plumber to correct any rattles, knocks, or other annoying noises that may ring through the house when water is running. Invest in a can of lubricating oil to eliminate any creaking doors and loosen any stuck windows.

Design

Examine the major rooms in the house to see how minor changes of furniture or lighting might improve the room's appearance. You may be able to enhance the appearance of the house with throw pillows, scatter rugs, and other decorative pieces that you may be able to acquire at reasonably low cost.

Leaks and Other Damages

If a prospective buyer sees signs of leaking—either on the ceilings or around sinks, toilets, tubs, or showers—he will immediately start tallying up many hundreds of dollars in repair bills to correct a problem, which he will assume still exists. If a leak has long since been repaired, but evidence of it still shows on the surface, get it covered up. If the leak still exists, get it corrected. If nothing else, any sign of a leak gives a would-be buyer a better bargaining position.

What Financing Will You Offer?

The availability of financing is as important to the buyer as is the asking price. In these years of high and rapidly fluctuating interest rates, any seller should be prepared to explore a wide range of "creative financing" possibilities, always with the advice of a good real estate agent and a lawyer. Chapter 9 explores some of these creative financing possibilities.

Is Your Mortgage Assumable?

As noted earlier, you should determine as quickly as possible whether or not your mortgage can be assumed, and under what conditions. If your mortgage is not assumable, you should inquire of local lenders what types of financing plans might be available to a credit-worthy buyer. Take these steps before you start showing the house; let your real estate agent be your guide.

Will You Take Back "Paper"?

Whether by choice or by necessity, you may find yourself having to take a buyer's promise to pay rather than his cash. This will be in the form of a first or second mortgage, which should be drawn up by a lawyer. If it is necessary for you to carry the buyer's promise to pay, negotiate an interest rate as close as the current going interest rate through conventional lenders as possible. It is also advisable to keep the duration of such mortgages at a minimum. Try to get the buyer to accept a term of three years or less. At the end of that time he'd be responsible for obtaining new financing on his own. If a buyer insists on a longer repayment program, you should negotiate a higher interest rate as consideration for granting him extra time.

All of these negotiations will, of course, be dependent on your level of anxiety to sell. The more anxious you are to sell, the less room you'll have to negotiate the terms of any paper you may be taking back.

Tax Implications When You Sell Your Home

If you sell your home at a profit, that profit may be subject to income taxes in the year in which you sell. If you sell your property and suffer a loss, the loss is not deductible. But there are important tax provisions that can allow you to postpone the payment of taxes or eliminate them altogether. As with most tax laws, the specific regulations that apply to these situations can be very complex, and professional assistance is advisable.

You have to assume that the Internal Revenue Service will be aware of the fact that you've moved simply by virtue of the new address on your next year's tax return. Your move, of course, may not necessarily mean that you have sold a residence. You may have moved from a rental unit or you may not actually have sold your house. But if you have sold a house, the pertinent facts must be reported on your tax return.

There are two types of tax breaks that can benefit sellers of homes. They are:

☐ The "rollover," which is available to sellers of any age; and

☐ The exclusion, which is available only to sellers aged 55 or over.

The Rollover

If you sell your house at a profit, the tax on the profit may be postponed if, within 24 months from the date of sale, you buy and occupy another principal residence the cost of which equals or exceeds the "adjusted sales price" of the old residence. The 24-month time limit works in both directions: You can buy the new house as much as 24 months before or 24 months after the date you sell your old house.

If the purchase price of your new residence is less than the sale price of the old residence, a portion of the profit will be taxable during that year. If you do not purchase a new principal residence—say you move into an apartment—the profit will be taxable during the year in which you sold. See the current Internal Revenue Service regulations for their specific definitions of the gain that is subject to taxes. If you qualify for this rollover, you should complete Form 2119 and attach it to your income-tax return.

The Exclusion

If either spouse is 55 years of age at the time you sell your home at a profit, you can exclude up to $125,000 worth of profit from taxation altogether. In order to qualify for this exclusion of taxation, you must have owned and occupied the house as your principal residence for at least three of the five years preceding the day of sale.

The exclusion is a once-in-a-lifetime privilege. But the rollover can be used over and over again, until such time as you sell your home and do not purchase another one, at which time the taxes will become due on all aggregate profits realized in prior years.

The matter can be quite complex and professional tax counseling should be sought. Example: The Renaldi's bought a home 20 years ago and sold it five years ago at a profit of $70,000. They bought another home at that time and thus took advantage of the rollover to postpone the payment of taxes on the $70,000 profit. Today, with Mr. Renaldi past the age of 55, they are selling their current home and will realize a profit of $60,000. Their total accumulated profit on the two homes is thus $130,000. If they are now planning on buying another home of equal or greater value than their current home, they can choose between the rollover and the exclusion. If they choose the rollover, the tax on the accumulated $130,000 profit will continue to be postponed until such time as they sell their new home and do not buy another one. At that time, they can choose the exclusion if they wish.

If they choose the exclusion now, then $125,000 of the $130,000 will be excluded from taxation, and the remaining $5,000 will be subject to taxation. It would make sense for them to choose this alternative if they are not now buying another house. But if they are buying another house, they would have to carefully estimate what the future might hold for them with respect to a potential profit on the sale of the new house.

If, instead of selling your house, you convert it to a rental property, different tax rules apply. If you rent it for a limited period of time—such as one year—and then sell it, it may still be considered your principal residence and the rollover or exclusion rules may still apply. However, if you convert it to an ongoing income property for an indefinite period of time, the Internal Revenue Service may consider that it is no longer your personal residence, and upon a sale the taxes would be payable on any profit during the year of sale.

Moving Expenses

Whether you're buying or selling a house, you're going to be moving. Moving involves many important considerations. Whether you decide to hire a moving company or do it yourself will probably depend on the number of household goods you'll be moving, the distance, and the time of year (a do-it-yourself move during the snowy season can involve more travail than you'd expect).

If your move is within the boundaries of your state, the moving company will not be controlled by the Interstate Commerce Commission. Customarily, such moves (intrastate) are charged on an hourly basis, plus time and materials for any packing that you hire the mover to do for you.

If you hire a moving company for an interstate move (from one state into another), you'll find yourself in the midst of a deregulation process. Rates were formerly strictly controlled on interstate moves by the Interstate Commerce Commission. But the government has gradually been deregulating the moving industry, and shopping for the best deal will be a more worthwhile endeavor than it was during the days of total regulation. Generally, interstate moves of equal weight and equal distance will cost roughly the same with most moving companies. There may be important differences in the overall cost of the move based on the amount of packing and unpacking you wish the movers to do. These rates will vary from company to company. You may wish to pack your own non-breakables and have the moving company pack the more fragile items, such as glassware, china, lamps and so on.

Representatives of moving companies can give you estimates on the cost of your move, but bear in mind that these are only estimates and not generally firm bids. The actual cost can't be determined until the van is loaded and weighed prior to its departure. Moving-company representatives are required to give you Interstate Commerce Commission information that spells out your rights as a shipper of household goods. Be certain to read and understand the information in that document, as it informs you as to your rights and the recourse you have if something goes wrong.

Tax Deduction of Moving Expenses

A major portion of your moving expenses (for which you are not reimbursed by your employer) may be tax deductible. Because moving expenses can amount to a considerable sum of money, you should keep a careful record of all such expenses and take advantage of whatever the law allows. In order to deduct moving expenses you must meet two tests: the distance test and the work test.

The Distance Test

As illustrated by Figure 12-1, measure the distance between your former home and your former place of work. Let's call that distance A and say it's 10 miles. Now measure the distance between your former home and your new place of work. Let's call that distance B and say it's 50 miles.

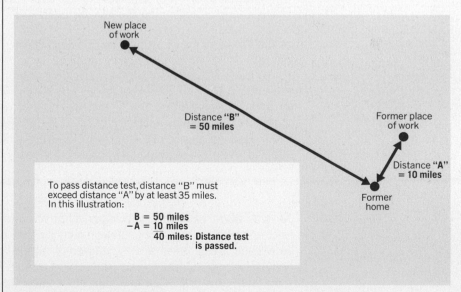

Figure 12-1   Distance test.

The law requires that the difference between distance B and distance A be at least 35 miles. If it is, you pass the distance test. Note that the distance test does not refer to the location of your new *residence* but rather to the location of your new *place of work*.

The Work Test

During the 12-month period immediately following your move, you must be employed full time for at least 39 weeks in order to pass the work test. If you're self-employed, you must be employed full time for at least 39 weeks during the first 12 months immediately following the move and you must also be employed full time for at least 78 weeks of the 24-month period immediately following the move.

If you meet both the distance test and the work test, the following expenses of your move may be deductible.

1. Travel expenses including meals and lodging for yourself and your family while enroute from your old residence to your new residence.
2. The costs of moving your household goods and personal effects.
3. The costs of househunting trips before you moved, including transportation, meals, and lodging.
4. The cost of temporary quarters at your new location if such are needed for up to 30 days after you've started your work.
5. The costs of selling your residence or settling your lease at your old location, and the cost of purchasing a residence or acquiring a new lease at the new location. These costs can include brokerage commissions, attorney's fees, "points" on your home financing, and similar expenses incidental to the sale or purchase of a house.

The deductibility of these expenses is based on the presumption that you will be working in your new location.

There are limits to the amount you can deduct. Items 3, 4, and 5 are limited to a total of $3,000 of which no more than $1,500 may be used for househunting trips (item 3) and the cost of temporary quarters (item 4). Tax counsel is advisable before you undertake your move to alert you to all possible expenses that might be deductible in accordance with specific Internal Revenue Service regulations in effect at the time you move.

**Terminating
a Lease**

Tenants don't have to worry about all of the ramifications of a sale of a residence. (That fact alone is why many people prefer to remain tenants indefinitely.) But there are a number of things to consider even if you have been renting, be it an apartment, a mobile home, or a house.

As far in advance of your leaving as possible, read your lease carefully. Be certain that you know when the lease terminates. Watch out for any clause that would create an automatic renewal of the lease. Such a clause may read, "Unless either party gives notice to the other in writing of his intention to cancel this lease, the lease will automatically renew for another year upon [date]." This means simply that if you don't want the lease to renew automatically, you must give proper notice to the landlord in writing before a certain date. If you fail to do this, the landlord can technically hold you liable for another year's rent.

If you have given the landlord a security deposit, what does the lease state about getting it back? Are you to apply it to the last month's rent? Is it to be held beyond the end of the lease to cover the landlord for anything you may owe him? The same holds true for breakage and cleaning deposits. Many states have laws that stipulate when, and under what conditions, a landlord is to return a tenant's rental deposit. Know in advance what your rights are in this regard so that you won't have to forfeit any money.

If you're planning to move before your lease has expired, does your lease give you the right to sublet the apartment? If you want to leave well in advance of the termination date, you can recoup considerable costs if you do sublet. Your lease should state what privileges you have in this regard. Bear in mind, however, that subletting can have its problems. If you do sublet, you should be certain that the subtenants are responsible. They should sign an agreement assuming all of your obligations under the lease, including the obligation to repair at their own expense any damages they may cause.

If you wish to move far in advance of the termination date and either you don't wish to or cannot sublet, you should discuss a settlement price with the landlord. You can, of course, simply move out, continue to pay your rent, and hope that the landlord will rerent your apartment quickly. Generally, the law puts some burden on the landlord to try to rerent as quickly as possible, but you can't always depend on the landlord to be diligent in this respect. It may be possible to obtain a settlement under which you pay a lump sum to be released from all responsibilities under the lease. You are then free to go, and the landlord is free to rent the apartment.

If you are renting any appliances or furniture or have any services under contract for an apartment or a rented house, be certain to examine the rental documents. For example, if you have leased the furniture or large appliances, you'll want to be certain that you can terminate those contracts concurrently with leaving the apartment. The same holds true for extermination services, water-softener services, and any other ongoing maintenance agreements that you may have signed.

If you are paying your own utilities, arrange well in advance to have all utility meters read as of your final day of occupancy. Ask the utility companies—telephone, electric, gas, water—to bill you for the final reading and be sure that the landlord understands that the meters are to be returned to his name following your departure.

If you suspect that there may be *any* question whatsoever regarding the condition in which you are leaving the house or apartment, settle it with the landlord *before* you leave. Go over the property with the landlord and be certain that he agrees that everything is as it should be. Then ask the landlord to sign a brief letter stating that everything is in the proper condition.

Renters are entitled to the same tax deductions for moving expenses as are homeowners, provided they meet the same distance and work tests. The cost of settling your lease obligation with your landlord if you move before the end of the lease can be included as one of the deductible expenses.

Personal Action Checklist
A Guide for the Home Seller

This checklist should help you *set* and *get* the best possible price for your home. It may cost you some money to complete some of the items, but the expense could return itself many times over in a better price, and in a faster sale. You may need the assistance of your real estate agent. Some of the information needed can be found at your local tax assessor's office or at your county recorder's office.

☐ What has been the *actual* selling price of *comparable* homes in your area within the past few months?

☐ How long were those homes on the market before they sold?

☐ How does the actual selling price of those homes compare with the prices that the sellers were originally asking?

☐ Based on these comparable sales, what do you realistically think your home should sell for? (Take into account all plus and minus factors that your home may have, relative to the comparables.)

☐ How will your home appear to a would-be buyer? Ask some friends, and your real estate agent, to give you an honest opinion of:
The exterior (paint, trim, landscaping)
The entry (lighting, odors, a sense of clutter or of orderliness)
The kitchen (cleanliness, odors, does everything work the way it should?)
Closets, other storage areas (cluttered, or clean and spacious looking)
Bathrooms (squeeky clean is a *must*)
Other rooms (lighting, odors, traffic flow, condition of flooring and walls)
Mechanical elements, such as heater, appliances (Does everything work properly? Are there noises, odors, etc., that would be offensive?)

It's very difficult to see your own home as others might see it. Prospective buyers can be very persnickety, and first impressions—such as the items listed above—can make the difference between a "thanks but no thanks," and a "let's talk about the price."

Consumer Beware
Moving-day Headaches

Selling a home, or leaving an apartment, invariably involves one activity that many people regard with fear and loathing: Moving Day.

All major moving companies offer abundant literature on how to take the pain out of moving: how to do your own packing, how to complete a proper inventory of your goods, how to get the children out of your hair, and so on. Helpful though this literature may be, it may not prepare you for some of the common and uncommon pitfalls of moving. These include:

□ *The lowball estimate.* An overzealous sales representative from a moving company may give you an estimate on the cost of the move that is much lower than what you've received from other companies. This could be due to an honest error on the part of the salesperson; it could be due to your failure to disclose everything that you had planned to move; or it could be an intentional ploy by the salesperson to win your business. Remember: an estimate is just an estimate. The total cost of the move won't be known until everything is packed and the van is weighed. Which leads us to:

□ *"Bumping."* This term describes the practice whereby four burly 200-pound moving men sit in the back of the moving van while it's being weighed. And you pay for it. It may be a rare occurrence, but it can be costly. Interstate Commerce Commission regulations clearly state that you, the shipper, are entitled to be at the weighing of the truck. That can be a money-saving precaution to take.

□ *Schedule demolition.* Often, despite the best intentions, the day of pickup of your goods can be missed. And the day of delivery at your new destination can also be off target. These missed dates can cause chaos, not to mention considerable cost, if you have to live in a motel for a few days waiting for the van to arrive. Moving companies generally can't guarantee pickup and delivery dates unless, in some cases, you reserve exclusive use of a van. Your best protection against these scheduling problems is to anticipate that the worst will happen. Then if everything goes off smoothly, you'll be that much happier.

Part Four | Where the Money Is

13 | **Financial Institutions**

The notorious bank robber Willy Sutton was once asked by a reporter, "Why do you rob banks?" His reply: "That's where the money is."

Sutton's involvement with banks was a lot more clear cut than yours will be. Dealing with banks and other financial institutions—savings associations, credit unions, and so on—can be complicated in these rapidly changing days. But the dealings can be worthwhile in terms of handling your money matters and making your money grow. This chapter is designed to acquaint you with how financial institutions work, what they can do for you, and what your rights are as a user of their services. You'll learn about such matters as:

☐ Which institutions offer what services.

☐ How checking accounts work, and the advantages and pitfalls in using them.

☐ How to shop for the services you'll need.

☐ What laws protect you with regard to financial matters, and how to pursue your rights if they are violated.

Suppose you have some money in your hands and you have no immediate need or desire to spend it. What can you do with it? You have many choices. You can put it in your pocket, in the cookie jar, or under your mattress until you do need it. Or you can entrust that money to one of many financial institutions for a variety of purposes.

If you wanted to use that money to pay some of your debts, you could open a checking account at a financial institution. Then instead of having to deliver cash to each of your creditors, you could simply mail them a check to satisfy the debt. The check, in effect, allows the creditor to receive money from your checking account. You may wish to invest the money so that the total sum will assuredly increase until such time as you need it for other purposes. In such a case, you could establish a savings plan at a financial institution.

You may wish to speculate with the money in the hope that it might increase in the future. In this case you could establish an account with a stock brokerage firm—one type of financial institution. Or you might wish to put the money away for a very long time so as to provide an assured fund for yourself in later years or for your survivors upon your death. In such a case, you would contract for a life-insurance policy with an insurance company, yet another type of financial institution.

On the other hand, suppose you needed money—such as to buy a car or a house, to pay your taxes, to go on a vacation, or for any other purpose. If you couldn't borrow the money you needed from friends or relatives, you would approach a financial institution for the appropriate type of loan.

The Middlemen

Financial institutions play an important "middleman" role in the nation's economy and in your own personal financial situation.

At any given time, there are countless individuals (and businesses and governments) who have more money on hand than they need for their immediate purposes. At the same time, there are countless others who do not have the money they need for specific purposes.

Financial institutions act as middlemen by providing a safe place for those with excess money to keep it until they need it. At the same time, they supply services and loans to those who seek to borrow at a fair and reasonable cost.

The middleman views this activity as a business. He must acquire his raw material (other people's money) at the lowest possible price (competition considered.) And he must lend it out on the most prudent basis, taking into account the ability of the borrower to repay the money at the agreed-upon time. In order for a middleman to survive, he must make a profit. Thus, he must charge the borrower more for the use of the money than he has to pay to the investors entrusting him with their money.

Certain middlemen may not be acting as a business but as a service to members of an association. The members may have banded together to pool their excess money and provide for the needs of borrowers. Although it isn't important for the association to generate a profit, members must still generate enough income within the operation to pay for personnel and overhead needed to run the operation efficiently. This type of financial institution is typified by credit unions, which commonly represents employees of a specific company or members of a particular trade union.

A Decade of Change

Until the start of the 1980s, there was a clear distinction among the various types of financial institutions. Commercial banks specialized primarily in checking accounts, business loans, and consumer loans. Savings institutions specialized primarily in savings plans and home financing. Stock brokerage firms specialized primarily in buying and selling stocks, bonds, and other types of investments and speculations. Insurance companies specialized primarily in life-insurance products, pension arrangements, and annuities.

But in the early 1980s a number of factors began to blur these distinctions. A trend commenced which could, by the end of the decade, result in a number of giant financial "supermarkets," with each offering a wide variety of financial services that previously had been reserved to specific types of institutions.

Some of these factors and trends include the following:

☐ The passage, by Congress, of the Monetary Decontrol Act of 1980. This law created the Depository Institution Deregulation Committee (DIDC), whose job it is to remove governmental regulation from the banking and savings segments of the financial industry. Governmental regulations targeted for removal include limits on the interest that institutions can pay on various types of savings plans and restrictions on the types of loans that various institutions can make.

☐ The acquisition of some types of financial institutions by other types. Early examples include the takeover by American Express (International banking, credit cards, travelers checks) of Shearson Loeb Rhodes (stockbrokerage); the takeover by Prudential Life Insurance of Bache Group (stockbrokerage); the takeover by Phibro (commodity trading) of Salomon Brothers (investment banking). Such combinations could be the foundations upon which the giant financial supermarkets of the 1990s are built.

☐ The inevitable spread of banking and savings institutions across state lines. Prior to the 1980s, these financial institutions, except in rare instances, were limited to operating within their state or county boundaries. Their expansion beyond those boundaries, whether through legislation, holding companies, acquisitions, mergers, or even electronic terminals further foretells the eventual development of the nationwide giants.

☐ Development of competing services by specific institutions. Stock brokerage firms have created "cash management" accounts, which provide all-in-one checking/investing/borrowing capability for its customers. Banks and savings institutions, in retaliation, have moved to set up stock brokerage and other types of investment services. Money market mutual funds offer checking account privileges. Insurance companies offer investment programs combined with check-writing privileges. Credit card companies and banks offer life insurance. Savings institutions offer property insurance. And the list goes on. Where it will stop, nobody knows.

These developments will make the financial industry more competitive, and that can mean more choices, more services, and more advantages for the *alert* consumer.

Since the ultimate size, shape, location, and names of these future financial supermarkets are as yet unknown, this chapter will concentrate on the basic types of institutions that you would commonly use and that will still remain on a local level even after the national giants have planted

Commercial Banks

their roots. We'll concentrate primarily on institutions offering banking and lending services. The ramifications of stockbrokerage and insurance will be covered in the respective chapters on those subjects.

There are roughly 15,000 commercial banks in the United States. Total assets of these commercial banks exceed $1 trillion. Commercial banks run the gamut from small country institutions to giant banks in such major cities as New York, Chicago, San Francisco, and Los Angeles. Of all the commercial banks in the United States, the 50 largest control roughly one-third of all deposits and the remaining banks control the other two-thirds.

Commercial banks are often referred to as "full service" institutions. They offer a broad range of services including checking accounts, savings accounts, trust facilities, and virtually all types of loans.

Subject to the expansionary trends mentioned earlier, commercial banks are generally limited to doing business within their state boundaries. They may be chartered by the state government or by the federal government to operate within a particular state. If a commercial bank is state chartered, it will be controlled and regulated by the State Banking Commission. If a commercial bank is federally chartered, it will be controlled and regulated by the Comptroller of the Currency. (If a bank is federally chartered, it will have the word "national" in its name—such as First National Bank. Or it will have the initials N.A.—National Association—after its name.) Most major banks, and many smaller banks, are also members of the Federal Reserve system, which exerts additional controls and regulations on the nation's banking industry.

Deposits in commercial banks are insured by the Federal Deposit Insurance Corporation (FDIC) for up to $100,000 per account in the event of the bank's failure. (The amount of insurance per account has increased periodically since the 1960s and could be increased again.) The FDIC is a federal agency that constantly scrutinizes the operations of all banks it insures for the protection of the depositors and the community. All federally insured banks pay an annual premium to the FDIC and the total is set aside as a reserve to be used to pay off the depositors should a bank be liquidated. In addition to its own funds, the FDIC can call upon the U.S. Treasury for additional money to back up its guarantee to depositors. The strength of the FDIC lies, not just with its funds, but also with its constant surveillance and expertise in determining when banks are in trouble and intervening as swiftly as possible to prevent financial loss.

In addition to FDIC examination, banks may also be examined by state or federal authorities, depending on their charter. They are also examined by their own internal auditors and commonly by outside independent auditors on orders from the bank's own Board of Directors. Examinations are generally by surprise and are very rigorous. All cash is counted. All loans are scrutinized in detail, including original credit information, current payment status, and prospects for ultimate full payment. Where loans seem to be in jeopardy, the examiners will notify the bank officials. If an excess of loans seem to be in jeopardy, the examiners will instruct the bank to take whatever steps are appropriate to correct the situation. The results of examinations are kept confidential between the examiners and the bank's officials. But examiners will follow up to determine whether or not the bank has taken necessary corrective steps to keep the operation in healthy condition.

Mutual Savings Banks

Mutual savings banks are few in number (about 500 of them located in roughly one dozen states, generally throughout New England and the Northeast, plus Ohio, Minnesota, Oregon, and Washington). But they are substantial in size, controlling almost $150 billion in assets. Mutual savings banks are state chartered and are insured by the Federal Deposit Insurance Corporation, which examines them as it does commercial banks. The major part of the business of mutual savings banks is savings plans and loans on real property—mortgages and home-improvement loans. Deregulation in the financial industry, though, has allowed mutual savings banks to extend their scope of business to include checking accounts and various types of consumer loans.

Savings and Loan Associations

There are about 5000 savings and loan associations throughout the nation. Like commercial banks, they may be either federally or state chartered. Traditionally, savings and loan associations concentrated their business in savings plans and home loans, but the new era of deregulation has given them powers to offer checking accounts and various consumer loans. Total assets of America's savings and loan associations are approximately $400 billion, and they are the largest mortgage lenders, with approximately $300 billion outstanding in mortgage loans. Savings and loan associations are insured by the Federal Savings and Loan Insurance Corporation (FSLIC), which acts in a manner similar to the Federal Deposit Insurance Corporation.

Credit Unions

Because credit unions don't advertise the way commercial banks and savings and loan associations do, they're not as familiar to the public as those other institutions. But credit unions are playing an increasingly important role in the American financial system. They are associations of individuals who have a common bond—they work for the same employer, they belong to the same religious order, or they are members of the same union or trade association. Credit unions are not operated for profit; further, they are tax exempt. They are operated solely for the benefit of their membership, which is open generally to all individuals who meet their requirements.

Credit unions accept savings accounts and may pay slightly higher interest than other institutions. This is possible because they do not have the profit motive, generally are located in very modest quarters, and do not have to pay any federal income taxes. Credit unions in some areas may make loans to their members at a rate slightly more favorable than that charged elsewhere. Loans usually are of the installment variety.

There are currently about 23,000 credit unions throughout the United States, supported by over 30 million members. Their assets total roughly $40 billion. In recent years, credit unions have been gaining the authority to offer a form of checking account, which would add another measure of competition to the overall banking industry.

Slightly more than one-half of all the credit unions are federally chartered and the balance are state chartered. Insurance on credit union accounts is available through the National Credit Union Administration (NCUA).

Consumer Finance or "Small Loan" Companies

These are private businesses, operating generally under state licensing, that make small loans available to credit-worthy seekers. Consumer finance companies do not accept public deposits. They obtain their money by borrowing from larger institutions such as banks and insurance companies. A small number of these companies have branches throughout the entire country, but most are limited to individual states or cities in their sphere of operation.

Merchant Lenders and Credit Card Companies

Technically, these are not financial institutions in the same sense as banks and savings and loan associations are. But they do provide a financial service to many millions of Americans: making credit available virtually at the request of the customer. A merchant lender, generally, is a retail or service establishment that will accept a customer's IOU as payment for goods sold or services rendered. In other words, rather than pay cash, the customer can "charge it."

Commonly, the customer will sign an agreement in which he or she agrees to make payments over a specified period of time with an agreed-on rate of interest. In effect, the merchant lender is lending the money to the customer to enable the customer to buy the product. Many merchants do this strictly as a convenience for their customers and to be in line with services that their competitors might offer. Often the merchant lender will sell the customer's loan agreement to another financial institution, such as a bank or a consumer finance company, so that it can get its money right away. In some cases the merchant lender will retain the loan agreement, and the customer will make payments directly to the merchant instead of to the third-party institution.

Some companies—such as gasoline companies, hotels and motels, airlines—operate nationally. To induce the public to use their services and products, they will issue credit cards to credit-worthy applicants. These credit cards allow the users to charge their purchases, thus creating a loan from the issuing company. The loan will be repayable based on the terms contained in the original credit card agreement.

Another form of quasi-financial institution is the credit card company: American Express, Diner's Club, and Carte Blanche are the prime examples. They have made arrangements with many thousands of businesses across the nation and around the world to accept their credit cards in lieu of cash. When a purchase is made by a customer on a credit card charge, the credit card company makes payment to the specific merchant and then seeks repayment of the amount borrowed by the customer. The credit card company is thus acting strictly as a middleman between the merchant and the customer. Most commercial banks also issue various forms of credit cards—BankAmericard (VISA) and Mastercard. When a purchase is made with a bank credit card, the bank pays the merchant and seeks repayment directly from the customer.

Services Available at Financial Institutions

The following financial services are those commonly found at larger commercial banks. They may also be available at smaller banks, savings and loan associations, mutual savings banks, and credit unions.

1. Checking accounts
2. Savings accounts
3. Safe deposit boxes
4. Trust departments
5. Installment loans
6. Credit cards
7. Business loans
8. Mortgage loans
9. Special checks
10. Notarial services
11. Electronic banking
12. Collection services
13. International banking facilities
14. Investment departments

Let's now take a closer look at what these services consist of. *Note:* Savings accounts (passbooks and certificates of deposit) are briefly noted here and are discussed in greater length in the chapter on fixed income investments. Installment, credit card, and business loans are dealt with in the chapter Credit and Borrowing, and mortgages are discussed fully in the chapters on housing.

Checking Accounts

It would be both inconvenient and risky if we had to conduct all our financial transactions with cash. Inconvenient if for no other reason than the sheer massive volume of cash that would have to be available in all segments of the economy at all times; risky because a loss of cash is irreplaceable.

Checks, simply stated, act as a substitute for cash. Checks are more convenient and the risk of loss is virtually eliminated.

The efficiency of our checking system is founded on a combination of mutual trust and law. We have grown accustomed to accepting these money substitutes as having the value represented; and in those rare cases when the document proves invalid, there are laws that can punish those who have violated the law and the trust between the parties.

How Checking Accounts Work

Bob lives in Phoenix, Arizona, and works for the Ajax Supermarket. Each day the supermarket gathers up all the money it has collected from its customers and deposits the money in its checking account at the Arizona National Bank. The essential agreement between the bank and the store is as follows: the bank agrees to hold the money safely for the store and to pay out the money to any persons that the store directs them to make payments to. The store will then issue checks to its employees for their wages, checks to the landlord for the rent on the building, checks to suppliers for the food that it obtains from them, and so on.

The checks order the bank to make payment to the holder of the check. That's the essence of the words "pay to the order of" that appear on all checks. The check—the order to pay—must be signed by a properly authorized representative of the store. The bank will have obtained copies of all the authorized signatures permitted on the checks and can compare those signatures with the signatures on the checks if they wish to determine the validity of the order to pay.

Bob's weekly paycheck, after all deductions have been taken out for income taxes, Social Security, and fringe benefits, looks like this (Figure 13-1):

"Negotiating" a Check

Bob now holds a piece of paper that is worth $250 to him. The piece of paper is a legal document in which the Ajax Supermarket instructs the Arizona National Bank to pay to the order of Bob Rosefsky the sum of $250. The check is thus known as an "order instrument." How can Bob then translate that piece of paper into real money? He can cash the check, he can deposit the check into his own account, or he can use the check to pay a debt or pay for a purchase.

Cashing the Check Bob takes the check to a branch of the Arizona National Bank, identifies himself, and asks for cash in exchange for the check. But before the bank will give Bob the cash, they will want him to acknowledge that he has in fact received the money. The bank must do this to prove that it has fulfilled the order given it by the supermarket. Bob acknowledges that he receives the cash by signing his name across the back of the check. This is known as a "blank endorsement." Bob receives his money; the bank has proof that it has properly fulfilled the

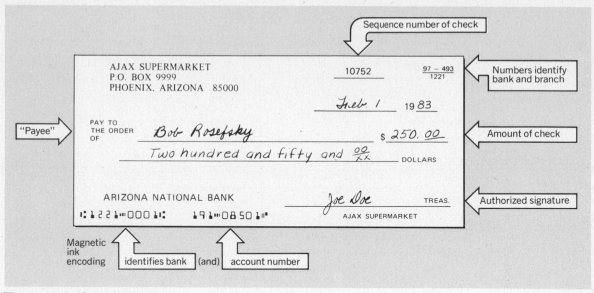

Figure 13-1   Sample check.

order given it. And as the check is processed internally, the supermarket's account with the bank will be reduced by $250 as a result of cashing the check.

Note this important precaution with respect to a blank endorsement: A blank endorsement converts the check from an order instrument into a "bearer instrument." A check containing a blank endorsement can theoretically be cashed by anyone who is the bearer or holder of it. In other words, if Bob endorsed the check in blank when he received it, and it dropped out of his pocket on the way to the bank and was found by a dishonest person, that dishonest person could likely cash the check and Bob would be out $250. A check should be endorsed in blank only at the time the money is received.

Depositing the Check   Bob can deposit the check to his own checking account at the Citizens Bank of Phoenix. To do so, he must properly endorse the check and fill out a deposit slip. He may endorse the check in blank, as if he were cashing it. Or, more prudently, he can put a restrictive endorsement on the check. A restrictive endorsement would read, "For deposit only to acct #007-085844," followed·by his signature. A restrictive endorsement simply restricts what can be done with the check. In this particular case it can only be deposited to Bob's specific account. If a restrictively endorsed check were lost, a finder would have a very difficult time doing anything with it.

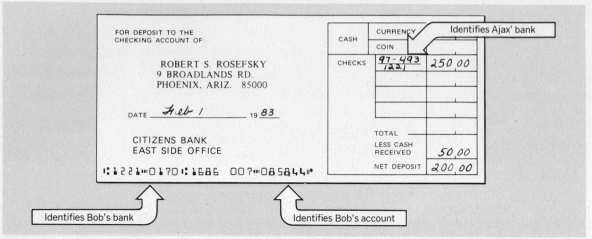

Figure 13-2   Deposit slip.

Figure 13-2 is a sample illustration of a deposit slip. Deposit slips will commonly be preprinted with the name and address of the account holder. The person making the deposit will write in the identifying number of the bank upon which the check is drawn—in this case 97-493—and the amount of the deposits, $250. When the deposit is processed, the receiving bank will encode its own identifying number as well as the identifying number of Bob's account, as shown in the illustration.

"Clearing" the Check

If Bob does deposit the check in his own bank, his bank technically doesn't know whether or not the check is any good. They simply have no way of knowing whether or not the Ajax Supermarket has money in its account at that time to honor the check. They could thus say to Bob, "Technically, we can't permit you to take money out against this check until we're sure that it has 'cleared,' that is, been honored by the bank on which it's drawn, Arizona National."

Bob's bank will actually send the check to the store's bank, where it will be processed. The Arizona National Bank does not notify Bob's bank that the check was good. Bob's bank will know that the check was good and was honored only if they do *not* get it back from the Arizona National Bank. If, in fact, the supermarket did not have enough money in its account to clear the check, the Arizona National Bank will return it to Bob's bank with a note that it was dishonored or that it "bounced," in this case for lack of sufficient funds.

Because both banks are in the same city, it customarily will only take one or two days for the check to go from one bank to the other. Thus,

Bob's bank can be reasonably sure that the check has cleared if it hasn't heard otherwise within two or three days—the time it would take for the check to go round trip, if in fact, that was its fate. In common practice, Bob's bank knows that he has been depositing these checks from the Ajax Supermarket for many years and that there has never been a problem. Thus, they would probably allow him to draw against those funds without waiting for the check to be cleared by the originating bank.

While a check is in the clearing process—which can be upwards of one to two weeks if it was written on a bank in a distant part of the country—the funds are considered "uncollected" by the bank. Example: Bob receives a check for $1,000 from his cousin Bernie in Binghamton, New York. Bob deposits it to his account at the Citizens Bank of Phoenix. Bob's bank knows that it will take roughly one week for the check to return to Bernie's bank in Binghamton. If the check is to bounce, it will take another week before Bob's bank finds out about it. Or if the check does not bounce, Bob's bank will still want to wait that additional week to be assured that it hasn't in fact bounced. Bob's bank thus regards that $1000 as "uncollected funds" for a period of two weeks. But Bob thinks he has $1000 in the bank, and he writes a check for $700 to a local used-car dealer as down payment on a car. The car dealer takes Bob's check into Bob's bank the next day, where it bounces. Bob has drawn a check against uncollected funds and the check will not be honored. Not only will this cost Bob a few dollars for the bounced check fee, but it will also cause him considerable embarrassment.

One should determine whether a bank will honor funds deposited to one's account immediately, or if the funds will not be honored, one should determine how long it will be before it's safe to write checks against such deposits.

Using the Check to Pay Debts or for Purchases

Bob owes $250 to his friend Gary in Taos, New Mexico. He wants to use his paycheck to settle his debt to Gary. He thus puts a "special endorsement" on the back of his check, which would read, "Pay to the order of Gary Smith," followed by his signature. A special endorsement gives only the named party the right to collect the amount of the check, or to negotiate the check on to a subsequent holder. When Gary receives the check, he will endorse it by signing his own name below Bob's signature, and the check will eventually come back to the original bank, where it presumably will be honored.

(Though Bob technically could have paid off his debt in this fashion, it might have been unwise for him to do so. It would have been better for him to deposit the store's check into his own account and then draw his own check payable directly to Gary. He would ultimately receive back his canceled check and would thus have adequate proof that Gary had received the payment and that the debt was paid. As it is, the store will

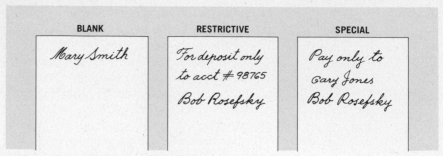

Figure 13-3   Types of endorsements.

get the check back and Bob will have to seek the store's help in verifying that Gary received the money.)

Figure 13-3 shows samples of blank, restrictive, and the special endorsements as outlined in the foregoing.

Following are some additional aspects of checking accounts that you should be aware of:

Stopping Payment

The treasurer of the Ajax Supermarket learns that the computer has erroneously issued a check to one of the store's meat suppliers. The check is for $500 more than it should be, and the treasurer is concerned that the meat supplier will cash the check and will refuse to refund the excess $500 because there had been an ongoing dispute between them over a previous bill. The treasurer wants to stop the check before the meat supplier can cash it at his bank.

It's literally a race against time. The proper course for the treasurer is to go to his bank, Arizona National, and issue a "stop payment" order. He must inform the bank in writing as to the amount of the check, the date it was issued, and to whom it was paid, and then sign the order. This done, the bank will then refuse to allow payment on the check when it is presented. But if the meat supplier gets to the bank first and is able to cash the check, he will have the money in hand and it will then be a hassle between the supplier and the store as to who is entitled to the money.

Once a proper stop payment order has been filed with the bank, the bank might be responsible to the store if they make payment on the check in error. Thus, once a stop payment order has been signed, the bank alerts all of its tellers and the appropriate bookkeeper on the Ajax account to refuse payment should the check be presented. If a stop payment order is conducted verbally and the proper documents haven't been signed, the bank might not be responsible if it does pay the check. Banks customarily charge a few dollars for the processing of a stop payment order.

Overdrafts

We previously noted the problems that can arise when a checking account customer writes checks against uncollected funds. The same costs and embarrassments can occur if one writes checks when there simply isn't enough money in the account to cover the checks. This is a case of being "overdrawn." If a customer overdraws an account too frequently, he or she could jeopardize credit standing with the bank. In some instances, a bank may pay a check even though it would overdraw the account. This may occur because the customer is in good standing, rarely has overdrawn, and the overdraft is for a relatively small amount. The bank isn't worried about getting its money, and rather than put the customer to any inconvenience, the bank will allow the check to be paid.

In other cases, banks offer overdraft privileges to their customers. If a check overdraws an account, the bank will automatically lend the customer at least enough money to cover the overdraft and will deposit that loaned money into the customer's checking account. The loan must then be repaid at a specified rate of interest. This program can be convenient and eliminate embarrassment, but it can also be at least as costly as basic overdraft charges. It might also act as too great a temptation for the customer who lacks the discipline to keep a checking account in the proper balance.

Keeping Track of Your Account

The register, or stub, is where the checking account customer keeps a record of all deposits and checks. The register should be updated immediately with each transaction. One of the most frequent causes of overdrawn accounts and other errors is customer failure to enter deposits and checks. If you neglect to enter a check transaction in your register, you run the risk of forgetting that transaction and subsequently overdrawing. Registers come in several forms. Figure 13-4 shows some sample registers, indicating how transactions are noted in them.

The Statement and Reconciliation

Periodically—usually monthly—the bank returns a statement to each of its checking account customers. This statement contains an itemized listing of all transactions made on the account and includes all checks written and cleared during the previous month as well as all deposit slips. In that way, the customer has written verification of every transaction. The bank also makes a microfilm record of all items, which the customer can refer to if necessary.

The statement also contains instructions for determining that the balance shown by the bank matches the balance shown in the customer's account. This is known as "reconciling" the account. Figure 13-5 illustrates an example of a monthly account reconciliation.

CHECK #	DATE	CHECK ISSUED TO (or description of deposit)	AMOUNT OF CHECK	AMOUNT OF DEPOSIT	BALANCE
a.					139.90
143	2/21	To *Joes Gas Sta* / For *Gas*	7.75		CHECK OR DEP. 7.75 / BAL. 132.15
Dep	2/27	To *(Net Paycheck)* / For		200.00	CHECK OR DEP. 200.00 / BAL. 332.15
144	3/15	To *Electric Co.* / For *Feb. bill*	28.10		CHECK OR DEP. 28.10 / BAL. 304.05
145	3/15	To *Saving & Loan* / For *March p. mt.*	242.00		CHECK OR DEP. 242.00 / BAL. 62.05

b.

CHECK # 144	DATE 3/5
TO *Electric Co.* *Feb. bill*	
BALANCE	332.15
CHECK	28.10
DEPOSIT	
NEW BAL.	304.05

CHECK # 145	DATE 3/5
TO *Saving & Loan* *March p. mt.*	
BALANCE	304.05
CHECK	242.00
DEPOSIT	
NEW BAL.	62.05

Figure 13-4   (a) Sample checkbook register.
(b) Sample checkbook stubs.

Shopping for Checking Accounts

Prior to 1981, except in a few northeastern states, checking account customers could not earn interest on the money that they had deposited in their checking accounts. All that changed when Congress authorized the negotiable order of withdrawal (NOW) accounts at the start of 1981. Checking account customers throughout the country now have a choice of checking account concepts: those which do not pay interest and those which do. While it would seem reasonable to assume that the interest-bearing checking accounts are the better choice, that isn't necessarily the case. In evaluating checking account plans, it's necessary to take into account the following factors:

□ The minimum balance you must keep in your account in order to earn interest;

1. Arrange canceled checks and deposit slips by number or date.
2. Check them off in your checkbook, verifying each amount as you proceed.
3. *Add* to your checkbook any deposits or other credits recorded on this statement that you have not already added.
4. *Subtract* from your checkbook any checks or other charges recorded on this statement that you have not already subtracted.
5. List at right each check you have written that is not yet paid by bank (does not show on statement). Total them, and enter total on line 10.

CHECKS NOT YET PAID		
DATE	#	AMOUNT
3/8	149	52.50
3/9	150	7.50
3/10	151	10.00
TOTAL		70.00

6. List any deposits you have made that do not show on statement, and enter total on line 8.

DEPOSITS NOT YET CREDITED	
DATE	AMOUNT
3/10	100.00
TOTAL	100.00

7. Ending balance as shown on statement. $ 182.00
8. Add total from line 6.   +   100.00
9. Subtotal.   282.00
10. Subtract total from line 5.   −   70.00
11. This total should be the same as the balance in your checkbook. $ 212.00

Figure 13-5   Sample reconciliation of checking account.

    □ The extra interest you could earn if funds were placed in a higher yielding account, other than the checking account itself;

    □ How much of the earned interest would be offset by the service charges;

    □ The range of other services that you might be entitled to at a given institution;

    □ The overall convenience and relationships you can establish by dealing with a particular institution.

Plans—both non-interest bearing and interest bearing—will differ from institution to institution and from time to time. In non-interest-bearing checking accounts you will likely have a choice between two types of plans: the minimum balance account, which will entitle you to no-service-charge checking provided you keep a minimum balance in the account; and the per-item account, which will cost you a fixed amount for each check written plus perhaps a monthly basic service charge regardless of the amount you keep in your account.

With the interest-bearing accounts, you will be required to keep a certain minimum balance in an account in order to qualify for the earned interest and possibly also for cost-free service. The minimum balance may have to be kept in the checking account itself, or you may be able to qualify by keeping the minimum balance in a savings plan with the institution. And if the institution does impose a charge for each check written, the total monthly service charges could exceed the amount of interest you earn, depending on the number of checks you write in an average month.

The Personal Action Checklist at the end of this chapter will help you decide which plans available in your community offer the lowest cost (or highest income) in your own individual case.

Savings Accounts

Savings accounts are available at commercial banks, mutual savings banks, savings and loan associations, and credit unions. Generally, they take one of two forms: passbook accounts and savings certificates of deposit (CD).

Unlike checking accounts, where money flows in and out constantly, savings accounts are relatively inactive. They're used as a device to accumulate money over a long period of time.

Financial institutions are willing to pay savings accounts customers for the use of their money. The payment is referred to as "interest." In effect, customers are lending their money to the institution and the institution is paying interest for the loan.

Passbook Accounts

The most common type of savings account is the passbook account. A passbook account may be opened with any amount of money, and the customer may make deposits to or withdrawals from the account as desired. (Some institutions might limit the number of withdrawals permitted in a month or in a quarter, and if that number is exceeded, the institution might levy a modest service charge.) Passbook savings account customers will usually receive a small booklet, or passbook, in which each deposit and withdrawal is entered and in which the interest earned on the account is added to the customer's balance.*

*A variation of the passbook account is the statement account, in which a monthly or quarterly statement is mailed to the customer. The statement reflects all transactions in the account for the preceding period.

**Certificates
of Deposit**

Increasing in popularity in recent years has been the savings certificate or CD. This is a contractual agreement between customer and institution whereby the customer agrees to leave a certain sum of money with the bank for a fixed period of time—perhaps as short as 90 days or as long as ten years. Certificates generally pay a higher rate of interest to the customer than passbook accounts because the institution is assured that it will have the fixed sum of money available for lending for a known period of time. If a certificate customer wishes to withdraw funds before the agreed-on time has elapsed, he or she will suffer a penalty. Check to determine current penalty regulations before you open a certificate account.

Competition is keen among institutions for savings accounts of all types. Generally, mutual savings banks, savings and loan associations, and credit unions pay a slightly higher rate of interest to savers than commercial banks. To offset that possible disadvantage, commercial banks offer a broader range of services.

Because many consider savings accounts as a form of investment, they are treated more fully in chapter 16.

**Safe Deposit
Facilities**

Safe deposit boxes provide the ultimate security for valuable items and documents that cannot be replaced or duplicated. Financial institutions that rent safe deposit facilities will make boxes of varying sizes available, generally on a yearly rental basis. The amount of the rent depends on the size of the box. The person or persons renting safe deposit facilities must sign a signature card at the time the box is rented and then only those persons who have signed the cards are permitted entree to the box. A key is given to safe deposit customers and it must be presented in addition to signing the entry form. It takes a combination of two keys—the one held by the customer and the one held by the institution—to allow entry into a box. If the customer loses a key, the likelihood is that the institution will have to drill the door open, probably at the customer's expense. Naturally, access to the box is available only during normal banking hours.

Some institutions may offer safe deposit box facilities at a reduced charge for customers who utilize other services.

Trust Services

Trust departments are usually found in larger commercial banks. The basic function of a trust department is to act as a trusted custodian of money or property for customers who require such services.

One very frequent use of trust services arises when an individual dies and directs that property go to his survivors "in trust." He will have established an agreement with the bank to act as trustee of the stated money and property. The trust department will then be responsible for investing the money prudently, for managing property (such as real estate), for selling any securities or properties that it deems proper to sell, for assisting with the necessary tax returns and other accounting matters on behalf of the trust, and for distributing the proceeds in accordance with the wishes of the individual who established the trust. Charges are levied for trust services depending on the total value of assets in the trust and the complexity of instructions that the trust department must follow. See the chapter on estate planning for further discussion of trusts.

Loans

See chapter 14, Credit and Borrowing, for a full discussion.

Mortgages

See chapter 9, Financing a Home, for detailed information.

Special Checks

Travelers checks provide a safe and convenient means of having funds available when one is traveling—in the United States, where personal checks may not be acceptable outside your own home community, and particularly in foreign countries where neither personal checks nor American dollars may be acceptable as exchange. Travelers checks can be purchased at most financial institutions in denominations of $10, $20, $50, and $100. The common charge is $1 per $100 worth of travelers checks. The most popular brands of travelers checks are issued by the American Express Company, Citicorp, Thomas Cook and Sons, and Bank of America and are readily accepted by most hotels, restaurants, and merchants throughout the world; they also can be changed into local currency at banks in foreign nations. If lost, they can be replaced at offices of the issuing agencies, or by mail, as directed in the instructions included with each packet of travelers checks. Some institutions may offer the travelers checks at less than the normal cost to customers who make use of other services.

Money orders are a form of check that one purchases at financial institutions (and at United States Post Offices) usually for payment of bills, or for any other personal needs. Money orders can be purchased in any denomination. They generally cost more than checks, and one must go to the institution in order to purchase one; thus, they aren't nearly as convenient as a checking account. They might be suitable for someone who issues very few checks each month, but if more than a handful of checks are issued, it might be cheaper to use a checking account instead of purchasing money orders.

If you're entering into an important transaction—such as the sale of your home—and you want to be absolutely certain that the check you receive from the other party will be good, you might want to require that the party give you a Cashier's Check or a Certified Check instead of a normal personal check. A Cashier's Check is a check drawn on the bank's own funds. A Certified Check is an individual's check that the bank has certified (in effect, guaranteed) that the funds are indeed in the account. Similarly, you might be required to present a Cashier's Check or Certified Check in certain situations. Assuming that you do have adequate funds in your account, the bank can accommodate these requests quickly and at little or no fee, depending on your status as a customer.

Notarial Services

We often have to sign documents requiring that our signature be "notarized." This service is performed by a notary public, and most financial institutions have a notary public on their staff available to serve their customers. The purpose of notarization is to verify that the signature is indeed that of the person indicated. When a signature is to be notarized, the document must be signed in the presence of the notary, and the notary must know that the signer is who he represents himself to be. Many institutions do not charge for notarial services, particularly for their own customers. Notarial services can also be obtained through law firms, governmental offices, insurance agencies, and other businesses.

Electronic Banking

Many commercial banks throughout the nation have begun installing electronic tellers—machines that offer 24-hour service on a variety of transactions: withdrawals, deposits, loan payments, and transfers from one account to another. Customers wishing to utilize these services are generally issued a plastic card with a secret code number assigned to it, thus preventing anyone except the authorized user from making use of the card. Currently, banks do not charge for this electronic banking service, because most consider it a competitive tool to attract accounts. It does offer considerable convenience, particularly to individuals who might find it difficult to do their banking during normal banking hours. Industry observers have speculated that someday electronic tellers may replace human tellers for most simple transactions. Although the technology certainly exists to accomplish this, it's far from certain whether the American public is willing to accept machines in place of the human element in their common financial transactions.

Collection Services

Business and commercial accounts are more likely to make use of this little-known service. For example, a landlord who lives in a distant city may find it more convenient for tenants to make their rent payments to the local bank, which will in turn deposit the payments into the landlord's account in that bank. He may feel that there's a psychological advantage that gets the rent paid more promptly if the payments are made to a local bank rather than to some distant address. Charges are made in accordance with the volume of service rendered.

International Banking

This is predominantly a service for the business executive, found in larger commercial banks. As American business spreads throughout the world, the need has arisen for banking services to exchange foreign currency for American currency, to establish business contacts in foreign countries, and to assist with the various business negotiations and transactions taking place between American and foreign firms.

Investment Department

As noted earlier, what banks don't lend out to the public or keep in reserve, they invest, usually in high-quality government and corporate bond issues. Many individual investors who seek those types of securities find it more convenient and less costly to acquire them through their bank investment department rather than through stock brokerage firms. Anyone contemplating investing in government or corporate securities would do well to inquire at their local bank to see whether their investment department can provide service comparable to or better than local brokerage firms.

Laws that Govern Financial Institutions and Their Transactions

Financial institutions, and the transactions that emanate from them, are governed by a complex system of state and federal laws. As noted earlier, each institution is given its original license to operate, either by the state in which it is located or by the federal government. The respective government then generally oversees and regulates the operation of the institution, including periodic audits and examinations to ascertain whether the institution is complying with governmental guidelines. Additional state regulations that institutions must comply with include laws of negotiable instruments (an important aspect of which is the concept of the "holder in due course"), laws of usury, and laws regarding secured transactions. Federal laws with which institutions must comply include the Truth in Lending Law, the Fair Credit Reporting Law, the Fair Credit Billing Law, and the Equal Credit Opportunity Law. Let's examine each of these.

The Negotiable Instruments Laws

The negotiable instruments laws refer to instruments—such as checks, promissory notes (IOUs)—that are negotiated—sold, exchanged, and otherwise passed from hand to hand. Each state has its own laws of negotiable instruments, but they all tend to be quite similar. In essence, negotiable instruments laws determine what constitutes a valid negotiable instrument and what does not. They also may set forth the penalties involved when one attempts to transact an instrument that is not negotiable. A check is a good example of a negotiable instrument. It carries an unconditional order to pay a fixed sum of money to the holder; it's dated; and the person who has drawn the check has signed it. If a check does not contain any of these elements—such as the signature of the drawer—it could be construed as being nonnegotiable and need not be processed in the manner that valid checks are processed. In short, it could be returned to the person who drew the check and the intended transaction would thus not occur.

Another example would be a promissory note: you buy a TV set from a local appliance dealer, and instead of paying cash for it, you sign a promissory note in which you agree to make payments over a specific period of time. The promissory note is payable directly to the dealer. The dealer in turn sells your promissory note to a local bank or finance company so that he can get his money out. You then end up making your payments to the bank. The bank has become a *holder* of your negotiable instrument *in the due course of business,* assuming that the instrument has been properly created and executed. If you had neglected to sign it, the TV dealer would not have been able to sell it to the bank. If the TV dealer had not properly endorsed it, the bank would not have bought it from him.

We noted in the above example that the bank had become a holder of your promissory note (or negotiable instrument) in the due course of business. The bank, in such a case, is referred to as the "holder in due course" and this brings up one of the more important aspects of the law of negotiable instruments. Let's follow the example a little further. After you've taken possession of the television set, you find it doesn't work properly. The store refuses to make adjustments, claiming, perhaps, that you have somehow damaged or abused the set. You disagree, of course, and claim that you shouldn't have to pay for something that doesn't perform as you expected it would. You inform the store that you intend to refuse making payments until they have honored the warranty and put the set in proper working order. The store owner smiles and shrugs and tells you that that's out of his hands: your promissory note has been sold to the bank, and it's the bank that you owe money to, not the store. "Settle it up with them," the store owner tells you.

You inform the bank of this situation, and that you don't intend to make any payments. But they tell you you're out of luck: you owe them the money regardless of any claim you have against the store. They are, as they say, a holder in due course of your legitimate promissory note, and they bought that promissory note regardless of any claims or disputes that might have existed between you and the store.

The disadvantage to the buyer is obvious: the strongest defense—withholding payment for an unsatisfactory product—is effectively cut off by the operation of the holder in due course doctrine.

On the other hand, the lender's viewpoint is not without some merit, in effect: "If we had to make certain that every buyer was totally satisfied with his or her purchase before we got involved with the financing, the wheels of commerce could grind to a halt. We simply don't have the time, nor does the consumer want to absorb the expense of having the lender make certain that everyone is happy before the money changes hands. Granted there are abuses, but they are extremely rare in relation to the volume of transactions that occur in which there is no complaint of any kind."

Throughout the 1960s and 1970s, the abuses began to come to the attention of consumer-protection agencies. A few states passed regulations that put limits on the holder in due course doctrine, and eventually, in May 1976, the Federal Trade Commission acted to impose limits to the doctrine on a nationwide basis.

Under the new regulations, most consumer credit contracts must contain a notice stating that the holder of the contract or promissory note will be subject to the same claims and defenses that the buyer could have asserted against the seller.

The wary buyer of goods should thus become aware of the protections that the law now allows and should rapidly assert his or her rights if there is the least suspicion that they may be violated.

Usury Laws

Each state has its own laws of usury. The usury laws dictate the maximum rate of interest that can be charged for various types of loans.

You should determine what the maximum interest rates allowable for various categories of loans are in your own state.

If a lender charges an excessive, or usurious, rate of interest on a loan or on any kind of financing, he may be subject to penalties. The borrower, or debtor, in a usurious transaction should determine what his or her rights are in such a case and take appropriate action.

In most states the laws of usury apply to individuals only. Corporations do not have the same measure of protection when they borrow.

Secured Transactions Laws

You purchase an automobile and arrange for financing through your local bank. In the common transaction, you will sign documents that give the bank the right to take back your car if you fail to make the payments as promised. As a result of your signing these documents and the bank's recording of them in the appropriate governmental office, the bank has what is known as a "security interest" in your new automobile.

By recording the security agreements, the bank has put all other parties on notice that it has a first lien on that particular property. Years later, when you pay off the loan, the bank should release that security interest by completing and filing the appropriate papers at that time.

Secured transaction laws are slightly different in each state, but they all derive from one uniform recommended law called the Uniform Commercial Code. These state laws describe how a lender goes about protecting his security interest in a property and how he must release that security interest when the loan is eventually paid off. The loan does not dictate when or if a borrower must put up security for a given loan nor how much security should be put up. That's between the borrower and the lender. The law does, however, describe the means by which each party is protected in such a transaction.

The Federal Laws: Truth in Lending

Congress passed the Truth in Lending Law in July 1969. The main purpose of the Truth in Lending Law (also referred to as Regulation Z) is to inform borrowers and consumers of the exact cost of credit so that they can compare costs offered by various credit sources.

The Truth in Lending Law is very broad in scope. It applies to virtually all issuers of credit, including commercial banks, savings and loan associations, credit unions, consumer finance companies, residential mortgage brokers, department stores, automobile dealers, furniture and appliance dealers, artisans (such as electricians and plumbers), and professionals (such as doctors, dentists, and lawyers). If these parties, or any others issuing credit to the public, extend credit for personal, family, household, or agricultural uses, or for real estate transactions, they must comply with the regulations of the Truth in Lending Law. (Credit transactions in excess of $25,000, except for real estate transactions, may be excluded from coverage of the law.)

The main objective of the Truth in Lending Law is to establish a uniform means of quoting credit costs. Prior to the passage of this law, grantors of credit frequently quoted interest costs in a variety of different forms—add-on, discount, simple, per month, per year, and so on. This variety of quoting costs made it quite difficult for the typical consumer to compare the true costs between one lender or credit grantor and another. It was, in a sense, like trying to compare apples with oranges.

The Truth in Lending Law dictates that any grantor of credit must clearly set forth the *total finance charges* that the customer must pay, directly or indirectly, in order to obtain the desired credit. The finance charges can include any of the following costs: interest, loan fees, finders fees, service charges, "points" (commonly, the added fees charged in a residential mortgage transaction), appraisal fees, premiums for credit life or health insurance, the cost of any investigation or credit reports.

It should be noted that certain costs involved in some loan transactions need not be counted in the finance charge. These include taxes, license fees, registration fees, title fees, and some real estate closing fees.

In addition to stating the total dollar amount of finance charges, the credit grantor must also express the cost in terms of a percentage. This is known as the *annual percentage rate* or *APR*. A formula was devised whereby all finance charges could be translated into APR, and it is the APR that must be quoted by all credit grantors. Technically, the APR formula now requires all lenders and credit grantors to quote credit costs using the same mathematics. APR, then, is the pure way of comparing credit costs between different lenders.

The Truth in Lending Law does not fix the interest rates that may be charged on credit. That's between the lender and the borrower within the limitations of state usury laws. But where interest or other finance charges are involved, the law states that the cost must be expressed in terms of APR.

The provisions of the Truth in Lending Law apply, not only to installment loans granted by lenders or to credit contracts, but also to what is known as "open-end credit." Open-end credit is generally that form of credit granted with credit cards and revolving charge accounts in retail stores, and check overdraft plans in banks. Detailed information about the finance charges and the APR must also be given to users of this form of credit.

Figure 13-6 is an example of a typical disclosure statement showing the various aspects of the credit transaction as referred to in the Truth in Lending Law.

If, in order to borrow money, you have to put up your home as collateral for the loan, the Truth in Lending Law requires that the lender give you a three-day period in which you can elect to cancel or rescind the transaction by sending proper notice to the lender. (This does not apply in cases where you are borrowing money to buy the home initially.) The purpose of this three-day "cooling off" period is to protect borrowers who might have second thoughts about a transaction, particularly when they might have received a high-pressure sales pitch or misleading promises. If you do elect to cancel such a transaction and proper notice is given to the lender, you are entitled to a return of any down payment you have given the lender or merchant.

Although the Truth in Lending Law sets forth a means of comparing credit wisely and prudently, it does not necessarily instruct the consumer how to make a decision on which lender to do business with. The cost of credit is not the only factor that must be considered in making a borrowing decision. Thus, while two credit grantors may offer varying APRs on a specific loan application—such as automobile financing—the lowest rate may not ultimately prove to be the best arrangement for the borrower. For example, if a local bank offers an APR slightly higher than an out-of-town credit firm, the borrower might still be better off doing business with the local bank, where other services and considerations may be provided that wouldn't be found at the out-of-town institution. The Truth in Lending Law goes a long way toward helping the consumer, but the consumer must ultimately weigh other factors in making his or her decision.

The Truth in Lending Law also sets forth regulations regarding the use of credit cards, the liability for their unauthorized use, and the means by which credit may be advertised.

The Fair Credit Billing Law

The Fair Credit Billing Law was passed in October 1974 as an amendment to the Truth in Lending Law. It was designed to put an end to the frustration that certain credit customers have when they receive a bill that contains an error and then cannot get the error properly corrected. It pertains to open-end credit—credit arising out of revolving charge accounts, checking overdraft plans, and credit card obligations. It does *not* apply to normal installment loans or purchases that are paid in accordance with a set schedule of installments.

The Fair Credit Billing Law covers only billing errors on your periodic statement. Billing errors are those that might arise as a result of the following: charges that you did not make or charges made by a person not allowed to use your account; charges billed with the wrong descrip-

DISCLOSURE STATEMENT

_____
(BANK)

_____
(OFFICE)

_____
(ADDRESS)

TRANSACTION: PROPOSED LOAN — NONREAL PROPERTY			
Amount	Security	Purpose	Type of Loan
$_____ Nonrescindable transaction	Not secured by real property	Consumer or agricultural	

NAMES AND ADDRESSES OF BORROWERS:

_____

_____

_____

The following disclosures are made pursuant to the Consumer Credit Protection Act by the above-named Bank (herein called Bank) to the Borrower(s) named herein (herein collectively called Borrower) in connection with the proposed loan described herein (herein called Loan):

1. AMOUNT OF CREDIT (excluding any Prepaid Finance Charge (Item 3) and Required Deposit Balance (Item 4)

(a) Net loan proceeds .... $_____

(b) Charges included in Amount Financed

  (1) Insurance premiums

    Credit life (if not required) .... $_____

    Credit disability (if not required) .... $_____

    Property .... $_____

    Liability .... $_____

  (2) _____ .... $_____

  (3) Charges, if any, itemized under Column A of Item 2 .... $_____

  AMOUNT FINANCED (Total) .... $_____

2. CERTAIN CHARGES NOT INCLUDED IN FINANCE CHARGE (Item 6)

(a) Fees to public officials for determining, perfecting, releasing or satisfying security	A Included in Amount Financed	B Not included in Amount Financed
(1) Recorder	$	$
(2) Secretary of State	$	$
(3) _____	$	$
(b) Fees imposed by law		
(1) License	$	$
(2) Certificate of title	$	$
(3) Registration	$	$
(c) _____	$	$
Total (enter at Item 1(b)(3))	$	

3. FINANCE CHARGES PAID SEPARATELY OR WITHHELD

	A Paid Separately	B Withheld from Loan Proceeds
(a) Loan fee	$	$
(b) Commitment fee	$	$
(c) Appraisal fees	$	$
(d) Investigation fees (_____)	$	$
(e) Credit report fees	$	$
(f) Notary fees	$	$
(g) Document preparation fees	$	$
(h) Insurance premiums Required credit life	$	$
Required credit disability	$	$
(i) _____	$	$
(j) _____	$	$
(k) _____	$	$
	$	$
Total	$	$

PREPAID FINANCE CHARGE (Col. A plus B) $_____

4. REQUIRED DEPOSIT BALANCE .... $_____

5. TOTAL PREPAID FINANCE CHARGE AND REQUIRED DEPOSIT BALANCE .... $_____

6. AMOUNTS INCLUDED IN FINANCE CHARGE

(a) Interest at_____% per annum on _____ .... $_____

(b) Interest added on of $_____ per $100 of Loan per annum .... $_____

(c) Flat charge .... $_____

(d) _____ .... $_____

(e) _____ .... $_____

(f) Charges, if any, itemized in Item 3 .... $_____

FINANCE CHARGE (Total) .... $_____

Any interest included in the Finance Charge accrues from date of advance, except that if a series of advances is to be made pursuant to written agreement, interest accrues on each such advance from date thereof and has been computed until maturity of the Loan in accordance with the estimated or approximate dates and amounts of advances as furnished by Borrower.

7. TOTAL OF PAYMENTS .... $_____

Payable in_____payment(s) as follows [Note any Balloon Payment(s)]:

_____

_____

_____

_____

_____

_____

8. ANNUAL PERCENTAGE RATE _____%

9. LATE PAYMENT CHARGE is payable on any payment in default for_____days in an amount equal to_____

10. PREPAYMENT CREDIT. Upon prepayment of the Loan in full, Borrower will be entitled to a rebate of any unearned (prepaid) (precomputed) interest_____

11. PREPAYMENT CHARGE. Upon partial or full prepayment of the Loan _____

12. SECURITY. Loan is to be secured by a security agreement covering the property described_____

and by an assignment of rights under insurance policies thereon as required by Bank, all as described in the security agreement(s). The security agreement(s) (will) (will not) cover (certain) after acquired property, and (will) (will not) secure future and other indebtedness. Loan is to be subject to a lien under Civil Code §3054 on personal property of Borrower in Bank's possession. Except as may be provided above, Loan is not to be secured as a result of any existing agreement between Bank and any Borrower or other person, any such agreement to the contrary notwithstanding.

INSURANCE

ANY PROPERTY OR LIABILITY INSURANCE TO BE WRITTEN IN CONNECTION WITH THE LOAN MAY BE OBTAINED BY BORROWER THROUGH ANY PERSON OF HIS CHOICE, provided, however, that Bank may for reasonable cause refuse to accept an insurer on any such insurance which is required by Bank. Such insurance may ☐ not be obtained from or through Bank ☐ be obtained through Bank at the cost set forth in a separate Insurance Statement furnished by Bank.

[Complete if credit insurance may be written but is not required] CREDIT LIFE AND CREDIT DISABILITY INSURANCE ARE NOT REQUIRED TO OBTAIN THE LOAN. No charge is to be made for such insurance and none is to be provided unless Borrower to be insured thereunder signs and dates the statement below. If obtained through Bank, the cost for credit life insurance will be $_____and for credit disability insurance will be $_____

I desire credit ☐ life and ☐ disability insurance.

_____ _____
(DATE) (SIGNATURE)

●IMPORTANT NOTE: ASTERISK DENOTES THAT AMOUNT INDICATED IS AN ESTIMATE.

Borrower acknowledges reading and receiving a duplicate of this Disclosure Statement and that he has not entered into any agreement with Bank for the making or payment of the Loan; and if the Loan is to be made in a series of advances pursuant to written agreement, approves the Annual Percentage Rate and method of computing the Finance Charge set forth above, and all the terms of that proposed agreement. THIS IS NOT AN OFFER OR COMMITMENT TO LEND OR TO PROVIDE INSURANCE.

_____ By _____ _____
(DATE)   (BANK)   (BORROWER)

_____
(BORROWER)

TL-4 (7-69 REV)

Figure 13-6 Sample disclosure statement.

tions, amount, or date; charges for property or services that you did not accept or that were not delivered as agreed; failures to credit your accounts for payments or for goods you have returned; accounting errors, such as arithmetic mistakes in computing finance charges; billings for which you request an explanation or written proof of purchase; and failures to mail or deliver a billing statement to your current address provided you gave at least ten days' notice of any change of address.

The law does not cover disputes over the quality of goods that you have received. In certain cases, however, you might be able to withhold payment under the Fair Credit Billing Law if you have purchased merchandise or services on a credit card and the goods or services prove to be unsatisfactory. In effect, if you would have had the right to withhold payment from the seller of the merchandise, you might also be able to withhold payment for that merchandise from your credit card account. The law won't help you settle the dispute, but it could give you the right to withhold payment while the dispute is being settled.

The Fair Credit Billing Law requires that open-end creditors give a notice summarizing the dispute settlement procedures to all customers who have active accounts or who open new accounts after October 28, 1975. After the first notice, additional copies must be provided to customers every six months.

The dispute settlement procedures regarding a billing error, as outlined by the Federal Trade Commission, are as follows.

1. *How you notify the creditor of a billing error.* If you think your bill is wrong, or if you need more information about an item on your bill, here's what you must do to preserve your rights under the law. On a sheet of paper separate from the bill, write the following: your name and account number; a description of the error and an explanation of why you think it's an error; a request for whatever added information you may think you need, including a copy of the charge slip; the dollar amount of the suspected error, and any other information you think will help the creditor to identify you or the reason for your complaint or inquiry. This would include your address and photocopies of the bill itself and the charge in question.

Send your billing error notice to the address on the bill listed after the words: "Send inquiries to," or similar wording indicating the proper address.

Mail it as soon as you can, but in any case early enough to reach the creditor within 60 days after the bill was mailed to you.

Do not simply notify the creditor by telephone. This will not necessarily protect your rights under the law. The proper way to protect your rights is to notify the creditor in writing.

2. *What the creditor must do.* The creditor must acknowledge all letters pointing out possible errors within 30 days of receipt of such letters,

unless the creditor is able to correct your bill during that 30 days. Within 90 days after receiving your letter, the creditor must either correct the error or explain why he, the creditor, believes the bill is correct. Once the creditor has explained the bill, the creditor has no further obligation to you even though you still believe there is an error, except as provided in 5 below.

3. *How you are protected from collection and bad credit reports.* After the creditor has been notified, neither the creditor nor an attorney nor a collection agency may send you collection letters or take other collection action regarding the amount in dispute. But periodic *statements* may be sent to you, and the disputed amount can be applied against your credit limit. You cannot be threatened with damage to your credit rating or sued for the amount in question, nor can the disputed amount be reported to a credit bureau or other creditors as being delinquent until the creditor has answered your inquiry. However, you remain obligated to pay whatever portion of your bill is not in dispute.

4. *What happens if the dispute is settled?* If it is determined that the creditor has made a mistake on your bill, you will not have to pay any finance charges on any disputed amount. If it turns out that the creditor has not made an error, you may have to pay finance charges on the amount in dispute, and you will have to make up any missed minimum or required payments on the disputed amount. Unless you have agreed that your bill was correct, the creditor must send you a written notification of what you owe. If it is determined that the creditor did make a mistake in billing the disputed amount, you must be given the same amount of time to pay as you are normally given for undisputed amounts before any more finance charges or late payment charges on the disputed amount can be charged to you.

5. *What happens if the dispute is not settled?* If the creditor's explanation does not satisfy you and you notify the creditor in writing within ten days after you receive his explanation that you still refuse to pay the disputed amount, the creditor may report you to credit bureaus and other creditors and may pursue regular collection procedures. But the creditor must also report that you do not think you owe any money, and the creditor must let you know to whom such reports were made. Once the matter has been settled between you and the creditor, the creditor must notify those to whom he had reported you as being delinquent.

6. *How the creditor can be penalized for not following the procedure.* If the creditor does not follow these rules, the creditor is not allowed to collect the first $50 of the disputed amount and finance charges, even if the bill turns out to be correct.

7. *When can you withhold payment for faulty goods or services purchased with a credit card?* If you have a problem with property or services purchased with a credit card, you may have the right not to pay the remaining amount due on them if you first try, in good faith, to return the item or give the merchant a chance to correct the problem. There are two limitations on this right: (a) you must have bought the item or services in your home state, or if not within your home state, within 100 miles of your current mailing address; and (b) the purchase price must have been more than $50. However, the above two limitations do not apply if the merchant is owned or operated by the creditor, or if the creditor mailed you the advertisement for the property or services.

In brief, the Fair Credit Billing Law gives you the right of extensive protection against alleged errors in billing. But you must exercise your rights as they are stated in the law. If you fail to do so, you may have waived those rights. Further, if the creditor is in error or does not follow the instructions regarding the law, it's up to you to take the steps to protect yourself accordingly.

The most important aspect of the Fair Credit Billing Law is the dispute procedure. There are some additional protections offered the public by the Fair Credit Billing Law. They include:

☐ If an open-end credit customer is given a time period within which to pay a bill without a finance charge, the creditor must mail or deliver the bill to the customer at least 14 days before the end of that time period.

☐ An open-end creditor must credit a customer's account with payments as of the date that they are received, unless not doing so would not cause extra charges.

☐ Open-end creditors must promptly credit any customer overpayment to the account and, if requested by the customer, must promptly refund the overpayment.

☐ Open-end creditors must, when the merchant accepts returns, credit a customer's account promptly for any refunds on returns.

☐ Under the Fair Credit Billing Law, merchants may, if they wish, grant discounts to customers for paying by cash instead of by credit card.

The Fair Credit Reporting Act

The Fair Credit Reporting Act, which went into effect in April 1971, is designed to give access to any information that may be on file at local credit bureaus regarding your own individual credit history. It also enables you to take steps to correct erroneous or outdated material that may be in your file.

It should be noted, contrary to what many people think, that credit reporting agencies are *not* governmental agencies. They are generally private firms, operating either on their own or as a cooperative of various merchants and lenders within the community. It is their job to accumulate appropriate credit information on individuals and make it available to their respective participating members. Most individuals aren't aware of it, but when we make application for credit of various kinds and sign our name to the application, we are giving permission to the lender to seek any information about us at the local credit bureau and to relay any information obtained on us to the bureau. This clause will normally be contained in the loan application statement. Easy access to credit information on the citizens of a community makes it easier and more convenient for credit to be granted to credit-worthy seekers. To this extent, the local credit bureau, as a clearinghouse of information, serves a most valuable purpose. But there have been abuses within that industry, as in any industry, and the Fair Credit Reporting Act was designed to correct those abuses.

Under the Fair Credit Reporting Act, you can, on presenting proper identification, learn the contents of your file at your local credit bureau. The identification requirements are for the borrower's own protection. This aspect of the law would eliminate the chance of a stranger walking into a credit bureau claiming to be you and viewing your credit file.

Regarding erroneous information, you can request the bureau to reinvestigate any items you question. If the information is found to be inaccurate or cannot be verified, it will be deleted. If the reinvestigation doesn't resolve the problem, you can write a brief statement explaining your position, and the statement will be included in all future credit reports. If an item is deleted or a statement added, you can request that the bureau so notify anyone who has received regular credit reports on you during the last six months.

If you've been denied credit during the past 30 days because of a report from the credit bureau, or if you've received a collection notice from a department affiliated with the credit bureau, the law states that you're not to be charged for viewing your file. If the above doesn't apply, a reasonable charge can be imposed for the privilege of viewing your file.

Information in your credit file that is adverse may not be disclosed to creditors after seven years have elapsed—except if you have had a bankruptcy in your past. That information may remain in your file and be available to inquirers for up to 14 years.

As with the other laws, the Fair Credit Reporting Act gives the rights to the individual, but it's up to the individual to see that those rights are obtained when deserved. The credit bureau will not call you to tell you what's in your file. It's wise to examine your credit file every few years to make sure it does not contain any adverse information. Through nobody's fault, adverse or incorrect information can find its way into an individual credit file. Mix-ups in names and addresses can occur—whether via computer or human error—and erroneous information can be released without your knowledge. Viewing your credit file for potential errors or inaccuracies is a simple and inexpensive way to facilitate all your credit and borrowing needs.

The Equal Credit Opportunity Law

The Equal Credit Opportunity Law went into effect in October 1975. Essentially, it's designed to prevent any discrimination in the granting of credit regarding sex or marital status of any person applying for credit.

In the most general sense, this law was designed to correct an apparent abuse that often prevented women from receiving credit to which they might otherwise be entitled. Highlights of the law include the following.

☐ Creditors must not discriminate against any applicant on the basis of sex or marital status in any phase of a credit transaction.

☐ Creditors must not make any statement to any applicant that would discourage a reasonable person from applying for credit because of sex or marital status.

☐ Creditors must not demand information about an applicant's child-bearing intentions or capability and may not ask about birth-control practices.

☐ Creditors must open separate accounts for husbands and wives if requested and if both are credit worthy.

☐ Creditors must consider alimony and child-support payments as they would any other source of income in assessing credit worthiness if the applicant wishes to rely on those means of income.

☐ Creditors must not consider sex or marital status in any system of evaluating credit worthiness.

☐ Creditors must allow applicants to open or maintain accounts in their birth-given name if they so desire.

☐ Creditors must require a co-signature of both spouses on loans only if the same requirement is imposed on all similarly qualified applicants without regard to sex or marital status.

☐ Creditors must give the reason why credit has been denied or terminated when asked by the applicant.

☐ Creditors must not terminate or change the conditions of any credit solely on the basis of a change in marital status while a person is using or is liable for an account.

☐ However, a creditor may require reapplication on a change in marital status where the credit has been granted to an applicant based on income that was solely earned by the applicant's spouse.

☐ Creditors must include a notice of the right to equal credit opportunity on written application forms, together with the name of the federal agency that supervises compliance.

☐ Creditors must report all information on joint credit accounts opened after November 1, 1976, in the name of both spouses if both spouses use the account or are liable for it.

Fair Debt Collection Practices Act

This federal law, which went into effect March 20, 1978, prohibits abusive, deceptive, and unfair debt-collection practices. Since financial institutions frequently employ outside debt-collection firms to collect on delinquent loan payments, this new law can affect your rights with respect to banks, finance companies, other lenders, or any firms or persons that have extended credit to you. The law covers personal, family, and household debts, including loans, charge accounts, medical bills, and the like. Here, in brief, is how the law works:

☐ A debt collector may contact you in person, by mail, telephone, or telegram, but it should not be at unusual places or times, such as before 8 A.M. or after 9 P.M. A debt collector may *not* contact you at work if your employer disapproves. A debt collector may contact any other person for the purpose of trying to locate you, but if he does so he may not tell the other person anything other than that he is trying to contact you. If you have an attorney, he must contact only your attorney. The debt collector must not tell anybody else that you owe money; should not talk to any person more than once; should not use a postcard; and should not put anything on an envelope or in a letter to others that identifies the writer as a debt collector.

☐ Within five days after you are first contacted by a debt collector he must send you *written notice* telling you the amount of money you owe, the name of the creditor, and what to do if you feel you do not owe the money.

☐ If you feel you do not owe the money, you must inform the debt collector, in writing, within 30 days after he has first contacted you. He may then not contact you again except: (1) if he sends you proof of the debt, such as a copy of the bill, in which case he can begin collection proceedings again; or (2) to notify you that certain specific action will be taken, but only if, in fact, he usually does take such action. In short, you can stop the debt collector from constantly harassing you if you properly notify him in writing to stop.

☐ A debt collector may not use false, deceptive, threatening, or abusive statements to induce you to pay. He may not threaten to take any legal action which he in fact cannot legally take. He may not send you anything that looks like an official document, which might be sent by a court or agency of any government.

If a debt collector violates the law, you have the right to sue him in a state or federal court within one year after the law was violated. You can recover damages, court costs, and attorney's fees (if you win, of course).

Table 13-1	**Federal Enforcement Agencies**
National banks	Comptroller of the Currency Washington, D.C. 20219
State member banks	Federal Reserve Bank serving the area in which the State member bank is located.
Non-member insured banks	Federal Deposit Insurance Corporation Supervising Examiner for the District in which the non-member insured bank is located.
Savings institutions insured by the FSLIC and members of the FHLB system (except for savings banks insured by FDIC)	The FHLB's Supervisory Agent in the Federal Home Loan Bank District in which the institution is located.
Federal credit unions	Regional Office of the National Credit Union Administration, serving the area in which the Federal Credit Union is located.
Creditors subject to Civil Aeronautics Board	Director, Bureau of Enforcement Civil Aeronautics Board 1825 Connecticut Avenue, N.W. Washington, D.C. 20428
Creditors subject to Interstate Commerce Commission	Office of Proceedings Interstate Commerce Commission Washington, D.C. 20523
Creditors subject to Packers and Stockyards Act	Nearest Packers and Stockyards Administration area supervisor.
Retail, department stores, consumer finance companies, all other creditors, and all non-bank credit card issuers	Federal Trade Commission Washington, D.C. 20580
Small business investment companies	U.S. Small Business Administration 1441 L Street, N.W. Washington, D.C. 20416
Brokers and dealers	Securities and Exchange Commission Washington, D.C. 20549
Federal land banks, federal land bank associations, federal intermediate credit banks, and production credit associations	Farm Credit Administration 490 L'Enfant Plaza, S.W. Washington, D.C. 20578

If a debt collector has violated the law with respect to a group of persons, that group can sue and recover money for damages up to $500,000.

If you feel that your rights under this law have been violated, you should contact the appropriate agency from the list in Table 13-1. These agencies use your complaints to decide which companies to investigate. You should also notify the debt-collection agency that you intend to contact the appropriate governmental unit. Many states also have their own debt-collection laws. Contact your State Attorney General's Office to determine your rights under the laws of your state.

Enforcement of the Federal Laws

Generally, the Federal Trade Commission administers all the foregoing federal laws regarding retail firms, department stores, consumer finance companies, all other creditors, and all non-bank credit card issuers. Table 13-1 indicates which federal agency enforces the various federal laws regarding credit and borrowing.

Personal Action Checklist
Earnings and Costs of Checking Accounts

This is designed to help you compare the costs of various checking account plans—particularly those which pay interest (NOW accounts). As with so many other of our day-to-day concerns, the lowest price is not always the best price.

	Plan A	Plan B	Plan C
☐ How much do you have to keep in the account in order to earn interest; in order to avoid charges for your checking account?	_____	_____	_____
☐ Is the above amount an *average* per month (or quarter), or is it a fixed dollar minimum?	_____	_____	_____
☐ Can you keep the minimum balance in an account other than the checking account itself, such as a savings certificate?	_____	_____	_____
☐ What charges will you incur if your required minimum balance drops below the set level?	_____	_____	_____
Basic monthly charge?	_____	_____	_____
Charge per check written?	_____	_____	_____
☐ Based on your past history (if you've had a checking account previously), what type of average balance would you expect to keep in your account?	_____	_____	_____
How many checks would you write per month?	_____	_____	_____
☐ If you've not had a checking account before, estimate the above items very carefully.	_____	_____	_____
☐ Based on above estimates, how much do you expect you'll earn (interest income less monthly charges) with this plan?	_____	_____	_____
☐ Business hours of institution?	_____	_____	_____
Open Saturdays?	_____	_____	_____
Automatic teller service available?	_____	_____	_____
☐ Convenience in getting to and from the institution.	_____	_____	_____
☐ Personal feelings about the institution: helpfulness of staff, other services offered, etc.	_____	_____	_____

Consumer Beware
Mistaken Identity

In the mid 1970s a company called Lincoln Thrift and Loan Association, based in Phoenix, Arizona, grew rapidly by offering investors a higher rate of interest than they could get at local banks and savings and loan associations. Investors were told that their accounts were "insured," and that the "insurance" was overseen by the State of Arizona.

In virtually all respects, Lincoln Thrift looked like a bank (or savings and loan association); it advertised in the same style; it had branches and tellers, and as was the custom then, it gave away gifts for new accounts.

But it was not what it seemed to be.

Shortly before Christmas day in 1975 the roughly 20,000 customers of Lincoln Thrift received shocking news: state authorities had closed the business. It had made an excessive number of bad loans, and there were accusations that the company management had pocketed large sums for its own private use.

And, worst of all, the insurance company that was supposedly protecting the accounts was insolvent too. It was not, as it had appeared, a quasi-governmental agency. The insurance company was owned by the same people who owned the thrift and loan company. If two birds in flight are tied together and you shoot one down, both will fall.

The customers had invested almost $60 million with Lincoln Thrift. For many, it was their life savings. And not a penny of it was actually insured.

It took years for government-appointed trustees to unravel the mess and collect on whatever loans they could. By the early 1980s, customers had finally received about 40 cents for every dollar they had invested. Needless to say, they earned no interest at all during that time. It's not likely that they'll ever collect more than that.

There are many thrift and loan companies throughout the nation. Failures are relatively rare. Lincoln Thrift is an uncommon, but gruesome, experience.

The facts, and the need for caution and prudence, speak for themselves.

14 | Credit and Borrowing

Imagine what would happen to our economy if it weren't possible to borrow money. Everything would grind to a halt: people couldn't buy cars, houses, appliances until they had accumulated enough cash to do so. Similarly, businesses and governments would be hard pressed to create new facilities, purchase needed equipment, expand their ongoing programs.

We live in a credit (borrowing) society. Making wise use of your ability to borrow can enhance your life. Abusing your credit can be very harmful. This chapter will explore the wise and unwise uses of credit and will guide you in the ways that credit techniques work. You'll learn:

☐ How to evaluate how much borrowing you can afford to do, and under what circumstances.

☐ Where to seek the credit you need, and how to best assure you'll get the money you need.

☐ How to structure your borrowing to best suit your ability to repay your loans.

☐ How to avoid the dangers of credit abuse.

☐ Where to look for help if you have credit problems.

Buy Now, Pay Later

Most of us take the "buy now, pay later" aspect of our economy for granted. But it was not always so.

It wasn't until about 1916, with the development of a phenomenon called the Morris Plan, that the individual working person could borrow from banks and other financial institutions. Prior to that, businesses, governments, and wealthy individuals were the predominant borrowers. Their loans were generally on a "demand" or "time" basis. A demand loan would be repayable in its entirety upon the demand of the lender. A time loan would be repayable after the passage of the stated amount of time. If the borrower wished, and the lender were willing, such loans could be renewed for an additional period of time, once the borrower had paid the interest due. It was generally felt that if the working man borrowed on such a basis, he would spend the borrowed funds on goods and services and would not be able to repay the lump sum at the agreed-on time.

Then, in 1916, a man named Arthur Morris devised a plan that would enable the individual working man to borrow money that he needed for his immediate purposes. Today, Mr. Morris' plan seems commonplace, but it was a revolutionary concept when originally devised.

The key to his idea—which came to be known as the "Morris Plan"—was that a loan could be repaid in monthly installments over a fixed period of time. The Morris Plan was the origin, and grandfather, of the installment loan, the time payment plan, the revolving charge account, the credit card loan, and all other forms of borrowing that we are accustomed to.

Morris' reasoning was simple enough: although it might be difficult for the typical worker to repay one large lump sum, if the individual was prudent and well employed, he or she should be able to set aside a fixed amount each month to apply to the debt. This type of debt would command a higher rate of interest from the borrower, and the lender would have a constant inflow of money as payments were made each month on the loans, thus enabling the lender to keep putting the available money back to work on a constant basis.

The Morris Plan was scoffed at by the established institutions, but Morris had faith that his plan represented a reasonable and prudent way to lend money to the working class and to make a profit in the process.

From an initial institution in Virginia, the Morris Plan proved itself. Within a few years there were scores of Morris Plan institutions in operation around the country. In many states they became known as "industrial banks" because they were designed to fill the needs of industrial workers—factory employees and the like.

Commercial banks soon saw the advantages and profits in making such loans, and merchants began to accept the installment IOUs of customers for many products. The buy now, pay later years were on their way.

The Morris Plan, and all that developed from it, proved successful on more than one level. By putting borrowing power into the hands of millions of American workers, more goods could be manufactured and sold. This, in turn, helped to create more jobs, which in turn created more income for more people. This then enabled a much larger segment of the population to borrow and buy.

The assembly line concept might never have been successful if there weren't people waiting with cash at the end to buy the products coming off the line. The Morris Plan and the installment loan created the availability of that cash to keep the lines moving and growing.

Today, there are very few adults in America who do not carry one of the descendants of the Morris Plan with them in their wallets or purses: the credit card. The credit card, in effect, allows a holder to write a personal installment loan—within limits—whenever and wherever he or she chooses. Just as Mr. Morris and his plan were originally scoffed at as being imprudent, the credit cards are often damned as being an evil temptation to squander money.

Understanding the workings of credit and borrowing is essential to any individual or family who wishes to manage their personal and financial affairs wisely. Let's now take a closer look at these workings and how they can be put to proper and sensible use.

What Is Credit?

Credit—the ability to borrow—is not a right. It's a privilege earned through careful planning and faithful performance. Good credit, properly used, can be a most valuable asset. Wise borrowers will have studied their own financial situation with great care. They will know the difference between needs and luxuries. They will know within pennies their ability to repay. They will know how to approach the lender, what to ask for, what not, and what to expect. They will resist the temptations that scream out "Buy me now!" and "Easy credit!"

They will have carefully defined their *access to credit, credit needs,* and *credit capacity.* And they will keep each in proper perspective and balance. Let's take a closer look at these three important elements of credit.

Access to Credit

Access to credit refers to the amount of credit readily available to you, through such means as charge accounts, credit cards, and installment loans. Access to credit is, of course, directly related to lender and merchant willingness to grant credit. That in turn depends on your past performance, income, other debts, work, and the purposes for which you may wish to borrow.

Credit Needs

Credit needs refer to the various needs you may have that can or should be fulfilled through borrowing. Common needs for borrowing include purchasing an automobile; revolving charge accounts at your department stores so that a large clothing purchase, for example, can be paid for over an extended period of time, thus making it easier on the monthly budget; home improvements; personal emergencies. *Note:* We are referring to *needs,* not luxuries. Most of us would like to obtain certain luxury items and indeed may be able to through the use of credit. But using credit to acquire luxuries, as opposed to using credit fo fulfill needs, can be dangerous. If your available credit is used excessively to obtain luxuries, you can cut off your access to credit for the more important needs.

Credit Capacity

Capacity for credit refers to the amount of borrowing you can realistically handle within your current situation of income and other expenses, as well as your future situation regarding anticipated income and other expenses.

Many people sometimes find themselves having access to more credit than they realistically need. (Or they may have needs for credit that are in excess of their credit capacity.) For example, Charlie and Charlotte estimate that they have access to roughly $15,000 worth of credit. Based on past experience, they're confident that their bank would lend them up to $5000 without collateral if necessary. The sum total of all of their credit cards and charge accounts would allow them to go into additional debt of about $5000. And a representative of a lending firm has told them that the equity in their house would allow them to borrow another $5000—if, naturally, they were willing to give a second mortgage on the house. Their current credit needs are much more modest. Their automobile is all paid off and next year they'll need a new one. They estimate that they might need between $4000 and $5000 for this purpose. Over and above that, their credit needs don't exceed $1000—to be used in their charge accounts to even out the monthly cost of clothing and home necessities.

Currently, then, their capacity for credit exceeds their credit needs. They can easily carry the projected needed debts within their current income and expense structure. However, Charlie and Charlotte are well aware that in three years their oldest child will be starting college. They haven't saved for his tuition and other expenses, and they expect to borrow quite heavily to meet those expenses. Thus, in three years, their credit capacity for debts other than the college expenses will be sharply limited. But their normal credit needs will continue. Their needs, then, will probably exceed their capacity. If they plan properly in advance, they can keep everything in a sensible balance and get through the squeeze. But if they abuse the access to credit that they have and use it for luxuries rather than needs, or even obtain more than is necessary for their needs, they can be in trouble in a few years.

We often have access to more credit than we need because credit is sometimes granted too indiscriminately. When we apply for a loan at a bank, the loan officer scrutinizes our overall financial situation and generally will not permit us to borrow more than we are capable of handling. But when we acquire credit cards and charge accounts, the scrutiny is not as severe. If we succumb to the easy temptation to let the credit card or charge account debts mount up, we can find ourselves in a severe financial crisis.

Each individual and family should, at least every two or three years, visit a lending officer at a financial institution and review their access to credit, needs for credit, and credit capacity for the present and the next three to five years. Only by such a periodic review can credit be put to the most satisfying and economical use. Everyone's situation changes at least slightly over the years, and so too will their credit situation.

Credit Sources

Installment loans for a variety of purposes are available at banks, savings and loan associations, credit unions, and consumer finance (small loan) companies. As a general rule, the cost of borrowing at these various institutions will tend to be highest at the consumer finance companies. Interest rates at credit unions will tend to be equal to, or possibly slightly less than, those at banks and savings and loan associations.

"Dealer financing" is another common source of credit. When you purchase such items as automobiles, furniture, and appliances, the dealer may be able to arrange financing for you. The dealer may extend the loan to you directly, or he may place your loan with one of the financial institutions mentioned above. When a dealer places financing with another institution, it's common for him to get a fee for doing so. Before you accept a dealer financing arrangement, you should compare the cost of such an arrangement with the costs you'd be charged if you dealt directly with a lender of your own choice.

Charge accounts are frequently used as a source of credit. Department stores, for example, will approve "open-end" credit arrangements with credit-worthy customers. This will allow you to charge purchases at the store up to a certain maximum limit. You'll be expected to pay at least a minimum amount each month toward your debt. If you don't pay your charge account debts in full each month, you'll be charged interest for the balance left owing. This interest charge is usually based on the average amount outstanding in your account during the prior month.

Credit cards have become one of the most popular sources of credit. The most common types of credit cards are those offered by banks and savings and loan associations: Mastercard and VISA. These cards are honored extensively throughout the United States and in foreign countries at all types of retail establishments. "Travel and entertainment" cards (American Express, Diners Club, Carte Blanche) are commonly used for business purposes at hotels and restaurants. Airlines and gasoline companies also issue credit cards for use in obtaining their specific products and services.

If a credit card applicant is deemed worthy, he or she will be granted a "line of credit" by the credit card company. That is, a maximum amount will be established that the individual can charge against the card. The card user will then be expected to pay at least a certain monthly minimum amount toward the accumulated debt, and any debt unpaid will be charged interest. As with charge accounts, the interest is usually calculated on the average balance in the account during the prior month. Most issuing institutions will also charge an annual fee for the use of the credit card. Interest costs on credit card usage tend to be higher than interest costs on a direct installment loan made at a bank.

Undisciplined use of credit cards and charge accounts tends to create some of the more serious financial problems that individuals find themselves trapped in. It's much easier to pay the minimum monthly amount than to pay off the entire month's charges. But this will mean that heavy interest costs are added to your debt, and those costs keep mounting over the months (and perhaps even years) that you take to pay off the debt. And the ease of using credit cards—at almost any time or any place you desire—compounds the problem by adding new debts to the existing debt you've already charged against your card. Credit cards can be a convenience, and if you pay off the full month's charges immediately, you might not incur any interest costs at all. But if you take the line of least resistance, paying only the minimum monthly amount, you'll sooner or later find yourself looking at a mountain of debt that can be very difficult to pay off without causing serious disruptions to your overall financial status.

Credit Reporting

The promptness with which you pay your existing debts will affect your ability to borrow in the future. Your performance record is known as your "credit history." Information that makes up your credit history is compiled by a credit bureau. Credit bureaus exist in every community for the purpose of gathering information on the credit performance of individuals in that community. See the discussion in chapter 13 on the Fair Credit Reporting Act. That federal law controls what credit bureaus can and cannot do, and what your rights are with respect to your credit history.

Figure 14-1 illustrates what a typical credit report looks like.

How the Cost of Credit Is Figured

Simple Interest

The fee you pay for the use of someone else's money is called interest. Interest rates are expressed as a percentage of the amount borrowed, and for a given period of time. For example: if you were borrowing $1000 for one year, and the interest rate was 10 percent per year, you would pay a fee of $100 (10 percent of $1000) for the use of the money for a period of one year. If you were borrowing $1000 and the interest rate was expressed as 1 percent per month, you would pay a fee of $10 per month (1 percent of $1000 equals $10), or a total over the year of $120 in interest. In these examples, you would have the use of the entire $1000 for the full period, be it one year or one month. This calculation is what is commonly known as "simple interest."

Loans calculated on a simple interest basis are loans that are generally repayable in one lump sum at a specific time, such as 30, 60, 90, or 120 days hence. Or the loan may be repayable on the demand of the lender. Businesses generally borrow on a simple interest basis, and some individuals may also be able to borrow on that basis. (The expression "prime rate" refers to the simple interest rate that banks charge their most credit-worthy borrowers. Prime rate loans in theory are the safest and lowest risk loans that lenders make. Thus, the prime rate is the lowest interest rate that a lender will offer. Borrowers who do not have the financial strength and credit worthiness of prime rate borrowers will pay a higher rate of interest. As the prime rate moves up and down, as it tends to do regularly, other interest rates usually follow.)

Of more concern to the average individual is the mode of calculating interest on installment and open-end credit. Installment loans are those that are repayable in equal monthly installments; open-end credit refers to debts generated through charge accounts, credit card accounts, and

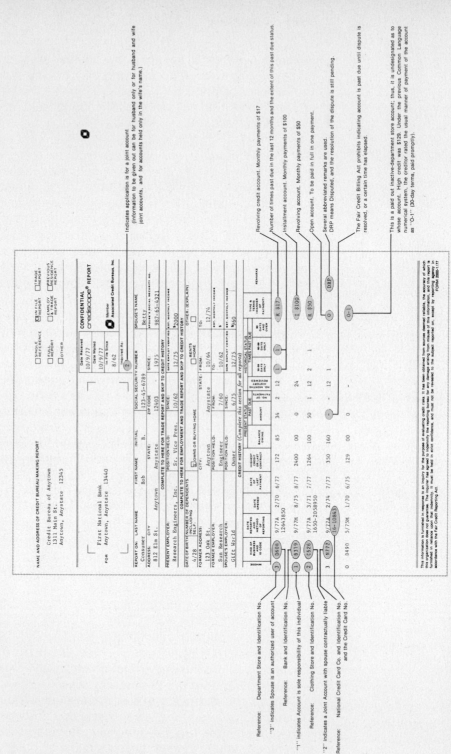

Figure 14-1 Sample Credit Bureau Report.

checking account overdraft accounts. In an open-end account, you will be billed for a minimum monthly payment, based on the total amount of the current balance you owe.

Add-on Interest

Probably the most common way of calculating interest in an installment loan is the "add-on" method. Here's how it works. Say you want to borrow $1000 for 12 months, and the rate is 6 percent add-on per year. Your rental fee for the use of the bank's money will be 6 percent of $1000, or $60. The lender will then add the $60 on to the $1000 worth of principal, making a total of $1060.

That sum, $1060, is divided by 12, giving you 12 equal monthly payments of $88.33 each. Thus, with the add-on loan, you receive the $1000 in cash and, over the course of one year, you will repay $1060. It sounds like simple interest, but it is really quite different. In the simple interest loan, you have the use of the full $1000 for the full one year. Under the installment method, such as add-on, you have the use of the full $1000 only during the first month of the loan, at the end of which you make your first payment. During the second month, therefore, you have the use of only 11/12 of the money, and proportionately less each month until the final month, when you have the use of only 1/12 of the money. In effect, then, you are paying $60 rental but you don't have the use of all the money all the time as you would in the simple interest loan. However, you do have the use of whatever it is you obtained with the money you borrowed—be it a car, an appliance, or whatever.

What if the loan is for more than one year? In the add-on method, the interest rate would be multiplied by the number of years. For example: if you are borrowing $1000 for two years at a 6 percent per year add-on rate, your total interest obligation would be $120 over the full two-year period. (6 percent per year, or $60 per year, times two years equals $120.)

Discount Interest

Another way of figuring interest on installment loans is the "discount" method. A loan that will, like the add-on loan, net the borrower $1,000 for 12 months at a 6 percent discount per year rate works like this: working from a prefigured chart, the lender notes that 6 percent of $1064 equals $63.84. Let's round that off to $64 for ease in figuring. A promissory note is signed for $1064, and the lender "discounts," or subtracts the interest from that, leaving you with $1,000 in cash. The $1064 is divided by 12, giving you 12 equal monthly payments of $88.66. You receive $1000. You repay $1064. Comparing the discount with the add-on method, you can see that the discount results in a slightly higher cost to the borrower and a slightly higher return to the lender. In other words, in the above examples, the 6 percent discount method will cost the borrower $4 more per year than will the 6 percent add-on method.

How Interest Costs Are Expressed: APR

Prior to the passage of the Truth in Lending Law in 1969, a borrower could be very easily confused or misled by the manner in which interest rates were quoted. A borrower shopping around for credit might be quoted from different sources rates of 10 percent on a specific loan request. But is it 10 percent add-on? 10 percent discount? 10 percent simple? 10 percent per year? 10 percent per month? Lenders would not always divulge the full facts and borrowers often didn't inquire. The Truth in Lending Law was designed to put an end to this confusion. Under the Truth in Lending Law, lenders and grantors of credit may *calculate* their interest rate and other finance charges in any way they want (within the limitations of the state's usury laws). But no matter how those rates are calculated, they must be *expressed* in terms of annual percentage rate (APR). The Federal Trade Commission has prepared extensive tables by which any lender can convert add-on or discount rates to APR terms. Table 14-1 shows the conversion of add-on rates for common installment loans to APR, based on the FTC Tables.

For example, a 6 percent per year add-on rate for a 24-month loan is equal to an APR of 11.13. A 6 percent per year add-on rate for 36-month loan is equal to an APR of 11.08.

Under the Truth in Lending Law all lenders are required to quote their rates only in terms of APR, even though many of them may still calculate their rates on an add-on or discount basis.

Variable Rates

Most installment loans are written at a fixed rate of interest. If you sign up for a three-year loan at 14 percent APR, that interest rate will not fluctuate for the full three years of the loan.

When variable-rate mortgage loans for home financing became more commonplace in the early 1980s, some lenders announced plans to offer variable-rate installment loans, such as for car purchases, home improvements, and the like. In such cases, the interest rate could vary, or "float" up and down during the life of the loan. With a floating or variable-rate

Table 14-1

Converting Add-on to APR

Term (Months)	Add-on Rates (in Percentages)			
	$5\frac{1}{2}$	6	$6\frac{1}{2}$	7
12	10.00% APR	10.90% APR	11.79% APR	12.68% APR
18	10.18	11.08	11.98	12.87
24	10.23	11.13	12.12	12.91
30	10.23	11.12	12.00	12.88
36	10.20	11.08	11.96	12.83
48	10.11	10.97	11.83	12.68
60	10.01	10.85	11.68	12.50

installment loan, it would be impossible to know your total interest expense at the time you obtained the loan. It could be more costly than a fixed-rate loan or less costly. You wouldn't know until the end of the term.

Since the life of most installment loans is relatively short (three to five years or less), it's not likely that the floating-rate installment loan will become as common as the variable-rate mortgage loan. But you should be aware of it. For purposes of this chapter, we'll discuss only the fixed-rate type of loans where your true cost of credit can be known in advance.

Open-end Credit

In the typical installment loan, the borrower receives a lump sum of money and pays it back in equal installments. In open-end credit, that's not necessarily the case. If, for example, you have a credit card account and you have not paid all of your charges, you will be carrying an "open-end loan." Open-end means, in effect, that you can, at will, add to that debt by making additional charges, or diminish it by making payments. Because the total balance you owe at any given time can fluctuate almost daily, the APR is normally calculated on the average balance owed throughout the monthly billing period. The APR rate will be expressed on the billing statement each month.

The Truth in Lending Law requires finance charges to be quoted as APR for installment loans and open-end credit. The Truth in Lending Law does not apply to simple interest loans or to loans repayable in four installments or less.

Figuring Your Installment Loan Costs

The APR gives us the means of comparing the *rate* and *costs* of various loan quotations. To determine how the actual *dollar cost* of any given loan is arrived at, it may be necessary to convert the APR back into the original calculating method, most frequently the add-on method.

The following formulas and tables will enable you to figure the actual dollar cost of an installment loan. If you have been quoted an APR rate, use the conversion table (Table 14-1) to find the equivalent add-on rate. (Space does not permit the inclusion of the entire add-on to APR conversions. Your banker can assist you in finding other conversion figures based on current rates being charged.)

Note: where "monthly payments" are referred to, they include principal and interest only. Extra amounts that might be paid for insurance, recording fees, and other charges should be determined from the lender and added in accordingly. Also, many of the figures used in the charts are rounded off for purposes of simplicity; consequently, figures you might obtain from other sources could differ slightly.

Table 14-2, the Interest Cost Finder for Installment Loans, is the basic tool we'll use to find the dollar costs of typical installment loans. Here's how it works:

Table 14-2 | **Interest Cost Finder for Installment Loans**

No. of Months in Loan	"Add-on" Rate—Per Annum (in Percentages)				
	6	$6\frac{1}{2}$	7	$7\frac{1}{2}$	8
12	.06	.065	.07	.075	.08
15	.075	.081	.088	.094	.10
18	.09	.098	.105	.113	.12
21	.105	.114	.122	.132	.14
24	.12	.13	.14	.15	.16
27	.135	.146	.157	.169	.18
30	.15	.162	.175	.187	.20
33	.165	.179	.192	.206	.22
36	.18	.195	.21	.225	.24
39	.195	.211	.227	.244	.26
42	.21	.227	.245	.262	.28
45	.225	.244	.262	.281	.30
48	.24	.26	.28	.30	.32
54	.27	.292	.315	.337	.36
60	.30	.325	.35	.375	.40

1. Determine how much money you want to borrow. Let's say it's $1000. We'll call that M.

2. Assume that you want the money (M) for a 24-month period, and that the going rate is 11.13 APR. The conversion table (Table 14-1) indicates that an 11.13 APR is equal to a 6 percent add-on rate for a 24-month term. Now turn to the Interest Cost Finder chart (Table 14-2) and find the factor on the chart where the 6 percent add-on column meets the 24-month column. The number there is .12, and we'll call that the factor (F).

3. Multiply the factor (.12) by the money ($1000). The answer is $120. That's your interest cost, and we'll call that I.

4. Now add the money (M) and the interest (I). The total is $1120, which is the total debt you'll have to repay. We'll call that D.

5. Divide the debt (D) by the number of months (24) and your answer is $46.67. That is your monthly payment, which we'll call P.

Thus, we have three formulas that can be used to determine the interest cost in dollars, the total debt, and the monthly payment for any loan within the limits of the chart:

Formula One: Interest (I) = Money (M) × Factor from chart (F).

Formula Two: Total debt (D) = Money (M) + Interest (I).

Formula Three: Monthly payment (P) = Debt (D) ÷ Number of months.

Here's another example using these formulas. How much will the monthly payments be on a loan of $2000 for 30 months at an APR of 12.88?

Using the add-on to APR conversion table, we find that on a 30-month loan a 12.88 APR is equal to a 7 percent add-on rate. Using the Interest Cost Finder table, we find that a 7 percent add-on rate on a 30-month loan gives us a factor (F) of .175.

Now we turn to Formula One: $I = M \times F$
$I = 2000 \times .175$
$I = \$350$. That's your interest cost.

Formula Two: $D = M + I$
$D = \$2000 + \$350$
$D = \$2350$. That's your total debt that you must repay.

Formula Three: $P = D \div$ Number of months
$P = \$2350 \div 30$
$P = \$78.33$. That's your monthly payment for interest and principal.

Additional Financing Costs

Many lenders may offer or suggest that you obtain credit insurance as a part of your installment loan transaction. There are two common types of credit insurance: life and health. If you obtain credit life insurance as a part of the transaction, the insurance will pay off any remaining balance on the loan should the borrower die before the loan is paid off. The borrower's survivors need not, therefore, pay the remaining balance on the loan.

If you obtain health insurance as a part of your loan transaction, the insurance company will make your payments for you in the event you become disabled for an extended period of time due to poor health or an accident. Credit health policies may differ from lender to lender regarding the initial waiting period involved before the insurance takes effect. In other words, if the waiting period is 15 days, then you must be disabled for more than 15 days before the insurance will take effect. In this case, if you are disabled for, say, 25 days altogether, the insurance will protect you for 10 days out of that month. They will, in effect, make roughly one-third of your monthly payment for you.

If your loan does include charges for life or health insurance, the lender, in effect, is lending you the amount of the premium for that insurance in advance. The amount of such premiums should, therefore, be added to the "M" before you start using the above formulas. In other words, if in the earlier example the life-insurance premium is $30, that amount should be added to the money you need, bringing the total of M to $2030. Your interest costs would then increase accordingly, which would change the results in the other formulas slightly.

Paying Off an Installment Loan Ahead of Schedule

Loan officers frequently have to resolve a perplexing dispute that arises when customers wish to pay off their installment loans ahead of schedule. Here's a typical situation. Charlie had borrowed $5000 for a 36-month term. The interest cost for the three years was $900, which, when added to the $5000, gave Charlie a total debt of $5900, and monthly payments of $164. Eighteen months have elapsed, and Charlie has accumulated some unexpected funds and wishes to use them to pay off his installment loan. Against the original debt of $5900, Charlie has, during these first 18 months, made payments totaling $2952. That would reduce his debt to $2948.

Charlie then figures that since he's halfway through the loan, he should pay half of the interest that he originally committed to, or $450. Subtracting the $450 from the $2948, Charlie calculates that he owes the bank $2498 to wipe the loan off the books. But the bank figures differently. They figure that Charlie is entitled to get back only 25.7 percent of the original $900, or $231. In other words, of the $900 Charlie was originally committed to pay, the bank is charging him 74.3 percent of that amount, or $669. In effect, then, $231 of his original interest commitment would be "rebated" to him. This would make his payoff figure $2717. Charlie is enraged to learn that he owes the bank $219 more than he had expected to. What happened to that $219? The Rule of 78s happened.

The Rule of 78s

It was noted earlier that in the typical installment loan the borrower has the use of the full original amount borrowed only during the first month of the loan. Then, as the borrower makes periodic payments, he or she has the use of progressively less and less of the original amount of the loan. That's the basis for the so-called Rule of 78s which is used to determine how each month's payment is broken down into interest and principal.

In an installment loan, the borrower commits himself to pay a certain amount of interest over the term of the loan. If he pays off the full balance of the loan before the full term elapses, the borrower is entitled to get back a portion of his interest cost, plus a portion of any other rebatable charges such as insurance. But the borrower does not get back an amount directly proportional to the amount of time the loan has run. As in Charlie's case, if you have a 36-month loan, and you pay it off at the end of 18 months, your interest rebate does not equal one-half of the original amount of interest, even though one-half of the loan has elapsed.

Here's an example of the rule of 78s in action.

On a 12-month loan, the borrower has the use of all the money during the first month. She then makes her first payment. During the second month she has the use of only 11/12 of the money. For the third month it becomes 10/12. And so on until the last month when she has the use of only 1/12 of the money.

Because the borrower has the use of more money in the earlier months, she has to pay proportionately more for it. Actually, the borrower has the use of 12 times more money in the first month than in the last month.

In the Rule of 78s, the sum of the number of months in a 12-month loan equals 78 (1 + 2 + 3 + 4 . . . to 12 = 78). During the first month

Credit and Borrowing

of a 12-month loan, you're charged with 12/78 of the total interest. During the second month of a 12-month loan you're charged with an additional 11/78 of the total interest. During the third month of a 12-month loan, you're charged with an additional 10/78 of the total interest. The last month you'd be charged with 1/78. The total of the 12 fractions is 78/78, or 100 percent of the total interest.

If, therefore, you paid off a 12-month loan at the end of six months, you'd be charged for 57/78 of the total interest owed (12 + 11 + 10 + 9 + 8 + 7 = 57). Your rebate would be the remaining 21/78, or about 27 percent of the original interest charged to you. If the original interest had been $60, you'd thus be rebated about $16.

For loans of other than 12 months' duration, the key number becomes the sum total of the number of months. For example: you've signed up for a 24-month loan, and you come into a windfall that will allow you to pay it off at the end of six months. The sum of the numbers one through 24 equals 300. During the first month of the loan you are charged for 24/300 of the total interest. During the second month, you are charged for 23/300 of the total interest. During the third month you are charged for 22/300 of the total interest—and so on until the sixth month has elapsed. During the first six months of the 24-month loan you will thus be charged for a total of 129/300 of the original amount of interest (24 + 23 + 22 + 21 + 20 + 19 = 129). That fraction converts to 43 percent. In other words, you are being charged for 43 percent of the original interest amount, which means you'd get a rebate of 57 percent of the original full interest if you pay the loan off at the end of six months.

Table 14-3 converts the fractions into percentages to enable you to figure the rebate on loans ranging from 12 to 60 months at six-month intervals. For loans set to run for other terms than those shown in the table, your banker can give you a precise rebate breakdown. A good working knowledge of installment loans and how rebates are figured can be most important in determining when, how, and why you should consolidate loans, refinance them, or pay them off. Here's how you can figure the rebates on any loans included in the table.

1. Determine the total interest you have been charged for the loan.
2. Decide at what point you want to figure the rebate—say, after nine months of a 24-month loan. Locate the factor on the rebate chart where the column "loan has run—9 months" meets the row "original term of loan—24 months." That factor is 40 percent, which is the percentage of your interest charge that you will get back or that will be credited to you if you pay off a 24-month loan after nine months have run.
3. Multiply your original interest cost by the rebate percentage to get the actual dollars to be rebated.

4. From your original total debt, subtract the amount of payments made so far. Then subtract the dollar amount of your rebate. The final total is your payoff figure.

Figuring Payoff

Here's an example using this formula. You had originally borrowed $2000 repayable in 30 months. The interest cost was $250, making your total debt $2250. Monthly payments are $75. You want to pay off the balance due after nine months. What will your rebate and your payoff amount be? (*Note:* The rebate schedule is the same for all interest rates.)

1. The percent of your total original interest that will be rebated to you is 49.7 percent. That's where the 30-month column (original term of loan) meets the nine-month row (number of months loan has run).
2. Your rebate is $124.24 (49.7 percent of $250).
3. Your payoff figure is $1450.75. From the original total debt of $2250 you subtract $675, representing the nine payments you made at $75 each. From that sum you further subtract the $124.25 that is your rebate. In other words, your payoff figure is your *original debt* less *payments made to date* less *rebate due you.*

Other rebatable charges, such as insurance premiums, are figured on the same basis. Thus, if you had a life-insurance premium charge on the above loan of $30, you would receive a rebate of that charge of $14.91 (49.7 percent of $30).

Does it make sense to pay off an installment loan early? In the above example, the borrower presumably found himself with a windfall of $1450. Even though his loan was only 30 percent paid off (nine months out of 30), more than half the total interest he was committed to pay has been used up. If he uses the $1450 to pay off the loan, he'll save about $125, representing the remaining interest he's obliged to pay. If, though, he puts that $1450 into a savings account, it will earn roughly $150 over the next 24 months.

On the other hand, if he pays off the loan early and puts the $75 per month into a savings account—instead of paying it on the loan—he'll build up a comparable-sized nest egg at the end of 21 months. Much of the decision depends on individual human nature. It might be easier to put away the lump sum in a savings account and thus realize a sizable nest egg at the end of the period than to deposit $75 each month into the savings account.

Refinancing an Installment Loan

Having the money to pay off an installment loan is a pleasant dilemma rarely faced. Much more frequent is the desire to refinance the loan, perhaps to reduce the monthly payments. The Rule of 78s applies in this situation just as it would in an early payoff. Following the above example,

Table 14-3 | **Rebate Schedule from the Rule of 78s (Showing Percentage of Finance Charge to Be Rebated)**

No. of Months Loan Has Run	Original Term of Loan							
	12 Months	18 Months	24 Months	30 Months	36 Months	42 Months	48 Months	60 Months
1	84.6	89.5	92.0	93.5	94.6	95.3	95.9	96.7
2	70.5	79.5	84.3	87.3	89.3	90.8	91.9	93.5
3	57.7	70.2	77.0	81.3	84.2	86.4	88.0	90.3
4	46.1	61.4	70.0	75.5	79.3	82.1	84.2	87.2
5	35.9	53.2	63.3	69.9	74.5	77.8	80.4	84.1
6	26.9	45.6	57.0	64.5	69.8	73.7	76.8	81.1
7	19.2	38.6	51.0	59.3	65.3	69.8	73.2	78.2
8	12.8	32.2	45.3	54.4	61.0	65.9	69.7	75.3
9	7.7	26.3	40.0	49.7	56.8	62.1	66.3	72.5
10	3.8	21.0	35.0	45.2	52.7	58.5	63.0	69.7
11	1.3	16.4	30.3	40.9	48.8	54.9	59.8	66.9
12	—0—	12.3	26.0	36.8	45.0	51.5	56.6	64.3
13		8.8	22.0	32.9	41.4	48.2	53.6	61.6
14		5.8	18.3	29.2	38.0	45.0	50.6	59.1
15		3.5	15.0	25.8	34.7	41.9	47.7	56.6
16		1.7	12.0	22.6	31.5	38.9	44.9	54.1
17		.58	9.3	19.6	28.5	36.0	42.2	51.7
18		—0—	7.0	16.8	25.7	33.2	39.5	49.3
19			5.0	14.2	23.0	30.6	37.0	47.0
20			3.3	11.8	20.4	28.0	34.5	44.8
21			2.0	9.7	18.0	25.6	32.1	42.6
22			1.0	7.7	15.8	23.3	29.8	40.5
23			.33	6.0	13.7	21.0	27.6	38.4
24			—0—	4.5	11.7	18.9	25.5	36.4
25				3.2	9.9	16.9	23.5	34.4
26				2.1	8.3	15.1	21.5	32.5
27				1.3	6.8	13.3	19.6	30.7
28				.65	5.4	11.6	17.9	28.8
29				.22	4.2	10.1	16.2	27.1
30				—0—	3.1	8.6	14.5	25.4

an individual might wish to refinance the original $2000 loan after nine of the 30 months had elapsed. As the formula indicates, he would have a balance owing of $1450. Assuming that he wished to refinance that balance for a new 36-month term at an 11.08 APR (6 percent add-on), the earlier tables indicate that he would have to oblige himself for an additional $261 in interest. The $261 added to the $1450 remaining pay-off figure would give a new debt of $1711 and monthly payments (interest and principal) of $47.53. He thus reduces his monthly payments by almost $30 but in so doing incurs added interest expense and an ongoing

Table 14-3 | **Rebate Schedule from the Rule of 78s (Showing Percentage of Finance Charge to Be Rebated)** *(Continued)*

No. of Months Loan Has Run	Original Term of Loan							
	12 Months	18 Months	24 Months	30 Months	36 Months	42 Months	48 Months	60 Months
31					2.2	7.3	13.0	23.8
32					1.5	6.1	11.6	22.2
33					.90	5.0	10.2	20.7
34					.45	4.0	8.9	19.2
35					.15	3.1	7.7	17.8
36					—0—	2.3	6.6	16.4
37						1.7	5.6	15.1
38						1.1	4.7	13.8
39						.66	3.8	12.6
40						.33	3.1	11.5
41						.11	2.4	10.4
42						—0—	1.8	9.3
43							1.3	8.4
44							.85	7.4
45							.51	6.6
46							.26	5.7
47							.09	5.0
48							—0—	4.3
49								3.6
50								3.0
51								2.5
52								2.0
53								1.5
54								1.1
55								.82
56								.55
57								.33
58								.16
59								.05
60								—0—

debt for 15 additional months. Whether or not it's wise to do this would depend on personal circumstances, and refinancing of a debt in such a manner should be done only after counseling with a loan officer. To extend the debt could create a bottleneck years down the road when other credit needs arise.

Increasing an Installment Loan

As with refinancing, individuals will frequently want to add a new sum of money to their credit line. For example, in the above situation assume that the borrower wished to acquire another $1000. He did not wish to take out a separate new loan, but wanted to add the $1000 to his existing installment loan to run for a period of 36 months. His payoff balance on the original loan is $1450. To that the lender adds the $1000 new money and then must add the interest onto that. Assuming an 11.08 APR (6 percent add-on), the additional interest would be $441. This would give him a total debt of $2891 with monthly payments of $80.30. For roughly $5 more than he is now paying each month, he has another $1000 cash in hand. But, as with the refinancing, he has stretched his payment schedule out for an additional 36 months—15 months longer than he was otherwise obliged to make payments for. And, as with refinancing, adding on to debt in this manner should be done only after adequate consultation.

Shopping for Loans

Interest Rates

A slight difference in the interest rate on an installment loan can have a considerable impact on the overall cost for the term of the loan. Table 14-4 illustrates the effect of varying interest rates on a sampling of different loans. You can work out similar charts for loans of different amounts and terms by using the Interest Cost Finder formula referred to earlier.

Table 14-4

Comparing Interest Costs

APR (Percent)	Add-on (Percent)	Total Interest	Total to Be Repaid	Monthly Payments
on a Loan of $1000 for 12 Months				
10.00	$5\frac{1}{2}$	$ 55	$1055	$ 87.92
10.90	6	60	1060	88.33
11.79	$6\frac{1}{2}$	65	1065	88.75
12.68	7	70	1070	89.33
on a loan of $2000 for 24 months				
10.23	$5\frac{1}{2}$	$220	$2220	$ 92.50
11.13	6	240	2240	93.33
12.12	$6\frac{1}{2}$	260	2260	94.16
12.91	7	280	2280	95.00
on a loan of $3000 for 36 months				
10.20	$5\frac{1}{2}$	$495	$3495	$ 97.08
11.08	6	540	3540	98.33
11.96	$6\frac{1}{2}$	585	3585	99.58
12.83	7	630	3630	100.83

Table 14-5 | **Effect of Down Payment on Loan Costs on a $3000 Purchase, at 11.08 Percent APR (6 Percent Add-on), for a 36-Month Loan**

Down Payment	Amount of Loan	Total Interest Cost	Total to Be Repaid	Monthly Payment
0	$3000	$540	$3540	$98.33
$ 300	2700	484	3184	88.44
500	2500	450	2950	81.94
800	2200	396	2596	72.11
1000	2000	360	2360	65.55
1200	1800	326	2126	59.05
1500	1500	270	1770	49.16

The Effect of Down Payment Size

To the extent that you borrow to buy anything, the cost of borrowing can add as much as 10 to 30 percent to the cost of the item. The less you can borrow, the less interest you'll be paying, and the lower your monthly payment and overall obligation.

The question may arise as to whether or not one is better off financing the whole amount of a purchase, and putting the available down payment dollars into a savings account where it can earn interest. Generally, when you're starting from scratch with an installment loan, before the Rule of 78s comes into play, you probably wouldn't do as well in going for the larger financing. Because a savings account pays less than what you must pay a lender for a loan, you'd probably be better off applying your available cash toward the purchase price and reducing the amount of the loan accordingly.

Table 14-5 illustrates the dollar effect of varying down payments on a specific loan. You can work out similar charts for loans of different amounts by using the Interest Cost Finder formula.

How Long Should Your Loan Run?

The amount of time, or term, of an installment loan can affect overall costs considerably. The longer the term, the lower the monthly payments and the higher the interest costs. Do the lower payments make up for the higher interest costs? Table 14-6 illustrates the effect of different terms on loans of varying sizes.

There are other basic guidelines helpful in determining how long an installment loan should run. Generally speaking, the life of the loan should not exceed the expected life use of the product or service you're borrowing for. Also, when one borrows for a recurring need, the loan should be paid off before the need occurs again. Examples of recurring loans include those for the payment of taxes, vacations, winter expenses, or automobiles.

Table 14-6 | The Effect of Different Terms on Loan Costs*

Amount Borrowed	Term of Loan (Months)	Total Interest Cost	Total to Be Repaid	Monthly Payment
$1000	12	$ 60	$1060	$ 88.33
1000	18	90	1090	60.55
1000	24	120	1120	46.67
1000	30	150	1150	38.33
1000	36	180	1180	32.77
2000	12	240	2240	93.33
2000	18	300	2300	76.67
2000	24	360	2360	65.55
2000	30	420	2420	57.62
2000	36	480	2480	51.67
3000	12	360	3360	140.00
3000	18	540	3540	98.33
3000	24	630	3630	86.42
3000	30	720	3720	77.50
3000	36	900	3900	65.00

*All loans are calculated at 6 percent add-on per year; APR will vary according to length of loan.

For example, say you borrow $600 on June 1 for a summer vacation. With a 12-month loan, you'll be all paid up by the next summer. But with an 18-month loan, you'll be paying for this year's vacation well into next fall. If you were to borrow again in June of next year for that year's vacation, you'd have a few hundred dollars of this year's loan still unpaid if you had taken the 18-month plan. If you then combined the remaining old balance and the new loan for yet another 18-month loan, you could still be paying for part of this year's vacation three years from now. This is an example of "pyramiding," and it can be a dangerous practice.

Car loans should be geared to the time you expect to retain the car. If you trade every two years, for example, your loan should be paid off within that period. Running the loan longer than the life of the car makes the borrower prone to the risk of pyramiding. In recent years, four-year car loans (and in isolated cases, five-year car loans) have begun to appear, partly because of the desire to keep payments lower while the cost of buying and operating a car goes higher. Unless certain that the car will be retained for at least the life of that loan, one should be very aware of the pyramiding problem that can arise by obtaining a new car before paying off the old one.

Major household items, such as large appliances, might not need replacing for a decade or more. But they should not be financed for as long as they will last. These debts should be eliminated as quickly as your budget will allow in order to make room for other borrowing needs and to keep your interest expenses down. Most lenders won't exceed a few years for such loans anyway, but avoid the temptation of becoming involved in longer plans that might allow for lower monthly payments. The interest cost will be that much higher, and you could still be paying off a loan when you'd rather have that credit capacity available for some other purpose.

One-shot loans, such as those for special events (weddings, etc.), special trips, and other nonrecurring personal needs should also be paid up as quickly as your budget will allow. The needs won't recur, but taking such a loan for too long a term can clutter up your future borrowing capacity and have you paying more interest than may be wise.

Home improvements, particularly major additions such as patios, pool, extra rooms, and so on, can get a bit tricky. These items can easily run into many thousands of dollars, and common installment financing plans run to five years, occasionally longer. For the most part, these improvements become a part of the house—you won't take them with you when you move. You may recapture all or a better part of the cost when you sell the house.

When these improvements are integral to the house, you might find it better to add the cost on to your mortgage if you can. Check with your mortgage lender to evaluate cost and feasibility. For example, a $4000 home improvement loan for five years could entail monthly payments of roughly $83. If you added that same amount to a mortgage that had 20 years left to run, the monthly payments would be about $35. If you expect to be selling the house within about ten years or less, it could be better to add the home improvement costs to your mortgage.

Twenty Do's and Don'ts When You Shop for a Loan

Two very important aspects of an individual financial program are gaining access to the *credit* you'll need for the various purposes you have in mind; and obtaining the *guidance* to help you use your credit wisely. Both of these important assets can be acquired through lending officers at your local financial institutions. It's worth the time involved to interview a number of these individuals to find one with whom you seem to be able to communicate openly and constructively. A loan officer can be an important ally in helping you achieve your financial goals, short term and long term. But a word of warning: loan officers are often transferred to other departments and one day you may find your friendly favorite helper no longer at the desk. It's always wise, therefore, to make an effort to know more than one loan officer so that there can be some continuity on a personal level between yourself and the institution.

The following list of basic suggestions can help you communicate better with your lender and make the best use of the credit available.

1. Do all of your shopping and homework beforehand. Whenever possible, know exactly what you're going to borrow for, how the money will be used, and what the total needs will be.

   Borrowers often ask a loan officer, "How much can I borrow to buy a new car?" or "How much can I borrow to buy a new house?" Unless the loan officer has a detailed familiarity with your individual credit history, it can be difficult to answer such questions.

   When you finally make your application, remember that the loan officer can serve you best when your specific needs are clearly stated. A loan application with question marks on it simply cannot be processed as readily as a completed one.

2. Make sure all your other credit accounts are up to date before you apply for credit. If necessary, check with each creditor and with your local credit bureau. The Federal Fair Credit Reporting Act permits you to see your credit file (there may be a modest fee involved), and it's wise to review your file every few years to make certain it contains no erroneous items. If there are errors, the law stipulates how they can be corrected. If you have credit accounts that are not up to date, it would be wise to update them before you make your application. A credit history showing late accounts may not kill your chances of getting a loan, but it could well cause delays and aggravation.

3. Get an idea of the rates charged by various lenders. This can be done quickly, discreetly, and, if you wish, anonymously. Be certain that any quotes you receive are expressed in terms of APR (Annual Percentage Rate) and determine what the total dollar charges are for interest and any other fees the lender may impose.

   In comparing interest rates, remember that the interest rate isn't the only item you're shopping for. You might be able to obtain a more attractive interest rate if you make a larger down payment on the purchase in question, and you may have to inquire whether or not this is possible. You also might get a more attractive interest rate if you are a customer of the institution in other departments. Service and convenience must also be considered.

   Should you finance directly through an institution or through a dealer that offers access to financing? Financing through the dealer can often be a time-saving convenience and rates may be comparable to those of local institutions. But it may be more important to have the personal contact directly with a local institution. The institution may be able to help you in a number of other ways, whereas the dealer-financed situation could place you in the hands of an out-of-town institution or a local institution where you're nothing more than a number on a computer. The personal relationship is important, and you may lose that with dealer financing.

4. Before you make your loan application, prepare a list of all your other debts, including the name of each creditor, purpose of the loan, original amount borrowed, current amount owed, and the monthly payment. This will make the loan officer's job much easier, and your application simpler to process. Divulge all pertinent credit information, even if you think it may not look good. The lender will probably discover it anyway, and if you haven't mentioned difficult accounts, the lender is liable to wonder why. Also, when you've compiled the list of all your debts and payments, double-check that this new debt you're seeking can be properly taken care of within your current and future budget.

5. Inquire in advance whether the lender has any specific requirements or taboos. Some lenders have strict requirements regarding the borrower's years on the job, period of residence in the community, and minimum down payment for specific purchases.

6. Be sure to tell the loan officer clearly and specifically just what the money is for. The more concise you are, the more the officer will be able to advise you if it appears you might be going overboard on a certain debt, since loan officers listen to dozens of requests each day.

7. Make sure your requested time for loan repayment does not exceed the use period of whatever you're borrowing for. If you let the lender know you've considered this, it will demonstrate your prudence and could enhance your application and relationship with the lender.

8. Be prepared to discuss your budget in detail. The loan officer wants assurance that there will be money available to pay off the loan, and if he or she doesn't see room in your current budget for the repayment, your request might be declined—and perhaps wisely so. If you plan to trim other expenses to make room for this debt, or if you are anticipating a higher income in the future, discuss these factors with the loan officer.

9. Bring your spouse, if you have one, to complete the application and sign all the necessary papers. Granted, under the Federal Equal Credit Opportunity Laws it may no longer be necessary for both spouses to sign credit agreements. That may satisfy many people, but traditional prudence still dictates that debt is a family obligation—morally if not legally—and both partners should have a full and complete understanding of their involvements.

10. Don't be embarrassed to seek the loan officer's specific advice on related financial matters. It's part of the job, and he or she might be able to discover and solve other money problems in ways you aren't aware of.

11. Don't try to get a better interest rate by telling a loan officer that you can do better elsewhere. Chances are you'll be told to go ahead and do so. And if you can do better elsewhere, you might as well. It doesn't hurt to ask if rates are flexible, but petty bickering will very likely gain nothing and may well lose a potential ally—the loan officer.

12. Don't caution the loan officer not to check a certain credit reference. If there is a problem or a dispute with one of your other creditors, clear it up in advance. If you raise suspicions in the loan officer's mind, he or she will undoubtedly take steps to find out what it's all about.

13. Don't act as if you're doing the lender a favor by coming to him. And don't make it appear that the lender is doing you one by making you a loan. This is a business deal and should be treated as such by both sides.

14. Don't be disturbed if the loan officer asks you to do your other business such as your savings or checking account, with his or her institution. This is part of the job. Very often, a loan applicant may be upset by such suggestions and this can destroy an otherwise good relationship. A simple "I'll be happy to consider it" should suffice if you don't want to change at the moment.

15. Don't fret if the loan officer starts "selling" life or health insurance for your loan. It's very common, and the cost is not unreasonable. If, after you understand their program, you still don't want it, merely decline politely. The loan officer should know that a "hard sell" is not becoming, nor is it liable to win friends or influence people.

16. Don't expect the loan officer to tell you whether your intentions regarding your borrowing are wise. If you aren't sure of the wisdom of your loan, maybe you shouldn't be asking for it.

17. Don't be surprised, however, if the loan officer does volunteer to question your wisdom. You may be absolutely certain in your own mind, but you may have overlooked something. The loan officer is in the business of evaluating personal financial decisions, and his professional knowledge might enable him to correct or amplify your thinking. The officer might be able to suggest other alternatives, some of which might provide a better solution than the one you're seeking.

18. Don't wait until the last minute to apply for a loan. Anticipate your needs far enough in advance to take care of all the details. If other matters hinge on whether or not you get the loan, keep the other parties informed of your progress. Careful and thoughtful planning in this regard can prevent serious problems.

19. Don't demand an answer to your application within a certain time. You have a right to have your papers processed promptly, assuming that everything is in order. The lender will make every effort to do

so. But delays, such as receiving an incomplete report from the credit bureau, can happen.

Often, too, an application may have to be considered by the loan committee. The loan officer isn't "passing the buck" when he or she refers an application to the loan committee. Your request may be for more than he has authority to approve, or he may just want to get other opinions on a puzzling point in the application. The committee can often be very helpful simply by giving the borrower the benefit of all its best collective thinking.

When you make your application, the officer should be able to give you a fairly good idea of how long it will take to process. Perhaps he can speed it up a bit for you if circumstances warrant. But if you give him a deadline—an "or else"—you might antagonize him.

20. Don't balk if the loan officer asks you for a co-maker or collateral to support a given loan request. He's trying to help you get your loan, but lending policies may require security. You may not want to comply, but rather than argue about it (which won't help matters), ask for an explanation.

There is often room for compromise. A request for collateral or a co-maker doesn't necessarily mean your credit isn't good. There just might not be enough of it—due to your age, job tenure, and so on. Remember—the loan officer doesn't have to ask you for the extra security. He or she can turn you down flat, but may not want to. It doesn't hurt to inquire if the request for collateral or a co-signer can be altered, so that the co-signer is obliged for only a part of the loan, or the loan is only partly collateralized.

Credit Abuses

Pyramiding

As noted earlier, pyramiding occurs when a loan for a recurring purpose has not been paid off by the time the purpose recurs. Let's look at a specific example.

Otto has been in the habit of trading his cars every three years. He's always taken three-year car loans, so that the loan has been paid off each time he buys a new car. This year a fancy new model catches his eye and he's determined to buy it. He'll need $5000 over and above his trade-in on his old car, but he can only afford payments of roughly $130 per month. His banker tells him that the interest on a three-year loan for $5000 would be $900, making the total debt $5900, and the monthly payments approximately $164. The dealer tells Otto that they can arrange financing for a four-year term and that the payments would only be $129 per month. (The interest would be $1200, making the total debt $6200.)

Otto prudently realizes that if he's financing the car for four years he should keep the car for that time. Even though that's contrary to his habit, he vows he will do this.

Three years later: Otto has dutifully made 36 monthly payments of $129 each, reducing his original balance from $6200 to $1556. An advertisement lures him into the automobile dealer's showroom, where he promptly falls in love with a brand new model. He realizes he shouldn't trade for at least another year, until the loan is paid off, but habit and desire get the best of him.

After allowing for the rebate due on his existing loan, his payoff figure is $1447. (A rebate would be $79: 6.6 percent of the original $1200 interest obligation—see the rebate tables.) Naturally, inflation has boosted the price of the cars, and in order to acquire the new model, Otto will need $6000 over and above his trade-in. The $6000, added to the payoff figure on the previous loan, means that Otto will have to borrow $7477. In order to afford the car, he'll have to obligate himself for another four-year loan, which means added interest of $1795, bringing the total debt to $9272—48 monthly payments of $193 each.

Three years later: Otto has made his payments of $193 for 36 months, reducing his original balance of $9272 to $2324. Another advertisement almost lures him into the auto dealer's showroom again, but first Otto does some arithmetic.

Over the previous six years, he has paid $2916 in interest for his loans ($1200 for the first loan plus $1795 for the second one, less $79 rebate on the first loan when he refinanced). In addition to having paid $2916 in interest, he still has a debt of $2324.

Otto calculates the arithmetic if he had stayed with his three-year financing plans. His interest cost for the first three-year loan would have been $900, and the loan would have been paid up at the end of three years. If he had bought the next new car at the end of three years, he would have needed a loan of $6,000, which would have meant an interest cost of $1080, giving him a total debt of $7080, with monthly payments of $197 (compared with the $193 he was paying for the second four-year car loan). After the second 36 months, he would have been all paid off. By using the two three-year plans, Otto's total interest expense would have been $1980, and he'd have no debt remaining. As it is, his interest expense has been almost $1000 greater and he still has a debt remaining of $2324.

Table 14-7 illustrates the effect of Otto's pyramiding.

Where does Otto now stand after six years of unwitting pyramiding? If he wants to buy a new-model car (whose price has gone up to $7,000 over and above the trade-in), and wishes to revert to the more prudent three-year financing, he'll have a total debt to finance of $10,863. This would be made up of the $7000 needed for the new car plus $2206 to pay off the old debt (the $2,324 debt remaining less a rebate of $118), plus an added interest cost of $1657. The payments for a three-year loan at this point will be $302!

Table 14-7   Effects of Installment Loan Pyramiding

	Amount Borrowed	Interest Cost	Total Debt	Monthly Payments	No. of Months	"Payoff" After 36 Months
Otto's first loan	$5,000	$1,200	$ 6,200	$129	48	$1,477
Second loan, 36 months later	7,477	1,795	9,272	193	48	2,206
Status after six years, if Otto borrowed $7000 for a 36-month term	9,206	1,657	10,863	302	36	0

If Otto had not been pyramiding and wanted to buy the $7000 car at the end of six years, his interest cost would be $1260 for a 36-month loan and the monthly payments would be $229.

As Otto's case illustrates, pyramiding can be a costly mistake, whether it originates innocently or as a result of lack of financial discipline. Otto took undue advantage of his access to credit, and exceeded both needs and capacity to borrow.

The pyramiding trap is equally as dangerous, if not more so, regarding credit cards and charge accounts. For example, an individual runs up $50 in gasoline bills for her car during a month. She charges them on a credit card. At the end of the month the bill comes in and rather than pay the full $50, which isn't necessary if she chooses to let the credit line run, she decides to send in only the minimum payment, say $10.

The same thing happens the next month: $50 worth of gas bills and a $10 payment. And so on throughout the year. Unless the individual comes to her senses, she could be paying for her January gas in December and even well into the following year. The interest costs continue to mount, adding between 15 and 25 percent per year to the cost of the goods so purchased.

The simple way to avoid pyramiding is to remember that an installment loan or an open-end credit account should be eliminated before the need to borrow for the same purpose occurs again.

Ballooning

Which is more appealing: a 12-month loan for $1000 with monthly payments of $88.33, or the same loan with monthly payments of only $60? The temptation is to take the loan with the smaller monthly payments, but obviously there's a catch—with the smaller monthly payments there will be one very large payment at the end of the loan, for the loan is to run for only 12 months. In this particular case, after making payments for 11 months at $60 each, the borrower will still owe roughly $400 in the twelfth month. This is what's known as a "balloon" payment, and it can be dangerous. If the borrower isn't equipped to meet the large payment, it may be necessary to refinance that payment and incur additional interest costs. Although the Truth in Lending Law requires lenders to disclose the Annual Percentage Rate and the total costs involved in making the loan, there may not be adequate disclosure regarding the size of the monthly payments. Any borrower should make certain that he or she knows whether or not there are balloon payments at the end of the loan. Unless there are compelling circumstances for a balloon payment program, prudence generally dictates sticking to the typical repayment budget with equal monthly payments.

Oversecuring

If you were borrowing $1000 to pay for your summer vacation, it would not seem wise to have to put up your car, your house, your bank account, and all of your other assets as security for that loan. Reputable lenders would certainly not require such collateral. But it can happen that some lenders may seek more security than reasonable for certain loans. This security may include a general assignment of your wages and your personal property. If a borrower does pledge those assets to obtain a loan, the legal aspect is that the lender can take action to recover those assets should the loan become delinquent. The individual borrower must determine when collateral is required for a loan and that that collateral is reasonable, proper, and not excessive. If it is excessive, the borrower is putting assets in jeopardy, which could create severe future problems. The borrower should determine exactly what collateral is being given to the lender and if more is being required than seems necessary, the borrower would do well to shop around at other institutions.

Loan Sharks

Despite all the consumer-protection laws and publicized warnings, there will always be loan sharks as long as there are people willing to pay exorbitant fees for borrowed funds. Loan sharks operate outside the limits of the law. Their interest rates are generally far above what the state usury laws allow and their collection techniques have been well publicized. If anyone becomes involved with a loan shark, he or she can expect to bear what could be severe consequences. Before entering such a situation, an individual should consult a banker or attorney to determine the legal methods that may alleviate his or her debt problems.

Loan Consolidation

The appeal is almost irresistible: "Why suffer along with all those big monthly payments when you can consolidate all your debts into one loan with a much smaller monthly payment?"

If a family or an individual has accumulated too much debt, loan consolidation seems a logical and convenient way out of the crisis. It's a line of least resistance too often taken by borrowers not aware of the potential pitfalls. Poorly planned, or impulsively embarked on, a consolidation loan

Table 14-8 | **Loan Consolidation: Charlie and Charlotte's Debts**

Loan	Current Balance	Monthly Payment	Months to Run	"Payoff" Figure Now
Car	$1180	$ 98.33	12	$1117
Home improvement	930	51.67	18	860
Personal	363	60.55	6	352
Total		$210.55		$2330

can cause more ultimate troubles than the original loans did. Sound, prudent planning might provide other, more suitable alternatives. Using the following example of a loan consolidation program, and consulting the interest finders and rebate formulas, you can plan any consolidation and judge its value.

Charlie and Charlotte have the following loans:

1. A car loan, whose original total amount was $3540, including interest of $540. The loan has run for 24 months, and has 12 months to go. Monthly payments are $98.33.

2. A home improvement loan that originally totaled $2480, of which interest was $480. The loan has already run for 30 months and has 18 months to run. The monthly payments are $51.67.

3. A personal loan, originally totaling $1090 of which interest was $90. Twelve months of the loan have already expired with six months still to run. Monthly payments are $60.55.

Table 14-8 illustrates Charlie and Charlotte's debts and how much they would need to pay them all off.

Charlie and Charlotte need roughly $2330 to pay off their existing debts. At an interest rate of 11.08 APR (6 percent add-on), they can obtain a loan of that amount for three years, which would entail an added $419 in interest, giving them a total new debt of $2749. Their 36 monthly payments would be $76.30 each, compared with the $210.55 they're now paying.

It seems like an easy way out of what to them has become a serious jam. But is it wise? Is it worth it? If they wait just six more months, the personal loan will be all paid off, reducing their monthly payments to $150. In 12 months the car loan will be paid off, reducing their payments to $51.67. And in 18 months the home improvement loan will be paid, eliminating their monthly payments altogether.

The consolidation loan will have cost them an additional $419 in interest and will require payments of $76.36 for 36 more months. During the next 36 months Charlie and Charlotte will in all likelihood have new reasons to acquire debt. Rather than consolidating their loans, they might be far better off in the long run if they could simply tighten their belts and continue with their current debt load. It will be lightened considerably in just six months.

If proper loan planning is done in the beginning, the need for a consolidation loan might never occur. If this need does occur, careful communications with a lending officer are necessary if a sensible consolidation plan is to be arrived at.

Cures for Overindebtedness

As the above example indicates, Charlie and Charlotte might be candidates for a severe case of overindebtedness. The problem, if not promptly treated, can lead to serious impairment of one's credit history, and can complicate—if not prevent—the ability to obtain credit for many months or possibly years, or it might force the borrower into obtaining credit through sources that specialize in higher risk situations, and charge higher interest rates accordingly.

The first symptom of overindebtedness is late payments. Not only will late payment entail late charges, which can be as much as 5 percent of the amount of the payment (the law varies from state to state), but it can also result in a bad rating on your credit history.

Borrowers who *anticipate* that they might be running into a delinquency problem should act *before* the actual delinquency occurs. Borrowers in such straits should visit *in person,* not by phone or by mail, with the creditors in question and explain the overall circumstances. It might be possible to arrange a different payment date that would be more convenient; or to remake the loan on favorable terms; or get a temporary reduction in payments; and it might even be possible to have late charges waived if your reason for delinquency is acceptable to the creditor.

It's up to the borrower to keep the lender informed of the circumstances. If the lender doesn't know what the borrower's problems are, he could rightfully assume that the borrower is being willfully delinquent. The borrower is subject to the terms of a legal contract—the promissory note—and it's the borrower's job to persuade the lender to amend the terms to alleviate the problem.

Frequently, lenders will attempt to communicate with the delinquent borrowers to determine the causes for the problem and when and how it might be resolved. It's always better for the borrower to take the initiative and contact the lender before the lender has to resort to these steps, for by that time the lender may consider that the account is in a "collection" status, which will appear, in all likelihood, on the borrower's credit history.

If the borrower has not complied with the terms of the loan agreement, the lender may deem that the borrower is in default. In that case the lender can commence whatever legal remedies have been reserved to him in the loan agreement. If collateral has been pledged for the loan, the lender can take steps to recover the collateral and sell it to pay off the loan. If a co-signer is involved in the loan, the lender can look to the co-signer for payment. In some instances the lender may be able to attach, or garnish, the borrower's wages.

Even if a debt situation has decayed to the point of default, it is still valuable for a borrower to make every effort to work out a satisfactory arrangement with the lender. If such an arrangement can be worked out and the borrower can perform accordingly, the situation might be alleviated. But, often, by the time a loan account falls into the default category, there is such ill will between the parties that a borrower makes no attempt to solve the problem.

Debt-Counseling Services

In many communities, lending institutions cooperate to create a debt-counseling service to assist people in financial trouble. In many communities this is known as the Consumer Credit Counseling Agency. See your banker for more details on such services available in your community. The agency usually contacts your creditors and gets them to hold off on their collection procedures while you make an effort to reorganize your financial matters. You'll have to make a show of good faith by making some regular periodic payments. If the counselors have been successful, those payments will be smaller than what your normal payments would have been.

(Be on guard against some commercial firms who offer debt-reduction services. Federal and state consumer-protection agencies have reported numerous cases of such firms charging excessively for those services rendered; in many cases the firms simply disappear with the customers' money and no debt reduction is accomplished.)

If a debt-counseling service of good repute is not available to you or not capable of helping you, the next step might be to visit with an attorney who can arrange for an Assignment for the Benefit of Creditors. This is similar to the services offered by the debt-counseling firms in that it tries to convince creditors to accept a smaller monthly payment until the full debt is paid off.

Bankruptcy

The ultimate way out of overindebtedness is bankruptcy. If you come to this ultimate move, you should seek the aid of an attorney. Bankruptcy is a last resort for solving debt problems, and whatever the reasons for declaring it, bankruptcy can remain on your credit history for as long as ten years.

Many lenders will attempt to rehabilitate a bankrupt family or individual, particularly if the reasons for bankruptcy were beyond their control. But an ex-bankrupt can still find it difficult to obtain the kind of credit needed for his or her lifestyle. Indeed, bankruptcy often requires individuals to seriously reduce the quality of their life for an extended period of time.

Bankruptcy laws are federal laws, though state laws may apply in determining the property that can be exempted from the bankruptcy proceedings. There are two basic bankruptcy proceedings for individuals:

Chapter 13, otherwise known as the "wage-earner plan," and Chapter 7, often referred to as "straight bankruptcy."

Chapter 13

Under Chapter 13, the debtor, under the supervision of a referee and the federal bankruptcy court, works out a plan for the repayment of outstanding debts. In effect, this wage-earner plan keeps creditors from getting at your wages and your property while giving you time to work out a timely payment of outstanding debts. (A similar plan for businesses is known as Chapter 11, wherein the businessman attempts to reorganize his affairs to satisfy his debts while his creditors are kept at bay.)

A Chapter 13 proceeding generally carries less stigma than does a Chapter 7 proceeding.

Chapter 7

This is known as straight bankruptcy. In this proceeding, your debts are discharged, or eliminated altogether. Bankruptcy laws were revised in late 1979 to make it easier for individuals to declare Chapter 7 and to protect more of the debtor's property from the creditors' claims. Under Chapter 7 declaration, certain of the debtor's property can be exempted from creditors' claims. A debtor can choose whether to take the exemption allowed under federal law or exemptions that might be allowed under his state laws. For example, federal law allows a bankrupt couple to exempt up to $15,000 worth of equity in their home plus additional exemptions for personal property, clothing, and automobile. The Chapter 7 bankruptcy can be filed only once every six years. (A debtor can file a new Chapter 13 proceeding once he has completed payments based on a prior Chapter 13 proceeding.)

Sometimes personal catastrophe requires an individual to undergo bankruptcy proceeding. Sometimes, however, it is nothing more than the undisciplined use of credit that leaves an individual with little choice but to declare bankruptcy. The public at large has little sympathy for individuals who spend their way into bankruptcy. Know before you proceed that the spectre of bankruptcy will haunt you for years to come.

Discipline

Making wise use of your ability to borrow can enhance your life. Imprudence can result in financial and emotional disaster. The lure of easy money—through charge accounts, credit cards, and other "cash-in-a-flash" enticements—can become addictive. Younger individuals, less experienced at the complexities of handling a budget, can more easily be trapped in the credit bind. It's at the earliest stages of using credit that a firm sense of discipline must be imposed on oneself. Only you can determine for yourself the amount of debt you're comfortably able to carry, considering your other financial needs and desires. But there is one unshakable rule that will apply to your use of credit: For every dollar you borrow (or charge) you will be adding 15 to 25 cents to the cost of your credit purchase. It can be difficult enough to make ends meet without adding such a heavy cost load to your already weighty burdens.

Personal Action Checklist
Comparing Loan Costs

It *can* pay to shop around for the best interest rate available on loans—such as car loans, home improvement loans, and any other personal or business borrowing needs. Loan sources include, not only banks and savings associations, but also credit unions, dealers, and some insurance companies. Employers, relatives, and friends might also be sources. This checklist will aid you in comparing the pertinent terms of most common personal loans.

	Lender A	Lender B	Lender C
☐ Down payment required?	_____	_____	_____
☐ Monthly repayment programs available?	_____	_____	_____
☐ Collateral required?	_____	_____	_____
☐ Co-signer required? And if so, when, and under what circumstances, can co-signer be released from the obligation?	_____	_____	_____
☐ Annual Percentage Rate (APR)?	_____	_____	_____
☐ Monthly payments required?	_____	_____	_____
☐ Total interest cost for life of loan?	_____	_____	_____
☐ Late charges, if any?	_____	_____	_____
☐ Will a better APR be offered if you maintain other accounts with the lender? (You'll probably have to ask, but it can be worth it.)	_____	_____	_____
☐ Cost of credit life insurance (if you desire it)?	_____	_____	_____
☐ Cost of credit health insurance (if you desire it)?	_____	_____	_____
☐ If you pay off the loan early, are rebates of interest based on the Rule of 78s, or on some other formula? Ask and compare.	_____	_____	_____
☐ For credit cards and charge accounts, what is the APR? Is it based on average prior monthly balance, or some other formula? Ask and compare.	_____	_____	_____

Consumer Beware
A Captive Audience

The furniture store advertisement made Fran and Pat very happy: "EASY CREDIT! NO MONEY DOWN! PAST CREDIT PROBLEMS ARE NO PROBLEM FOR US!"

Fran and Pat wanted to set up housekeeping, and neither of them ever having had any credit before, they feared that they wouldn't be able to buy a stick of furniture on their slender budget.

The Easy Credit store took excellent care of them, including setting up a two-year financing plan to pay for their purchases. They knew the interest rate was exceptionally high, but at least they were able to furnish their apartment as they had wanted to.

They made every payment on time for two years. Then, wanting some additional furniture, they approached a local bank seeking the money. Their hope was to get out from under the excessive interest costs that the furniture store had charged them.

They proudly gave the furniture store as a credit reference. But on checking their file at the local credit bureau, the bank could find no reference to the furniture store loan. The bank turned down Fran and Pat's request. Dejected, they felt they had no choice but to return to the original furniture store and accept their high interest financing for their additional purchases.

But the loan officer at the bank had smelled something fishy, and he did some investigation. He discovered that the furniture store made a practice of never divulging the good payment records of customers. In that way they succeeded in building a captive audience of borrowers: people who were unwary enough to seek credit elsewhere, who felt that the store and the loan company affiliated with it were their only source of borrowing.

The matter was called to the attention of the Federal Trade Commission, and their threat of investigation put a stop to this unfair, but not necessarily illegal, practice. Pat and Fran got their loan from the bank.

"Easy credit" is a myth. If it's that easy to get, it will be very hard to repay: the interest cost will be inordinately high, and collection procedures very harsh if payments aren't made promptly.

Part Five | Making Your Money Grow

15 | Making Your Money Grow: An Overview

A question often asked of financial advisors is: "How should I put my money to work?"

Answers that astute advisors should give are: "What do you want your money to do for you? Do you want it to give you a temporary surge of excitement by putting it to work in a gambling, or risky, situation? Do you want it to grow steadily and safely for you over a number of years? How much risk do you want to take? How long can you leave it alone until you need it?" And so on.

Until one's investment objectives are clearly known, it's difficult to establish sensible investment (or speculative) activities. This chapter will introduce you to the concepts that must be understood if you are to construct a meaningful program of making your money grow. It will give you an understanding of:

☐ How different investment opportunities can be compared.
☐ How the growth of your money can be affected by taxes.
☐ How to acquire specific investment information and counsel.

Further, it will give you a basic foundation to enable you to better understand the more specific investment techniques discussed in subsequent chapters.

Today Dollars and Tomorrow Dollars

One of the most essential parts of anyone's financial program involves putting away dollars that you don't need today so that they can be available to you in the future. Some of the many different ways we can go about accumulating tomorrow dollars will involve a relatively high degree of risk, others, a relatively low degree. Some ways might offer a relatively comfortable measure of protection against inflation while others may grant little or none. Some ways may seem simple, others complicated; some require luck, others prudence.

The challenge is to find the right program that will enable you to accumulate the needed amount of future dollars safely, comfortably, and in such a manner that the accumulation program does not interfere with your ability to pursue your current needs and desires.

The relative importance of your own personal future needs and desires will be a major factor in shaping what accumulation techniques you choose. In the opening of this book we discussed the importance of establishing future goals, and each individual was urged to set specific targets subject to the inevitable changes that will occur as we mature, and as our needs and objectives change. Now let's examine the specific vehicles you can utilize to help reach your specific destinations.

Automatic Accumulating

In shaping our long-range accumulation program we must remember that some tomorrow dollars are being created automatically as a result of other transactions we may be making. For example, a homeowner makes monthly payments on a mortgage. A portion of those payments is applied toward interest on the debt, and a portion is applied to reducing the debt. Eventually, when the house is sold or refinanced, that portion of the payments that had been applied to the debt may be recaptured in cash. This recaptured money is commonly referred to as "equity." It's a form of automatic accumulating.

Another form of automatic accumulating can occur with life insurance. Here a breadwinner is putting away today dollars to be used by the survivors after his or her death. In ordinary life-insurance policies, the policy will also build certain values that allow the policy owner to either cash in the policy at a later date or borrow against it or convert the values into other forms of insurance. The insured is building these future values as an automatic part of paying the life-insurance premium.

Deductions from our paycheck represent another form of accumulation of future dollars. Social Security taxes are automatically deducted from the paycheck of everyone covered by the system and in many cases pension and profit-sharing plan contributions are also deducted. Thus, we are joining with our employers and our government to create a pool of future dollars. We may have little or no control over how these tomorrow dollars are being put to use, but we do have some reasonable assurances as to how much will be available to us at the preestablished time when we're entitled to retrieve them.

Active Accumulating

Active accumulating of future dollars can take two broad forms. First, we can lend our dollars to another person or institution with the understanding that they will pay us interest for the use of our money. This type of accumulating is referred to as "fixed income investing," and a savings account is perhaps the most familiar form of accumulating dollars within this category.

A savings account is, in effect, a loan to a financial institution, accompanied by an agreement stating that the institution will pay us "rental" for the use of our money—interest.

We may also make "loans" to governments and corporations. A U.S. savings bond (series EE bond) is an example of one of the many kinds of loans that we can make to the federal government. Loans made to cities and states are referred to as municipal bonds. Loans made to corporations are referred to as corporate bonds.

These forms of accumulating future dollars normally carry a high degree of assurance that we will get all of our money back plus the agreed-upon interest at the agreed-upon time. When we entrust our money, we receive a binding legal contract from the debtor that promises to pay us what we are due, regardless of whether or not the debtor operates efficiently or profitably. If the debtor should fail, the interest and principal due us might be in jeopardy. Although there have been remote instances of corporations and municipalities defaulting on their debts, defaults by the federal government have never happened, nor have insured accounts in federally insured banks and savings institutions ever lost money as a result of the failure of the institution.

When we lend or entrust our money to others in these forms, we're minimizing both the risk of loss and the chance of gain, and in return we're getting a fairly assured program that will take us to our appointed destination on time.

The other broad form of active accumulating of future dollars is to buy something that we hope will generate income, and also possibly increase in value while we own it. As owners, either in part or in whole, we have a stake in another entity—an equity.

We buy a portion of ownership in a company, hoping that the company will be profitable and that it will distribute a portion of its profits to its owners. We also hope that the company will prosper and that the value of our ownership interest will increase, allowing us to sell it at a profit in the future.

We may invest in real estate, hoping to operate that property so that it shows a profit and further hoping that the property will increase in value and allow us to reap a profit when we sell. Similarly, we may invest in our own business interest where, in addition to earnings and profits, we may also be able to pay ourselves a living. When we invest our money in a piece of ownership of another entity, there may be many outside forces that can shape the destiny of our future dollars.

The distinction between lending or entrusting our money to reliable debtors on one hand and buying something with our dollars is critical. When we lend, we have a binding legal contract that promises us the return of our principal. When we buy with our dollars, we are owners and we have to take our chances in the marketplace and with the forces beyond our control that we can get back our money at any time we wish. This distinction should always be remembered in establishing any kind of accumulation program.

The following are additional factors to bear in mind when establishing our long-range tomorrow dollars program. They include the risk/reward rule, liquidity, yield, pledge value, hedge value, and income tax implications.

Investment Criteria

Safety: The Risk/Reward Rule

This rule is simple and has virtually no known exceptions. It's this: The bigger the possible reward, the higher the risk. The more conservative individual may look at this axiom a bit differently: The safer my money, the less return I'll have to be satisfied with. And yet a third, and perhaps more elemental viewpoint: In planning a program of savings and investments (commonly known as a portfolio), much depends on whether you'd rather eat well or sleep well.

Liquidity

Liquidity refers to how quickly and conveniently you can retrieve your money and at what cost, if any. Often a price may have to be paid for liquidity.

For example, in a regular savings account, you can get all of your money plus accrued interest immediately, simply by making the request in the proper fashion to the institution. But with a savings certificate—in which you have placed your money with the institution for an agreed upon minimum amount of time—you might have to forfeit a portion of your interest and principal if you want to get your money out right away. But generally the certificate will pay you a higher rate of interest than the regular passbook savings account.

In other words, the passbook savings account is more liquid than the savings certificate, but at a price. The passbook account offers a lower rate of return in exchange for the ability to get your cash out that much more readily.

The need for liquidity varies from portfolio to portfolio. If you're putting the money away for the long term and are confident that you won't need it for an extended period of time, you can afford to give up liquidity in favor of higher return. On the other hand, if you think you'll need the money sooner, you may feel better forgoing the higher return for the chance of being able to get at your money in a hurry. The amount of liquidity that you need, or are willing to forgo, depends on the nature and timing of your own individual goals.

Yield

Generally, yield refers to how much money your savings or investments will earn for you. For example, if a savings account is paying 6 percent interest per year and you put $100 into the account, you will receive $6 during the first year that your $100 is in the account. Your yield may be expressed as "6 percent" or as "$6 per $100 per year." The term "yield" is often used interchangeably with "return" and "return on investment."

In making any form of investment, you should determine not only what yield you can expect immediately, but whether or not that yield will continue, for how long, and what degree of fluctuation it might be subject to.

If you put your money into long-term corporate or government or municipal bonds, you are assured of a constant yield for the amount of time you own the bonds, assuming that the debtor continues to pay the interest promised. The actual face value of the bond may fluctuate up and down during the time that you own it, and you may sell the bond for more or less than what you originally paid for it. But the actual income you receive for the term of your ownership will remain constant. If you buy a government bond for $1000 that promises to pay 8 percent per year, you will receive $80 for each year that you own the bond, regardless of whether the face value of the bond increases or decreases, which it might.

Passbook savings accounts might be somewhat subject to minor fluctuations in yield over the years.

If you buy a share of ownership in a company—stock—and that company distributes a portion of its profits to its owners—dividends—your yield, or return, is expressed as the amount of dividend dollars you receive. If you pay $100 for a stock and during the first year of your ownership the company pays you $5 in dividends, your yield can be expressed as 5 percent or $5 per $100 per year, based on your purchase price.

Many companies have long histories of dividend payment records, and many also increase their dividends from time to time. Even more companies have erratic dividend payment histories, while some companies pay none at all. If a company runs into hard times, a dividend payment record may suddenly halt. On the other hand, if a company suddenly has a surge in business, it may start to pay dividends unexpectedly. Investing in the stock market, then, offers a broad range of yield possibilities.

An investment in real estate also offers a wide range of yield potential. If you own a property and it's leased for a long term to respectable tenants, and those tenants are responsible for paying escalating costs such as property taxes and utilities, your yield (total income less total expenses) could remain quite constant for long periods of time. On the other hand, if you have less reliable tenants and you as the owner are required to pay those escalating operating costs, your yield could be far less constant and far less satisfactory.

Following the risk/reward rule, you'll find that the more respectable tenants will bargain for and receive a lower rental rate than the less reliable tenants. Although your rental income may therefore be higher from the less respectable tenants, the chances of it ceasing or being eroded by vacancies and added costs are that much greater.

Gain and Loss

It's important to keep a clear distinction between yield and gain or loss. For example, you buy stock for $100 and during the first year of ownership it pays a dividend of $5. But at the end of the year you sell the stock for $120. You have realized a gain of $20 on your investment, plus a dividend of $5, for a total overall increase in your fund of $25. Would this be considered a yield of 25 percent? Technically no. It is indeed an overall gain of 25 percent, but it comes from two different sources: the dividend yield of 5 percent and the increase in value of 20 percent.

Similarly, if you sold the stock at year end for $80, you still would have had a dividend yield of 5 percent, but you would have suffered a loss of $20, or 20 percent of your original investment.

Generally, in embarking on an investment program, the expected yield is a relatively known quantity—at least with savings accounts, bonds, and stocks with good dividend payment history. The aspect of possible gain or loss, particularly with stocks, is a relatively unknown factor, if not totally unknown. In building toward a specific future goal, a relatively predictable yield can be a far more useful aspect than the relatively unknown gain or loss. The prudent investor should structure his or her program accordingly.

Pledge Value

You may, from time to time, have an unexpected need for money: to take advantage of a once-in-a-lifetime bargain; to pay pressing bills; to help out someone in need; to pay for expensive repairs. You may not have the cash on hand, and it thus becomes necessary for you to borrow the needed money. The quickest, and sometimes the cheapest, way to borrow money is to pledge your investments as collateral for such a loan. The "pledge value" of any investment is a measurement of what percent of the value of the investment you can borrow, how quickly you can get the money, and how much will it cost you.

Savings accounts—both passbook and certificate—have the highest level of pledge value among the common types of investments. Most depositors can usually borrow virtually all of the money in their savings account at favorable rates, without any delay. This can be an excellent device for obtaining short-term funds in a hurry and may be preferable to actually invading the savings account or cashing in the certificate.

Because stocks are prone to fluctuation in value, they have a somewhat lower pledge value than savings accounts. The amount you can borrow from your banker against any given stockholdings will depend on the quality of the stock itself. You can also borrow from your broker—on a "margin" account. In either case of course you have to surrender the certificate as collateral for the loan.

Good-quality real estate has a high pledge value, but because of the nature of the documentation required in borrowing against real estate, the process can be costly and time consuming. This, in effect, detracts from real estate's otherwise good pledge value.

Hedge Value

Investors must be concerned over the ability of their investments to withstand the effects of inflation. The common expression is "hedging against inflation." This aspect of investing, then, may be called the "hedge value" of an investment.

Historically, it has been claimed that the stock market always provided a good hedge against inflation. In theory, as prices rise, so do profits for a company, and so thus do their stock prices. However, in recent years that historical theory has been thrown into much doubt as the stock market—on the whole—has often failed to respond to the upward pressures of rising prices. But whether the stock market is a good hedge against inflation or not, the problem is that there are thousands of stocks from which to choose. The average investor might find that selecting the right one for inflation protection is more of a challenge than he or she is prepared for.

Savings accounts have long been accused of having no protection against inflation because the principal amount invested doesn't grow except for periodic additions of interest to the account. Although it is true that the principal does not increase on its own, there is some protection against inflation because interest rates paid on savings plans will tend to rise in line with rising costs. By the same token, interest rates paid on savings plans may also decrease in the face of decreasing costs.

Real estate has long been considered a good hedge against inflation, but again this depends on the nature of the property, the management of the property, and the trend in the community in which the property is located.

In short, there is no form of investment with a guaranteed hedge against inflation. But there is one important caution to note regarding the psychology of inflation. This has been particularly true since the early 1970s, when double-digit inflation became commonplace.

In recent years thousands of small investors let themselves be convinced and conned by wily salespeople that inflation was destroying their life savings. Invariably, the salesman would offer a "better deal." But the better deal was frequently a very risky, if not downright fraudulent, situation in which the frightened investors lost all or a portion of their life savings. In other words, fear of inflation caused them to lose much more money than they might have lost through inflation itself. This kind of thinking is still very prevalent today.

Tax Implications

Tax regulations are constantly changing. All investors—large and small—must pay constant attention to the tax implications of the various types of investments available to them. Tax implications divide investments into three broad categories:

☐ *Taxable investments.* These are investments in which, except as noted below, all of your income will be taxed in the year in which it is earned.

☐ *Tax-deferred or tax-sheltered investments.* With these investments, the payment of taxes on income earned can be delayed until some future time.

☐ *Tax-exempt investments.* All or a substantial portion of your income from these investments is tax free.

Taxable Investments

Income you earn from savings plans and from corporate and U.S. Government bonds is subject to taxation. So are dividends earned from investments in stocks. But to encourage investment in these areas, Congress has been making some exceptions in recent years. For example, on tax returns filed in 1982 (for 1981 income) couples filing a joint tax return were entitled to exclude up to $400 of interest or dividends from their taxable income. Check to determine what exclusions from this type of income are allowable in tax years after 1982. (With respect to U.S. Government bonds, interest earned on them is exempt from any state income taxes you might be subject to.)

With respect to stocks and other capital assets, if you sell them at a profit after holding them for the appropriate amount of time (12 months), that gain is considered a "long-term capital gain" and the profit is subject to taxation at capital gains rates. Capital gains rates are lower than ordinary rates so although such income is taxable, it is not fully taxable in the sense of being taxed at ordinary income rates.

Tax-deferred, or Tax-sheltered, Investments

The best example of a tax-deferred investment is the Individual Retirement Account, or IRA, which allows workers to invest money each year for their retirement. The amount they invest in the plan each year is a form of tax deduction, thus reducing their immediate tax obligation to the government. Further, the earnings on these funds are not taxed each year. However, when the money is withdrawn, which cannot be before age 59½ (without penalty), the taxes on the withdrawn money must then be paid. The presumption is that when money is withdrawn on retirement, the individual investor will be in a much lower tax bracket than at the time the contributions were made. Thus, there can be a considerable tax break. Moreover, all of the money contributed into the fund has been allowed to work without being subject to taxation, which can again make a substantial difference in an overall nest egg over the long term. The Keogh plan, for self-employed individuals, is another example of a tax-deferred investment. IRA and Keogh plans will be discussed in more detail in chapter 16.

In a tax-sheltered investment, some of the income received is offset by some of the expenses incurred in maintaining the investment. The effect is to reduce the amount of income that is subject to taxes. However, when a tax-sheltered investment is later sold, some taxes will become payable. The most common form of tax-sheltered investment is real estate. Because buildings physically depreciate, tax laws allow real estate investors to deduct a "depreciation" factor from their income. This depreciation factor does not represent an actual loss in value on the building, but rather a paper loss. Indeed, the building may be increasing in value even while the owner is deducting depreciation on his tax return. The depreciation factor offsets income that the building may be earning, thus reducing the amount of taxable income that the owner has to pay. When the building is sold, though, the tax payable by the investor on any profit will be affected by the amount of depreciation he has deducted in earlier years. (Depreciation does not apply with respect to one's residence.) This aspect of investing is discussed in more detail in chapter 18.

Tax-exempt Investments

When local governments, such as cities and states, borrow money, investors do not have to pay federal income taxes on the interest they receive. These investments are known as municipal bonds and the income the investor receives is referred to as "tax exempt." That income is simply not reported on your tax return and no taxes are paid on it. There are two exceptions: If you invest in municipal bonds and sell the bonds at a profit, the profit itself is taxable, even though the interest you earned while you owned them is not taxable. Also, if you invest in municipal bonds issued by a government unit outside of your state of residence, the interest earned will be subject to any state income taxes you might have to pay. For example, if a California investor buys a municipal bond issued by the city of San Diego, the interest he earns will be exempt from both federal and California income taxes. But if that same investor buys a municipal bond issued by the city of Houston, the interest he earns will be exempt only from federal taxes. He will have to pay California income taxes on that interest. Tax-exempt investments, including all-savers certificates will be discussed in greater detail in chapter 16.

Investigation

"Investigate before you invest" is one of the essential maxims to remember when putting your money to work. An equally important statement all too frequently overlooked is "investigate before you un-invest." Homework is a necessity before you place your funds in any kind of situation, and there's no form of investment for which homework can't and shouldn't be done. But the homework doesn't stop once you've made the investment.

Knowing when to get out of a situation is as important as knowing when to get in. "But," many say, "I don't want to become a slave to my investment. I don't want to have to worry about it. I just want to be able to put it away and have it grow and deliver what I'm seeking without the worry or the constant checking."

All well and good—but beware that such a course may result in a diminished nest egg compared to what it might have been. The decision is up to each individual; you don't have to become a fanatic. But you're planting a tree and you want it to bear the most and the best possible fruit. This involves care, nurturing, and an awareness of all steps you can take to improve your crop. In short, your ability to prosper will depend largely on your willingness to work. And your need to work will be minimized by your initial efforts in understanding how the various forms of investments function and what they can and cannot do for you.

Sources of Information

There is more literature published every year on investments than on any other subject with the possible exceptions of dieting and sex. It's impossible to keep up with the outpouring: hundreds of books, thousands of magazines and newspaper articles, tens of thousands of reports and analyses published by stock brokerage firms and investment advisory firms. Where is one to begin? Following is a selection of useful literature and courses that can assist you in learning more about your investment opportunities.

Books

Books run the gamut from the "doom and gloom" variety to the "how to get rich overnight" variety. The former tend to preach that the end of the world is rapidly approaching and that unorthodox investments are called for to cope with the calamity. The latter type tend to lure investors toward highly speculative types of portfolios. Between these two extremes there are a number of worthwhile books published each year on basic money management and investment programs. Sample them at your local library or bookstore and read one or two a year to give yourself some diversity in views and tactics. The problem, in general, with books—including this one—is that there is a considerable amount of time between the writing and the publication and many of the ideas presented can be outdated before the book is in the stores.

One book that is updated annually is *Dun and Bradstreet's Guide to Your Investments,* published by Lippincott and Crowell. It covers a wide range of investment opportunities and is as up to date as publication schedules can allow in the book industry. Specific investment suggestions offered in the Dun and Bradstreet book should be checked for current facts with your banker, stockbroker, or other investment adviser.

Magazines

Newsweek and *U.S. News and World Report,* both weeklies, contain good current information and informative columns on finance and investing. *Forbes* is published every other week and is directed to an audience of businessmen and investors. It is most highly recommended as a source of specific information and general guidelines on a wide variety of investment techniques. *Financial World,* a weekly, contains in-depth articles on specific stock opportunities and much statistical information. *Fortune* (every two weeks) and *Business Week* (weekly) are both examples of excellent financial journalism, but are directed more to the businessman than to the relatively inexperienced investor. If any of these periodicals prompt you to be interested in a specific investment situation, check with your stockbroker for more detailed information. Also worthwhile are *Money* and *Changing Times.*

Newspapers

The *Wall Street Journal,* read daily and thoroughly, is the best of all possible tools to keep you alert not only to specific investments but to the state of the economy as well. The business pages of your local newspaper are a necessary supplement to the *Journal.*

Seminars and Courses

Local community colleges, universities, and financial firms often conduct programs geared to the investor's needs. Such programs will normally be announced in the catalogues published by the schools and in newspaper articles or advertisements. Many seminars conducted by private firms and financial institutions are geared to obtaining clientele or to selling specific investments to attendees. Many of these programs can be extremely expensive. If so, try to find a book that covers the subject just as well for a fraction of the price. If it is the type of program where clientele will be solicited, prepare yourself as you go in for a sales pitch and act accordingly.

Sources of Investable Funds

All sources of investable funds must be accurately evaluated. You have little or no control over the inactive investment activities that you're now engaged in, such as building the equity in your home, your life-insurance policies, your pension or profit-sharing programs, or your Social Security. But these funds can become actively investable at some future time, and you must, in line with your goals, determine how much will be available and when. These sources may not materialize for many years, but it's senseless to play guessing games about their amounts. Reasonable estimates, periodically revised, will be needed to help assure that you reach your goals. Check periodically with your employer and with your local Social Security Office to determine what you can reasonably expect from those respective sources.

Discretionary Income

The major source for active investment funds is your discretionary income—the difference between what you take home in earnings and what you currently spend for all your present needs. "But," say the majority, "I'm just living hand to mouth as it is. By the time everything is deducted from my paycheck and I keep up with rising costs and allow some modest improvements in my lifestyle, there's barely a penny left to put away."

Or, as is also said: "There's too much month left at the end of the money." True enough, and in many cases there's little you can do about it. However, a close examination of your current living style, in comparison with your *desired future* living style, is in order. Investable funds can be provided by creating disposable income. And disposable income can be created by cutting down on current expenditures or by increasing current income. Simply translated, this means additional work and/or belt-tightening. Whether you wish to do either depends on how closely your *existing* investment program meets your targeted goals. If your current program is adequate, there may be no need to either increase your income or tighten your belt. If, though, the development of your nest egg will not be adequate to meet your targeted goals, you may have to consider one of these two steps to expand your discretionary income. The alternative, of course, is to cut down on future goals. But that, perhaps, is the most dangerous course of all.

Consider that the most critical goal for most individuals and families is to have enough income to live in the desired style when work ceases and retirement begins. If, when that time rolls around, you don't have what you had hoped you might have, *you don't get to do it over*. You're locked in. Again, it's up to each individual: how much, if anything, are you willing to sacrifice in your current lifestyle in order to assure a future lifestyle? When you can approximate an answer to that question, you'll be more readily able to determine what adjustments you want to make in your current discretionary income.

Inheritances and Gifts

Other sources of investable funds can include inheritances and gifts. This is a touchy area that must be handled delicately, but nevertheless must be faced. A great many people will receive inheritances from parents and other family members, and the amount may be token or may be considerable. It may occur soon, or it may not occur for many, many years. The amount ultimately received can have an important bearing on your own overall plans. If you know or can determine what can reasonably be expected in the way of an inheritance, you may want to adjust your existing investment program or your current lifestyle accordingly.

What We'll Explore

We'll now examine the most common types of investments available: what they are, how they work, and their respective features regarding yield, liquidity, safety, hedge value, pledge value, taxation, and investigation.

There are no specific rights or wrongs in structuring an investment portfolio. Each must be tailored to the needs, both present and future, of a particular individual or family. And it must be structured with the thought that those needs can and probably will change over the years. Thus, although the discussions are presented from a relatively conservative viewpoint, there's ample room for disagreement.

Personal Action Checklist
Sources of Your
"Tomorrow Dollars"

Where will the money come from to allow you to meet your future goals? This is an exercise to help make you more aware of the potential sources of your "tomorrow dollars." Assume that you plan to retire in five years (or that there is some other defined goal that you hope to accomplish at that time). Evaluate the following possible sources of money, and see how close you come to meeting your estimated needs. If there is a short-fall, how will you make up the difference?

	Lump sum available	Monthly income, if lump sum is invested at 10 percent annual interest
☐ Pension proceeds	_____	_____
☐ Profit-sharing plan	_____	_____
☐ Social Security	_____	_____
☐ Equity in your home (after setting aside enough to provide satisfactory living quarters)	_____	_____
☐ Cash or loan value in your life-insurance policies	_____	_____
☐ Existing investment programs (savings, bonds, etc.)	_____	_____
☐ Existing speculative programs (stocks, metals, commodities, etc.)	_____	_____
☐ Inheritances realistically expected	_____	_____
☐ Discretionary income (the excess of current income over current expenses, which could be put to work to create a source of "tomorrow dollars"	_____	_____
☐ Miscellaneous: collections, works of art, and so on, that could be sold	_____	_____

Consumer Beware
No "Do-overs"

There's no greater shock than, on nearing retirement, learning that you won't have enough money to live in the manner you'd hoped for. At that age, and in those circumstances, you don't get a do-over. You can't go back 10 or 20 or 30 years and start again to build a nest egg. This interview illustrates the plight:

"When I finished school I bounced around from job to job for many years. I was out for fun, and the real future seemed too far off to worry about. Then, in my early 30s, I found a job that looked good for the long run. There was no pension plan, but the pay was good and I was able to live like I wanted to. I still didn't look beyond the following week. I just assumed that I'd always have a good income, and that Social Security would take care of me after that.

"Some years later the company offered an investment plan to the employees. If we put in a certain amount each month, they'd add a chunk of their own. They advised us to take advantage of it, to build for our future, but I couldn't see cutting back on my lifestyle by salting away money for 10 or 20 years.

"Did I mess up! Retirement is just a few years away now, and I don't have a penny to show for all the years I put in with the company. I just checked with my Social Security office and found that my monthly check will barely cover the rent on my apartment. What I had thought would be adequate has been chopped into little pieces by inflation.

"I really don't know what I'm going to do. The thought of going on welfare just makes me sick. I guess I'll just have to trim my sails and keep on working till they drag me out.

"When I was younger I used to like a song that had a line in it: 'Let's forget about tomorrow for tomorrow never comes.' Back then, that song suited me just fine. But oh how I hate the thought of it today."

Nobody—no employer, no government, no mystical "they"—will take better care of you than you can yourself. If you don't take care of yourself, don't expect that anyone else will do it for you.

16 | Making Your Money Grow: The Money Market

Prior to the mid 1960s, the average person had very few safe choices for investing his or her money. The most common methods were passbook savings accounts and government savings bonds. Today, however, the choices are many and varied. New techniques are constantly emerging. Confusion reigns. But you need *not* be perplexed by all of the different offerings. You *can* distinguish clearly what each of them offers you. And you *can* choose which is best for you. That's the purpose of this chapter:

☐ To describe how different savings techniques work.
☐ To help you evaluate the opportunities available to you in certificates, bonds, mutual funds, and other situations.
☐ To acquaint you with certain tax-favored retirement plans.
☐ And, overall, to help you shape your own investment program using these various devices.

Chapter 15 described the two basic ways of making your money grow. One way is to lend it to others, in return for which you receive a fee known as interest. The other way is to buy something (such as stock or real estate) and hope that you can sell it later for more than you paid for it. During the time that you own such an entity you may also receive a share of the entity's profits, if in fact it is profitable.

There is a critical distinction between the two basic techniques. With the former—lending—you will have an agreement with the borrower (financial institution, corporation, government) that will state that you are entitled to have all of your invested money returned, either upon your demand or at some future time. The agreement will also state the amount of interest you are to receive. That amount of interest either will be fixed at a certain level or will be subject to variation. If the interest rate is variable, there may or may not be limits as to how high or how low the rate may go. In summary, you are assured of getting all of your money back (assuming that the borrower remains healthy) and you are assured of getting at least some interest.

When you buy something, you do not have assurances of getting all of your money back or getting any return on your money during the period of ownership. If you are fortunate, your investment might increase many times in value. If you are unfortunate, your investment could wither and even disappear altogether. But there is no way of knowing when you make the investment what the future will hold.

The distinction between the two techniques could then be most succinctly described as: security versus risk.

A conservative investment philosophy would dictate that you safeguard your future by using secure techniques. Once you have embarked on a well-disciplined plan to create such a foundation for your future security, you might then want to consider using the risk techniques. If you are fortunate, the risk techniques could later enhance your future; if you are unfortunate in your choice of risk investments, your future could suffer.

Let's now explore the various ways of lending your money so as to assure your future security. In the broad sense, the arena in which you find these opportunities is known as "the money market."

What Is the Money Market?

The money market is not a place but a concept. In a general sense, when IOUs and money change hands, money market transactions have thus taken place. When you open a savings account or buy a savings bond, you have entered into a money market transaction: you have loaned your money to a bank or to the government and you have received their promise to repay you. In a more technical sense, the money market refers to certain transactions involving short-term government and corporate bonds. See the later discussion on money market mutual funds for more detail.

Some types of money market investments have traditionally been known as "fixed income investments." However, as the concept of variable interest rates becomes more widespread, the traditional forms of fixed income investments bode not to be as "fixed" as they formerly were. Interest rates on various investments will be more likely to fluctuate up and down; or a guaranteed fixed rate may be fixed for a much shorter period of time than was formerly customary.

The term *money market instruments* has become more commonplace in our language. Money market instruments are the various forms of money market investments: certificates of deposit, bonds, repurchase agreements, bankers' acceptances, commercial paper. These various instruments will be described in more detail throughout this chapter.

How Is Interest Figured?

As noted, interest is the fee a borrower pays in order to have the use of someone else's money. Interest is normally expressed as a percentage of the total amount borrowed, calculated on a yearly basis. In other words, if you were to make an investment of $1000 at a 6 percent annual interest rate, you would receive $60 over the course of one year. If you were to remain with that investment for only half a year, you would receive $30 in interest. If you stayed with it for two years, you would receive $120. That's the simple part.

Aside from the rate of interest, there are two other aspects in calculating your true return that can have a distinct effect on your overall investment: the compounding of interest and the crediting of interest to your account.

Compounding

The compounding of interest means that the interest you earn stays in your account and begins to earn interest itself. Following the above example, if you earned $60 in interest during the course of one year (on a $1000 investment at a 6 percent annual rate) and you left that $60 in the account, you would then have $1060 to work for you during the second year. During the second year, your $1060 would earn $63.60. And so it would go for future years: you have an ever-increasing amount of money working for you because the interest is left in the account to compound.

In many types of accounts, interest is compounded more frequently than once a year. Quarterly compounding is very common, as is daily compounding. With quarterly compounding, the interest you earn during each quarter of the year is added to your original principal balance. Table 16-1 illustrates this. During the first quarter of the year, with your $1000 investment at 6 percent, you earn $15 (that is, one-fourth of $60). At the start of the second quarter, you have $1015 working for you, which will earn $15.23. That $15.23 earned during the second quarter is added to the $1015 of principal, thus you have $1030.23 at work for you during the third quarter. With daily compounding, 1/365 of your total annual interest is added to your account each day. As Table 16-1 illustrates, more frequent compounding means a higher return to the investor.

Table 16-1

Comparison of Compounding Methods—6 Percent Annual rate

		$1000	
		Quarterly Compounding	Annual Compounding
First Year	1st $\frac{1}{4}$	$1000.00 earns $15.00	
	2nd $\frac{1}{4}$	1015.00 earns 15.23	
	3rd $\frac{1}{4}$	1030.23 earns 15.45	
	4th $\frac{1}{4}$	1045.68 earns 15.69	$1000 earns $60
	Balance at work, end of first year	$1061.37	$1060
Second Year	1st $\frac{1}{4}$	$1061.37 earns $15.92	
	2nd $\frac{1}{4}$	1077.29 earns 16.15	
	3rd $\frac{1}{4}$	1093.44 earns 16.40	
	4th $\frac{1}{4}$	1109.84 earns 16.64	$1060 earns $63.60
	Balance at work, end of second year	$1126.48	$1123.60

Passbook savings accounts are the most common type of investment in which compounding takes place. But some investments do not offer compounding: corporate bonds, for example, will pay you interest twice a year by check directly from the company. If you don't reinvest that interest on your own, it will not be working for you.

Crediting of Interest to Your Account

Savings plans can differ with respect to the manner in which interest is actually credited to your account. Many institutions will credit you with interest from the day a deposit is made until the day the deposit is withdrawn. For example, if you made a deposit in such an institution on January 15 and withdrew the total balance on December 15, you would earn interest for the full 11 months that the money was in the account. However, some institutions use different methods of crediting the interest to your account. For example, an institution might require that the money remain in your account for a full calendar quarter in order to earn interest. Thus, if you made a deposit on January 15, you would not earn any interest for the entire first quarter of the year. You would start earning interest at the beginning of the second quarter, April 1. Also, if you withdrew the money on December 15, you would forfeit interest for the entire fourth quarter of the year since you withdrew it before the end of the full calendar quarter. In such a case, even though your money was with the institution for a full 11 months, you would be earning interest for only six months—the second quarter and the third quarter.

Another method of calculating interest uses the low balance in any quarter as the amount on which interest is computed. For example, you start the first quarter of the year with $1000 in your account. On January 15 you withdraw $600 to pay bills until your income tax refund comes in. The refund comes in on February 15 and you put the money back into your account. During that first quarter of the year, you will be credited for interest on only $400 even though you had $1000 in the account for the majority of the time. In a day-of-deposit-to-day-of-withdrawal account, the interest would be calculated on the balance in your account each given day of the quarter, and you wouldn't suffer as you do in the low-balance type of calculation.

Determining the true yield on a money-market investment requires more than just examining the rate of interest being paid. You must examine the frequency of compounding and crediting of interest to the account as well.

Tables 16-2 and 16-3 illustrate how your money will grow over various periods of time at different rates of interest, compounded annually.

Types of Money Market Investments

The variety of money-market investment opportunities is staggering by comparison to just 20 years ago. As borrowers compete ever more aggressively for investors' dollars, new techniques, and new twists on old techniques, are emerging at a rapid pace. The selection of opportunities

Table 16-2

How Does Your Money Grow? No. 1

If you invest
$1000 per year
at this rate of
interest . . .　　　　　　. . . you'll have this much after this number of years

	5 Years	10 Years	15 Years	20 Years
6 percent	$5,980	$13,970	$24,570	$ 38,990
8 percent	6,340	15,650	29,320	49,420
10 percent	6,710	17,530	34,960	63,000
12 percent	7,120	19,650	41,750	80,700
14 percent	7,540	22,040	49,980	103,770

Note: This table does *not* take into account income taxes on yearly interest earnings.

Table 16-3

How Does Your Money Grow? No. 2

If you make a
one-time investment
of $1000 at this
rate of interest . . .　　　　. . . you'll have this much after this number of years

	5 Years	10 Years	15 Years	20 Years
6 percent	$1,340	$1,790	$2,400	3,210
8 percent	1,470	2,160	3,170	4,660
10 percent	1,610	2,590	4,180	6,720
12 percent	1,760	3,110	5,470	9,650
14 percent	1,960	3,710	7,400	14,960

Note: This table does *not* take into effect income taxes on yearly interest earnings.

Example: To better understand the power of compounding, look at where the 10-year column crosses the 10 percent row. $1000 will have grown to $2590. In other words, your investment will have increased by $1590 over 10 years, or an *average per year* of $159. That means, in effect, that you have enjoyed an *average* annual growth (noncompounded) of 15.9 percent.

available to you today might be still broader and more varied than the selection which follows.

Passbook Savings Accounts

A passbook savings account is an "open-end" agreement between the customer and the financial institution. The customer is free to put in as much money as desired at any given time and can take out as much as he or she wishes at any given time. While the money is in the account, it will earn interest in accordance with the agreement set forth between the institution and the investor. The institution may reserve the right to alter the interest rate being paid upon giving proper notice to its investors. The form of notice should be set forth in the rules and regulations of the passbook account.

Some institutions may offer special types of passbook accounts which are a cross between a passbook and a time certificate. These accounts will have a fixed maturity, but the customer may be able to add or withdraw certain sums from the account periodically.

Passbook accounts are commonly available at banks, savings and loan associations, and credit unions. The Federal Deposit Insurance Corporation (FDIC) offers insurance on $100,000 per account for all accounts—checking and savings—in commercial banks and in mutual savings banks. Similar protection is available in savings and loan associations through the Federal Savings and Loan Insurance Corporation (FSLIC). Federally insured credit unions are insured under the National Credit Union Administration (NCUA) program. In some states, state-chartered institutions and thrift companies do not offer the federal insurance, and although many of these institutions may be sound and well managed, occasional abuses do occur, resulting in the depositors' funds being lost by a failure of the institution. Institutions insured by federal government agencies must post prominent notices of that fact in their place of business and in their advertising.

The maximum interest that can be paid on passbook savings accounts has been fixed by federal law. However, in 1980, a congressionally appointed committee proposed steps that would gradually phase out interest-rate ceilings on passbook savings accounts. It's anticipated that by 1986, there will be no ceilings on passbook savings accounts and that competition alone will determine what interest rate investors can obtain in this type of account.

Investment Criteria

☐ *Yield.* Passbook savings accounts have traditionally given the lowest yield of all money market instruments. However, this may change as the aforementioned ceilings are lifted. To determine the true yield, it's important for the investor to be aware of the annual interest rate payable as well as the frequency of compounding and crediting of interest to the account.

☐ *Liquidity.* Passbook savings accounts are as liquid an investment as one can make short of storing the money in a cookie jar. You can withdraw your entire principal at any time simply by submitting your passbook and the appropriate withdrawal slip. If interest is not credited daily to your passbook account, you could sacrifice some interest if you withdrew funds prior to the end of the calendar quarter.

☐ *Safety.* Savings accounts insured by the federal government have the highest degree of safety.

☐ *Hedge value.* Savings accounts offer little protection against rising prices except to the extent that the interest you earn will likely increase as inflation continues.

☐ *Pledge value.* Savings accounts have a very high degree of pledge value. You can normally borrow up to 90 percent of the total amount in your account at favorable rates by presenting your passbook to a loan officer and signing simple documents.

☐ *Tax implications.* Historically, all interest earned on passbook accounts has been fully subject to federal income taxes. But, as noted in chapter 25, some interest earned may be exempt from taxes starting in 1985.

Certificates of Deposit

Certificates of deposit (or CDs, as they are often called) are fixed contracts for a specific amount of money to run for a specific length of time and to pay a fixed interest rate. Some newer forms of certificates offer a variable rate of interest. A certificate of deposit may be for as short as 90 days, or for as long as ten years, perhaps even longer. The interest rate payable on any certificate will depend on general interest rate conditions at the time the investment is made.

Once a fixed-interest certificate of deposit investment is made, the interest rate agreed to will be in effect throughout the life of the certificate, even though the general rates may change subsequently. For example, on Monday, you obtain a 30-month certificate of deposit from a local bank with an interest rate set at 12 percent per annum. You are guaranteed that 12 percent rate for the life of the certificate. On Tuesday, the same bank announces that from that day onward they will pay $11\frac{1}{2}$ percent on all 30-month certificates. That change will not affect you. It will only affect people who obtain certificates from Tuesday onward until any other change in the interest rate is made. By the same token, if on Tuesday the bank should announce an increase in the certificate rate, you will not be able to take advantage of the higher rate since you committed to a firm contract on Monday at the 12 percent rate.

Penalties

Since certificates of deposit are firm contracts for a set amount of time, you can expect to be penalized if you want to withdraw money from your certificate account before the maturity date. For example, in 1980 governmental regulations imposed a penalty of three months' worth of interest on all certificates of less than one year's duration and a penalty of six months' worth of interest for longer certificates. In the event that such certificates had not been in existence long enough to have earned the respective three months' or six months' worth of interest, the principal deposit could be tapped to make up the difference. For example, you contract for a six-month certificate of deposit for $10,000 at a 12 percent interest rate. You would thus earn $100 per month in interest. One month after you obtain the certificate you decide you need the money for some other purpose, and you cash in the certificate. Your penalty, as noted, would be three months' worth of interest, or $300. But after the passage of only one month, you've earned only $100 worth of interest. Thus, the bank would deduct the other $200 from your principal investment leaving you with $9800 after having cashed in your certificate prematurely.

Check with your banker or savings and loan official to determine the current penalties on early withdrawals from certificates of deposit.

Renewal

Commonly, when a certificate of deposit reaches its maturity, the institution will renew it for another term at the interest rate then prevailing. For example, you have a six-month certificate that was obtained at a 12 percent interest rate. Today the certificate is maturing and the current interest rate on such certificates is 10 percent. Unless you instruct the institution to the contrary, they will automatically renew your certificate at the now current 10 percent rate. Some institutions, however, will not automatically renew certificates: they may instead place the funds into a passbook savings account lacking your instructions to the contrary. In such a case you would be likely to earn a much lower rate of interest than what a renewed certificate would have paid. Whether institutions automatically renew certificates or automatically put the proceeds into a passbook account, they will give you a seven-day grace period on the expiration of the original certificate. During that seven days, you will continue to earn interest at the then-prevailing rate. At the end of the seven days the automatic conversion will occur.

Here is a common problem that arises when investors fail to pay attention to the renewal provisions of their certificates. Your six-month certificate will mature on the fifteenth of the month. At the end of the seven-day grace period—the twenty-second—your certificate will automatically renew for another six months. You have every intention of getting to the bank on or before the twenty-second to take the money out so that you can put it to some other use. But you get distracted and don't get around to doing this until the twenty-third of the month. By that time the certificate has already renewed, and if you now want to take out the money, you will have to pay the penalty as noted above. On a large certificate, a few days' delay can cost hundreds of dollars in lost interest.

Choices

While certificates of any amount or length of time are possible, following is a sampling of some of the more popular types of certificates of deposit. Check with your local financial institutions now to determine what other possibilities are available to you.

Six-month or Treasury Bill Certificates   A brief historical background is in order to explain this terminology. When the U.S. government borrows money for a short term—less than one year—the IOUs it gives to investors are called treasury bills. An investor must have at least $10,000 to purchase a U.S. government treasury bill. Common maturities for treasury bills are three months and six months. In the latter 1970s, investors were finding much more attractive opportunities in U.S. government treasury bills than they were at their local banks and savings and loan associations. Investors therefore began to withdraw their money from the local institutions to invest with the government. This drain on local banking deposits posed a serious threat to the financial industry and to the economy, and so permission was given for the banks and savings and loans to offer a competing investment to the treasury bill. This competing investment would have basically the same terms as the treasury bill: a six-month maturity, a minimum $10,000 deposit, and an interest rate comparable to what the federal government paid on its six-month borrowings. Since this new type of investment was so similar to the actual U.S. government treasury bill, financial institutions who offered such investments referred to them as "treasury bill certificates," or "T-bill certificates" for short. Some institutions referred to these six-month certificates as "money market certificates."

There has been a great deal of confusion in the public between treasury bills on the one hand and treasury bill certificates on the other hand. Treasury bills are a direct investment with the United States Government obtainable through the Federal Reserve Bank or through stockbrokers. Treasury bill certificates are certificates of deposit obtained through banks, savings and loan associations, and credit unions. In the former, you're lending your money directly to the United States Government. In the latter, you're lending your money directly to a local financial institution. Interest that you receive on a treasury bill is exempt from state income taxes and local income taxes but is fully taxable at the federal level. Interest received on a treasury bill certificate is fully taxable—city, state, and federal. There may be slight differences in the interest rate obtainable through treasury bills as compared with treasury bill certificates.

As originally devised, regulations on these six-month certificates would not permit interest to be compounded. Check whether this regulation has been amended. If a certificate is cashed in prior to its maturity date, it will be subject to currently prevailing penalty provisions.

Small-saver Certificates   These were introduced in 1980. They have a maturity of 30 months, and there is no minimum deposit required. They can be opened for any amount of money, though many institutions have imposed a $100 minimum just to simplify bookkeeping matters. At the time they were introduced, small-saver certificates paid an interest rate of roughly double the interest that could be obtained on passbook savings accounts and thus were very attractive to savers with small accounts who were willing to lock away the money for the 30-month required term.

As with the six-month certificates, the small-saver certificates are subject to penalty upon early withdrawal. But unlike the six-month certificates, the small-saver certificates were originally designed to allow interest to compound over the life of the certificate.

Jumbo Certificates   On all certificates of deposit under $100,000, the maximum interest rate that the institution can pay is fixed by law. But on certificates in excess of $100,000 the interest rate is negotiable between the investor and the institution. These are known as jumbo certificates. They commonly will range in duration from 30 days to one year with the interest rate being determined by current conditions in the overall money market. Commonly, interest rates on jumbo certificates can be considerably higher than those on smaller certificates. Investors with enough money available to consider jumbo certificates should check current rates with a number of local institutions to determine the best deal available at any given time.

All-savers Certificates   Tax law changes in 1981 introduced a new form of certificate commonly referred to as the all-savers certificate. As originally designed by Congress, investors in all-savers certificates can earn tax-exempt interest: up to $1000 worth for those who file a single tax return; up to $2000 for those who file a joint tax return. These certificates were to be available from October 1, 1981, until December 31, 1982, although some observers suspect that Congress will extend the concept beyond that cut-off date. Certificates are to run for 12 months, and there are severe penalties if the principal is withdrawn prior to maturity. As originally designed, the tax-exempt earnings were to have been a once-in-a-lifetime opportunity. If Congress extends the all-saver plan beyond 1982, however, the chance to earn additional tax-exempt interest might be available to investors.

Investment Criteria

☐ *Yield.* You are certain of receiving the yield you bargained for by virtue of your contract with the financial institution. Beware, however, of potentially misleading advertising with respect to six-month certificates. Advertising for six-month certificates often quotes two different interest rates: the actual yield and the "annualized" yield. The actual yield refers to the actual interest rate that will be paid for the six-month term. For example, if you contract for a $10,000 six-month certificate at 12 percent interest, you will receive $600 for your six-month investment (12 percent of $10,000 is $1200, and half of that—six months' worth—is $600). The quoted so-called annualized yield refers to the return you *would get* if, in fact, you renewed the certificate at the same rate as you originally obtained. However, there is no way of knowing what your renewal rate will be at the end of six months. It could be higher. It could be lower. The annualized rate is based on supposition, not on actuality.

☐ *Liquidity.* The liquidity of certificates of deposit is somewhat impaired as a result of the penalty provisions for early withdrawal. It is possible, however, and often advisable, to borrow against a certificate rather than cash it in should you have an immediate need for some of the money.

☐ *Safety.* As with passbook savings accounts, certificates at federally insured institutions are protected by the federal insurance programs up to $100,000 per account. Thus, certificates are considered to be at the highest level with respect to safety.

☐ *Hedge value.* Since the interest rate on certificates is fixed and will not rise with inflationary trends, the hedge value of certificates is minimal.

☐ *Pledge value.* As with passbook savings accounts, certificates can be used as collateral for borrowing. Many institutions will guarantee a fixed interest rate should you wish to borrow against a certificate. Such an interest rate might be 1 percent over and above what you're receiving on your certificate. In other words, if you are receiving 12 percent interest and you wish to borrow against your certificate, you would have to pay 13 percent per year for borrowing any of your funds. As noted, this could be a cheaper way of getting to your funds than by cashing in the certificate prematurely and suffering a heavy penalty.

☐ *Tax implications.* Except to the extent that the Internal Revenue Service will allow you to exclude income earned on certificates (see savings passbook tax implications), your interest income on certificates is fully taxable at the federal and local levels.

Bonds

Just as you often borrow money—to buy a car, to fix up your home, to pay your bills, or to refinance existing older debts—businesses and governments likewise borrow money for similar needs. They may borrow for a long term, upwards of 40 years, or for a short term, a few years or even a few months. When they borrow for a long term, the IOU that they issue is referred to as a bond. Short-term IOUs may be referred to as bills, notes, and, in the case of corporate short-term IOUs, "commercial paper."

There are three major categories of bonds—federal government, local government, and corporate. And there are three kinds of ways that an investor can get involved in bonds: directly, semidirectly, and indirectly.

You can buy various bonds *directly* through a stockbroker, and in some cases through the investment department of major banks. You can invest in them *semidirectly* through mutual funds that specialize in various bonds. The mutual funds pool the investments of many individuals and spread them out over a wide assortment of different issues. This is something that the ordinary investor can't do individually.

And although you may not be aware of it, you *already* have *indirect* investments in the bond market. If you have a bank account, an insurance policy, or pension fund, it's very likely that some of your money is already invested in the bond market—and that in itself is a good reason for you to become familiar with the workings of bonds.

Corporate Bonds

Under the overall heading of corporate bonds are included the IOUs issued by railroads, public utilities (such as local electric and gas companies), and industrial firms (manufacturers, service companies such as airlines, retailing firms). Broadly speaking, there are two classifications of corporate bonds: straight and convertible. The straight bond is a simple long-term IOU of the issuing company, wherein a fixed interest rate is agreed to be paid to the investor. The convertible bond carries with it the right for the holder to convert the bond into shares of that same company's common stock. Convertible bonds, or convertible debentures as they're sometimes called, are discussed in more detail later in this chapter.

Corporate bonds can usually be bought in denominations of $1000, and the commission payable to a stockbroker is generally much less than when buying stock. Further, when you buy a bond at its initial offering (and this applies to government and municipal bonds as well as corporate bonds), there's usually no commission to pay. Likewise, if you hold a bond until maturity, and it's redeemed directly by the issuer, there'll be no commission to pay.

How to Read Bond Quotations

Many major daily newspapers carry bond quotations, as does the *Wall Street Journal. Barron's,* a financial newspaper issued weekly, also contains a full listing of traded corporate bonds.

In bond price quotations, the number quoted is the selling price of the bond expressed as a percentage of its face value. Thus, if a $1000 bond is currently selling for $950, the quotation would appear as "95," which is 95 percent of its face value. Similarly, a bond selling for $985 would be quoted as "$98\frac{1}{2}$" which is 98.5 percent of its face value.

An example: In 1950 the XYZ Company borrowed some money from public investors and issued their bonds as IOUs. These bonds contained a promise to pay 4 percent interest per year for 40 years to everyone who bought the bonds, issued in $1000 denominations. The bonds would thus mature in the year 1990, at which time the XYZ Company would pay all holders of the bonds $1000 for each $1000 bond. Over the years, investors traded the bonds back and forth among each other. Due to market conditions, that bond today sells for $950. The quote in the newspaper would look like this, on a day when there was no fluctuation in its price:

Bond	Hi	Low	Last
XYZ 4s 90	95	95	95

This bond would be referred to as the XYZ Company 4s of 90. The 4s refers to the original interest rate that the company agreed to pay, or 4 percent; the 90 refers to the year of maturity, 1990; the three 95 figures refer to the high, low, and closing prices for the day. (Remember we said that the price didn't fluctuate on this particular day.)

How Bond Yields Are Figured

Bonds have three different yields, and the difference must be clearly understood. (This is equally true for government and municipal bonds.)

The following description does not take into account brokerage commissions or income taxes payable on bond interest received.

Coupon Yield   Referring back to the earlier example of the XYZ 4s of 90, the 4 percent interest that the company originally agreed to pay is known as the *coupon rate.* In other words, the company guarantees that it will pay $40 each year (usually in semiannual installments) to each holder of each $1000 bond. The bond may fluctuate in price up and down, but the holder will continue to get $40 per year for each $1000 bond held, regardless of the price of the bond.

Current Yield   We noted that the bond was quoted at $950 on a given day. If an investor purchased a $1000 bond for $950 and received $40 per year in interest from the company, the actual *current yield* is 4.2 percent ($40 on $950, which is your actual investment). If, on the other hand, you had paid $1050 for the bond, your *current yield* would be roughly 3.7 percent ($40 is 3.7% of $1050, which is your actual investment).

Yield to Maturity   The third concept of yield is called the *yield to maturity,* and it's a bit more difficult to understand. Say that you buy a $1000 face value bond for $950, and you buy it exactly one year before its maturity date. Assume that it's paying the same 4 percent per year as the bond quoted above. When the bond matures one year after your purchase date, you get back the full face amount, or $1000. That's $50 more than you paid for it, and that $50 is considered a capital gain. Also, you're going to get the $40 in interest during the year you hold the bond. Altogether you will receive $90 in one year for your $950 investment, or a *yield to maturity* of just over 9.4 percent.

If, however, you purchased the bond five years before maturity date, that $50 gain would be prorated over the remaining five years. Thus, you would be getting the $40 each year in interest plus an eventual extra $50 on redemption, which is equal to an extra $10 on average each year, assuming that you hold the bond until maturity. Your annual average *yield to maturity* would then be approximately $50 each year, or about 5.2 percent of your initial $950 investment.

How Bonds Fluctuate in Value

The above illustration discusses a bond whose original price has fluctuated in value. Why do bond prices fluctuate? At the time XYZ Company borrowed the money back in 1950, the prevailing interest rates for companies of XYZ's caliber seeking loans of that particular size for that particular duration was 4 percent per year. A company of higher credit standing than XYZ might have been able to borrow at a somewhat lower interest rate. And a company with a lesser credit worthiness might have had to pay a higher one. But for XYZ, at that time, 4 percent was the going rate.

The general rule in the bond market is that bond *prices* tend to move in the *opposite* direction of *interest rates*.

Let's say that by 1960 the prevailing interest rates for companies of XYZ's size and quality had increased to 5 percent. In other words, if XYZ wanted to borrow in 1960, they'd have to pay 5 percent for their money instead of the 4 percent they had contracted for ten years previously. If you had originally bought a $1000 XYZ bond in 1950, what would that bond be worth in 1960 when the prevailing interest rate had increased from 4 percent to 5 percent?

If you wanted to sell it, you'd have to take less than the $1,000 you had paid. Why? Because another investor could go into the new bond market and buy a new issue at 5 percent getting $50 per year on a $1000 investment. Why then should he pay you $1000 and get only $40 per year for his investment? For this reason, your $1000 bond might now only be worth $880 to $900. If you wanted to sell it in 1960, you'd have to take a loss of $100 to $120. That's because a buyer in 1960 would be seeking 5 percent on his investment and, in order to achieve a 5 percent return on your older bond, would be willing to pay you only the lesser amount for it.

By 1970, prevailing interest rates for a company of XYZ's size and quality have jumped to 7 percent. That means that if XYZ were borrowing in 1970, they would have to pay 7 percent interest on their money for a long-term loan. This would mean that your $1000 bond bought in 1950 might only be worth about $750. If an investor paid you $750 for your $1000 bond in 1970, he'd receive $40 in interest per year, plus an average of $12.50 per year once the bond matured in 1990—assuming it was held until 1990. At that time he'll get his full $1000 from XYZ company. (He'll receive $250 more than he paid for the bond on maturity, which is an average of $12.50 per year.) Thus, he'd be getting roughly $52.50 per year, on average, and that would equal 7 percent on his $750 investment.

The value of your bond has thus slipped from $1000 in 1950 to $750 in 1970.

By 1980, prevailing interest rates for a company of XYZ's size and quality jumped to 12 percent. That means that if XYZ were borrowing in 1980, they would have to pay 12 percent interest on their money for a long-term loan. What, then, has happened to the value of the original bond issued in 1950? An investor in 1980 could obtain a bond similar in quality to XYZ's and earn 12 percent interest, or $120 on a $1000 investment. If that investor wanted to earn 12 percent on the original 1950 XYZ bond, he might be willing to pay only about $340 for it. (A $40 annual return on a $340 investment would be about 12 percent.) Does this mean that a bond that was originally worth $1000 is now worth only about $340? In some cases, yes. And that in fact is the type of thing that happened to the bond market commencing in the late 1970s when interest rates on bonds started to rise at a very rapid rate.

However, in this case the situation isn't necessarily that grim. Why? Because now the bond is beginning to approach its maturity date of 1990. Now, an investor is more likely to be looking at the yield to maturity mentioned above. Thus, in 1980, an investor might be willing to pay close to $600 for that original XYZ bond, particularly if he's planning on holding the bond until its maturity in 1990. If he pays $600 for it in 1980, he will get $1000 back in 1990—a $400 gain or an average per year gain of $40. Adding the $40 per year to the $40 per year interest, he'll be receiving $80 per year on average. An average annual return of $80 on an investment of $600 gives an average annual yield to maturity of about 13 percent.

Thus, while the general rule is that bond prices move in the opposite direction of interest rates, the situation changes as the maturity of the bond gets closer, when the price of the bond tends to move toward its face value regardless of what is happening with interest rates. This phenomenon illustrates an interesting investment opportunity. Where a good-quality corporate bond is selling at a discount (below its face value) and is nearing maturity, there are definite advantages to the investor. The yield to maturity may be attractive, and the investor will also achieve favorable tax benefits, for the difference between his purchase price and redemption price will be considered capital gains, taxable at a much lower rate than is ordinary income. Further, upon redemption of the bond by the issuing company, there are no commissions to be paid by the investor. Investors seeking a relatively assured yield over a three- to five-year period, with attractive capital gains taxation and minimal commissions, would do well to explore these opportunities.

We've looked at an example of how a bond price declines in the face of rising interest rates until some indeterminate time, when, nearing maturity, the redemption date begins to draw the price of the bond back up to face value. The same situation holds true if interest rates decline: bond prices then tend to rise for the same reason, and they may well rise above face value. Again, there will be an indeterminate point at which the redemption date will begin to draw the price of the bond back down to face value. For example, say that a bond had been selling at a premium—more than face value—or $1050. As maturity nears, the holder of the bond knows that the company will pay off only $1000 for the bond and will see the price begin to slide from the $1050 toward the $1000 to be paid off at maturity.

Another factor that can affect the bond price is the change in the quality of the issuing company. If the company falls on hard times financially, investors may become pessimistic about the company's ability to meet its debts and the interest due thereon. This can have a negative effect on the value of the company's bonds. Naturally, in such cases, the stock of the company will have also been affected, most likely in a more drastic fashion than the bond. Similarly, an improvement in the financial status of the issuer can have an upward effect on the value of the bond.

Although the yield on a bond can be accurately calculated at the time it's purchased, an investor must, for reasons noted above, be well aware that the total *value* of an investment can fluctuate over a long period of time. Bond prices will tend to fluctuate more slowly and gradually than will stock prices, but this can mean that an investor might get caught in a downtrend for a longer period and suffer a loss if the need arises to sell the bond. The closer a bond is to maturity at the time it's purchased, the less that risk. If a bond is purchased at a price *above* face value, the investor must be aware that as maturity approaches, the value of the bond will *drop* to meet the ultimate redemption price. This obvious effect on the ultimate yield must be taken into account at the time of purchase.

Sinking Fund and Call Privileges

When corporations borrow money, they typically do something most individuals and families should be well advised to do. They set up what is called a "sinking fund" out of which they will eventually pay off the bond. They put aside so much money each year toward the eventual redemption of that bond and actually use those monies to pay off the investors, either at maturity, or in advance of maturity if market conditions so dictate. For example, a company has issued a bond paying 7 percent interest per year. After the passage of a number of years, the interest rates prevalent throughout the economy have dropped to 6 percent. The company sees an opportunity to refinance the existing IOUs and drop their interest rate from 7 percent to 6 percent, thus cutting their interest expense considerably. In order to take advantage of this possible occurrence, many bonds have written into them a "call privilege," which means that the company has the right to call in the existing bonds and pay off the holders at an agreed-on price.

A would-be investor in corporate bonds should determine what call privilege or protection exists. Because a bond is usually a relatively long-term investment, it would be to the investor's advantage to know that the company can't call the bond for at least five to ten years.

Corporate Bond Ratings

There are thousands of corporate bonds available to investors at any given time. How is one to determine the relative quality of so many bonds? Corporate bonds are rated according to quality by two companies: Standard and Poor's, and Moody's. Both rating systems are very similar, taking into account the basic financial strength of the corporation and its ability to pay the interest on its debts. Highest-rated bonds offer the lowest rate of interest and the lowest risk to investors. Following is a brief summary of the Standard and Poor's ratings:

AAA: highest-grade obligations
AA: high-grade obligations
A: upper-medium grade obligations
BBB: medium-grade obligations

BB: lower-medium grade obligations

B: speculative obligations

CCC–CC: outright speculations with the lower rating denoting the more speculative

C: no interest is being paid

DDD–D: all such bonds are in default with the rating indicating the relative salvage value

The ratings companies keep a watch on the financial status of all bond issuers, and if there is a change in the financial strength of a company, its rating will be changed accordingly. For more specific details on the ratings, refer to the monthly rating books published by the two companies, available at stockbrokerage firms and at most local libraries.

Investment Criteria

☐ *Yield*. With higher rated companies, you have a very high assurance of receiving the yield (interest payment) that you have bargained for. With lower rated companies, the yield may be in doubt.

☐ *Liquidity*. The major bond exchanges (New York and American) maintain a ready market for buyers and sellers of bonds. But depending on the specific issue and the number of bonds being bought and sold, it could take from a few minutes to a few days to effect a transaction.

☐ *Safety*. The higher the rating of the bond and the closer it is to maturity, the safer your investment. As noted, bond prices can fluctuate substantially in value, moving in the opposite direction from interest rates. In the last few years the bond market in general has undergone severe fluctuations compared to the relatively minor fluctuations prior to the late 1970s. There is no way of knowing if or when the bond market will return to its relatively stable days of old.

☐ *Hedge value*. If a bond is bought at or near face value, there is little protection against inflation. As prices move upward—interest rates being among those prices—bonds will likely decrease in value, as noted above. Thus, the hedge value might be considered negative. If, on the other hand, a bond is bought below face value and maturity is approaching, the bond price will move upward as maturity nears, thus offering a measure of protection against rising prices.

☐ *Pledge value*. The amount that one can borrow against bonds and the interest rate paid on such a loan depends on the quality of the bond as determined by the rating services. Generally, well-rated bonds provide ample opportunity for pledging at reasonably favorable interest rates. However, if a bond has decreased in value, the amount that can be borrowed against it will decrease proportionately.

☐ *Tax implications*. Except to the extent that interest earned can be excluded from taxable income (see passbook savings accounts), interest earned on corporate bonds is taxable. If a bond is sold at a higher price than what was paid for it and the bond had been held for the requisite capital-gains period, the profit on the transaction is subject to capital-gains taxes, which are lower than ordinary income taxes. A bond sold at a loss, when held for the requisite capital-gains period, will qualify for a long-term capital loss. The further implications of capital gains and losses will be discussed in chapter 26, Tax-saving Strategies.

U.S. Government Bonds

The federal government is the biggest borrower of them all. Federal IOUs range from the common savings bond for as low as $25.00 to the multimillion dollar obligations issued frequently by the U.S. Treasury. The federal government even borrows from itself. For example, the Social Security Administration invests its own funds in U.S. Treasury IOUs. Federal government obligations are further broken down into three subcategories: U.S. Treasury borrowings, federal agency borrowings, and savings bonds.

U.S. Treasury

The U.S. Treasury borrows frequently on a short-term, medium-term, and long-term basis. Short-term obligations are called treasury bills, and their maturities range from three months to one year. Medium-term obligations are called treasury notes, with maturities ranging from one to seven years. Long-term issues are called treasury bonds, with maturities ranging from five to 30 years. Any of these treasury debts can be obtained at a nominal commission through a stockbroker or the investment department of a bank, or directly from the Federal Reserve Bank at no commission. The prices and yields of all U.S. Treasury obligations are listed daily in the *Wall Street Journal* in a column titled: "Treasury issues: Bonds, notes, bills."

Federal Agency Securities

A number of federal government agencies are frequent borrowers of large sums of money. The money they borrow is generally pumped back into the economy to subsidize such things as mortgage loans for home buyers and farm loans for the agricultural industry. Investments are available in a wide range of maturities. Short-term obligations, usually for a year or less, are commonly called "notes." Medium-term obligations, which may run from one to five years, are commonly referred to as "debentures." Long-term obligations that run from five to 25 years are referred to as "bonds." Some of the more popularly traded federal agency obligations are issued by the Federal National Mortgage Association, the Federal Home Loan Bank, Banks for Cooperatives, Federal Land Banks, and Federal Intermediate Credit Banks.

The prices and current yields (before commissions) of treasury obligations and agency obligations are quoted daily in the *Wall Street Journal* under the heading "Government, agency, and miscellaneous securities."

Savings Bonds

Savings bonds are the most commonly known and popular form of bonds issued by the federal government. Prior to 1980 savings bonds were referred to as Series E bonds and Series H bonds. Since 1980 they have been called Series EE bonds and Series HH bonds.

When you buy an EE bond, you pay less than the face value for it. For example, you pay $25 for an EE bond which, at maturity, will be worth its face value of $50. The difference between what you pay and what you ultimately receive is the interest that the bond will have earned. Table 16-4 shows the purchase price and redemption price (face value) of all other EE bonds.

The true interest that can be earned on EE bonds depends on how long the bonds are held. The longer they are held, the higher interest an investor will earn. In mid 1980, Congress permitted the U.S. Treasury to increase the interest paid on EE bonds as often as once every six months if the Treasury saw fit to do so. From early 1980 until mid 1981, the Treasury increased the rate on EE bonds from 6 percent to 9 percent and also shortened the maturity from 11 years to 9 years. Your local bank can tell you about further changes in the interest rate and maturity since 1981.

Any changes in the interest rate on EE bonds also will affect all outstanding E bonds. Whatever rate EE bonds are paying will also be paid on E bonds. (Note that once the older E bonds reach their fortieth birthday, they will stop paying interest. An E bond issued during January 1943 will cease paying interest in January 1983 and so on.)

EE bonds can not be redeemed during the first six months after they are issued. But after that time they can be redeemed at most financial institutions, which have schedules issued by the government indicating the redemption values. Bonds redeemed before maturity will not receive as high an interest rate as bonds held to maturity. Neither E bonds nor EE bonds can be sold or transferred to another individual, and they cannot be used as collateral or security for a loan. This is also true of H bonds.

Table 16-4

Purchase Price	Redemption Price (Face Value)
$37.50	$75.00
50.00	100.00
100.00	200.00
250.00	500.00
500.00	1,000.00
2,500.00	5,000.00
5,000.00	10,000.00

HH bonds (H bonds prior to 1980) are issued in denominations of $500, $1000, $5000, and $10,000. With HH bonds you receive interest checks twice each year from the government, starting six months after the issue date. HH bonds can be redeemed after six months from the issue date.

EE and E bonds offer an attractive tax benefit to investors. While the bonds earn some interest each year, you have the option of paying taxes on the interest earned each year or delaying the payment of taxes on interest earned until you ultimately cash in the bonds. In other words, you are effectively able to earn interest free of taxes for as long as you own the bonds. You can delay cashing in the bonds until you are in a low-income year—such as upon retirement—and thus save considerably on the taxes you'd have otherwise paid on regular taxable investments during higher-income years.

Another attractive tax benefit can be obtained if bonds are issued in the names of children or other individuals whose incomes are so low that they pay little or no income taxes. Being registered in the names of non-income-tax payers, the bonds are thus virtually tax-exempt investments and can be an ideal way to accumulate a nest egg for a child's education or other needs.

The taxation of interest earned on E and EE bonds can be delayed by converting those bonds to HH bonds. By converting to HH bonds, you spread the tax bite out over the life of the HH bond. For example, over the years you've accumulated E and EE bonds that today have a cash value of $10,000. Your cost of these bonds was originally $6000. By cashing them in today, you'll have to pay taxes this year on interest earned of $4000. But if you convert those old bonds into a $10,000 HH bond, you will be subject to taxes only on the interest earnings of the HH bonds each year that you hold them, for as long as ten years. When you finally cash in the HH bonds, you will then be obliged to pay taxes on the original interest earned of $4000. In effect, you are deferring the payment of these taxes for as much as ten years by converting to HH bonds.

Investment Criteria

□ *Yield.*   On regular government bonds and agency bonds you are certain to get the yield you are promised. On EE and HH bonds, your yield may actually increase, subject to the dictates of the U. S. Treasury. Remember that to get the full yield on EE and HH bonds, you must hold them until their full maturity.

□ *Liquidity.*   There is an active market on most government and agency issues which would allow you to cash in your holdings prior to maturity if you so wished. Commissions on such transactions are generally less than commissions on stock transactions. As mentioned earlier, EE and HH bonds cannot be cashed in until six months after the date of purchase.

□ *Safety.* Government issues are considered to be in the highest safety category. To the ultimate skeptic, it's safe to presume that before the government falls, everything else will have fallen long since.

□ *Hedge value.* An investor in long-term government issues has virtually no protection against inflation. The rate of income is fixed, and the fluctuations in the value of the bond are relatively minor. Traders in shorter-term government IOUs can realize better protection against inflation, for as their issues mature, they can move into new issues whose interest rates would reflect prevailing trends throughout the country. If interest rates have moved up, the short-term trader can thus take advantage of higher new rates at the time of reinvesting.

□ *Pledge value.* EE bonds and HH bonds cannot be pledged as security for a loan; they thus have no pledge value. Other government agency bonds can be pledged as security, usually at a very high percentage of their value. Because of the high safety of such bonds, the pledge value would be greater than for corporate bonds of equal size and maturity.

□ *Tax implications.* As indicated in the discussion on passbook savings accounts, certain interest earned on government bonds may be excluded from income for tax purposes. Over and above any such exclusions, interest earned on government bonds is subject to federal taxation, but not to state or local taxation. Tax aspects of EE and HH bonds have been noted earlier.

Municipal Bonds

States, cities, towns, water districts, school districts, sewer districts, highway authorities, and a variety of other local entities have periodic needs to borrow funds. The interest that these bonds pay has been deemed exempt from federal income-tax obligations. This, of course, benefits the local residents of the particular jurisdictions. It makes the cost of building and maintaining schools, roads, sewers, whatever, cheaper than if the holders of the municipal bonds had to pay income taxes on the interest they earned. If the bonds were not tax exempt, they would have to be issued at a higher interest rate, resulting in higher interest costs that would be passed along to taxpayers.

There are two major types of municipal bonds: general obligation bonds and revenue bonds. The general obligation bonds are backed by the taxing authority of the locality. The revenue bonds are backed by the revenues produced by the entity, such as toll roads on a highway-authority bond, or water-usage fees on a water-revenue bond.

Tax Exemption

The most notable aspect of municipal bonds is that the interest they pay investors is exempt from the investors' federal income taxes. Interest earned is also exempt from state income taxes if the investor lives in the state in which the bond is issued. However, if you buy a municipal bond and later sell it at a profit, that profit is subject to full federal and state income taxes. If such a bond has been held for the minimum capital-gains holding period, the taxation will be at the capital-gains rate, which is lower than the ordinary income rate.

Here's an example of how the tax-exempt aspect works. If a couple filing a joint return has a top income rate of 36 percent, a tax-exempt bond paying 8 percent interest will give them the same return as a taxable bond paying $12\frac{1}{2}$ percent interest. Table 16-5 gives a comparison of tax-exempt yields and taxable yields.

Although tax exemption of municipal bonds is attractive, municipal bonds are not for everyone. Taxpayers in higher brackets can benefit considerably, but taxpayers in lower brackets may not be better off with municipal bonds than with taxable securities, particularly when the commission costs of buying and selling such bonds are taken into account.

Municipal Bond Quotations

Quotations on the prices and yields of municipal bonds are not available in daily newspapers. An investor would have to contact a stockbroker for specific details on the prices and yields of any municipal bonds.

Municipal Bond Ratings

Municipal bonds are rated by the same two services that rate corporate bonds, Standard and Poor's and Moody's. As with the corporate bonds, these ratings services examine the financial status of the municipalities, and the ratings compare the relative qualities of the various issues. The formats in both ratings systems is similar. Following is a brief summary of the Standard and Poor ratings.

AAA: highest quality
AA: high grade
A: good grade

Table 16-5

Comparison of Yields: Tax-exempt versus Taxable Securities

		... a tax exempt yield of		
If you are in this tax bracket ...	6 percent	7 percent	8 percent	9 percent
		will net you the same as a taxable yield of		
19 percent	7.4	8.6	9.9	11.1
32 percent	8.8	10.3	11.8	13.2
36 percent	9.4	10.9	12.5	14.1
42 percent	10.3	12.1	13.8	15.5
54 percent	13.0	15.2	17.4	19.6

Example: A taxpayer in the 32 percent tax bracket (joint taxable income of roughly $25,000 to $30,000) will earn the same, after paying taxes, on a taxable investment yielding 11.8 percent as he will earn on a tax-exempt investment yielding 8 percent.

BBB: medium grade
BB: speculative grade
B: low grade
D: default

As with corporate bonds, if the financial condition of a municipality changes, so will its rating. Higher ratings mean a lower return to investors and a lower risk. Check with the rating services for more specific details.

Investment Criteria

☐ *Yield.* In higher rated municipal bonds you are assured of receiving the yield you bargained for. Lowest rated bonds may be subject to a termination of interest payments, such as happened with New York City bonds in the late 1970s.

☐ *Liquidity.* Trading in municipal bonds is not nearly as active for the small investor as in stocks and corporate bonds. Thus, an investor wishing to sell municipal bond holdings may have to wait until a willing buyer comes along, which could be a matter of days or weeks if a specific price is sought. The seller may have to settle for a lesser price in order to find a willing buyer.

☐ *Safety.* As with corporate bonds, the higher the rating of a municipal bond, the higher the safety level. Municipal bonds, like corporate bonds, are subject to the same fluctuations caused by interest-rate changes. Indeed, the traditionally stable municipal bond market has undergone relatively severe fluctuations in recent years in conjunction with interest-rate changes. Thus, the long-term investor in municipal bonds must be concerned over getting caught in a long-term down-swing in the value of his holdings should interest rates move upward from the time he bought the bonds.

There have been innovations—and more will be created—to protect municipal bond investors from these fluctuations. One type is called the "floating rate bond" in which the interest rate will float up and down within set limits, based on U.S. Treasury rates. Because the interest rate floats, the principal balance of the investment should remain relatively stable. Another innovation is the so-called option tender bond in which the holder has the option, or privilege, of cashing in the bond with the original issuer after some years from the date of issue. The investor can cash such bonds in at the original issue price. Check with stockbrokers for more details on these and other innovations in municipal bonds.

☐ *Hedge value.* Municipal bonds offer a rather indirect protection against inflation. Although the bond itself pays a fixed rate of income for as long as one holds it, the tax-exempt factor can be translated into some protection against inflation for the investor whose income is on the rise. As your income increases, you move into ever-higher tax brackets.

The higher the tax bracket you're in, the greater the tax advantage the municipal bond affords you.

☐ *Pledge value.*   Holders of municipal bonds should be able to borrow against their holdings without much difficulty. The percentage of the total value that they can borrow and the interest rate they'll have to pay will depend on the quality of the issue itself as well as its current price level. The higher the quality, the higher percentage of face value you may be able to borrow.

Miscellaneous Money Market Investments

Over the last decade, the ingenuity of the financial marketplace has been particularly bright with respect to the creation of new and unusual forms of fixed income investment. Some of the concepts outlined here have long been the domain of big-money investors. But as the competition for investment dollars has heightened, the concepts have been enlarged to allow the small investor access to these techniques. Over the years, some will capture the public attention, some will fail to, and new techniques will continually be emerging.

Mutual Funds

The mutual fund concept has found great favor with the public at large. Mutual fund companies and stockbrokerage firms pool the investments of many small investors and put that money to work in a variety of ways. Example: As explained earlier, the jumbo certificate of deposit is one which exceeds $100,000 and pays a considerably higher rate of interest to investors than do smaller certificates. If 100 investors could pool $1000 each, they could buy one jumbo certificate for $100,000 and reap a higher return on their investment. But rounding up all these small investors and taking care of the paperwork is a costly and cumbersome procedure for an individual to undertake. The mutual funds have the machinery to handle such detail work with much greater efficiency. Naturally, they charge for their service, but if they are efficient in their investment techniques, the small investor can still reap greater rewards through mutual funds than he might on his own.

Until recent years, mutual funds concentrated primarily on common stocks, but now there are many mutual fund opportunities in the fixed income arena. They encompass corporate bonds, municipal bonds, and money market instruments.

The number of mutual funds of all types may soon exceed 1000. They are all different, though they can be broken down into categories of similarity. Mutual funds do not offer investors any kind of magic formula. The managers of the funds are capable of making good judgments and bad judgments just like the individual investor. So before summarizing some of the major types of fixed income mutual funds, it would be in order to examine some of the main distinctions among mutual funds.

☐ *Closed Versus Open.*   The vast majority of mutual funds are "open-ended." The managers of the fund are continually buying and selling securities at whatever pace they see fit. Thus the composition of the overall fund is constantly changing. The ability to buy and sell allows the fund managers to adjust to changing market conditions. It also expands the possibility of the managers making wise decisions *and* *un*wise decisions. Open-end funds are often known also as "managed funds." There are also a small number of "closed-end" funds that trade in bonds. These function similarly to open-ended funds, but they will generally not repurchase their own shares from the public. Shares in closed-end funds are traded on the stock market.

Yet another type of pooled investment is the *unit trust.* Unlike investment funds that are constantly buying and selling securities, the unit trust will buy a group of securities and hold them until maturity. The income with a unit trust is thus more certain than it is with a managed fund, but the value of each share is susceptible to the ups and downs of the market—remember, interest rates and bond prices move in opposite directions.

☐ *Load Versus No-load.*   This refers to the commission price an investor pays to buy shares in a mutual fund. A "load" can be as much as 8 or 9 percent of the initial investment. In other words, in a typical $8\frac{1}{2}$ load fund, $8\frac{1}{2}$ percent of the investor's initial investment will go to pay the brokerage commission. On a $1000 investment, $85 goes toward commissions and only $915 goes to work for the investor. A no-load fund implies that there is no commission to pay when acquiring the investment. But there may be other charges incurred over the life of the investment with both load and no-load funds.

☐ *Maintenance and Service Charges.*   In addition to the loading commission, mutual funds will charge some kind of monthly or annual service fee. Commonly, the service fee is based on a percentage of the fund's assets. Some funds may also take a fee based on the earnings of the fund during the year. These fees may be deducted from the total fund assets or directly from each individual account. Either way, they are an added cost that can affect your yield.

☐ *Fund Objectives.*   With fixed income mutual funds, the most common objective is to generate maximum income for the investors. (The common stock mutual funds' objectives fall into a broader spectrum ranging from income to speculative growth.) But there can be a distinct difference in the level of income and safety sought by various funds. This will largely be a factor of the distribution of the invested assets.

☐ *Distribution of Investments.*   How will a fund invest the money it receives from individual investors? Differences can be considerable. Some funds will go for the highest quality investments available. This will mean the highest possible level of safety for investors but a lower level of income than can be obtained from funds that seek out lesser quality investments. It's necessary to determine the broad makeup of the portfolios of a number of funds before making an investment decision.

☐ *Minimum Investment Required.* As a broad average the minimum initial investment required in fixed income mutual funds is $1000. There may be a few with a lower initial amount, and there are some with a higher initial required investment. After the initial investment, investors may make additional investments in smaller amounts.

☐ *Extra Privileges.* Many mutual funds are a part of a family of other mutual funds. The owner of shares in such funds may therefore have the privilege of exchanging all or a portion of their shares for shares in another fund managed by the same investment advisory group. For example, you might switch from a corporate bond fund into a common stock fund or vice versa, at a minimal charge. Reinvestment privileges—whereby your earnings are automatically reinvested in additional shares of the fund—are commonplace, usually at no extra charge. Withdrawal privileges—taking out a fixed amount each month or each quarter—are also available, with some minimal restrictions as to the amount that can be withdrawn.

☐ *Investment Criteria.* The investment criteria of a given fixed income mutual fund will be approximately the same with regard to yield, liquidity, safety, hedge values, and pledge values as for that specific type of instrument. In other words, a mutual fund that concentrates exclusively on long-term corporate bonds will have the same investment criteria as individual corporate bonds and so on. There is one important difference, however. The value of the investment criteria depends largely on the investor's own individual ability to interpret changes, trends, and concepts. Theoretically, the professional money managers are better able to do this than individuals. It follows, theoretically, that an investor who is seeking high income may do well, but a professional money manager may be able to do better, and so on.

The mutual fund concept allows an investor to spread his risk over many securities rather than place all of his eggs in one basket. But a careful evaluation of the objectives, the management, and the overall risks involved is as necessary with a mutual fund as it is with a single investment and a specific issue. Investors are advised to read a number of prospectuses of various mutual fund offerings so as to distinguish among the various criteria noted above.

Following is a summary of major types of fixed income mutual funds as well as brief descriptions of additional innovative fixed income investments.

Corporate Bond Funds

These funds invest in a wide variety of corporate bonds: high quality, low quality, long term, short term. The range of possibilities is vast and it is essential to examine the prospectuses to determine the level of risk and income that an investor can expect.

Tax-exempt Municipal Funds

These mutual funds invest predominantely in municipal bonds—those whose income payable to investors is exempt from federal income taxes. The range of quality and risk is not as wide as with corporate bonds, but a range does exist. As with buying municipal bonds, investors should be aware that not all of the income will necessarily be exempt from federal income taxes. If, for example, a mutual fund buys a bond and sells it later for a profit, that portion of the profit that is distributed to shareholders will be considered taxable. Further, interest income from a mutual bond fund can be taxable on the local level (state and city). And as the prospectuses for these funds will disclose, many funds will not invest 100 percent of their assets in tax-exempt municipals. They reserve the right to invest a small portion in other types of instruments that might be taxable. On the whole, however, the major portion of income on such funds would be tax exempt. It would be wise to check with one's tax adviser to determine if tax-exempt mutual funds make sense in any given individual situation.

Money Market Mutual Funds

In the early 1980s the money market mutual funds were the hottest phenomenon in the entire financial marketplace. The popularity of these funds has been based on their ability to give small investors access to high-interest-rate money market instruments, such as treasury bills, jumbo certificates, and the like. Important aspects of money market mutual funds are:

☐ They are flexible. Investors can get out at any time without penalty.

☐ Return on these funds will vary from day to day, as interest rates fluctuate. Thus, an investor will never know what his actual return will be over a long run. (With certificates of deposit, investors are assured a fixed rate for a fixed period of time.)

☐ Fees are reasonably low compared with other types of mutual funds. However, in many funds, the individual broker or salesman that one deals with may receive little or no commission himself. This has caused many brokers to shun small investors' business in money market funds. For those brokers who don't shun such business, the next item can prove a problem for investors:

☐ In virtually all money market mutual funds, the investor will be dealing with a salesman or a stockbroker. Sooner or later that investor should expect to receive a call from the salesman or broker suggesting that the investor get out of the money market fund and into something else. If the investor isn't prepared for that sales pitch, he may find himself making a switch that could prove profitable or unprofitable. In short, an investor might find himself being wooed from a highly secure position into a speculative position. This is not necessarily bad, but the investor should be aware of the potential before he makes his investment.

☐ Shares in money market mutual funds are not insured like bank accounts, but the bulk of money market fund investments are in highly secure instruments such as government issues and bank certificates.

☐ Many large brokerage firms will offer to tie in money market investments with checking accounts and credit card availabilities. In effect, a portion of your checking account balance that isn't needed for immediate use can be invested in the brokerage firm's money market fund where it can earn a high rate of interest. The minimum deposits required for such services and the cost of such services should be carefully examined by prospective investors.

Following are some other types of money market investments which may be available to individual investors directly, or may be included in a mutual fund portfolio.

Repurchase Agreements

Financial institutions often have to borrow large sums of money for very short periods of time, from a few days to a few months. They may borrow from each other; they may borrow from the government (from the Federal Reserve Bank in the case of commercial banks and from the Federal Home Loan Bank in the case of savings and loan associations). Or they may issue what are known as repurchase agreements or "repos." In a repurchase agreement, a bank will sell securities that it owns to outside investors and will give those outside investors a promise that it will repurchase the securities within a fixed period of time at a higher price than the investors paid for them. For example: Bank X may sell $1 million worth of its own government securities to investor Y. The bank promises to repurchase those securities 90 days later for $1,025,000. That $25,000 represents the lender's "profit," which is equal to an annual yield of 10 percent on the invested money.

In many communities, financial institutions have offered small parcels of repurchase agreements to small investors. In other words, instead of selling a single $1 million security to a single investor, it will break the $1 million down into 1000 pieces worth $1000 each and will offer those small pieces to individual investors. Commonly, repurchase agreements in this form run for 89 days or less and pay a yield to investors considerably higher than what their passbook savings accounts will pay. Repurchase agreements are technically not bank accounts and, thus, are not covered by the federal insurance. However, investors are protected by owning a share in the high-quality securities which the institution is selling and rebuying. In theory, if a financial institution defaulted on a repurchase agreement, the individual investors would have the right to sell the underlying security in order to get their money back.

Repurchase agreements can be profitable to financial institutions. They "borrow" from individual investors and in turn reinvest that borrowed money at a higher rate of return in the money market. The difference between what they earn on their own investment and what they pay the small investor is their profit. The repurchase agreement plan allows a financial institution to compete more effectively with the money market mutual funds for investors' dollars.

Bankers Acceptances

Say an American company sells a product to a Japanese company for $200,000.00. The Japanese company gives a written promise to pay for the goods upon delivery, which is expected to be in six months. The American company doesn't want to wait for its money, so it takes the Japanese company's promise to pay to a bank. The bank examines the credentials of the Japanese company and agrees to buy its promise to pay from the American company at a certain price. The bank has thus, in effect, "accepted" the Japanese promise to pay. The bank may then turn around and sell this IOU to investors. The instrument is known as a bankers acceptance. In effect, the investor is buying the promise to pay of a foreign company. The investor is secured to the extent that a bank or other financial institution was willing to take the risk itself. Bankers acceptances tend to pay an attractive rate of interest for short-term investments. Some financial institutions have parceled out bankers acceptances in small lots, similar to their technique with repurchase agreements, thus making portions of bankers acceptances available to small investors. Many money market mutual funds also will have bankers acceptances in their portfolios.

Commercial Paper

When corporations borrow for a long term, as discussed, their promises to pay are called corporate bonds. Often, corporations will borrow for a short period of time—such as a few months. Short-term corporate borrowings are referred to as "commercial paper," and their quality tends to follow the quality of the corporation's bonds. As the bond is rated, so commonly will the commercial paper be rated. See the discussion on bond ratings for more detail. Money market mutual funds will frequently carry sizable amounts of commercial paper in their portfolios.

Commodity-backed Bonds

These are relatively rare but could become commonplace. In a commodity-backed bond, the corporation borrowing money gives the investor a choice of being paid off either in cash or in the particular product that the company makes or sells. The first popular commodity-backed bond was issued in 1980 by the Sunshine Mining Company, one of the nation's largest silver mining firms. In addition to paying interest, the bonds offer investors the option of redeeming their bonds in either cash or silver. The interest rate payable on the bonds was considerably lower than what the company would have had to pay on a normal bond. But investors were willing to take the chance with the lower rate of interest in the hope that the amount of silver they could eventually receive would be worth much more than the face value of the bond. The guaranteed rate of interest, albeit on the low side, gave investors a level of fixed income security; and the opportunity to redeem in silver added an element of speculation. The ultimate potential for commodity-backed bonds in a vast range of goods and services is yet to be determined.

Floating-rate Bonds

As discussed previously, interest rates and bond prices move in opposite directions. As a result of this phenomenon, the prices of bonds fell drastically in the late 1970s and early 1980s as interest rates rose to record high levels. This had the obvious effect of discouraging investors from entering into the bond market.

To ease investor concern, a number of floating-rate bond issues were created. In a floating-rate situation, the interest rate can be adjusted upward and downward in line with the general interest trends. Because the interest rate is adjusted periodically, the value of the bond should remain fairly stable. Thus, investors will give up some of the potential interest return in exchange for the safety of their principal.

Floating-rate bonds are available in both taxable and tax-exempt forms. Among the taxable floating-rate notes, the most popular ones have been issued by banks, with Citicorp being the leader in the field. In the tax-exempt area, numerous local governments and industrial development authorities have found an eager market for floating-rate bonds and notes.

In floating-rate issues, the fluctuations in interest rates are tied to interest rates that the government pays when it borrows money, and there is generally a maximum above which the rate cannot go and a minimum below which it cannot go.

Convertible Bonds

These issues (sometimes called convertible debentures) are corporate bonds that give the owner the right to convert the bonds into common stock of the issuing company. Here's an example: XYZ Corporation issues a convertible bond with a selling price of $1000. The bond pays an interest rate of 10 percent—$100 per year. That rate is fixed for the life of the bond. An owner of the bond has the right to convert his bond into 50 shares of XYZ common stock, which is now selling for $20 per share and paying a $2 per share dividend. Thus, the income from 50 shares of the common stock is $100 per year, the same as the bond. At this point, the $1000 bond and the 50 shares of common stock are equal in value. There would seem to be no point in converting from the bond to the stock. However, an investor may be hopeful that the dividend on the stock could increase, say from $2 to $3 per share. If, in fact, that happened and the investor converted from the bond to the stock, he would increase his yield from $100 per year to $150 per year. The interest rate on the bond is fixed, but since the dividend rate on the stock is not fixed, an investor who is willing to speculate on increased dividends could find convertible bonds profitable.

On the other hand, the bond is eventually going to be worth $1000 upon maturity. The investor knows that for sure. The stock could drop to a much lower level than its conversion value. If an investor does convert, he is taking a chance that the stock will decrease in value and he could suffer a considerable loss.

During the holding period, prior to a decision to convert, the bond and the stock will tend to move up and down on a fairly parallel course. Once the investor has converted from the bond to the stock, he is stuck. He can't convert back to the bond again if his expectations do not work out.

Yields on Money Market Securities

The Personal Action Checklist at the end of this chapter will help you to compare the current yields on the most common types of money market securities. Since these yields change frequently, you should compare them at the time you are ready to make a specific investment.

Tax-deferred Fixed Income Investing: IRA and Keogh Plans

Individual Retirement Accounts (IRA) and Keogh plans are commonly referred to as do-it-yourself pension programs. Both plans allow qualified participants very attractive income-tax benefits. Because IRA and Keogh investments are commonly placed in fixed income "money market" programs, it's appropriate to discuss them in detail at this point.

How They Work

Effective tax year 1982, all workers are eligible for IRA plans. An IRA participant can invest each year up to $2000, or 100 percent of his or her income from work, whichever is less. (Example: If someone earns $10,000 from work in a year, the maximum IRA contribution will be $2000. If someone earns $1500 in a year from work, the maximum contribution will be $1500.)

If an IRA participant has a nonworking spouse, the maximum annual contribution can be as much as $2250, if the couple opens what is known as a "spousal" IRA account. If both husband and wife qualify, each can contribute the full maximum amount in a given year. Thus, it's possible for a working couple to invest as much as $4000 in their IRA plans.

The amount of the annual investment is tax deductible to the participant. Technically, it's listed as an "adjustment" on the tax return, but the effect is the same as if it were a deduction. The deduction thus is available even though the individual does not itemize his or her deductions. Also, investments in an IRA fund will earn income on a tax-deferred basis.

Keogh plans are available to self-employed individuals. The maximum amount of an annual Keogh investment is $15,000 or 15 percent of income from work, whichever is less. (Example: A self-employed individual earns $50,000 in a year. The maximum Keogh investment allowable will be 15 percent of that amount or $7,500. Another self-employed individual earns $200,000 in a year. The maximum Keogh investment allowable will be $15,000 for that year.) As with IRA plans, Keogh investments are tax deductible to the participant. If a self-employed individual has employees, he or she must make contributions on behalf of certain of those employees.

Except in cases of death or disability, IRA and Keogh investments cannot be withdrawn before the age of $59\frac{1}{2}$. If withdrawals are made before that age, a penalty will be payable to the government in addition to any taxes that are owed on the withdrawn funds. In both plans, a withdrawal program must begin by age $70\frac{1}{2}$.

When the funds—both the original investment and the earnings thereon—are withdrawn, taxes will be payable on the amounts withdrawn in the years in which the money is withdrawn. The theory behind IRA and Keogh is that money will not be withdrawn until retirement, at which time the participant will be in a lower tax bracket.

The combination of deductibility of the annual investment and tax-deferred earnings on the invested funds offers a very attractive double tax advantage to IRA and Keogh participants. Table 16-6 compares the growth of a nest egg in an IRA or Keogh plan over a long term, compared with the growth in a fully taxable form of investment.

Setting up a Plan   Both IRA and Keogh plans can be set up relatively simply at banks, savings institutions, stockbrokerage firms, and mutual fund companies. The Keogh plan will likely require more paper work than the IRA. An IRA or Keogh participant should shop around to determine what types of plans are available. IRA and Keogh investments are for retirement purposes and should not be a subject of speculation. Stockbrokerage firms offer IRA and Keogh plans that can be self-directed by the participants;

Table 16-6

If you put away $1000 a year for this many years, at an 8 percent annual return . . .	. . . and you were in the 40 percent tax bracket, this is how much you'd end up with	
	in a taxable plan (after taxes)	in an IRA or Keogh plan
5 years	$ 3,461	$ 6,335
10 years	7,835	15,645
15 years	13,366	29,323
20 years	20,356	49,421
25 years	29,195	78,951
30 years	40,369	122,341

Note: Upon withdrawing from the IRA or Keogh plan, some taxes would then be payable from these amounts. Amount payable would depend on your tax bracket at that time, presumably lower because you'd be in retirement.

that is, you can instruct the broker as to how your money is to be put to work. But be aware that if undue risk is taken, it can have a hazardous effect on your retirement nest egg.

It should be noted that you are not required to make a contribution to either plan every year; you are simply limited to the maximum amount that you can invest in a given year. Also, you are permitted to alter your IRA or Keogh plan investment mode from time to time. Check locally for current regulations on these and other matters. Since the conception of Keogh plans (1960) and IRA plans (1974), Congress has periodically increased the maximum allowable annual investment. It is possible that that trend will continue and that in future years higher limits will be permissible.

In addition to do-it-yourself IRA plans, the law allows employers to set up various programs to which they can contribute on your behalf and to which you can also make supplemental contributions that will qualify for the IRA deductions.

The IRA Rollover

One of the most important, and most frequently overlooked, aspects of the IRA program is the so-called rollover. This can be very valuable to individuals who are moving from one job to another and to individuals who are receiving a lump-sum pension benefit at retirement.

If you are leaving a job and your employer owes you pension or profit-sharing benefits, you might have to pay substantial taxes when you receive those benefits. But you can defer payment of those taxes by placing the proceeds of your pension or profit-sharing benefits into an IRA rollover account, which you can establish as you would a regular IRA account. You must do so within 60 days of receipt of the benefits. Once you have put the money into an IRA rollover account, you defer payment of taxes that would otherwise have been due on that money until such time as you later withdraw the funds for your own use.

The IRA rollover can also be used to transport your pension or profit-sharing benefits from one employer to a new one, assuming the new employer is willing to allow you to do so. If that's the case, the proceeds from the old employer should be placed into an IRA rollover and then, at the appropriate time, withdrawn from the IRA rollover and placed into the new employer's pension or profit-sharing plan. By so doing you also defer payment of taxes that would have otherwise been due on that money.

Finally, if you are retiring and receiving a lump-sum benefit that you do not need immediately, you can place that money into a rollover and defer taxes until you later do withdraw that money for your own personal purposes.

Personal Action Checklist
Comparing Current Income Opportunities

It's expected that savings opportunities will become more and more competitive, as the financial industry gradually adjusts to the congressionally mandated deregulation of interest rates. Whereas in the past, virtually all institutions paid comparable rates of interest, the emerging deregulation is expected to offer the public a mind-boggling assortment of choices. Following are what will be among the more popular choices, along with criteria that can help you evaluate which is best for your specific current situation.

	Annual rate (percent)	Yield, after compounding and taxes	Maturity	Penalty*	Safety†
☐ U.S. Treasury issues					
3 month	_____	_____	_____	_____	_____
6 month	_____	_____	_____	_____	_____
12 month	_____	_____	_____	_____	_____
24 month	_____	_____	_____	_____	_____
36 month	_____	_____	_____	_____	_____
☐ U.S. Agency issues					
under one year to maturity	_____	_____	_____	_____	_____
2 to 5 years to maturity	_____	_____	_____	_____	_____
☐ Certificates of deposit					
6 months	_____	_____	_____	_____	_____
12 months	_____	_____	_____	_____	_____
30 months	_____	_____	_____	_____	_____
48 months	_____	_____	_____	_____	_____
☐ Corporate bonds, commercial paper					
under 3 years to maturity	_____	_____	_____	_____	_____
3 to 6 years to maturity	_____	_____	_____	_____	_____
☐ Repurchase agreements	_____	_____	_____	_____	_____
☐ Special tax-protected investments					
tax-exempt savings	_____	_____	_____	_____	_____
tax-deferred IRA and Keogh plans	_____	_____	_____	_____	_____
tax-exempt municipal notes and bonds	_____	_____	_____	_____	_____
tax-deferred annuities	_____	_____	_____	_____	_____

*Penalty refers to any loss of interest or principal if any principal is withdrawn prior to the maturity of the investment.
†Safety refers to the level of security: governmental insurance, quality of the issuing company, and so on. Evaluate as per discussion in this chapter, plus any up-to-date developments that would have a bearing on safety.

Consumer Beware
"It Seemed Like a Good Idea at the Time"

In 1969–70 the yields on high-quality corporate bonds rose to unexpectedly high levels: in the 8 to 9 percent range. Many stockbrokers and investment advisers counseled clients seeking high income to acquire these bonds. Double-digit inflation had not yet reared its ugly head; and professional money people would have laughed in disbelief had anyone suggested that similar-type bonds would offer roughly twice the yield a decade later.

Those who invested in such bonds then did not concern themselves with the fact that many of the bonds did not reach maturity until after the year 2000. And many of the investors then were senior citizens, who looked to the returns on the bonds as a supplement to their retirement income. "If worse came to worst," they rationalized, "we can always cash the bonds in if we need the money for something else."

All things considered, the investments appeared to make sense: high income (at least for those days); solid security; and a liquid market so you could cash in if need be. As so many rueful investors were to note later, "It seemed like a good idea at the time."

As interest rates soared in the early 1980s, the market value of these bonds plummeted. Many dropped to 50 to 60 percent of their face value, which would mean a stunning loss for investors who wanted to sell. And the 8 to 9 percent income seemed paltry after almost ten years of unrelenting inflation.

Of course, the bonds will be worth their full face value when they reach maturity. But to the investors who have to wait another 20 years to recover their full investment, the prospects are definitely not heartening.

Those who do their homework may find that they can swap these low-value bonds for higher yielding bonds that are closer to maturity, and combining the tax loss with the higher income at least improves their situations somewhat. But many of them simply throw up their hands and say, "I hope at least my grandchildren will enjoy the money."

Prudence dictates keeping fixed income maturities within a fairly short term—not to exceed three to five years, unless special circumstances dictate otherwise. By keeping maturities short, you gain flexibility. And now, more than ever, flexibility is an invaluable tool to help you keep up with rapidly changing times.

17 | Making Your Money Grow: The Stock Market

This chapter continues our exploration of ways you can make your money grow—hopefully. The stock market involves aspects of risk not found in "money" market investments. The nature of those risks are not always understood by would-be investors/speculators. If the risks aren't understood, serious damage can be done to your financial well-being. To help you understand and evaluate those risks, we'll examine:

☐ What makes the stock market tick.

☐ How to understand the language and the numbers of the stock market.

☐ What motivates various kinds of people to put their money to work in the stock market, the better to help you identify and understand your own motivations.

☐ Specific techniques that you can use within the arena of the stock market.

☐ Evaluating the professional help available to you through stockbrokers.

Stock Ownership as a Form of Investing

In the previous chapter on money market investing we explored the possibilities of creating future wealth by "lending" your money to another entity, receiving in turn a promise to pay a fee (interest) for the use of your money, plus the promise to return it at an agreed-on time. These promises are legally binding obligations of the debtor or institution.

Stock ownership as a form of investment is quite different. With stock ownership, the investor has become a part owner of a business enterprise and has no promise (legal or otherwise) that he will receive any fee for the use of his money, or that anyone will be obliged to pay him any or all of his money back at any future time. He is dependent on the profitability of the business venture to generate a return on his investment and to create the possibility of a gain should he later wish to sell the investment.

Lending Versus Buying

What's the difference between lending your money to a business (investing in a corporate bond) and buying a portion of ownership in the business (buying stock)? Businesses often need money to develop new products, expand their facilities, buy new equipment, modernize, and for other job-creating activities. Some of the money needed may come from the profits that the business generates, but this isn't always enough. In order to acquire large sums of money relatively quickly, a business will either borrow from investors (issue corporate bonds) or will sell a portion of itself to investors (issue stock). The former route is frequently referred to as the debt market, the latter as the equity market.

Regarding its debt, the company has a legal obligation to pay interest to the investors and to return the principal sum at the agreed-on time. With equity, or stock, the company has no such legal obligation. *If* profits are in fact generated, the company *may* distribute a portion of the profits to the stockholders. The company is under no obligation to buy the stock back from a stockholder. If a stockholder wants to sell the stock, he or she hopes to find a buyer willing to pay an attractive price.

The important priority to note in comparing debt with stock ownership is that debt service (interest) *must* be paid *before* profits are tallied. Profits are the dollars left over after the business has paid all of its obligations, among which may be the payments due on its debts.

The same holds true when a business is terminated, either voluntarily or otherwise. In such a procedure, commonly called a liquidation, everything that the company owns is converted into cash. Out of that pool of cash, all of the company's debts are paid, including any bonds that may be outstanding. What's left over is split up between the stockholders. In other words, creditors have priority over stockholders in liquidation as well as in the day-to-day operation of a business.

The profitability of any kind of business venture depends on a great many factors, including management of the business, nature of the competition, overall ups and downs in the nation's economy as well as for a particular category of industry, and the totally unpredictable quirks and whims of the investing public. It's this last element—the whims and quirks of the investing public—that makes the stock market a series of unending dilemmas. In the stock market, you are not just necessarily betting on how profitably the company can perform; you are also betting on how *other* people think the company might perform.

The Primary Market Versus the Secondary Market

Distinction should be made between the primary or new issues market and the secondary market. The primary market is that aspect of stock trading in which companies raise money from the investing public. Once the money has been raised and shares of ownership in the companies have been issued to the investors, the stock is traded in the secondary market. Only a tiny percentage of all stock transactions are primary market transactions; the vast majority are on the secondary market.

The primary market serves a critically important purpose in the economy of the nation: it provides ready access for companies to raise money for expansion, research, and other worthwhile purposes. The secondary market is often looked upon as little more than a gambling casino. There is, however, an important purpose for the secondary market: without the secondary market, the primary market could not exist. Businesses could not raise money by selling stock if the investors did not know that they could readily sell their stock at a fair price. Thus, despite the often speculative aspect of the secondary market, our economy would severely flounder without it.

Possibilities Versus Probabilities

Virtually every transaction in the stock market, every purchase and every sale of every share, is essentially a disagreement. The sellers want to get out because they don't think the stock offers them satisfactory income or potential any longer. The buyers want to get in because they feel the stock *does* offer satisfactory income or profit potential. In other words, the two parties disagree about the potential of the stock.

The stock market offers a vast spectrum of possibilities. The challenge is to find that small cluster of possibilities that can help achieve your stated objectives. But note the word *possibilities*. In the fixed income investment area, we're dealing with the realm of *probabilities*—in the stock market it's *possibilities*.

In your own personal life, you have a spectrum of future needs and desires: some probable and some possible. It's *probable* that you're going to retire some day and need adequate money to live on. It's *possible* that some day you might be in a position to enjoy a trip around the world. Goals that are probable or fixed or certain need appropriate techniques if they are to be achieved. Those techniques tend to fall into the fixed income investment spectrum. You can't afford to take chances that you will or will not achieve those fixed and necessary goals. You have to be certain that they will be reached, or at least as certain as you can be.

Other goals that are less certain may be appropriately sought after by the *less certain* investment techniques, principally the stock market, *but not until after you have established a disciplined program that you feel confident will put you on the path to achieving your fixed goals.*

In other words, get a reasonable program under way that will take you to your fixed destinations. If you still have funds available to invest after you've put enough away toward those top priorities, you might want to consider the more speculative techniques to help you achieve lesser priority goals—goals that if not achieved will not cause you to really suffer.

For a more vivid comparison of the difference between fixed income investing and "ownership" investing, let's look at the following scale, which represents the likelihood of achieving stated objectives.

1. Relatively total certainty
2. Fairly certain
3. Highly probable
4. Probable
5. Highly possible

6. Possible

7. Relatively uncertain

8. No degree of certainty

The objective: to put away X dollars today and know that you will have Y dollars at some future date.

The better quality ranges of the fixed income types of investment will fall into the top half of the scale, from one to four. The better quality range of stocks will fall in the middle, from three to six. Although many high-quality stocks have a very strong assurance of continuity of dividends, they are, nonetheless, subject to the fluctuations in value that can have an important bearing on your overall nest egg. Consider, for example, what many think to be the bellwether of all stocks: American Telephone and Telegraph. Its dividends have been increasing over the years, but the stock was selling for about $70 per share in the mid 1960s, below $40 in the mid 1970s, and around $55 in the early 1980s.

The majority of investments in the stock market would fall in the four to seven range and a considerable number would be in the six to eight range. A small number of lower rated fixed income securities might fall into the bottom half of the scale, but the risk in such securities is much more self-evident because of the ongoing ratings of the securities.

For the balance of this chapter, we'll examine in greater detail some of the inner workings of the stock market. In no way at all should any of the discussion be construed as recommendations to buy, sell, or hold any types of securities; it is to help you determine whether or not the stock market offers the opportunities that will help you meet your goals, to understand how the mechanism works, and to motivate you to do further independent research to find those specific areas that will provide you with the returns you're seeking.

Cautions

As you read and discuss the material on the stock market, bear in mind the following cautions.

1. Aided by sophisticated computers, millions of workhours are spent every day studying every movement, jiggle, and quiver of the stock market. Yet no one can predict with any degree of certainty what direction the market as a whole, or any individual stock, is liable to take even a minute or two from now.

2. There have probably been more statistics compiled about the stock market, and more books written about it, than perhaps any other phenomenon on earth. Yet it continues to be one of the most confusing, mystifying, and frustrating subjects we deal with.

3. The stock market touches our day-to-day life in more ways than we can imagine, yet we are powerless to control it in even the slightest way. Even though you may have never had anything to do directly with the market and don't intend to ever have anything to do with it, it can still affect you. If the company that employs you is traded on the stock market, swings in the value of the stock can affect the future profitability of the company and possibly the future of your job. If your employer or boss is a stock market trader, his or her success or failure in the market on a day-to-day basis can have an affect on his or her personality and attitude, which in turn can affect yours. If your pension fund or profit-sharing fund has money invested in the stock market, the investment expertise of those who manage those funds can have a profound bearing on your future.

4. There is no person, no book, no system, no computer, that can *assure* you of making money in the stock market. The stock market can play an important function as an integral part of establishing your future security. But unless one approaches it with the proper frame of mind, the proper expertise, and the proper degree of skepticism, its traps and pitfalls can destroy the very best intentions.

How a Business Operates

A brief look at how a corporation functions will assist you in understanding the workings of the stock market.

A corporation is a legal entity in its own right. Each separate state has its own specific laws governing how a corporation may be created and how it can be run. Like a person, a corporation can own, buy, or sell property; it can be taxed; it can sue and be sued; and it can conduct business.

A corporation is owned by its stockholders. Operating within the framework of applicable laws, the stockholders determine what they wish their corporation to do. But, particularly with corporations that have a great many stockholders, it is cumbersome for the stockholders to meet and consult over every item of corporate business. Thus, the stockholders elect a group of representatives who will act on their behalf in setting basic policy and direction for the corporation. This group of representatives is referred to as the *directors*.

In turn, the directors will choose a group of individuals to carry out the day-to-day and month-to-month operations of the business. These people are called the *officers* of the corporation. The chief officer of a corporation is commonly called the President. (Many large corporations also have other titles of high magnitude that may be equal to or greater in power than the President, such as Chief Executive Officer.) Under the President, and answering directly to him or her, will be an array of Vice Presidents, each with their own area of tasks, obligations, and responsibilities. Other officers of the corporation will commonly include the Treasurer, the Secretary, and the Comptroller, and each of these may have an additional hierarchy of assistants.

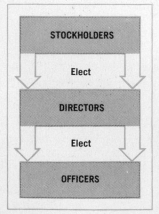

The stockholders generally meet once each year, at which time they are informed of the progress and future potential of the corporation. It's at the annual meeting that the stockholders select the directors, who in turn select the officers. If an individual stockholder is unable to attend this annual meeting, he or she will receive a "proxy," a voting authorization on which one can indicate the selection of directors and one's choice on a number of issues on which stockholders have been asked to express an opinion or a vote.

Commonly, the Board of Directors will recommend to the stockholders a slate of nominees for the board for the forthcoming year. If ownership has been pleased with the job that management has done, the board's recommendations will usually be followed. If ownership has not been pleased with management's performance, a struggle might ensue. One or more directors may be voted out, and one or more proposed policies may be rejected by the stockholders. It is the rule rather than the exception in most large corporations that the stockholders will comply with the recommendations of the Board of Directors. Stockholders assume that management knows best, even though there may have been some setbacks during the year, or they may simply not care to express any contrary views when completing their proxy vote. In recent years, though, the annual meetings of many major corporations have been enlivened by sharp discussions between ownership and management regarding corporate responsibility in the fields of discrimination, pollution, and political practices. As a result, many corporations have adopted policies in keeping with stockholder wishes to amend their stance or create a new stance in line with these highly visible public issues.

How the Stock Markets Operate

An individual's share of ownership in a corporation is represented by the stock certificate, which stipulates how many shares the individual owns. The value of each share, and thus of one's overall sum total of shares, is determined by a number of factors: profitability of the company, future potential for the company, amount of dividends the company is paying, and, broadly, what the public at large thinks it's worth. If a stockholder wishes to sell his stock, he must find a buyer who's willing to pay the asking price. If an investor wishes to buy stock, he must find a willing seller. In small local corporations, word of mouth may be all that's needed to find the respective buyer or seller, if one is to be found. But with large corporations, particularly those with hundreds of thousands or millions of shares outstanding, this would be impractical. If a would-be investor in stocks did not feel confident that he could sell his shares quickly and efficiently, he would likely be discouraged from making the investment in the first place.

Thus, throughout the nation and the world, exchanges long ago came into being to provide a ready marketplace for both buyers and sellers. The most familiar is the New York Stock Exchange, located in lower

Manhattan, in an area commonly referred to as Wall Street. Other major exchanges include the American Stock Exchange and the Pacific Stock Exchange.

The stock exchanges are basically a form of auction in which buyers and sellers try to achieve the best buying or selling price. An investor who wishes to buy or sell stock places an order with a local stockbroker who works for a firm who owns a "seat" on an exchange. The order is relayed from the local broker's office to the firm's facilities on the floor of the exchange. In some cases, the brokerage firm may fill the order itself. In other cases, the order may be referred to a "specialist" on the floor of the exchange. Each individual stock traded on any given exchange is represented by a specialist whose job it is to match certain buy and sell orders and to keep an orderly marketplace for the stock he represents. In order to do so, he may be required to actually buy or sell stocks from his own account.

When the order is filled, word is relayed back to the local brokerage firm, who informs the customer of the results. Written confirmation of the transaction follows shortly thereafter.

The Prospectus

Before a stock can be publicly traded (including on an exchange), it must comply with certain governmental regulations. If a stock is to be sold only to the residents of the specific state in which the company is located, the company must comply with local state regulations. If it is to be traded broadly, beyond state boundaries and across the nation, it must comply with requirements of the federal agency that oversees such matters, the Securities and Exchange Commission (SEC).

The federal regulations require a company to disclose a variety of facts relating to its operation including the identity and experience of its management, its debts, its legal affairs, its overall financial status, and the potential risks that an investor might face in investing in the company. All of this information—usually spelled out at great length in cumbersome legal jargon—is contained in a document called the prospectus.

A prospectus is required when a company initially sells its stock, or when it issues subsequent securities, including stocks or bonds. Once the initial prospectus has been issued, a company need not issue subsequent ones unless it offers additional securities at a later date. Thus, while the prospectus is an important tool for the investor, if it is substantially out of date (as most are), its value can be diminished. Yet it still might serve as important background material and should not be ignored.

Corporations do issue annual reports for the stockholders and for the SEC that contain more up-to-date information than the prospectus. A would-be investor should examine the annual reports, and it would be wise to compare these reports with the original prospectus, if for no other reason than to determine how well the company has met its originally stated objectives.

One critical aspect of the prospectus must be emphasized: Investors often believe that because a company has filed a prospectus with the SEC, the strength of the federal government stands behind that stock and in effect Washington has somehow bestowed its blessings on the company and its stock. Nothing could be further from the truth. On the front cover of each prospectus is this often overlooked statement:

These securities have not been approved or disapproved by the Securities and Exchange Commission, nor has the Commission passed on the accuracy or adequacy of this prospectus. Any representation to the contrary is a criminal offense.

That statement means exactly what it says: The government does not in any way stand behind any of the statements made in the prospectus. The government does not say whether the information in the prospectus is accurate or adequate, but corporations found to have included inaccurate or inadequate or improper statements in their prospectus are subject to criminal prosecution. Further, anyone who tells you that the government has approved the issue or any of the specific details can also be subject to criminal prosecution. Thus, if a company lies in its prospectus in order to raise more money through the sale of stock, and stockholders are subsequently damaged as a result of the deception, it is possible that criminal and civil prosecution could result in an order requiring the corporation to reimburse the deceived stockholders. But if there's no money available to make such reimbursement, all is for naught.

Investors Insurance

The government does offer one measure of protection to investors, through the Security Investors Protection Corporation (SIPC).

When scores of banks folded as a result of the Great Depression in 1929–1935, the government acted to create an insurance program that would prevent a recurrence of such a disaster. The Federal Deposit Insurance Corporation came into being to insure bank depositors against the institution's failure. But until 1970, there was no comparable protection for investors who entrusted their funds to stockbrokerage firms. A severe stock market collapse in 1969–1970 caused a number of brokerage firms to fail. Many more, on the brink of imminent failure, were absorbed by larger and healthier firms. As a result of the near panic that ensued, the government, in conjunction with the securities industry, took steps to create the SIPC, which would insure investors' accounts for the value of any securities or funds held by their brokerage firm in the event of a failure of such a firm. Most major firms currently provide this protection to their customers, but some smaller firms may not. (*Note:* The insurance does *not* protect against the value of any stock going down.)

Keeping the Records

The shares of most major corporations are traded by the hundreds or thousands every business day. It's not uncommon for over 40 million shares of stock to change hands in a single day on the New York Stock

Exchange alone. This total volume is made up of many thousands of individual transactions, representing handfuls or major blocks of shares. Smaller corporations whose shares are seldom traded may hire clerical help to administer the necessary bookwork involved in periodically amending the list of stockholders. But most major corporations hire "transfer agents" to take care of this burdensome task. Transfer agents are usually affiliated with major banks.

When you buy or sell shares of a stock, the transfer agent will be notified accordingly, and your name will either be placed on or removed from the list of stockholders of that corporation. As dividends become payable, the transfer agent will see to it that the dividend is transmitted to you, or to your account with the stockbroker.

When you buy stock, you have the choice of obtaining the certificate registered in your own name (or in the name of whatever parties you choose as owners, such as husband and wife jointly); or you may prefer to have the broker retain custody of the stock. In that case, the stock would be listed "in street name"—technically it is in the broker's name and possession, but he is holding it for your account. Some investors may prefer to obtain the certificate in their own hands, aware of the fact that they should make proper safekeeping arrangements for it. Other investors prefer the convenience of having it remain in the broker's custody. In such cases the investor will receive a monthly statement from the broker indicating the status of the account and which securities are being held in his or her name.

Each buy and sell transaction will be followed up by a written confirmation that indicates the date of the transaction, the price for which the security was bought or sold, the amount of the broker's commission and any appropriate taxes, and the net amount due to the broker or to the investor from the broker. These confirmation slips should be retained by the investor, for they will contain information helpful in determining future gains or losses on the stock. The confirmation slips also indicate the "settlement date," which is the day by which the payment must be made and the stock delivered.

Executing an Order

Once you have opened an account with a broker by signing the necessary papers, you can execute orders, that is, instruct your broker to buy or sell on your behalf. (If the individual broker with whom you regularly deal is not available at the time you wish to place an order, you can always place an order through another representative of the firm.)

Orders to buy or sell stock can take many different forms. Here are the major types:

Market Orders If you instruct your broker to buy or sell "at the market," he will then buy or sell your shares at whatever the going market price might be. He should, of course, try to get the best possible price, but it may not be exactly what you had in mind. For example, XYZ is currently selling at $50 per share, and you instruct your broker to buy 100 shares "at the market." At the moment your order reaches the floor, the best possible price for those shares may have risen to $51 per share. That's what you would end up paying. On the other hand, if you instructed your broker to sell 100 shares "at the market," the best possible price available when your order reaches the floor might be $49, and that's what you'd get. It could also work the other way around. You might be able to buy at a lower price than you had anticipated or sell at a higher price.

Limit Orders   A limit order sets a maximum or minimum price on the sale or purchase of shares. For example, you purchased 100 shares of XYZ at $50 per share. You have made up your mind that if it reaches $55 per share, you want to sell and take your profits, and if it drops to $45 per share, you want to sell and cut your losses. You can place a limit order at $55 per share, and that order would be executed only when the stock can be sold at $55 per share. If the stock never reaches that level, the limit order will never be completed. If you want to buy stock, a limit order can also be used. Say you wish to buy 100 shares of XYZ if the price drops to $45 per share. You place a limit order with your broker, and if and when XYZ hits $45 per share, your order will be executed. If the stock never does hit that price, your order won't be executed.

Time Orders   A time order can be attached to a limit order. It adds a time deadline to the limit order. A time order may be for a day, or for any number of days. One common type of time order is called a "good this week" order (GTW). This order will remain in effect until the end of the calendar week. Example: You would like to buy 100 shares of XYZ for $45 per share, but only if XYZ hits $45 per share before the end of this week. You would thus instruct your broker to enter a combined limit order and time order. If XYZ does hit $45 per share before the end of the week, your order will be executed. If not, then you will not have bought the stock. Another form of time order is called the "open order," or "good till canceled" (GTC) order. It is a standing order to buy or sell at a fixed price until you, the investor, cancel the order or until it is actually executed at that price.

Fill or Kill Orders   This is an order to buy or sell at a fixed price immediately. Example: You wish to sell 100 shares of XYZ at $55 per share. With a fill or kill order, if your broker cannot execute immediately at that price, the order will be canceled.

Most orders to buy and sell stock are handled by telephone. It's important, therefore, to make certain that your broker has followed your instructions explicitly, particularly concerning the number of shares you're selling or buying, the price at which you wish to buy or sell, and the specific type of order you're giving him. These specifics should be repeated between you and the broker and you should make immediate written note of them and he should do the same.

Who Invests in the Stock Market and What Are They Seeking?

The vast diversity of stock market investors can be broken down into three broad categories: by objective, by size, and by type.

Investors by Objective

What is an investor seeking when he buys stocks? It could be any one, or a combination, of the following: short-term growth, long-term growth, income, and "no foggy idea." Let's look at each in turn.

Short-term Growth   This objective might be best described as "out to make a fast buck." If this is your objective, you might be as well served by your nearest racetrack or gambling casino as by the stock market. Humorist Will Rogers had some good advice for those who dive into the stock market looking for the fast buck: "It's easy to be successful in the stock market. You just buy stock, and when it goes up you sell it. And if it don't go up, don't buy it."

Long-term Growth   This more prudent objective is more likely to reward the patient investor who has done the necessary homework. The most immediate advantage of a long-term growth objective is that when a stock has been held for the minimum 12-month holding period, profits are then taxed at a long-term capital-gains rate, which is a lower rate than for short-term gains. The investor whose objective is long-term growth will analyze industries and specific companies whose long-term future looks healthy and profitable and will select his investments accordingly. If he selects wisely and luckily and is willing to wait long enough, he may well realize his objectives.

Income   Many investors get involved in the stock market with the main objective of receiving income in the form of dividends. While the dividends they earn might not be as rewarding as what they could have earned in money market investments, there is also the secondary hope that the stocks will increase in value over a period of time.

The investor whose objectives are balanced between growth and income is perhaps the one who is approaching the market most intelligently. He is the investor who will set a target for upside potential and downside potential. He might, for example, define his objective as a 15 percent annual return (after brokerage commissions) on his investment—

perhaps 7 percent might come through receipt of dividends and the other 8 percent through increase in the value of his shares. Say that XYZ Company is selling at $50 per share and is paying a $3.50 per share dividend per year. That's equal to a 7 percent return in the form of dividends. If, during his first year of ownership of XYZ, the price moves from $50 to $54 per share—an 8 percent increase during the year—he will have realized his 15 percent objective. By the same token, he would also set a downside limit. If XYZ drops to $45 per share, he'll get out at that price and thus shelter himself from any further losses. There are no strict rules of thumb as to what a desirable balance is. Many of one's objectives in this area must relate to what can be attained with the same investable dollars in the money market. If you know that you can attain a 15 percent return on a guaranteed money market instrument, then why take a chance on a 15 percent objective in the stock market? You could do better, or you could do worse. But if 15 percent is your aim and you can get it for certain in the money market, it might be best to take it that way and wait to play the stock market another day.

"No Foggy Idea"   This well may represent the majority of stock market investors. In short, they haven't the foggiest idea what their objectives are. They're not sure why they bought what they bought when they bought it. And they have no notion as to when or why they should sell. Their only hope for success in the market is good luck.

Investors by Size

Within the size categories there are individuals and institutions—or, put another way, small investors and large investors. Individual investors (as well as groups of them such as in investment clubs) and small organizations generally trade in small blocks of stock. Blocks of 100 shares are referred to as round lots; blocks of less than 100 shares are referred to as odd lots, and such transactions may carry a slightly higher brokerage commission—called the "odd lot differential"—than round lot trades.

The large investors, such as pension and profit-sharing funds, mutual funds, trust funds, large corporations, insurance companies, and the like, often trade in very large blocks—many thousands of shares at a time. Large block trades can disrupt the normal flow of supply and demand of shares and can thus cause considerable fluctuations in the price of a given stock at the time that such an order to buy or sell is placed.

The existence, side by side, of the small investor and the large investor has been referred to as the "two-tier market." From the end of World War II until the late 1960s, the securities industry had vigorously wooed the small investor all across the nation. Small investors responded by the millions and became part owners of American business. They were particularly welcomed in the stock market, not only because of the commissions they generated for the brokerage firms, but also because the large mass of small investors tended to exert a stabilizing influence on the market movement as a whole.

But the stock market debacles of 1969–1970 and 1974–1975 chased many small investors away from the stock market, leaving an inordinately heavy portion of the trading to be done by the large investors. This has contributed to a much more volatile market: day-to-day fluctuations in prices tend to be much broader than they had been during the 1950s and 1960s, thus casting an even more uncertain aspect on the fate of anyone's investment.

Investors by Type

The following are brief descriptions of eight broad categories of investors. They may represent individuals or institutions. They are all together in the market at the same time, all expressing a constant flow of opinions that may be in total accord or total discord with their colleagues. Generally there is enough disagreement to keep most prices on a relatively even keel most of the time. Let's take a closer look at the cast of characters.

The Novice

The novice isn't really sure what he's doing. His obvious motivation is to "make money," but he's not really certain how, or if, he will. If he has done any studying at all, it's probably been only superficial; most likely he has involved himself in the market because of the suggestion of someone else, and he's probably followed the suggestion at its face value. He may fancy himself an investor, but his real status is more akin to that of a blind bettor.

The Insider

There are three types: the way-insider, the fringe-insider, and the pretend-insider. The way-insider is a person on intimate terms with the day-to-day operation of the corporation—an officer, an employee, a director, or a major stockholder. He will be privy to information not yet available to the public that, when released to the public, can have a good or bad effect on the stock of the company. He may know, for example, that a potentially profitable deal is about to be completed; or that a sharp loss is about to be announced; or that an important new product is about to be introduced; or that an unsuccessful old product is about to be withdrawn from the market. Based on his inside information, he may buy shares of the company's stock, anticipating that the impending announcement will cause a price rise. Or he may sell in the anticipation that the news will cause a drop. If his information is accurate and the announcement has the effect he anticipates, he could reap a substantial profit, or avoid a sharp loss by selling out his existing holdings.

The fringe-insider may have indirect or delayed access to the intimate information available to the way-insider. He may, for example, be the stockbroker for the way-insider, or a close friend, associate, or relative. He may be a supplier to or a buyer from the company. He may be a professional advisor (lawyer, accountant) of a way-insider. He will likely obtain the valuable inside information sometime after the way-insider has obtained it. Perhaps he will learn of the important facts in time to act on his own behalf, perhaps not. He doesn't really know for sure what will happen, but if he does receive what he believes to be valid insider information, he's very likely to act on it.

The pretend-insider is another step or two, or more, removed from the fringe-insider. He is in the "friend of a friend" category. By the time he gets the information, the upswing or downswing may have long since occurred. But he won't necessarily be aware of that. Having just obtained what he believes to be a valid company secret, he's still likely to act on it, even though it's long after the fact. The pretend-insider is a victim of that common children's party game: the first person whispers a phrase into the ear of the second, who then must repeat what he or she heard to the third person, and so on. By the time it reaches the last person, the original statement is usually drastically changed.

Trading on inside information is illegal. It's not supposed to happen, but it does, and the Securities and Exchange Commission admits that enforcement of their insider-information rules is extremely difficult. Even though certain insiders are required to report their buy and sell transactions, it is still very difficult to discover and prove wrongdoing in this area of stock market trading. Illegal though it may be, and successful or unsuccessful though it may be, it does exert a distinct effect on specific stocks and to a lesser extent on the market as a whole.

The Hunch Player

He will probably be an active trader, and possibly a seasoned veteran of the stock market. He may be convinced that all the study in the world is for naught, because the quirks and whims of fellow investors are imponderable and have more of an effect on the value of any given stock than the true value of the company itself. He'll listen to tipsters avidly, if not actively seeking them out. Much of his trading will be based on what can best be described as hunches: a gut reaction, a voice in the night, an omen. It he's canny to the ways of the market and has observed in enough detail the minute ebbs and flows of prices over the years, he might be fortunate enough to generate a trading profit during periods when the market is moving upward; and he may be astute enough to stay away from the market when it's in a general downtrend. His investment objectives tend to be without any long-range plan or pattern: he just wants to make what he can when he can.

The Theory Trader

Though often mistaken for the hunch player, the theory trader bases his transactions on one or more specific theories that may be directly tied to something as tangible as governmental statistics, or as intangible as trends in international currency fluctuations. Though they may be small in number, the theory traders can be very influential when their theories prove correct; however, they also have a way of disappearing temporarily when their theories have proven incorrect. Many theory traders will often be found reading stock market advisory newsletters, generally the wellspring of their information and decisions. Because they paid a steep price for these advisory letters, they assume the information has to be correct—otherwise it wouldn't be so expensive.

The Sentimentalist

This well-intentioned group of investors may place their money in stocks of companies that they work for or that are located in their hometown. Sentimentality or loyalty will be their primary reason for investing. Emotionally, it's like rooting for the hometown team to win; but rationally this can amount to nothing more than total speculation.

The Technical Analyst

The technical analyst (sometimes called "chartist") is a serious student of the stock market. Essentially, technical analysts closely follow, and chart, specific short-, medium-, and long-term trends in individual stocks, in groups of stocks, and in the market movement as a whole. Technical analysts, as a group, have come up with a dazzling array of indicators that supposedly give signals to buy and sell. There are market peaks and market troughs; there are bellwether stocks that purportedly lead the way in one direction or another; high ratios and low ratios; moving averages; overbought and oversold indexes; and charts that plot every conceivable squiggle a given stock may be subject to. (More detailed information on these various techniques can be obtained through the dozens of books available on the subject, and through brokers.)

But in spite of all the information available, the problem is that the meticulously plotted signals of the analysts are often invalidated by the actions of other traders, who pay no attention to these signals. Further, the analysts don't necessarily agree with each other as to which signal means what and often come up with conflicting signals.

The Fundamentalist

The fundamentalist is the serious investor who has done his homework and who is willing to continue to do the necessary homework. He has learned how to analyze the financial statements of the companies he is interested in investing in, and he has learned how to seek out the basic sound fundamental value of each company. He's not a trader: he'll be willing to wait years for the fundamental value of the company to prove itself in terms of price appreciation and dividend payments. He realizes that his market decisions are subject to the actions of all the other types of investors, but he feels confident that his prudent and rational analysis of the facts at hand will survive the whims and flutters caused by other types of investors.

The fundamentalist knows that there's no such thing as a sure thing in the stock market but is willing to take the time necessary to find the best things available. He'll analyze profit-and-loss statements, dividend-payment records, the amount the company has earned on its invested capital, profit margins, the ratio of the company's assets to its liabilities and debts, and what the trends are in the company's overall performance over recent years. He'll have studied the industry as a whole to determine if it is healthy or failing, and whether or not it appears to have a chance to grow at a more rapid rate than the economy as a whole. He'll shun advice from tipsters. He won't play hunches, he won't let sentimentality get the best of him. And he won't subscribe to any theories that are not rooted in accurate financial analysis of the companies he's considering investing in.

The Prudent Investor

The prudent investor is the fundamentalist-plus. Plus what? Perhaps plus a bit of technical analyst, for many of the analytical devices can be helpful in the fundamentalist approach. Perhaps also plus a tiny bit of the hunch player, for even the most prudent investor will occasionally need the intestinal fortitude that is second nature to the hunch player to survive unexpected turns for the worse. Further, the prudent investor will have most of the following attributes.

☐ He will have a firm, crystal-clear understanding of his current financial situation and of his overall investment objectives. He will convey this understanding to his stockbroker and will make a joint commitment with the broker to stick with the stated objectives. If the prudent investor wants the benefit of the broker's expertise, he must give the broker proper instructions. Without that basic understanding between investor and broker, both may be groping in the dark. Periodically, with the broker's aid, the prudent investor will review his objectives and determine whether or not they are still reasonable in view of the unpredictable nature of the stock market. Can they still be obtained, and if so, at what potential risk? Or should the objectives be revised, particularly in light of changing financial circumstances?

☐ The prudent investor will clearly define his own role. Is he an investor or is he a trader? The investor, broadly speaking, is putting his money to work and he's willing to let it do the job over the needed span of time. The trader is working his money and he must have the know-how to cope with weekly, daily, and hourly fluctuations and trends. A prudent investor can be a little bit of both, but to do so he must keep his more prudent investment funds and his more speculative trading funds strictly segregated. When the two start to mingle, objectives can get derailed swiftly.

☐ The prudent investor will do his homework. Investment decisions are ultimately the investor's, not the broker's. There are thousands of securities, no two alike, and no human being can keep track of the fine points of more than a few dozen at a time. A broker can give the investor research tools and an opinion, but the investor must reach his own conclusions. And sound conclusions require work.

☐ The prudent investor will avoid the natural quirk of human nature that leads one to want to recover losses as quickly as they may have occurred. This can lead an investor out of one speculative situation into another. When an unexpected loss occurs, it is time for research and cool thinking, not guessing games and gut reaction. Desire to recoup quickly can deter a prudent investor from basic objectives. It can turn one from an investor into a speculator, a role that might not be suitable.

☐ The prudent investor who finds himself holding a stock at a loss will ask himself: would it be consistent with my investment objectives to purchase that same stock today at its current price? If so, that may be a sign to continue holding the stock. If not, what other security would be more consistent with the stated investment objectives?

☐ The prudent investor will look back to learn from his past mistakes. Why did he buy or sell too soon or too late? Did he listen to a tip? Did he play a hunch? Did he panic? The ability to recognize one's own mistakes and benefit from them is a rare quality, one worth cultivating by the prudent investor if he doesn't already possess it.

☐ When a prudent investor invests in a stock, he will determine, at that time, when he will be likely to sell. He will set limits for himself and will stick to them, barring unforeseen conditions that may dictate otherwise. He will have determined how much of a loss he's willing to take in order to acquire a certain gain. He'll be well acquainted with, and willing to abide by, that old maxim of the investment community: Take your profits when you can, and cut your losses when you can.

☐ The prudent investor will be well aware of the value of a good night's sleep. Or, for that matter, of a good day's work. Distractions and frustrations caused by involvement in the stock market can detract one from one's own personal productivity and one's pleasures. Whatever gains an investor may be chasing may not, under keen analysis, be worth it in terms of lost time and lost efficiency in other endeavors. In other words, if your involvement with your investment portfolio begins to interfere with your personal life, whatever gains you may achieve may not, in the long run, have been worth it.

☐ The prudent investor will not waste his time or his money chasing after systems that purport to "beat the market." There are none. And there aren't any books, brokers, newsletters, analysts, chartists, economists, or tipsters who know anything more about where the market is headed than you do. If there were, we'd have heard about them long before now.

Basic Stock Market Information

The daily trading activity of all of the major stock exchanges is contained in fairly complete detail in the *Wall Street Journal* each day. A number of stocks will be traded on more than one exchange, and their listings will be contained generally in the larger exchange on which they're traded.

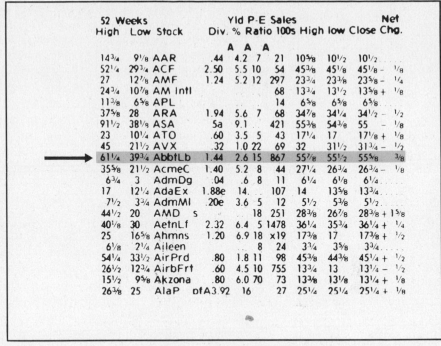

52 Weeks				Yld	P-E	Sales				Net
High	Low	Stock	Div.	%	Ratio	100s	High	low	Close	Chg.
		A A A								
14³⁄₄	9¹⁄₈	AAR	.44	4.2	7	21	10⅝	10¹⁄₂	10¹⁄₂	. . . .
52¹⁄₄	29³⁄₄	ACF	2.50	5.5	10	54	45³⁄₈	45¹⁄₈	45¹⁄₈ –	¹⁄₈
27	12⅞	AMF	1.24	5.2	12	297	23³⁄₄	23³⁄₈	23⅝ –	¹⁄₄
24³⁄₄	10⅞	AM Intl				68	13³⁄₄	13¹⁄₂	13⅝ +	¹⁄₈
11³⁄₈	6⅝	APL				14	6⅝	6⅝	6⅝	.
37⅝	28	ARA	1.94	5.6	7	68	34⅞	34¹⁄₄	34¹⁄₂ –	¹⁄₂
91¹⁄₂	38¹⁄₈	ASA	5a	9.1		421	55³⁄₈	54³⁄₈	55 –	¹⁄₈
23	10¹⁄₄	ATO	.60	3.5	5	43	17¹⁄₄	17	17¹⁄₈ +	¹⁄₈
45	21¹⁄₂	AVX	.32	1.0	22	69	32	31¹⁄₂	31³⁄₄ –	¹⁄₂
61¹⁄₄	39³⁄₄	AbbtLb	1.44	2.6	15	867	55⅞	55¹⁄₂	55⅝	⅜
35⅝	21¹⁄₂	AcmeC	1.40	5.2	8	44	27¹⁄₄	26³⁄₄	26³⁄₄ –	¹⁄₈
6³⁄₄	3	AdmDg	.04	.6	8	11	6¹⁄₄	6¹⁄₈	6¹⁄₄	. . . .
17	12¹⁄₄	AdaEx	1.88e	14.		107	14	13⅝	13³⁄₄	. . . .
7¹⁄₂	3³⁄₄	AdmMl	.20e	3.6	5	12	5¹⁄₂	5³⁄₈	5¹⁄₂	.
44¹⁄₂	20	AMD s		. .		18	251	28³⁄₈	26⅞	28³⁄₈ + 1⅝
40¹⁄₈	30	AetnLf	2.32	6.4	5	1478	36¹⁄₄	35³⁄₄	36¹⁄₄ +	¹⁄₄
25	16⅝	Ahmns	1.20	6.9	18	x19	17³⁄₈	17	17³⁄₈ +	¹⁄₂
6¹⁄₈	2¹⁄₄	Aileen			8	24	3³⁄₄	3⅝	3³⁄₄	. . . .
54¹⁄₄	33¹⁄₂	AirPrd	.80	1.8	11	98	45³⁄₈	44³⁄₈	45¹⁄₄ +	¹⁄₂
26¹⁄₂	12³⁄₄	AirbFrt	.60	4.5	10	755	13³⁄₄	13	13¹⁄₄ –	¹⁄₂
15¹⁄₂	9⅝	Akzona	.80	6.0	70	73	13³⁄₈	13¹⁄₈	13¹⁄₄ +	¹⁄₈
26³⁄₈	25	AlaP	pfA3.92	16		27	25¹⁄₄	25¹⁄₄	25¹⁄₄ +	¹⁄₈

Figure 17-1   New York Stock Exchange Listing from the *Wall Street Journal*.

Price Quotations

Many local daily newspapers also carry extensive listings, though many are abbreviated from the full listings used in the *Wall Street Journal*.

Figure 17-1 shows a sample New York Stock Exchange listing from the *Wall Street Journal*. Let's examine the details more closely. The tenth listing is "AbbtLb" which stands for Abbott Laboratories, a major manufacturer of various health-care products. (All companies traded on the exchange carry an abbreviation or trading symbol. Abbott's is ABT. The abbreviation does not show in the newspaper stock quotations.)

□ *52 Weeks High Low.* This listing indicates that during the previous 52 weeks Abbott Laboratories sold at a high of 61¼ ($61.25) per share and at a low of 39¾ ($39.75) per share. (When fractions appear in quotes they are referring to fractions of a dollar. Thus, ⅛ equals 12.5¢; ¼ equals 25¢; and so on.) The purpose of the high/low listings is to give you some idea as to the stock's recent trading history. The past history has absolutely no bearing on what the future values of the stock might be.

□ *Dividend (Div.)* The dividend column indicates the rate of dividend paid based on the most recent quarterly dividend. It is not necessarily an indication of dividends that will be paid in the future. Abbott Laboratories paid a dividend in the prior year of 1.44, which means $1.44 per share. An investor would have to dig more deeply to determine the likelihood of any company continuing its indicated rate of dividend for the foreseeable future. The *Wall Street Journal* listings do contain some explanatory notes that may bear on the regularity of dividend payments. You'll note, for example, that a few lines down, AdaEx shows a dividend of 1.88e. The small *e*, according to the explanatory note, indicates that the dividend was "declared or paid in the preceding 12 months," which could indicate that while that was the actual payment history, there may be reason to believe that it is not the normal regular expected dividend. The full explanatory notes, as contained in the *Wall Street Journal*, are shown in Figure 17-2.

☐ *Yield % (Yld).* This indicates the yield, in percentage terms, that you would receive if you bought the stock at its current price (55⅝) and received the dividend of $1.44; $1.44 is roughly 2.6% of $55.62. As you look down these sample listings you can see the wide range of yields that the stocks return to investors in the form of dividends.

☐ *Price earnings ratio (P-E Ratio).* The price-earnings ratio is arrived at by simple arithmetic, but determining its meaning is a bit more mystic. The specific figure, which is 15 in the case of Abbott Laboratories, is the result of dividing the *price* per share of the stock by the *earnings* per share of the stock. If a company earned $1 million during a year, and it had 1 million shares of stock outstanding, its earnings per share

---

EXPLANATORY NOTES
(For New York and American Exchange listed issues)

Sales figures are unofficial.

The 52-Week High and Low columns show the highest and the lowest price of the stock in consolidated trading during the preceding 52 weeks plus the current week, but not the current trading day.

u—Indicates a new 52-week high. d—Indicates a new 52-week low.

s—Split or stock dividend of 25 per cent or more in the past 52 weeks. The high-low range is adjusted from the old stock. Dividend begins with the date of split or stock dividend.

n—New issue in the past 52 weeks. The high-low range begins with the start of trading in the new issue and does not cover the entire 52-week period.

g—Dividend or earnings in Canadian money. Stock trades in U.S. dollars. No yield or PE shown unless stated in U.S. money.

Unless otherwise noted, rates of dividends in the foregoing table are annual disbursements based on the last quarterly or semi-annual declaration. Special or extra dividends or payments not designated as regular are identified in the following footnotes.

a—Also extra or extras. b—Annual rate plus stock dividend. c—Liquidating dividend. e—Declared or paid in preceding 12 months. i—Declared or paid after stock dividend or split up. j—Paid this year, dividend omitted, deferred or no action taken at last dividend meeting. k—Declared or paid this year, an accumulative issue with dividends in arrears. r—Declared or paid in preceding 12 months plus stock dividend. t—Paid in stock in preceding 12 months, estimated cash value on ex-dividend or ex-distribution date.

x—Ex-dividend or ex-rights. y—Ex-dividend and sales in full. z—Sales in full.

wd—When distributed. wi—When issued. ww—With warrants. xw—Without warrants.

vj—In bankruptcy or receivership or being reorganized under the Bankruptcy Act, or securities assumed by such companies.

Figure 17-2   Explanatory notes for New York Stock Exchange Listing from the *Wall Street Journal*.

would be $1. If that same stock were selling for $10 per share, its price-earnings ratio would be 10 to 1 ($10 market price to $1 worth of earnings), or simply 10.

The earnings referred to in the P-E ratio quotes are the actual latest available earnings or the best estimated earnings of the company for a one-year period. The prudent investor will determine whether or not the P-E ratio reflects actual past earnings or estimated future earnings. If the ratio reflects actual earnings, it's a picture of reality. If it reflects future estimated earnings, one must gauge the accuracy of the estimate in order to determine the validity of the ratio itself.

For example, say that a stock is selling for $48 per share, and that its *actual* earnings for the *past* year were $3 per share. This would give it a P-E ratio of 16. *Estimates* of earnings for the *forthcoming* year are $4 per share. This would give the stock a P-E ratio of 12.

What does the P-E ratio mean? As with other stock market "indicators," it is, at best, a broad and general yardstick, essentially indicating the relative conservatism or speculation involved in a given stock. The lower the P-E ratio, the more conservative the investment, and the higher the P-E ratio, the more speculative. But note: this is only a broad general measure and does not necessarily mean that a stock with a low P-E ratio will perform better or worse than one with a high P-E ratio. In the lower P-E brackets, investors are looking more closely at the true investment value of the stock: the actual earnings of the company.

Regarding some stocks, an investor may feel that their actual or currently projected earnings do not truly reflect the ultimate potential of the stock, or the ultimate potential of what other investors may be willing to pay for the stock. Based on this kind of optimism, they may be willing to pay far more for one stock than another, and as the price goes up, so does the P-E ratio. Thus, in the higher P-E brackets, investors are speculating, not so much on what the company itself may truly earn, but on what other investors might be willing to bid for the stock.

☐ *Sales 100s.* This indicates the amount of activity in the trading of the stock for the prior day. Abbott Laboratories shows 867 under this column, which means that a total of 86,700 shares were traded during the prior day. Market analysts will keep an eye on the sales volume of specific stocks, looking for the unusual. If a stock normally has a trading volume within a fairly close range from day to day, and suddenly there seems to be a great surge or a tapering off of activity, this could signal that something out of the ordinary might be happening with the value of the stock. Unfortunately, there's no way to know for sure what the happening might be, or whether it will have a plus or minus effect on the stock. If the stock seems to be moving upward on heavy volume, it would indicate a high degree of buying interest—investors willing to take the plunge. On the other hand, if the stock moves downward in high volume trading, it would indicate a desire of investors to unload.

The only problem is that you never know until it's too late whether you're getting on or off the rollercoaster at the right point.

☐ *High/Low/Close.* These columns indicate the high, low, and closing prices per share for the previous day's trading. During the previous day, for example, Abbott Laboratories traded at a high of 55⅞ ($55.875) and a low of 55½ ($55.50). It closed out the day at 55⅝ ($55.625). During that day a trader might have bought or sold at prices anywhere within that range.

☐ *Net change.* Abbott Laboratories closed down ⅜ ($.375) from the close of the previous day. In other words, the value of the stock dropped by $.375 per share from where it had been at its last trade on the prior trading day.

Other Published Listings

More detailed information on specific stocks can be found in *Barron's,* a weekly newspaper, and in the stock guides published monthly and quarterly by Standard and Poor's and Moody's. *Barron's* is commonly available at newsstands, and the stock guides are available at brokerage firms and at most public libraries. The added information consists of historical high and low trading, dividend history and dividend payment dates, the financial status of the company, and a history of its earnings per share. The prudent investor will not rely simply on the daily newspaper quotation, but will make extensive use of these more detailed published statistics.

Brokers Quotations

Aided by computers, brokers at local brokerage firms are equipped with video terminals that can display up-to-the-second price fluctuations as well as detailed information on any given quoted stock. In addition, the "ticker tape," now computerized, flashes on a large screen each transaction for each stock that's sold on the respective exchanges.

Stock Market Averages

"How's the market doing?"
  "Up two."
  Or you may hear a news broadcaster report, "The market was down nine points today in heavy trading. Analysts attribute the decline to investors' concern over the impending automobile workers' strike."

The Dow Jones Industrial Average

What do these cryptic sayings mean? The statements "up two" and "down nine" refer to the daily fluctuations in the Dow Jones Industrial Averages, or DJIA. This is the oldest and most commonly referred to measurement of stock market prices. But it does not reflect the movements of all stocks; rather, it refers only to the movement of 30 major industrial stocks. The Dow Jones company, which publishes the *Wall Street Journal, Barron's,* and many other financial publications, has historically used these 30 major corporations to reflect the "essence" of the market as a whole. The average is arrived at by tallying the prices of the 30 stocks within the averages and dividing the total by a divisor that takes into account previous stock splits and stock dividends. The divisor is changed from time to time as any of the companies within the group of 30 declares stock splits or stock dividends. Although other companies have devised more broad-based averages over the years, the DJIA has remained the favorite indicator of most investors.

In addition to the Dow Jones Industrial Average, there are two other Dow Jones averages: 20 transportation stocks for the transportation averages, and 15 utility stocks for the utility averages. These, respectively, reflect movements within those areas: transportation companies and utility companies.

Standard and Poor's Stock Price Index

The Standard and Poor's Corporation maintains an index of 500 major corporations: industrials, utilities, financial and transportation. All of these stocks are listed on the New York Stock Exchange. Although the Standard and Poor's index represents a much broader spectrum of listed securities, it has not achieved the popularity of the DJIA. Moody's, the other company that lists ratings and statistical data on securities, also maintains an index of 125 industrial corporations listed on the New York Stock Exchange.

New York Stock Exchange Common Stock Index

This index is maintained by the New York Stock Exchange itself and covers all of the common stocks listed on that exchange.

Classification of Stocks

Stocks can be classified in a number of ways: by "personality," by objective, and by industry grouping.

☐ *By "personality."* Vague though this classification may seem, it can be a worthwhile investment guideline. The basic personalities of stocks are either "blue-chip" or "glamour." Blue-chip stocks are those which are considered to be major, solid companies with relatively stable stock prices and regular dividend-payment histories—in other words, the more conservative of the vast realm of companies. The glamour issues are those which have recently attracted a lot of investor interest, in large measure because they have experienced a high volatility in price, tending toward the upward side. These are the more speculative issues. The price fluctuations are likely to be much more drastic and the payment of dividends more questionable than with the blue-chips.

☐ *By objective.* For investors whose objective is income, there are income stocks: those which pay a relatively high level of dividend. For investors whose objective is growth, there are growth stocks: those which have recently had spurts in value above and beyond the broad average of stocks as a whole. If you investigate carefully, there is a reasonable assurance that you can find an income stock whose dividend payment level is likely to continue or increase. But there is absolutely no way that you can find a growth stock whose future growth will necessarily match its past growth.

□ *By industry grouping.* Despite the profitability (or lack thereof) of any specific company, the value of its stock may be drastically affected by the performance of the overall industrial group into which it falls. For example, a major retailer, such as Sears, may have a very strong financial position. But because of an impending recession, retailers as a whole (of which Sears is one) may have a gloomy outlook. Thus, despite Sears' individual potential, the investment community may frown upon Sears because it belongs to an industrial group whose future is in doubt, at least for the near term.

Many different factors can affect industry groups in one way while not affecting other groups as noticeably. Sharply rising fuel prices can have a negative effect on the airline industry, but perhaps little or no effect on the electronics industry. Rising interest rates can have a negative effect on the construction industry, and possibly a positive effect on the banking industry. A severe drought can have a negative effective on the food industry, and no effect on the chemical industry. Theoretically, but not necessarily, these external factors will affect each specific company within an industrial group. Well-managed companies that are able to anticipate correctly what these outside factors may be can weather the problems and capitalize on the good breaks. The overriding problem is that the investor doesn't know whether his company has done well or poorly until after the fact.

Following is a sampling of major industrial groups:

Drugs, cosmetics, and health care	Metal producers
Beverages	Electrical
Aerospace	Financial
Chemicals	Automotive
Metal-product manufacturers	Foods
Construction	Electronics
Apparel	Machinery and equipment

Dividends

A dividend is that portion of a company's profit paid out to its owners, or stockholders. Dividends are commonly paid in cash, but in some instances a corporation may issue additional shares of stock as a form of dividend. This is known as a stock dividend, and the recipient of a stock dividend is free to sell these shares for cash or to retain the investment.

The value of a dividend is usually referred to as the "yield." The yield is the percentage return you're getting on your money, and it's figured very simply by dividing the stock's annual dividend by its price. If a stock is selling at $50 per share and it pays an annual dividend of $2 per share, its *apparent* yield is 4 percent (2 divided by 50 equals .04). We use the word *apparent* because the yield does not take into account the commission that you'll have to pay when you buy the stock or when you sell it. The commissions must be considered to come up with a more accurate yield figure.

Further, if you do not hold the stock for at least a full annual cycle, you won't receive the apparent yield. For example, say the above stock paid its dividend quarterly on the first day of January, April, July, and October. It would pay 50¢ for each share four times a year, for a total of $2. If you bought the stock on January 2 and sold it during the subsequent December, you'd have received only three of the four dividend payments, or $1.50, even though you had held the stock for almost 12 full months. You would not have received the first dividend, payable on January 1, because you were not a "stockholder of record" on the date called for. In such a case, your yield would be only 3 percent, before the payment of both commissions.

Dividend payments are announced, or "declared," by the Board of Directors of the company at its regular meetings. Here's how it works: At their February meeting the Board of Directors of XYZ Company declares that they will pay a dividend on April 1 to stockholders "of record" as of March 5. If you are recorded on the books of the corporation as being a stockholder as of March 5, you'll be entitled to receive the April 1 dividend even though you sell your stock between March 5 and April 1. The reason for the time lag is to give the company enough time to get an accurate list of all its stockholders, in anticipation of the payment date, so that checks can be prepared and other necessary book work done.

Ex-dividend Date

What if, following the above example, you instructed your broker to buy XYZ stock on March 2? Would you be entitled to the dividend? Probably not. It usually takes four or five days from the time of an order until you are officially registered on the books of a corporation as an owner of the stock. Thus, the stock exchanges, in listing dividends payable on stocks, generally note that a stock is "ex-dividend" about four or five days prior to the *record* date. When a stock is quoted "ex-dividend," it means that if you buy the stock at that time you won't get the next dividend that has been declared by the company. Following along with the above example, XYZ might be quoted as "ex-dividend" on March 1—five days before the record date. Anybody who buys the stock from March 1 onward will not receive the dividend payable in April.

The prudent investor, particularly one bargaining for a known return on invested capital, will pay close attention to the history of dividend payments of any company that he's thinking of investing in. These records can be found in the Moody's and Standard and Poor's guides, or directly from the broker. Some companies have long histories of regular dividends, many of which increase periodically as earnings increase. Some companies pay no dividends, and other companies pay erratically. Companies that pay small or no or erratic dividends tend to fall more into the speculative category of investment. The steady dividend payers are more conservative.

Unlike the movement of a stock's price, which is subject to countless and often indefinable pressures, the dividend payment rate is generally well rooted in the company's earnings and in its willingness to spread those earnings out among its stockholders. Earnings that are not distributed to stockholders are retained within the company (and are referred to as "retained earnings") for investment within the company itself. Those retained earnings may be used as a cushion against troublesome economic times or to create new facilities, which in turn can create new jobs and new products, which can create additional earnings for stockholders.

Commissions

Brokerage commissions are the fees received by brokerage firms for handling your transactions when you buy and sell stock. Prior to 1976, commission structures were quite uniform among all various major brokers. Pressure from the government to break up what was considered a form of price fixing resulted in a wider spectrum of commission charges, depending on such matters as the size of the transaction, the price of the stock, and the total volume of business a given investor does with the brokerage firm during the year. Further, since that time, a number of "discount" brokers have emerged on the scene, offering strictly the execution of orders, and not offering, as major firms do, the full range of research services, custodial services, and the like. The discount firms give the investor an opportunity to transact at lower commission rates. But many investors may feel more comfortable with the size and backup facilities of major firms.

Abuses exist in all industries, and the securities industry is no exception. A common abuse is called "churning." Churning exists when a broker convinces an investor to continually buy and sell securities, with the net result being large commissions generated for the broker, to the possible detriment of the investor's account. Prudent investors will have committed themselves in all likelihood to ride with their investments for a protracted period of time and likely will not succumb to the intrigues of churning, which demands frequent in and out trading.

Long and Short

When an investor buys stock, hoping for an increase in value as well as receipt of dividends, he or she is "buying long." This is the most common type of transaction, constituting the vast majority of all trades on the exchanges.

But what if an investor thinks a stock may go down in value? There is a technique called "selling short" that enables an investor to seek a profit as a stock declines in value.

Selling short is a sophisticated and risky transaction. Here's how it works. Let's say you think that XYZ, which is now selling at $10 per share, is due to slump in price. You want to "sell it short," or bet that it will decline.

In effect, you borrow 100 shares from your broker and you sell them on the open market at the $10 price. You now have $1000 cash in hand (before commissions) and you owe your broker 100 shares of XYZ.

If the stock then dipped to, say, $6 per share, you in effect buy 100 shares at the going market price, for $600, and return the 100 shares to your broker. You took in $1000, then paid out $600 so you're $400 ahead as a result—again, before commissions.

The broker will have obtained the "borrowed" stock usually from his firm's supply of customers' stock that they are holding. You, as the short seller, must have cash or unmargined stock in your account before you can initiate a short sale. This is to assure the broker that you have available funds to repay the stock you've borrowed from him, and those funds are effectively tied up during the life of the transaction.

The element of risk involved in short selling can indeed be frightening. On a regular, or long, transaction, your ultimate loss is limited. If you bought XYZ long at $10 per share, and XYZ goes bankrupt, you can lose only the $10 per share. That's it. It can't go any lower than zero.

But if you sell a stock short at $10 per share, and it goes up instead of down, your loss can run on indefinitely. Say you bought 100 shares short at $10, and then the stock runs up to $50 per share. If you wanted to get out then, you'd have to shell out $5000 to buy enough to pay back your broker the shares you owe him, for a net loss of $4000. If you decide to wait, hoping for a drop, and it goes up another $10 to $60 per share, your loss is even greater. Such run-ups may be rare, but the risk is there.

One further problem with selling short: If you're holding stock in a long position, you receive any dividends the stock pays. But if you're in a short position, you are obliged to pay the dividends to the broker since you technically owe him the stock itself. This can add to your losses or cut into your hoped-for gains.

Prudent investors would not find themselves comfortable with short selling.

Capital Gains

Property that is held for investment purposes, such as stocks and bonds, is considered a "capital asset" under the federal income tax laws. As such, it may be subject to special tax treatment when you realize a gain from the sale of such assets.

If you have owned such property as stocks for a long enough period of time and you then sell it at a gain, that is considered a "long-term capital gain." The long-term holding period is one year. In other words, if you own a stock for at least one year before you sell it and you then have a gain on the sale, that gain is taxed at a lesser rate than your normal income-tax rate would be.

Buying on Margin

Buying on margin is a means of buying stock on credit. The rate of margin varies from time to time, depending on overall economic conditions throughout the nation and the condition of the stock market. The Federal Reserve Board sets the margin rate. If the margin rate is 40 percent, you can buy stock by putting up only 40 percent of the total purchase price. The remaining 60 percent you borrow from the broker using the stock as collateral for the loan. Say that XYZ is selling at $30 per share, and you wish to buy 100 shares. The margin rate at that time is 40 percent. You can thus buy $3000 worth of XYZ by putting up $1200 in cash and borrowing the remaining $1800 from the broker. Let's say further that at that time the interest rate that you'll pay your broker on the margin account is 10 percent, which means that during the course of the year you'll owe him $180 in interest on the $1800 margin loan.

If XYZ goes to $35 per share at the end of one year and you sell, you have realized a profit of $500, less the $180 in interest, for a net (before commissions) of $320. But you've only invested $1200 of your own cash at the outset, so your return of $320 is equivalent to a yield of 26.7 percent for the year, not counting commissions or dividends. If you had invested the full $3000 and realized a $500 gain, your rate of return would have been 16.7 percent before commissions. This is what's known as "leverage." The gain on a sale and the rate of return on the dividends are magnified by the fact that you have less of your own money at work for you.

However, margin buying can be very dangerous, particularly if the stock declines in value. If you had purchased XYZ normally—that is, unmargined—for $3000 and it had dipped to $25 per share, you'd have a loss of $500. But if you bought it on the margin account, your loss would be increased by the amount of interest you would have to pay on the loan. In the above example, your total loss would come to $680.

Another potential danger in buying on margin is the possibility of a "margin call." If the margin rate is 40 percent, as in the above example, you can buy stock by putting up 40 percent of the amount required. The broker lends you the other 60 percent. On the $3000 transaction, the broker will originally lend you the $1800 and you put up the other $1200. But in a margin arrangement, the amount of your loan with the broker may not exceed the margin level—in this case 60 percent of the value of the stock. If the stock should drop to $20 per share, or a total value of $2000, the maximum amount of loan that the broker would be willing to extend to you would therefore be $1200. Since your original loan from the broker was for $1800, he will, in such an event, call you to inform you that you have to reduce your loan from $1800 to $1200. In other words, you have to come up with fresh cash to keep your account solvent with the broker. This is what's known as a margin call, and if an investor isn't prepared with the necessary cash in the event of a drop in the price of the stock, he ought not get involved in that kind of trading. In all, trading on margin is a highly speculative form of investing.

Stock Splits and Stock Dividends

Occasionally a company will issue a stock dividend to its stockholders. This may be instead of or in addition to a cash dividend. For example, if a company declares a 10 percent stock dividend, it will give all of its stockholders one share of additional stock for each ten shares already owned. A 100 percent stock dividend means that stockholders will get one new share for every one already owned. In effect, this doubles the amount of shares of stock outstanding. Frequently, companies will continue to pay the same amount of dividend in dollars after a stock dividend. This has the effect of increasing the return to the investor because he has more shares of stock earning dividends for him.

Table 17-1 illustrates the before and after status of a 10 percent stock dividend. In this case, the effect of the stock dividend is to increase the value of the investment and the dividend income—assuming that the stock retains its predividend market value.

Table 17-1

10 Percent Stock Dividend—Before and After

	Before	After
You own	100 shares	110 shares
Current value per share	$50	$50
Current total value	$5000	$5500
Annual dividend per share	$5.	$5.
Total dividend income per year	$500	$550

A company will "split" its stock when it wishes to get more shares of stock out into the marketplace, and also perhaps to bring the price of the stock down into a more attractive range. For example, a two-for-one stock split means that you will end up owning two shares of stock for every one that you had owned originally. Generally, though, when a stock is split, its price will be split accordingly, as will its dividend. If a stock was selling for $50 per share and was paying a $2 per year dividend, it will, after a two-for-one split, probably sell for $25 per share, and the dividend will be $1 per share. Thus, your actual net worth as an owner of that stock will not necessarily have changed as a result of the split.

Table 17-2 illustrates the before and after effects of a 100 percent stock split.

Table 17-2

100 Percent Stock Split—Before and After

	Before	After
You own	100 shares	200 shares
Current price per share	$50	$25
Total value	$5000	$5000
Dividend per share	$5.	$2.50
Total dividend income per year	$500	$500

A stock split is often taken as a sign of optimism: investors are anxious to buy shares, and when the price has been effectively lowered, more investors will be able to get involved with the company. A buying surge often tends to boost the value of a stock; thus a stock split is viewed by traders as a sign of a possible upswing in a given stock. Often this is the case, but it is not necessarily so. Sometimes there are rumors of a stock split, but the split may never actually occur. This can cause wild gyrations in the value of a given stock.

Preferred Stocks

Preferred stock is a separate class of stock from common stock, which has been the type under discussion until this point. If a company has bonds outstanding, the bondholders have to be paid before any dividends can be paid to any common stockholders. If a company also has preferred stock outstanding, the holders of the preferred stock also are entitled to preference over the common stockholders. This is the derivation of the name "preferred." In other words, if a corporation has bonds *and* preferred stock *and* common stock outstanding, the bond holders are first paid the interest due them, then the preferred stockholders are paid their dividends, then the common stockholders receive their dividends.

Preferred stock generally pays a higher rate of return on dividends than does common stock, and the preferred stock is less subject to fluctuation than the common stock.*

Cumulative Preferred

Most preferred stocks are "cumulative." This means that unpaid dividends will accumulate and the preferred shareholders must be paid in full on all back unpaid dividends before common stockholders can be paid any of their dividends. For example, a company has preferred stock outstanding, on which it has set a fixed dividend rate of $3 per share. The dividend rate on its common stock has been $2 per share. The company runs into hard times and for three years pays no dividends. In the fourth year it realizes a healthy profit. Before common stockholders can receive any dividends, the preferred shareholders must be paid $9 for each of their shares for the back accumulated dividends that had not been paid.

Callable Preferred

Some preferred shares will have a "call price." This means that the company can redeem the preferred shares at a stated price. If the preferred should reach $28 per share and the call price is $25 per share, the owner will suffer a loss if the company does call, or redeem, the stock. If the call price is above the actual selling price, the owner is in no danger of losing, as long as the call price remains above the selling price. An

*For these reasons they tend to appeal more to conservative and relatively sophisticated investors.

investor in preferred stock should always determine what call privileges exist regarding the stock.

In stock listings, preferreds are indicated by a "PF" following the name of the company.

Convertible Preferred

Like convertible bonds, noted in a previous chapter, convertible preferred stock may be converted into shares of the company's common stock at an agreed-upon ratio. And as with convertible bonds, the price of convertible preferred stock tends to fluctuate in tandem to the common stock, but the fluctuations are generally not as great as with the common stock. Thus, convertible preferreds are considered to offer attractive advantages: a relatively high rate of return on one's investment (from the dividends paid on the preferred stock); a chance to convert into the common stock if the common stock starts to rise rapidly; and a downside cushion of protection since the preferred stock will tend not to drop as rapidly or as deeply as the common stock might if prices begin to fall.

Here's an example of how a convertible preferred situation might work. (The same kind of thinking applies to convertible bonds.)

Say that XYZ preferred stock is selling at $50 per share and is paying a $5 per share dividend. Owners of those shares have the right to convert to one share XYZ common stock, which is selling at $40 per share and paying a $4 per share dividend. At those prices, there's obviously no apparent reason to convert from the preferred to the common: an investor would be losing money and dividend income as well. But if XYZ common stock gets "hot" and starts to move upward in value rapidly, the *general tendency* is for the common stock to rise more swiftly than the preferred. An owner of the preferred might then decide to sell the more conservative preferred or convert to the more volatile common stock with hopes of realizing a more handsome profit.

On the other hand, if XYZ common takes a downturn, it's likely to go down farther and faster than the preferred. In such an event, the preferred holder will retain his preferred.*

Convertibles are a sophisticated area of investing that require further study on the part of any interested student. Ample literature is available from most stockbrokerage firms.

Warrants

On occasion, when a company is issuing a bond or preferred stock, it may offer "warrants" to purchasers of the bonds or preferred shares as an extra inducement to get them to invest. The warrant will entitle them to purchase shares of common stock at a fixed price for a set period of time. In other words, if the common stock is selling at $20 per share at the time the bonds or preferred shares are issued, the warrant might

---

*The only way an investor can switch his common stock holdings to preferred stock is to actually sell the common and buy the preferred. The commission costs in doing so could offset any advantages in making such a move.

entitle the holder to acquire a share of common stock at $25. The issuing company will fix the life of the warrant, which may be a few months or a number of years.

Warrants are totally speculative. The owner of a warrant does not have any ownership in the corporation unless or until he or she exercises the warrant—that is, trades it in for the share of stock to which one is entitled. The owner of a warrant receives no dividends and has no voting rights in the company.

Here's an example of how a warrant might work. If the warrant gives the holder the right to purchase a share of common stock at $25 per share, the warrant theoretically has no value whatsoever until the common stock is selling for over $25 per share. If the common stock rises to $27 per share, the warrant might then become worth $2 per share, or slightly more if the market is generally optimistic about the future of the common stock. In other words, one could buy a warrant for $2 per share, which would give him or her the right to buy the common stock at $25 per share. The $2 investment in a warrant would indeed bear fruit if the stock went to $30 per share, for the value of the warrant would rise accordingly. The investor would reap a $3 profit over and above the $2 investment. A warrant, in other words, enables an investor to partake in the comparable price rise potential of the common stock without investing all of the money needed for the common stock purchase. In the above case, it would take $2500 to purchase 100 shares of the common stock outright. But 100 warrants might be purchased for $100 to $200, depending on the price of the common stock.

The ultimate danger with warrants is that they expire at a fixed point. Once they expire, they are worthless. If the warrant never rises to the exercise price, or above the price at which you purchased, then your investment is totally and completely gone. Your loss is complete. Warrants represent a speculative level of trading, and the prudent investor would not normally be attracted to such modes.

Stock Option Trading

Trading in stock options is a fairly new and sophisticated form of investing, which can range from highly speculative to staunchly conservative. The volume of stock option trading has expanded phenomenally since the concept was first introduced on major exchanges in the early 1970s. We will now examine the basic concepts of stock option trading, and readers who find the technique appealing will want to seek further information from stockbrokers about specific option-trading possibilities.

Placing a Bet

There are two main ways to gamble at the racetrack. First, you can buy a horse and enter it in races. If your horse wins, you will receive the winner's purse. If the horse never wins, you can recoup some of your investment by selling it, by training it to pull a plow, or by putting it out to stud. In other words, even if your initial gamble never pays off (the horse never wins), the horse still has some residual value.

Second, you can place bets on other people's horses. The life of your bet will be approximately two minutes—the time it takes to run the race. If the horse you bet on wins, you win. If the horse you bet on loses, your betting ticket is instantly and permanently worthless. In short, there is no residual value on the bet.

The situation is very similar in the stock market: there are two basic ways you can gamble. First, you can buy stock and hope that it increases in value. If it does, you win. If it doesn't, there is still some residual value in the form of dividends and the selling price that you might receive.

Second, you can place a bet that the stock will increase in value. You can do this without actually having to buy the stock itself. You place your bet by buying what is known as an option. An option, in effect, is a bet on the stock. And like a bet on a horse, the option has a limited life— upwards of nine months at the maximum—after which it will become worthless.

This is a very oversimplified view of stock option trading, but hopefully it will have clarified some of the confusion about what an option is. Option trading is to stock trading what horse betting is to horse owning. Let's take a closer look at how it works.

Calls and Puts

The most common type of option trading is betting that a given stock will increase in value. Technically this is known as a "call" option. It is also possible to bet that a stock will decrease in value. You can place such a bet by buying what is known as a "put" option. For purposes of this discussion and for the sake of clarity, we'll restrict the material to call options.

Option Quotations

Table 17-3 shows how options are quoted in the *Wall Street Journal:*

This quotation refers to option trading in the stock of XYZ Company. As the column on the far left indicates, the actual price per share of XYZ common stock closed the prior day at $41 on the New York Stock Exchange. The rest of the quote illustrates nine potential "bets" that can be placed on the future of XYZ's stock.

Look at the bottom line in the quotation—XYZ 45. Let's assume that we are now in late November. You have a hunch that XYZ will rise from its current level of $41 per share to $45 per share by next January. You'd like to bet on your hunch. You can do so by buying the stock itself, but

Table 17-3

Option NY Close	Strike Price	Jan.	Apr.	July
XYZ	35	7	8	9
41	40	$3\frac{1}{2}$	$4\frac{1}{2}$	5
41	45	2	3	4

to buy 100 shares will cost you $4100. Or you can buy an option. As the January column indicates, you can buy January options for $2. Contracts are sold in 100-share lots, so a 100-share option contract would cost you $200.

If you bought 100 shares of the stock for $4100 and it moved up to $4500 by January, you'd have reaped a profit of $400 (before commissions). If you bought a 100-share option contract for $200 and XYZ moved to $45 per share by say, December, the value of the option would have increased by $4 per share, or $400 for 100 shares, to roughly $600, and you'd have a $400 profit (again before commissions) on a bet of only $200.

But note this critical difference: If you had bought the stock and the price did *not* rise, you would *still own* the stock *indefinitely* and you'd still be entitled to any dividends that the stock paid. However, with the option, if the bet doesn't work out, the option expires at the established date and you own nothing after that time.

The cost of your bet is known as the "premium." The price at which you have the right to buy the stock—45 in this example—is known as the "strike price." The expiration is generally the third Friday in the month indicated. (Technically, the option gives you the right to buy the shares of the stock at the strike price. But since the commissions involved in doing so would take a big bite out of your potential profit, most option traders simply sell the option itself to another interested buyer rather than convert their option into the actual shares of the stock.)

Let's say you weren't quite as optimistic about XYZ going to $45 per share by January. But you thought it might reach that level before the following April. In that case, you could buy an option for a premium of $3 per share, or $300 for a 100-share contract. If you wanted to have until July to see whether the price moved up, a 100-share contract would cost $400. The longer the life of the option, the higher the price. This is because you have more time for the stock to reach the desired level. In effect, you're paying an added premium for the extra time.

Buying call options is highly speculative. Once you've bought an option, you receive no dividends on your invested money and the clock is running against you: The option becomes valueless upon the expiration date. It's like the betting ticket on the horse that didn't finish in the money.

Selling Options

Who do racetrack bettors buy their bets *from?* They buy them from the racetrack owners who have very carefully calculated that they will keep a portion of every bet for their own overhead and profit (not to mention taxes). For every dollar that is bet, the racetrack may pay back only about 80¢ in winnings to the bettors. Over the days and months and years the track knows that it can't lose. That's why it's better to own a racetrack than bet at one. And the same philosophy holds true with option trading: it's better to sell options than to buy them.

From whom do option buyers buy their contracts? They buy them from option *sellers*—people who already own the given shares of stock and who are willing to sell them to buyers at a specific price.

Referring back to the quotations, let's assume that you had purchased 100 shares of XYZ some time ago for $35 per share. You've been happy with the stock and with the dividends that it has paid, yet you'd be willing to part with the stock if it hit $45 per share. That would mean a $10 per share profit to you.

The option exchanges offer you intriguing possibilities. As the quotations indicate, you, as the owner of XYZ, can sell someone else the right to buy your 100 shares any time between now and next January, and you'll receive a $200 premium in exchange. Or you can sell an April contract for $300, a July contract for $400. If you sell an option and it is never exercised, you get to keep the whole premium. You also get to keep any dividends that are paid on the stock during the life of the option. That's like the racetrack keeping a portion of each bet for its own purposes. If the option is exercised, you must give up your stock at the strike price—$45 per share in the current example. But you have expressed a willingness to do that—to take a $10 per share profit—as part of your overall investment philosophy. If the option is not exercised, you can sell yet another one and keep the premium. If the option is exercised and you give up the stock, you have the $4500 to reinvest as you see fit. (None of these transactions take brokerage commissions into account.)

As this example indicates, selling options can be a sound and secure way for owners of stocks to increase their return substantially without increasing their risk. As long as you are willing to let go of your stock at a fixed higher price than you paid for it, you literally have everything to gain and nothing to lose by selling options on stocks you already own. If you plan to make new investments on stocks for the purpose of selling options against those stocks, you of course take upon yourself the basic risk inherent in any stock investment: the potential fluctuations in value that could work for or against you. Since this discussion was intended as nothing more than a brief overview of option-trading possibilities, interested investors should seek further information of specific techniques from their stockbroker.

Rating the Stocks

Like bonds, stocks are ranked and rated by both Standard and Poor's and Moody's. The following excerpts from the Standard and Poor's explanation of their rating system not only is informational but also serves as a guide to the prudent investor in the quest to determine the relative value of stocks within the broad selection available.

Earnings and dividends rankings for stocks. The relative "quality" of common stocks cannot be measured, as is the quality of bonds, in terms of the degree of protection for principal and dividends. Never-

theless, the investment process obviously involves the assessment of numerous factors—such as product and industry position, the multi-faceted aspects of managerial capability, corporate financial policy and resources—that makes some common stocks more highly esteemed than others.

Earnings and dividends performance is the end result of the interplay of these factors, and thus over the long run the record of this performance has a considerable bearing on relative quality. Growth and stability of earnings and dividends are therefore the key elements of Standard and Poor's common stock rankings, which are designed to capsulize the nature of this record in a single symbol. The rankings, however, do not pretend to reflect all other factors, tangible and intangible, that also bear on stock quality.

The Standard and Poor's rankings for common stocks are as follows:

A+	Highest
A	High
A−	Good
B+	Medium
B	Speculative
B−	Highly speculative
C	Marginal
D	In reorganization

Preferred stock ratings, according to Standard and Poor's, represent a "considered judgment of the relative security of dividends but are not indicative of the protection of principal from market fluctuations." These ratings are as follows:

AAA	Prime
AA	High grade
A	Sound
BBB	Medium grade
BB	Lower grade
B	Speculative
C	Nonpaying

Refer to the respective ratings themselves for more detail and information on this important aspect of evaluating one's investment alternatives.

Dividend Reinvestment Plans

Dividends are usually paid to stockholders quarterly. If you own 100 shares of XYZ and it is paying a dividend of $5 per share, you will receive a total of $500 in dividends during the year, but you will receive them in quarterly checks of $125 each. That money is yours to do with as you please—to spend or to reinvest. But many investors get lazy about reinvesting their dividend earnings and often find themselves spending these checks on nonessentials. By doing so, they can erode the potential size of their future nest egg.

Many companies offer an interesting alternative to sending quarterly dividend checks. They offer automatic dividend reinvestment plans in which your dividend is used to purchase additional shares of stock in the company. If an investor has faith in the company and wishes to acquire additional shares at virtually no out-of-pocket cost and with no effort, the dividend reinvestment plan is an ideal way in which to proceed. There are some special advantages to the automatic dividend reinvestment plans depending on the specific company. Brokerage commissions are very low or nonexistent. If the amount of your dividend check is not sufficient to buy a full share of stock, fractional shares can be purchased and added to your account. And some companies even offer a discount on the purchase price as compared to the going market rate that you'd otherwise have to pay.

Companies that offer automatic dividend reinvestment plans will notify stockholders of the availability. To sign up for the plan, the investor merely fills out the simple form the company will send him. From that point on, dividends are reinvested automatically and customers will receive a quarterly statement of the account. The company will retain the actual additional shares purchased and the investor can cash them in at any time by notifying the company.

Following is an example of how a dividend reinvestment plan can work. Assume you own 100 shares of XYZ with a value of $50 per share and an annual dividend of $5 per share. Assume for the sake of this illustration that the price of the stock and the amount of the dividend do not vary over the years. (In fact, both prices will vary, and those fluctuations can affect the dividend reinvestment plan.) The example is set forth on an annual basis rather than a quarterly basis for simplicity. As you can see (Table 17-4), in the first year your 100 shares will earn $500 worth of dividends. Those dividends in turn will buy ten additional shares of stock giving you a total of 110 shares going to work for you at the start of the second year. Note that during the fourth year, you would have earned $665.50 in dividends on your original investment of $5000. Your return has increased because you have more shares working for you earning dividends. In essence, then, the automatic dividend reinvestment plan does for your stockholding what compounding interest does for your money-market investments.

Of course, there's no way of knowing what the ultimate value of your reinvested dividends will be. If the price of the stock increases over the years and the dividends remain level, each dividend will buy fewer shares

Table 17-4 | **Dividend Reinvestment Plan**

		100 Shares of XYZ, Value $50 per Share, Dividend $5		
Year	Shares owned, start of year	Dividend earned . . .	. . . buys this many new shares . . .	. . . giving you this many total shares by year end.
1	100	$500	10	110
2	110	$550	11	121
3	121	$605	12.1	133.1
4	133.1	$665.50	13.31	146.41

of new stock. If the stock decreases in value and the dividends remain level, each dividend will buy more shares of stock. And if the dividend itself increases, the purchasing power of your plan will increase as well.

Following is a brief list of some of the companies that have offered dividend reinvestment plans. Check with a stockbroker to determine the current status of available plans.

Allied Chemical   IBM
American Brands   Mobil Corp.
AT&T   Nabisco
Bristol-Meyers   Penney (J.C.)
CBS, Inc.   PepsiCo
Colgate-Palmolive   Pillsbury
DuPont (E.I.)   RCA
Eastman Kodak   Sears
Exxon   Texaco
General Electric   U.S. Steel
General Motors   Xerox
Goodyear Tire

Price and Value: What Can Affect the Worth of a Stock?

The distinction between *price* and *value* is as important in the stock market as in any other form of commerce. A patch of barren land in the middle of the desert may sell at a very low price, say, $10 an acre, because it seems to have no value. But if there is oil underneath that patch of land, the value can be astronomically high, even though the price was very low.

On the other hand, that same barren patch may have absolutely no value—no oil or anything else hidden beneath it. But a fast-talking pitchman can sell the land to a gullible investor, leading him to believe it is a future oil well, a future retirement villa, a potential gold mine, or whatever. In this case, the price may be astronomically high in comparison with the value.

In all of our normal acquisition of the goods we buy, we attempt to make sure that we're getting good value for the money we pay; that value and price are compatible.

In the stock market, we have to maintain the same vigil, for very easily the price and value of a stock can take off in opposite directions. We might speculate on a stock with little intrinsic value, but because of a speculative fever the price of the stock may jump and reap a bonanza. Or we may invest in a stock with sturdy and dependable values only to find that a reverse form of speculation has condemned the stock to a severe plunge, and our money with it.

There are many factors that can have a direct effect on the *value* of a given stock; and there are many that can have a direct effect on the *price,* although those factors technically have no bearing on the underlying value.

Value

The underlying value of a stock is related to the profitability of the company in selling its product and services to its customers. The essential factors involved are the expertise of management; the cost of its raw materials (which can be affected by weather conditions, labor costs, strikes, and delivery problems); the efficiency in producing its finished product from the raw materials (which can likewise be affected by the foregoing elements of labor, weather, and gremlins); and by the efficiency with which it delivers the finished product to the market, at a price and in a package the public is willing to accept.

Further, with a great many of our major companies now involved in international commerce, international factors must also be considered. These can include fluctuations in currencies between various nations, international politics, trade and tariff regulations, and the same unpredictability regarding weather and labor strife that we have in America, but compounded by the distance and difficulty in communicating between the various parties.

Price

Following are some of the important elements that, although they do not affect the underlying value of the company, can have a distinct bearing on the price of the stock.

☐ When a new issue of a stock is being offered to the public, the level of persuasion exerted by the sales agents for the brokerage firms can have a bearing on the price of that issue for some time to come. If the market is receptive to a new issue, the price of the new issue may gravitate upward and remain there for an extended period. If the market is cold to the agent's persuasions, or if the persuasions themselves are cold, the new issue may sink and remain depressed for an extended period of time.

☐ The general health and outlook of the national economy can give a boost to the market as a whole, and sometimes to specific stocks, or it can have a depressing effect if the news is bad.

☐ Financial analysts periodically examine major listed companies to determine the true valuation of the company. The reports by the financial analysts are often reacted to vigorously by the investing public. Optimistic reports can have a positive effect on a stock, and pessimistic ones can have a depressing effect. The reports of financial analysts are far from infallible. In determining, or attempting to determine, the true underlying value of a company, they can, by even minor errors or misstatements, have a sharp effect on the price of the stock.

☐ A large investor, such as an institution, might be persuaded to make a substantial investment in a company. A major investment could be a sign of optimism for other investors. On the other hand, if a major investor pulls out of a situation, for whatever reason, this could be construed as a sign of pessimism. There's no way to know what might have persuaded a large investor to get involved or disengaged from a specific situation, but the large block of stock that changes hands is sure to affect the price, at least for a short term.

☐ One of the great imponderables is competition. The threat of formidable competition can have a depressant effect on the stock of a given company; the fading of competition can have a bouyant effect.

☐ The rumor mill is always a potentially troublesome source of information (or misinformation) that can affect the price of a stock. Wall Street is a tight little community, and word can get around very fast. In all likelihood, the day-to-day ebb and flow of rumors is perhaps one of the most prevalent forces in shaping the daily fluctuations of the market.

Mutual Funds in the Stock Market

Stock market mutual funds pool the dollars of many small investors and place them in a broad portfolio of various stocks. There are hundreds of different stock mutual funds offering a wide variety of choices to the investor. There are "performance" funds, whose objective is to create as rapid a growth pattern as possible. These funds tend to be more speculative, taking chances on stocks that fund management sees as having a quick short-term potential rise. There are growth funds that are geared more to long-term steady growth, with a lesser emphasis on dividend income. There are income funds whose primary objective is to generate maximum current dividend income. And there are growth/income funds that attempt to achieve a balance between growth and income factors.

The primary task of the investor seeking mutual funds as a vehicle is to determine whether the fund's objectives are in line with his or her own: short-term growth, long-term growth, income, or a combination. These objectives are spelled out in the fund prospectus, which must be read prior to making any investment decision.

Once a group of appropriate funds is selected, the investor must then review all of the pertinent factors that can shape one's investment future: costs involved in buying into the fund, annual charges for management or maintenance, the history of the fund in meeting its stated objectives.

Sales costs (loading fees) vary considerably with stock mutual funds, from as much as 8½ percent of the investment to as little as zero (no load). Similarly, annual or monthly maintenance and management fees vary considerably. In many cases, the load funds (those with a sales charge) may charge a lesser annual fee than do the no-load funds, and proponents of the load funds claim that this difference over the long pull offsets the initial commission factor. Debate has ranged long and furious over which is better—load funds or no-load funds. Proponents of each side can find specific groups of funds over specific periods of time in which their viewpoint prevailed. There is no simple answer. Like the stock market itself, there's an element of speculation even in choosing one type of fund over another.

Mutual funds are quoted daily in the *Wall Street Journal* as well as in many local daily newspapers, weekly in *Barron's,* and annually in *Forbes* magazine. *Forbes* devotes an entire issue (usually in August) to the mutual fund industry. It rates the funds based on their performance in general up and down markets, giving a perceptive analysis of how various funds have performed during periods of boom and adversity. Another good service is "Investment Companies," by A. Weisenberger.

The daily listings of mutual funds quote the "net asset value" (NAV), the offering price, and the net asset value change. The net asset value of a mutual fund is the actual value per share. It's arrived at by dividing the total assets of the fund by the total number of shares outstanding. If a fund has $10 million in total assets, and 1 million shares outstanding, the net asset value per share will be $10.

The offering price is the price that an investor would have to pay for shares in a particular fund. If the fund is a no-load fund, "N.L." will be indicated in the offering price. If the fund is a load fund, the offering price will be higher than the net asset value price, with the difference being the commission charges. For example, a fund may show a net asset value (NAV) of $12.68, and an offering price of $13.86. The investor pays $13.86 for each share, currently carrying an actual market value of $12.68. The difference of $1.18 represents the loading charge. $1.18 is 8½ percent of $13.86. But as a percentage of your money that's actually going to work for you, it is 1.18/12.68, or 9.3 percent.

Another fund shows a net asset value of $7.70 and an offering price of $8.28. The 58¢ difference is the loading charge, which is equal to 7 percent of the dollars invested. A no-load fund will sell at the same price per share as the net asset value.

Mutual funds have had a spotty history. They reached the peak of their popularity in the mid and late 1960s, during years when the stock market was generally moving upward. A number of "performance" funds performed spectacularly during those years, some of them doubling, tripling, and quadrupling investors' money within very short periods. This caught the public attention and many other more conservatively oriented funds began to try to match these performance records in order to attract investor dollars. Investors who had thought they were embarking on relatively conservative courses found their fund management deviating from initial objectives. Those were the years of the "performance cult," and the performance funds became known as "go-go funds." Investors poured their money by the billions into these funds, persuaded by convincing sales pitches that the funds would go up forever with no end in sight. But there was an end, and it came rather suddenly in 1969–1970 when the stock market went into a severe tumble and with it most of the mutual funds. Many investors had just gotten in at the tail end, and they were the hardest hit, watching their investments dwindle rapidly as the market plunge continued.

The problem was compounded when large numbers of investors began to cash in their shares rather than suffer further losses. When an investor sells shares of stock owned individually, he or she sells to another willing buyer. But when a mutual fund shareholder wants to cash in shares, the mutual fund is obliged to buy them back directly from the investor. Thus, the mutual fund must have cash on hand to redeem shares. If they don't have adequate reserves, they may have to sell off some of their existing stockholdings in order to generate the cash. The surge of redemptions, or cash-ins, following the market decline in 1969–1970 made it necessary for a great many funds to sell off stockholdings at severe losses. As the assets of the fund thus dwindled due to redemptions by investors, the funds were unable to generate new investments when the market began to move upward again in 1971–1972. Throughout the mutual fund industry as a whole, monthly redemptions (cash-ins) began to exceed new sales with regularity. For a period of 20 consecutive months, from early 1975 until late 1976, the mutual fund industry had an excess of redemptions over sales every month.

Perhaps the biggest disappointment in the mutual funds industry arose as a result of a feeling by investors that they were paying a fee to have their money professionally managed, whether that fee was in the initial commission charge or in the annual maintenance charges. If an investor buys stocks individually and loses, he can only blame himself and perhaps his broker. But when an investor is led to believe that professional management firms are handling his nest egg, and for a not inconsiderable fee, he casts the blame directly on the fund management during adverse times. And disappointment and word of mouth are quick to spread.

The concept of the mutual fund is a valid one, and there are ample numbers of sound management firms that can handle the public's money effectively. Mistakes have been made by both the public and the mutual fund managers, and more mistakes will happen in the future. But if all parties have learned from their previous errors, the mutual fund as a constructive means of achieving objectives can still be a valuable investment alternative for many individuals and families. Careful study must be done, and each investor must be wary of being "sold" whatever the sales agent is pitching.

Choosing Your Broker: A Guide Through the Investment Jungle

All of the above dilemmas are difficult enough for the advanced investor to cope with, let alone the novice. The choice of the right broker can be an invaluable aid in helping to evaluate the various factors an investor is faced with. There is no assurance that the broker will know the truth or falsity of any given rumor or will be able to evaluate the long-term implications of a new competitor entering the market or an old one leaving it. And a broker can't spend as much time on your account as you might want him to, for he does have other customers. But the good broker, wisely chosen, can direct you to sources of information that can assist you in making a proper decision and can steer you away from unreliable sources.

Choose your broker carefully, remembering at all times that *you* must make the ultimate decisions based on his recommendations and advice. A good broker can be a valuable ally in helping you meet your objectives, but only if you and the broker take the time to state those objectives clearly, and only if he then steadfastly assists you in meeting them.

Remember that a broker, with rare exception, earns his living by executing trades. He gets a commission on each trade, whether you're winning or losing. In other words, if he's going to eat, you've got to trade. If you invest a given sum of money in a given stock and instruct the broker to stash it away and forget about it for five or ten years and then tell him that's all the market investing you plan on doing, it's no wonder he wouldn't regard you as his favorite customer. Granted, he'll make his commission on your initial investment, and if he's still around when you cash in, he'll make another commission on the sale. But meanwhile your money is sitting idle as far as he's concerned, and he knows he's not going to make anything from you.

Naturally, any broker wants his customers to do well because this enhances his own professional image in the community, and each satisfied customer is like a walking, talking billboard. Many brokers can string along a losing customer for a period of time, blaming the continuing losses on market conditions, international news, and a variety of other factors beyond his control. True or not? It depends. There are indeed many factors beyond the control of any brokerage firm; but there are also many that could work to the broker's advantage yet are overlooked.

The broker may not be keeping close enough tabs on all of his customers' various accounts, and may neglect to advise you to buy or sell at an advantageous time. He may be too prone to listening to unfounded rumors and passing them along to his customers. He may not be making adequate use of research materials available in his firm and through other sources. He may be spending too much time hustling and too little time learning. And because there have been all too many lean periods for the brokerage industry in recent years, he may be so worried about where his next meal is coming from that he neglects the application of his own expertise to his customers' needs.

Consider these criteria in choosing your broker: how closely his investment philosophy parallels yours; his reputation for integrity and hard work, which you can learn from other customers who have used his services; the amount and continuity of his schooling, scholarship, and research; his willingness to spend time with you in learning or helping you to set your own goals and the amount of time he will subsequently spend in seeking out the best means of achieving these goals; and finally, faith—something that can't be described, shopped for, or catalogued. It's just got to be there and you'll know it when it is or isn't.

Personal Action Checklist
Playing the "Paper Game" with the Stock Market

The "Paper Game" is a harmless—and free—way to acquaint yourself with the ups and downs, the trials and tribulations, of the stock market. Play the Paper Game for six months or a year, and you'll have gained a good idea of whether it's the kind of place you want to send your money off to work for you.

   The rules of the Paper Game are very simple:

1. Select any ten companies whose stock is traded on the New York Stock Exchange. Pick whichever you like. We'll call this assortment Group A. Make believe that you buy 100 shares of each.

2. Put a recent listing of the New York Exchange stocks on a wall, and throw ten darts at it. Make believe that you buy 100 shares of each of the companies nearest whose names the darts landed. We'll call this assortment Group B.

3. Take a few minutes each day to record the changes in all 20 stocks. You may sell any Group A stocks any time you want, but you must buy another 100 shares of another company selling for about the same price. You may also sell Group B shares whenever you like, replacing them with another company determined by a throw of the dart—keep throwing until you hit a company selling for about the same price per share as the one you sold.

4. You must deduct the cost of all brokerage commissions—on both purchases and sales—from your total portfolio.

5. Add to your portfolio the total of all dividends you would have received if you really owned the stocks.

6. At the end of the designated time span—six months or a year—tally up the results. How did you do? How did you like it? How would you have felt doing this with real money?

   (For simplicity purposes, don't bother to consider reinvestment of dividends, or the tax consequences of profits or losses. But remember, of course, that those items must be considered in the real stock market game.)

   The following tally sheet can be used to keep track of your progress.

	Purchase price	Commission	Sale price	Commission	Dividends	Gain/ loss
Group A stocks						
1.	_____	_____	_____	_____	_____	_____
2.	_____	_____	_____	_____	_____	_____
3.	_____	_____	_____	_____	_____	_____
. . . through 10.	_____	_____	_____	_____	_____	_____
Group B stocks						
1.	_____	_____	_____	_____	_____	_____
2.	_____	_____	_____	_____	_____	_____
3.	_____	_____	_____	_____	_____	_____
. . . through 10.	_____	_____	_____	_____	_____	_____

Consumer Beware
The Poseidon Adventure

As we mentioned before, Will Rogers had the perfect plan for succeeding in the stock market: "You buy a stock," he said, "and when it goes up, you sell it. And if it don't go up . . . don't buy it."

Easier said than done, of course, for the mystique of the stock market is based on the expectation that any stock one buys will indeed increase in value. Such expectations can easily be compared with wearing rose-colored glasses, with believing only what you want to believe, with shunning sound research in favor of hot tips and hunches.

These trends are especially dangerous when we hear that a company has just been awarded a big contract, or has just hired a genius away from the competition, or is rumored to be unveiling a hot new product, or has just made a new discovery. Hypnotized speculators, old pro and novice alike, don't always stop to analyze whether or not this supposedly good news can be translated into *profitability* for the company.

In keeping with the law of gravity ("What goes up must come down"), it's appropriate to note the story of Poseidon, Ltd., an otherwise lackluster Australian mining firm whose stock was selling for about one dollar per share in 1969. They came across a major discovery of nickel in the western wilderness of that continent, and when word got out the stock began to skyrocket, rising from one dollar to $350 per share in less than one year!

Then came a slight problem: getting the nickel out of the ground *profitably.* The next few years proved to be a horror of ghastly proportion for Poseidon, Ltd., and its eager investors. Even though the price of nickel (and thus Poseidon's potential profits) had more than doubled from $1.05 per pound in 1969 to $2.40 per pound in the mid 1970s; and even though the Australian government subsidized the mining effort with a $24.7 million loan; and even though they brought in the nation's leading nickel mining firm as an expert partner; Poseidon could not get the nickel out of the ground *profitably.*

The stock slid as the troubles mounted. In late 1976 it was again selling at one dollar per share. Deep in debt and demoralized, Poseidon then gave up the ghost and went into receivership.

Many profited on the upswing, no doubt. But fortunes were lost on the plunge. Those with good timing and good luck breathed a sigh of relief as they took their profits and ran. As for the losers—they probably wished they could have followed Will Rogers' advice.

18 | Making Your Money Grow: Real Estate

Real estate investing has a certain allure not found in other types of investing. Perhaps it goes back to our prehistoric roots as territorial creatures who seek out and protect their "turf." With most other types of investments, your only tangible evidence of your money is a piece of paper: a stock certificate, a savings document, a bond. But with real estate you own all (or part) of something very real: land, buildings. These are things you can walk on, plant, live in. You can say, "This is mine," and point to something of substance. Indeed, there is even an emotional attachment—for better or for worse—to a piece of real property.

And therein may lie a serious flaw: Personal feelings and prudent investment decisions don't always go hand in hand. The former can be dangerous to the latter. This chapter takes a cold, hard look at real estate investing—its advantages, its pitfalls, its myths, and its realities. After reading it you should be able to:

□ Distinguish between the various types of real estate investment techniques.

□ Know how the depreciation factor provides particularly attractive tax advantages to the real estate investor.

□ Evaluate investment opportunities in group-type situations.

□ Understand the time and expertise needed to pursue real estate investment and ownership properly.

Myths and Facts About Real Estate Investing

Property values have been increasing at a rapid rate throughout most of the country, and as those values increase, the mystique about investing in real estate grows, too. Fostered by a myriad of "get-rich-quick" books and seminars, and by the proud boastings of investors who claim to have "made a killing" in real estate, the mystique takes on dangerous proportions for the uninformed would-be real estate investor. Let's first examine some of the myths and some of the facts about investing in real estate.

Myth: Real estate is easy; anybody can make money at it.

Facts: Successful real estate investing always has been, and always will be, a venture requiring a considerable amount of expertise. As in any kind of investment endeavor, there will always be a handful of lucky ones who make it look easy to others. But those are definitely the exception, not the rule. Real estate is a fast track: experts profit at the expense of novices. The experts know when to buy, when to sell, how to finance, and how to manage property properly. And even the experts can make mistakes. Expertise in real estate investing can take years to achieve. It requires the ability to deal efficiently and profitably with tenants, tax assessors, lenders, insurance agents, contractors, lawyers, appraisers, and other prospective buyers and sellers. The novice real estate investor, lured by the myth of fast and easy money, is apt to make serious mistakes and incur serious losses.

Myth: Real estate offers an assured return on your investment.

Facts: Real estate investing is very much like the stock market in that there are an infinite number of variables which can, in fact, make an assured return on your investment very questionable: a tenant defaults, seriously curtailing your income. Your furnace or central air-conditioning unit self-destructs, leaving you with a multi-thousand dollar repair bill. The taxes on real estate in your community double in a short period of time. A visitor to your building trips on a piece of broken flooring material and sues you for five times the amount of your public liability insurance. The neighborhood in which your building is located begins to deteriorate seriously. An unexpected rerouting of traffic makes your building far less attractive to would-be good-quality tenants. Your city passes a rent-control ordinance.

Events such as these, and countless others, can have a very negative effect on your expected investment return. There are, of course, events that can have a positive effect: an improvement in the neighborhood, a favorable rerouting of traffic, and so on. But the fact remains that there are many unknowns in the real estate–investment field. The primary caution to be aware of is this: People who are selling real estate investments have an obvious vested interest in convincing you, the buyer, that there is an attractive and assured return awaiting you if you make the investment. Those promises may be realizable for only a short time until the unknowns begin to be felt. Any would-be investor in real estate must approach any given project with a keen awareness of the potential unknowns that can drastically affect return.

Myth: Real estate investment offers assured profits.

Facts: The aforementioned factors that can have an effect on your anticipated return can have as serious an effect on your anticipated profit. Further, real estate is cyclical. There are up periods and there are flat or down periods. It's impossible to predict the cycles in any particular community.

Real estate investment is also subject to the failure of the "Greater Fool theory." The Greater Fool theory states that if you buy something, at whatever price, sooner or later a greater fool than yourself will come along and buy it from you at an even higher price. The failure of the Greater

Fool theory occurs when a community runs out of greater fools. Sooner or later, there will be no greater fools left to buy from you at a higher price. Then you're stuck.

Also be aware of the fact that in any type of investment—and real estate is certainly no exception—winners always boast, but losers are never heard from. This contributes to the myth of profitability in real estate investing. Winners not only boast, they exaggerate. Even lies are not unheard of. Losers tend to keep their mouths shut. They don't want to admit to their own errors, stupidity, or lack of judgment. Thus, you'll hear an excessive amount of good news and a sore lack of bad news from people who have tried their hand in real estate. Be advised accordingly.

Myth: You don't need any money to invest in real estate. You can buy property with "no money down."

Facts: Perhaps more money has been made selling books and expensive seminars on this subject than will ever be made in the real estate deals themselves. The simple and inexpensive secret behind these books and seminars is this: Yes, you can buy real estate with no money down. All you have to do is find a seller who is willing to sell you his property with no money down; or find a lender who is willing to lend you 100 percent of the purchase price. Or any combination of the two. Those feats are not easily accomplished. And there's a very high degree of probability that if a seller is willing to sell for no money down, the purchase price you pay may be much higher than the property is really worth. Likewise, if a lender is willing to lend you 100 percent of the purchase price, the interest rate you'll have to pay could be excessive. Real estate experts and wheeler-dealers may be able to accomplish this, but the novice can be on dangerously thin ice in attempting to work such techniques.

The Good Points

Despite these pitfalls, real estate can provide an attractive investment vehicle to the individual who is willing to do the necessary homework and put forth the necessary energy in keeping up with his investment. If the local marketplace is properly researched, if the premises and legal documents are properly scrutinized, and if the required amount of time and patience are devoted to the project, real estate can be very productive over the long run. One of the most attractive aspects of some kinds of real estate investment is the tax deduction that is allowed for the physical depreciation of the building. In a well structured investment, this factor not only can render the income from the real estate investment free of income taxes but may also shelter the investor's other income from real estate taxes. This factor will be discussed in more detail in the section on income-producing real estate.

A World of Opportunities

There are four major categories of real estate–related investments plus one category that allows you to invest as part of a group. The categories are as follows:

□ *Income-producing real estate.* You purchase a building with the intent of renting it out to tenants, and thereby realizing income. At some later date you may sell the building and realize a profit on the sale as well.

□ *Vacant-land investing.* You buy unimproved land with the intent of either renting it out or selling it at some future date at a profit.

□ *Turnover investing.* You buy a property with the intent of reselling it as soon as possible at a profit. Income is a secondary consideration.

□ *Mortgage investing.* You, in effect, lend other people money with the loan being secured by real estate. You don't actually acquire an ownership interest in the property at the time you make the investment, but you might if the borrower defaults. Thus, it's essential that you know the values that apply to the underlying real estate that is collateral for the loan you've made.

□ *Group ventures.* You pool your money with that of other investors in any or all of the above categories. Group ventures can include real estate investment trusts, syndications, and partnerships.

The whole world is made up of real estate, and opportunity exists in every country in which the free enterprise system is at work. Common sense, however, dictates that the closer to home you invest, the more knowledge and control you will have with respect to your investment. Let us now examine the basic categories of real estate investment.

Income-producing Real Estate

The primary objective in investing in income-producing real estate is to earn income on your investment and to the extent possible obtain tax sheltering of that income through the depreciation deduction. But, as noted earlier, there are many factors that can affect the flow of income. Here are some of the main factors that must be considered:

Factors That Can Affect Income-producing Property Investments

The Quality and Type of Tenants

In residential property, for example, consider the problems involved in an apartment complex that rents primarily to "the swinging single" crowd, particularly if it's in the vicinity of a university. An owner can expect a relatively high rate of turnover, and with each turnover comes the chance of a vacancy and the possible need to repaint and refurbish each apartment as it's vacated. On the other hand, an apartment complex catering to married couples or older persons might experience a relatively low rate of turnover, thus minimizing the chance for vacancies and the need for refurbishment. Applying the reward/risk rule, which relates as much to real estate as it does to any other form of investment, the properties with the higher chance of turnover and higher refurbishing costs should carry a proportionately higher rent than the more stable properties.

In commercial properties there is a broad spectrum of possible tenants that could occupy any given space, limited only by the landlord's willingness to accept certain types of tenants and zoning ordinances that might control the usage permitted in certain locales. Consider, for example, the possible uses that can occur in a small neighborhood shopping center—a popular type of moderate real estate investment for small to medium-sized investors. A given space might be occupied by a business or professional firm, such as an insurance agency. It will have relatively little public traffic and will need no special plumbing, electrical, or drainage installations. The same property might be occupied by a coffee shop or a tavern, which could have a high level of public traffic that can contribute to the more rapid deterioration of the premises; in addition, such installations need specialized plumbing, plus electrical and drainage connections that might not be suitable to other tenants who would want to occupy the space after the coffee shop or tavern moved out. Further, these uses could generate smoke and possible fire hazards that could increase the insurance rates on the building and of the adjoining tenants.

Two similar businesses, one new and one established, can have very different meanings to the landlord. The established business will have a seasoned clientele and, theoretically, a more dependable credit history, which the landlord should study in making rental decisions. Even though the owner of the new business may have good credit, he or she may be undercapitalized and unable to cover obligations during the usually difficult first two to three years of business. Thus, the landlord might face a vacancy far in advance of expectations. And as in residential projects, commercial vacancies mean not only a temporary loss of rent, but the likely need to refurbish to make the premises attractive to new would-be tenants.

The credit worthiness of a prospective tenant is not to be overlooked. When entering into a legitimate business venture, such as a lease, the landlord can and should check with the local credit bureau to determine the tenant's credit worthiness. A sloppy credit history might indicate a number of possible actions the landlord should consider: He might want to decline renting to that particular tenant altogether; he might feel the credit problems justify asking a higher rent; he might seek a co-signer to insure payment of the rent; he might request a substantial rental deposit, as well as a breakage and cleaning deposit, from the tenant to help assure that the rent will be paid or, if it isn't, that the landlord will at least be partly compensated for a period of vacancy that he might have to endure before he can rerent the premises.

A tenant who is tardy with rent can cause more than one problem. In addition to the headache and aggravation that the landlord must undergo in collecting overdue rent, the landlord might have to dip into his own funds to meet *his* monthly payments as they fall due. If the landlord has to borrow money to meet his own obligations on the building while awaiting past-due rents, the interest cost for such borrowed funds can substantially eat into his return on the property itself.

The Nature and the Quality of the Building

The potential risks and rewards for the landlord are directly related to the quality, location, and nature of the building itself. As in buying a house (chapter 8), the would-be investor in income-producing real estate must pay explicit attention to all the various mechanical and structural details of the building. If not familiar with building construction, it would behoove the investor to hire a construction specialist to provide a detailed inspection and report on the building. A building with hidden defects can cause serious and costly problems for the unsuspecting landlord; one in good physical condition will keep risk at a minimum and cut down problems of maintenance, repairs, and replacements. Many investors in real estate are content to take the word of the seller or the real estate agent representing the seller concerning condition of the building. The more prudent investors will determine on their own, with professional assistance, that the building does meet the standards they are seeking.

Location is important to the would-be investor; one must determine whether or not traffic patterns or changes in adjoining neighborhoods can have an effect on the investment. An attractive gas station, motel, shopping center, or restaurant on a heavily trafficked thoroughfare might seem most appealing. But if a new highway diverts all the traffic away from the street, the result can be disastrous. A neighborhood shopping center might seem to offer attractive possibilities; but when a bigger and better shopping center is constructed a few blocks away the unaware investor may regret the day he signed his down-payment check.

There are several sources that the prudent investor can use to determine the continuity of the status of the proposed location. The local zoning map discloses what uses are permitted in which areas of the city. If adverse uses exist in close proximity, or could possibly exist, the investor should be forewarned. A visit with the local and state agencies that control traffic and highway patterns might reveal whether any changes in these patterns or street routings are anticipated. A check with local real estate firms might reveal new developments pending within the trading area of the subject property that could have either a good or bad effect on the investment.

The nature of the building must also be considered. Many buildings are limited by their size, shape, and type of construction in the uses to which they can be put. Food franchise buildings often fall into this category; they might prove very unadaptable to other uses should the original tenant move out. On the other hand, some buildings are easily converted to suit many different purposes. The more limited the use of a given building, the more difficult it may be to find tenants and maintain the level of investment return sought.

The Tax Base

The tax base is the aggregate of buildings (and their taxpayers) in a given community that provide the local real property tax payments that flow into the city coffers. Many cities have been having severe problems with their tax base in recent years; some are older with shrinking populations; others are in financial distress.

Before entering into any real estate investment, the prudent investor will visit with the local tax assessor to determine the recent history of property taxation in the community and the projected future. In order to evaluate properly the cash flow on a given investment situation, the investor must bear in mind the likely cost of property taxes over a relatively long term—or at least as long as he or she plans to own the building. An investor may be able to blunt rising taxes by requiring tenants to pay some or all of the taxes. But not all tenants will agree to such conditions, and in that case, the landlord will have to absorb the higher taxes and should be prepared in advance to do so.

Utility Costs

Before the energy crisis little thought was given by real estate investors to the cost of electricity and fuel for heating. Those costs rarely changed from year to year and in cases where the landlord was responsible for electricity and heat the effect was relatively small. However, since the crisis, utility costs have been leaping upward rapidly. Although it's difficult for anyone to predict what level the costs might ultimately reach, the prudent real estate investor must be ready for whatever comes.

A landlord obliged to provide utilities for tenants would thus do well to consider negotiating a "utility stop" clause in any new leases and lease renewals. This clause would provide that the landlord pay for utilities up to an agreed-on amount; any usage of electricity or fuel over and above that amount is absorbed by the tenant. This not only offers some protection against rising utility costs but also serves as a caution to the tenant not to be wasteful.

Management of the Property

Management, in the overall sense, includes the leasing of premises when they become vacant, collection of rentals, supervision of repairs and maintenance as needed, maintaining good public relations with the tenants, and taking the steps needed to improve the investment.

A skilled property manager can be a very valuable ally for the real estate investor. In addition to day-to-day operations, a manager is in close touch with the general real estate market within the community and might be able to spot potential tenants or buyers. A manager's experience helps detect the need for preventive maintenance that can avoid serious repair or replacement costs. And—perhaps most valuable—the manager absorbs the headaches inherent in real estate ownership: dealing with tenants, with repair and service personnel, with tax assessors, lawyers, accountants, and so on. In short, the property manager removes the personal problems from this type of investment and leaves the owner with a much more simple and clear-cut situation.

One of the most serious mistakes made by real estate investors, particularly novices, is attempting to tackle management alone, without any outside professional assistance. Unlike those investments in which your money is at work for you and there's not much you can do to change what's happening, real estate requires direct involvement. The efficiency of that involvement can make a bad deal good, or its lack can make a good deal turn bad.

In assuming the task of managing one's own property, the investor must have a reasonably good working knowledge of how a building and all of its mechanical components function. When mechanical equipment fails or needs to be replaced, or when other work has to be done on a building, a good deal of comparison shopping, pricing, and evaluating may be in order. This can be very time-consuming, and a wrong decision may prove costly.

In addition to repair and replacement of the building and its components, the owner will be subjected to a continuing barrage of sales persons who offer a variety of products and services.

An owner will have to take the time to listen to the various salespeople offering these products. Discerning the best buy for the money and the purpose is a task requiring experience and a sharp head for figures. A two-year supply of fluorescent lightbulbs may be offered at a discount, and indeed might be an attractive purchase. But how will this affect the owner's cash flow if the bulbs have to be paid for in advance; what will it cost to store them until they're needed; are there better deals elsewhere? If the owner doesn't have the head or temperament for such matters, professional management would be recommended.

Financing

The mechanics of financing income property are generally the same as financing one's own home. The investor (unless paying all cash) gives a down payment to the seller of the property and either assumes an existing mortgage or obtains a mortgage loan from outside sources.

But there the similarity fades, for the real estate investor must arrange financing geared to his or her investment objectives: obtaining a satisfactory return on invested capital. If the mortgage payments are so high that, when combined with the other expenses of operating the property, there is no cash flow available to the investor, he or she is involved in a totally speculative situation—hoping that someday the property will be sold at a substantial profit. Some investors prefer to pay off any mortgage debt as rapidly as possible so that when the debt is finally eliminated, the cash flow on the property will be all that much greater.

The prudent investor, however, will seek a good return on invested capital (the cash down payment) and to that end will attempt to structure the mortgage so that there is adequate cash flow to meet objectives. Clauses in a mortgage that allow the lender to increase the interest, and thus the total monthly payment, can have an obvious effect on the investor's cash flow, and such clauses should be closely scrutinized. If there are interest-rate escalation clauses, the owner will have to be prepared to adjust rents accordingly if he or she wants to maintain a constant rate of cash flow.

The real estate investor may also need large sums of money at indeterminate future dates in order to accomplish major renovations and repairs. If possible, the investor will negotiate with the mortgage lender to obtain such funds by adding them on to the existing mortgage, hopefully at favorable terms.

When a lender is considering a mortgage loan application on income property, he or she will examine, not only the owner's credit worthiness, but the caliber of tenants that currently occupy the building. The owner's ability to make payments on the mortgage is, of course, directly related to the ability of the tenants to make their regular rental payments. The better the tenants, the more favorable terms the borrower should be able to negotiate with the lender. Better quality tenants will, as noted earlier, be able to bargain for a lower rental from the landlord. The landlord can make up this difference by seeking the most favorable terms on his mortgage payments.

The Lease

At the heart of any real estate investment is the lease: the agreement between the investor/owner and the tenant/user. Whether the property is commercial, residential, or a combination, the specific terms of the lease can have an important bearing on the investor's overall success. Residential leases tend to be shorter and simpler, usually running for a period of not more than one or two years. Commercial leases can be more complex, and because the property might be usable in many different ways by different tenants, a variety of clauses should be carefully considered by the investor. In either case, residential or commercial, the prudent investor will see to it that an attorney prepares a lease best suited to the investor's interests.

The following are some of the more important terms that should be evaluated, particularly in commercial leases.

Length of the Lease   Is there any ideal length of time for a lease? Not really. As noted above, residential leases usually only run for one or two years, sometimes slightly longer. But for commercial leases it's quite a different story. The tenant will want to know that he or she has the right to use the property at a fixed rental rate for as long as the property is profitable. If it ceases to be profitable, for whatever reason, the tenant will probably want to depart. On the other hand, if the landlord feels the space could be rented out more profitably after the passage of time, he may wish to replace the tenant or increase the tenant's rental.

A preferred situation for a tenant would be to have a medium-term lease—say, three to five years—with options to renew at agreed-on rentals. This offers the tenant both flexibility and fixed overhead. But this might not be to the landlord's advantage. By giving a tenant the privilege to renew, he is effectively taking the property off the market for the length of the original term and possibly the period of renewal.

Customarily, where renewal clauses exist, the tenant is obliged to give notice of intention to renew two or three months prior to the expiration of the lease. Technically, the landlord does not know until notice is given whether or not the space will be available after the expiration of the lease. The landlord can certainly make inquiry, but tenants are legally not obliged to express their intentions to renew or depart until the time stated in the lease agreement. Where there are no renewal privileges, the landlord knows exactly when he can expect the premises to be vacated and can begin seeking new tenants with an assurance of when they can take occupancy. Or the landlord can renegotiate the lease with the existing tenant and hope that conditions will permit an equal or better rental on the renewal term.

The landlord should bear in mind that because a tenant has a right of renewal at an agreed-on rental this does *not* guarantee that the tenant will pay that rental. Renewal date may roll around and the tenant may want to continue in the space, but at a reduced rental. This can put the landlord in a predicament, for he now has a relatively short period of time in which to try to find a better tenant for the premises. Working out such problems often comes down to nothing more than plain old hard-nosed bargaining, the outcome of which will generally depend on the condition of the local real estate market at that time. If there's a surplus of tenants looking for space, the landlord is in a better position and vice versa. There's no way of knowing what these conditions will be like years in advance, so the parties just have to be prepared to cope with the situation as it arises.

An alternative position—part way between a renewal option and no renewal option—is a lease with a *right of first refusal to renew*. Here's how such a clause might operate: the tenant is paying, say, $300 per month for a two-year period. At the end of the two years, the tenant has a right of first refusal to renew the lease at $400 per month. During the initial two years, the landlord still has the right to offer the property to other potential tenants, but before he can lease it, he must allow the initial tenant to meet or beat any bona fide rental offered by another would-be tenant. The offer must be acted on within a specified period.

With six months to go before the end of the initial two years, the landlord finds a new tenant who is willing to pay $450 a month for the space. Before the landlord can make a deal with this tenant, he must first offer it back to his original tenant, who has, say, ten days in which to meet or beat the $450 offer. If the tenant wishes to equal the offer, the space is his for a renewal term. If not, the new tenant will take over the space at the expiration of the original term. If the landlord does not come up with any other bona fide offers, the original tenant can renew for the originally agreed-on $400 per month.

This device offers a measure of protection to both parties. The landlord can still offer his property for rent to the highest bidder, subject to the tenant's rights, and the tenant has the ability to remain on the premises at a rental that should be in line with current market conditions.

Another important factor to consider concerning the length of a lease is that mortgage financing can depend on the term of the lease. A long-term lease—ten or more years—with a well-qualified tenant will be more attractive to a mortgage lender than a short-term one. The lender is obviously better protected on the longer term lease, assuming that the credit worthiness of the tenant meets the lender's standards otherwise. Thus, a landlord might have to offer a longer term than he otherwise might in order to satisfy the requirements of the mortgage lender and get the best financing terms available. All of these elements must be weighed and balanced before decisions are made, and before leases are signed.

The Rental Rate   In most cases, market conditions will determine the probable amount of rental a given tenant will pay. In commercial rentals, the rent is often expressed in terms of "per square foot per year." A space of 1000 square feet rents for $500 per month, or $6000 per year. The rental is thus quoted as $6 per square foot per year. In the jargon of real estate agents, it might be referred to as "$6 a foot."

Commercial rentals are also referred to as "gross" or "net." In a gross lease, the landlord is responsible for virtually all operating costs on the property, including real estate taxes, utilities, maintenance, cleaning, and generally servicing the premises. In a net lease, the tenant is responsible for most of these expenses. There is no precise definition of a gross lease or net lease, for circumstances and practices may differ from area to area, and one slight amendment to a lease can tend to change the definition of gross or net. But the jargon of the trade does refer to what's commonly called a "net-net-net" lease, which customarily requires the tenant to pay for absolutely everything except for the owner's own mortgage payments.

With a gross lease the landlord will receive a considerably higher monthly payment from the tenant. But out of that payment he has to meet all of his related expenses and obligations on the building. The landlord who wants a minimum of involvement in the operation of the building will prefer the most net lease he can get, preferably the net-net-net lease. Some tenants may prefer a net-net-net lease because they can more directly control the operating expenses on the building and end up paying less money for their occupancy costs. Whether gross or net, someone does have to take care of the operation of the property, be it landlord or tenant, which will take time—an ultimate cost to somebody. A landlord with a net-net-net lease is less likely to need a property management firm than one with a gross lease.

Rental payments may be fixed for the term of the lease, or they may escalate upward in line with rising prices or simply by agreement between the parties. In addition to the basic flat rent, commercial leases often have percentage clauses.

A percentage clause will state that the tenant must pay additional rent to the landlord in an amount equal to an agreed-upon percentage of the volume of business the tenant does. For example: The tenant may be required to pay 6 percent of all gross income in excess of, say, $100,000 per year. In such a case, if the tenant's business does not gross over $100,000 in a year, the percentage clause will not go into effect. But if the tenant generates $150,000 of volume, the percentage lease will require the tenant to pay 6 percent of $50,000 or $3000 in additional rent for that year. The existence and terms of a percentage clause are a matter of negotiation between the parties. If a landlord feels that a tenant's business prospects are good, the landlord may prefer a lower base rent with a percentage clause. A more conservative landlord may simply prefer a higher base rent and no percentage clause. A percentage lease allows the landlord the right to look at the books and records of the tenant so that the correct amount of the payment can be determined.

Use of the Property   The lease stipulates the purposes for which the premises can be used by the tenant, or by any subtenants, if there is a right of sublease. If, for example, a tenant rents a store property for a retail shoe business, the landlord does not want the tenant, or a subtenant, to later change the premises to a tavern.

In addition, particularly in a multiple-occupancy situation such as a shopping center, the tenant may request a "noncompetition" clause. This would prevent the landlord from allowing other spaces in the center to be rented to competitors. The landlord will have to evaluate such a request in light of current market conditions, his eagerness to rent the space, and the rent that the tenant is willing to pay.

Repairs and Restorations   The lease should stipulate who is responsible for each and every kind of repair. Customarily, the tenants are responsible for making minor interior repairs, and the landlord is responsible for structural repairs and matters affecting mechanical equipment, such as the heating plant and the air-conditioning unit. Of course, the parties can agree to any combination of who does what and who pays for what. A prudent landlord might prefer that the tenant pay for certain repairs, but that the landlord will see to the actual work. By so doing, the landlord can choose the firm to do the repair work and might get a better level of satisfaction than by having the tenant make the choice.

A restoration clause is again subject to negotiation between the parties. This clause would require the tenant to restore the premises to its original condition at the time he or she first took occupancy. If tenants have made renovations within the premises, they will have to see to it, at their own expense, that the property is brought back to its original condition unless the landlord later agrees otherwise. If a restoration clause is agreed on between the parties, it would be necessary for them to include a careful description of the premises at the time of the start of occupancy (including colored photographs as an added precaution) to assure that the amount of restoration needed is also agreed on.

Default   What if the tenant doesn't live up to the agreement? He or she may damage the property and not repair it. Or the tenant may leave in the middle of a lease and try to escape making further payments. The lease should clearly state that the tenant remains responsible for any default, although including such a clause within a lease does not necessarily mean that the tenant will automatically make good on a default. The landlord must still pursue his rights, through the courts if necessary, to gain satisfaction.

As a measure of protection against default, the prudent real estate investor will insist upon a rental deposit and a breakage and damage deposit from a tenant. The rental deposit, usually designated as the last month's rent on the lease, assures that the landlord will have at least some cash in hand should the tenant skip. The breakage and damages deposit will protect the landlord to some extent in the event that the tenant neglects to make such repairs. But it should be clearly understood that the amount of the rental deposit and the breakage and damage deposit are not the limit of the tenant's obligation. He or she will still be obliged to make whatever payments are due over and above the amount of the deposits.

**"Compounding"
Your Income**

In fixed income investments your earned interest can be automatically reinvested in your account and go to work for you. This is known as compounding interest. The same ends can be accomplished in the stock market, through either a dividend reinvestment plan or a mutual fund that pumps your earnings back into additional shares of the fund. But can you "compound" your earnings in a real estate investment? In a sense, yes, at least to a certain extent. Prudent real estate investors realize that a portion of their income should be reinvested back into the property, by way of refurbishing and modernization. The net effect of this *should* be to generate higher income from tenants of the property.

It's not as simple or as automatic as the compounded interest on your savings account, and it requires some expertise to know which dollars can generate additional rentals. The investor may prefer to take all income out and invest it in some other fashion, if in fact he or she is not spending it. But the investor should examine the possibilities of reinvesting the money in the property before making an ultimate decision.

For example, a tenant might agree to an increase of $20 per month if the landlord repaints the premises. The paint job might cost $1000, but the landlord will be getting an additional $240 per year for the balance of the lease. That's a 24 percent return on the investment, which shouldn't be tossed off lightly. Other modes of refurbishing might be more or less profitable to the landlord, and much will depend on negotiations between landlord and tenant. The prudent investor will be continually on the alert for ways to increase income by plowing profits back into the property.

An Example

Let's look at a very simple example of an income-producing real estate investment. You buy a small commercial building for $150,000, giving a down payment of $10,000 and assuming a mortgage for $140,000. Monthly payments on the mortgage are $1680. In addition to the mortgage payment, your other expenses total $500 per month (including property taxes, fire insurance, and other miscellaneous items).

Your total monthly costs are, therefore, $2180. Your tenants pay you a monthly rental of $2200, and the tenants pay all of the utilities and necessary repairs on the building. The difference between your income and your expenses is, therefore, $20 per month, or $240 per year. You've invested $10,000 of your own money so a $240 per year return represents a 2.4 percent yield to you. Admittedly, that's rather puny. But now let's take into account the previously mentioned depreciation deduction available to real estate investors.

The Depreciation Deduction

Over the years, just about everything weakens or deteriorates or depreciates. It's as true of buildings and mechanical equipment as it is of human bodies. But even while something is physically depreciating, it can be appreciating in actual market value. A 20-year-old human body is more sturdy than a 50-year-old one, but the 50-year-old one is capable of generating many times the annual income of the 20-year-old one. Likewise with property: A building that sold for $50,000 20 years ago might be worth $150,000 in today's market, even though it is not as sound physically.

Federal tax laws recognize that property does depreciate physically and that it can simultaneously appreciate in monetary value. Tax laws have been devised to take both of these phenomena into account.

Those who invest in property (machinery as well as real estate) for the purpose of producing income are allowed to show a "loss" on their income-tax forms to reflect the supposed physical deterioration of that property. Technically this "loss" is a deduction for depreciation: the amount in question reduces the amount of income that is otherwise subject to taxation.

Referring back to the example: The building in question cost $150,000. Of this total amount, it would be fair to allocate $30,000 toward the land and $120,000 toward the structure. (Land itself is not depreciable. Only the structure is depreciable.) Internal Revenue guidelines suggest that the building, at the time you bought it, had a remaining useful life of 20 years. In fact, it might survive for a century or more, but investors are happy to use the shorter IRS estimates or attempt to justify life spans even shorter than what IRS guidelines suggest.

Using the common "straight-line" method of depreciation, you as the owner of the building will be able to claim a deduction for depreciation of $6000 for each year you own the building ($6000 times 20 years equals $120,000, the total depreciable value of the building). Remember that during your first year of ownership of the building you had a cash-flow income of $240 (income less expenses). In addition to that cash-flow income, you now take into account the affect of the depreciation deduction of $6000. That $6000 is deducted from your otherwise taxable income. If you are in the 30 percent tax bracket, that $6000 means that you pay $1800 less in taxes than you otherwise would have paid had you not owned the building. The depreciation deduction "shelters" your other income from taxation. This is why real estate is commonly referred to as a tax-sheltered form of investing.

So now we are looking at a cash-flow income of $240 plus taxes saved of $1800, or a total benefit of $2040. That is a 20.4 percent return on your invested $10,000. That's the impact of the depreciation deduction. The higher tax bracket an investor is in, the greater the benefits of the deduction. Note also that there are other methods of calculating the depreciation deduction. The straight-line method referred to allows an equal amount every year for the remaining life of the property. Other methods allow a larger deduction in the earlier years and a smaller deduction in later years. The choice of methods depends on the specific aspects of each deal and the investor's tax situation. Tax law changes effective in 1982 make it possible for a structure to be depreciated within 15 years. Regulations are complex and the assistance of a professional tax counselor is advised before undertaking a depreciation schedule on a real estate investment.

Now the Bad News   You paid $150,000 for the building. Say that you own the building for ten years and you take a depreciation deduction of $6000 for each of those ten years or a total of $60,000 in depreciation. At the end of ten years you have the opportunity to sell the property for $250,000. Naturally, you'll have to pay a tax on your profit.

What is the extent of that profit? You paid $150,000 and received $250,000 for an apparent profit of $100,000. But that's not the amount you'll have to pay taxes on. Because you took $60,000 worth of depreciation while you owned the building, tax laws require that your cost basis be reduced by that amount; in other words to $90,000. The profit that will be subject to taxes will then be the difference between your selling price ($250,000) and your cost as adjusted by the amount of depreciation you took ($90,000). You will thus be taxed on a profit of $160,000, not the apparent profit of $100,000. This will obviously mean a substantially higher tax bill.

However, this is no reason for real estate investors to despair. During the ten years that you owned the building you were sheltering ordinary income at a considerable savings. The tax payable on the profit when you sell the building is at capital-gains rates, which are much lower than ordinary income rates. So even though you may have to pay a somewhat higher tax when you eventually sell a property, you will have reaped considerable benefits during the period of ownership. *Note:* Tax laws are always subject to change, and prior to any anticipated real estate investment you should determine what current laws and regulations are on the subject of depreciation as well as any other applicable laws that could affect your investment.

Investing in Vacant Land

Investing in vacant, or raw, land can be one of the most extreme forms of speculation. We do hear of "killings" made in land by investors; and we hear statements, such as the one Will Rogers made, "You ought to buy land, cuz they ain't gonna print no more of it." But success in raw land investment, for the most part, remains the province of the skilled professional who has the expertise, the capital, and the selling skills needed to turn a profit most of the time. *Note* "most of the time." Even the skilled professional will have setbacks.

Other forms of investment pay a form of income to the investor—interest on fixed income investments, dividends on stocks, rentals on income properties. But raw land requires the investor to be constantly *paying out* money: real estate taxes, public liability insurance, and money for necessary signs and security. Further, the investor in raw land has put his or her capital beyond reach until the land is actually sold. It's extremely difficult to borrow against raw land, and if one does, then the interest expense has to be added to the other expenses.

An investment in raw land will usually take one of two forms. It may be land that you hope to use some day for your own purposes, such as for building a summer home, a retirement home, or a principal residence. Or an investment in raw land may be for the purpose of a hoped-for profit on a subsequent resale, with the possibility of rental income in the interim, such as from farmers.

Land for Personal Use

Buying land for future personal use can make sense as an investment if a number of criteria are met. If you are certain that you want to eventually build a particular type of home at a specific location; and if you are certain that the price you pay for the land today will be less than what you'll have to pay for it at some future point (considering the ongoing cost of owning the land, as noted above); and if you are certain that the specific piece of land, or anything comparable to it, will not be available at the future date you plan on building, then it might be wise to put your money into the land today. If, in fact, your anticipations prove to have been correct—

that at some future time you still do wish to build a home, the price of the lot has increased tremendously, and you wouldn't have been able to purchase anything comparable—then you may score a successful investment. But if your building plans change, or if the land does not go up in price as you had thought it would, or if many other comparable lots are still available to you at a lesser price, then your investment may have been in vain.

"Known" Land

There's a much better chance for success in such an investment if you're dealing with known land—that is, land that exists in a community with which you're familiar and on which you can get professional estimates from real estate professionals concerning probable future value. Known land also implies that you are certain of the availability of utilities, sewers, roadways, schools, shopping, and other necessary facilities.

"Unknown" Land

Uncounted millions of dollars are lost every year by people who sign contracts and checks to buy parcels of unknown land—generally, land in distant places that is being sold as part of a development program for the creation of a "new city," a resort, or a retirement village. Although there are legitimate developments in all parts of the country, the abuses, intentional or otherwise, that have arisen have been all too frequent.

Anyone considering investing in raw land for future personal use, particularly if it's unknown land, must observe the following cautions.

See the Land   It's necessary to actually view the land, and walk it from corner to corner, before you sign any documents. The majority of people who have been bilked on such deals haven't done this. Fancy brochures and high-pressure sales pitches lead them to believe that they may be getting an idyllic lot in an ongoing development, when in fact they may be buying a barren patch of wasteland.

Hire an Attorney Before You Sign Anything   The attorney should help you determine whether the land you saw is the land you'll actually be buying. He or she will also scrutinize the other documents involved and help you ascertain exactly what you can expect for the money you're paying. If you sign documents before you have had legal counsel, it may be too late for the attorney to help you. If you're planning on spending many thousands of dollars for a piece of land that you hope to use in the future, it's only prudent to make sure that you're actually getting what you're paying for, and an attorney is the proper party to give you that assurance.

Read the Property Report   If a developer is selling land on an interstate basis—to buyers in many states—federal law requires the provision to prospective buyers of a Property Report. The Property Report must contain certain information prescribed by the Interstate Land Sales Act, a federal law. If a developer fails to provide the Property Report within the prescribed time limits, the buyer might be entitled to revoke the contract and obtain a refund.

Investing in Land Seeking a Future Profit

Here, too, we must consider the difference between known land and unknown land. All of the above cautions regarding unknown land bought for future personal use apply equally, if not more so, to land purchased in the hope of a future profit on resale. Indeed, many of the lots sold for personal use are sold with the following inducement: "Even if you never do decide to build on the lot, you can always sell it for a profit." This obvious appeal to everyone's greed has been eminently successful. Personal case histories abound of people who have bought such lots, vaguely anticipating that they might build a home on them some day, but with the principal motivation of "turning a quick profit" when enough years had passed. Their disappointment was immeasurable when they later learned they couldn't sell their land, or even give it away.

Regarding known land—land located within a community with which you're familiar and within which you can get expert appraisals and advice—there are additional cautions to follow if a successful investment program is to be realized.

Appraisal

Success in a raw land investment depends on two critical decisions: the price you pay for the land, and the price you get when you sell. Before an investment is made, the prudent investor will obtain an appraisal on the land at its current market value and at least a reasoned estimate as to its potential future worth.

The seller's asking *price* may or may not bear a resemblance to the current market *value*. Current market value is determined by the sale of comparable property, which can be put to comparable uses in comparable neighborhoods. A real estate agent or a professional appraiser can assist you in determining these facts. The professional can also advise you about the elements that may or may not contribute to the increase in value of the property, such as improving traffic patterns, increasing population trends, the stability of the tax base, the scarceness of such land for designated uses, and the attractiveness of the terms on which you can buy and later sell.

Tests

If you buy a piece of raw land with the hope to sell it to someone at a profit, you have to consider the likelihood that that ultimate buyer will want to erect a building on the property. If he is a prudent buyer, he will want to be certain that the land is adequate for the use he intends. The buyer may thus require that certain tests be conducted on the land and may expect you, as the owner/investor, to bear their costs. On the other hand, you as the owner/investor, anticipating the possibility of such necessary tests, may want to do them on your own well in advance. The availability of the appropriate test results might enhance your ability to sell the land. But the costs of the tests have to be taken into account.

The soil test determines the bearing capacity of the soil. In other words, how much of a building load can the soil withstand? The soil may be compact enough, and of the right composition, to support a small, one-story cinder-block or brick building, without needing any expensive footing or foundations. On the other hand, the soil may not be proper to support a multistory building without getting into expensive substructures.

Percolation tests determine the drainage capacity of the land—how much rainfall and moisture the land can absorb without turning into a swamp or a sea of mud. The condition of the ground in this respect can obviously have a bearing on the use of the land and the cost of constructing a building on the land.

Surveys

Although not technically tests, the boundary survey and the topographical survey will assure a would-be buyer/builder of the true boundaries of the property and of the precise slopes that may exist on the property. If there is, for example, too much slope to the property, a prospective builder might be faced with expensive land-moving costs, and those costs could be reflected in a price that a buyer is willing to pay for the property.

The prudent investor in raw land might deem it wise to have these tests made, even before making his purchase, so as to determine the ultimate usability of the property and/or the cost of making it most usable to most prospective buyers.

Dollars and Cents

If a parcel of raw land doubles in price within the short space of five years, an investor might break even. Here's the arithmetic. Say that an investor pays $10,000 in cash for a piece of vacant land. He is forgoing a return on his money of, conservatively, $600 per year. That's how much he could have earned by simply investing the money in a savings certificate insured by the federal government. In addition, he may have the following typical expenses: property taxes, $500; insurance (mainly for public liability, to avoid lawsuits if anyone is hurt while crossing the property), $200; signs, advertising, and security, $200. (These figures are just rough estimates, but within the bounds of probability.) His total annual expenses (including lost interest) are thus $1500, or a total over five years of $7500.

Assume that five years later he is able to sell the property for $20,000. If he has used a real estate agent to find a buyer—which is likely—his commission to the real estate agent will be 10 percent of the selling price, or $2000. In addition, he'll probably have expenses related to the sale, particularly legal fees and recording costs that can easily total $500. His total expenses then are $10,000—$1500 per year for five years, or $7500, plus the $2500 at the time of sale. His selling price of $20,000 thus results in a net of $10,000. Over a five-year span, the property has doubled in value and the investor has broken even.

This example may be pessimistic, but it's intended to provide a would-be investor the kind of "what if" arithmetic one faces before making a decision. The time to evaluate this very clear risk is before making any commitments to invest in raw land. Once the commitment is made, you can't get out of it as you could selling a share of stock or cashing in a savings certificate. You're stuck with it until a buyer comes along, and if that buyer isn't willing to meet your price, you may have to take whatever is offered. And the longer you hold on, the more it costs.

"Turnover" Investing

Probably somewhat more speculative than higher quality income property investing, and probably less speculative than raw land investing, is the purchase of existing homes for subsequent resale. It's a tricky business requiring expertise, hard work, and patience. But many small investors have found handsome profits in such endeavors, so that they have become semi-businesses rather than just investment modes.

Many opportunities exist involving homes that need refurbishing, and these might prove particularly attractive to the investor with repair talents. Such talents will allow you to make reasonably accurate estimates of what renovations might be needed, how much they'll cost, and how much they can boost the potential selling price. A few hundred dollars wisely spent on paint or paneling or flooring, for example, could increase the potential selling price by a thousand dollars or more.

The overall procedure involves seeking out houses that have good underlying basic value but can be bought for less than the normal market price, perhaps because the owners have had financial difficulties and are anxious to get out.

The success of any venture will depend on the investor's ability to buy right and to finance right.

Buying Right

Buying right requires the careful evaluation of the neighborhood as well as of the physical structure itself. A run-down house in an area of better homes could command a handsome price if it's spruced up to be on a par with its surroundings. Another run-down house might offer little or no profit potential regardless of how much you do, because the general neighborhood isn't that desirable. Remember that your buyers are looking for location as well as a house itself, and the selling price is affected accordingly.

There are three major sources where an investor might find attractive situations. First, you can scout around privately for people who are hard pressed to sell, because of either time or money pressures. The more pressure on them, the better the deal you might strike. Word of mouth, or simply driving around looking for "for sale" signs are ways of discovering such opportunities. Advertising is another way. The seller may place a classified ad with a tipoff that indicates a good buy; or you, as the investor, can advertise under the "homes wanted" or similar classifications in the want ad pages.

A second source would be real estate agents in your area. Make it known to a number of them that you're in the market for such houses, and ask them to contact you if they spot any. Often, agents might be reluctant to take a listing on run-down houses from the seller, but if they know they have a possible buyer, they could put you on to a number of opportunities.

A third source would be banks and savings and loan institutions that have taken back properties on foreclosures and that don't relish owning a lot of unused residential property. This possibility deserves particularly careful attention because you might well find a source of automatic financing when you later sell to another party.

Financing Right

If you've bought right, and if you've refurbished correctly, your chances of finding a willing buyer who will pay you the sought-after profit will be greatly enhanced if you can offer the property fully financed. This means that a credit-worthy buyer can step right into a mortgage situation for which you have made prior arrangements. In order to make such arrangements it will be necessary to develop a relationship with a mortgage lender, or lenders, in your community who will be willing to cooperate with you in such transactions. As part of the negotiations involved in setting up such a relationship, you may have to guarantee all or part of any given loan that is arranged on behalf of your buyer. Although this can improve your potential profitability in the sale of the house, it does put you on the hook for an extended period, and you should be particularly careful that the buyer pays an adequate down payment and that his credit history justifies your assuming that possible risk. As noted earlier, many mortgage lenders in the community may have an inventory of used homes that they'd be willing to sell at attractive prices to investors willing to fix them up and offer them for resale. In such cases, they might be willing to cooperate in advance in making commitments for long-term financing to credit-worthy buyers.

The Profit Margin

Perhaps the biggest challenge in this kind of investment is building enough of a profit margin into the deal to cover your initial expenses, as well as your continuing expenses, and yet not price the property out of the market. The investor must be well aware that once renovations are completed and the property is on the market, time can start working against him or her. Every month that goes by in which the house remains unsold means added costs—interest, taxes, insurance, advertising, and so on. As these costs mount, the investor, for lack of a buyer, might drop the price. As the expenses rise and the asking price drops, the investor might succumb to a feeling of panic. That's the worst danger. The difference between what you will pay out for the purchase, the renovations, and the continuing expenses and what you'll take in at the time of sale must be most carefully estimated.

A well-structured deal offers the opportunity for substantial profit if a buyer is found in the early months, but as time goes by, profitability rapidly erodes. This risk must be well considered by anyone investing in homes for resale purposes.

Investing in Mortgages

Technically, mortgages are not really real estate investments, but many people think of them as such. These investments fall more aptly into the fixed income category: you're actually buying someone else's IOU with a piece of real estate as security for the IOU. But because you could end up owning the real estate if the borrower defaults on the mortgage payments, it can, and perhaps should, be considered within the overall category of a real estate investment.

The prudent investor must scrutinize the value of the property itself as much as he must scrutinize the credit worthiness of the borrower. In effect, he or she must exercise the same precautions that a bank would in making an original mortgage loan: appraising the property, determining the credit status of the borrower, and seeing to it that there is adequate protection regarding title and property insurance. The assistance of an attorney is necessary for preparing all the required documents, and the cost of the legal service must be taken into account. It's not unusual in private mortgage investing for the costs of legal matters and related documentation to be passed along to the borrower. In addition, the private mortgage lender might be able to impose extra fees or "points" in much the same way that institutional lenders do.

Prior to becoming an investor in mortgages, it would be valuable to meet existing mortgage brokers in your community and determine what the current going prices and interest rates are. You might even, as a would-be investor in mortgages, prefer to deal through such brokers before you embark on your own. The mortgage brokers will, in effect, place your money for you in mortgage situations and will take a fee for their service. Most communities have a number of private mortgage brokers who are always looking for funds that they can invest, content to take a service fee for their efforts. You can find them listed in the Yellow Pages of your telephone directory and in the classified section of your newspaper, usually under the heading "Money to Lend."

A mortgage investment can take one of three forms.

"Taking Back" a Mortgage

If you sell property that you own and agree to accept the buyer's IOU in full or partial payment thereof, this is commonly known as "taking back" a mortgage. The buyer of the property becomes obligated to you to make the monthly payments called for in the mortgage agreement. Many people who sell their homes or business properties don't have immediate use for the full proceeds and might prefer to let the money stay in the property as a form of investment.

Initiating a New Mortgage

This is very much like the above situation, except that instead of taking back a mortgage on a property that you own, you are making a new mortgage loan to an individual who is buying a different property. The interest rate, costs, and added fees that you as an investor can generate out of the deal are subject to negotiation between the parties. Some important cautions are in order, though, if the deal is to be structured to your best advantage.

First, you must determine why the individual is not able to obtain conventional financing through a normal lending institution. If it's because his or her credit status is weak, you might be asking for trouble. In such cases, you might be able to command a higher interest rate (subject to state usury laws) because you are taking on a higher than normal risk. Or the property buyer may simply not have enough down payment to meet the requirements of the institution, even though the credit status is perfectly acceptable. This is a lesser risk, but one that you should evaluate nonetheless.

An individual may also find that you are offering better terms than the local institutions offer. For example, the current going rate at banks might be 14 percent and you might be willing to take back or grant a new mortgage at a 12 percent interest rate. The bank might not be satisfied with that lower return, but you might be perfectly pleased with it.

Another caution must be noted regarding the term of the mortgage. Mortgages commonly can run for 20 to 30 years, and a large institution can absorb that long-term debt easily into its overall loan portfolio, for it has a substantial amount of short-term loans outstanding to balance off the long-term one with regard to cash flow. But you as an individual don't have that advantage, and a 20- to 30-year term might be far longer than you care to have your money tied up. To offset that problem, it is possible to structure the mortgage so that payments are based on a long-term payout, but you reserve the right to have the full balance come due at some much shorter point, perhaps five to ten years hence. This matter, too, is subject to negotiation between the parties. The borrower may not like the prospect of having to refinance at the end of five years, but may be willing to go along if there is no other choice or if, all things considered, it's still a better deal than can be found elsewhere.

Your documents should be structured so that the borrower (the property owner) cannot sell the property to another party without your express permission. For obvious reasons you would not want him to sell the property to a person whose credit status is unacceptable. You might permit him to do so on the condition that he remain liable for the debt in case the other party to whom he sold defaulted. A subsequent buyer of the house whose credit history is unacceptable may damage the premises in some way, or decrease its value, so as to jeopardize your investment.

In establishing the interest rate on a new mortgage or a "taken back" mortgage, you might also want to consider what many institutional lenders are doing: putting in clauses that permit them to alter the interest rate, when and if interest rates in general throughout the country change. This matter was discussed in more detail in chapter 9, where it was described from the borrower's viewpoint. As a potential investor in mortgages, consider the same factors, but from the lender's viewpoint.

Buying Mortgages at "Discount"

There's an active market in most communities in this type of investment.

Some years ago Murphy bought Johnson's house and Johnson took back a mortgage from Murphy at a 10 percent interest rate. Today Murphy still owes Johnson $40,000 on that mortgage, and payments are to run for another ten years. Johnson needs money now. He can't wait ten years to collect what is owed him. Johnson approaches you to sell you Murphy's IOU. You know that Murphy is very credit worthy and that the value of the property is more than ample to cover your investment. But comparable investments are available today that will give you a yield of 14 percent. So why would you buy Murphy's IOU, which pays only 10 percent?

You might offer to buy Murphy's IOU at a "discount," that is, for less than the face value. Depending on how anxious Johnson is to get cash, he might be willing to sell you the $40,000 IOU for, say, $30,000. If such a deal is made, you will receive 10 percent on the amount of capital you have at work, and you will also, over the ten-year period, receive an additional $10,000 over and above what you invested. The attractiveness of this kind of investing depends on the original interest rate on the mortgage, the amount of discount you can negotiate, and the true yield that results from the combination of the interest rate and the discount.

Return of Principal

There's one catch in investing in mortgages that investors aren't always aware of. Each monthly payment that you receive contains some interest and some of your own investment that you're getting back. Review the section on mortgage financing in chapter 9 to refresh your recollection of how this aspect of mortgages works. Since you're receiving a small part of your investment back each month, that means that you have less and less of your original investment working for you as the months go by. Unless you take steps each month to reinvest your principal, your ultimate return won't be as much as you had thought it might be.

For example, you invest $10,000 in a mortgage paying 12 percent interest for ten years. You will receive monthly payments of $143.50. Over the full ten years those payments will total $17,220. You will have received, therefore, $7,220 more than you had invested. Divide that figure by ten (for ten years) and you come up with an average annual return of $722, which is equal to a 7.22 percent return on your original investment of $10,000. What happened to the 12 percent return that you were expecting? Each month, as you received the checks from the borrower, your original $10,000 investment dwindled since you were getting some of it back. In short, the whole $10,000 wasn't working for you all the time. In order to have kept it working for you, you would have had to reinvest the principal portion of each monthly payment as you received it. In all likelihood the only way you could invest such small monthly sums safely would be in a passbook savings account where your return would be far lower than 12 percent.

Lending institutions such as banks and savings and loan associations can avoid this problem because, as the money comes in, they are constantly relending all of it. As an individual you can't do that. If you are dealing through a mortgage broker for your mortgage investments, on the other hand, he can pool all of his various investors' payments as they come in and put them back to work in new mortgages. This advantage might offset the fee that you have to pay the broker for keeping your money at work for you at the highest possible yield. But if you do deal with a broker, it is essential that you find one whose investment and payment record is totally reliable. His or her reputation should be checked most thoroughly before you get involved.

Group Investing

There are two ways that a small investor can pool his or her money with that of other small investors to get involved in real estate and take advantage of the depreciation laws discussed earlier.

Syndication

The first of these is syndication. Usually, a promoter, or syndicator, will embark on a single major project such as an apartment complex or a shopping center. Shares will be parceled out in denominations of $5000, $10,000, and so on to small investors who wish to become involved in the project. The promoter will likely take a fee for efforts in organizing the syndicate and may also share in the profits of the project. These syndicates are usually structured so that the promoters reserve to themselves all control over the management of the funds and the property, and the investors have no say in the matter.

Real estate syndications will often take the form of a limited partnership in which individual small investors are known as "limited partners" and the promoters are known as "general partners." Syndications and limited partnerships are not without risks—indeed, in many cases the risks can be very high. Often, unwary or gullible investors will allow themselves to believe grossly exaggerated profit and income potentials on such deals, only to find that such rewards never materialize. The prudent investor in a syndication will take every precaution, including viewing and appraising the property, making certain that all legal documents are in order, and determining the reputation and reliability of the organizers of the syndication or partnership.

Real Estate Investment Trusts (REITs)

These are specialized forms of investment programs set up under the federal tax laws to allow small investors access to the real estate investment market. A REIT is like a mutual fund. It will pool the money of small investors to acquire a variety of real estate investments, and as long as it adheres to Internal Revenue Service regulations, it can pass its profits, income, and depreciation deductions along to individual investors. The REITs tend to be much larger and more broadly based than syndicates, which usually restrict their deals to one or a few individual properties. REITs are available in shares of stock comparable to buying stock in a company itself. Since REIT shares are sold on stock exchanges, not only is the value of REITs affected by the income and profitability of the real estate interests they own, but they are also subject, to some extent, to the whims of the stock market. Because of this, the REITs lose much of their element of certainty for prudent investors.

Excessive speculation by many REITs during the 1970s caused many of them to go bankrupt and others to incur severe losses for investors. By the early 1980s it began to appear that the concept of the REIT might be undergoing a revival. Potential investors should carefully examine the prospectus of a REIT to determine the nature and type of investments it is making and what the potential returns are.

Private Partnerships

Because so many real estate investments require a fairly large down payment, an individual might wish to seek one or more partners on a particular venture.

Although partnership arrangements can make real estate investments available to the smaller investor, there are obvious problems. All of the individuals involved must be firmly committed to the same long-term objectives. For example, investment partners must determine how much of the income will be pumped back into the property for refurbishing and modernization. They must determine who will be responsible for managerial duties, bookkeeping, taking care of tenant problems, and all other matters relating to the investment.

If one partner wants to sell out, will he or she be required to offer the share to the other partners first, and if so, on what terms? What kind of vote will it take to determine whether the property should be sold or refinanced?

The natural human tendency is not to worry about such matters until they arise. This can be foolhardy, for nothing can stand between friends and business associates more distinctly than disagreement over money. All possible items of dispute, including those noted above, should be reduced to a binding contract among the parties at the inception of the deal. A contract can't eliminate the disputes, but it can minimize them.

To Learn More

This chapter has offered only rudimentary guidelines on real estate investing. If you contemplate becoming seriously involved in real estate investing, it would be advisable for you to take the courses and exams given in your state leading up to the licensing as a salesman and as a broker. Check with your local County Board of Realtors to determine how these courses of instructions can be obtained.

Personal Action Checklist
Income Property Evaluator

Before undertaking an investment in income property, a careful analysis must be made of both the cash-flow situation and the condition of the property. Even if you're not contemplating such an investment now, it could be educational to conduct such a survey on an income property for sale in your area. The following analysis sheet will help get you started. Further analysis as to the specific investment advantages should be done with the help of your accountant and real estate agent.

☐ General condition of building, including foundation, walls, roof, landscaping.

☐ Specific condition of "working" aspects, including plumbing, heating, air conditioning, electrical system, elevators, appliances.

☐ Current rental income (all sources).

☐ Are there any controls on raising rentals?

☐ Potential rental income within 12 months, 24 months, 36 months.

☐ Current operating expenses.

☐ Do leases provide that tenants absorb any portion of operating expenses?

☐ Potential total operating expenses within 12 months, 24 months, 36 months (allow for likely increases in property taxes, insurance, maintenance, etc.).

☐ How do current property taxes compare with those of comparable buildings in the same area? If higher, how much could be saved in taxes by way of a successful assessment protest?

☐ General condition of immediate neighborhood.

☐ Is trend declining or improving?

☐ Are nearby traffic patterns likely to remain stable, or might they be changed? If changed, will that be to the benefit or detriment of the property and the ability to attract tenants?

☐ Can existing mortgage be assumed by buyer? At what interest rate?

☐ What is the cost of interest for new financing, if needed?

☐ What type of secondary financing will be needed?

☐ Will seller make secondary financing available? At what interest rate? Terms?

☐ What is the estimated management time and money needed to run the property efficiently (in hours and dollars per week)?

The above information, at the very least, will be needed if a sound investment decision is to be made.

Consumer Beware
The $100 Million Misunderstanding

The Lockwoods knew that they didn't have the time or the expertise to invest in real estate. But the salesman was offering them something that seemed just as good: an investment in second mortgages (or trust deeds, as they're called in California, where this scandal occurred in 1981).

In a nutshell, it would work like this: Mr. Jones wanted to borrow $40,000. He owned a home worth $120,000, and there was a first mortgage on the home of $30,000. He would give the Lockwoods a second mortgage on the home as security for the loan. The Lockwoods would be amply protected, for the home was worth much more than the total of the liens against it (the first and second mortgages, which would total $70,000).

Mr. Jones was so anxious to have this loan that he was willing to pay an astonishing 28 percent interest per year for three years, after which he'd have to pay the loan off, presumably through either refinancing or winning the Irish Sweepstakes. The salesman would take a percentage for his fee, leaving the Lockwoods with a neat 25 percent annual return on their $40,000 investment.

Less than one year later the Lockwoods found that they were among the 6,000 victims of a $100,000,000 swindle—perhaps the biggest of its kind in history.

They had taken the salesman's word for everything. This is what they learned when they investigated the matter on their own: They didn't have a second mortgage on the house. They had an *eighth* mortgage. The house wasn't worth $120,000, but more like $90,000. And the total amount of loans against the house was $430,000! Theirs being eighth in line, they knew quickly that their investment was lost forever. Jones, it seems, was a front for the promoter.

Victims of the defunct company had invested from a few thousand dollars to hundreds of thousands. The promoter behind the scheme allegedly spirited away tens of millions of dollars. Court proceedings are still underway as of this writing, but it's likely that when the dust clears, less than 20 cents on the dollar will be recovered by the average victim.

A combination of the classic Ponzi scheme (see chapter 5) and blatant take-the-money-and-run tactics, this misadventure at least served to dispel the then-prevailing myth that investment in California real estate—whether directly or indirectly—was a "can't lose" proposition.

19 | Making Your Money Grow: Other Opportunities

Beyond the money market, the stock market, and the real estate market, there is a whole galaxy of opportunities for making your money grow—or shrink. Some methods can be offshoots of hobbies such as collecting coins, stamps, bubble gum cards, beer cans, autographs, and commemorative medallions. Still others are of a much more serious nature such as commodities, equipment leasing, or investing in a business or franchise. The range of possibilities and risks is infinite. This chapter will examine some of the more common varieties of this broad range of investment and speculation possibilities, in particular:

☐ How to evaluate an investment in a small business.

☐ The pros and cons of speculating in such things as commodities, precious metal, and gems.

☐ The craze for collectibles: is it right for you?

☐ Overall, the importance of realizing that these relatively uncommon techniques require a certain level of expertise. Luck and the assurances of smooth-talking salespersons won't be enough.

Investing in Small Businesses

Existing Businesses

Many people will come across opportunities to invest in small local existing businesses, becoming involved either as a "silent partner" or an "active partner," or actually buying a business outright and becoming sole proprietor. An existing business may be seeking fresh capital for expansion or renovation or for the purchase of machinery or other equipment. The owner may prefer to seek private financing rather than bank financing so as to cut down on the interest cost. The owner might prefer to offer a share of the profits to an investor rather than be obliged to pay interest on a loan. Or an owner may wish to sell all or a part of his interest for a variety of reasons. He may be anticipating retirement; he may be ill; he may just wish to move on to something else; or he might be trying to get out from under a bad situation.

In any of the above instances, a would-be investor in a going business must do extensive and detailed investigation and will need the assistance of a lawyer and an accountant. Here is a checklist of matters that the prudent investor must examine with the aid of those professional assistants.

How Will Funds Be Used?

If the business is seeking funds for expansion, renovation, or new equipment, how will the funds specifically be put to use? What are the prospects of the new capital being able to generate added profits? Often, small businesses will overexpand, anticipating substantial additional business when little or none actually results. Or the cost of the expansion will be too great to permit increased profits. There's a high level of risk in such investments, and the would-be investor should turn to outside sources for help. The Small Business Administration office in your community can direct you to sources of information on specific types of businesses, how they function, and how profitable they might be. Such background information would be advisable for the prudent investor in any kind of business investment situation.

Why Is a Business Being Sold?

If all or a part of a business is being sold, you must determine the reasons for the sale. Is it a genuine case of retirement, illness, dissatisfaction with an associate, or lack of a successor? Or is there some problem that might not be visible on the surface? With the aid of your accountant, you should examine at least three years of the business's operating statements, as well as three years of its federal and state income tax returns. You should attempt to trace the flow of income and expenses to determine whether you can spot any trends that could indicate danger ahead.

You should obtain a credit report on the business and on the principal owners to determine if they have been meeting their obligations. These obligations would include the payment to suppliers, lease payments, utilities, and taxes. If you spot any pattern of delinquency in meeting obligations, you might be looking at a danger sign. The pattern might indicate, for example, that the owner has been subsidizing the business out of his own pocket, and these subsidies might not show up in the business's operating statement. The owner may have considered such transactions to be private loans to himself and not entered them in his books. Although you as a buyer would not necessarily have to repay those loans, you would find, in short order, that the business was not capable of maintaining itself without further subsidy from you.

Other reasons for selling a business might include threat of future competition. The owner may be aware of plans for a major shopping center near the retail outlet and want to sell out while the selling is good rather than risk being wiped out by the competition. Local realtors in the area might be familiar with such pending plans, and they could aid you in making your long-term projections concerning the future profitability of the business. In addition to competition, there are other developments that might affect your investment, such as changes in highway routings, nearby construction projects whose noise and dirt could be troublesome for an extended period of time, or zoning changes that could permit uses of land and buildings near your premises that would be incompatible with your business.

If you're considering investing in a business that relies on a particular product for its success (such as a brand name item that the business may have a territorial exclusive on), determine whether or not that particular product will continue to be available to you, and if at a relatively predictable price.

Determine whether or not there are any claims or law suits pending against the business, such as tax liens, claims for refunds, lawsuits arising out of unpaid obligations or damages suffered by individuals for which there is no insurance to cover the cost.

Find out whether the business has maintained a good record with the local Better Business Bureau and any other consumer-protection agencies in the community. You don't want to discover after the fact that a business has a bad public image, which can seriously detract from your investment. Determine whether the business has met all of its federal, state, and local government obligations including proper payment of federal and state withholding taxes, unemployment insurance taxes, workers' compensation insurance premiums, and all necessary filings regarding its business status with all appropriate agencies.

"Goodwill"

If you will be replacing the existing owner in the day-to-day operation of the business, either totally or partially, you'll want to determine how much of the business's success (or lack thereof) may be due to the owner's presence. Does he, for example, have a large loyal following that may disappear when he is no longer there on a day-to-day basis? Such a situation could jeopardize your investment. On the other hand, you might be able to determine that the existing owner has a bad public image and that by replacing him or her the business can actually improve, thus enhancing your investment.

The Lease

Your attorney should review the lease on the premises to determine how well protected you are. How long does the lease run and what kind of renewal options do you have? What provisions are there for increases in the basic rent or in the cost of utilities, property taxes, and maintenance? To what extent will you be responsible for repairs? Will there be any percentage clauses requiring you to pay a portion of your gross business volume to the landlord as additional rent? If a landlord owns additional space, for example, in a shopping center, do you have any rights to expand into such space should you so desire, and if so, at what cost? Further, are you protected against the landlord allowing undue competition to rent space near you in the same center?

How Much to Pay for a Going Business

There are many elements to consider when determining how much of an investment is justifiable in an existing business. There is the hope for expanded profits as the business enlarges and improves in its efficiency.

There is a hope for a profit on a later resale. There is the matter of a salary that one might gain from becoming active in the business.

But the ultimate question is: What kind of return will you get on your invested capital? The potential increased profits and the potential profit on a later sale are speculative, and the prudent investor will not be satisfied with mere hopes and promises. The question of a salary is not truly an investment concern. If you do earn a salary from becoming involved in the business, theoretically you'll be giving up some other form of earning to take over the tasks of running the business. If you're moonlighting while retaining your existing work, it's true that you'll have increased your income as a result of your involvement, but you can always moonlight without making a substantial investment in an existing business.

Thus, the question of return on investment becomes all-important, and this can be arrived at, with the help of your accountant, by examining the books closely to determine how much money is left after all expenses, including the business's own taxes and any salary paid to you, have been paid.

Depending on economic times, America's major corporations have an average return on invested capital per year ranging between 10 and 15 percent. If a local business investment doesn't generate at least 10 percent, you might do better to look elsewhere for a source of investing your funds. If the business promises a return of greater than 15 percent, there may be undue risks attached to the investment.

The Legal Documents

With the aid of your lawyer, you will enter into a contractual agreement with the seller or borrower. The contract will spell out all of the rights and obligations of the parties, particularly regarding the ongoing management of the business. The contract will stipulate how any profits are to be split and how any losses are to be made up. The contract should also give you protection if you later determine that the seller or borrower made misrepresentations to you about the business.

If by becoming involved in the business you are becoming liable for any of the business's debts, you should make arrangements with the creditors so that the extent of your obligation is clearly understood. You should also see to it that you are properly protected as an individual regarding the business's lease on its premises, as well as on all insurance policies relating to the operation of the business, including fire and public liability insurance. If the business provides group health, life, or other insurance, and if it provides a pension or profit-sharing plan, you should also see to it that all documents are in order to protect you to the extent that you and your associate have agreed on. These things will not take care of themselves. Many documents may have to be amended to assure that you are getting what you have bargained for and what you're entitled to.

Investing in a New Business

Starting up a business from scratch, either on your own or through such means as a franchise arrangement, does not fall into the investment category at all. It's pure speculation. There can be no assurance whatsoever of your getting any kind of return on the money you put into such a venture. You could reap a bonanza, and you could go broke in short order.

Yet many will regard such situations as a form of investment. Indeed, during the 1960s and 1970s, thousands of Americans invested millions of dollars in franchises and distributorships, and a very high percentage of them are still bemoaning the loss of a life's savings as a result of imprudent or impulsive reactions to high-pressure sales pitches.

It's one thing to dive into an *existing* business where there is some record of the business's success available for your examination, and established clientele, patients, customers, what have you. But to start from scratch, where you have nothing on which to base even estimates, can be extremely hazardous.

Some major national franchises, on the order of McDonald's, Kentucky Fried Chicken, and the like, have indeed produced many successful investor/restauranteur/operators. But for each McDonald's there were dozens of "Beauty Burgers" that proved to be a disaster for one and all. Of course, each new franchise operation that comes along envisions itself as the next McDonald's, and they sell as such to the would-be investors. This is where dreams are turned into nightmares. Proceed, if you must, with complete awareness of the risks that you face, and remember that the salesperson is trying to sell you something on which he or she will make a profit. There's no assurance that you too will make a profit, or ever see your money again.

If you're starting up your own business from scratch, be well aware that, on average, it takes from two to three years before a typical new business venture begins seeing a profit. This is not a casual warning but a fact of life. Many businesses will fail because they were not adequately capitalized at the outset. The owner may have gotten an overdose of glamour and failed to see the realities of running a business.

In any kind of new business venture, the efforts of your legal, insurance, and accounting advisors are essential before you proceed with any expenditure of funds. And bear in mind this simple but important caution: if you're prepared to risk it all on a new business venture, you have to be prepared to lose it all.

Gambling in Commodities

Like raw land and new business ventures, the commodity market represents a form of pure speculation. It's one of the most volatile, unpredictable, and high-pressure gambling devices yet devised. Next to a commodity exchange, a Las Vegas casino might seem tame by comparison.

In the commodity or "futures" market, you are betting on the future prices of a variety of crops, metals, and international currencies. In the middle of March, for example, you can place a bet on what wheat or corn might be selling for next September; what hogs and cattle will be worth in December; what the future price of sugar or orange juice or cocoa might be a few or many months hence. You can, in effect, buy a contract for the future delivery of 5000 bushels of wheat on the Chicago Board of Trade (which also deals in corn, soybeans, soybean oil, oats, silver, and plywood).

Or you can buy a contract for the future delivery of 40,000 pounds of cattle, which is traded on the Chicago Mercantile Exchange (which also trades in hogs, pork bellies, fresh eggs, russet potatoes). The New York Coffee and Sugar Exchange will sell you a contract for the future delivery of 112,000 pounds of sugar or 37,500 pounds of coffee, and the New York Cocoa Exchange will sell you contracts for 30,000 pounds of cocoa.

The International Monetary Market (an adjunct of the Chicago Mercantile Exchange) deals in foreign currencies, trading contracts for Mexican pesos, Swiss francs, British pounds, Canadian dollars, German deutsche marks, and Japanese yen, as well as U.S. treasury bills. If you think you know what any of those commodities might be worth a month, six months, or a year from now, the commodity exchanges offer plenty of action where you can place your bets.

The chances of any bet succeeding are based, not only on how the other bettors are betting, but on such other totally unpredictable factors as weather conditions, crop blights, the law of supply and demand, governmental and international politics, major shifts in the world's economy, minor shifts in the economy of any given nation, and even consumer boycotts.

In 1974, for example, American homemakers, shocked at the sharply rising cost of beef, boycotted that product. They simply cut back on their buying. Cattle breeders, with millions of tons of ready-for-market cattle on their hands, found the demand for their product sharply dropping, and with it the price. As the market price of beef dropped, speculators in beef futures (those who had bet on the future price of beef) were taking a beating. Other speculators may have profited mightily when sugar prices skyrocketed in 1975, when coffee prices skyrocketed in 1976 as a result of frozen crops in Brazil, when orange juice prices skyrocketed in 1977 as a result of unexpected freezes in the Florida citrus groves, and when peanut oil prices soared in 1981 as a result of a severe drought in the peanut producing state of Georgia. But for every profit, there is probably a corresponding loss.

Any student interested in learning more about speculating in the commodity markets can obtain abundant material through a stockbroker or through the respective Exchanges.

Commodity Funds

If the commodities market intrigues you, but the high level of risk frightens you, you might find commodity funds more to your liking. Commodity funds pool small investors' money and bet it on a diversified selection of commodities. In effect, commodity funds act like mutual funds, but technically they are a form of limited partnership.

Commodity funds can be somewhat less risky than direct speculations in commodities because of the diversification that is probably not available to an individual speculating on his own. Further, or at least it is hoped, professional management of the fund should be capable of making better decisions than the individual would be.

Commodity funds also purport to offer the individual better protection against the margin calls than he would have on his own. A substantial amount of commodity trading is done on "margin": Investors put up only a small percentage of the total cost of the contract that they're buying. If the price of the commodity drops, the investor either must sell his contract at a loss or come up with additional money to protect his interest. The effect of this is that an investor in commodities can lose more than his original investment. Review the section on margin buying in chapter 17 for more detail on the mechanics of such trading.

The commodity funds set aside a substantial portion of their overall assets to meet such margin demands, thus insulating the individual investors from having to come up with more money. This means that not all of your invested money is going to work in commodity contracts; the part that is set aside by the fund will be put to work in more stable investments such as U.S. government securities where they can earn interest until needed for margin calls.

Commodity fund investors should be wary of the costs and commissions that they will incur by investing in the fund. It's not unusual for total costs, including management fees, brokerage commissions, and incentive fees, to total as much as 20 to 30 percent per year. That means that the investor won't make any money at all until after the fund has earned enough to cover those fees.

The prospectus of any commodity fund should be read thoroughly before an investment decision is made. In examining the prospectus, the investor should determine the extent of diversification of the funds' assets; the experience of the portfolio manager; and the ability to get your money out when you want it.

Foreign Exchange and Deposits

The foreign exchange market is closely related to the commodity market: You bet on the future value of the money of other countries. The foreign exchange market is also every bit as risky as the commodity market.

The value of the money of most other countries always fluctuates with respect to the U.S. dollar. Today, for example, you might be able to buy a British pound for $2.10. Next month that pound might cost you $2.15, or $1.95. If you bought a contract for pounds on the foreign exchange markets, you might be able to reap a profit if pounds became more valuable in the future, but you'd suffer a loss if the value of the pound dropped.

Why do the values fluctuate? Think for a moment of Great Britain as a company whose stock is traded on the exchange. Countries, like companies, have their ups and downs—financially, politically, and in the eyes of speculators. If Great Britain's economy is being well managed, the value of its money should remain stable, or improve, with respect to the dollar. If its economy is being poorly managed (high inflation, high unemployment, a balance of payments deficit), the value of its money may decrease with respect to the dollar. Buying foreign currency is, in effect, like buying "stock" in that country. Your gamble is subject to the financial integrity of the country and to the whims of speculators who may or may not know more about that country's fortunes than you do.

The exchange that specializes in foreign exchange is the Chicago International Monetary Market, which trades in most major currencies, including the British pound, the Japanese yen, the Canadian dollar, the Swiss franc, and the German deutsche mark.

Another form of speculating in foreign markets is to open bank accounts in the other countries. Canada and Mexico have been popular because of their proximity to the United States. With a bank account, the investor can earn interest while awaiting his potential profit; or the earning of interest can offset a potential loss. But this form of speculating has risks of its own. In order to open foreign bank accounts, your dollars have to be converted into the currency of the other country. That will involve some cost. Also, when you terminate your investment, the foreign currency will have to be converted back to U.S. dollars at another cost. Further, while your money is sitting in the foreign bank, it is subject to the rules and valuations of that other country—and you may be totally unaware of the passage of regulations that could affect your money. Canada, for example, has made a practice of taking 15 percent of all earnings from such accounts to pay for Canadian taxes. Furthermore, you don't have the benefit of the U.S. federal insurance when your money is deposited in a foreign bank account. Overall, your lack of familiarity with local customs and banking regulations in other countries adds to the general risk of foreign exchange and bank deposits.

Precious Metals

Gold and silver (and to a similar extent, platinum) are nothing more than blatant and extremely risky speculations. This was made clear at the start of the 1980s and matters aren't likely to change for the rest of the decade. Witness: In the early months of 1980, gold soared from a year earlier level of about $250 an ounce to over $825 an ounce. At the same time, silver reached $50 an ounce from its year earlier level of about $10 an ounce. In early 1982, gold had plummeted to under $330 an ounce—a loss of more than 60 percent to those who had bought it at its peak. And there were many who had done so. The silver debacle was much more swift. One wealthy Texas family, the Hunts, had virtually cornered the silver market in early 1980, borrowing heavily to do so. When their ability to repay those debts came into doubt, the price of silver plunged by 80 percent within just a few months. Many small investors were wiped out.

The gold and silver fever was started and maintained by a handful of commentators known as "gold bugs." In lectures, broadcasts, and newsletters the gold bugs touted the get-rich-quick capabilities of speculating in precious metals. It became a self-fulfilling prophecy. Enough investors started clamoring to buy the metals, and the price began to climb. The word spread rapidly, and before long totally uninformed individuals were cashing in their savings to buy gold and silver.

The gold bugs devised a curiously morbid campaign to keep the fever going: there will always be misery in the world, and as misery increases, so will the price of gold. The underlying theory to this campaign was that in nations suffering from wars and other international tensions, wealthy individuals would convert their cash holdings into gold, convinced that the gold would survive any international crisis, whereas their own nation's currency might not. Indeed, this can be true in some cases. But it is generally an imprudent reason for an investor to put his money into gold. As long as this campaign lasts, speculators in gold will be looking to profit in direct relation to human suffering. In time, this theory will prove to be invalid (as most investment theories ultimately do). But until that day, many innocent investors will be lured into wild speculative ventures in gold and silver that they have no business being involved in.

A Losing Proposition

If you bought gold for, say, $500, and the price soared by 50 percent over a three-year span to $750, and you then sold it, you would have made a bad deal!

Here's the arithmetic that most gold buyers overlook: When you buy or sell gold, you have to pay sales commissions and possibly sales taxes and assay costs. (A buyer may demand an assay, which is a test to determine whether the metal is really gold, and to what extent.) It's not unreasonable to expect those costs to be 10 percent when you buy, and 10 percent when you sell. Thus, in the example given, you would pay $50 when you bought and $75 when you sold, for a total of $125. Subtracting those costs from the $750 selling price, you end up $625.

On the other hand, if you invested your $500 in a guaranteed savings plan paying 10 percent interest, with no commissions to pay, your money would grow to over $650 over a three-year span. In short, because of the costs of buying gold, and because your money isn't earning anything for you while you own gold, you would, as in this example, be better off with the old tried and true savings plan.

The above example is based on the assumption that you had bought real gold! Sadly, the gold marketplace is ridden with fraudulent dealers who pass off gold-plated lead, counterfeit coins, and phony contracts for future delivery in quantities that may never be determined fully. The same precautions apply equally to silver and platinum.

If you must speculate in precious metals, it is imperative that you deal only with firms whose reputations are totally reliable. Particularly avoid dealing with strangers over the telephone or through the mail. Whomever you deal with, keep in mind the following standards of measurement and use them to be certain that you're getting what you bargained for.

Gold and silver are weighed in troy ounces. There are 31 grams to a troy ounce; and there are 480 grains to a troy ounce. It can be dangerous to confuse grains and grams and ounces.

What is referred to as pure gold is known as 24 karat gold. Anything less than 24 karat gold means that gold is mixed with another metal. Thus, 18 karat gold is 18/24 (or 75 percent) real pure gold and 25 percent other metal; 12 karat gold is 1/2 pure gold and 1/2 other metal. Similarly, what is referred to as "sterling silver" is not pure silver, but rather roughly 92.5 percent silver and the rest other metal.

The prices for these metals that are commonly quoted do not refer to a single ounce but to a much larger quantity. This price is known as the "spot" price and gold is quoted in 100 troy-ounce lots, silver in 5000 troy-ounce lots. You would, then, expect to pay a higher price per ounce for quantities under the spot level.

Where to Speculate

☐ *Commodity exchanges.* You can bet on the future value of precious metals on a number of commodity exchanges. Gold is traded on the New York Commodity Exchange and the International Monetary Market (part of the Chicago Mercantile Exchange). Platinum is traded on the New York Mercantile Exchange. Silver is traded on the New York Commodity Exchange and the Chicago Board of Trade. Most major stockbrokerage firms can place these bets for you.

☐ *Mining companies.* Rather than buy the metals themselves, you can buy stock in the companies that mine them. Again, stockbrokerage firms can handle the transactions for you. Mining stocks can be every bit as speculative as the metals themselves, but many do pay dividends so that your money is earning something for you as long as you own the stock.

☐ *Certificates.* Some large banks have gotten into the precious-metals business. They will buy and hold for you a certain sum of gold and silver and will give you a certificate representing your interest in the metals. They will, of course, charge appropriate fees for these services.

☐ *Coins.* Many nations, including the United States, have minted gold coins over the years. Some of them are older and, if in good condition, may have collector value over and above the gold value itself. To determine the true value of any such investment, you should seek the assistance of a reputable coin dealer. Many other gold coin opportunities are newly minted—such as the South African Krugerrand, the Canadian Maple Leaf, and the American Arts Commemorative Medallion offered through the U.S. Post Office. Any potential collector value of these coins is questionable at best and is probably not realizable for many years. All coins are subject to counterfeiting.

☐ *Jewelry.* All gold jewelry manufactured in the United States is by law required to have the correct karat content stamped on the piece. But this law is not rigidly enforced. The best protection is to deal with reputable jewelers. Speculating in gold by way of jewelry purchases is probably the least feasible in terms of making money, for you will pay the dealer's markup plus the cost of any artistry that has gone into making the piece. It's unlikely that you'd be able to recapture those costs unless the value of gold itself triples or quadruples within a fairly short period of time. But at least jewelry can be worn, and if you appreciate that aspect of it, you'll receive at least some ego benefits, if not financial benefits.

One final caution: Trading in gold and silver—except on the commodity exchanges—is virtually totally unregulated. That means you'll have no governmental agency to turn to for help if you find you've been bilked.

Strategic Metals

For better or for worse, the so-called strategic metals will make a lot of investment headlines in the 1980s. Strategic metals, in the broad sense, include such things as cobalt, manganese, iridium, molybdenum, and chromium. These are metals which, at least currently, are considered important to our national defense and industrial production, but which we must import from other countries in large quantities. Advances in technology could render some currently strategic metals not so strategic in the future; and other insignificant metals and chemicals could become very important in the future.

As with the precious metals, the strategic metals are often touted as easy paths to getting rich quick by the same kinds of promoters who push gold and silver. As with gold and silver, the strategic metals investments are highly speculative and subject to the same kind of self-fulfilling prophecy. Speculators who have the good luck to get in right and get out right might make fast money. But the strategic-metals course is no place for the prudent investor who wants to build a solid foundation.

Stockbrokers can direct you to all of the speculations available in the field of strategic metals, such as companies which mine the metals. And the same precautions hold true for strategics as for the precious metals: Deal only with people whose reputations are totally reliable and not with strangers. That means only that you have less chance of being defrauded, not that you'll have a better chance of making a profit.

Gemstones

Speculating in metals might almost seem prudent when compared with speculating in gemstones. Trading in gemstones without the assistance of a totally reliable professional (jeweler or gemologist) is absolutely fool-hardy.

The most popular form of gemstone speculation has been in diamonds. But speculation in colored gemstones (rubies, emeralds, sapphires primarily) is expected to surge during the 1980s. These speculative opportunities are not restricted to big-money investors. Many plans are devised to appeal to small and medium-sized investors. And many of these plans are rife with danger.

Gemstones are as unlike each other as snowflakes. If you examined 1000 diamonds (or emeralds or rubies or sapphires), it's highly doubtful that you would find any two alike. They can vary not only in size and color but in basic quality, from priceless to pure junk. If you buy any gemstone sight unseen, you could be getting the junk. To buy any gemstone without first having it independently appraised by a reputable jeweler or gemologist is extremely hazardous.

Whether it's your intent to speculate in gemstones or to acquire them as jewelry pieces, you should be aware of the characteristics that contribute to their value or lack thereof. Diamonds are considered to be the most easily appraised of all gemstones. Colored gemstones are more difficult to accurately appraise because of the wider range of colors and chemical compositions in them. But even with diamonds, experts can vary by as much as 10 to 20 percent in their estimate of value.

Diamonds are evaluated in accordance with the four "C's." Colored gemstones use similar formulas. The four C's are color, clarity, cut, and carat weight.

☐ *Color.* Diamonds can range in color from the highly regarded "pure blue-white" to murky yellows. The better the color, the higher the value. Gemologists can grade the color of a diamond by use of a spectroscope. Even slight differences in the color grade can make a substantial difference in the value of a given stone.

☐ *Cut.* Raw diamonds (in the rough) will be cut into various sizes and shapes. The more highly valued cuts are those which permit the maximum brilliance of light to refract through the stone. The depth of the stone and the faceting contribute to brilliance or lack thereof. The shape of the finished stone can also bear on its value. Common shapes are emerald cut (rectangular), oval cut, square cut, round cut, and marquise (pointed oval). The perfection and proportion of the cut can make a stone worth more or less. Further, some shapes are more popular than others for jewelry purposes, and that too can affect the value. Gemologists can measure the preciseness of the cut of any diamond and grade it numerically.

☐ *Clarity.* When looked at under a magnifying glass or microscope, impurities in a diamond will appear. (Some may even be visible to the naked eye.) The highest clarity diamonds are those with the fewest imperfections or flaws. Clarity is also measured numerically by gemologists.

□ *Carat weight.* There's a lot of confusion between *karat* and *carat. Karat,* as noted above in the discussion on gold, measures the percentage of pure gold in a given item. *Carat* is an actual unit of weight. Thus, a diamond might weigh—on an actual scale—one carat, or two carats, and so on. A carat is divided into 100 points. Thus, a 25-point diamond is equal to one-quarter of a carat. As between two diamonds equal in color, cut, and clarity, the heavier one (carat weight) will be the more valuable. But a one-carat stone of high quality in terms of color, cut, and clarity could be worth vastly more than a three-carat stone whose cut, color, or clarity is poor. Also, a single stone is worth more than an aggregate of smaller stones of equal quality and total weight. Thus, a single one-carat stone will be worth more than four 25-point stones of equal quality.

Those are the basic guidelines for determining the value of gemstones. Proceed at your own risk.

Collectibles

The possibilities are limitless: from old comic books to Chinese jade, from antique buttons to hubcaps, and everything in between. Whether prudent investment or wild speculation, the field of collectibles offers a measure of personal satisfaction in the hobby aspects of the endeavor. Thus it is difficult to evaluate the financial considerations of collecting: If you get enough pleasure out of accumulating beer cans, movie posters, or original Picasso oil paintings, then perhaps the money doesn't matter.

But whether your objectives in collecting are personal, financial, or any combination thereof, there are some basic precautions to observe lest you be separated from too much money needlessly.

□ Coins and stamps are the most popular forms of collectibles. There is abundant information published on both of these areas, and the novice should take advantage of that literature. Before buying and before selling, the most current price lists should be consulted. If major transactions are contemplated, an outside appraisal can be inexpensive insurance to protect a large investment.

□ Many forms of collectibles cannot readily be converted into cash. The more exotic the items, the fewer potential buyers there may be. Finding a buyer for a collection, or part of a collection, may require considerable time and expense—such as advertising in specialized publications that deal with those types of items (antique magazines and the like).

□ Lacking ready buyers, such as are commonly available in the areas of coins and stamps, collectors of such things as art may have to turn to dealers and galleries in order to convert their collectibles into cash.

A dealer is likely to pay only about half of the item's retail value, and that could mean a loss to the collector. On the other hand, some dealers might be willing to take an item on consignment. He won't promise you any price, but he'll offer it to his clientele and take a commission for his effort. The commission may range from 10 to 25 percent. If he's not successful in selling it, you take it back. If any valuables are left with any kind of dealer on consignment, an agreement should be entered into setting forth the nature of the consignment and the responsibility in case the item is damaged, lost, or stolen.

☐ Many collectibles go through fads. They may be hot one year, cold the next. If you get involved in a fad collectible that is on the wane, you could end up a big loser, but if you're lucky enough to get in on the rise, you could be a big winner. The gambling element is self-evident.

☐ All collectibles require some level of expertise. Much of that expertise can be acquired by studying; much of it only by trial and error. Before embarking on a program of collectibles, therefore, do whatever studying you can and then proceed with caution until you feel confident of your ability to know when and what to buy, and when and what to sell.

Equipment Leasing

This is very much like real estate investing except that instead of buying buildings and leasing them to tenants, you buy equipment and lease it to users. The advantage is the same as in real estate: the equipment is subject to a depreciation deduction, which can shelter your income. Review the section on real estate to refresh yourself on the implications of the depreciation deduction.

Depreciation schedules for personal property have been amended by the income-tax law changes made in 1981. An interested investor should review those changes with his professional tax counselor with respect to any equipment-leasing program he might become involved in.

In many respects, equipment leasing is even more attractive than real estate. Most equipment can be depreciated more rapidly than real estate; thus the tax advantage is more attractive than with real estate. Whereas a building may have a useful life of ten years or more, many types of equipment can be depreciated on one's tax return in five years or less.

Although equipment leasing has long been the province of large investment companies, it is available to the small investor. Here's how it works: Someone you know needs a particular piece of equipment—an automobile, a typewriter, store fixtures, power tools, and so on. He doesn't have the cash to buy that equipment, or doesn't want to finance it. You buy the equipment and lease it to him. The rental he pays you is income to you. If you have borrowed on your own to buy the equipment, the interest you pay on the loan can offset all or part of the rental income in terms of taxes. You as the owner of the equipment can take the depreciation deduction on your tax return. At the end of the original lease term, the item has a "salvage value." You can either renew the lease with the user, or you can sell the equipment and pay a capital-gains tax on the difference between the salvage value and your selling price.

Cautions: Deal with people you know. Check the credit of any individual to whom you are leasing equipment. Have a lawyer draw up a simple lease agreement between yourself and the user to protect your interests.

Private Lending

While not generally thought of as such, lending money to individuals or businesses is a form of investment. Whether they approach you or you approach them, the same precautions are in order: Establish terms (interest rate, repayment date) that will be fair and reasonable. Check the credit of the borrower to determine the level of risk you are undertaking. If you feel that the borrower's signature alone on the promissory note does not adequately protect you, seek either collateral or a co-signer for the loan. Be certain that you know the financial status of the borrower: What other debts does he have? What kind of income sources does he have? And, all things considered, from what sources will he be able to make repayment on the loan? Have a properly drawn promissory note signed by the borrower, setting forth all the appropriate terms including your rights should the borrower default on the payments. A lawyer is the right person to do this for you.

In short, take all the same precautions that a bank would take on the making of a loan. If you find yourself faced with the prospect of making a private loan, a chat with your own banker could be helpful to make sure you protect yourself adequately. In addition to having the banker show you the specifics of the loan procedure, it might be wise to inquire whether the banker would be willing to make the loan himself or to buy the loan from you should you later wish to sell the borrower's IOU. If the banker balks at either prospect, he probably sees some flaw in the loan that you might want to know about. Are you willing to take a risk that the bank would not?

Knowledge

Whether you're investing in the money market, the stock market, the real estate market, any of these assorted miscellaneous investments/speculations, or any new things that may come along, the best investment of all is your own investment in knowledge. The world of money is changing at an increasingly rapid pace: taxes, interest rates, governmental regulations, the emergence of new techniques are all in a state of flux. Further, your own individual circumstances are also changing. You can't afford to ignore this outpouring of new information. If you want to make your money grow, you must fertilize it. And knowledge is the best fertilizer.

Personal Action Checklist
Playing the "Paper Game" with Commodities

The rules for the Paper Game were set forth in the Personal Action Checklist at the end of chapter 17. It's highly advised that a similar exercise be conducted before you embark on any ventures in the commodity markets.

As with the stock market Paper Game, choose ten commodities on your own and ten at random (use darts or any other method). A full range of commodity quotations is available daily in the *Wall Street Journal* and in many major local daily papers.

Follow the same rules as set forth in the chapter 17 Game. Assume that you are paying full price (not borrowing) to buy each commodity contract. Remember that if you have not sold your contract by its maturity date, your contract will become worthless.

Track each item for at least six months, on a daily basis. Determine, as best you can, what causes the price fluctuations: weather conditions, international events, whatever.

Use the tally sheet to keep record of your overall success.

Group A Commodities	Purchase price	Commission	Maturity date	Sale price	Commission	Gain/ loss
1.	_____	_____	_____	_____	_____	_____
2.	_____	_____	_____	_____	_____	_____
3.	_____	_____	_____	_____	_____	_____
. . . through 10	_____	_____	_____	_____	_____	_____
Group B Commodities						
1.	_____	_____	_____	_____	_____	_____
2.	_____	_____	_____	_____	_____	_____
3.	_____	_____	_____	_____	_____	_____
. . . through 10	_____	_____	_____	_____	_____	_____

Consumer Beware
The Big Print Giveth . . .
The Small Print Taketh Away

The small newspaper ads were indeed intriguing:

"BUY A SILVER INGOT FOR $7 . . ."
"BUY A GOLD COIN FOR $10 . . ."
"RUBIES, SAPPHIRES, EMERALDS, ONLY $5 EACH . . ."
"GENUINE DIAMOND . . . $10 . . . CALL THIS NUMBER TOLL FREE . . ."

They've appeared in newspapers and magazines across the nation. Many of the ads are from the same company. Others are copycats. All, according to consumer-protection authorities, raked in money, while operating within the letter, if not the spirit, of the law.

Public misunderstanding as to the true value of precious metals and gemstones led countless investors, collectors, and curiosity seekers to waste good money on these offerings. Virtually without exception, they paid many times what the items were actually worth. In many cases, the items were totally without value.

Yet the ads, for at least some of the offerings, did contain enough detail to give a wary reader a clue to what they'd get for their money.

The ad for the $10 gold coin noted, in the small print, that the coin contained ".174 grams" of 14 karat gold. As this chapter has indicated, 14 karat gold is $14/24$ pure gold, and there are 31 grams in a troy ounce. Simple arithmetic would then indicate that for $10, a purchaser would actually be getting about $2 worth of gold, based on the price of gold at the time the ad appeared.

Similarly, the silver ingot for $7 offered one gram. Silver, at that time, was selling for about $12 per ounce so a buyer was paying roughly 15 times more than the item was worth.

Samples of the rubies, emeralds, and sapphires—examined by certified gemologists—revealed that they were considered "junk" stones, worth a few cents apiece if anything. And the $10 genuine diamond? The small print noted that it was ".25 points" in size, or one-quarter of one point. There are 100 points to a carat, so this stone was one-four-hundredth of a carat in size. The gemologists noted that six to eight such stones could fit on the head of a pin. Value? None.

The initial lesson to those who fell for the ads may not have been that costly. But their names ended up on numerous "sucker" mailing lists. And sooner or later they'll get taken for big money.

Part Six | Protecting What You Work For

20 | Life Insurance

Most everyone owns some life insurance, in one form or another. But nobody likes to talk about life insurance, and few people like to be confronted by someone who is selling life insurance. What is this strange product that most of us own but don't want to think about?

Life insurance, despite its ominous overtones, can play an extremely important role in your overall financial plan. This chapter, without taking any sides and without trying to sell anything, should enable you to:

☐ Understand how life insurance policies work.

☐ Distinguish between different types of policies, their benefits, and their costs.

☐ Gain a working knowledge of the terms and clauses of a life insurance policy, so that you can communicate effectively with sales personnel if and when the need arises.

☐ Determine whether you do need life insurance as a part of your plan and, if so, how much and what type.

☐ Learn how to deal with insurance agents and get the most from them.

Coping with Risk

Life is full of surprises—risks—that we don't adequately anticipate or prepare for. Some of these risks we accept willingly: driving a car, taking on a new job, investing or betting our money. Others may be strictly a matter of fate: illness, natural disaster, an employer going bankrupt.

When an event occurs for which we have not been adequately prepared, we may suffer disappointment, wasted time, physical harm, and financial loss. The danger inherent in many risks can be avoided or minimized simply by taking some minimal evasive or defensive actions.

There are many events, though, whose occurrence we can neither foresee nor control. They happen in spite of our most precautionary efforts. But we can take steps, prior to their happening, to reduce the loss that we would otherwise suffer by, in effect, hiring others who will be willing, for a fee, to reimburse us for losses that we suffer.

In earlier chapters we examined automobile insurance and homeowners (and tenants) insurance. Those types of insurance reimburse us for damages suffered to our cars and our dwellings and also reimburse persons who suffer losses arising from automobile accidents and accidents in the home. We may never suffer losses with respect to our car or our dwelling, but we still need the insurance to protect us just in case.

Life insurance is designed to provide money to the survivors of an insured person when that person dies. That is an event which will certainly occur, but we never know when. If the breadwinner of a young and growing family dies prematurely, life insurance will, in effect, reimburse the survivors for lost earnings, thus enabling them to continue to live in relative comfort and security. If an insured person dies at or after the normal life-expectancy age, the proceeds of the insurance may be needed to pay estate taxes, to provide support for a surviving spouse, to allow the insured's business to continue, or to simply add to the wealth of the survivors. Now let's take a look at the basic mechanics of life insurance, but first of insurance in general as a device to protect us against risk.

Insurance Is Protection Against Risk

That is what insurance is all about. Example: On an average given day, 1000 skiers will run a slope and one will end up in the hospital. The cost of hospitalization may be $1000. You never know whether that injured skier will be yourself or one of the 999 others. If it should be you, it will cost you $1000. But if each skier chipped in $1 to cover the cost of that day's accident—whoever it might happen to—you have eliminated your risk at a very insignificant cost. For the price of $1, you may have saved yourself $1000. You may run the slope 1000 times and never be hurt, but actual experience indicates that that's not likely.

If all the skiers aren't willing to chip into a mutual kitty to protect themselves, some enterprising business executive will offer to make the arrangements for them. He will point out the risks that each skier faces, will arrange to collect and hold all of the money in safekeeping, and will see to it that the proceeds are paid out to the injured parties as the injuries occur. For this service, he is entitled to a fee; thus, instead of charging $1 per skier, he may charge $1.05 or $1.10—whatever he and the skiers agree his services are worth. In so doing, he is acting as a one-man insurance company.

That, in a nutshell, is how the insurance industry operates. The insurance company will determine the probability of risk in many given situations, such as a house burning down, an automobile crashing, a person dying before the normal life expectancy, and so on. The company will further determine how much money it must collect from each individual to properly protect those individuals should the stated risk occur. That money will be invested prudently, so that the fund can grow, until it comes time to pay benefits to people who have suffered the risks. These calculations are known as the "actuarial" phase of insurance. The money that's taken in from each individual is called a "premium," and the money paid out to individuals who do suffer the stated risks is called "benefits." The portion of each premium dollar set aside to pay future benefits is called the "reserve."

Part of each premium dollar that is received by the insurance company is used to pay the agents for their work in selling the insurance to the public. Part of it is set aside to pay for the buildings that the insurance company occupies, the machines and computers they need, the clerical help, the supplies, the advertising, and the educational material.

When an individual, or a business, enters into an agreement with an insurance company regarding a specific risk, the parties sign a contract that sets forth all the specific rights, duties, and obligations of the parties. This contract is called an "insurance policy." Its specific details are discussed later.

Why Life Insurance?

Victor is 40 years old with a wife and two teenage children. He's in good health and makes about $25,000 per year with good prospects for improvement. He wants to be certain that his children have a good college education, but meeting his monthly mortgage payments hasn't allowed him to put much money aside for college expenses. Even though Victor's life expectancy is about 35 years, he's very much aware of the possibility—however remote—that he could die tomorrow. Contemplating this possibility, Victor thinks, "If I did die suddenly, where would the money come from to keep my family reasonably comfortable and provide for the college education? I'd need an immediate nest egg of about $100,000. If they invested that wisely, the income and some of the principal could take care of their needs for quite a long time. But right now I'd have trouble raising the price of a Big Mac let alone $100,000."

Instant Solution?

How can Victor resolve this dilemma? He might be lucky enough to beat multimillion-to-one odds and win a lottery. Or he could start stashing money away in a savings plan; at the rate of $100 per month, he'd have accomplished his goal in just under 25 years. These aren't very satisfactory solutions.

To solve his problem, Victor needs an immediate and guaranteed way to create an umbrella of protection for his family. That is the main purpose of life insurance.

Life insurance can be created instantly (or, more correctly, in the simple few weeks it takes to process an application). Rather than take chances on a lottery ticket or wait decades for a savings fund to build up, Victor can create the level of protection that he wants immediately through life insurance.

Further, the protection is guaranteed as long as the premiums on the policy are paid. Victor might also be prompted to consider the desirability of life insurance for his spouse and children. If the spouse works, and if the family is dependent on her income to maintain their standard of living, it might be wise for the family to consider insuring her life so as to provide a source of income that would be lost in the event of her premature death. In some cases, insurance on the life of a nonworking spouse can be utilized to pay the costs of a terminal illness if those costs are not covered by a health insurance plan; and if the spouse's estate is subject to estate taxes, life insurance proceeds can also be used to pay those taxes in lieu of having to sell other assets to cover the estate-tax obligation. The primary objective of a family's life insurance portfolio should be the replacement of a source of income in the event of the breadwinner's death.

With respect to the children, the actual *need* for life insurance is relatively minimal. Some parents may, however, wish to commence a life insurance portfolio for their children to assure a low premium base for later years. Such a plan may be costly to the parents while the children are young, but when the children later take over the policies on their own, they will have a distinct advantage in that the premiums are lower than they would be for new policies taken out at the current age, and there will be some cash and conversion values already built up in the policies.

On learning how the dilemmas can be solved, Victor (and you) are likely to ask, "Can I afford to do it?" But a more appropriate question might be, "Can I afford *not* to do it?" The material that follows will help you answer these questions and will give you guidelines that will be useful in establishing any life insurance program you deem suitable for your own needs.

The Basic Elements of Life Insurance

Simply put, a life insurance policy is a contract between an individual and a life insurance company. The individual agrees to pay premiums, in return for which the insurance company guarantees to pay a certain amount of money to the beneficiaries named in the contract upon the death of the insured party. But not so simply put, life insurance policies are as different as snowflakes. There are over 1800 life insurance companies in the United States and virtually all of them offer a wide array of different types of policies. Further, the mathematics of life insurance can differ widely depending on the age of the insured at the time that the policy is purchased, the amount of coverage, the type of coverage, and the specific terms of the contract. Perhaps the most visible common thread that runs through all life insurance contracts is the fact that the younger you are when you initiate a contract, the lower your annual costs will be. Let us now examine some of the major diversities in life insurance.

Kinds of Companies: Stock and Mutual

There are basically two different kinds of life insurance companies: stock companies and mutual companies. Stock companies are owned by stockholders, in much the same fashion as stockholders own other companies such as General Motors, American Telephone and Telegraph, and so on. The stockholders of these companies elect the Board of Directors to run the company. If the company is run profitably, the stockholders of those companies will likely receive dividends on their stock, again in much the same way as stockholders of industrial companies.

Mutual companies, on the other hand, are in effect owned by their policyholders. The policyholders elect the Board of Directors, who manage the company. In a mutual company, where the premium income exceeds the expenses (benefits paid and other expenses) by a certain amount, the policyholders/owners will receive back a portion of the excess needed to meet expenses. These sums are also referred to as "dividends," but they are technically not the same thing as dividends received on common stock.

"Par" and "Nonpar" Policies

The kinds of policies issued by mutual companies, wherein dividends are paid to policyholders, are referred to as "participating" policies—the policyholders participate in a distribution of excess income over expenses.

Stock companies generally do not pay such dividends to their policyholders. These policies are referred to as "nonparticipating." In some instances, however, stock companies do issue participating policies.

Participating and nonparticipating policies are commonly referred to as "par" and "nonpar."

The difference between stock and mutual companies may be better understood by referring back to the earlier example of the skiers. The skiers who banded together on their own to chip in $1 for each run formed a kind of mutual company. The skiers who declined to do this on their own and were approached by an outside business executive who would do it for them took part in a stock company.

Premiums on par policies will customarily be higher than premiums on nonpar policies, all other things being equal. But the owner of a par policy has the hope of receiving dividends each year that may be used to offset the cost of the premium. Very possibly the amount of dividends received by a par policyholder could reduce the out-of-pocket cost of his or her insurance to a lower level than what an equal nonpar policy would cost. For example, an individual shopping for a life insurance policy may find that two policies of equal face value, one par and one nonpar, have annual premiums of $300 and $250. If, over a period of time, the par policy pays a dividend of $60 per year, then the par policy will end up being less expensive than the nonpar policy. But insurance companies cannot give any guarantee of what dividends will be paid in any given year. It will depend on their actual experience of premium dollars received and expense and benefit dollars paid out. (Technically these dividends are considered as a return of overpayment of premium. As such they are not considered taxable income by the IRS.)

How Is Life Insurance Acquired?

Life insurance is generally acquired in one of three ways: group plans, private plans, and credit plans.

Group Plans

Group life insurance is designed for large groups of people in similar circumstances. Your employer, for example, may provide a group life insurance plan for all employees who meet the necessary requirements of tenure on the job. Group insurance may also be issued to members of social organizations, professional organizations, and unions. Frequently, group life insurance is issued in relatively small amounts, and the insured individuals may not be required to take physical examinations to prove the state of their health. The group insurance policy will cover all eligible employees, and each participating individual will receive a copy of the master policy, or an outline of it. In some cases, the employer or union may pay the premiums for all of the individuals; in other cases, such as with professional associations, each individual makes his or her own payment.

When an individual ceases to be a member of the group, his insurance may terminate. But in many cases it's possible for the individual to make arrangements to continue the coverage, provided he makes the necessary premium payments on his own.

Because administration costs on a group policy can be much lower than those connected with many individual policies, the premium cost to the insured individuals in a group plan is generally lower than what it would be in a private plan.

Private Plans

Private insurance is contracted for directly between the individual and the insurance company. Depending on the issuing company and the amount of insurance involved, a physical examination of the insured may be required.

Credit Plans

When you borrow money, the lender may offer you a program of life insurance that is designed to pay off any balance on the loan should you die before the loan is paid off. This is available in mortgage loans, as well as in small personal installment loans, such as for an automobile or home improvements. The amount of the insurance coverage decreases as the balance on the loan decreases. (This is known as "decreasing term" insurance.) In a long-term mortgage, the insured will generally make payments on the policy each year. In the shorter term installment loans, the insured will generally pay the full premium in one lump sum at the inception of the loan. Frequently, the amount of the insurance premium is added to the amount of the loan so that the insured is not out-of-pocket anything at the outset.

Types of Life Insurance

Basic types of life insurance are generally either permanent or temporary. Permanent insurance is designed to run permanently: that is, for the life of the insured individual. This type of insurance is commonly known as *ordinary insurance* or *straight insurance* or *whole life insurance.*

Temporary insurance is designed to run for a specific period of time, such as one year, five years, or ten years. This is known as *term insurance.* At the end of the term specified in the contract, the insurance ceases. However, in renewable term policies the insured has the right to renew for an additional term; however, it will be at a different premium rate. Term policies may also be convertible to ordinary policies.

A third type of life insurance is the *annuity*, wherein the insured is guaranteed a fixed monthly payment, which will begin at a specified time and will last for the agreed-on length of time. Let's take a closer look at these various types of life insurance.

Permanent Insurance

Permanent insurance is a lifetime contract. You agree to pay a fixed-level premium and the insurance company agrees to deliver a stated sum of money upon your death, or, in certain cases, at some earlier time. If the money is to become payable at a date prior to death, the insured may elect to receive it in a lump sum at that date or may elect to have the company pay in periodic installments, which would include an agreed-on amount of interest. The insurance company can also hold the money (paying interest on it) for as long as the insured lives, and then pay it to the beneficiaries. The rate of interest that an insurance company will pay on monies held for the benefit of the insured or survivors will be specifically set forth in the contract.

In addition to the benefits payable on the death of the insured (or earlier, if called for), the permanent policy will also build up "cash values," also referred to as "nonforfeiture values." These values will permit the insured to terminate the policy and obtain either cash or some other form of insurance, if desired at some later time. These values are discussed in more detail later.

Examples of permanent insurance include:

1. You agree to pay the stated premiums for, say, 20 years. At the end of that period the policy will be "paid up"—the full face value will be payable on death, and you don't have to pay any more premiums. This policy would be referred to as a limited pay plan or, in this case, "20-pay life": 20 years of payments pays it up in full.

2. You agree to pay the stated premiums for the remainder of your life. Upon death, the full face value will be payable. This policy would be referred to as "whole life" policy.

3. You agree to make certain premium payments, and the full face value then becomes available to you in cash at a stated age, say 65. If you don't elect to take the cash, you can exercise other options, as noted above, such as installment payments or having the company hold it for you plus interest, for later payment to yourself or to your beneficiaries in the case of your death. Such a policy is of the endowment species, and might be referred to as "endowment at age 65."

The amount of premiums involved for these various policies will differ considerably. For example, in the "20-pay life" policy, the insurance company must accumulate from the insured all the premiums it will need to make the necessary payments on the death of the insured. It only has

20 years in which to do so, even though the life expectancy of the individual may be much longer. Consequently, the insurance company must charge a higher premium for this kind of insurance than it would for whole life, for it has fewer years in which to accumulate the needed funds.

In the endowment policy, the full face value will become payable to the insured when he or she reaches a specific age. The person may live many years after that. In such a case, the insurance company has fewer years in which to accumulate the needed funds in which to pay off the face value than it would on a whole life policy, so again it must command a higher premium to meet its own obligations.

Term Insurance

Term insurance is "pure" insurance. You obtain a fixed amount of protection at a fixed annual price for a limited amount of time. For example, a 25-year-old might be able to obtain a term policy for $25,000 for five years at an annual premium of $100 per year. Most term policies are renewable: that is, the individual can renew his protection for an additional term, but at a higher annual premium, since he is older. Thus, the 25-year-old, on reaching 30, might find that his $25,000 worth of protection will now cost him $120 per year. To renew for another five-year term at age 35, the annual premium might go to $150 per year. As he gets older still, the cost of his annual premiums will increase at greater rates upon each renewal.

With rare exceptions, term insurance policies do not build up any of the cash or nonforfeiture values found in permanent policies.

Many term insurance policies contain a right to convert to a permanent insurance policy at stated times. Depending on the company and the amount of insurance, the insured may or may not have to take a physical examination, either upon initiating or renewing the term policy or on converting it to a permanent policy.

Because term insurance does not have any cash value buildup as a rule, it is the least expensive among all forms regarding initial out-of-pocket premium expenses. But as term insurance is renewed at ever-increasing ages—and thereby at ever increasing rates—the ultimate out-of-pocket expenses can reach, and possibly exceed, those of permanent life.

As indicated earlier, another, and still cheaper, form of term insurance is decreasing term insurance, which accompanies mortgage loans and installment loans. Such insurance is cheaper because the amount of actual insurance decreases each year as the balance on the loan decreases.

Annuities

We've noted that the main emphasis of life insurance is to provide a fixed sum of money to the beneficiaries when the insured party dies. In some cases, however, the insured may retrieve monies paid into the policy while still alive. This occurs in the case of an endowment policy or an ordinary life policy when the insured takes advantage of the cash values that he or she may borrow against or use to convert the policy to another form, or simply cash in the existing policy.

An annuity is technically not an insurance policy. It is designed basically to provide a source of income to an individual who purchases such a contract. This individual is called the *annuitant.* Although technically not an insurance policy, an annuity is sold as a major product of insurance companies. In some cases there may be death benefits with annuities. The buyer of an annuity contract pays money to the insurance company either in one lump sum or in periodic payments over a number of months or years. The insurance company then agrees to pay back to the contract holder a sum of money each month for an agreed-on amount of time.

That sum of money may be fixed in the contract (a fixed-dollar annuity) or may vary (a variable annuity), but there is a guaranteed minimum. With a fixed-dollar annuity the funds are invested conservatively—predominantly in government and corporate bonds as well as mortgages—and the company can thus assure the amount of monthly payments to the annuitant.

In the variable annuity, a substantial portion of the money is invested in the stock market. The theory is that the stock market can provide protection against inflation. If the theory works, the annuitant may get more back than he or she might have received under a fixed-dollar annuity. The annuitant is guaranteed at least a certain minimum back from the insurance company. Variable annuities rise and decline in popularity as the stock market rises and declines.

Here's a brief description of the common types of payment programs available with annuities.

☐ *A straight life annuity.* Payments used to buy an annuity are called a "consideration," not premiums as in normal life insurance. In a straight life annuity, once you have made your payments, you will begin to receive the agreed-on monthly sum at the agreed-on date. Annuities will usually begin payments on retirement. In a straight life annuity, the payments last for as long as you live. If an annuitant dies one month after the payments have commenced, no further payments will be made to any party. If the annuitant lives far beyond the normal life expectancy, he or she will continue to receive the monthly payments from the insurance company, even if they have to pay out much more than they received at the outset from the annuitant. The company, in effect, is taking the risk that the annuitant will live no longer than the life expectancy.

☐ *Annuity with installments certain.* This type of annuity is set up to provide monthly payments for a fixed period of time—perhaps ten or 20 years. If an annuitant dies before the agreed-on time has elapsed, his beneficiary will continue to receive the payments until the term finally elapses.

☐ *Refund annuities.* If an annuitant dies before receiving back all the money paid in, then his beneficiary will get back the balance still due. It may be in installments or in one lump sum, depending on the agreement between the parties.

☐ *Joint and survivor annuity.* This can cover two people, such as a husband and a wife. When one dies, the other continues to receive the payments until the agreed-on fund or the length of time has been exhausted.

Certain tax advantages can be obtained through annuities. While the insurance company is holding your funds, they are investing the money and it will be earning interest and/or dividends. Generally, you do not have to pay income taxes on the earnings while the insurance company is holding the money for you. Once you do begin to receive the annuity payments, the interest that has been earned is taxable. But, presumably, you will have retired and you'll be in a lower tax bracket—thus the tax bite will be far less than it would have been if you had had to pay taxes on the income while you were still actively working.

Many pension funds are set up through annuities. If you are making payments to a pension fund, you won't have to pay income taxes on the annuities payments as you receive them with regard to that portion that you yourself have contributed. True, it really amounts to getting your money back without having to pay taxes on it, but it could have been earning tax-free interest for an extended period of time, so the tax advantage is not inconsiderable.

In the chapter on fixed income investments we discuss the Individual Retirement Account and the Keogh plan. Both of these plans can be funded through annuities, in which case the amount that you contribute each year to your program will be tax deductible on your income-tax return; in addition, the funds will continue to earn on a tax-free basis until they begin to pay out to the annuitants.

Generally speaking, annuities might be considered a fixed income form of investment offered by insurance companies. The fixed-dollar annuity guarantees a fixed income for the agreed-on amount of time, and the variable annuity guarantees at least a minimum level of income with the chance of reaping more if market investments are correct. Some individuals may prefer to assure themselves a future source of income via annuities rather than through the stock market, where the level of security is always questionable. But the return offered by annuities may not be as attractive as that available through other forms of fixed income securities, such as bonds and savings plans.

The Parties to an Insurance Policy

There can be as many as five parties involved in an insurance policy contract: the owner of the policy; the person whose life is insured; the beneficiary; the contingent beneficiary; and the company itself. In a great many cases the owner and the insured are one and the same party. In many instances a contingent beneficiary will not be named in the policy. The roles of each of these five parties are important to an overall understanding of life insurance. Let's take a closer look at each of them.

The Insured

This is the person whose life is insured by the policy. It is on the death of the insured that the proceeds are paid. The insured may also be the owner of the policy, but it is possible for the insured and the owner to be different parties.

The Owner

The owner is perhaps the most important person referred to in the policy, for it is the owner who has the power to exercise various options within the policy, including naming and changing the beneficiary and making loans against the policy or cashing in the policy.

Consider Harold and Esther Klein. Harold applies for a life insurance policy on himself and retains ownership in his own name. He names Esther as the beneficiary. In this case, Harold is both the insured and the owner. Harold could also make application for the policy with himself as the insured and Esther as the owner. Alternatively Harold could name himself initially as both insured and owner, but at some later point decide to transfer ownership to Esther.

Here are other examples of the owner and the insured not being the same party: Arthur is a valuable employee, so his boss takes out a policy on Arthur's life payable to the company. The premium is also paid by the company. This is to protect the company in the event of Arthur's death—it would alleviate, for example, the cost of training a replacement and the expense of getting along temporarily without Arthur's services. This is generally known as "key man" insurance. The company is the owner of the policy and Arthur is the insured.

Jose needs a loan from his bank. The bank, in conjunction with making a loan, may offer Jose a life insurance policy, with the proceeds payable to the bank in the event of Jose's death. As discussed earlier, this is known as "credit life insurance." In such a case, the bank is the owner of the policy and Jose is the insured. (The bank will also be named as the beneficiary of the policy.)

The owner has important powers regarding a life insurance policy. The owner can assign the policy to a creditor. For example, Jose, instead of buying a new credit life policy, assigns an existing policy to the bank to protect the bank in the event of Jose's death before the loan is paid off. Should Jose die before the loan is paid off, the bank will receive the proceeds of the policy; should Jose default on the loan before his death, the bank would have the right to take whatever cash values exist in the policy. (An assignment is valid only if the insurance company has been properly notified and has accepted the assignment.)

The owner, and only the owner, can change the beneficiary of the policy, assuming that that right has been reserved in the original policy.

The owner can transfer ownership from himself to another party, and this might be wise in certain instances of estate planning.

The owner can exercise the nonforfeiture provisions in the policy.

The owner can dictate the manner in which the face amount will be payable to the beneficiary, where a choice exists.

It is only the owner who can make these changes, and they must be done in accord with the insurance company's stipulations in the contract. The insured cannot exercise these powers unless the insured is also the owner. If Harold conveys a life insurance policy on his own life to Esther as the owner—either as a result of an estate planning recommendation or as a gift or any other reason—then it is Esther, and Esther only, who can exercise the various rights granted in the policy. As long as Harold retains ownership, only he can exercise those rights.

The Beneficiary

The beneficiary is the one who receives the stated payments to be made on the death of the insured. The choice of the beneficiary is up to the owner of the policy, who, as noted above, may be the same party as the insured. The beneficiary may be one or more persons, a charity, a business concern, or the estate of the insured.

Contingent Beneficiary

There is always the possibility that the originally named beneficiary will die before the insured. The owner of the policy can name a contingent beneficiary, who will take the place of the original beneficiary if he or she dies before the insured. If no contingent beneficiaries are named, the terms of the policy will probably set forth how the proceeds will then be distributed. As with the original beneficiary, the contingent beneficiary can also be one or more persons, a charity, a business concern, the estate of the insured, or any other recipient the owner wishes to name.

The Company

The company is, of course, the insurance company with whom you are entering into the contract. You, as the insurance buyer, will deal with a representative of the company—either an agent connected directly with the company or an independent agent who may represent a number of various companies. Once you have entered into the contract, you may or may not see that agent again. It all depends on the level of service he wishes to provide and the prospective sales he may feel he can generate from you and your family. Generally, the agent is the primary representative of the company as far as the insured is concerned, and the party to whom the insured should turn when any question arises. Some companies maintain service offices in communities throughout the nation to handle questions, problems, and complaints. Otherwise, you will turn to the agent directly.

The Life Insurance Contract and Its Clauses

A life insurance policy is a legally binding contract once it has been properly signed by the necessary parties—the owner and the company. The policy, as a legal contract, sets forth all the rights, duties, and obligations of the parties to the contract. The only way the contract can be amended is by agreement between the parties. If an agreement is reached, it must be set forth in writing and attached to the policy. Changes to a life insurance policy—or any other kind of insurance policy—are called endorsements or riders.

The Application

An important part of a policy itself is the application, which is the questionnaire that the applicant for the insurance must fill in to have the policy issued. The application contains pertinent information about the individual applying for insurance, including medical data. If the application contains false or misleading information and the insurance company issues the policy not knowing this, the policy might later be voided if the insurance company docs learn the truth. For example, an individual applying for life insurance may have recently had a severe heart attack but states that he is in perfectly good health. If he can somehow prevent the insurance company from learning of his physical condition and the policy is granted, he has entered into the agreement on false premises, and the policy might be voided if the company learns of the circumstances within the stated time limit.

Insurance companies go to considerable lengths to assure that they will not be defrauded. Physical examinations will be conducted, and interviews of neighbors may be undertaken to learn an individual's personal habits. All doctors that the applicant has seen in the past few years may be questioned by the insurance company to determine the reason for seeing these doctors.

In recent years, an organization known as the Medical Information Bureau has assisted the insurance industry in minimizing fraudulent applications. Currently, in most cases, when one applies for life, health, or disability insurance, he or she will sign a statement giving the insurance company permission to relay all health information to the Medical Information Bureau (MIB) and seek out any information that may exist there relative to the individual's health. The computer banks of the MIB can reveal information on you that you may not have been aware anyone knew. By reducing fraudulent applications, the insurance industry is able to reduce the claims that it otherwise might have had to pay out and thus can offer a lower premium base to the vast majority of the public dealing on an honest and forthright basis.

Recent life insurance statistics reveal that of all applications made for life insurance in the United States, only 3 percent are declined. Eighty-five percent of all applications have policies issued at the standard risk levels, and 4 percent of the applications have policies issued at extra risk levels. (Extra risk policies may be issued in cases where there is an obvious health problem but not one so great that the company will refuse the coverage. They will accept coverage, but usually at a higher premium level or in some cases, particularly in health insurance policies, will exclude certain physical conditions.) Eight percent of all applications are approved by the company but are not accepted by the applicants.

The Face Amount, or Face Value

This is the amount of money due the beneficiary on the death of the insured. The face amount is set forth on the policy, and it is what we usually refer to when we talk about the amount of an insurance policy. For example, if we say a "$10,000 life insurance policy," we're talking about the face value of the policy.

It is possible that the beneficiary could receive more or less than the original face value. The beneficiary may receive more than face value if a double indemnity clause was activated in the policy. The beneficiary may also receive more than the face value if the owner had applied dividends that he or she had received toward the purchase of additional insurance.

The face value might be decreased if the owner has borrowed against the policy and has not paid off these loans. In some policies, the face value may change (usually decreasing) when the insured reaches a stated age.

Double Indemnity, or Accidental Death Benefit

A double indemnity clause, which is generally available at an additional premium, provides for the payment of double the face amount in the event of accidental death as opposed to natural death.

Incontestable Clause

Commonly, the insurance company will have a set period of time, usually two years, during which it must take issue with any suspected false or misleading information contained in the application. During that initial two-year period, a company may contest statements made by the applicant and can void the policy if improper statements were made. But once the two years have elapsed, the company can no longer contest any statements.

Guaranteed Insurability

Some policies will, for an additional premium, guarantee you the right to increase the face value of the policy within certain limits and within fixed times, regardless of your health. The cost of obtaining this guarantee should be carefully evaluated.

Premium and Mode of Payments

The policy contract will spell out how much the premiums are on the policy and how they can be made. The policyholder may elect to pay premiums annually, semiannually, quarterly, or monthly. The more frequent the mode of payment, the more costly it will be for both the insurance company and the insured. Monthly or quarterly payments might be more convenient to an individual's budget, but the individual should be aware of the probable added cost in paying more frequently than once a year.

Lapse, Grace Period, and Reinstatement

The general agreement in a life insurance policy is that the company will pay the face value to the beneficiary as long as the policy remains "in force." The term *in force* means that the owner of the policy has continued to meet his obligations: he has made his premium payments regularly and without fail. If a policyholder does not meet premium obligations, the policy can lapse. When a policy lapses, it is terminated. There is no more insurance.

Unless financial circumstances leave little or no alternative, it can be most imprudent to let a policy lapse. Money paid in up to the date of lapse will be forfeited, and an individual may find that if he or she wishes to obtain life insurance at a later time, it will cost more because of increased age; and in some cases, because of the onset of physical problems, the person may not be able to get the insurance at all. He or she may fall into that small but important 3 percent of all applications that are turned down by the company.

Lapsing of policies is not in the best interests of insurance companies either. They stay in business because of the continuity of insurance programs, not their termination. The insurance industry has structured the typical life insurance policy so that a lapse does not occur that easily or that automatically.

If a premium is not paid by the stated due date, the policyholder will have a "grace period" of usually 31 days, during which he or she can still make payment and continue the policy in force without any penalty. As the end of the grace period approaches, the policyholder will usually be notified, either in person by the agent or through the mail from the company itself, concerning the approaching deadline.

If payment still has not been made by the end of the grace period, many permanent policies have an automatic cash loan provision. If cash values have already begun to build up in the policy and there is enough to cover the payment of one premium, the company will automatically borrow against those values and use the proceeds to pay the premium and thus continue the policy in force for another period. If there are no cash values in the policy—either it's a term policy with no cash values or it's an ordinary life policy not yet old enough to have adequate cash values—the policy will then lapse.

Even after a lapse has occurred, the policyholder has a limited time within which to exercise his or her rights to "reinstate" the policy. If a policyholder wishes to reinstate the policy, he or she may have to take a new physical examination or may simply sign a statement about health conditions. Which approach taken will depend on the amount of the face value and the company's general regulations in that regard. If the company is satisfied about the state of the insured's health and if the person pays all back premiums and any interest owing thereon, the policy can then be reinstated.

Waiver of Premium

This protection is available at a slight additional cost to most life insurance policies. It provides that if the insured is totally disabled, the need to make premium payments will be waived. In other words, the insurance can continue in force, without the insured having to make premium payments during the period of disability. It's like a miniature income disability policy built into the life insurance policy itself. But note that the definition of "totally disabled" may differ from policy to policy. It might, for example, be defined as "unable to work in a job for which you were trained" or "unable to work at all." The difference can be important.

Conversion Values

Conversion (or nonforfeiture) values become available to policyholders under permanent life insurance policies. The amount of the values builds up as you pay your premiums over the years, but the rate of build-up will vary from policy to policy. In shopping for an insurance policy, the prudent individual will carefully compare the rate of growth and relative size of these values. Policy A may have a lower premium than policy B for the same face value. Thus, policy A may seem to be the better value. But policy B may have a higher level of conversion values, which could be of considerable importance to the policyholder many years later. Thus, what you get for your premium dollar isn't just the face value of the policy. These other values must be considered most carefully.

Here's how conversion values work. If you cease paying your premiums by choice or otherwise, these conversion values will allow you to convert your policy into a number of alternative plans.

Cashing In   You can cash in the policy. You then receive the amount of cash set forth in the Cash Value table (which is usually the same as the Loan Value).

Borrowing   You can borrow against the policy, usually up to the amount stipulated in the Loan Value table. For policies issued before the mid-1960s, a policyholder usually can borrow at the very attractive rate of 5 percent per year. Policies issued in more recent years will carry a higher borrowing rate, but it still might be a very attractive rate compared with what one would have to pay for a simple interest loan at a lending institution.

Borrowing against a life insurance policy may be quick and convenient and inexpensive, but it's not always prudent. The act of borrowing is simple: notify the company of your wishes, sign the appropriate papers, and receive a check shortly thereafter. Repayment is up to you: you need not repay the principal at all; but you must pay interest annually. If you do not repay the principal, the face value will be diminished by the amount of the outstanding loan at the time of the insured's death. For example, if the face value on a given policy was $10,000 and the owner borrowed $1000 against it, then died before repaying the loan, the beneficiary would receive only $9000.

Some policyholders have found it wise to borrow against their policies at the available low rates and use those funds for investment. This can be done either prudently or imprudently. If the purpose of the life insurance program is protection of the family—the most common and reasonable purpose—you can enhance that protection by investing borrowed proceeds in conservative situations, such as bonds and savings accounts. The owner of a seasoned policy could, for example, borrow against the policy and pay a 5 percent interest rate, then deposit the funds in an insured savings certificate paying, say, 12 percent. The difference between what one has borrowed and what one earns on an investment is additional income.

On the other hand, one might borrow those funds and speculate with them. In doing so, one risks losing the funds, thereby impairing the overall degree of protection.

Converting to Extended Term Insurance   You can convert your existing program to "extended term insurance." With such insurance, you will be covered for the same original face value of the policy, but only for *a limited period of time* rather than for the rest of your life, had you continued the policy in force.

Converting to Paid-up Insurance   You can convert to "paid-up insurance." If you cease paying premiums, you can still be covered for a *portion* of the face value for as long as the original policy would have protected you.

Automatic Premium Loan   This provision, as noted earlier, will allow the company to borrow against your loan values automatically in order to make premium payments that you have neglected to make.

Nonforfeiture Tables

Each policy will contain a "Table of Nonforfeiture Values" indicating the precise level of these values at specific points. Table 20-1 is an abbreviated sample of the normally much longer table of nonforfeiture values. Nonforfeiture values are based on the age of the insured at the time the policy is taken out. Values will vary from company to company and from one type of policy to another.

Here's how the tables work. The face amount of the insurance policy is $10,000 and the age of the insured at the time the policy was taken out was 25. At the end of the tenth policy year (when the insured is 35), he will have $1340 worth of cash/loan values. That means he can stop

Table 20-1 | **Nonforfeiture Values, Sample Policy, $10,000 Face Value**

End of Policy Year	Cash or Loan Value	Paid-up Insurance	Extended Term Insurance
5	$ 590	$1410	14 yrs. 48 days
10	$1340	$2900	20 yrs. 310 days
15	$2100	$4130	22 yrs. 288 days
20	$2890	$5180	22 yrs. 303 days

making payments, cash in the policy, terminating the insurance altogether, and have $1340 cash in hand. Or he can borrow that much against the policy at the interest rate stated in the policy, and otherwise continue the policy in force by continuing to pay annual premiums.

If he wishes to convert to paid-up insurance, he will, at the end of the tenth policy year, have the right to convert to a permanent policy with a face value of $2900. That means he no longer need pay any premiums, and he's protected for the rest of his life for $2900 in face value. The last column indicates the extended term insurance provisions. At the end of ten years this individual could convert to extended term, in which case he would be covered for the full face amount ($10,000) for 20 years and 310 days. At the end of that time, the coverage would cease altogether.

In order to take advantage of any of the nonforfeiture provisions, the insurance company should be notified of your intention, and you should receive documentation that verifies exactly what steps you're taking. It would be advisable in any case to discuss the ramifications of making such a move with your insurance agent and any other financial advisors before you actually proceed.

Dividend Options

Earlier in this chapter we noted that some types of life insurance policies—particularly those issued by mutual life insurance companies—pay dividends to policyholders. If you own such a policy, you'll probably have a number of choices as to the manner in which those dividends are paid. You may wish to receive the dividends in cash to do with as you please; you may want to apply the dividends toward the next premium due on the insurance policy; you may let the premium "ride" with the insurance company where it will draw a rate of interest set forth in the insurance policy; or you may use the dividends to purchase additional life insurance.

An annual statement from your insurance company will indicate what dividends are payable to you and will instruct you how to choose the mode in which the dividends will be applied. If you have any questions, discuss the matter with your agent.

Settlement Options

Policyholders may also have options concerning the manner in which the payment of proceeds will be made. These are called "settlement options." In many cases, the beneficiary of the policy may decide how the monies are to be paid out—either in a lump sum or spread out over a period of time (in which case interest will be paid on the proceeds that remain in the company's control).

In some plans, the owner of the policy may determine how the proceeds are to be paid out, and only the owner will be able to amend that plan. For example, a husband may determine that he does not wish his wife to have the entire proceeds in one lump sum. He may then dictate that she is to receive periodic payments; or perhaps he may determine that the wife as beneficiary will receive the interest only, and that a subsequent beneficiary on the death of the wife will receive the full proceeds. Each policy will spell out exactly what options are available and how to go about choosing them and changing them.

Buying Life Insurance: Who Needs It, and How Much?

When we're hungry, we go to the market and buy the food we need. We don't have to wait for someone to tell us that our stomachs need refilling. Not so with life insurance. The need is not as clear cut. Indeed, contemplating the need for life insurance reminds us of our own mortality, and it's no surprise that human nature would short circuit such thoughts.

With life insurance, many of us have to be told of the need, but we frequently don't take any action to satisfy that need until a representative of the insurance company comes knocking at our door offering us a package of insurance programs. The problem is further compounded by the fact that the agent may talk in terms that we don't fully understand; and he or she may be a person whose presence we don't find pleasant or comfortable.

Despite these negative aspects, sound personal financial planning demands that life insurance be at least carefully investigated as a part of one's overall financial foundation. Not everyone needs life insurance, but everyone should at least examine how life insurance can function with respect to his own long-term needs and objectives.

Who needs life insurance? In short, if you want to protect or enhance the financial welfare of anyone who is dependent on you, and your existing assets aren't adequate to provide the desired level of protection, you need life insurance. That is, you need it if you want to get the job done quickly and assuredly.

The extent of your need can be more easily determined if the possible times of death are examined. These times can be: prematurely, or in accordance with normal life expectations. Life insurance may also be needed to resolve estate tax and business situations.

On Premature Death

Victor's case, discussed earlier, is a typical example of how life insurance can fill a need: protecting a family against the sudden and permanent loss of the main source of the family income.

Two basic approaches can be taken. First, you can embark upon a program of term insurance. This would be the less costly way to provide the umbrella of protection for a limited period of time until the need for that protection ceased—the children are grown and you have created other assets to take care of your surviving spouse.

The other way would be to create a program of permanent insurance. This would be more costly for the present but could be cheaper over the long run. The umbrella of protection would be there for as long as you needed it, and when the need was no longer there, the values that had accumulated in the policy could be put to other uses. Alternatively, the policy could remain intact to provide an enhancement of the wealth of your survivors upon a later death. Depending on your spendable dollars, a combination of the two approaches might work out best for you.

Some years ago, a major national insurance company used an advertising slogan that very aptly pinpoints what any would-be insurance buyer must be aware of: "There's nobody else like you." You, and your family, as you are today and as you may be in the future, are unique. Your needs, desires, aspirations, life expectancy, and goals are yours alone. An insurance program that might be perfect for your neighbor might be improper for you. Only through careful planning—based on your own unique situation—can you develop your own proper individual program.

On a Normal Death

Once the basic protection for your family has been accounted for, how much more life insurance, if any, do you want to create for the benefit of your ultimate survivors? How much of your current income should be directed toward that end? This is a very personal decision that can't be answered with a simple formula. Some people may feel an actual need to create an inheritance for their survivors. Some may have a desire but not the money to do so. Others may give it no thought whatsoever. But if you do have the need, or even the desire, life insurance is an assured way to fill that need.

Tax and Business Purposes

Chapters 23 and 24 will help you determine whether your heirs are facing the prospect of federal estate taxes on your death. If they are, life insurance can commonly be used to assist survivors in meeting that tax obligation. Life insurance provides instant cash to meet such debts. Lacking the needed cash, survivors might be faced with having to sell other assets—house, investments—in order to pay the taxes. Having to sell off those other assets, particularly if they are income producing, could provide a hardship for the survivors. Life insurance eliminates the need to sell off other assets.

Similarly, business interests can be protected by life insurance. If, for example, you are the sole proprietor or a partner in a small business, your death could cause the business to have to terminate. If, however, there are life insurance proceeds payable to the business, those proceeds, which are not taxable to the recipient, could be used to hire a replacement for you so that the business could keep running or could provide a fund of cash to allow for an orderly liquidation of the business. Either way, your survivors can be protected by that immediate infusion of cash into the business.

How Much Insurance Is Needed?

The first task in evaluating how much insurance is needed by any individual is to determine, as noted earlier, who is going to be protected by the insurance program and to what extent? These are your goals, and you must define them most specifically in order to reach dollar figures. For example, do you want to insure that the children will have at least half of their college tuition guaranteed in the event of your premature death? 75 percent? 100 percent? Are they on their own after that? Or do you want them to have a nest egg to help get them started in their chosen career? These are individual questions that only you can answer.

Now comes the time for some thoughtful arithmetic. You must determine, as accurately as possible, the following:

1. What might be the possible extent of "final" expenses? These would be expenses arising as a result of death, and they would include the possible uninsured costs of a terminal illness, burial expenses, estate taxes, and a certain sum to help survivors get through the early difficult time of adjustment. In evaluating these matters, one must also take into account the extent of one's health insurance coverage for a costly terminal illness—an item of considerable expense. If you feel you're amply protected against such costs through your health insurance program, you need not necessarily include them as part of your life insurance planning.

2. How much existing debt—mortgages, personal loans, and so on— might the survivors have to pay? Obviously, the amount of your indebtedness can fluctuate considerably from year to year. If you don't now own a house, you won't have to worry about a mortgage being paid off. But if you buy a house tomorrow, there will be a sizable debt that will eventually have to be paid. And if you don't want the family to sell the house to eliminate the debt, you might wish to cover such contingencies through life insurance. Careful planning will cover existing debts, with flexibility retained to increase or decrease as future circumstances warrant.

3. How much per year will the survivors need to maintain themselves in whatever style of living you and they feel would be suitable? Looking

at this question in terms of the husband/breadwinner, consideration must be given to the possibilities of the wife remarrying, of her going to work, of children going to work, of other potential sources of income materializing or failing to materialize. Elimination of the husband's own cost of living—food, clothing, recreation, and so on—must also be evaluated. It would probably be simplest to base estimates on a continuation of the current lifestyle, with allowance for possible upward or downward adjustments.

4. Beyond the immediate annual cost of living, estimate the extraordinary expenses that survivors will face, and how much of those expenses you want to assure them of being able to meet. Such expenses might include education, weddings, having a stake to go into business on their own, and so on.

5. For how many years would you want them to continue your particular lifestyle on a worry-free basis?

6. What benefits will be provided by Social Security? A visit with your nearest Social Security office can provide this information.

7. Inventory all current assets, paying particular attention to current market value, potential future value, liquidity (how easily and at what cost the assets can be converted into cash), and the earning potential of any assets. Outline a program showing when certain assets could, or should, be converted to cash to meet family needs. Such a program should also show which nonearning assets might be converted to earning ones. (*Example:* Should that vacant lot you bought for speculation or as a site for your future summer home be sold and the money put to work as an earning asset?)

8. Evaluate what other realistic sources of income there might be in the future, such as inheritances or scholarships. You can't count on these sources materializing, but you should be aware of the possibility.

9. Evaluate current life insurance programs, including group plans and any others. Determine what the proceeds could earn annually if they were conservatively invested, and determine how long the proceeds would last if the principal were invaded by a certain amount each year. (The savings charts in the chapter on fixed income investments can assist you with this.) Evaluate all your other assets in the same manner. This information might not be easy to compile and you may want the help of an accountant, or perhaps your insurance agent could assist you impartially and objectively. Even though it may be difficult to obtain, this information is essential for an intelligent plan to evolve.

A Case History

When you've surveyed your data, the gaps can be measured and the alternatives for filling those gaps can come into focus.

Let's examine a fairly simple case. This exercise illustrates the basic type of thinking you should go through to estimate your own life insurance needs.

Phillip is married, has a 12-year-old child, and earns $2000 a month after taxes. His wife does not work but is capable of doing so should the need arise.

Phillip's current financial status is as follows:

☐ He owns his home, which has a current market value of $90,000. He owes $60,000 on a mortgage with monthly payments of $620.
☐ He has $5000 in a savings plan.
☐ He has $10,000 in the profit-sharing plan at work. This could be payable immediately to his survivors in the event of his death.
☐ He owns two cars, both used, with a current total value of $8000.
☐ He has a life insurance policy, with a face value of $30,000.
☐ His debts, in addition to his mortgage, consist of bank loans totaling $5000. Monthly payments are $300.

Phillip has estimated his financial status if he were to die suddenly. He has determined that his existing health and burial insurance programs would take care of all of his final expenses. His wife and child would need approximately $1720 a month to live on. They would receive $300 from Social Security, leaving them with a need for $1420 a month. (This would cover the mortgage payment of $620; the bank payments of $300; and other living expenses, $500.)

If he died now, Phillip would not want his wife to sell the house at this time. She could, though, make use of the savings account, the profit-sharing plan, and the life insurance proceeds, which would total $45,000.

For purposes of this exercise, Phillip and his insurance agent have estimated that that $45,000 could be invested conservatively to yield 10 percent after taxes, or $4500 a year or $375 per month. That income would be interest only; it would not involve dipping into the principal amount. If the surviving spouse were to establish a program of dipping into the $45,000 principal, plus interest, she could realize a monthly income of $594 for ten years or $483 for 15 years, at the end of which times the total sum would be used up. This is illustrated in Table 20-2. (See also Table 22-5.)

As the table illustrates, the interest income on a $60,000 investment coupled with the interest income on the existing $45,000 fund would generate interest income of $875 per month. If the widow were to embark on the ten-year payout program, she would have an income of $1387 per month. This is roughly what she would need to cover her basic needs assuming that she did not work at all.

After ten years, when the total funds had been dissipated, the child would have graduated from college or would otherwise be embarked on his career and the equity in the house would be considerably greater

Table 20-2 | **Income Sources**

	Interest only	10-year payout	15-year payout
From existing $45,000	$375*	$ 594	$ 483
From extra $60,000	500*	793	645
Total income available	$875*	$1387	$1128

*Principal amount always remains intact

than it is now, allowing the widow the opportunity to refinance or sell in order to establish a source of living funds.

In summary: Phillip has calculated that to establish at least a minimal level of income for his wife and child, he'd have to create an investable fund of at least $60,000 which, added to his existing sources, could be tapped over a ten-year period. If either his wife or his child worked, that would provide them additional comfort. If Phillip created a larger investable fund, that would of course offer greater security.

Phillip's situation is a relatively uncomplicated one. If he were concerned about such matters as estate taxes, creating a substantial college tuition fund, protecting a business interest, or any other matter beyond the ordinary, his need for insurance would have been much greater. Now, having solved the relatively uncomplicated matter of how much insurance he needs, Phillip must tackle the far more perplexing matter of what kind of insurance to buy.

What to Buy

Buying life insurance is a lot like buying a car. You can choose a subcompact with no frills or you can go lavish and splurge on a fancy sedan with all the trimmings. The sticker price isn't always the determining factor in what you will buy. If you need a car just to hop back and forth to the office or the shopping center, the subcompact might certainly make the most sense. But if you're a traveling salesman and expect to be driving thousands of miles every week, it may well be worth the added price to buy the luxury car so that the physical comfort of the automobile reduces the wear and tear on your body. There's no easy answer.

Life insurance is just as complicated. You, or Phillip, could go for the stripped-down term policy or for a "loaded" whole life policy. Both have pluses, both have minuses.

Consumerists and the life insurance industry have been arguing bitterly for years about the relative costs and comparisons of features of life insurance policies. The matter is extraordinarily complicated. The whole issue is made even more muddy by the basic underlying argument between term-insurance advocates and whole life–insurance advocates. But mind boggling though it is, some life insurance shopping is essential before you embark on a plan of your own.

For an excellent starting point, refer to the February 1980 and March 1980 issues of *Consumer Reports* magazine, which should be available at your local public library. Those two issues contain an extended special report analyzing life insurance policies, companies, and costs. Bear in mind, though, that by the time you read those reports, many of the companies may have changed their price structures. Nevertheless, the reports will give you some beginning guidelines as to choosing companies and policies.

By way of briefly excerpting those reports, Tables 20-3 and 20-4 illustrate the high and low initial premiums on a variety of policies. The dif-

Table 20-3 | **Term Policies**

		Low	High
Age 25	$ 25,000 Par	$ 52	$ 134
	25,000 Nonpar	68	128
	100,000 Par	182	414
	100,000 Nonpar	201	473
Age 35	$ 25,000 Par	$ 62	$ 173
	25,000 Nonpar	82	149
	100,000 Par	210	665
	100,000 Nonpar	225	568
Age 45	$ 25,000 Par	$126	$ 300
	25,000 Nonpar	145	266
	100,000 Par	435	1173
	100,000 Nonpar	453	1028

Table 20-4 | **Whole Life (Cash Value) Policies**

		Low	High
Age 25	$ 25,000 Par	$ 236	$ 475
	25,000 Nonpar	187	353
	100,000 Par	999	1841
	100,000 Nonpar	658	1375
Age 35	$ 25,000 Par	$ 350	$ 637
	25,000 Nonpar	316	485
	100,000 Par	1461	2487
	100,000 Nonpar	1162	1909
Age 45	$ 25,000 Par	$ 549	$ 921
	25,000 Nonpar	550	726
	100,000 Par	2408	3613
	100,000 Nonpar	2068	2872

Note: These premium costs represent only the first year. For more accurate comparisons you must also take into account renewal premiums (for term policies), dividend payments anticipated (for participating policies), and cash value and conversion value build-ups (for whole life policies).

ferences in premium costs for seemingly equal policies are, you're sure to agree, astonishing.

These tables illustrate the differences only in the initial premium on the given policies—that is, the premium paid during the first year. With the whole life policies, the premium remains the same for the life of the policy.

Insurance company analysts maintain that premium cost alone is not enough upon which to base a wise shopping decision. They have projected other methods of determining the true value, one of the main ones being the "cost adjusted" method. This method assumes that you will terminate the policy after a number of years, and it evaluates the cash you'd have on hand after that time, taking into account premiums you've paid over the years. This method might be valid if in fact everybody did terminate their policies at that time, but obviously not everyone does.

It's not the province of this textbook to tell you which insurance policy to buy any more than it is to tell you which automobile to buy. You've been shown the tools to use to evaluate insurance programs, and the homework and shopping will be up to you. To try to do battle with the analysts would not leave room in this book for any other subjects to be discussed. You will be helped, not so much by charts and graphs and complicated analyses of cost comparisons, but by a good agent, whose value will be discussed shortly.

The prudent insurance buyer will want to make sure that he or she has chosen a company whose reputation is established. If a would-be buyer has any questions or doubts about the stability of any given insurance company, reference should be made to *Best's Insurance Reports* and *Best's Recommended Life Insurance Companies,* which are available at most major libraries. Reference might also be made to the insurance department in your state.

The Importance of the Agent

There is no such thing as a typical insurance agent. His training might range from minimal to the rigorous demands of the courses leading to the CLU (Chartered Life Underwriter) designation. His experience might encompass weeks or decades. His income level can range from paltry to six figures. And his personality, sales techniques, and sense of ethics can run the full spectrum of human potential.

There will be many trying to seek you out. If you can find the right agent, you've made a valuable catch. But how do you know what to look for? Before we get into a shopping list, let's take a quick look at some of the dilemmas in the industry.

Dilemma No. 1   The insurance agent makes his living by selling insurance policies. Proper counseling may be of equal or greater value to you than the policy itself, but the agent doesn't make a penny unless he makes a sale. Needless to say, good counseling can produce a good sale, but it might not.

Any agent, therefore, finds himself taking a calculated risk on how much time he'll spend with any given prospect in counseling sessions. This can result in counseling and selling efforts becoming intermingled, to the point where you might not be able to tell them apart. With the agent's help, you should define your protection goals and recognize the gaps between what you have and what you need, and what various alternatives there are that can help you fill those gaps to reach your goals. Those items are the subject of counseling. Once that's in hand, it's time to get into the specifics of various policies.

If the agent is not willing to take the time you need to understand your goals, you might not be getting the service you need. And the agent might not take the time if he's not confident that there will be a sale as a result. This dilemma is perhaps best resolved by open and frank communications at the outset: "Mr. Agent, this is what I have to learn from you before I will even consider doing business with you. If you're willing to teach me what I think I have to know, I may well be a customer, but there's no guarantee. If you're willing to proceed on those terms, fine. If not, perhaps it would be best if we didn't waste each other's time."

Dilemma No. 2   With rare exception, people closer to the top of the economic ladder have better access to more sophisticated insurance counseling than those closer to the bottom. This, for better or worse, is the way of our world.

It might take an agent the same, or more, time to sell a $10,000 policy to a working family as it would to sell a $100,000 policy to an executive. The reward to the agent for his time is obviously drastically different. Further, the agent who is going for the big sale will probably have to be better equipped to handle the more sophisticated problems wealthy prospects will have. People on the lower rungs of the economic ladder also need more sound advice, but it may be more difficult for them to get it.

The more an individual learns about life insurance, the better able he or she will be to take advantage of whatever advice is given, and the better prepared to seek and understand the more sophisticated advice that could be of greater value.

Dilemma No. 3   Each of us has so many dollars to spend. Some of those dollars will be spent on our current needs and some will be put away to cover future needs and desires. There are many institutions that would like to take care of our future dollars for us—insurance companies, mutual funds, banks, savings institutions, stockbrokers. They all make their living by putting our future dollars to use until we need them, and the competition is keen to get access to these dollars.

In varying degrees, each of these giant industries has become envious of the success of the others. Some segments of the life insurance industry have reacted, for example, by putting mutual funds in the same attaché case as their insurance policies. The funds might be good, so might the policies. Mixing them together too much may not be.

With all these financial industries competing with each other for our future dollars, it's essential that we keep a clear distinction between insuring and investing. Each has its separate set of purposes and goal-fulfillment abilities. Insurance offers certainty; some forms of investment offer a measure of certainty, others offer little more than possibility.

Keeping these dilemmas firmly in mind, what then do you look for in an insurance agent?

As in choosing any professional advisor, you must have trust in his ability, confidence in his training, and knowledge of his integrity. You don't usually get these on a hunch or a first impression, though it's not impossible. Personal familiarity, recommendations from others, and reputation in the community are indicators. The individual who comes on with a hard sell after his first "how do you do?" may have the same program to offer you as the agent who holds his fire until after the proper rapport has been established. The choice is up to you.

What are the agent's credentials, background, training, and prior experience? Does the agent represent only one company, or does he, as is the case with independent agents, represent the products of a number of different companies? These are important factors to determine and evaluate. It is, of course, possible for an eager-to-get-established novice to serve you just as well as an old pro. But the Perennial Job Hopper is liable to leave you with some loose ends hanging.

The CLU

In evaluating an agent's credentials, the question of whether he is a CLU (Chartered Life Underwriter) might arise. A CLU is an insurance agent who has been through a rigorous course of instruction to better equip him to serve his public and make his living. Only a small percentage of agents are CLUs. The time and educational requirements may scare off many from pursuing the credential. These educational requirements include five separate courses on economics, taxes, estate planning and conservation, corporate law, contract law, pensions and profit-sharing plans, accounting, and the technical aspects of life insurance itself.

Each course requires about 60 hours of classroom work, plus abundant outside homework. On completing the courses, each agent then must pass a four-hour written exam on each of the five subjects.

A CLU doesn't have any product or secret policies to offer you that other agents don't have, but he does possess the education that might enable him to better determine your needs and find the right policy to satisfy those needs. (Certainly, there are many fine agents who do not have the CLU designation who can serve your needs most adequately.)

In dealing with a CLU, you are working with an individual who has invested hundreds of hours of his own time to become more expert in his own field. That fact alone might cause many insurance shoppers to lean in favor of doing business with a CLU.

Remember that no insurance agent, CLU or not, can make a living unless he sells policies. The amount of time he can give to counseling any client is limited. But the *quality* of counseling is important, perhaps more so than the amount of time given it. And that might well be where the CLU has another edge.

A major portion of your efforts must be directed to meeting and evaluating a number of prospective agents. The difference between *choosing* an agent and *being chosen by* an agent can be very important. The selection process is up to you, and if you make the most of it, you'll get the most from it. This may seem an undue amount of work simply to buy an insurance policy. But remember that you are not buying a simple product that you'll use today and be done with tomorrow. You're striving to build a structure that will shelter you and your family for many years. If it's built right, it will last, it will perform, and it will have been worth the time and the money involved.

Personal Action Checklist
Life Insurance Policy Comparisons

Shopping for life insurance can be very confusing. Companies differ. Specific policies differ. Salespeople differ. Decisions are often made on the basis of the personality of the salesperson or on the "name brand" reputation of the company. These aren't necessarily improper decisions, but close attention must, of course, be paid to the actual coverage you're obtaining and its cost. The following comparison chart will help you keep a close eye on the numbers themselves.

	Policy A	Policy B	Policy C
☐ Annual premium for a $10,000 straight life policy at your current age.	_____	_____	_____
☐ Participating or nonparticipating.	_____	_____	_____
☐ If participating, what would have been the dividend paid during the past year?	_____	_____	_____
☐ If participating, what is the company's estimate of dividend for the coming year?	_____	_____	_____
☐ If dividends are left to accumulate with the company, what interest rate will they earn?	_____	_____	_____
☐ Total premium cost over the next 10 years (excluding dividends, since their actual amount won't be known until each year occurs).	_____	_____	_____
☐ At the end of ten years, what will be your:			
Cash/loan value?	_____	_____	_____
Paid up conversion value?	_____	_____	_____
Extended term conversion value?	_____	_____	_____
☐ Total premium cost over next 20 years.	_____	_____	_____
☐ At the end of 20 years, what will be your:			
Cash/loan value?	_____	_____	_____
Paid up conversion value?	_____	_____	_____
Extended term conversion value?	_____	_____	_____
☐ At what interest rate can you borrow against the policy?	_____	_____	_____

Ask the help of the respective agents in analyzing and evaluating the difference you find in these numbers. What special features might justify higher costs or lower values?

Consumer Beware
Now You See It . . .
Now You Don't

Shopping for life insurance can be one of the most perplexing exercises you'll ever undertake. Policies are available in a bewildering assortment, with different costs, different values, different options. Yet the life insurance industry is relatively clean when it comes to complaints about consumer abuses.

Most complaints revolve around misunderstandings as to the terms and benefits of the policies. An example: V.S. bought what he thought was an endowment policy when his first child was born. He understood—or was led to believe, he states—that after making payments for 20 years he'd be entitled to a lump sum of $5000, which he'd use to pay for his child's college education.

But after dutifully making his payments for 20 years, he was shocked to learn that he could get only about $2000 in cash. He had bought, it turned out, a whole life policy instead of an endowment policy. Did the agent who sold him the policy mislead him? There was no way of proving it, for the agent had long since died, but it did appear that the agent would not have earned a higher commission for himself by misrepresenting the program. So the matter is best relegated to the "unfortunate misunderstanding" category.

On the other hand, a blatant fraud did occur in a campaign to sell life insurance to senior citizens who would have thought themselves uninsurable because of their age. Not only that: the premiums were amazingly low. The oldsters were urged to name their grandchildren as beneficiaries of the policies. When investigators uncovered the scam, they found that legal insurance policies had been written, but the grandchildren had been named as the *insured* parties, and the grandparents had been named as beneficiaries—just the reverse of what the sales pitch had promised.

Understanding of the terms, conditions, and benefits of life insurance is essential if you are to create a program that will meet your targeted needs.

21 | Health and Income Insurance

Health and income insurance protect us against the costly ravages of medical problems. Most of us have some form of health insurance through group plans at work. And most of us also have some type of sick pay program that will provide at least some income for a while if we're off work due to illness or accident. But are these forms of protection adequate in view of today's extraordinarily high costs of health care? This chapter will enable you to:

☐ Evaluate the extent of your current health and income protection.
☐ Determine whether you should acquire added protection on your own.
☐ Understand how health and income insurance policies work, and what you should acquire for your own benefit.
☐ Compare the costs and benefits available in different types of policies.
☐ Be aware and take advantage of health and income insurance programs available through various governmental agencies.

Insurance When the Risk May Not Occur

There is a very distinct and important difference between life insurance and the other common forms of personal insurance. With life insurance, as long as the policy remains in force, the company must pay the agreed-on benefits to the designated beneficiary at a fixed date: the death of the insured. There is no question that the risk being insured against—the death of the insured—will occur. Because of the broad base of statistical information available, the insurance company is able to make a reasonably accurate estimate as to when that date will probably be. And the insurance company knows precisely how much it must then pay.

With the other common forms of personal insurance—health, income, property, and public liability—the risk that is being insured against may not occur. If it does, it might occur tomorrow or ten years from now. When it does occur, the company may have to pay a token amount to the insured, or a moderate or substantial sum. There may be a dispute as to whether or not anything should be paid.

With life insurance, you know for certain that a fixed sum of money will be available to you or your beneficiaries. With the other forms of insurance, the money you pay out may never be seen again. Human nature may lead us to think—perhaps dangerously so—that these kinds of risks will occur to others but never to us. We thus would never be out of pocket as a result of such occurrences, and perhaps we should therefore keep our costs for such insurance to a minimum.

In many respects, the potential losses that can be suffered as a result of risks relating to health, income, property, and public liability can be far more devastating than when a breadwinner dies leaving no life insurance. Vague and unpredictable though these risks may be, it would indeed be imprudent to fail to acquire the appropriate level of protection that can prevent a financial disaster.

The basic mechanics are generally the same for life insurance and the other forms of personal insurance. A contract (policy) is entered into between the insured party and the insurance company. The contract sets forth all of the rights and obligations of the parties, including the stated risks that are insured, as well as precise definitions of all the appropriate terms in the policy that can have a bearing on the rights of the parties. The insurance company holds and invests the premium dollars until claims have to be paid.

But the claim procedures with these other forms of personal insurance can often be much more complicated than with life insurance. When an insured individual dies, the company is notified of the death and makes the payment. But in the other forms of insurance, there may be many questions about the status of the insured or of the injured parties, and the extent of damages suffered may be subject to question.

Presenting a claim for payment with these various types of personal insurance may require filling out numerous and extensive forms. The information you submit on the forms may be subject to further investigation by the insurance company to determine the validity of the claims.

Although the vast majority of all claims are clearly defined in insurance contracts and are paid in accordance with the company's obligations, there is a continuing burden on the insured individual to comply with the requirements for getting satisfaction and for seeing to it that the full measure of the claim is clearly stated and received.

Health Insurance

The average American family might spend as much in a given year on hot dogs and breakfast cereals as it spends (directly or via fringe benefits) on health insurance. If the hot dogs are too fatty or the cereal is nonnutritive, nobody will suffer any great loss. But if money spent on health insurance—either privately or through an employer—isn't wisely planned and maintained, the results can be catastrophic.

The Gap

Currently, out of every $3 spent on private health care and health insurance premiums, only about $1 is returned to the public in the form of health insurance benefits. The other $2 is out of pocket. This is in spite of the fact that close to 90 percent of the working population is covered by one or more plans of health insurance.

Why should there be such a tremendous gap between what we pay for medical expenses and protective insurance, and what we get back in insurance benefits? Many individuals simply prefer to take their chances that they will not be exposed to risk, rather than spend a lot of money for insurance protection. Others may think they are protected by an existing health insurance program when in fact they are far less protected than they believe. Many people are adequately protected for minor and probable medical expenses, but are unprotected for the major catastrophic expenses. Many insurance policies do not increase their benefits at the same rate that health and medical expenses have been skyrocketing in recent years.

One of the single most frequent causes for financial distress is poor health and the lack of proper protection against medical expenses. Many segments of the population have been so poorly protected that the government has intervened—at enormous expense to taxpayers—to provide forms of basic medical care for those segments. Medicare is designed to take care of a substantial portion of medical expenses for the elderly; Medicaid, as administered by the various states and supported by the federal government, does the same service for those economically distressed. Further, for many years, the federal government has been debating the merits of a form of national health insurance to protect the population at large.

Whether or not the government sees fit to close the medical expense gaps for those who don't do this on their own, the prudent individual and family will see that their welfare is protected by designing and maintaining a sensible health insurance plan.

Reasons for the Gap

The following case histories illustrate some typical situations wherein people learn the hard way about the coverage gap in their health insurance programs.

Arthur's Case History   Arthur considered himself in the peak of health and never paid much attention to the sick-pay policies of his employer. It wasn't until a co-worker suffered an injury and was laid up for four months that he realized how vulnerable he was. Through his co-worker he learned that the employer would provide full pay for the first two weeks of any disability, then half pay for another month and a half, then nothing. After two months of disability, the co-worker had ceased to receive any income, and the total cost of his disability and recuperation put his family into a critical financial bind.

Arthur was thus a ripe prospect for an advertisement that offered "$200 a week extra cash when you're hospitalized . . . and $100 a week when you are recuperating at home!" Those were the two-inch-high letters that caught his eye. He skimmed over the small print in the advertisement, for it seemed too complicated. He bought the policy, and, even though he had ten days in which to return it if he wasn't satisfied, the small print in the policy also seemed too complicated. He retained the policy, assured that he was protected come what may.

A freak accident landed him in the hospital with a broken hip a few months later. Arthur was hospitalized for three weeks, and sent in his claim for $600, and received a check shortly thereafter. This was in addition to the sick-pay benefits he was receiving from his employer.

But he was in for a long siege of convalescence and rehabilitation, and wasn't able to return to work for ten weeks after he left the hospital. Three weeks after leaving the hospital he submitted another claim for the $100 per week that was due him, and again he got a check immediately.

Now the sick-pay benefits from his employment were near an end, but Arthur was not aware that his insurance policy benefits were also at an end. After another month, Arthur filed a claim for his $100 per week, but this time the insurance company notified him that he was entitled to no more benefits.

The small print that he had skimmed over and had not understood explained that the recuperative benefits were payable for no longer than the time he spent in the hospital. Three weeks in the hospital would entitle him to three weeks of at-home benefits. But no more. He had thought that the benefits would be payable for as long as any recuperation lasted, but the policy said otherwise. The remaining weeks of recuperation, with no source of income at all, made a serious dent in Arthur's savings account.

Brian's Case History   Brian was a bright business executive who was keenly aware of his family's need for protection against medical expenses. Ten years earlier, he had carefully shopped around for and had obtained a comprehensive medical insurance program. He filed the policy away, satisfied that he had insulated himself from any problem in the medical expense field, particularly major catastrophes. And he was fortunate, for ten years elapsed with no major health-care obligations. He dutifully paid his premiums, but, being a busy man, never took the time to review the coverage offerred by the policy, even though he was aware that medical costs were steadily rising.

Then his wife developed some strange intestinal pains, and the seige began—tests, x-rays, specialists, surgery, hospitals, drugs, postoperative care, nurses, consultations, more drugs, more x-rays, more tests, more nurses. But Brian never had a worry about getting it all paid for.

Finally, the doctor pronounced his wife cured, and Brian started to add up the bills. His ten-year-old policy had provided $25 a day toward the hospital room. That had seemed ample ten years ago, but today the cost was in excess of $300 a day. The surgical schedule in the policy allowed $100 for the needed operation, but the surgeon's bill now was $800. And so it went throughout all of the specific items Brian had to pay.

The insurance company paid fully and promptly, but the total payments that Brian received were only a fraction of the total bills. Brian realized too late what a costly error he had made by not periodically reviewing and updating his policy. For the sake of a few minutes every few years, he could have saved many thousands of dollars that were now gone forever.

Cora's Case History   Cora was widowed a few years ago, and though she was left with adequate income, she had no protection against medical expenses. Cora was not yet old enough to be eligible for Medicare, but she was old enough to believe what her friends told her about the cost and difficulty of obtaining health insurance at her age. She inquired of a few agents and found, indeed, that what her friends said was true. It was a costly proposition to acquire adequate protection, and she feared dipping into her limited sources of income to obtain that protection.

Like Arthur, she was ripe for the lure of an advertisement offering a medical insurance plan that "required no medical exam . . . absolutely no age limit." Cora mailed in the coupon attached to the ad, and a few days later was visited by an aggressive sales agent who, after scaring her with tales of what might happen to her, sold her a medical and hospital expense plan that, he said, would give her all the protection she might need.

Time passed, and an old kidney ailment came back to haunt Cora. She had all but forgotten about the condition, since she thought it had been cured many years ago.

She submitted her claim to the insurance company and was shocked to learn that they would not pay her anything. She was told that preexisting conditions weren't covered in the policy. Any condition that developed after she had acquired the insurance policy would be covered but none that had existed previously and recurred would be covered. Cora had been totally unaware of this clause. As a gesture of goodwill, the insurance company offered to return all the premiums she had paid in. But that was a small token compared to the medical expenses she had incurred. Her assets drained by the uninsured illness, Cora had to turn to public welfare.

**Big Print/
Small Print**

The big print giveth and the small print taketh away. As the case histories illustrate, a clear understanding of precisely what the insurance contract states is essential if an individual is to have protection. And this requires reading the small print, and understanding it. If the small print is too garbled by legal mumbo-jumbo, seek the assistance of the insurance agent, your family doctor, and any friends or associates who may be helpful. Sadly, many documents—particularly insurance policies—that we must understand to protect our financial situations are not worded in the language of the common person, but in the language of the lawyer.

To an extent this is necessary, for the wording must clearly define the legal obligations and rights of the parties. Some companies have attempted to present the contractual matters in a more easily understandable format, but not enough are doing so. Even when they are, the client does not always take the time to read beyond the big print to see what the small print says and means.

The big print says: "We will pay you up to $5000 if you are hospitalized because of illness or accident." But the small print says: "Payments shall not exceed $500 in any given year."

The big print says: "No more worries about surgical expense! We will pay you up to $10,000 on your surgical bills." The small print says, in effect, that the $10,000 is the outside maximum payable over the entire life of the contract. Any single claims are subject to a precise schedule of benefits, which may provide payments well below the actual costs. Furthermore, coverage may be for the surgeon's bill only and not cover such things as anesthetic, operating room fees, assistant surgeon, surgical nurse, and recuperative costs.

The big print says: "This policy is guaranteed renewable!" The small print says: "Guaranteed renewable to age 65 only, and annual renewals will be made at premium rates in effect at the time of renewal."

The Contracts

Before we delve into the specifics of different kinds of medical costs and the forms of insurance you can obtain, it is necessary to have an overall understanding of the workings of the contracts themselves.

The following precautions are necessary.

☐ Compare a number of plans in detail. Lay out a chart, perhaps, itemizing each point of coverage for each kind of insurance protection: for how much and how long are you covered? What exceptions or exclusions or limitations are there? What will the premium costs be? Only by doing this can you really get an accurate comparison of what the policies will offer you.

☐ Examine the policy carefully before you buy it. If an agent won't provide you with a copy of the policy he is selling, you can find other agents who will. Without a copy of the policy, you are buying big print, but getting small print.

☐ Examine the policy after you buy it. Conditions may have been imposed on the contract as a result of information contained in your application.

☐ Before you buy any policy, determine what actual current costs are in your area for various forms of medical care. This can be done with a few phone calls—to your local medical society, your doctor, and a local hospital. If the policy benefits aren't in line with actual costs, you'll find yourself footing the balance of the bill on your own.

☐ Review policies periodically, be they group, Blue Cross/Blue Shield, or individual. Old policies can be out of touch with current costs and may need updating or supplementing. Many policies contain riders that permit you to increase your limits from time to time. You may want to take advantage of these rights.

☐ Remember that it is the policy itself, and not what the sales agent says, that spells out the obligations of the insurance company. If, later on, the company refuses to pay a claim, you'll get nowhere if you tell them, "But the agent said . . ."

☐ Be well aware that the policy that seems the cheapest isn't always the best.

☐ Don't be fooled by some of the wording and language that may appear in mail order or promotional insurance advertisements. Many private companies will attempt to lure buyers by using slogans, replicas, and names that sound like government-sponsored programs. Examples may include such wording as "Medi-Care," "Veterans Insurance Division," "Armed Forces Policy," and so on. Envelopes may be created to resemble official U.S. government envelopes. Plans offered by these companies may be legitimate, but the sales approach is less than ethical and you could end up paying for far more than what you are actually getting. If you have any questions, check out the reputation of the insurance company. One source of such information is *Best's* directory, a rating service that will probably be available at your local library. Your local agent may also have a copy, and may be able to help you in deciphering the language in *Best's.* Other information sources include your state Insurance Department, your local Better Business Bureau, the National Council of Better Business Bureaus, and the Bureau of Deceptive Practices of the Federal Trade Commission (Washington, D.C.).

Understanding Health-care Costs and Risks

The first step in building a sound program of protection is to determine precisely what your existing health insurance coverage consists of. If you are protected under a group plan at work, the personnel office at your place of employment should be able to help you understand the precise limits of your coverage.

If you are privately insured, you may have to depend on your agent for help in understanding the details. If a policy—be it group or private—has not been updated within the last year or two, or if it does not contain automatic escalation clauses that increase the benefits in line with increasing costs, it will likely be necessary to amend your policy or find supplemental policies that will bring your level of coverage up to a par with current actual costs.

In addition to determining what existing coverage you have, you'll also want to evaluate what this coverage is costing you and how much more you can afford for added protection.

Health-care costs and the risks you'll be facing can be broken down into three ranges: minor, heavier, heaviest.

Minor Expenses

In the first range are the necessary minor expenses: periodic checkups for all family members, the inevitable smattering of doctor bills for injuries and common illnesses, prescriptions, first aid, and the like. Do you need insurance to cover these relatively minor predictable costs? Are you just swapping dollars with the insurance company—dollars that might better be spent protecting you against the major, unpredictable, possibly crippling costs? No two individuals are alike. Some may prefer to budget these costs in their normal expense program. Others may want the security of insurance even though, over the long pull, it's possible that they may be spending more on premiums than they will get back in benefits. In any event, it's worth looking at your current program to determine whether or not you are covered for expenses that you'd rather take your chances on, and save the administration costs that go to the insurance company.

Heavier Expenses

The second range of health-care costs involve the heavier, less predictable situations that entail hospitalization, extensive doctor bills, and surgery. These situations, in turn, can lead to loss of income due to the length of disability. In addition to out-of-pocket medical expenses and lost income, the convalescent expenses connected with such medical situations can be considerable.

Heaviest Expenses

Major diseases and injuries can entail expenses that swiftly mount into the many thousands of dollars. The initial expense is often followed by protracted periods of disability in which no work can be done and no income received. In addition to conditions that threaten life itself, many impose limitations on one's ability to work and otherwise function normally in society. It is this area of health-care problems—often referred to as "catastrophic"—that has been the primary focus of recent government attention looking to establish some form of federal protection for the public against such costs.

Slightly more than half of the American population has adequate or good protection against catastrophic medical costs. The balance is unprotected or has less than adequate protection.

Although it's logical to assume that a major disability to the family breadwinner would be most damaging (largely due to loss of income), a similar fate befalling any individual can be nearly as severe.

The difficulty in predicting potential costs increases from the first level of health care (the necessary minor expenses) up to this highest level. Fortunately, the health insurance industry in America has devised a variety of programs that can be tailored to fit our available budgets and help us achieve the necessary circle of protection that we're seeking.

Basic Hospital, Surgical, and Physician Insurance

These three forms of insurance protection cover three different areas of medical costs. Frequently, they are lumped together in one type of basic policy, such as in group programs and Blue Cross/Blue Shield programs. If an individual has more than one plan—such as a group plan at work plus a private plan—care must be taken to determine that coverage does not overlap or, in other words, that you are not protected for the same expense twice. Some policies will not pay you benefits if you have received benefits from another policy. Further, duplication of coverage means that you're paying more in premiums than you need to.

Hospital Insurance

Hospital insurance is designed to reimburse you for hospital expenses: room and board, nursing, minor supplies, and perhaps x-rays, tests, and medications. The major item—room and board—may be limited to a maximum amount per day, for a maximum number of days. The other items may also be limited to specific dollar amounts. In evaluating the adequacy of hospital insurance, you must take into account the following:

□ What are the actual going rates at hospitals in your area, particularly the one you'd use if the need arose? What are the costs for a private room, a semiprivate room, and a ward? What about emergency room costs? Intensive-care unit costs? To what extent would the proposed insurance plan cover these costs?

□ Do your local hospitals anticipate raising their rates and, if so, to what levels? It can be assumed that hospital expenses will increase in the future. If you want complete coverage, does your plan contain provisions that allow you to increase the benefits for hospital care expenses? Would it make sense to pay an added premium to obtain higher coverages if such coverages can in fact be obtained?

□ Is the hospital you'd use covered under the proposed insurance plan? Some hospitals may be excluded from certain kinds of insurance policies, and you must determine this in advance.

□ Must you be an "inpatient" in order to be covered? That is, do you actually have to be registered in the hospital as a patient? Is there coverage for emergency room treatment and for outpatient visits?

□ For how many days of hospital stay are you fully covered?

□ Are you covered for any cause that may put you in the hospital, or are there exclusions? For example, mental disorders may not be covered, even if you are hospitalized.

□ Are there extra benefits for intensive care? These costs can be considerable, and not all policies will protect an individual against intensive-care confinement. If the policy offers optional intensive-care coverage, what is the cost, and what are the limitations?

□ Must you be in the hospital for a minimum number of days in order to be covered, or are you covered from the very first day? This type of clause is generally referred to as a "waiting period." Bear in mind that the average hospital stay is only about eight days. If there is a waiting period that leaves you unprotected for the first six or seven days, you'll recover very little for an eight-day stay, and you'll actually be out of pocket for the days during the waiting period.

☐ What limitations are there for such miscellaneous expenses as x-rays, radiation treatments, lab tests, nurses, anesthesia, oxygen, traction gear, plasma, ambulance costs, drugs, and medications? How does the protection offered by the policy actually compare with current going costs for these items?

☐ What benefits are payable, if any, for nursing care? Benefits may cover only a certain number of hours per day of nursing care, or they may offer 24-hour coverage. There also might be limitations on the hourly amount payable for nursing care regardless of the number of hours and other limitations regarding the type of nurse that you'll be reimbursed for.

Surgical Insurance

Surgical insurance pays for surgeon's fees and related expenses such as anesthesia, operating room fees, and assistant surgeons. Surgical policies may also provide some coverage for postoperative care and follow-up surgery if needed. Surgical benefits are usually tied to a specific schedule, and related expenses are often expressed as a percentage of the fee allowable to the surgeon. For example, a surgeon may be allowed as much as $400 for a specific type of surgery. The policy may further state that an assistant surgeon will be paid up to, say, 15 percent of the surgeon's fee, which would mean that $60 would be payable toward the fees of the assistant surgeon.

In analyzing the surgery-insurance aspect of your protection program, you must consider the following:

☐ What are the current going rates for various surgical services in your area? For comparison purposes, ask your family doctor or your local medical society for approximate surgical fees for some of the most frequent surgical procedures such as: stitching of lacerations; setting a fracture; setting a dislocation; tonsillectomy; appendectomy; hysterectomy; and childbirth. How do the surgical benefits of the insurance policy compare with actual current costs?

☐ A surgical procedure may require more than one incision. Or you may have two more operations through the same incision. Determine what the extent of coverage would be in such cases. If an incision has to be reopened for further surgery related to the original cause, would this be partially or totally covered in your policy?

☐ How much is allowed for the cost of assistant surgeon, anesthetist, surgical nurses, and operating room fees, and do the benefits payable compare with the current costs in your area?

☐ In order for surgery to be covered in your policy, must the surgery be done in the hospital? Some minor surgery may be done in a doctor's office, and this may or may not qualify for coverage under the policy. Further, a great deal of surgery is now being performed in ambulatory-care facilities. These are not hospitals, but they are equipped with virtually all surgical facilities and are designed so that the patient spends a minimum amount of time in them. It's a fairly new phenomenon, and you must determine whether any older policy, or a new policy, will provide coverage for surgery conducted in such situations.

☐ In many policies, the surgical schedule may be connected with the room rate schedule for the hospital portion of the policy. In other words, you would be entitled to a higher schedule of surgical fees if you select a higher schedule of room rate protection. Do you have the right to increase the surgical benefits at any time in the future? If so, to what limits?

Physician Insurance

Generally, physician insurance, or basic medical insurance, is designed to pay doctor bills for hospital visits, office visits, and house calls. There may be a dollar limit per visit, and there may be a limit to the number of visits that will be paid for. All plans differ. In determining the breadth of coverage offered by your physician insurance, you must determine the following:

☐ What are the actual going rates for doctors' visits in your area, including office visits, house calls, hospital calls, "overtime" visits (such as nights, weekends, and holidays), telephone consultations. Consider the costs involved, not just with your regular doctor, but with specialists as well, such as pediatrician; ear, nose, throat; internist; eye; skin; obstetrics and gynecology; and surgeons (for nonsurgical consultations).

☐ How much will your plan pay for each type of visit with each type of doctor, and how many visits will be paid for per family per illness or accident, and per year? There may be limitations in all these respects. Two seemingly identical policies may pay the same amount per doctor visit, but one may be much more strictly limited in the number of visits that will be covered during a given period of time.

☐ Will you receive benefits for diagnostic as well as for treatment calls?

☐ Are there any limitations concerning the type of doctors that you'll be covered for? For example, will you be covered for visits with chiropractors, osteopaths, podiatrists? To what extent would you be covered for eyeglasses? For prescriptions?

☐ What about dental coverage? In recent years, dental protection has increased considerably, particularly in group policies. Although a group policy is something that's made available to you, and your only choice is to accept or reject it, many people will want supplementary insurance beyond what their group policy offers, for both dental and medical purposes. Thus, it's important to understand what even a group policy will provide regarding these professional services.

Major Medical Insurance

A major medical policy—or "major med" as it's frequently called—is designed to protect you against the major, unexpected, and catastrophic medical expenses that seem to be so commonplace. The basic philosophy behind major med insurance is that you, the insured, will pay some of the minor costs on your own (either out of pocket or through the basic hospital/physician/surgery protection), and the major med coverage will then pay all or a substantial portion of the heavier costs. The initial costs that you yourself absorb are referred to as the "deductible." For example, a major med policy may have a $500 deductible per family per year. This would mean that the major med coverage would not come into effect until after the family had paid $500 worth of eligible expenses during that year. In such a case, if one individual used up the deductible, then all of the other family members would be eligible for the major med protection.

Another form of deductible might be, for example, $100 per person per year. In such a case, any member of the family would become eligible for the major medical coverage once he or she had incurred $100 worth of eligible expenses during the year. But the other members of the family would not become eligible until *each of them* had accumulated his or her own expenses up to the deductible amount.

Once the deductible has been met, the typical major med policy will pay 80 percent of all additional costs, and the insured will have to pay the other 20 percent. (Some major med policies may split this on a 90/10 basis, and a few might even pick up 100 percent of all costs over and above the deductible.)

Most major med policies will also have schedules for room rates and for surgical benefits similar to those contained in the basic policies. The company's obligation to pay, say, 80 percent over and above the deductible may be limited by these specific room rates and surgical benefit schedules. If a major med policy has a $50-a-day limit on hospital rooms, that's all it will pay, even though the policy otherwise states that it will pay 80 percent of your costs over and above the deductible. Where specifically excluded, the hospital room and surgical benefits will not fall into that 80 percent payment obligation of the insurance company. Many policyholders overlook this very important clause and are distressed to learn that the major medical plan has not paid all that they thought it would.

There will also be a maximum ceiling—a top limit of total expenses that the policy will pay. If, for example, the maximum is $25,000, then that's all the company will pay, and the insured will have to absorb any costs exceeding that.

How It Works

Here's an example of how a typical major medical policy works. The policy calls for an annual deductible of $500, with the company then paying 80 percent of all qualifying expenses above the $500 deductible, up to a total of $25,000.

The insured party, Mr. Ramez, has a 60-day hospital seige resulting from a severe heart condition. His total expenses are $26,000, including hospital room and board, x-rays, private nurse, cardiologist fees, physician's fees, lab tests, and so on. Mr. Ramez has to pay the first $500 worth of expenses, and the insurance company pays 80 percent of the next $25,500, or $20,400, subject to room rate and surgical rate limits. Mr. Ramez has to pay the remaining 20 percent, or $5100. The total out-of-pocket costs for Mr. Ramez are $5600—the initial $500 deductible and the remaining 20 percent of the excess over the deductible, which was $5100.

Mr. Ramez has now eaten into the maximum benefits payable under the policy, reducing his available protection by $20,400: from $25,000, the original limit, to $4600.

If Mr. Ramez had a basic protection package—surgical/hospital/physician—in addition to the major medical plan, that would have reimbursed him for a portion of the $5600 he was out of pocket. But the limitations in the basic plan might not have protected him adequately for the major portion of the total expenses.

Depending on the type of policy, the costs, and the family's financial circumstances, it might be advisable for some families to forgo the basic coverage and use those premium dollars to pay for a sound major medical insurance program.

Some homework is essential in buying a good major med policy. From company to company, and even within the same company, the coverage can vary widely. Here are some of the factors to consider and compare when shopping for a major med plan:

☐ How much is the deductible? Does the deductible apply per family or per person? What expenses can be applied toward the deductible and what expenses cannot?

☐ Does the deductible run for the full year regardless of the claims that may be made against the policy? Or does a new deductible start after each claim is paid? The latter situation might provide far less coverage, particularly if one person has more than one claim in a given year.

☐ How much above the deductible will the company pay—70 percent, 80 percent, 90 percent, 100 percent? This can make a considerable difference both in the level of protection you're receiving and in the premium you'll pay for the coverage.

☐ What is the maximum amount that the company will pay, and is it per person, per family, per claim, per year? If the maximum is used up, does it terminate the policy altogether? In some policies the maximum can be replenished over a period of time, thus allowing continued coverage.

☐ How much expense can you afford without major medical insurance? Determine the maximum limits on your basic insurance plan, and talk with your doctor to get an idea of the possible costs involved in major situations, such as heart disease, cancer, lung disease, and the effects of major fractures or other disabling accidents. How well prepared are you, between your existing assets and your existing basic insurance, to stand the cost of any such major medical catastrophe?

☐ How long does the "benefit period" run? The benefit period is the amount of time that benefits will be payable once the deductible has been covered. For example, a major med policy may state that the benefit period will run for one year. That means that if you incur medical expenses, the policy will pay benefits owing to you for up to one year. At the end of the one-year period, you must accumulate a new deductible before a new benefit period will begin to run again.

General Health Insurance Provisions

There are a number of provisions that can appear in any of the foregoing insurance policies that can affect your rights. They should be given careful attention when choosing a policy. The more important of these provisions are:

☐ *Maternity benefits.* What is covered and what is not? How much of a waiting period is there before maternity benefits will be payable? Maternity benefits may be optional, and obviously if you anticipate the birth of children, you'd want to take advantage of the insurance protection. If you've had coverage for maternity benefits in an ongoing policy, and you have reached a point of not having any more children, you should look into deleting that area of coverage from your policy because it can be costly. How will complications arising from pregnancy be treated—under obstetrical surgery benefits, under maternity benefits, or as regular sickness benefits?

☐ *Dependents.* To what extent are dependents, particularly children, covered? If children are born to you or adopted by you after your plan has begun, will they be covered and to what extent? If you have children now who may be incapacitated—mentally or physically—will they be covered by the plan, and with what limitations and up to what age? Until what age are children generally covered under your policies? Once they have passed that age, will they be permitted to continue coverage either on their own or under your wing, by the payment of an additional premium?

☐ *Waiver of premium.* As in life insurance policies, if you become totally disabled, a waiver of premium clause will protect you: there will be no need to make premium payments during the period of such disability.

Do your health insurance plans carry such a provision, and if so, at what cost?

☐ *Termination.* This can be particularly important in group health insurance situations. If you leave the job, presumably your protection under the group plan would cease. Will the insurance company allow you to maintain your protection individually once you have left, and if so at what cost? The extent of coverage offered by group plans can differ widely. If you have comprehensive coverage under an existing group plan, and you are anticipating changing jobs, will your new employer offer you comparable coverage? If not, you'll probably want to supplement the group coverage with a private plan. The costs of doing this should be anticipated before a job change occurs, since the cost can be considerable and may offset what seems to be a higher earning level at a new job.

☐ *Preexisting conditions.* As Cora's case history illustrated, many policies will not provide coverage for conditions that have already been known to exist. Some policies will permit coverage of these preexisting conditions after the passage of time, sometimes one year, but more likely two years. If you do have any known preexisting conditions that are even remotely likely to recur, this clause can be critical to your overall protection package.

☐ *Excluded or rated risks.* Many policies will not provide coverage for certain stated risks, such as injuries occurring during acts of war or riots. Other policies may exclude coverage from more likely risks, such as the onset of mental illness and the costs connected thereto. Still other plans might offer full protection, but at a higher premium cost if the individual is deemed to be risk-prone, either as a result of a preexisting condition or as a result of occupation. These specifications should be clearly understood before entering into a policy agreement.

☐ *Renewability and cancelability.* If a policy is guaranteed noncancelable and renewable, you have the right to renew it on its expiration. If a policy is cancelable by the company, or if you do not have a right to renew, the insurance company could terminate your insurance at the end of the policy term or could renew at a higher rate than you had been paying. In a guaranteed renewable policy, though, the rate can be increased only if the entire class of insured have had their rates increased. The company cannot single just you out for an increase. Generally, policies that are noncancelable and guaranteed renewable will cost more than those that can be canceled or be denied renewal. You're paying more money for the assurance of continued protection, but that expense may well be worth as much as any other facet of your health insurance policy.

☐ *Grace period, lapse, and reinstatement.* If you don't pay your premium on the due date, what grace period is there during which you can still pay the premium and continue coverage? Is there a penalty? If the policy does lapse, what rights, if any, are there to have the policy reinstated? If a policy has lapsed, the insurance company may examine your recent medical history as a stipulation for permitting reinstatement. If they determine that you have suffered certain conditions, they may allow reinstatement only if those conditions, or recurrence of them, are excluded from coverage. Consequently, it can be most imprudent to allow a health insurance program to lapse, particularly if such a condition has occurred during the time you've been covered.

Other Forms of Health Insurance Protection

In addition to the basic forms of medical insurance, there are other modes of protection that may be available. One—the health maintenance organization (HMO)—can offer a fairly comprehensive package. Others, such as Workers' Compensation, offer only a limited level of coverage.

Health Maintenance Organizations (HMOs)

HMOs are a form of prepaid medical-care facility. Instead of paying premiums to an insurance company and then being reimbursed later, if and when medical expenses occur, with the HMO you pay in advance a fixed amount each month, for which you are entitled to a broad range of medical services. Generally, you use the doctors and facilities provided by the HMO, rather than choosing your own. Preventive medicine is at the heart of the philosophy behind HMOs—regular checkups for all family members are covered by the overall fee you pay. It is hoped that major expenses can be avoided by early diagnosis and treatment of various diseases. HMOs have their own schedules of how much treatment is provided for what types of need; additional fees may be payable to the HMO for treatment and care beyond the normal maintenance programs. HMOs are a fairly new phenomenon. A handful have existed throughout the country for a number of decades, but it wasn't until the mid 1970s, when the federal government encouraged their development with substantial grants, that they began to proliferate. They are still relatively few in number, and the financial stability of some has not yet been proven. Some HMOs are backed by major insurance companies, and it would seem reasonable that their financial stability offers a greater level of assurance to subscribers.

Workers' Compensation

If you are injured at work, or if you contract an illness related to your work, you will likely be protected by state Workers' Compensation laws. These laws provide a fixed schedule of benefits for medical care and certain disability income benefits, as well as rehabilitation expense reimbursements. Each individual should consult the personnel office where he or she works to determine the extent of coverage provided by Workers' Compensation.

Medicare

Medicare is a health insurance program administered by the Social Security Administration designed to protect citizens 65 years of age and over. The costs of and the benefits provided by Medicare are amended from time to time, and anyone currently eligible for Medicare, or soon to become eligible, should check with the local Social Security office to determine what current costs and benefits are.

There are two aspects of Medicare: hospital insurance (the basic plan), and medical insurance (supplementary plan). These are referred to as "Part A" and "Part B."

Persons eligible for Medicare must pay an initial deductible amount with Part A, and a monthly premium in order to be protected by the medical insurance coverage, Part B. Part A, after the deductible has been paid, covers the bulk of the cost of hospital services and extended-care facilities, including rooms, meals, nursing, and certain drugs and supplies. Part B is designed to defray the cost of doctors' services, as well as related medical expenses for such things as x-rays, various equipment, laboratory fees, and so on. Medicare will cover a major percentage of these various expenses, but the insured may be responsible for a certain percentage as well. Part A, the hospitalization insurance, is also limited to a specific number of days.

Many older citizens have had the mistaken belief that Medicare is the ultimate protection for them against health-care expenses in their later years. Although Medicare does cover a substantial portion of normal medical expenses, many people have found themselves still heavily burdened by costs not covered by the program. A number of supplemental programs are available through major insurance companies, and any existing or prospective Medicare recipients should explore the advisability of obtaining some supplemental protection.

Do not mistake comprehensive supplemental health care programs for the often heavily promoted hospital supplemental programs, which offer "tax-free cash while you're in the hospital." Those programs offer cash payments only during periods of hospitalization, usually on a per-day basis. The lure of "$1200 a month cash while you're in the hospital" may seem attractive, but it's far less so when you realize that you're being paid only $40 per day, and that if there's a waiting period of, say, six days, and you end up in the hospital for eight days, you'll end up with only $80 in benefits, a far cry from $1200. These hospital supplemental plans can fill a very minor portion of the gap, but they should not be relied on as being any form of full-fledged comprehensive protection.

Medical Coverage in Homeowner's and Automobile Insurance

These other forms of personal insurance may contain medical payment plans that will reimburse you for certain medical expenses if guests are injured in your home or anyone is injured in your automobile. The amount of such protection may be minimal or extensive, depending on the premium you're willing to pay in your homeowners or auto insurance policies. Although they provide only a limited health protection plan, they can fill small gaps, and should not be overlooked as part of your overall package.

"Dread Disease" Insurance

Some health insurance companies have, in recent years, offered "dread disease" policies to protect you against costs incurred by such scourges as cancer. Numerous reports of scare tactics in the marketing of this type of insurance have prompted many state insurance departments to investigate these plans. In evaluating any such plans, you should determine whether or not the coverage offered duplicates what you already have in your major medical program. Also determine whether or not you can obtain the same coverage offered by the dread disease plan by expanding the limits of your major medical coverage, perhaps at a lower cost.

The Agent

As with life insurance, the agent who handles your health insurance program can be a valuable ally. He or she can assist you in determining the coverage gaps that you face and present a variety of ways by which these gaps can be covered within the budget you have available. If you're covered only by a group plan, it would be advisable for you to meet with a representative of the company carrying that plan and seek assistance in judging the extent of protection offered and ascertaining the gaps that remain.

The same general suggestions regarding a life insurance agent hold true with health insurance and the other forms of personal insurance. The agent who is willing to take the time to study your needs, who can communicate clearly and simply, and who is staffed to provide the measure of service you expect for the dollars you're paying is a most important professional within your overall financial structure.

Income Insurance

How long could you get by without any income? One week? One month? Six months? A year? What other sources could you call on for funds to live on? Your savings account? Your investments? The equity in your home? Friends or relatives or institutions who might lend you money?

Income can be lost in one of four ways: quitting your job, being fired, being laid off, or being laid up due to physical disabilities. With the possible exception of quitting your job, all of these occurrences are totally unpredictable.

Loss of work due to physical disability can mean more than simply lost income. With the disability may come added expenses of rehabilitation, recuperation, medicine and drugs, nursing, and other miscellaneous medical costs. Further, there can be intangible costs: the psychological depression that the laid-up breadwinner may suffer, the extra demands imposed on other members of the family, the natural worry over what prospects the future holds.

Existing Programs

There are a number of existing programs that give a moderate degree of protection against lost income. But for many people these programs won't be enough, and they will want to examine the opportunities offered by private disability income insurance policies. Before we delve into the specifics of that kind of personal insurance, let's briefly examine some of the other ongoing programs that may already be protecting your income.

Sick-pay Plans

The sick-pay plan at your place of employment should be examined to determine the level of protection it offers. Some employers have a set policy on how much sick pay they will provide for ill or injured employees. Others, particularly in smaller concerns, may "play it by ear" when an employee is unable to work due to physical disability. It would be sheer folly not to take the time to learn what your employer's program is regarding sick pay, for this is the core of your basic income-protection plan. A private plan, should you acquire one, must be tailored around and built on the foundation of your employer's sick-pay program.

Workers' Compensation

Workers' Compensation offers a measure of disability income to workers who are injured on the job or who contract an illness that is job related. But, needless to say, you could be physically disabled from causes not related to your work, in which case Workers' Compensation would be of no help to you. Through your personnel office, determine what Workers' Compensation benefits for disability income would be, because this, along with the sick-pay plan, is an important consideration in structuring any private plan for your ultimate protection.

Social Security

If you become totally disabled—that is, "unable to engage in any substantial gainful activity," according to the Social Security laws—you may be eligible for monthly benefits under the Social Security system. You can obtain more specific details from your local Social Security office.

Unemployment Insurance

Unemployment insurance offers a measure of income if you are laid off from work. Your state Unemployment Office can assist you in learning what benefits are payable and for how long. You will be expected to seek out other work if you are receiving unemployment benefits, and you may waive your rights to the benefits if you do not comply with state regulations.

Waiver of Premium Clauses

Waiver of premium provisions in your life insurance and health insurance policies can protect you, at least to the extent of those obligations. If you are disabled and unable to work, the premiums for those policies would be automatically paid for you. This is only a minimal level of protection, but it would at least assure that those important payments were being met, so that you do not further jeopardize your overall financial situation.

Credit Health Insurance

This is similar to credit life insurance, which is obtained in conjunction with a loan to pay off the loan in the event of the borrower's death. With credit health insurance, if you are disabled and unable to work, the loan payments will be made for you during the period of disability. The same protection may be available with your home mortgage. The cost of such insurance, and the benefits payable, will vary from lender to lender. If you believe this is valuable protection, you should determine the costs and the benefits available from various sources at the time you are negotiating the loans.

Evaluating Your Needs for Disability Income Insurance

In order to determine how much, if any, disability income insurance you may need, you must evaluate the foregoing sources of protection as well as the other personal sources of available income. These latter sources would include the ability of other family members to work and generate income; the size of your personal savings and investments and how much you'd be willing to dip into them and for how long; other assets that may be converted into cash such as the equity in your house, the cash values in your life insurance, plus vested rights in profit-sharing and pension funds that you may be able to get access to; part-time or temporary work that you yourself could do that could help reduce the strain; and loans or gifts from family, friends, associates.

Some of these sources you may dip into without hesitation. Others you might not want to utilize until all else failed. This is an individual matter that you must examine and resolve yourself. Once you have made a reasonable determination of outside sources of supplementary income, you can begin to examine closely the benefits available from private disability income policies.

Private Disability Income Policies and How They Work

Like life insurance and health insurance, disability income insurance is available in a vast variety of sizes and shapes. You may obtain an individual policy directly through a company, or you may obtain a policy on a group basis, such as through a professional association, a union, or a trade group.

Depending on your age, your occupation, and your income, you may be required to take a physical examination for a policy to be approved. The cost of the disability income policy can also vary depending on your age, income, and occupation.

The Waiting Period

One of the most important factors in shaping a disability income policy is the waiting period—the amount of time that you have to be disabled before the insurance will begin to pay benefits. It's possible to obtain a policy that will begin payment of benefits on the very first day of disability due to accident. Or you might obtain a policy with a waiting period of 15, 30, 60, 90 days, or even longer. Waiting periods may differ for accidental disability, and disability caused by illness (usually a seven-day minimum wait). Obviously, the shorter the waiting period, the higher the premium, for the company will become obliged to pay you all that much sooner. This is why it's so important to know what your sick-pay plan is at work. If your sick-pay plan will cover you fully or substantially for, say

30 days, there's not much point in beginning the disability plan until after 30 days of disability have elapsed. You can do so, of course, but you'll be paying a substantially higher premium, and you may not recover in disability benefits what the premium will cost you. Once your sick-pay benefits have been exhausted, you might want to look to your ready sources of other income before you begin the disability plan. If your sick-pay plan will last 30 days and readily available other sources can provide for another 30 days' worth of income, it might make sense to have the disability plan begin after 60 days from the date of the disabling incident.

Total Disability and Partial Disability

Disability income policies agree to pay you a flat fixed monthly amount in the event that you are totally disabled. Should you be partially disabled, the company will pay you a portion, usually half, of the full total disability benefit. The definition of total disability can be very important. If, in order to receive total disability benefits you must be totally unable to perform *any kind* of work, it may be more difficult to obtain such benefits. Many people who become disabled are unable to perform their normal job, but still may be able to perform other jobs on a limited basis.

If the definition of total disability states that you are not able to perform *your own specific tasks,* you might be more readily able to obtain total disability benefits. In this case it would not matter that you could perform other duties. The important distinction is whether or not you can perform your own normal duties in order to be considered totally disabled.

You should also determine whether the policy requires you to be either bedridden, home-bound, or under the care of a physician in order to maintain continuing benefits, whether total or partial. As with all insurance, the more liberal the benefits, the higher the premiums. You're probably getting more protection, thus you're paying extra dollars for the desired security.

How Much Protection?

Once the disability payments begin, how long will they continue? One year? Five years? Ten years? Lifetime? Policies may differ widely in this respect, as will the cost of the policy. There may also be maximum limitations on how much the policy will pay you over a lifetime. Many income disability policies will cease paying benefits or will curtail the benefits once you have reached age 65, even though you may still be working. Naturally, when you do cease work, it can be expected that the disability income policy will also cease, since it's designed to protect you against lost income.

Benefits that you receive from a disability income policy are not subject to income taxes. Thus, it's not necessary for you to try to obtain a monthly benefit that's equal to your actual income.

Some disability income policies will offer extra benefits in the event of a loss of a limb or limbs or loss of eyesight. Some will also offer death benefits.

All things considered, a sound program of disability income protection is similar to a sound program of medical expense protection. You may determine that you'd be better off dollar-wise taking your own chances on short-term minor disabilities and using the available premium dollars to amply protect yourself against the major long-term crippling disabilities. As with other forms of personal insurance, the right agent will help you evaluate your needs and illustrate the alternatives you have for protecting yourself against the probable risks.

Personal Action Checklist
Health-Care Costs and Insurance Coverage

As noted in this chapter, there is often a considerable gap between an individual's health insurance coverage and the actual cost of specific health care. This gap is frequently due to the fact that a health policy, whether a group or private, is simply not up to date with rising health-care costs.

The cost of closing the gap comes out of your own pocket. It can be foolhardy to be underinsured, and yet it can be costly to have too much insurance. A proper balance must be struck: what risks are you willing to assume on your own, and what risks do you want to buy insurance to cover?

With the help of your doctor and local hospital, obtain reasonable estimates of the following health-care items, and compare those costs with your coverage. The size of the gap will then become clear to you, and you can begin to take steps to close it on a cost-efficient basis.

Health-care items	Actual current costs	Your current coverage	Limits on your coverage	The gap
☐ Visit to doctor's office	_____	_____	_____	_____
☐ House call by doctor	_____	_____	_____	_____
☐ One-day in hospital				
Semi-private room	_____	_____	_____	_____
Private room	_____	_____	_____	_____
Ward	_____	_____	_____	_____
☐ One-day private nurse care	_____	_____	_____	_____
☐ Selected surgical fees:				
Suturing a laceration	_____	_____	_____	_____
Tonsillectomy	_____	_____	_____	_____
Appendectomy	_____	_____	_____	_____
Hysterectomy	_____	_____	_____	_____
Setting a simple fracture	_____	_____	_____	_____
Childbirth	_____	_____	_____	_____

Continued on next page

Health-care items	Actual current costs	Your current coverage	Limits on your coverage	The gap
☐ Assistant surgeon fees	————	————	————	————
☐ Operating room fees	————	————	————	————
☐ Anesthetist fees	————	————	————	————
☐ Postoperative surgical visits	————	————	————	————
☐ Ambulance costs	————	————	————	————
☐ X-rays	————	————	————	————
☐ Pharmacy items	————	————	————	————

Obviously, this is only a small sampling of potential medical expenses, but it should get you started thinking about what constitutes a well-rounded program. Update this worksheet every two or three years.

Consumer Beware
An Experiment with Mail-order Insurance

Health and disability insurance are heavily marketed through the mail, via ads in newspapers, and on television. Firms that sell mail-order policies maintain that their product can be less costly to consumers because mail-order selling is cheaper, per customer, than selling directly through agents. As an experiment, I responded to a number of mail-order insurance offerings. My survey was not scientific, but the results were convincing. You might want to try a survey of your own before you commit yourself to buying health or disability insurance through the mail. These were the results:

Inquiry No. 1. Eight weeks after sending in the coupon I had still received no reply. Had I really been in need of the insurance, or had I suffered any malady that could have given rise to a claim, I would have been out of luck.

Inquiry No. 2. I received a policy by return mail, and the bills for it started flowing in. It was a disability income policy, and I compared it in detail with other plans received directly from agents. The agents' plans all offered far broader coverage for about the same cost.

Inquiry No. 3. I never received a policy from the company, but I did receive bills urging me to pay the premium before my "valuable coverage" (whatever that may have been) lapsed and left me unprotected.

Inquiry No. 4. In response to the coupon, an agent called on me without an appointment. He was personable and tried to be helpful, but would not talk about any of the limitations on the policy unless I asked him directly. He seemed surprised that I knew to ask such pertinent questions, and in some cases he wasn't sure of the answers. He had no literature to leave with me and said there was absolutely no way for me to see a sample policy unless I signed up with him. Then, he said, I would have ten days to cancel if I wanted to. His main concern was to sign me up on the spot. Can't blame him for trying.

Inquiry No. 5. Again, an agent called without an appointment. The interview was similar to the one above. He did leave some vague literature, but no sample policy. "It simply can't be done," he stated. My express wish to study and compare the policy terms at my own leisure fell on deaf ears.

Inquiry No. 6. Same as No. 5: they would not provide me with a sample of the policy.

Even with a cancellation privilege, insurance is not a product to be bought sight unseen. All too often one doesn't exert the effort to cancel an inadequate policy, and the risk is then that you think you're protected when in fact you are drastically underprotected.

22 | Financial Planning for Later Years

Inside every person there's an echo of 10 or 20 or 30 years ago, when the younger self did something very right—or very wrong—and that action now has a very distinct effect on the older self. "If only I hadn't let that fast-talking salesman con me into that bum of a deal with my whole life's savings." "If only I had started to salt away money for retirement when I was 30, instead of now, when I'm 60." "If only I had paid attention to my pension benefits before I quit that job in a huff." So it goes.

Your years of financial maturity may seem far off, but the planning you do now, and the actions you take now, can have a most decisive effect on your security, or lack thereof, when that time does come. This chapter is intended to motivate you to think of the eventuality of that day and to ignite an awareness of:

☐ Your housing needs as your family begins to diminish.

☐ Your sources of income when work ceases.

☐ Your legal rights under your pension plan.

☐ Your capabilities of combating a seemingly permanent state of inflation.

☐ Your responsibilities to your future self and to your future family. How will you meet them?

Reaching Financial Maturity

There comes a time—it's different for everyone—when we reach a plateau that might be referred to as "financial maturity." This time, particularly for families, generally coincides with those years when children have grown up and moved out on their own. It's a period when we find ourselves looking at our personal and financial affairs from a new perspective. Many of our needs have changed, and many previously long-term, vague goals now begin to achieve sharper focus.

As we reach financial maturity our needs and attitudes toward a great many important financial matters are in a state of change. These matters include housing, investing, insurance, use of leisure time, and the ultimate direction of our working career. Many of the financial decisions we make in our 20s and 30s can have a profound bearing on our ability to fulfill goals during the mature years. Thus, thinking about and making plans for the years of financial maturity should begin at the earliest possible time.

The most dangerous course is to totally ignore the future. We live in an age of instant gratification, constantly urged and teased into buying things for the here and now. If we succumb to such urges excessively, we can end up ruining tomorrow for the sake of today. Tomorrow *will* come and we must be ready for it.

Let's take a close look at some of the major elements of financial planning for the later years, so that alternate choices can be properly envisioned and anticipated. We can only conjure with possibilities and probabilities; specific solutions will be strictly up to each individual and family.

Housing

"This is the old homestead. This is where we raised our family. This is where we feel comfortable. It's almost all paid for, why should we move?"

Or, "Without the children, we don't need this house to rattle around in any longer. Do we sell or do we stay, and what are the ramifications of either choice? If we sell, do we find another place in our present community or do we move to a new community? Do we find another house? A condominium? An apartment?"

Our housing requirements are often drastically altered with the onset of financial maturity, and our personal feelings may easily stand between us and many thousands of dollars that could help provide added security and comfort in the years beyond.

The dilemma is simple enough: retaining the old "family homestead" with its comforts and its memories, or exchanging it for another dwelling that may be more practical and economical.

Most homeowning couples in their 40s and 50s will have substantial equity in their homes. In addition to what they have paid in on their mortgage debt, the value of the property itself will probably have increased considerably. But as long as that equity is tied up in the house, it's not working for you—except to provide a roof over your head. You may be perfectly content with that roof and not wish for any other pleasures the equity may be able to buy for you. However, by selling or refinancing the house, you could avail yourself of the means to provide personal satisfactions previously unavailable because your money was tied up in the property. In addition to equity dollars, sufficient thought must be given to the costs involved in maintaining a home.

Further, one of the main financial advantages in homeownership—the deductibility of mortgage interest and real estate taxes—may be of far less value to you in the later years, particularly on retirement, than they had been in the earlier years. All these considerations must be carefully evaluated.

Let's examine the case of the Johnson family to see what alternatives faced them. The basic thinking in this example can be used to determine the specific dollar advantages in almost any other situation.

Mr. and Mrs. Johnson are in their mid 50s. Their children have moved out on their own and the large family home they purchased 15 years ago is now far too big for just the two of them. They've started to think seriously about retirement—planned for ten years hence—and they realize that their home represents their single biggest asset as well as their single largest monthly expense. They are puzzled about whether they should keep the house or sell it. And if they sell it, should they rent a dwelling or should they buy another?

Their house originally cost them $75,000. When they bought it, they paid $15,000 as a down payment and obtained a 30-year mortgage for $60,000 at 8 percent interest. The monthly payments on the mortgage totaled $440. Today, with 15 years yet to pay on the mortgage, they still owe roughly $48,000.

If they sold their house today, they could get $150,000, after selling expenses such as brokerage commissions. Thus, if they were to sell it and pay off their existing mortgage, they would have a $102,000 cash-in-hand nest egg to do with as they please. (Since the Johnsons would presumably be 55 or over at the time they sold the house, up to $125,000 of profit on the sale would be excluded from taxation. See chapter 12 for a more detailed explanation of this tax situation.) In addition to their current mortgage expense of $440, they have real estate taxes averaging $120 per month, property insurance costs of $40 per month, utility costs averaging $120 per month, and maintenance expenses averaging $80 per month. Their total outlay for shelter is, therefore, $800 per month.

Staying as Is

Let's assume that the Johnsons are willing to spend $800 per month for their basic shelter. They realize that inflation will boost their property taxes, insurance, utilities, and maintenance costs. But because they have a fixed-rate mortgage, the monthly mortgage payment will not be affected by inflation. Table 22-1 illustrates the approximate effect of inflation on their monthly housing outlay ten and 15 years from now.

They realize that they can only guess at the long-term impact of infla-

Table 22-1 | **Monthly Housing Outlay—Existing Home**

	Now	In 10 Years	In 15 Years
Mortgage	$440	$440	0
Property taxes	120	200	240
Insurance	40	70	80
Utilities	80	130	160
Maintenance	80	130	160
Total	$800	$970	$640

tion, but for purposes of this exercise, they have assumed that inflation will double those costs in 15 years. If the Johnsons decide to remain in the house indefinitely, their outlay will have crept up to $970 ten years from now, the time at which Mr. Johnson plans to retire. Anticipating that his wages will continue to increase between now and retirement, he has no worries about being able to handle that increased monthly housing outlay. Fifteen years from now, the mortgage will be all paid off, and as Table 22-1 indicates, their monthly outlay will drop to about $640.

Staying put seems to be the simplest course for the Johnsons, for it would involve no need to sell their home and look for another dwelling, nor would they have to worry about any financial manipulations. But is staying put the best course for them? What are their other choices?

Becoming Renters

If they sold the house now, they could rent either an apartment or another house. Instead of spending the $800 per month on the mortgage and housing expenses, they could apply it toward their rental. By selling, they'd also have $102,000 in cash to spend or invest as they saw fit. If they couldn't find a rental situation for $800 a month that pleased them, they could invest the $102,000 and use some of the income from that investment toward their rental.

If, for example, they invested the $102,000 in a plan that yielded 8 percent after taxes, that would generate $680 per month income for them. That, added to their current monthly housing outlay of $800, would allow them to spend $1480 per month on rent. And they would always have their $102,000 nest egg intact to do with as they pleased in the future.

If the rental increased on their apartment, it's fair to assume that the availiable yields on a $102,000 investment would also increase proportionately, thus allowing them to maintain a fairly level standard of housing over the long term.

Buying Another Dwelling

Another alternative would be to *buy* another dwelling—house, townhouse, or condominium—with the proceeds of the sale on their existing home. Let's say that the Johnsons find a new but smaller dwelling with a $100,000 price tag. They put $40,000 of their total $102,000 nest egg toward a down payment on the new house, and sign up for a $60,000 mortgage for 15 years at 12 percent. The new monthly mortgage payments would be $720. Let's assume that the taxes, insurance, utilities, and maintenance costs would be lower in their new dwelling because it's a more modest property.

Assume that those new monthly expenses are $100 for property taxes, $30 for insurance, $60 for utilities, and $60 for maintenance. This brings the grand monthly total outlay to $970—$170 more than they have currently been paying. Table 22-2 illustrates what their current outlay in a new smaller house would be for the present, and for ten and 15 years hence.

Table 22-2   **Monthly Housing Outlay—New, Smaller House**

	Now	In 10 Years	In 15 Years
Mortgage	$720	$ 720	0
Property taxes	100	160	200
Insurance	30	50	60
Utilities	60	100	120
Maintenance	60	100	120
Total	$970	$1130	$500

NOTE: Projections are based on an approximate annual inflation rate of 6 percent for property taxes, insurance, utilities and maintenance costs.

Remember that the Johnsons have $62,000 left over from the sale of their previous house. Assume that they put that to work in an investment that will earn them 8 percent after taxes, or roughly $410 per month. They can apply that income toward their housing expense and still leave the $62,000 nest egg intact for future use. Table 22-3 shows the net housing cost for the Johnsons in their new home, assuming that they apply the income from their investment toward these costs.

Table 22-3   **Net Housing Costs—New, Smaller House**

	Now	In 10 Years	In 15 Years
Base costs (from Table 22-2)	$970	$1130	$500
Income from $62,000 investment	410	410	410
Net housing cost, after applying investment income	$560	$ 720	$ 90

Currently, their net housing costs would be $560 per month. That's $240 per month less than what they now have budgeted for housing. They could, if they wish, begin an additional investment program with that $240 per month and create an even larger nest egg for their retirement years.

What About Refinancing?

If the Johnsons decided to stay put for the time being, would it make sense for them to refinance their existing mortgage? Unless the current interest rates are equal to or less than the original 8 percent interest rate on their existing mortgage, a refinancing at this time would be of relatively little benefit. Assume they were to refinance their existing $48,000 mortgage for a new period of 30 years at 12 percent interest per year. Their monthly mortgage payments would actually *increase* by about $54 per month, to $493 per month. Obviously, there's no advantage to such a move. However, if they wait another five years, the balance on their existing mortgage will have dropped to about $38,000. If they refinance at that time for a new 30-year term at 12 percent interest, their monthly mortgage payments would then drop to about $390 per month, or $50 per month less than what they are currently paying. Individual circumstances will vary, as will interest rates, and careful calculations will be necessary to determine the value of refinancing at any particular time.

Profit Potential

The Johnsons face yet another perplexity in trying to reach a decision: What profit potential might they be giving up if they sell their existing house? The house has doubled in value in the past 15 years. Will it double again in the next 15 years? If they sell now and become renters, would they then be giving up a veritable small fortune that they could reap in the future by selling later? On the other hand, if they sell now, and buy another house, what is the profit potential on that other house? Could it be more or less than the potential on the existing house?

If the Johnsons are risk takers, they might prefer to hold on to their existing house and take their chances on what the future housing market might bring. If they are more conservative, they might prefer to establish a workable plan that will ignore the unknown elements and give them a greater sense of security for the years to come.

There is no rule of thumb as to which choice is best for any given family. But there are choices to be made, and those choices should be evaluated clearly, with professional help, wherever uncertainty emerges.

Investing

Our investment attitudes and tactics will likely undergo a considerable change as we reach the plateau of financial maturity. Until now, we've been concerned with generating capital to meet the heavy expenses of housing, educating the children, and other family needs. Now, with those needs substantially accomplished, we turn to the philosophy of preservation of capital. While we were younger, we could afford to make mistakes and still recoup. Now we may be at an age when the specter of a financial loss via investments is more fearsome: we may have neither the time nor the ability to recoup.

The advantages of fixed income investing, as opposed to more speculative forms, become clearer. Although many individuals are just reaching their peak earning years at this stage, the feasibility of taking risks is diminishing. We simply have less time to recover from a poor risk. Anticipating some future time when work may cease, we begin to realize the importance of preserving our capital so that there will be adequate funds available. This does not imply that all attempts to generate capital in more speculative modes should be abandoned altogether. But the risk factor must be examined more closely and should be considered with much more respect than it may have been a decade or two earlier.

A portfolio of fixed income investments to preserve capital can take many shapes. Perhaps the line of least resistance is to take whatever lump sum you may have accumulated and put it into a long-term high-yielding bond or savings certificate and forget about it for as many years as it has to run. This minimizes the need to have your nose buried in the *Wall Street Journal,* keeping tabs on your capital and constantly looking for better opportunities. If you're locked into a given situation, you may regret it later if better opportunities do present themselves. On the other hand, nothing better may come along, and you'll be very content to ride it out with your locked-in situation.

But the prudent investor in the mature years must be aware of the value of liquidity and flexibility. To obtain liquidity and flexibility in the fixed income portfolio, one must consider the advantages of building a portfolio based on *staggered maturities.*

What are staggered maturities? Instead of investing a whole lump sum for one long period, the investor would break up the lump sum into perhaps three or four or five nearly equal segments and invest them for different lengths. For example, you have a $10,000 lump sum that you want to put into fixed income securities. Consider breaking it into four equal parts of $2500 each and investing each of the four segments for a different maturity: one segment for one year, one for two years, one for three years, and one for four years. Within each time span, you can take advantage of the highest yielding security available. Then as each segment matures, starting in one year, you can redirect that money into whatever is best at that time, considering safety and yield.

With a portfolio like this, you'd have one-quarter of your total nest egg roll over every year. In some years you might have to take a lesser yield than you had previously been earning on that segment because of a drop in overall interest rates. In other years you might be able to obtain a better return. With a program of staggered maturities (not exceeding a five- or six-year maximum) you're going to have a higher degree of control and liquidity with your nest egg, which could bring you a greater sense of satisfaction and financial return.

Overall, as noted in the chapter on fixed income investing, the fixed income portfolio allows you to predict with a reasonable degree of certainty how much money you will have available at any given future point. By sticking to fixed income investments with shorter maturities, you can avoid the problem of being caught in a long-term downtrend of prices on such fixed income securities as bonds. If you need to tap your nest egg, you will have minimized any worry that the value will have shrunk because of fluctuations in those securities.

Insurance

Financial maturity brings accompanying changes in our insurance program. We may have had a life insurance program designed to protect our family in the event of the premature death of the breadwinner. Now the family is on its own and we may have far better uses for those premium dollars. Moreover, because age renders us more susceptible to the risks of injury and illness, we must be increasingly concerned with our ability to cope with such circumstances both psychologically and financially.

Life insurance programs begun when one is in the 20s and 30s can have a most important effect on financial status in the 50s and 60s. If a young person is willing to sacrifice a bit of current pleasures for the sake of greater security and comfort in the future, he or she can create a life insurance program that will serve well in the later years. In the chapter on life insurance, we examined some of the deliberations and alternatives facing the young person in making a choice of various kinds of life insurance programs. Let's now look at the effect of one particular choice decades later.

When Joe was 30, he embarked on a straight life insurance program by buying a policy with a face value of $50,000. His annual premium for this life insurance protection was $653. From the very first day the policy was issued, Joe and his family had the peace of mind in knowing that $50,000 would be payable to his family in the event of Joe's death. Joe has lived a full and healthy life, and today, 20 years later, he is pleased to observe the nonforfeiture values in his life insurance program.

Table 22-4 illustrates the status of Joe's policy (See chapter 20, Life Insurance, for a more detailed explanation of how these nonforfeiture values work.) When Joe is 50, and the policy is 20 years old, Joe looks at his life insurance needs quite differently than he did when he commenced the policy. His children are grown now and there is not as much need for immediate cash to take care of his family in the event of Joe's death.

At age 50, Joe will have paid premiums totaling $13,060. The policy now has a cash surrender value of $14,450. In other words, Joe can cash in the policy and receive back *more* than what he has paid in. If he invests the $14,450 at 8 percent per year, he will have a return of $1156 per year, leaving his $14,450 nest egg intact. The net results: For the past 20 years he has guaranteed his family a substantial lump sum of money—$50,000—in the event of his premature death. Now, instead of being out-of-pocket $653 for premiums each year, he can have an added income

Table 22-4 | **Joe's Life Insurance**

At Age	Total Premiums Paid to Date	Nonforfeiture Values		
		Cash/Loan Value	Paid-up Insurance	Extended Term
50	$13,060	$14,450	$28,550	19 years, 103 days
65	22,855	27,550	39,950	14 years, 160 days

NOTE: Policies will differ with respect to these values.

of $1156 per year plus a cash nest egg of $14,450. If he cashes in the policy, the $50,000 coverage will terminate. Joe may also elect to borrow the $14,450 from the company. On an older policy such as Joe's, this can be done at an interest rate of 5 percent. Joe can then turn around and invest the borrowed funds at, say, 8 percent, and the difference between what he earns at 8 percent and what he pays at 5 percent will be money in his pocket. In the meantime, choosing this alternative, the policy will remain in force, except that in the event of Joe's death, the proceeds payable will be the face value of the policy minus any loans outstanding against the policy.

Joe's other alternatives are to convert the policy to a paid-up or an extended-term status. If he chooses the paid-up method, he can cease paying the annual $653 premium and will have a life insurance policy with a face value of $28,550, paid up for the rest of his life. He doesn't have to pay any more premiums, and, on his death, his survivors will receive that sum. If he converts to extended-term insurance, he will be able to stop paying premiums and still be insured for the full $50,000 face value for a period of 19 years, 103 days—until he's almost 70.

What if Joe continues to pay on the policy and keep it in force until he reaches age 65? He will have paid in a total of $22,855 in premiums and he will have a cash value of $27,550. The other conversion values for that age are indicated in Table 22-4.

The important thing is that the 30-year-old Joe did in fact create the program that the 50-year-old Joe or the 65-year-old Joe can now either continue or convert to suit current needs. The young man created a liquid and flexible package that the older man can benefit from.

Health insurance is also important. Many individuals reach retirement age and find that leaving their job means the cessation of a group insurance plan that had given them the protection they've needed throughout their working years. Now they might become totally dependent on Medicare and on costly supplemental programs. The person who had taken out a good supplemental or major med program in the younger years can leave a legacy for the older one: a well-rounded program that can continue beyond the cessation of work and provide abundant protection to the older family during years when they might be most susceptible to the crippling costs of medical care.

Activities and Idleness

Our personal activities and leisure pleasures may undergo substantial alteration when we reach financial maturity. Much of our free time in the younger years may have been devoted to family affairs or community activities. We may also find that our contemporaries are shifting from old patterns into new ones, and there's a natural need to pursue various interests jointly with friends.

One very serious problem arises from neglecting to develop outside interests that will provide a measure of satisfaction and constructiveness in later years. In spite of all the money one may have accumulated, the loneliness, boredom, and helplessness that can attack are overpowering.

To Work or to Retire

As financial maturity begins, so starts our thinking about how long we wish to continue working. This might be the most drastic forthcoming change of all.

If you intend to continue working, either voluntarily or out of necessity, what kind of employment might be available to someone with your skills, desires, experience, and needs? If mandatory retirement is not in your future, when will you voluntarily want to begin to taper off and how quickly? Will you want to take some new direction in your career, albeit at a later age? Will you want to try that certain something that you'd always wished you could do?

The earlier you can start shaping those thoughts into something tangible the better. If you anticipate a work activity that will take some investment on your part, the earlier you can start setting aside the necessary funds the better you'll be able to accomplish your desires. If no investment will be needed, you'll have all that much more time to establish extra reserve funds to see you through should the business venture not work out.

Some Particular Thoughts for the Older Single Person

The single person reaching financial maturity has some considerations slightly different from those of the married person. (By single we're referring generally to someone who does not have a family dependent on him or her and does not plan to have one in the future.) The single individual might easily justify spending more of his or her disposable income on personal pleasures than the married person. But the single person must be every bit as aware as the married person of the impending future and, unchecked by a constant companion, should avoid developing spendthrift habits that could be regretted later on.

Regarding insurance, the single person probably has fewer concerns and fewer budgetary obligations. A single who does not have a family dependent on him or her has obviously little need for life insurance and can allocate those dollars elsewhere. To the extent that a single wants to leave an inheritance to anyone, life insurance does provide a good vehicle for that purpose, as it does for a married person. But if insurance is simply for the welfare of surviving dependents, the single may choose to do without such protection.

Many singles may have life insurance policies acquired many years ago. If the original need for the insurance has diminished, the single might do well to examine the conversion privileges in the policies, as noted earlier in the case of Joe.

In health and disability insurance, the single has some other matters to be concerned about. Being alone, only one person's health has to be insured. This can represent a savings on premiums compared to what the couple and the family will pay. But if disability strikes, the single can be at a disadvantage—long-term convalescence can be a costly and time-consuming proposition. With a couple, the well spouse can assume many of the obligations and duties that the single might have to pay someone to do. Housekeeping, shopping, nursing care, and the like must be considered, and the costs can run high. It's essential for the single to maintain a comprehensive insurance program that will protect him or her in the event of long-term disability.

A single facing a long-term disability may be involved in some problems that need a lawyer's attention. If you are unable to act on your own behalf, for whatever reason, someone trusted should be allowed to step into your shoes and take care of important matters for you. These matters could be as simple as writing or endorsing checks, or as complex as selling a home. The Power of Attorney can be a valuable tool for the single, particularly in the event of an extended disability.

A Power of Attorney need not be given just to a lawyer; it can be granted to anyone you choose. But a lawyer should definitely draw up the documents. A Power can be limited to specifically stated acts or can be general in scope. A general Power of Attorney is very broad and should be entered into only in the most compelling circumstances. Your lawyer can give you more details.

Financial Arrangements for the Later Years

How much will you have to live on when your active working career tapers off and/or ceases altogether?

Before we take a closer look at some of the specific details involved in planning your retirement budget, we must discuss one very frequent comment: "Whatever we have to live on, it won't be enough because inflation will eat away at it."

We occasionally hear horror stories of elderly people forced to turn to public welfare or to pet food in order to survive during their later years. Such stories may be true and sad indeed, but they represent only an extremely small fraction of all those who have entered their later years, the vast majority of whom are able to live comfortably and contentedly within their fixed income. The prudent individual who has planned properly and saved scrupulously should not have these fears.

The Specter of Inflation

Inflation can be a specter, particularly if the ability to work has diminished or disappeared. But it can be coped with.

Upon reaching the later years, many individuals reduce their living expenses and thus blunt the effects of inflation. Moving to smaller quarters, moderating clothing needs, having only one car can sharply reduce financial needs. Many families will have paid off the mortgage on their home, and many will terminate or convert existing life insurance programs. These steps can create additional spendable dollars previously applied toward these purposes.

Beyond what a family or an individual does unconsciously to meet its diminished needs, they might also take some conscious steps to cut back so that their disposable income can still provide satisfaction. A review of any budget can reveal minor excesses that can be reduced or curtailed without materially affecting lifestyle.

The effects of inflation can also be blunted on the income side. Social Security payments are scheduled to increase in line with Consumer Price Index fluctuations, and many pensions also have escalation clauses tied to rising prices. Furthermore, as costs move upward, so inevitably do yields available on secure fixed income investments. If inflation starts to nibble away at a nest egg, the proper shifts into higher yielding investments can offset the inflationary bite.

Shaping the Budget

There are two primary sources of sustenance that must be considered in detail: income and principal. Income is money received from all sources such as Social Security, pensions, investments, and work. Principal is accumulated money working for you that may be dipped into for living purposes as the need arises. Until an individual or family determines how much it wants to spend, it can't adequately determine how much, if any, principal will meet their needs. The obvious and prudent tendency is to attempt to live off income and keep principal in reserve until needed. A careful review of your savings and investment program is necessary. How much principal do you have? How well is it protected? Can you count on the projected income from principal? If not, how can you restructure your investment program to offer better protection?

The Income Sources

The farther you are from a termination of work, the more difficult it will be to get specific figures on the sources of income that will be available. But at least ten or 15 years before you anticipate retirement, you should begin to obtain some estimates of what might be expected. As the date approaches, you should check with regularity—at least every second year, tapering down to every year—in order to focus more clearly on the ultimate income figures. One very sad mistake is to conjure up in one's own mind what these income sources might be—those who guess too high can be grievously disappointed. The proper way to go about this is to check with the specific sources and get their most reasonable conclusions as to the true amount of dollars that will become available.

Income from Social Security

Social Security payments are increased periodically as the Consumer Price Index increases. Because there is absolutely no way of knowing what those fluctuations might be in the future, there is no way of predicting what your ultimate Social Security check might be. But a visit with your Social Security office can be helpful in instructing you about probable trends. The closer you get to actual retirement, the more closely the Social Security Administration can estimate your income.

Income from Pensions and Profit-sharing Plans

Visit with your employer's pension or profit-sharing plan administrator to determine as closely as possible what money you may have coming from those sources. What options do you have with those funds? Will you be paid a fixed monthly amount and, if so, for how long? Will you be able to obtain a lump sum payment; what will it be and when can you get it? Will payments continue beyond the death of the working spouse and be available to the surviving spouse and, if so, for how long? The Pension Reform Law, passed in 1974, makes many provisions for the benefit of pensioners-to-be. The appropriate details of that law are discussed later in this chapter.

Income from Investments

As retirement nears and the ability to earn income from work diminishes, you'll seek more assurance that a fixed amount will be available to meet your needs. The trend toward fixed income investments becomes more pronounced under these circumstances and the more you solidify such a program, the more clearly you'll be able to see the kind of return that you can expect once you have retired. The greater your need to know what your investment income sources will be, the more motivated you will become to create a portfolio that clearly defines the sources.

Income from Working

Many people will continue to work long after they are eligible to retire. They may go into business for themselves or take a full- or part-time job out of either choice or necessity. But the farther away you are from retirement, the more difficult it is to predict how much postretirement income you might earn from working, or for how long it might continue. With the earning potential from work so unpredictable, it would be prudent not to rely upon any such income for your basic support and well-being. It would be better to consider any such income as "icing on the cake" to provide for extra comforts and leisure activities during retirement.

Due to peculiarities in the income-tax laws and Social Security regulations, it is possible for some people to end up with more spendable income—after taxes—once they have retired as compared with before retirement. For example, when Bernie and Flora were both 64, they had a total income from their jobs of $20,000 per year. After all taxes and voluntary pension contributions were taken into account, they were left with a net spendable income of $12,500. The following year, they retired. Just to keep busy, they took part-time jobs, from which they earned $3000 during their first year of retirement. They received an additional $3000 for that year from a pension plan, and $7200 from Social Security. The Social Security income was not taxable. Considering all taxes on their sources of income, Bernie and Flora ended up with a net spendable income of $13,000 during their first year of retirement, even though their actual income from work was a fraction of what it had been during their working years. In other words, they had more spendable money after retirement than they did while they were still working.

Postretirement income from work can also be affected by Social Security regulations, which can reduce your benefits if you earn more than a set amount during a given year from work. Anyone planning to work after starting to receive Social Security benefits, must determine immediately what the effect of the earnings will be on benefits. For many years these regulations have penalized senior citizens who wish to continue being productive members of society. The laws, however, and the philosophy behind them, have been undergoing close scrutiny by the government, and drastic changes may be in the making. Gaining an awareness of the effect of income-tax and Social Security laws on postretirement income is a necessary step in preretirement planning.

The Principal Sources

The principal sources of future spendable dollars may be easier to estimate than income sources, particularly if an investment portfolio is in fixed income situations. The potential principal sources are the following.

Equity in Your Home

As noted earlier in this chapter, many people will sell their existing home or refinance an existing mortgage to get access to the dollars they've been paying in over the years on their mortgage. This equity can represent a substantial portion of anyone's ultimate future nest egg and should be estimated as carefully as possible, and as far in advance as feasible.

Life Insurance Values

Individuals with conversion values in their life insurance policies should determine precisely what those values currently are and what they will be in future years, assuming premium payments are continued until a conversion is made. Personal circumstances will dictate whether to continue the protection of the life insurance in full, convert it to one of the other forms of life insurance, or retrieve the cash that's available.

Pension and Profit-sharing Funds

If lump sum distributions are available instead of monthly payments, these should be counted in your overall sources of principal.

Business Interests

If you have an interest in a business, either wholly or partially, how might that be converted into investable funds, and at what time? How can you best sell out your business or professional interest and on what terms?

Anyone in these circumstances must recognize when a business or professional practice is at peak potential and reach a decision as to how much energy should be devoted to the business compared to other pursuits. A common problem arises when a business owner begins to feel a diminution in energies regarding operation of the business. As energies diminish, so can profitability and, in turn, the opportunity to reap the best possible price on a sale of the business. The sad end result can be that the business falls far short of being able to provide for the needs of the owner at the time of retirement because the ability to sell it has been so negatively affected.

Prudent planning may dictate that when the business owner or professional recognizes the peak potential in his or her occupation, the individual should immediately begin to consider the feasibility of a gradual phase-out. This generally would involve selling the business to a younger successor or turning over the reins to a family member.

Existing Investment Portfolio

This would include all money you now have invested. Some of it currently may not be offering any return—you are hoping for a gain in value to realize your ultimate rewards. As retirement approaches, you may deem it advisable to convert these nonearning assets into earning situations where you can specifically gauge how much will be available to you at future points.

Potential Inheritances

Realistically, try to estimate inheritances from family members in the foreseeable future. Will the funds be in cash, securities, property, or some other form? Will they be earning assets or nonearning assets, and what would be involved in converting them into situations best suited to your personal needs? For example, you might inherit a parcel of income-producing real estate. Although this could generate an attractive measure of income, you might not want to continue ownership of the building. It might be a great distance away from where you live or you simply may not have the desire or expertise to deal with income-producing real estate. What are the prospects of selling the building, and what sacrifice, if any, would be made in your income picture if you convert the property into cash or other securities? These considerations apply to any inherited assets, except perhaps cash.

How Much and for How Long?

Most of us face the ultimate dilemma in the later years: to have enough money available to live within a desired framework for an *indeterminate* time, and possess the security of having sufficient funds to take care of virtually any contingency. Life expectancy and health factors are unknown quantities, but the amount of money available should be known. If, after work has ceased, you can live comfortably on income alone, your later years should be relatively worry free. The dilemma is compounded in those many situations where principal has to be invaded, minimally or substantially, to provide for necessities and contingencies.

In many cases, it's necessary for a lifestyle to be trimmed in order to conserve enough principal to guarantee future comforts and necessities. Temptations to dip into principal should be examined carefully. When the principal is reduced, so is your earning power.

Let's say that you have a nest egg soundly invested, and you want to dip into it to increase your monthly spending money. How much, and for how long, can you dip into the nest egg before you deplete it? As Table 22-5 shows, starting with a lump sum nest egg of $30,000, you could withdraw $269 per month for 15 years. At the end of 15 years you would

Table 22-5 | **Dipping into Your Nest Egg**

Starting with a lump sum of . . .	. . . you can withdraw this much each month, for the stated number of years, reducing the lump sum to zero . . .				. . .or you can withdraw this much each month and always have the original nest egg intact.
	10 years	15 years	20 years	25 years	
$ 10,000	$ 116	$ 89	$ 77	$ 70	$ 59
15,000	174	134	116	106	88
20,000	232	179	155	141	118
25,000	290	224	193	176	142
30,000	348	269	232	212	179
40,000	464	359	310	282	237
50,000	580	448	386	352	285
60,000	696	538	464	424	360
80,000	928	718	620	564	467
100,000	1160	896	772	704	585

have depleted the nest egg. Or you could withdraw $179 per month indefinitely, and always have the original nest egg intact. (In this latter case you are withdrawing only the interest earned by your investment.) The table is based on an interest rate of 7 percent per year, compounded quarterly, before income-tax considerations.

The 1974 Pension Reform Law: How It Affects the Rights of Workers and Retirees

In September 1974, Congress passed the Employee Retirement Income Security Act of 1974, more commonly known as the Pension Reform Law or ERISA. The purpose of the law was to correct abuses that occurred in the administration of pension funds that resulted in pensioners being deprived of monies that were due them.

The administration of the law is under the jurisdiction of two governmental agencies: the Internal Revenue Service and the Department of Labor. Both agencies will be producing regulations and guidelines, and the courts undoubtedly will be interpreting the regulations and guidelines for years to come, so specific elements of the law are bound to be modified. The following discussion is intended to acquaint you with the overall concepts. Persons accumulating pension benefits subject to ERISA should determine from their employer exactly what their benefits will be and what their rights are under the law as it becomes amended.

What the Law Says

The law is aimed at those pension funds that are "qualified" under the Internal Revenue Service regulations. Qualified pension funds, generally, are those maintained in such a way as to allow the employer tax deductions for the cost of contributions, and allow the employee receiving the benefits not to have to report those contributions as income until the money in the fund is later withdrawn. About 50 million Americans are thus covered by the blanket protection of the law regarding pensions.

The Pension Reform Law does *not* require any company to start a pension plan. But if a company does begin one, it must meet the requirements of the law. Further, the law does *not* stipulate how much money an employer should pay in pension benefits for employees, nor how much, if any, an employee should contribute. But the law does establish that once promises are made regarding pension contributions, those promises must be kept.

If your employer does not have a pension or profit-sharing plan, you should still be aware of the benefits available under the law. You may change jobs and go to a company that does have a pension plan, or people close to you may be affected by the law, and your awareness of its benefits can be helpful to them.

The Pension Reform Law attempts to correct abuses in these main areas: vesting, funding, folding, reporting, and managing.

Vesting

Vesting refers to that point when your benefits are "locked up" or guaranteed as a result of the time you've spent on the job. Say you've worked for a company for many years and you leave, either to change jobs or to retire. When you try to collect your pension, you're told you hadn't been on the job long enough to receive a full pension. You had not worked long enough to have rights "vested" in your behalf.

The Pension Reform Law is designed to eliminate the problem of when you are entitled to how much money. To better understand what this means, let's follow the basic steps involved in obtaining pension benefits from a company.

First you must become eligible to participate in the plan. The law states that any employee who is at least 25 years old with at least one year on the payroll must be taken into the pension plan if the company has one.

Once you become eligible, the company credits a certain sum to your pension or profit-sharing account each year until you either leave the company or retire.

The next step in receiving the benefits is *vesting,* or locking up whatever accrued benefits have been set aside in your name.

The employer must choose one of three vesting plans and stand by it. This requirement is retroactive from January 1, 1976. Vesting programs for all who have worked since that date must fall into line with the new requirements.

The three vesting choices are the following.

1. At least 25 percent of all your accrued credits must be vested in your account after five years of service; then at least 5 percent per year must be vested for the next five years; then 10 percent per year must be vested after that until you're fully vested, which will be by the fifteenth year.

Table 22-6 shows an example of this vesting plan. It's based on the assumption that the employer is contributing $500 per year to an employee's pension fund account, once the employee has become eligible to participate in the plan. As you'll note, at the end of five years, 25 percent of the amount contributed up to that time has become vested. After the fifteenth year, 100 percent of whatever the employer contributes is vested—the employee will eventually get all that money.

2. The second choice is that the employer need not vest anything for the first ten years, but the employee must become 100 percent vested after ten years of service. In other words, if you work for nine years and then leave the job, you will lose all your accumulated rights to your pension. But if you work 11 years and then quit, you will still be entitled to those benefits accrued during those 11 years and can begin receiving them when you finally do reach retirement age, or sooner if the plan calls for an earlier payout.

3. The third choice is called the "rule of 45." You become 50 percent vested when the sum of your age and your years of service total 45. You become additionally vested by 10 percent each year after that until you become 100 percent vested.

One exception to the rule of 45 is that you must, in any event, have at least five years of service. Thus, if you join a company at age 44,

Table 22-6	**Vesting Choice No. 1—Example**		
Year	Total Amount Contributed	Percent Vested	Dollars Vested
1	$ 500	0	0
2	1000	0	0
3	1500	0	0
4	2000	0	0
5	2500	25	$ 625
6	3000	30	900
7	3500	35	1225
8	4000	40	1600
9	4500	45	2025
10	5000	50	2500
11	5550	60	3300
12	6000	70	4200
13	6500	80	5200
14	7000	90	6300
15	7500	100	7500

you don't fall under the rule of 45, when, after one year of service, you reach the 45 total. After five years of service, when you're 49, you would become 50 percent vested.

These vesting choices do not mean that you're entitled to a full pension once you've achieved full vesting. You may have to wait until you actually retire before any of the funds are available. In certain cases, an employer may be willing to pass on the vested funds to an employee in the event of an earlier termination. This must be determined directly with each employer in any specific individual case.

Note also that these vesting requirements refer to the *employer's* contribution to the pension fund. If you are making your own contribution, either directly or through payroll deduction, you are fully and immediately vested regarding those contributions.

An employer's plan must state which vesting alternative is being used. The employer must keep records of every employee's service and vesting. Each employee is entitled to a yearly statement from an employer concerning vesting and accrued benefit status. You must consult your employer to determine exactly what your benefits are under this important aspect of the Pension Reform Law.

Funding

Funding refers to putting enough money into the pension fund to meet the future promises to pay the benefits.

Say that XYZ Company has ten employees in its pension plan. By reasonable estimates, each of the ten employees will receive pension benefits of $50,000 over his or her lifetime after retirement. Let's assume that all ten employees retire on the same day and that they all request a single lump sum distribution of their benefits. On this mass retirement day, therefore, the XYZ pension fund should theoretically have at least $500,00 in it.

But what if the XYZ pension fund only has $200,000 in it? Why might this be so? Perhaps through some bookkeeping shenanigans or some imprudent investment, or perhaps due to a simple shortfall in the amount it was contributed, the company has missed the mark considerably. What then happens to the ten employees? They split up the $200,000 into lumps of $20,000 each and sit there in amazement wondering what happened to them.

The Pension Reform Law attempts to correct this possible abuse. It imposes very stringent requirements on all pension funds to put away the amount that they, according to reasonable expectations, will need to meet the targeted promises.

Despite the rigid requirements of the Pension Reform Law, a company may still violate the law and not properly fund enough money to meet its obligations. You may not discover this until the time for your retirement at which point, of course, it's too late.

Folding

A company for whom you've worked could also fold after you've already started receiving your pension benefits, thus putting those benefits in jeopardy.

The Pension Reform Law has created an insurance program that will guarantee retirees at least a *portion* of their benefits if their company folds. The law established the Pension Benefit Guarantee Corporation (PBGC) to administer this program.

This insurance program is intended to provide for benefits that are *vested*. If you become entitled to your benefits under the PBGC, the *most* you can receive is $750 a month. The actual amount you will receive depends on your highest paid five consecutive years while working for the company. The $750 limit is subject to change depending on future changes in the cost of living index.

In effect, the PBGC is like a safety net under the overall pension programs throughout America. But don't rely on it to the exclusion of any other safety nets that you might provide on your own through individual initiative and planning.

Reporting

The law has created these benefits and protections for the individual worker, but how is the average individual supposed to learn about them and keep up to date with them?

The law has seen to that too. Every eligible participant in a plan must be given a description of the plan plus a periodic summary of the plan "written in a manner calculated to be understood by the average plan participant." This summary must explain in detail the participant's rights and obligations under the plan. Additionally, the company must maintain open access to the latest annual report on the plan, and related documents must be available for examination by participating employees.

The written explanation shouldn't be treated lightly. You should study the booklet when you get it and ask questions if you don't understand. Sound financial planning requires that you know the exact status of your pension rights at all times.

Managing

The law sets stringent guidelines for the management of pension funds. It sets forth fiduciary duties, the punishment for their breach, prohibited transactions, and steps to avoid conflicts of interest between the respective parties. In short, it can be expected that the investment philosophy of pension funds will become much more conservative to comply with this requirement of the Pension Reform Law.

Pensions and Taxes

Individuals who are entitled to benefits under a pension or profit-sharing plan may be given the choice of receiving those benefits in one lump sum or in a long-term program of monthly payments. (This need not occur just at retirement, but can also occur at a much earlier age if an individual is leaving a job and has vested benefits due him or her.)

It's necessary for anyone in such a situation to do some careful arithmetic—perhaps with the help of an accountant—to determine which is the best long-term program. A prudent investment of the lump sum might generate a higher monthly income than the company's annuity program and could still leave all or part of the lump sum available for future needs.

Careful attention must also be paid to the tax implications on a lump sum payout. Income taxes will be due in the year in which the lump sum is received on that portion of the lump sum that represents the employer's contributions, as well as on the income that has been earned on all contributions. This tax bite can be considerable and can obviously cut into the earning potential of the lump sum distribution. But there are ways to defer the tax bite.

One way is to make use of the IRA Rollover. (The IRA—Individual Retirement Account—was discussed in detail in chapter 16.) If you deposit the taxable portion of a lump sum pension or profit-sharing payout into an IRA Rollover account within 60 days after you've received the lump sum, you thus defer the payment of taxes due on that amount until such future time as you withdraw the money from the IRA Rollover. Further, the funds invested in an IRA Rollover Plan will earn on a tax-deferred basis, again until money is withdrawn. If you withdraw money from an IRA Rollover before you reach 59½, you will have to pay a penalty to the U.S. government in addition to taxes then owing on the withdrawn sum. The penalty is waived in the event of death or disability. The withdrawal program must begin by age 70½. Funds invested in an IRA Rollover will earn on a tax-deferred basis until withdrawals are made.

The other way of deferring the taxation on a lump sum payout is known as the "ten-year averaging" program. You're eligible to choose this program if you have been in the pension or profit-sharing program for at least five years and if you receive the lump sum payout all in one year.

The advice of an accountant would be appropriate before making a choice between these various alternatives.

One Final Caution

The Pension Reform Law takes a lot of the guesswork out of how much a worker can expect to have on retirement. The provisions of the law can serve as an excellent planning guide for the 50 million American workers covered by pension plans. But a pension, unless it's most generous, should not be relied on solely as a means of support during retirement years. Regardless of what your pension rights might be, you still have to evaluate all other sources of income properly and structure your program in line with your needs. The pension may fall far short of fulfilling your needs, yet many people have made the mistake of assuming that it, plus Social Security, will be all they need. It's a mistake from which there may be no ability to recover.

Further, for the other 50 million individuals not currently covered by pensions, arrangements must be made to provide for necessary living funds when they do cease work. The IRA plan is a most attractive mode, along with other fixed income programs, plus the addition—where prudent—of more speculative techniques. The law can only help answer questions; it can't solve basic problems. For that, you must look primarily to yourself and to your own ability to do the necessary homework and planning.

Personal Action Checklist
Estimating Retirement Costs

Even though retirement may be a long way off for you, this exercise can help you envision changes in your financial situation once your working career has ceased. Assume you'll be retiring within the next few years. Estimate the changes in your income and expenses once that occurs. This will help you shape a workable budget for your retirement—something that most people don't do until it's too late.

	Now	Then
☐ After-tax income from work.	_____	_____
☐ After-tax income from investments.	_____	_____
☐ Social Security income.	_____	_____
☐ Pension, profit-sharing, IRA, or Keogh income (assume lump sum is invested at 10 percent annual income, and you're taking out only the income).	_____	_____
☐ Lump sum from any of the above, on hand for whenever you need it.	_____	_____
☐ Housing expenses, assuming you stay where you are.	_____	_____
☐ Housing expenses, assuming you move to smaller quarters.	_____	_____
☐ Extra income resulting from net gain on sale of home, after setting aside any down payment needed for purchase of new home.	_____	_____
☐ Transportation expenses (consider particularly that the "going-to-work" car may no longer be needed, or will be used much less).	_____	_____
☐ Clothing expenses.	_____	_____
☐ Food, both at home and out, considering work lunches.	_____	_____
☐ Entertainment.	_____	_____
☐ Insurance premiums (life, health, disability; retirement and Medicare often change one's insurance program considerably).	_____	_____

Consumer Beware
Excerpts from a Survey of Recent Retirees

"When I was 30 my employer told me that my pension plan would provide $511 per month at age 65. That, plus my Social Security, seemed enough to meet all my needs and allow my wife and me to have a leisurely and comfortable life at retirement. I left it at that and didn't make any other plans. We spent what we earned and lived well.

"Then came the blow. I was made to retire at age 62, at a $405 per month pension benefit. And times have changed! Not only am I getting more than $100 less than I expected, but the money I am getting doesn't go very far at all. If I had my life to live over again, I'd have anticipated this possibility and would have salted away some of my earnings in an investment program. . . . It can be a sad mistake to rely on a fixed pension program or Social Security alone. Nobody is going to take care of you later on better than you can take care of yourself."

———————

"I retired from my dental practice ten years ago, at age 62. We had no children, and quite honestly I never became involved in any hobbies or activities. Now I'm paying the price. . . . The worst part of retirement is too much time on your hands. Retirees should have hobbies or sports interests consistent with their health. The worst habit is getting bored and turning to the bottle."

———————

"Think young and resolve to be independent as long as you're able. Neither your children nor any organization owes you anything. If you think you've reached the age where now someone will take care of you, you're sadly mistaken. If you haven't long ago accepted the fact that only you are responsible for your future, then you're in for a rude awakening. Your family will keep in close touch, especially your children, but be prepared if they don't. They have their own lives to live and probably have their own problems. You'll be hurt and feel neglected, but don't throw their neglect up to them, for it will only alienate them. Let them see that you're happy."

———————

"Retire while you're still young enough to adapt to new surroundings. A sense of humor helps too."

———————

"Be as debt free as you can within the projected lifestyle you wish to enjoy. Interest on borrowings is a heavy drain."

———————

"Don't expect to be missed for long by former business associates and do not visit them unless invited. You should be realistic and accept the loss of clout gracefully."

———————

"The best advice is for the couple to get as mentally close together as when they were first married, and to remember that they cannot enjoy leisure without doing some work, nor can they enjoy pleasure without having some pain."

23 | Estate Planning: The Tools You'll Use

One of the most important—and most overlooked—aspects of personal financial concern is estate planning. It's important because it goes right to the heart of your financial structure, while you are living and upon your death. And it's overlooked because people don't like to think about their own mortality, let alone make plans regarding it.

Further, when people do investigate estate planning for their own purposes, they are often mystified and put off by the strange language and concepts that prevail in the field. As an introduction to the subject, we'll first examine the jargon and the tools used in the field of estate planning. This discussion will enable you to understand:

☐ What a *will* is, and how it works.
☐ Who are the various parties involved in an overall estate planning program, and what are their roles.
☐ Specific things that you can accomplish with a properly prepared estate plan.
☐ How you can, and should, utilize professional help in the creation of a sound estate plan.

Unexpected Problems

Barlow was 37 years old, in good health, and financially self-sufficient. All was well with him. Well, almost all.

Barlow's elderly widowed mother lived with him. She was in failing health, but relatively happy that she could live out her remaining days in comfort, close to her son and three beloved grandchildren. But this arrangement deeply troubled Barlow's wife, who was otherwise devoted to her husband and children. The wife was extremely bitter about having the mother live with them. She felt that it was an intrusion on her privacy and a negative influence on the children, and, perhaps most important, that the money Barlow had to spend for his mother's care was money that could have been spent by the wife for her own benefit. Barlow and his wife fought frequently and angrily over this issue. The wife had often expressed her preference that, given the choice, she would have the mother sent to the dismal county home for the aged so as to get rid of the whole problem.

Every Saturday morning, Barlow would play three sets of tennis with his old childhood friend, Murray. Murray was decidedly overweight, and Barlow constantly chided him that their Saturday morning exercise was the only thing that was keeping the obese Murray from an early grave. On one Saturday, with Barlow leading three games to one in the second set, Murray raced to the baseline to return a high lob. In midstep, he suddenly clutched at his chest, emitted a loud moan, and fell to the ground. He was declared dead on arrival at the emergency room, a victim of cardiac arrest.

It was weeks before Barlow recovered from the shock of his close friend's death. But one of the first things he was prompted to do when order returned to his life was to ask his lawyer one simple question: "Do I need a will?"

"Not necessarily," the lawyer responded.

"But I thought everyone should have a will," Barlow said perplexedly.

"If someone dies without a will," the lawyer responded, "the state in which he lives will determine how his wealth and property are to be distributed. This is what's known as the law of *intestacy*."

"What would happen to my wealth and property if *I* died without a will?" Barlow asked.

"Under the laws of our state—and each state has its own separate laws on this matter—your wife and children would split whatever there was. Your mother would get nothing," the lawyer noted.

Barlow felt a cold chill go through his body. Under these circumstances, he felt certain that his wife would immediately deliver his mother to the county home for the aged and that the wife would likely embark on a spending spree that could quickly erode the funds he had set aside for his children's college education.

Barlow expressed these fears to his lawyer, who in turn suggested that Barlow quickly embark upon an estate plan.

"Let us begin," said Barlow. "I had thought that such matters were best left to the later years. But I have learned now, the hard way, that it's time to do what's right."

This chapter, and the one that follows, are intended to acquaint you with the rudiments of estate planning. *It is not by any means a guide to preparing one's own estate plan.* But with the understanding that can be obtained by reading this material, you will be capable of discussing your own personal estate-planning matters with your lawyer, who is the properly qualified party for tending to the problems of estate planning.

A Minor Device to Aid in Your Reading

One of the most commonly used devices in estate planning is the "last will and testament," commonly called a "will." To minimize the confusion between a "will" and the other uses of the word ("I will follow my lawyer's advice"), "will," as used in this chapter, is typeset as follows: WILL.

What Is an Estate?

While a person is living, his or her "estate" is all that the person owns, less all of that person's debts. On the death of the person, the estate becomes a legal entity in its own right. When John Doe ceases to exist, the "estate of John Doe" comes into existence. This estate becomes the legal machinery that pays the estate taxes, distributes the property and money, and carries out all other legal wishes of the decedent.

If the decedent has executed the proper legal documents, most commonly a WILL, the activities of the estate will be carried out by the Executor, a person or an institution named by the decedent to carry out these functions. If the person has died without a WILL, the state in which he or she resided at the time of death will name an administrator who will be responsible for carrying out the laws of intestacy of that state as they apply to the individual's estate.

What Is Estate Planning?

Estate planning, simply stated, is the development of a program that will insure that any individual's last wishes are carried out regarding the estate.

We have two primary choices in distributing our estate. The first choice is to take steps on our own to insure that our wishes are *clearly stated,* that they will be *carried out,* and that they will receive the *full protection of the courts.*

There are many devices to establish the desired program. The most common is the preparation of a WILL. Other devices include life insurance, gifts, trusts, and simply spending it all, leaving nothing behind.

The second choice is to do nothing, in which case the laws of the state of residency at the time of death will determine the distribution of any estate.

In order to make a sensible choice between the two alternatives, we really have to understand the effects of each choice. If we exercise the first choice, and see that it's done properly, we can determine who will get what, and who will attend to the fulfillment of our wishes. On the other hand, if we choose not to take steps on our own, we owe it to ourselves and our families to know what the state laws are regarding distribution of an estate where there has been no other legal distribution set forth by the individual.

Each state has its own laws concerning this, known as "laws of intestacy." All state laws are somewhat similar, yet different. Each person must determine what the state laws of intestacy are, and how they might affect him or her.

The Rights Involved in Estate Planning

Rooted deeply in our legal tradition and its English origins are the rights of an individual to determine what will happen to his or her accumulated wealth upon the person's death. Our freedom is not total in this respect, but it is precious enough to take the fullest possible advantage of. Over the years, certain limitations have been placed on the overall freedom to distribute our accumulated wealth as we wish. For example, it was long ago determined that the federal government and some state governments would have a right to a certain share of our wealth. When the estate itself, as a legal entity, is required to pay taxes, these taxes are known as "estate taxes." The federal government levies estate taxes—though the 1981 Tax Reform Law has eliminated the federal estate taxation from all but a very small percentage of estates. Further, many states levy estate taxes.

In some states, those who *inherit* may become liable to pay taxes to the state. These are known as "inheritance taxes."

Our wishes may be limited because they are contrary to public policy. For example, a court may not carry out the wishes of a deceased person who leaves money to an individual on the condition that the individual marry or divorce a certain person or change religions or do or refrain from doing other things that society at large would deem improper or immoral.

Another form of limitation exists regarding surviving spouses. Laws differ from state to state in this respect, but, generally speaking, a surviving spouse has a right to at least a certain minimum portion of the deceased spouse's estate. If, for example, the laws of a specific state proclaim that a surviving spouse is entitled to at least one-third of the deceased spouse's estate, and the deceased spouse has expressed in his WILL that his widow will receive only 25 percent of the estate, the surviving widow has a "right of election against the WILL." In effect, she can disclaim that portion of the WILL that gives her only 25 percent, and, if everything else has been done in proper legal fashion, the spouse will then be entitled to the minimum allowed by the state, or one-third.

The overriding limitation on our freedom to distribute our wealth as we wish is that we must do so in accordance with the law. If we want the full protection of the courts, we have to play the game by the established rules.

The most obvious purpose of an estate plan is to determine who will get our money and property after our death. But there are other important purposes. In addition to distributing property, the legal documents of the estate plan can establish who will be responsible for carrying out the wishes of the deceased. If the individual has not named a party to do so, the courts will appoint one.

The proper use of an estate plan can minimize taxes; it can name guardians of orphaned children or other individuals previously under the guardianship of the deceased; and it can set forth specific instructions, such as funeral and burial procedures.

The deceased individual will of course never know the difference once dead, but he or she can live with a greater degree of peace of mind knowing that these wishes will be carried out because of a proper estate plan.

The Language of Estate Planning

The language of estate planning contains many strange words and phrases. Some people call it legal "mumbo-jumbo." Lawyers bandy these strange words about freely, not knowing whether their clients understand the meanings. To better understand the concepts of estate planning and to better prepare yourself to work with your own lawyer on your own plan, it's necessary that you grasp the meanings of the most common bits of jargon. Following is a brief glossary of the language of estate planning.

Testator (Female— Testatrix)

This is a person who makes out a WILL. When you ask your attorney to prepare your WILL for you, you are regarded as the testator or testatrix.

Decedent

A decedent is a person who has died. The testator eventually becomes the decedent.

Beneficiary

A beneficiary is one who receives an inheritance in the estate of a decedent. For example, your WILL may say, "I leave my summer cottage to my sister, Melba." Melba is thus a beneficiary of a portion of your estate, namely your summer cottage. But what if Melba should die before you? In your WILL, or in other estate documents, you can name a contingent beneficiary. A contingent beneficiary is one who takes the place of a named beneficiary who has already died. For example, "My summer cottage shall go to my sister, Melba, and if she dies before I do, it shall go to my other sister, Lucy." In this case, Melba is your beneficiary and Lucy becomes your contingent beneficiary in the event that Melba dies before you do. Had you not named a contingent beneficiary, the summer cottage may have passed through Melba's estate, to whomever she may have named to receive whatever she might have owned.

Bequest (Legacy)

A bequest is the specific property or money given to a beneficiary. In the above example, the bequest consists of the summer cottage.

Life Estate

A life estate is a form of bequest with some strings attached. To create a life estate, the WILL might read: "My summer cottage shall go to my sister Melba for as long as she lives, and on her death it shall go to the Boy Scouts of America, local chapter 123." In other words, Melba has the use of the cottage for her life, but she has no right to pass it on to anyone else on her death; at that time it will go the local Boy Scout chapter. You have given her a life estate in the summer cottage, and you have further directed who shall get it after her death.

**Executor (Female—
Executrix)**

This is a person, or an institution, that one names in a WILL to handle the affairs of the estate. Generally, the executor will be granted broad powers to allow him (or her or it) to carry out the directions of the WILL. For example, the executor commonly will be given the power to buy and sell properties and securities, and to do whatever else may be needed to carry out the wishes of the deceased as closely as possible. The executor may be entitled to receive a fee for his duties, but it is possible to arrange for an executor to serve without a fee. This will all depend on personal circumstances. The testator may request or require that the executor post a bond. This is a form of insurance that will protect the estate from financial harm at the hands of the executor.

The duties of the executor can be considerable. In addition to following the specific wishes of the decedent, he may also have responsibilities of a more personal nature to the family members. In all likelihood, the executor will need the assistance of a lawyer and an accountant in fulfilling all the needs of the estate, which can include the payment of estate taxes and income taxes when the estate has earned income on investments or properties prior to the disbursement of the funds to the ultimate beneficiaries. If an executor is unable or unwilling to fulfill his duties, the court will generally appoint a successor executor.

**Administrator
(Female—
Administratrix)**

If an individual dies without a WILL, the court will appoint a person or an institution to handle the affairs of the estate. This person is called the administrator or administratrix. Duties are similar to those of an executor, and the question of fees and bonds will probably be determined by the court.

Probate

Probate is a court proceeding in which the validity of a WILL is established. The term *probate* comes from a Latin word meaning "to prove" or "to examine and find good." If the WILL is properly drawn and executed and no one challenges its terms, the court will direct that the terms of the WILL be carried out. If a challenge arises that can't be settled by the parties, the WILL is thus "contested" and additional court proceedings might be needed.

As with other matters relating to the distribution of an estate, the laws of probate can differ from state to state. Generally, the attorney for the estate, acting in conjunction with the executor, will request that the appropriate court commence the probate proceedings. All potential heirs will have been notified and will be given the opportunity to accept or challenge the WILL as written. A would-be heir who wishes to challenge an otherwise valid WILL will have to do so at his or her own expense, which can be considerable.

A challenge to a WILL, or a contest, can be a most bitter and costly struggle. Even the most carefully planned and painstakingly drawn estate plan cannot guarantee that an outside party will not challenge it. But the chances of an outside party succeeding in such a challenge will be drastically reduced by virtue of the professional expertise that has gone into creating the plan.

Probate procedures are constructed so that frivolous claims or challenges will be quickly dismissed. In order for a challenge to be successful, the challenging party must have fairly clear and convincing proof that all or part of a WILL was invalid, or that the WILL being probated was not in fact the last WILL of the decedent.

The Will

A WILL is the most common form of device utilized in the formation of an estate plan. A simple WILL, which is adequate for most individuals, can be prepared quickly and inexpensively.

What Goes into a Will—the Basic Clauses

In a sense, a WILL is a form of contract: it is a legally binding document that sets forth certain rights and responsibilities of the parties and cannot be changed without the consent of at least the person who drew up the WILL. If the testator has had his WILL prepared in full compliance with the laws of his state, then, on his death, the executor has the responsibility for carrying out the stated wishes in the WILL, and the courts of the state are responsible for seeing to it that the rights of the survivors are given the full protection of the law.

The major clauses of a WILL that set forth primary responsibilities and rights are as follows.

The Introductory Clause

This generally is the opening clause of a WILL and should clearly and unmistakably state, "This is my last WILL and testament," or, "My WILL is as follows." It is essential that this clause establish that you are creating the WILL and that the document is in fact your WILL. If both you and the document are not clearly identified as to who and what they are, it's conceivable that another party might claim that this is not your actual WILL. For example, an individual might intend to create a WILL by writing a personal letter to his spouse, his children, or his attorney. He does not clearly identify the letter as being his purported WILL. In the letter he disinherits one of his children. After his death, the letter is introduced as being his actual WILL. The disinherited child, who would stand to gain considerably if there were no WILL (and the property passed through the laws of intestacy, which would assure each child a certain percentage of the estate) attacks the letter claiming that it is not in fact the true WILL of the deceased. The court will probably uphold the disinherited child, thus invalidating the purported WILL and requiring that the property pass through intestacy.

Revocation of Prior Wills

If an individual is creating a WILL, and has previously made another WILL, he should, assuming these are his wishes, clearly revoke the entire prior WILL by stating so clearly in the new WILL. If he does not do this, it's possible that the prior WILL, or at least portions thereof, might be included in the probate with his new WILL. If there are two WILLs, the latter one will generally control, except to the extent that the specific provision of the two WILLs are consistent with each other. But even this can cause unnecessary complications, which can be avoided by a clear revocation of the former WILL.

For example, a testator prepares a WILL in which he leaves a bequest of $10,000 to each of his grandchildren. At the time he drew the WILL he had two grandchildren. Many years later, he draws another WILL, but does not clearly revoke the earlier WILL. The new WILL contains the same clause giving $10,000 to each of his grandchildren. But now he has eight grandchildren, which means a total bequest to them all of $80,000. This is now a very substantial portion of his total estate. The question may well arise as to whether or not only the original two grandchildren were entitled to the $10,000 bequest or whether all eight are entitled to it. If all eight are entitled to it, other heirs might receive much less. The actual wording of the old WILL and the new WILL, perhaps with the assistance of the court in interpreting the clauses, will ultimately determine who gets what. But the example illustrates how confusion and disagreement can result where there are two WILLs that may convey the same intentions, but each with a substantially different effect on the overall estate.

Debts and Final Expenses

Before your survivors can receive their share of your estate, the remaining debts, funeral expenses, and taxes must be paid. Commonly, a testator will include a clause in his WILL instructing the executor to make all these appropriate payments. But even if there is no such clause, the executor will still be required to make them.

Each individual state law sets forth the *priority* of who gets what and in what order. If your state laws require that a "widow's allowance" be paid, that generally is the item of first priority. This is not the widow's ultimate share of the estate, but is usually a minimum allowance to enable her to get by for at least a short time. After the widow's allowance, the priorities generally run as follows: funeral expenses; expenses of a final illness; estate and other taxes due to the United States; state taxes; taxes of other political subdivisions within the state, such as cities and counties; then other debts owed by the decedent.

Creditors of the estate must generally file a claim against the estate if they wish to be paid. The executor may determine, or the testator may have instructed the executor accordingly, that certain claims are not valid. A testator cannot invalidate legitimate claims against his estate by simply stating in the WILL that those claims are not valid. However, if claims are in fact invalid, or even questionable, the executor's powers might result in eliminating such claims or minimizing them, particularly if the creditor does not wish to press the matter with the executor and the courts.

If, after all debts, taxes, funeral costs, and final illness expenses are paid, there is enough left in the estate to make payments to the survivors, such payments are then made in accordance with the "legacy clauses." If, however, these debts and expenses consume all that there is in the estate, then the survivors may receive nothing. In such a case, the estate is considered to be insolvent.

Legacy, or Bequest Clauses

These clauses determine which of your survivors gets how much. Broadly speaking, there are four ways in which property can pass on death to the survivors: through joint ownership with right of survivorship; through a specific bequest; through a general bequest; and through the residuary.

If property is owned in joint names—such as a home or a savings account—the property will pass to the survivor of the two joint owners on death, assuming that the ownership had been structured in that form. The WILL need not necessarily specify such matters, but it would probably be advantageous to make note of these items in the WILL to avoid possible misunderstanding.

A specific bequest, or legacy, will refer to a particular item or security. For example, a testator may bequeath to a child, "my stamp collection which is located in safe deposit box 1234 at the Fifth National Bank." The collection will pass to the survivor on the death of the testator, assuming that the testator still owns it at the time of death. If he no longer owns it, then obviously it cannot pass, and the gift will dissolve. The heir will receive nothing in its place unless the testator has specifically instructed the substitution of other items of value, or money, should he no longer own the collection. Further, if the subject of a specific bequest is not free and clear—it has been pledged, for example, as collateral for a loan—the heir will receive that property subject to the debt against it and will be responsible for paying off the debt unless the testator has instructed that he is to receive it free and clear. For example, the stamp collection may have been pledged as collateral for a loan. The collection is worth $10,000 and the balance on the loan is $2000. If the testator has not stated that the heir is to receive it free and clear, the heir can be responsible for paying the $2000 owed. If the testator has instructed that the heir should receive it free and clear, however, the $2000 debt will be paid out of other estate resources.

General legacies are those payable out of the general assets of the estate. Commonly, general legacies will be in the form of cash, such as "I bequeath to my housekeeper, Marsha Margolis, the sum of $3000."

Occasionally, there will be a form of legacy that is a cross between a specific and a general legacy. It's referred to as a "demonstrative legacy." For example, the testator instructs that his two nephews, Tom and Dick, each receive $3000 from the proceeds of the sale of his stamp collection, which is to be sold to the highest bidder at auction after his death. This may be construed as a demonstrative legacy. If the auction of the stamp collection brings only $5000, Tom and Dick might still be entitled to receive their full $3000 by dipping into the general assets of the estate for the remaining $500 apiece.

After all property has passed through either joint ownership, specific legacies, or general legacies, everything that's left is called the "residual." Commonly, this will represent the bulk of many estates. A typical residual clause might read as follows: "All the rest, remainder, and residual of my estate I hereby bequeath to my wife and children, to be divided equally among them." There may be further detailed instructions concerning the manner and timing of such distributions, including the possibility of trusts that would parcel out the payments over a specific period of time.

In planning a WILL program, it's essential that the testator and attorney discuss all these various provisions for distribution in detail. Further, as individual circumstances change over the years, these clauses should be reviewed to determine that the bequests are still what the testator wishes; and if the subjects of specific bequests are no longer owned by the testator, provisions should be made as desired for the proper substitution.

(Another minor definition should be noted: personal property generally passes through a WILL as a "bequest." When real estate is transferred, the transaction is commonly referred to as a "devise." For example, I bequeath to my son my diamond ring; and I devise to my daughter my summer cottage at the lake.)

Other elements of who gets what—and who doesn't—may include clauses of disinheritance; clauses that set forth a preference among various heirs; gifts to charitable causes; and clauses that release individuals from debts owed to the decedent.

Survivorship Clauses

Though rare, it can happen that a husband and wife will be killed in a common disaster, such as an automobile accident or an airplane crash. Each of their WILLs should have been created with this possibility in mind, particularly if there are minor children. The couple will want to determine who will be the guardians of the children in the event of such a disaster. If estate taxes are of concern to the couple, a survivorship clause should also set forth the sequence of the deaths (who is to have been presumed to have died first) in such a way as to minimize the effect of estate taxes.

Appointment Clauses

In this clause the testator will appoint the person or institution who will be the executor of the estate. Where personal circumstances dictate, a testator may also want to name an attorney for the estate to act in conjunction with the executor.

If other individuals—such as minor children or elderly parents—are dependent on the testator, the testator should also name the guardian for such individuals. This guardian will have the duties and responsibilities, and fee if any, that are specified in this appointment clause.

It's common for one spouse to name the other spouse as executor (or executrix). The testator wants to know that someone who is deeply concerned with the welfare of the survivors will be in charge of carrying out the duties of the executor. It should be noted, however, that the duties of the executor can be rigorous and demanding; the more complicated the estate, the more exacting the duties. A surviving spouse may not be equipped to handle many of the duties; thus, many prudent individuals will name an institution, such as a trust department of a bank, as a co-executor. The institution is fully staffed and capable of carrying out the specific legal and accounting responsibilities of the executorship, and in cases of substantial estates, such a co-executor should prove to be well worth the fees. The testator, in naming this co-executor, has the added peace of mind of knowing that the burden on the surviving spouse will be minimized; the personal concern will remain, with the added expertise of the financial institution.

The Execution

The final clauses of a WILL are very important. They are called the "testimonium clause" and the "attestation clause." The testimonium clause contains language in which the testator expresses that he or she is signing this document as his or her true last WILL and testament, as of the specific date on which the document is being executed. The attestation clause contains language in which the witnesses to the WILL agree that they have witnessed the signing of the WILL in each other's presence and in the presence of the testator on the specific date.

The combination of these two clauses should serve as ample proof that the document is in fact the last WILL and testament of the testator, that the document has been properly signed, and that the witnesses can verify all of this.

The execution of a WILL is a ritual that should follow the letter of the law. Each state's law determines how many witnesses should attest to the signing of the WILL by the testator. It is generally imprudent for any individual who may receive a share of the estate—either as a family member or as a recipient of a specific or general bequest—to act as a witness at the signing of the WILL.

In addition to the signing and witnessing at the end of the WILL, the attorney may have the testator and each witness sign or initial each separate page of the WILL. This may help serve as added proof that the WILL that is finally presented for probate is the true and complete total WILL of the testator.

Until the WILL is finally signed and witnessed, it is not in fact valid. Any attempt to shortcut the execution procedure might open the doors to anyone with thoughts of contesting the WILL if this person can prove that the WILL was not properly signed or witnessed by the appropriate parties.

Changing a Will

A WILL can be legally changed in one of two ways: it can be totally revoked by a brand new WILL, in which case the brand new WILL should expressly state that the former WILL is totally revoked, or minor changes can be effected by means of a brief document called a "codicil."

A WILL can *not* be legally amended by crossing out or adding words, by removing or adding pages, or by making erasures. A codicil should be drawn by an attorney and should be executed and witnessed in the same fashion as the original WILL itself. The codicil should then be attached to the WILL. If a WILL is amended in any way other than the creation of a new WILL or the creation of a properly executed codicil, it's all that much easier for anyone who wishes to contest the WILL to be successful. Further, a court might not admit to probate a WILL that has been changed by hand. Such improper changes could conceivably invalidate the entire WILL and could render the estate subject to the laws of intestacy. In short, a testator should not destroy all that he or she has created in the estate plan by making changes unless they are made in the proper, legally prescribed fashion.

Once a WILL has been drawn and executed, it's common for the attorney to keep the original in a safe or a fireproof file. You should keep a copy or two for your own reference, and if you've named a bank or other institution as executor or co-executor, the proper people there should also receive a copy for their files.

When Should a Will Be Amended?

A prudent individual should review his or her WILL and overall estate plan at least every three years. Depending on the extent of change in the individual's circumstances, revisions may or may not be called for. These are the common circumstances that might dictate the need to amend a WILL or any other portion of an estate plan:

☐ If the individual has moved to a different state, the WILL should be reviewed. Remember that the law of WILLs and estate distribution are state laws, and there can be slight or significant differences from one state to another. A change in state residence could therefore have a slight or significant impact on an estate plan. You won't know until you've had your plan reviewed by an attorney in your new state of residence.

☐ Changes in family circumstances might dictate the need to alter a WILL. Children may have grown up and moved out on their own. If one child has been particularly affluent and another has suffered economically, you might want to make provision to assist the less fortunate child. You may wish to add or delete charitable contributions, to amend your funeral and burial instructions, to add or delete specific bequests that you have made to individuals, and there is a myriad of other possibilities. The testator himself must see to it that changes are covered in the proper legal fashion.

☐ If there have been substantial changes in your assets and liabilities, a review of your WILL might indicate that changes are in order. If you have acquired substantially greater wealth since the original drawing of the WILL, this may dictate different modes of distribution to your heirs. If your estate has been diminished by financial reversals, appropriate changes might also be in order.

☐ If heirs named in your WILL have died before you, you might want to review the effect that would have on the distribution of your estate.

☐ If an executor or guardian named in the WILL has died or has become incapable of acting in the desired capacity, or if you simply no longer wish to have that person representing your interests, an amendment to your WILL would be in order.

☐ If tax laws change regarding estates, a review of your WILL would most certainly be in order. The changes wrought by the 1976 and 1981 Tax Reform Laws have a sweeping effect on millions of estate plans already in existence. Virtually all estate plans and WILLs prepared prior to the effective date of these Tax Laws should be at least reviewed by an attorney, and changes should be made where called for.

It's impossible to know when further changes may come about in the laws, and there are often court decisions that cast slightly new and different interpretations on existing laws. Any of these decisions could conceivably have an effect on your own estate distribution, and your attorney should be aware of such possible effects and advise you accordingly to make the appropriate changes.

Uncommon Wills

Occasionally a court will receive for probate a WILL that has been prepared by the testator in his own handwriting. It may or may not have the appropriate number of witnesses. A WILL that's prepared in the handwriting of the testator is called a "holographic WILL." Some states permit the probate of holographic WILLs under certain circumstances, but such WILLs are definitely not substitutes for WILLs prepared under proper legal guidelines. The courts recognize that individuals may be in dire circumstances and unable to acquire the proper legal counsel to prepare a totally valid WILL. Thus, allowances are made for the occasional probate of a holographic WILL.

In more extreme cases, a WILL may be spoken by the dying individual to another party or parties. Such a WILL, oral or spoken, is referred to as a "noncupative WILL." It's allowed only by some states, and then only under strictly defined conditions.

Neither a holographic WILL nor a noncupative WILL should be relied on as a substitute for a properly prepared WILL. A court may find such a WILL invalid and could throw the entire estate into a situation of intestacy. Where at all possible, proper legal assistance should be sought in creating a WILL. A store-bought WILL, with the blanks filled in, or a WILL prepared under the instructions of a "do-it-yourself" guidebook could prove to be totally futile and foolish. This is one of the most glaring forms of false economy—saving the legal fees involved in creating an estate plan could result in a far more costly and aggravating situation when a do-it-yourself WILL is either invalidated or contested with great bitterness by survivors or subjects the estate to unnecessary taxation.

Other Devices for Passing on One's Accumulated Wealth

In addition to the common WILL, there are other means whereby one may pass wealth to heirs and other generations. A trust is a "strings attached" way of passing money or property to another party.

Trusts

For example, you have the sum of $10,000 that you would like eventually to pass to your son, who is now 25 years old. But you're concerned that he might run through that money imprudently. You thus decide that until he reaches the age of 40, he should be entitled only to the income that the $10,000 will generate through investments.

When he reaches 40, he can have the entire amount. In order to accomplish this, you create a trust.

To be sure that your wishes are carried out without further concern on your part, you make an arrangement, for example, with your bank to administer the trust. The bank then becomes the "trustee." You deposit the $10,000 with the bank, which then agrees to invest it prudently and pay out the income to your son until he reaches the age of 40, at which time he will be paid the full principal amount.

That's an oversimplified view of the creation and function of a trust, but it's intended to make the point that passing money by trust is not an outright transfer. There are, as noted, strings attached. The trust agreement itself can stipulate just how much the beneficiary (your son) will get at what time and under what circumstances.

In the foregoing case, both parties involved in the trust are still living. This would be called an *inter vivos* trust, or a trust between the living.

A trust can also be established in one's WILL to take effect upon death. Instead of property passing outright to the beneficiary of the WILL, it may go in trust. For example, you might leave $10,000 in your WILL in trust for your son until he reaches the age of 40, with the full amount payable to him on that date. Where a trust is established in one's WILL to take effect on death, it's referred to as a "testamentary trust."

A trust can be revocable or irrevocable. A revocable trust is one that can be revoked or canceled. An irrevocable trust may not be canceled; it is permanent.

Under certain circumstances, trust arrangements may be desirable in place of a WILL or may be used in conjunction with a WILL. There is no fixed rule—it all depends on individual circumstances.

The law of trusts is complicated. A great deal can be accomplished with trusts, both in the control of property and in the minimization of estate taxes. An attempt at a do-it-yourself trust might be even more foolhardy than a do-it-yourself WILL because of the added complexities of the trust laws.

The trustee is the person or firm who has the duty of carrying out the directions of the trust. The trust document, which is a form of contract, spells out the trustee's powers and responsibilities. Many people prefer to use a financial institution as a trustee instead of an individual. Bank trust departments are operated by professionals, and there is an assurance of permanence. Such permanence has obvious advantages if a trust is designed to continue for many years. As with naming executors in a WILL, an individual might prefer to name both a corporate trustee (such as a bank) and a person close to the family as co-trustees.

Gifts

Making gifts of money or property is another form of estate planning. Gifts have long been popular with more wealthy individuals as a means of cutting down on their potential estate tax liability. By making gifts prior to death, money or property may escape taxation, wholly or partly. The overall desirability or feasibility of making gifts a part of an estate plan should be discussed in detail with professional advisors.

Insurance

For a great many families, life insurance is the predominant way of passing wealth from one generation to the next. Indeed, in families of lesser means, a life insurance program may be the only form of estate planning necessary. But it would be imprudent to rely on the existence of life insurance policies as a substitute for sound estate planning. Even the most modest estates should attempt a review with the proper professionals to determine what will occur on the death of each individual. Insurance can pass money from one generation to another, but it may not assure that the parties who need the money most, or who are most entitled to it, will get what the testator wishes. For example, an individual may have little estate other than life insurance policies, and if his children are named as beneficiaries, his widow may not receive what she needs for her own survival. If the children aren't willing or able to help her, she could be in dire straits. On the other hand, the widow could be the sole beneficiary of the life insurance policies, and the children could thus be deprived of funds that the individual wished them to have. These matters should be discussed with a life insurance agent, in conjunction with an attorney and accountant.

Joint Names

Putting property in joint names, such as husband and wife, often seems a simple and attractive way to insure that the surviving spouse will receive everything in the event of the other spouse's death. This may be true in many cases, but it can subject the total value of the estate to estate taxes that could have been avoided and may prevent the money from ultimately going where you had wished it to go. For families of more modest means, a joint-names program might suffice in many cases. It's not safe to make any assumptions about the ultimate distribution of an estate wherein everything is owned jointly—the advice of a competent attorney is still essential.

Other Uses of Estate Planning

At the beginning of this chapter, you were introduced to Barlow and his problems. Barlow followed his lawyer's advice and created an estate plan to pass his accumulated wealth and property to those he wished to have it. In addition to the distribution of wealth, Barlow also provided that his mother should remain in his home until it became no longer medically feasible for her to do so. He also established a trust program by which his wife and children would receive their inheritance over a period of years rather than in one lump sum. This arrangement, Barlow felt, would protect the interests of all concerned. Having thus created his estate plan, Barlow achieved a peace of mind that had eluded him for some time.

As Barlow's situation indicates, there are purposes of estate planning other than the distribution of one's accumulated wealth and property. An estate plan can be utilized to provide care for others, to manage money, to assure a continued lifestyle for the survivors, and to minimize taxation.

This chapter has reviewed the tools that one uses to create an estate plan. In the next chapter we will examine the objectives of estate planning and how the tools can be used to fulfill those objectives.

Personal Action Checklist
Distribution of Your Estate

Estate planning, properly done, should involve an attorney with expertise in the field. The assistance of an accountant and a life insurance agent can also be worthwhile. Even though federal estate taxes are scheduled to be phased out by 1986 (for all but a very small percentage of the population), there are still many important matters that must be resolved. Who will get what? How liquid are your assets? What provisions have you made to take care of the immediate and long-term needs of your survivors?

   The following checklist is designed to motivate you to commence a proper program of estate planning. It is based on the assumption that you will die tomorrow. You should acquaint yourself with your state's law of intestacy to learn what would happen if you died without a WILL or other satisfactory distribution arrangements (trusts, for example).

Your assets	Value	Who would get what?
☐ Your home	_____	_____
☐ Your personal possessions	_____	_____
☐ Proceeds of pension or profit-sharing plans	_____	_____
☐ Proceeds of life insurance policies	_____	_____
☐ Any debts owed you	_____	_____
☐ Your investment portfolio, specifically:		
Stocks	_____	_____
Bonds	_____	_____
Savings accounts	_____	_____
Real estate	_____	_____
Collections	_____	_____
Other	_____	_____
☐ Any business interests you may have	_____	_____

Consumer Beware
Interview with a Lawyer Who Has Done Extensive Work in Financial Counseling and Estate Planning: Part One

Q. What percentage of families actually go through a proper estate-planning program?

A. Very few. I would say it's probably under 5 percent.

Q. Why? Is it a matter of cost?

A. No, I don't think it's cost. For the average family the cost would not be at all great. A one- or two-hour interview plus the time to draw a simple WILL would be all that's entailed.

Q. Then what are the reasons most people don't get involved in estate planning?

A. I think superstition has a lot to do with it. Strange as it may seem, a lot of people feel that once they've prepared a WILL, they're going to walk out of the office and lightning will strike them. I know it sounds silly, but I and many other lawyers have seen that reaction all too often.

Many times we'll convince a client of the value of estate planning, and they'll have us go ahead and create a plan. Then, when it's time for them to come back to the office and sign the documents, they find dozens of excuses to cancel the appointment.

Again, it's probably a matter of superstition. And believe me, it can be expensive superstition. I've seen many cases where proper estate planning could have saved tens of thousands of dollars. And when I've spoken to families after a death, they're shocked to learn how much has to be paid in estate taxes, and how poorly the assets have been distributed.

When they ask why nothing had been done to prevent these chaotic situations, I explain that the deceased simply never got around to signing the WILL that had been prepared. You can't force them to sign, you know.

Q. Any other reasons?

A. Frankly, I'm afraid that I have to say that the legal profession in general has done a relatively poor job of acquainting the public with the advantages of estate planning. I certainly feel that the Bar Associations in each community and state can do more to educate the public concerning their rights and obligations.

Q. Where could this education be most effective?

A. Community colleges and four-year colleges are appropriate places for people to start learning the rudiments of estate planning. The younger the better, because estate planning is something that grows with you, and that you grow up with. If kids in school just learned what estate planning was all about, even if they never actually did anything, they would have a greater awareness of the needs and advantages of estate planning as they matured.

24 | Estate Planning: Achieving Your Objectives

This chapter continues the discussion on estate planning, more specifically directed to meeting actual objectives. It can be a mistake to think that an estate plan is something that pertains only to one's death. In fact, the creation of a sound estate plan can and should be an integral part of one's living plan. Overall, it's part of your goal-setting and goal-reaching endeavors discussed early in this book. The discussion that follows will assist you in doing your own planning by making you aware of:

☐ The consequences of inadequate or improper estate planning.

☐ The accomplishments that can be realized through sound estate planning.

☐ The ramifications of the federal estate tax, and the recent changes in the law that will affect the possibility of your estate being taxed.

☐ The importance of planning for the possible taxation on the estate of a surviving spouse.

☐ The worthiness of commencing your own estate planning at the earliest possible time, no matter what your age.

The Wrong Way

Nelson was a wealthy widower with two sons, Jeremy and Roger. Jeremy had taken over the family business and was dutiful, loyal, and devoted to his father. Roger, on the other hand, had a bitter argument with his father many years before and had run off to Paris. He had been there ever since, earning his living as a jazz guitarist. Nelson had long ago vowed that Roger would "never get a penny from me."

One reason for Nelson's wealth was that he carefully watched every penny that he spent. Thus it was that when he was ready to create an estate plan, he shunned the expense of a lawyer. Rather, he went to a local stationery store where, for $2, he bought a blank WILL form and proceeded to fill it out himself, leaving his entire estate to Jeremy. The blank WILL indicated that there were to be two witnesses to Nelson's signature. But since Nelson didn't want anyone other than Jeremy to know of this WILL, he had only Jeremy sign as a witness.

When Nelson died, Roger was shocked to learn that he had been disinherited by his father. Roger asked his lawyer to look into the matter, and after doing so, the lawyer recommended that Roger contest the WILL. If the WILL could be proved invalid, then Nelson's estate would be divided equally between Jeremy and Roger. The lawyer pointed out that there had been only one witness, whereas the state law requires two witnesses. Further, the only witness, Jeremy, was the heir to the entire estate, and that threw a further cloud over the validity of the WILL.

Under such circumstances, Roger could have an excellent chance of having the WILL invalidated, thereby upsetting Nelson's intent to disinherit him. By saving a small sum on legal fees, Nelson allowed half of his wealth to go where he had not intended it to go.

The Right Way

There is really only one proper way in which a desired estate plan should be implemented: with the aid of a capable lawyer. Any attempts—repeat, *any attempts*—at do-it-yourself estate planning can be fraught with danger. Last wishes may not be carried out as expressed; taxes may have to be paid when they could have been avoided; and survivors could be left in a variety of predicaments that could have been avoided.

Citizens of the United States have a very precious right: to pass a substantial portion of their acquired wealth to the survivors of their choice. These rights are protected by our courts. But in order to achieve their fullest protection, the wishes of any individual must be expressed in full and complete accordance with the law.

Each state has its own separate body of laws regarding how property passes from a deceased person to his survivors. In our highly mobile society, individuals move from state to state and may own property in states different from the one in which they live. Thus, it's possible to be affected by estate laws of more than one state.

Further, federal laws on estate taxation can have a bearing on the estate of any individual regardless of which state he or she lives in.

Thus, a lawyer, particularly one specializing in estate matters, is *the best* qualified party to tend to the problems of estate planning. He or she may see fit to call in other professionals—bankers, insurance agents, accountants—as the need arises.

The first necessary step in the creation of an estate plan is a visit with the chosen lawyer. During this initial meeting, you should disclose all of your assets, liabilities, and, most important, your estate-planning objectives. The lawyer will then be able to determine what estate-planning documents might be best suited to achieving your stated objectives.

What Should Your Estate Plan Accomplish?

Four main objectives should be kept in mind when creating or amending any estate plan.

1. To establish the proper distribution of assets and liquidity.

2. To establish a program of sound management of assets.

3. To provide for the assured continuation of a family's lifestyle in the event of death, disability, or retirement.

4. To minimize taxation. Three aspects of taxation must be taken into account: the federal gift and estate taxes that would come out of the overall estate assets; the taxes that the heirs may ultimately have to pay on inherited property; and, perhaps of slightly lesser concern, the income taxes that the estate may have to pay, if it has had earnings before the ultimate distribution of the assets to the heirs.

Let's now take a closer look at each objective.

Distribution and Liquidity

Distribution of one's assets and the liquidity of those assets go hand in hand. Distribution refers to "who gets what." Regardless of the size of your estate, you want to be certain that it will be distributed in the fashion you desire. Liquidity refers to the ability to put cash on the table as quickly as possible and with as little expense as possible. The more liquid one's assets, the easier it will be for everybody to get whatever it is they are to have. The most important reasons for having liquidity are to be able to provide for the immediate needs of one's survivors—spouse, children, and so on—and to be able to pay any estate taxes when they are due.

Mike's case illustrates the dangers in failing to make adequate provision for proper distribution and liquidity in one's estate.

Mike was a good provider, or so he had thought. Twenty years ago, when he was 40, Mike made some major changes in his life. He gave up his job as a plumber, and with a partner, Willy, he opened up a wholesale plumbing-supply firm. His only child, Maryanne, was soon to be married, so Mike and his wife, Sybil, decided to sell their home and buy an apartment house. They would live in one of the apartments. Mike also borrowed heavily to buy a large tract of vacant land 15 miles outside the city. He was confident that the city would grow in that direction, and that in 10 to 15 years this land would be extremely valuable as a site for a shopping center and new housing.

All of these things accomplished, Mike took one further step: He visited a lawyer to have a WILL prepared. For reasons that Mike had long-since forgotten, he left the land to his wife Sybil; the apartment house to his daughter, Maryanne; and his interest in the plumbing-supply business to be divided equally between Sybil and Maryanne. His lawyer advised him, and rightly so at that time, that his net worth was so low that there would not be any problem of estate taxes.

Twenty years later, this is the status of Mike's estate:

☐ Mike and Willy worked hard at their business and it prospered. Mike, with an easy and outgoing personality, was the "Mr. Outside" of the business. He took care of the sales, the customer relations, and the good will of the venture. Willy, on the other hand, was the "Mr. Inside." He took care of the books, the inventory, and the detail work, which Mike preferred not to handle. Both of them drew a decent wage from the business, and except for an occasional bonus, they pumped all of the profits back into the business. They were constantly improving their leased store and warehouse, updating their equipment, and expanding their lines. Twenty years after having begun the business, Mike was proud that he could draw a salary of $40,000 a year, upon which he and his wife could live comfortably. He was even more proud of the fact that he valued his share of the business at $200,000.

□ The apartment house also proved to be a good investment. It was a well-built building located in a desirable part of town. While it generated good rental income, Mike preferred to reinvest much of the income in improving the building rather than spending it for his own personal purposes. Today, after all expenses, the apartment house was generating $20,000 a year income, and if Mike wanted to sell it, he could reap $200,000 after all selling costs. He and his wife continued to live in the same apartment.

□ The vacant land didn't fare as well as Mike had hoped for, but his potential profit was still substantial. An anticipated highway was never built, and the community growth was not as rapid as Mike had expected. Had those things taken place, the land today might have been worth in excess of half a million dollars. Nonetheless, as the community grew, Mike felt that the land could now be sold in various parcels to net him $200,000.

□ Mike had no other assets of any consequence. All available income from the business and the apartment house were reinvested back into those entities, and Mike felt that his growing wealth precluded the need for any life insurance.

□ Daughter Maryanne's lot was not a happy one. She and her husband moved out of state, and while their marriage was basically happy, their financial situation was constantly in chaos. Mike had given them some financial help and guidance early in their marriage, but nothing seemed to change their wasteful, spendthrift ways. Many years ago, Mike had given up. He would no longer help them, and Maryanne felt very bitter and angry toward her parents because of this.

□ Mike was now a wealthy man—at least on paper. The value of his assets totaled $600,000. But in the 20 years since he had drawn his original WILL, he had never taken the time to reexamine it or change it in any way.

A Costly Failure to Plan

In spite of Mike's apparent wealth, his distribution of assets and lack of liquidity resulted in terrible turmoil upon his death. The problems Sybil faced were as follows:

□ The federal estate taxes due on Mike's estate were estimated at $100,000. Where would that money come from? Even after working out the best possible arrangements with the Internal Revenue Service,

Sybil was faced with the likelihood of having to either sell one of the assets or borrow against them, which would entail very expensive interest costs—costs that she could barely afford since there was little enough left for her to live on.

☐ An appraisal of the plumbing-supply business verified that, at the time of Mike's death, his interest was indeed worth $200,000. But no buyer could be found. Willy had become very difficult to deal with and without Mike's talents, the profitability of the business quickly declined. The income that Mike had been bringing home quickly shriveled to a fraction of what it had been. And that was the money that Sybil needed to live on.

☐ The apartment house had been willed to Maryanne, and she took the opportunity to get her revenge against her parents. She expressed her intention to sell the property as quickly as she could and pocket the profits. She told her mother that she could remain as a tenant in the building, but she'd have to pay rent like everyone else.

☐ In desperation, Sybil looked to the vacant land as her source of salvation. But in her grief, confusion, and anxiety, she was to be easily taken advantage of by any potential buyer. Given enough time and clear-headedness, she could have sold the land for a gain of $200,000. But under the circumstances, Sybil found herself accepting an offer for half that amount. And after paying the capital-gains taxes on the profit from the sale of the land, her nest egg was reduced even further.

Alternatives?   Mike's greatest error was his failure to review and update his estate plan. Had he done so periodically, he could have corrected the problems: total lack of liquidity and a distribution plan that gave the wrong things to the wrong people.

What else could Mike have done? He could have worked out an arrangement with Willy whereby Willy would buy out Mike's interest in the event of Mike's death. This could have been accomplished through a plan known as "key man" life insurance. It would work like this: Each partner would have his life insured for an agreed-upon amount—say, $200,000 in Mike's case. In the event of either partner's death, the life insurance proceeds would be paid to that partner's survivors, and the other partner would then gain the dead partner's interest in the business. In Mike's case, Willy would have ended up with total control of the business to do with as he pleased, and Sybil would have ended up with $200,000 cash to do with as she pleased.

By giving the apartment house to Sybil instead of Maryanne, Mike could have assured Sybil of the continuing rental income as well as a place to live rent free.

And by paying more attention to estate tax–avoidance techniques, Mike could have either reduced the tax liability on his estate or provided a more ready source of funds to pay whatever taxes were due. (Estate taxes will be discussed in more detail later in this chapter.)

It would have cost Mike relatively little to implement these or other alternatives. He, of course, is not around to feel the brunt of his planning errors. But his wife will have to live with them for the rest of her life.

Establishing a Program of Sound Management for Estate Assets

The bulk of Ned's estate consisted of life insurance and stocks. By the time Ned reached his mid-40s, he had accumulated a large enough estate to provide for his family in a most comfortable style, including education for the children and total peace of mind for his wife in the event he should die suddenly, as he unfortunately did.

Ned's plan had been carefully prepared, but he had made one major miscalculation. When left on her own, Ned's wife proved to be a very poor manager of money. Between her grief at having become a widow at such a young age and her lack of familiarity with the specifics of investments, Ned's estate was wiped out within a few short years.

Ned had at one time thought that because there was a sizable sum involved, he should arrange to have it flow through some form of managed program whereby the money would be allocated to the family as needed. But because of his faith in his wife and because of the cost involved in a managed program, he didn't do so.

Proper management of assets in an estate is a factor all too often overlooked, as is the distributional plan discussed in the case of Mike. Tales are legion of widows and children who have squandered money, been bilked, or were ill-advised.

The prudent individual planning an estate program must be aware of the need for sound management of assets for as long as the survivors will have use or need of those assets. Management can be accomplished in a number of ways. Assets can flow through a trust arrangement whereby income is paid to the survivors, and they can further have a right to tap the principal as and if the need arises for specific purposes. Insurance policies can be arranged so that the money is paid out over an extended period rather than in one lump sum. Similar extended withdrawal plans can be set up with annuities, mutual funds, and pension and profit-sharing plans. Whether a management program is set up formally, as through a life insurance company or a trust, or whether it's established by common consent among the parties, there is still no substitute for a basic knowledge on the part of family members about the nature of the assets of the estate, an awareness of the pitfalls that can jeopardize those assets, and a cool collected head to keep things on an even keel, particularly during the difficult early months and years following the death of the breadwinner. In short, education and knowledge are essential for a sound management plan.

As with all other elements of estate planning, the matter of management must be reviewed from time to time and amended as needed.

Assurance of Continued Lifestyle

Oliver worked out a fine estate plan, taking into account all the foregoing questions of distribution and management of assets. But his mistake came in viewing the estate plan as something that commenced at the time of death. His primary concern—the concern of many—was to provide ample funds so that his family could continue to live in their accustomed manner upon his death.

But he erred in failing to provide for that same lifestyle while he was still living. When Oliver first fell ill, his business associates continued to pay him a full salary for a number of months even though he was contributing nothing to the business. All his medical expenses were paid by a very comprehensive health insurance program. But after several months, his associates came to him and said they'd have to reduce his salary since the business was hurting by his continued sick-pay benefits and the loss of his energies.

Oliver could understand this and consented to it, feeling that he would soon be on the road to full recovery and at full earnings. But it didn't work out that way. A few months later his associates told him sadly that they would have to cut his salary down to a minimum level, and a few months after that it was terminated completely. Even though his medical expenses continued to be paid, there was no income, and Oliver had to start dipping into his reserves.

His illness lingered, and when he died three years later, the bulk of his estate had been used up. His heirs received virtually nothing. Oliver's case illustrates a most tangible problem that has very intangible solutions: an otherwise adequate estate demolished by unforeseen events. In Oliver's specific case, a solid program of life and disability insurance could have provided ample protection and allowed him to leave his estate much more intact. Those are insurable risks, but other occurrences are less insurable. A portfolio of investments can suddenly turn sour—stocks, real estate, business interests. The need to support elderly or disabled family members can drain one's assets suddenly and sharply.

Prudent individuals will insure against all foreseeable risks, within reason, without becoming "insurance poor." And they will further structure their portfolio of investments and business relationships to at least minimize the chaos that could result from unforeseen catastrophes.

Perhaps most important is to communicate with family members about the size and extent of the estate and what they can expect from it. They should be prepared for the contingencies they will face, realizing that the more knowledgeable they are, the better they will be able to cope on their own.

Minimizing Taxes

Carl had no worries about estate taxes. Two years ago, when he had his WILL prepared, his lawyer told him that his estate was not large enough to incur any estate taxes. At that time, Carl's total wealth was approximately $150,000: the equity in his house, which was worth $80,000; his investments valued at $20,000; his vested rights in a pension fund worth

$30,000; and his personal property worth $20,000. Carl signed his WILL, content that all his wealth would go as directed to his wife and children and none would go to the government.

But a lot can happen in a short period of time. Carl's wife ran off with Roger, a jazz guitarist from Paris, and Carl sued for divorce. His wife didn't contest the divorce—she was content to let Carl keep everything, including the three children. Further, and unbeknownst to Carl, his great-aunt Trudy had fallen critically ill and had included Carl in her WILL.

The $40,000 Hangover

On January 2 Carl awakened groggily—he had suffered through the previous day with a massive hangover due to overindulgence on New Year's Eve. Now that headache was gone, but a worse one awaited him in his mailbox. There he found two letters. One was from his lawyer informing him that the divorce proceedings had become final. The other was from a lawyer in Vermont telling him that his Aunt Trudy had died and that Carl was now the proud owner of one-third of Aunt Trudy's Vermont dairy farm, with his interest worth approximately $150,000.

The good news quickly turned to bad when Carl telephoned his lawyer to discuss these matters. "Alas," said the lawyer, "the value of the inheritance boosts your total worth to $300,000, and the divorce means that you can no longer take advantage of the important estate tax savings device known as the marital deduction. In other words," the lawyer cautioned, "if you were to die today, your estate would owe federal estate taxes of about $40,000."

Carl was dumbfounded. "How can that be?" he gasped. "When I went to bed last night, I could have died in my sleep and not owed Uncle Sam anything. Now I wake up in the morning and my estate could be in debt for $40,000 if I died today!"

Carl's lawyer then proceeded to explain to him how estate taxes work, and what can be done to minimize them or avoid them. What the lawyer told Carl is substantially what follows in the rest of this chapter.

How Estate Taxes Work

Not all estates will be subjected to estate taxes. But as Carl's case illustrates, an obligation to pay those taxes can arise unexpectedly. Or, more likely, the obligation to pay taxes can arise more gradually as one's wealth increases over the years due to inflation (such as in the value of one's house), appreciation in the value of one's investment portfolio, the addition of life insurance and pension benefits to one's net worth, and so on. If you are in your 20s or 30s today, your estate may seem too small to cause you concern about estate taxes. But as you reach your 40s, 50s, and 60s, your total wealth will likely increase by many times its current value, thus exposing you to estate taxation.

Sound financial planning dictates that continued attention be paid to one's potential estate tax liability. With proper advance planning, the costly bite of estate taxes can indeed be minimized.

Three Kinds of Taxes

Three possible kinds of taxes can arise when a person dies. They are:

1. *Estate taxes.* When a person dies, his or her "estate" becomes a legal entity. If the estate is large enough, the federal government will levy a tax on the value of the estate. The tax is to be paid out of the assets of the estate, generally before anything is distributed to the survivors. It often happens that an estate will have to sell investments or other property in order to pay the federal estate taxes. The federal estate tax is the biggest of all possible taxes arising on one's death, and it is the tax that will be discussed in greater detail in the sections that follow. In addition to the federal estate tax, some states also levy an estate tax.

2. *Inheritance taxes.* Some states levy an inheritance tax. This is a tax that is paid by those who receive inheritances. The basic difference between estate taxes and inheritance taxes are as follows: Estate taxes are paid out of the assets of the estate *before* anything is distributed to the heirs. Inheritance taxes are paid by the heirs *after* the estate has been distributed.

3. *Income taxes.* Many months, if not years, can elapse before an estate is distributed to all of the heirs. During that time, the assets of the estate may be invested and receive income. In such cases, the income received is subject to income taxes. A separate return must be filed for any such income earned by an estate. An inheritance that you receive is not subject to income taxes. If, say, you receive $10,000 from Uncle Willy's estate, the $10,000 is not considered taxable income to you. If you invest that $10,000 and earn $1,000 a year in interest, however, then the $1,000 income is subject to income taxes on your own personal return. If you receive property as an inheritance and you later sell that property at a profit, the profit is subject to income taxation.

The Federal Estate Tax

The following discussion incorporates the extensive changes in estate and gift-tax laws that went into effect at the start of 1982.

Beulah died in 1982. At the time of her death, Beulah owned a substantial interest in the family business and had a portfolio of investments that she had received as an inheritance from her parents. The total value of all assets that Beulah owned, including her personal effects, was $380,000.

Beulah's funeral expenses and the costs of administering her estate totaled $20,000. In her will, Beulah had made a charitable bequest to the Red Cross of $10,000 and a bequest to her husband of $50,000. The balance of her estate was distributed equally among her three children.

A few months later, after all the paperwork and proceedings were completed, Beulah's accountant notified her heirs that Beulah's estate owed $25,000 in federal estate taxes.

Table 24-1 illustrates how Beulah's estate tax was arrived at. Each of the items in Table 24-1 is numbered, and an explanation follows the table.

Table 24-1 | **Beulah's Estate**

1. *Gross estate*	$380,000
2. Less *deductible expenses and contributions*	− 30,000
3. *Adjusted gross estate*	350,000
4. Less *marital deduction*	− 50,000
5. *Taxable transfers*	300,000
6. *Tentative tax* on $300,000 = $87,800	
7. Less *credit* − 62,800	
8. *Tax due* $25,000	

1. The *gross estate* consists of everything that an individual owns or that is owed to the individual. This can include assets that may have been in joint names and that pass directly to the survivor of the jointly owned property. In Beulah's case, as noted, the *gross estate* totaled $380,000.

2. Certain *deductible expenses* are subtracted from the *gross estate*. These items can include funeral expenses, the costs of administering the estate, certain debts of the deceased person, and charitable bequests. In Beulah's case, these *deductible expenses* totaled $30,000.

3. After subtracting the *deductible expenses* from the *gross estate,* we arrive at the *adjusted gross estate,* which in Beulah's case was $350,000.

4. The *marital deduction* is one of the most important ways of reducing estate taxes. The *marital deduction* consists of that portion of an estate that is left, in proper legal fashion, to one's surviving spouse. For deaths occurring in 1982 or after, there is generally no limit as to the amount of *marital deduction* that can pass from one spouse to the other. This applies whether the transfer of wealth occurs before death or upon death. Note that gifts or bequests made to other family members, such as children or parents, do *not* qualify for the *marital deduction.* Only gifts or bequests made to the spouse qualify.

   Beulah could have made a bequest to her husband of her entire estate, but for reasons of her own choosing she only stipulated a $50,000 bequest.

5. Subtracting the *marital deduction* from the *adjusted gross estate* gives us the *taxable transfers.* This is the amount that is finally subject to the federal estate tax, and in Beulah's case it is $300,000. This is the amount upon which the *tentative tax* is calculated in accordance with Table 24-2.

6. Beulah's *taxable transfers* total $300,000. According to Table 24-2, the *tentative tax* due on that amount is $87,800. (In Table 24-2 note that where the *taxable transfers* are between $250,000 and $500,000 the tax is $70,800 plus 34 percent of the excess over $250,000. The excess figure is $50,000, and 34 percent of that is $17,000. Adding the $17,000 to the base $70,800, we arrive at a total of $87,800.)

Table 24-2	Federal Estate and Gift Tax Rates

Taxable Transfers (Via Gift or Estate, After All Proper Expenses, Deductions, Marital Deduction)	Tax Due (Before Credit)
Under $10,000	18 percent of Taxable Transfers
$10,000 to $20,000	$1,800 plus 20 percent of excess over $10,000
$20,000 to $40,000	$3,800 plus 22 percent of excess over $20,000
$40,000 to $60,000	$8,200 plus 24 percent of excess over $40,000
$60,000 to $80,000	$13,000 plus 26 percent of excess over $60,000
$80,000 to $100,000	$18,200 plus 28 percent of excess over $80,000
$100,000 to $150,000	$23,800 plus 30 percent of excess over $100,000
$150,000 to $250,000	$38,800 plus 32 percent of excess over $150,000
$250,000 to $500,000	$70,800 plus 34 percent of excess over $250,000
$500,000 to $750,000	$155,800 plus 37 percent of excess over $500,000
$750,000 to $1,000,000	$248,300 plus 39 percent of excess over $750,000
Over $1,000,000	For taxable transfers in excess of $1,000,000, a new schedule of rates will apply each year until 1985, when, for deaths occurring in that year and beyond, the maximum tax rate will be 50 percent on transfers in excess of $2,500,000.

7. All estates are entitled to a *credit* against the *tentative tax* due. For persons dying in 1982, the credit allowable was $62,800. (See Table 24-3.)

8. Subtracting the allowable *credit* from the *tentative tax* we arrive at a *tax due* of $25,000. The federal estate-tax return is to be filed within nine months of the individual's death. Extensions for payment can be arranged with the Internal Revenue Service.

The Credit Against Taxes

What would be the tax due (before credit) on a taxable transfer of $225,000? Referring to Table 24-2, you will see that the tax due on a taxable transfer between $150,000 and $250,000 is $38,800 plus 32 percent of the ex-

Table 24-3	Credit and Exempt Equivalents

Year	Credit	Exempt Equivalent
1982	$ 62,800	$225,000
1983	79,300	275,000
1984	96,300	325,000
1985	121,800	400,000
1986	155,800	500,000
1987 and later	192,800	600,000

cess over $150,000. The excess, in this case, is $75,000; 32 percent of that is $24,000, which, added to the base tax of $38,800, totals a tax due of $62,800. You will notice that that is the exact amount of the credit for deaths occurring in 1982. In other words, if a person dies in 1982 with taxable transfers (that's after all proper expenses, deductions, and marital deductions have been taken into account) up to $225,000, that estate will not be subject to federal estate taxes because the credit will equal the amount of tentative tax due. In short, for deaths occurring in 1982, taxable transfers of up to $225,000 are exempt from estate taxes.

The amount of the credit is scheduled to increase each year until 1987 when it will reach $192,800. This will result in an estate with taxable transfers totaling $600,000 being exempt from estate taxes. Table 24-3 sets forth the schedule of credits and the exempt equivalents through 1987.

Cutting Beulah's Estate Tax

If Beulah had made a bequest to her husband in the proper legal fashion of $125,000, her estate would not have had to pay any estate taxes. Why? Because such a bequest, qualifying for the marital deduction, would have reduced her taxable transfers to $225,000 and the tax due thereon would have been totally offset by the credit. It would thus seem a simple matter for virtually anyone to eliminate possible estate taxes by making a large enough marital deduction bequest to their surviving spouse to reduce the taxable transfers to a point where they would be offset by the credit.

However, it isn't always necessarily best to give the largest possible marital deduction to the surviving spouse. Much depends on individual circumstances, but the larger the marital deduction to the surviving spouse, the bigger the potential estate tax on the surviving spouse's estate when he or she dies. We'll examine the implications of the "second" estate tax—that on the surviving spouse's estate—later in this chapter.

Giving It Away

Beulah could also have eliminated the whole tax problem by giving away all or part of her wealth while she was still alive. Effective in 1982 and onward, an individual can make gifts to as many persons as he or she wishes, but if those gifts exceed $10,000 per recipient per year, the amount in excess of $10,000 is subject to taxation at the same rates as the estate tax rates. If both spouses join in making gifts, the annual amount that can be given per recipient without incurring tax liability is $20,000. (There is no annual limit with respect to gifts made to pay for the recipient's schooling or health-care costs.)

An estate that might otherwise be subject to taxation can be reduced considerably by making gifts over a period of years. Naturally, one does not want to make gifts imprudently, and the advice of your estate-planning lawyer should be sought before embarking on any program of gifts, whether to minors or to others.

Taxes on the Second Estate

In doing the estate planning necessary to minimize taxes, it's important to pay attention to the estate of a surviving spouse. If a surviving spouse does remarry, he or she may not wish the second spouse to share in the inherited estate. As is often the case, the surviving spouse would rather have his or her inherited estate pass on to his or her own children. This, of course, is an individual choice. But the effect of "cutting out" the second spouse is to eliminate the availability of the marital deduction and this, in turn, can increase the potential estate tax.

On the other hand, many remarried widows or widowers *do* want to pass some of their own inheritance to their second spouse. By doing so, they can also reduce estate taxes. Consider the case of Matilda and her three children, as shown in Table 24-4. Matilda inherited $400,000 from her first husband, Maurice. She then married Wilbur. Matilda invested the $400,000 wisely, and between Wilbur's income and her own income from the investments, she had no need to dip into her inheritance at all. Assuming, for the sake of simplicity, that on Matilda's death she would have an adjusted gross estate of $400,000, we can see in Table 24-4 the effect of three choices that Matilda might have made in planning her estate: leaving nothing to Wilbur; leaving $50,000 to Wilbur; and leaving $100,000 to Wilbur. (Assume that Matilda dies in 1982.)

As you can see, by making no bequest to Wilbur, Matilda's estate would be taxed heavily. Naturally, it's Matilda's choice as to who she wants to receive her money: the loved ones (Wilbur and the children) or the U.S. government.

Matilda could have gone yet a step farther and established a "life interest" for Wilbur, with the remainder passing to her children on Wilbur's death. For example, assume that their house was part of Matilda's estate. She could have given a life use of the house to Wilbur with the house passing to her three children on Wilbur's death. Wilbur's life interest in the house could have qualified as a marital-deduction bequest, assuming

Table 24-4 | **Matilda's Estate**

	Nothing to Wilbur	$50,000 to Wilbur	$100,000 to Wilbur
Adjusted gross estate	$400,000	$400,000	$400,000
Marital deduction	0	50,000	100,000
Taxable transfer	400,000	350,000	300,000
Estate tax (after credit)	59,000	42,000	25,000
Amount to children, after paying U.S. tax and bequest to Wilbur	(113,666 each) 341,000 total	(102,666 each) 308,000 total	(91,666 each) 275,000 total
Total amount to "loved ones"—Wilbur and children	341,000	358,000	375,000

that it was done in the proper legal fashion, and thus could have minimized further or even eliminated Matilda's estate taxes. Then, later, on Wilbur's death, her children will ultimately share in the proceeds of their father Maurice's original estate.

No Remarriage

What if a surviving spouse does not remarry? In such a case, of course, there would be no marital deduction available at all. The estate would be subject to maximum taxation unless the surviving spouse had taken other steps to minimize the tax burden.

The impact of the combined tax on the estates of both spouses is illustrated in Tables 24-5 and 24-6. Able, Baker, and Charlie all had identical estates. The only difference between them was the amount of the marital-deduction bequest to their wives. As Table 24-5 indicates, Able gave $100,000 to his wife; Baker gave $200,000 to his wife; and Charlie gave $400,000 to his wife. Assume that all three died in 1982.

Table 24-5

Able, Baker, and Charlie Estate Taxes

	Able	Baker	Charlie
Adjusted gross estate	$500,000	$500,000	$500,000
Less marital deduction	100,000	200,000	400,000
Taxable transfers	400,000	300,000	100,000
Tax due after credit	59,000	25,000	0

It would appear that Charlie's plan was the best of the three, since his estate wouldn't have to pay any taxes at all. But what will be the tax status of their respective widows' estates? Assume as illustrated in Table 24-6 as was the case with Matilda, that each of these three widows was able to live comfortably without dipping into her inheritance. Assume that they, too, all died in 1982 and that their adjusted gross estates equaled the amount of inheritance they had received from their husbands. Re-

Table 24-6

Widows Able, Baker, and Charlie Estate Taxes

	Mrs. Able	Mrs. Baker	Mrs. Charlie
Adjusted gross estate	$100,000	$200,000	$400,000
Less marital deduction	0	0	0
Taxable transfers	100,000	200,000	400,000
Tax due, after credit on her estate	0	0	59,000
Plus tax on his estate	59,000	25,000	0
Total federal estate taxes on both estates	59,000	25,000	59,000

member: the marital deduction is not available to them since they have not remarried.

As you can see, even though Charlie's estate had no tax liability, his wife was taxed heavily on her estate. Looking at the combined totals of these estates, it was the Bakers who got away with the least tax. There is no rule of thumb as to what is right. The objective of this phase of estate planning is to minimize taxes while still having the wealth going where one wants it to go. Proper planning requires the posing of a number of "what ifs."

Who Cares?

"What does all this have to do with me?" you may be asking. "All these huge amounts of money are more than what I'll ever expect to see in my life."

Not necessarily. Your total estate could reach dimensions that you might not dream of today. The value of your home, your life insurance, your pension benefits, and any inheritances you may receive can boost an otherwise untaxable estate into taxable status more quickly than you might think.

Further, while your own estate might not approach taxable ranges for many years, your parents or other family members might now be in a potentially taxable situation. Their lack of planning could expose their estate to taxes, which could, in turn, diminish your inheritance. Open and frank conversation among family members is always desirable on matters such as this, particularly when it involves retaining one's acquired wealth within the family unit, as opposed to sending it to the government.

With these thoughts in mind, let's briefly review some of the ways in which estate taxes can be minimized.

Tax Avoidance Devices

Estate planning specialists often recommend one, or a combination, of the following devices to minimize estate taxation. Individual circumstances, along with the advice of professionals, will help one determine what is best in any given individual case.

☐ Giving gifts has already been mentioned as a means of reducing one's estate and thereby the taxes thereon. Gifts may be either outright or in trust. When a gift is made in trust, the recipient may not be able to have full access to the gift until some future time. It may be possible for the donor of the gift to receive income that the gift generates. For example: a father may give a child, in trust, a gift of stock. The child may not be able to sell the stock until he or she reaches age 21. In the meantime, the dividends payable on the stock may still be received by the father. If a gift made in trust is revocable—that is, the donor has the right to take the gift back—then the gift may still be considered to be part of the donor's estate.

☐ Life insurance is a common way of passing wealth from one generation to another. A father may take out a life insurance policy and name his children as beneficiaries of the policy. If the father retains *ownership* in the policy, the value of the policy can be taxed as part of his estate. If the ownership of the policy resides in the wife or the children, however, then the value of the policy will not be taxed in the estate of the father.

☐ Certain U.S. Treasury bonds, commonly known as "flower bonds," may be used to pay estate taxes. It's possible to buy these bonds at less than their face value, but when they are used to pay estate taxes, their full face applies, even though they've been purchased for a lesser amount. For example, you might be able to buy a flower bond with a $1000 face value for, say, $750. If that bond was purchased before death and is used to pay estate taxes, the full $1000 value is credited against the tax, even though the bond cost only $750. These bonds pay a low rate of interest, so it's generally advisable to obtain them only when an individual's death is reasonably imminent and foreseeable. Otherwise, the tax advantages may be offset by the low rate of return payable on the bonds.

☐ Private annuities are a fairly complicated arrangement, usually between members of a family, whereby a child will purchase an asset from the parent, with a promise to pay for the purchase over an extended number of years. Such a plan, when properly constructed, has the effect of taking the value of the asset out of the estate of the parent. A private annuity should be entered into only upon the advice of legal and tax counsel.

☐ Ownership of properties in joint names will not necessarily relieve one's estate from taxation, though it may simplify the administration of an estate and thereby cut down on administrative costs.

It's Never Too Early

While estate planning is commonly thought of as an activity for senior citizens, you are never too young to consider the importance and benefits of estate planning. Thought should be given to estate planning when an individual marries and as children are born. Then, periodically, as the family grows, further consideration and review should be given to a plan at least every few years. As the family structure changes, so does the need for reviewing the plan. In addition to the financial benefits that can result from sound estate planning, the peace of mind that can be achieved cannot be denied.

Personal Action Checklist
Federal Estate Tax Estimator

Your estate might be subject to federal estate taxes. Perhaps more importantly, you may be an heir to an estate—such as your parents'—which might have to pay federal estate taxes. It could be a costly error to assume that you—either as deceased or as an heir—will not be exposed to those taxes. If the possibility of estate taxes exist in your situation, strategies can be put into motion, with the help of qualified professionals, to reduce potential taxes.

Using Tables 24-2 and 24-3, prepare an estimate of potential estate taxes for yourself and for anyone in whose estate you might be an heir. Prepare the estimate assuming death this year, and assuming death five years from now. For the five year projection, do your best to estimate the value at that time of all the assets of the estate.

	Death this year	Death in five years
1. Gross estate	_____	_____
2. Less deductible expenses and contributions	_____	_____
3. Adjusted gross estate	_____	_____
4. Less marital deduction	_____	_____
5. Taxable transfers	_____	_____
6. Tentative tax on total in line 5 (see Table 24-2)	_____	_____
7. Less credit (see Table 24-3)	_____	_____
8. Tax due	_____	_____

Consumer Beware
Interview with a Lawyer Who Has Done Extensive Work in Financial Counseling and Estate Planning: Part Two

Q. Is it just the breadwinner who needs an estate plan, or should both spouses become involved?

A. Without a doubt, both spouses should become involved. For the most part, the man is still the main breadwinner. But in ever-increasing numbers, women are contributing to the overall family income and accumulation of wealth. Further, the wife—and statistics indicate that every average American wife will probably be a widow for close to four years—should be aware of the implications of estate taxation and distribution of assets on her death.

Families must communicate openly and frankly about what they want to do with their accumulated wealth, however large or small it may be. For example, parents simply have to determine how much, if anything, they want to leave to their children, and how much they want to spend on their own pleasures when they can.

Q. That may be the biggest dilemma of all: how do parents determine what to leave their children and what to spend on themselves?

A. There is no formula, no pat answer. It's something that each family has to hammer out on its own. Some parents will struggle mightily to create such a large nest egg for their children that the children will never have any financial worries. This may be laudable, but it can be a detriment to the children. It all depends on the parents and the children. No two examples are identical. Everything returns to the need for communication. If children are brought up with a sense of values regarding self-sufficiency, they'll be more prone to strive for that regardless of what kind of nest egg may be waiting for them in the future. If children aren't made aware of the value of self-sufficiency, no amount of money will ever be able to resolve the frustrations they may be in for.

Q. Do you ever advise parents on how much they should strive to set aside for their children?

A. Not really. All you can really give children as they're growing up is love, devotion, a sense of ethics, and an awareness of self-worth. That, and a good education, and they're off on their own to do as they please anyway.

Q. Are you telling me, then, that an important part of estate planning is the communication between members of the family, with respect to growing up and making one's own pathway through life?

A. Yes I am. Most distinctly. Estate planning has its tax and accounting and legal aspects. But when you boil it all down, estate planning is *life* planning. It's putting the numbers and details on what you're doing with your life, your career, your whole process of maturing and raising a family. Your estate is more than simply your financial worth. In a sense, it's also your philosophy, your direction, your desire for achievement. It's attitudes, feelings, goals. Families would be better off and more in touch with themselves if they at least thought about such planning, rather than ignoring it, or feeling that it's something that only "rich people" do.

One of the most unfortunate aspects of estate planning is the name itself—estate planning. Perhaps if we had learned to call it "life planning," instead of something that seems to refer to death planning, we'd all be more willing to take advantage of it.

Part Seven | Income Taxes: How to Bite Back

25 | Income Taxes: How They Work

The Federal income tax has become an ever-present influence in the management of personal financial matters. Investment decisions, record-keeping disciplines, retirement planning, and just plain day-to-day budgetary matters are all affected, for better or for worse, by income-tax implications.

The Federal tax structure is not only complex; it is also extraordinarily changeable. Changes in the law and in the forms are virtually inevitable from year to year. And as the laws change, so, perhaps, must your own financial plans if you are to take advantage of what the law allows, or to escape any disadvantages that the law may impose. This chapter is not intended to be a step-by-step guide to filing your tax return. That information—in much more expanded form—is available in a variety of commercial publications. Rather, this chapter is designed to:

☐ Give you a basic understanding of how the income tax laws work.

☐ Illustrate the types of choices and decisions you can, and should, make in order to keep your taxes at a minimum.

☐ Assist you in using the tools available to complete your own tax filings each year.

Be Prepared

As you read this chapter you should have at hand the most current copies of the basic income tax forms, particularly the 1040 form and the schedules that accompany it. These forms are included in the instruction package the Internal Revenue Service (IRS) mails to all taxpayers each January. They are also available year-round at local IRS offices, and during the first few months of each year at most banks, savings associations, and post offices.

Specific examples of tax situations, and sample illustrations of segments of the tax forms, are included in this chapter for the purpose of giving you a general understanding of the laws and the forms. For the year in which you are studying this chapter, or doing your return, you must determine the current laws and how they apply to the current forms. You should complete the Personal Action Checklist at the end of this chapter before you read this chapter.

This chapter discusses Federal income taxes. Most states, and a few cities, also levy income taxes on their citizens. State and city tax formats generally follow the Federal format, so this chapter will also be helpful to you in understanding your local income tax situation.

The Importance of Knowing about Income Taxes

☐ In order for both Ralph and Marcia to work, they had to hire a baby-sitter to take care of their two small children. Like many people, they hated to do the work connected with filing their Federal income tax return. To minimize that work, they took a short cut and filed the simple 1040A form. But had they paid closer attention to their specific tax situation, they would have found that they could cut their tax bill by more than $1000 by claiming their child-care expenses as a *credit* against their tax! This would have required them to file the longer 1040 form, which might have taken them an extra hour or two of their time. Wouldn't it have been worth it?

☐ Jess moved from Detroit to Los Angeles to take a better job. His new employer paid one-half of his moving expenses, and Jess paid the other half out of his own pocket. He was so pleased with the new job that he didn't give a second thought to paying some of his own moving expenses. And when it came time for him to file his tax return, he overlooked the fact that he could have claimed those moving expenses as an *adjustment* to his income. This could have cut his tax bill by many hundreds of dollars—and it would have taken only a few minutes to enter the necessary information on the form.

☐ Connie and Gary did a lot of spending last year. They bought a new car, some new furniture, and new carpeting for three rooms in their home. When they completed their income tax return, they looked at the standard tax table that sets forth how much in sales taxes are deductible. Based on that table, they claimed a deduction for sales taxes of $350. Had they read the small print under that table, they would have realized that they could have taken *additional deductions* for the sales taxes on those major purchases, which could have saved them a few hundred dollars on their income taxes.

☐ Karl was a machinist. His boss required that Karl provide certain of his own tools needed for the job, as well as his own work clothes. The boss didn't reimburse Karl for these expenses, but Karl was otherwise happy with the job and didn't mind the expense. Nor did he pay attention to the tax laws, which would have allowed him a *deduction* for the unreimbursed cost of the tools and work clothes. By not claiming the deduction, Karl paid much more in income taxes than he'd actually had to.

☐ Brent was a traveling salesman. He returned from the road every Friday afternoon, and spent two or three hours sitting at his dining room table filling out his expense vouchers and doing other paperwork associated with his job. Another salesman had once told him that if he did work at home, he could claim a deduction on his tax return for the expense of having an office in his home. Brent thus figured that the use of his dining room table for a few hours each week was worth $2400 a year in deductible expense. Without seeking other advice, he claimed that amount on his tax return, which resulted in a tax savings of over $800. But Brent was more than a little dismayed when an auditor for the Internal Revenue Service called him in for a visit: the expense was being disallowed as an *improper deduction,* for it did not meet the very stringent guidelines for claiming office-at-home expenses. Brent had to pay up accordingly, plus interest and penalty.

□ Much to his surprise, Joel received an inheritance of $2000 upon the death of a long-lost uncle. Wanting to be perfectly legal and forthright about this windfall, Joel included it, but did not identify its source, as "other income" on his tax return. By doing so he increased his taxes by $600. But, he figured, he was still better off by $1400, and the IRS couldn't claim he was hiding income. In fact, the IRS assumed that the unspecified $2000 was legally taxable income, and they gladly accepted the extra $600 from Joel. But if Joel had done his homework before completing his tax return, he would have learned that inheritances are *nontaxable income.* He should *not* have reported it, and he should *not* have paid the tax. If he later realized his mistake, he could have filed an *amended return,* and gotten back the overpayment. But he never did realize the mistake. Nor did the government.

The Pervasiveness of Taxes in Our Lives

The above examples illustrate just a few of the hundreds of common situations in which income taxes raise an issue. And as the examples show, many people could be paying more in income taxes than they really have to. Or they may be courting costly problems by *not* paying the taxes they really do owe. With hundreds, perhaps even thousands, of dollars at stake in your own tax return, it's essential that you make yourself aware of all the possible ways to keep your taxes at the legal minimum. To an extent, a professional tax preparer can help you gain this awareness. But the preparer spends only a few hours a year with you. He may not think to ask, and you may not remember, all of the transactions you conducted during the year that could have tax consequences.

Your awareness of the tax laws will help you to be a better record keeper and a better manager of your financial affairs. The preparer can only work with the information you provide him. It's up to you to know which transactions have tax implications and to collect the necessary documentation that will enable you to support whatever claims you make on your return.

The income tax structure also requires that you make a number of important choices, such as which form to file, which filing status to choose, whether or not you should itemize your deductions, and so on. Making the wrong choice could mean paying higher taxes than necessary or running into a hassle with the IRS. If you make a choice that favors the government, you can *not* necessarily assume that they'll correct the matter for you. For example, if you choose not to itemize your deductions, when in fact doing so would lower your taxes, the IRS will not come back to you with the suggestion that you itemize. They'll gladly accept the extra taxes you've paid.

Let's examine the basic workings of the income tax structure and the ways in which you can make the correct decisions to legally minimize your taxes.

The Basic Concept of Income Taxes

Of all the income you receive in a year, only *some* of it is subject to income taxes. There are many ways that the total amount of your income can be *reduced* to find the taxable portion. And once that taxable portion is determined, there are ways to minimize the taxes you owe on that income.

Your assignment, should you choose to accept it, is to take advantage of all the ways you can to legally reduce your taxable income and the taxes thereon. Should you choose not to accept it, you'll pay more taxes than you may have to. When you glance at the tax forms, you may think that this is an impossible mission. It isn't, if you're willing to do a reasonable amount of disciplined homework, for which you can be amply rewarded.

Following, in brief, are the steps you'll take. We'll examine each one in more detail later.

1. Accurately list all of your income. Be sure to *exclude* any income that is *not* taxable. (See Joel's case, above, for one example of nontaxable income.)

2. From the total in Step 1, *subtract* expenses that are known as *adjustments to income*. Jess's case, noted earlier, is one such example.

3. Further *subtract* expenses that are known as *deductions*. Connie and Gary, as well as Karl, illustrate samples of deductions.

4. Figure all of the *exemptions* you're entitled to. Exemptions are generally members of your family and others who may be dependants. For each exemption you can further reduce your income that is subject to taxes. For example, if each exemption is worth $1000, a family of four can reduce their income by $4000.

Summing Up Midway

Let's stop briefly to review how these steps might work in an actual situation. Glenda and Mac have two young children. Last year they received $32,000: $30,000 was from work, and $2000 was tax-exempt interest from an investment. They had $3000 worth of adjustments and $5000 worth of deductions. Each valid exemption that year was worth $1000. Here's a rundown of Glenda and Mac's status, based on the four steps outlined above:

Income (excluding nontaxable income)		$30,000
Less: Adjustments	$3,000	
Deductions	5,000	
Exemptions (4 × $1000)	4,000	
Total subtractions		12,000
Income that is subject to taxes		$18,000

Thus you see that even though Glenda and Mac took in $32,000 during the year, only $18,000 is subject to taxes. But this will be so *only* if Glenda and Mac actually take the steps to accurately tally and include the proper subtractions when they prepare their return.

Now let's look at further steps that can be taken to minimize the actual taxes due on the income that is subject to taxes.

5. Choose the correct *filing status*. This relates to your marital and family situation. Given the same amount of taxable income, a person in one status might pay more, or less, tax than a person in another status. For example, two unmarried persons, Pat and Mike, each had a taxable income of $20,000 in a recent year. Pat chose a "single" filing status, and his tax was $3829. Mike, who was eligible to do so, chose "unmarried head of household" as his status, and his tax, on the same $20,000, was $3548. A difference of almost $300! If Pat was legally entitled to use the "head of household" status, he obviously should have done so.

6. Calculate what *credits* you're entitled to: Ralph and Marcia's case, noted earlier, showed you one type of possible credit. For every dollar's worth of credit you can claim, your tax bill is reduced by a dollar.

7. Determine if you're eligible for *income averaging*. If your income is much higher this year than it has been in the past four years, you may be able to pay your tax this year based on a five-year averaging of income, rather than on this year's high level of income. This can result in lower taxes this year.

Let's now return to Glenda and Mac, who had $18,000 worth of taxable income. How could steps (5), (6), and (7) affect their tax situation?

□ With respect to their *filing status,* they could choose to file separate returns or a joint return. Let's assume that of their total income from work, two-thirds of it was Glenda's and one-third of it was Mac's. In such a case, if they chose to file separate returns their total income taxes would be about $150 more than if they filed a joint return. (If their incomes had been equal, the total tax from separate returns would be about the same as from a joint return.)

☐ With respect to *credits,* assume that they had to pay a baby-sitter every day so they could go to work. As with Marcia and Ralph, this could entitle them to a credit against their taxes. In their case it was $300. But they would have to indicate this specifically on their tax form if they wanted to get the benefit of it.

☐ With respect to *income averaging,* their income in this year was much higher than in past years, since Glenda had not worked before this year. By filing the income averaging form they could have reduced their tax for the year by $75.

Here, then, is a summary of what Glenda and Mac could save if they took the proper steps:

	Tax savings
Choosing the right filing status	$150
Claiming the child-care credit	300
Income averaging	75
Total saved	$525

Combine these savings with the savings they realized as a result of claiming all proper *adjustments, deductions,* and *exemptions,* and their *total* savings—right way versus wrong way—could run into thousands of dollars!

A Walk Through the 1040

The previous discussion illustrated the *basic concept* of how income taxes are figured:

☐ Tallying your income that is subject to taxes;

☐ Reducing that total by the proper legal methods (adjustments, deductions, exemptions);

☐ Then figuring the lowest possible tax by choosing the right filing status, claiming all proper credits, and using income averaging whenever appropriate. (Other tax-reduction devices may also be of use to you. For details on those devices, talk to a professional tax preparer and see the information contained in the IRS and other commercial tax publications.)

Let's now see how these specific steps are taken on the tax forms themselves. Bear in mind that the laws and the forms change from year to year, thus this discussion must be general in nature.

Before proceeding, you should complete the *Personal Action Checklist* at the end of this chapter. It is designed to help you update many of the important specifics of the tax forms and laws, and will enhance your understanding of the current situation.

Who Must File?

Your first step, of course, is to determine whether or not you are legally required to file an income tax return for the past year.

Whether or not you are legally required to file a return will depend on three main factors: The amount of gross income you received during the year; whether or not you are married; and whether or not you or your spouse is over the age of 65. Depending on your age and marital status, there are different levels of gross income at which you will be required to file a return. You may not owe any taxes; indeed, you might be entitled to a refund. But you must file a return if you fall within the legal requirements. Determine what the minimum income requirements are for the current tax year. (If you've completed the Personal Action Checklist at the end of this chapter, you will have obtained this information as well as other specific data that are likely to change from year to year.)

There are a few other circumstances under which you might be required to file a return:

☐ If you are claimed as a dependent on someone else's tax return, such as your parents', you may be required to file your own tax return if you had a certain amount of *unearned* income during the year. (Unearned income is generally income from investments as opposed to earned income, which is income from work.)

☐ Even if your income for the year falls below the aforementioned minimum levels, you'll have to file a return if you owe certain other taxes outside the normal realm of income taxes. Such other taxes might include taxes on a distribution from an IRA account, or Social Security taxes on tips that you didn't report to your employer.

☐ If you are self-employed, either full time or part time, you will have to file a tax return if your net earnings from self-employment exceeded the fixed amount. This is so regardless of your age or marital status. Self-employed persons must also pay self-employment tax on the self-employment income. This is comparable to the Social Security tax that regular employees have withheld from their wages.

There are some circumstances when you may not be *required* to file a tax return, but *should* file one. These circumstances include the following:

☐ You may not have earned enough income to be required to pay taxes, but you did have income taxes withheld from your pay. If you file a tax return, you will be entitled to a refund of the taxes that were withheld from your pay. If you don't file a return, even though you're not required to, don't expect a refund.

☐ If you are entitled to the "earned income credit," you should file a return if you want to receive the money that is due you.

Check specific IRS instructions for the current year to determine the exact filing requirements as well as to clarify any other matters discussed in this chapter.

Which Form Should You Use?

The two common forms that individuals use to file their returns are the form 1040A, known as the "short form," and form 1040, known as the "long form." You *may* have a choice as to which one to use. The short form is simpler to complete, but if you use the short form, you are not permitted to claim most of the allowable *adjustments* and *credits*. Further, if you wish to itemize your deductions, you *must* use the longer form.

Also, depending on the amount and the source of your income, the laws might require you to use the long form. It's advisable to determine whether or not you can use the short form, if for no other reason than that it's easier to complete. But virtually all of the important tax-cutting advantages are available only through the long form. For the balance of this chapter, therefore, we'll be referring to the long-form provisions.

Choosing Your Filing Status

The first important choice you have to make in preparing your return is with respect to your filing status. The segment on the form looks like this:

Filing Status

1 _____ Single
2 _____ Married filing joint return
3 _____ Married filing separate return
4 _____ Head of household
5 _____ Qualifying widow(er) with dependent child

As you can see, there are five possible choices. Many taxpayers can qualify for more than one status, but choosing the wrong one can result in higher taxes. This was noted briefly earlier in the case of Glenda and Mac. The choices you have will depend on your marital status.

Married Taxpayers

Married taxpayers can choose to file separate returns or they can file together on a joint return. Generally speaking, if both spouses have approximately equal income, they may be able to achieve minor tax savings by filing separately. But if the spouses' earnings are unequal, it almost always will be to their benefit to file jointly. If you're in doubt, calculate your taxes both ways and choose the way that results in the lower tax.

If you were legally married on the last day of the year, you are considered to have been married for the whole year. If your spouse died at any time during the year, you also are considered to have been married for the whole year.

If married persons do choose to file separately, they both must do the same with respect to their deductions. They both must either itemize their deductions or they both must use the "standard deductions" (also known as the "zero bracket amount"). One spouse can't go one way and the other spouse the other way. This is often considered a disadvantage to filing separately.

There is a possible exception to this general rule: Even though you may be technically still married, if you live with your dependent child apart from your spouse, you may be considered unmarried if you meet certain tests. In such cases, you could file as a single taxpayer or as a head of household, and you will not have to itemize your deductions even if your spouse does, or you may itemize your deductions even if your spouse does not. In order to qualify for this unusual status, you must meet all four of the following tests: (1) You must file a separate return. (2) You must pay more than half the costs of keeping up your home for the tax year. (3) Your spouse did not live in your home at any time during the tax year. (4) Your home was, for more than six months of the year, the principal home of your child or step-child, whom you can claim as a dependent. If you can satisfy these four tests, you can file as a single person. If your home in test (4) was your child's principal home for the *whole* year, and all the other tests are met, you can then file as a "head of household," in which case your tax rate will be less than as a single person.

Unmarried Taxpayers

Unmarried taxpayers may be able to choose from the other three filing statuses: Single, Head of Household, and Qualifying Widow(er) with dependent child. Of these three choices, the single status will pay the highest tax, followed by the head of household and the qualifying widow(er). In one recent year, for example, an individual with a taxable income of $20,000 and two exemptions would have paid the following taxes, depending on their status.

Single	$3498
Head of Household	$3250
Qualifying Widow(er)	$2739

As you can see, choosing the correct legal status can make a considerable difference in the amount of taxes you'll have to pay.

Head of Household If you can qualify for this status, your tax rate will be lower than the single status or than the married-filing-a-separate-return status. In order to qualify you have to be unmarried on the last day of the year and you must have paid more than half the costs of keeping up a home that was the principal home for the *whole* year for any relatives whom you can claim as a dependent (see the later discussion on who qualifies as a dependent). These relatives can include your married children or grandchildren, your grandparents, your brothers and sisters, your in-laws, and blood-related aunts, uncles, nieces, and nephews. Note that these family members must actually have lived with you.

You can also qualify if unmarried children or grandchildren lived with you, even though they may not be technically your dependents. Further, you can qualify if your mother or father were your dependents, even though they did not actually live with you.

Check the current IRS instructions for the definitions of "keeping up a home," the "cost of keeping up a home," and other specific pertinent definitions and requirements.

Qualifying Widows and Widowers

People who qualify for this status pay at the same tax rate as married couples who file a joint return. That's the lowest rate of the five different statuses. If your spouse died in a preceding year, you can file as a qualifying widow or widower if you were entitled to file a joint return with your spouse for the year in which he or she died, *and* you did not remarry before the end of the current tax year. You must *also* have a child, step-child, or foster child who qualifies as your dependent for the year, and you must have paid more than half the costs of keeping up your home, which had to be the principal home of that child for the whole year.

Your Exemptions and Dependents

As was noted earlier, for every exemption you can legally claim, you are allowed to reduce your income that is subject to taxation. In one recent year the allowable amount was $1000 per exemption.

The section of the 1040 form wherein this information is placed looks like this:

Exemptions

☐ Yourself ☐ 65 or over ☐ Blind   Total boxes
☐ Spouse   ☐ 65 or over ☐ Blind   checked ☐

First names of dependent children who   Total
lived with you_____   children
_____   listed ☐

Other dependents

Name	Relation-ship	No. of months lived in your home	Did dep. have income of $ or more?	Did you provide more than ½ of dep. support?	Total other de-pendents ☐
___	___	___	___	___	
___	___	___	___	___	
___	___	___	___	___	
___	___	___	___	___	

Add numbers entered in boxes above ☐

Obviously, the more exemptions you can legally claim, the lower your taxes will be.

You are entitled to claim one exemption for yourself and, if you are married, you can claim one exemption for your spouse. You can claim *extra* exemptions if either spouse is over 65 years of age or legally blind in accordance with IRS regulations. In other words, if both spouses are over 65 and legally blind, they can claim six exemptions between them. You can claim an exemption for a spouse even if the spouse died during the year.

In addition to yourself and your spouse, you may claim additional exemptions for every person who is your legal dependent. (You cannot claim the extra age and blindness exemptions for a dependent—those apply to only yourself and your spouse.)

For the most part, children are the most commonly claimed dependents. But you are not limited just to children. Other persons, related or not, may qualify as dependents if all necessary tests are met. (Employed persons such as housekeepers, maids, and servants cannot be claimed as dependents.)

In order for a person to qualify as a dependent, he or she must meet *all* of the following five tests:

1. The support test
2. The gross income test
3. The member of household or relationship test
4. The citizenship test
5. The joint return test

The requirements in summary form are as follows. Check current regulations to determine the full extent of the tests.

1. *The support test.* You must provide more than half of the dependent's total support during the calendar year.

2. *The gross income test.* Generally, you may not claim a person as a dependent if that person had gross income during the year of a certain fixed amount. During one recent tax year that gross income amount was $1000. (Tax-exempt income, such as Social Security payments, is not included in gross income.) There are two main exceptions to this rule. The gross income test can be ignored if the person you claim as a dependent is your child and is either under 19 or is a full-time student, in accordance with IRS definitions. In other words, if your child was under 19 and earned over the legal maximum gross income for the year, that child can still be claimed as a dependent. Similarly, if the child was over 19 and earned more than the permitted maximum but was a full-time student, the child can still be claimed as a dependent.

3. *The member of household or relationship test.* Provided the other tests are met, a person who lives with you for the entire year and is a member of the household can qualify as a dependent, even though that person is not related to you.

Further, certain relatives can qualify as dependents even if they do not live with you, provided they meet all the other tests. These relatives can include children and grandchildren, parents and grandparents, brothers, sisters, step-family, and in-laws.

4. *The citizenship test.* To qualify as a dependent, the person must be a U.S. citizen or a resident of Canada or Mexico for some part of the calendar year in which your tax year begins.

5. *The joint return test.* If the person you wish to claim as a dependent has filed a joint return on his or her own with a spouse, then you cannot claim that person as a dependent. For example, you supported your daughter for the entire year while her husband was in the Armed Forces. The couple files a joint return. Even though your daughter may meet all the other tests, you may not claim her as a dependent.

The tax regulations are very specific as to what constitutes support of a dependent. Some expenses qualify while others do not. Check current regulations to be certain that you are proper in claiming your dependents. Note also that you cannot claim a partial dependent. Either someone meets the test or they don't.

Declaring Your Income

This is the area where you must declare all of your income that is legally taxable and you must, as noted earlier, take care *not* to report any income that is *not* taxable.

The *income* section of the 1040 form looks like this:

Income		
	Wages, salaries, tips, etc.	_____
Please attach	Interest income	_____
Copy B of your	Dividends	_____
Forms W-2 here.	Alimony received	_____
	Business income (or loss)	_____
	Capital gain (or loss)	_____
	Pensions, annuities, rents, royalties, partnerships, etc.	_____
	Other income (state nature and source)	_____
	Total Income	_____

The sample form above does *not* contain all of the possible income items. It has been abbreviated to include the more common types of income only. Check current regulations and forms to determine the full extent of reportable income.

Taxable Income

Let's take a more detailed look at each of these items of taxable income.

Wages, Salaries, Tips, etc For most taxpayers, this is the major source of taxable income. Early in the year, employees will have received copies of "W-2" forms from their employer. These forms will summarize the total amount of income earned during the taxable year and will indicate how much of those earnings have been withheld by the employer to pay income taxes, Social Security taxes, state income taxes, and any other withholdings that are required or voluntary. The amount of total income that shows on your W-2 form should be inserted on this line and a copy of the W-2 should be attached to this part of your form when you mail it in.

Interest Income On this line you place the total of all taxable interest you've earned during the year. The current form will dictate whether or not you are required to itemize all the sources of income on a separate schedule. Taxable interest generally includes interest you earn on regular deposits with banks, savings and loans, and credit unions (including interest-bearing checking accounts and certificates of deposit); also interest earned on mortgages, trust deeds, promissory notes, corporate bonds, and U.S. government bonds (except for Series E and EE savings bonds). With Series E or EE bonds you have the option of declaring the interest earned in a given year and paying taxes on it during that year or of deferring the taxation until you later cash the bonds.

Some types of interest earned are tax exempt. Interest earned on All-Savers Certificates are tax exempt up to the limits set by law. Those limits as originally passed by Congress in August 1981 were $1000 for individuals filing single returns and $2000 for people filing joint returns. Interest earned on municipal bonds is also tax exempt. However, if you purchased a municipal bond and later sold it at a profit, the profit itself is subject to taxation.

Some types of interest earned are not taxable in the year in which you earned it, but will be taxable in some future year. This is known as tax-deferred income. It includes interest earned from annuity plans, IRA plans, Keogh plans, and other pension and profit-sharing programs.

For tax years beginning 1985, you may be able to exclude a sizable amount of earned interest from taxation. The excludable interest will be referred to your "net interest." Your net interest is the difference between interest you *earn* during the year and interest you *pay* during the year for your consumer expenses. (Interest paid for business or home financing purposes is not included in this definition of interest expense.) Here's an example: In 1985 you earn $5000 in interest. During that year you also have interest expenses of $2500 of which $1200 is interest payments on your home financing. Your "net interest" expense for the year, therefore, would be $3700: $5000 interest income, less $1300 in consumer-type interest expense. The $1200 on the home financing does not count. There is a limit to the amount of net interest you can exclude from taxation. The excludable amount can not exceed 15 percent of the *lesser* of: (1) $3000 ($6000 on a joint return) or (2) your net interest for the year. Following the above example, and assuming that you file a joint return, your exclusion for that year would be $555. Why? 15 percent of $6000 is $900; 15 percent of your net interest, $3700, is $555. The excludable interest is limited to the *lesser* of these two figures, that being $555.

Dividend Income   Here you insert the total value of dividends you've received during the year. This can include dividends you receive on common stock ownership, ownership of mutual fund shares, and the value of dividends that have been reinvested in shares of common stock or a mutual fund. If the total amount of dividends you've received exceeds a certain limit, the form will indicate that you are to itemize all dividend income on a separate schedule. You may be allowed to exclude a certain portion of your dividend income from taxes. The form will indicate the current amount excludable.

If you invest in the stock of public utility corporations, you may be able to exclude from taxation a substantial portion of your dividend income from such companies. If, instead of taking your dividends from such utility corporations in the form of cash, you elect to receive your dividends in the form of additional shares of common stock, you can exclude from taxation up to $750 per year ($1500 on a joint return) of the value of such stock dividends. The tax laws of 1981 make this provision effective for tax years 1982 through 1985.

Tax laws state that any party who pays you more than $10 per year in interest or dividends must prepare a form 1099 that indicates the amount paid to you. A copy of this form is sent to you, and a copy is sent to the IRS. You should therefore assume that the IRS knows you received that particular amount of money; should you fail to report it on your tax return, you can expect to be questioned by the IRS.

Alimony Received   Alimony payments that you receive are considered fully taxable income. However, child-support money received is not considered taxable income. See current regulations for definitions of taxable alimony.

Separately Scheduled Income

If you receive certain other types of income, you will be required to complete additional detailed schedules. These types of income include:

Business Income or Loss—Schedule C   If you ran your own business, part time or full time, as a sole proprietor, you are required to complete Schedule C and show the income or loss from that business on the appropriate income line on the form. (If you operated the business as a partnership or a corporation, you'll have to file the appropriate partnership or corporate income forms.)

Capital Gains and Losses—Schedule D   If you sell a "capital asset," the gain or loss on such a sale is subject to a different tax treatment than is ordinary income, such as your wages. What is a "capital asset"? Generally speaking, any property you own is a capital asset, except property related to your business or other income-producing activities, such as inventory items, stock in trade, property that you offer for sale to customers, and the like.

The most common types of capital assets subject to this special treatment are investments: stocks, bonds, real estate. If you sell a capital asset less than one year after you bought it, any gain you realize will be fully taxable. This is known as a "short-term capital gain."

If, however, you hold a capital asset for more than one year before you sell it, any gain is then known as a "long-term capital gain," and the gain is subject to advantageous tax treatment: only 40 percent of the gain is taxable. Here's how it works: Assume you purchased shares of stock in XYZ Company and after a year had elapsed, you sold those shares and realized a gain of $1000. Only 40 percent of that gain, or $400, will be taxed. If, say, you're in the 30 percent tax bracket, your tax on that gain will thus be 30 percent of $400, or $120. By comparison, if you earned $1000 in fully taxable interest on a bond investment and you were in the 30 percent tax bracket, your tax would be 30 percent of the full $1000 income, or $300. If you suffer a loss on the sale of investment-type capital assets, a portion of the loss can be deducted from other income.

Property that you own for your personal use, such as your home, your automobile, your jewelry, and so on, is also considered a capital asset. A gain on the sale of such personal properties is treated similarly to gains on sales of investment-type capital assets. (Sales of personal residences are treated separately in certain circumstances. See chapter 12, Selling Your Home, for more details on such transactions.) With respect to *personal* capital assets sold at a loss, such losses are *not* deductible from other income.

Pensions, Annuities, Rents, Royalties, Partnerships—Schedule E   This schedule covers a number of possible income or loss areas.

☐ Pension and annuity income. If you received pension or annuity income that was *fully* taxable—that is, all the money came from your employer's contributions and from the fund's earnings—you will report that income on another line within the income section. If, though, you had pension or annuity income that is *not fully* taxable—that is, you made voluntary contributions to the funds—you will report that income in part 1 of Schedule E.

☐ Rent and royalty income or loss is reported in part 2 of Schedule E. Expenses and depreciations that pertain to rental income property must also be detailed in Schedule E.

☐ Income or losses from partnerships, estates, trusts, and small business corporations are reported in part 3 of Schedule E.

Miscellaneous Taxable Income   There are many types of income, other than those noted above, which are taxable. Included are:

☐ Fees for services you perform such as serving as a member of a jury, an election precinct official, a notary public, an executor or administrator of an estate, to name a few.

☐ Property you receive through barter. If you receive property in exchange for your services, you must include as income the fair market value of the property on the date you received it. If you received the services of another person in exchange for your services, that also will be taxable at its fair market value.

☐ Gambling winnings are taxable income. However, you can deduct gambling losses during the year up to the extent of your winnings. Winnings from lotteries and raffles are considered gambling winnings. If you win property other than cash, the fair market value of that property must be counted as taxable income.

☐ Prizes and awards received as a result of drawings, television or radio programs, beauty contests, and the like are taxable. So are awards and bonuses that you receive from your employer for your good work or your suggestions. As with gambling winnings, prizes in the form of property must be included in taxable income at their fair market value.

☐ Part or all of any unemployment insurance benefits that you receive might be taxable income. See the instructions in the form 1040 for specific details on the formula that determines how much, if any, of your unemployment insurance benefits are taxable.

It should be noted that this discussion on forms of taxable income does not include all such forms, but rather a sampling of the most common types of taxable income. You should refer to the 1040 instructions and your professional tax preparer to determine whether you have any taxable income over and above what has been mentioned here.

Nontaxable Income

You may receive nontaxable money from various sources. These items should not be reported on the income part of your 1040 form. Following is a sampling of the more common types of nontaxable income. As with the taxable items, you should check the 1040 instructions for more specific details as to revisions in the law.

☐ *Interest income.* As noted earlier, *some* types of interest income may be excludable. They include limited interest received on All-Savers Certificates, interest received on tax-exempt bonds, and interest which is otherwise excludable because of specific regulations in the tax laws.

☐ *Accident and health insurance proceeds.* Payments that you receive for the following are exempt from tax: Workers' Compensation payments; Black Lung benefit payments; Federal Employees Compensation Act benefits; damages received for injury or illness; benefits received under an accident or health insurance policy for which you paid the premiums; disability benefits received for loss of income; compensation you receive for permanent loss of a part of your body or a function of your body; and reimbursement for medical care.

☐ *Gifts and inheritances.* These are not considered income. But if the cash or property you received as a gift or inheritance generates income for you, then the income that is generated is taxable. If a gift or inheritance is paid to a trust fund instead of to you, the income you receive from the trust fund may be taxable to you.

☐ *Life insurance proceeds.* Payments made because of the death of the insured person are generally not taxable. There are some possible exceptions. If someone else turned a life insurance policy on their life over to you and you paid a price for the transfer of that policy, then proceeds payable to you as beneficiary may be taxable to you. Also, if proceeds of a life insurance policy are paid out in monthly installments and those monthly installments include interest from the insurance company, then the interest portion of the monthly payments are taxable to you.

☐ *Social Security benefits.* These are not considered taxable income.

☐ *Scholarships, fellowships, and grants.* Generally, money received in this form is not taxable if you are a candidate for a degree. There are, however, numerous technical exceptions and you should check the IRS regulations to be certain that you do report any portion of such income that may be taxable.

☐ *Prizes and awards.* These may be tax free if you meet certain requirements: the prize must be awarded in recognition of your past accomplishments in religious, charitable, scientific, educational, artistic, literary, or civic fields. In order for such monies to qualify as nontaxable income, you must also not have entered the contest on your own; rather you must have been selected as a possible recipient without any volunteering on your part. And you must not be required to perform future services as a condition of receiving the prize. Athletic awards do not qualify for tax-exempt status.

Total Income

In completing this portion of your 1040 form, you add up all the items that are considered taxable income. Be sure not to include items that are excludable from taxation. From this total income figure we will now begin the subtractions, the first being for *adjustments to income.*

Adjustments to Income

This is the first main category of expenses that can be used to reduce your total income figure. Items included in the adjustments category are often referred to as "deductions." But technically they are not deductions. You are entitled to claim these adjustment items even if you do not itemize your deductions. (See later discussion on itemized deductions.) The most common types of adjustments will appear on your 1040 form in the following manner:

Adjustments to Income

Moving expense	_____
Employee business expense	_____
Payments to IRA, Keogh plans	_____
Interest penalty on early withdrawal of savings	_____
Alimony paid	_____
Total Adjustments	_____

You may be required to fill out separate schedules or forms with respect to the claiming of some of these adjustments. The current 1040 will instruct you accordingly. Here's a brief rundown of these more common adjustment items.

Moving Expenses   If you moved during the past year to change jobs or start a new job, you may be entitled to claim some of your moving costs as an adjustment. See Chapter 12, Selling Your Home, for a more detailed discussion on the regulations that pertain to this item.

Employee Business Expenses   If you incur travel or transportation expenses for your employer, and your employer does not reimburse you for those expenses, you may claim them as adjustments. (Entertainment and gift expenses related to your business which are not reimbursed by your employer are treated separately from travel and transportation expenses. Entertainment and gift expenses are considered deductions and should be claimed under the "miscellaneous deduction" category on the Schedule A itemization of deductions.)

Payments to an IRA or Keogh Plan The investments you make in these retirement plans in a given year are entered on this line. Bear in mind that that for tax years beginning 1982, all workers, even those covered by pension plans, are eligible for IRA plans.

Interest Penalty on Early Withdrawal of Savings If you withdraw money from certain savings plans before those plans have matured, you will lose some of the interest you would otherwise have received. If this has happened to you during the past year, you should report the total amount of interest you *would* have received on the "interest income" line in the income section of the 1040; then you deduct the amount of the penalty as an adjustment to this line.

Alimony Paid As noted in the income section, alimony received is taxable income. On the other hand, alimony that is paid is an adjustment that can be used to reduce your total income.

Adjusted Gross Income

At this point you will total your adjustments and subtract them from the total income. The result is the "adjusted gross income."

Let's assume that Howard and Maggie had a total taxable income of $35,000 and adjustments totaling $3000. Their adjusted gross income would, therefore, be $32,000.

Deductions: To Itemize or Not to Itemize?

The tax law, in general, has identified certain types of expenses as being "deductible" from your income. These expenses include those for medical purposes, charitable contributions, taxes that you've paid, interest that you've paid, casualty or theft losses that you've suffered, and other expenses that are related to your ability to generate income.

Whether or not you have actually incurred such expenses, the law allows you to claim a certain fixed amount of such deductions anyway. This is known as the "standard deduction" or, in more recent years, as the "zero bracket amount." The amount of the standard deduction you're entitled to claim depends on your filing status. The amount is subject to change from year to year, but in one recent year the amounts of the standard deduction were as follows: for those filing joint returns, or for qualifying widows, the amount was $3400. For those claiming single status or head of household status, the amount was $2300. For married persons filing separate returns, the amount for each spouse was $1700.

Let's assume that during that particular year the Greenbaums did not actually incur one penny's expense for any of the deductible items: they had no medical expenses, they paid no interest, they paid no other taxes, they made no charitable contributions. Even though they had not incurred any expenses of a deductible nature, they would still be entitled to have claimed a $3400 standard deduction, which would reduce their income accordingly.

Your Choice

If you have, in fact, spent *more* on deductible items than the standard deduction allows, you are entitled to claim all of those expenses as deductions. But you must itemize each and every one of them and you must have proper evidence that you did in fact incur such expenses.

The choice is yours: You can take the easy route and claim the standard deduction, in which case you won't have to keep records of all the particular expenses and completing your tax form will be that much simpler; or you can keep all the proper records and tally up the deductible expenses to see what you actually did pay for such items. If your true deductible expenses exceed the standard deduction amount, it will pay you to itemize. The only way you can tell is to know for sure what your itemized expenses are. Many taxpayers take the shortcut of the standard deduction when in fact, had they itemized, they would have saved tens, hundreds, or even thousands of dollars.

How do you decide whether you should itemize or not? If you are a homeowner, it's very likely that you will have deductible expenses in excess of the standard deduction amount. For most homeowners, the interest expense on their mortgage and their real estate taxes alone will be close to, if not more than, the standard deduction amount.

If you're not a homeowner, you'll have to do some more careful estimating of your deductible expenses. The largest items are likely to be your state income taxes, interest you've paid on loans, sales taxes, and medical expenses that were not reimbursed by your employer or insurance. If those items approximate the amount of the standard deduction, it may be well worth your while to tally all of your deductible expenses, looking toward a greater total deduction than what the standard deduction would allow you.

The following discussion will help familiarize you with the types of expenses that are deductible. The more familiar you become with these expenses, the more readily you'll make note of them throughout the year in your checkbook or otherwise so as to be aware of them as deductible items on your tax return. By doing so, you'll begin to find the process of itemizing that much simpler.

If you do itemize your deductions, you will be required to complete Schedule A of the 1040 form. Here is an abbreviated example of Schedule A. Note that this form is subject to change from year to year. Use the current form and check current regulations to be certain you are claiming all proper deductions in the proper form.

Schedule A—Itemized Deductions

Medical and Dental Expenses

(follow formula on current version of Schedule A to arrive at proper deductions)

TOTAL MEDICAL   _____

Taxes

State and local income   _____
Real estate   _____
General sales   _____
Personal property   _____
Other (itemize)   _____
_____   _____
_____   _____
TOTAL TAXES   _____

Interest Expense

Home mortgage   _____
Credit and charge cards   _____
Other (itemize)   _____
_____   _____
_____   _____
_____   _____
TOTAL INTEREST   _____

Contributions

Cash contributions   _____
Other than cash   _____
TOTAL CONTRIBUTIONS   _____

Casualty or Theft Losses

a. Loss before reimbursement   _____
b. Insurance reimbursement   _____
c. Subtract line b from line a   _____
d. Subtract $100 from line c and enter here. This is the amount you can deduct   _____

Miscellaneous Deductions

Union dues   _____
Other (itemize)   _____
_____   _____
_____   _____
_____   _____
TOTAL MISCELLANEOUS DEDUCTIONS   _____

Summary of Itemized Deductions:

Total medical   _____
Total taxes   _____
Total interest   _____
Total casualty   _____
Total miscellaneous   _____
TOTAL DEDUCTIONS   _____

Following is a brief explanation of the common deductions that are included on Schedule A, plus many of the allowable deductions that are not included on Schedule A. Those that are not specifically listed on Schedule A are to be included under the category of "miscellaneous deductions."

Medical and Dental Expenses   Within certain limitations, you are allowed to deduct most medical, dental, and health insurance expenses for which you were not reimbursed by your insurance, your employer, or otherwise. Schedule A contains the formula that you must follow to determine the proper amount of deductions for these expenses.

Taxes   As you well know, the Federal Government is not the only agency that imposes taxes on you. As a general rule, most major taxes paid to state and local governments are deductible expenses on your Federal return. These deductible taxes include general sales taxes, personal property taxes, real estate taxes, state and local income taxes, and state transfer taxes on security transactions. (Some taxes and fees are *not* deductible, however. These include: federal gift, estate, and income taxes; motor vehicle taxes; cigarette, tobacco, and alcoholic beverage taxes; fines and penalties.)

Most of your major tax payments are readily identifiable: your property taxes, your state income taxes, and the like. But the state and local sales taxes you may have paid during the year can be very difficult to tally. The IRS has established a formula, based on the size of your family and the state in which you live, which sets forth an allowable sales tax deduction without having to submit any proof of the specific expenses. The allowable amounts are contained in a table in the IRS 1040 instruction booklet. If, in fact, you have incurred more sales taxes than what the table allows, you can claim such additional sales taxes as legal deductions, assuming that you can prove the expenses. This would come into play if you've made any major purchases during the year such as a car, a boat, major appliances or furniture, or any other costly, sales taxable items. The sales taxes on a car alone could exceed the recommended allowance in the sales tax tables. If you have made any such major purchases, be sure to keep the appropriate documents so that you can justify a claim for the additional sales tax deductions should you later be questioned by the Internal Revenue Service.

Interest Expense   All of your personal interest expenses can be deductible. These include the interest on your home mortgage, credit cards, charge accounts, installment loans, revolving credit accounts, tuition loans, insurance loans, and debts that you owe to other individuals. Also, if you pay "points"—extra fees for the use of a lender's money—in connection with obtaining home financing, those points are deductible as interest in the year in which you paid them.

Charitable Contributions   If you itemize your deductions, you can deduct your charitable contributions made to properly qualified charitable organizations. (See IRS regulations for definitions of qualified charities and for certain limitations that may apply with respect to the maximum amount you can deduct in a given year.) Contributions may be cash or property. If you give property such as clothing or books, the deduction should be an amount equal to the then fair market value of such property. In order to justify the charitable deductions, you should have proper documentation and appraisals. If you are actively involved in a charitable organization, you cannot deduct the value of your time contributed to the organization; but you can deduct out-of-pocket expenses that you incur on behalf of the charity.

If you do not itemize your overall deductions, you are still allowed to claim some of your contributions separately. In tax years 1982 and 1983, those who do not itemize their deductions will be allowed to deduct 25 percent of their charitable contributions up to a maximum of $25 for each year. For 1984, the 25 percent limit applies, but the maximum deduction allowable will be $75. For tax year 1985, 50 percent of charitable contributions may be deducted, and from 1986, 100 percent of charitable contributions may be deducted. This specific provision, enacted as part of the 1981 Tax Cut Laws, is due to terminate after the 1986 tax year.

Casualty or Theft Losses   If you suffer a sudden and unexpected loss or casualty, you can deduct the value of the loss less $100. (A possible exception may occur if the loss was due to your own gross negligence.)

For example, you're in an auto accident that results in $1000 worth of damage to your car. Your own insurance policy has a $250 deductible, which means that the insurance company will pay you $750. That leaves you out-of-pocket $250. You subtract the $100 IRS deductible, which results in your being able to claim a casualty loss of $150. The IRS $100 deductible applies to each incident of casualty or loss. Thus, if you had three instances similar to the automobile accident, you would have to apply the $100 IRS deductible to each incident, claiming any other unreimbursed losses as your deduction.

Deductible casualty losses may result from a number of different causes, including fire, hurricanes, tornadoes, floods, storms, sonic booms, and vandalism.

Nondeductible casualties will include car accidents when your own negligence caused the accident; breakage of household items, such as china and glassware, under normal conditions of use; damage done by a family pet; damage caused by termites, moths, plant disease; damage caused by progressive deterioration of your property.

Theft losses include those arising from burglary, robbery, larceny, and embezzlement. If, however, you simply misplace or lose money or property, that may not be considered a deductible theft loss.

Miscellaneous Deductions   In recent years, the Schedule A of IRS 1040 has listed only two specific miscellaneous deductions: union dues and tax return preparation fee. It contains space for "other" miscellaneous deductions and, indeed, there are many that can qualify. By not listing them it would seem that the IRS does not want to tip off taxpayers as to what those other deductions might be. Indeed, you have to seek them out for yourself.

Generally, other allowable deductions are related to the production or protection of your income. Here are some of the more common types of other deductions:

☐ It was noted earlier that unreimbursed costs of travel and transportation on behalf of your employer can be claimed as an adjustment to income, and that entertainment expenses you incur, not reimbursed by your employer, are eligible as miscellaneous deductions. You can also claim job-related deductions if you spend money, and are not reimbursed, for specialized work clothes and tools, plus the necessary costs for cleaning and maintaining them.

☐ If you maintain an office in your home, under the strict guidelines set forth by the IRS, you can claim a deduction for your home-office expenses. Note that the IRS is very touchy about such deductions and is likely to scrutinize your claim very closely. If your claimed expenses are not in line with the IRS regulations, your claim may be disallowed. Nonreimbursed costs for dues to professional or trade associations and subscriptions to publications are also deductible.

☐ Educational expenses, including tuition, books, supplies, lab fees, and necessary related travel may be deductible if you acquire the education in order to maintain or improve the skills needed on your *present* job. Education obtained in order to qualify you for a *new* position will not be deductible. Educational expenses can also be deductible if you incur them in order to meet your employer's requirements to keep your job.

☐ Aside from job-related expenses, expenses incurred to produce, collect, or protect other income can be deductible. Such expenses can include accounting, tax, and investment advice and publications; fees paid for investment services, including collection of rents or dividends, record keeping, and custodial expenses; safe deposit box rentals if the box is used to hold your securities; employee and related office expenses if you hire someone to manage your investment income; travel costs necessary for looking after your investments or for consulting with your attorney, accountant, or investment advisor related to the production of income; legal expenses if the issue involves your business or employment or income-producing property. (You can't deduct legal expenses for strictly personal matters, such as a divorce, a criminal matter, or a traffic infraction.)

As with all other types of deductions, these miscellaneous deductions must be properly documented so that you can prove their validity if you are questioned by the IRS.

☐ Starting in tax year 1982, there will be a special deduction for married couples with two working spouses: Part of the lesser-earning spouse's income will be deductible from the couple's combined joint income. For 1982 this deduction will be limited to 5 percent of the lesser-earning spouse's net income, up to $30,000. In other words, for that year the maximum deduction will be $1500 (5 percent of $30,000). For example, in 1982 one spouse earns $20,000 and the other earns $40,000, for a combined total of $60,000. Five percent of the lesser income, or $1000 (5 percent of $20,000 is $1000) will be deductible from their total $60,000 income. In effect this would reduce their taxable income from $60,000 to $59,000, and their tax would be lowered accordingly.

Starting in 1983 the deduction will be 10 percent of the lower-earning spouse's net income, up to $30,000. From that year onward, then, the maximum deduction will be $3000.

In calculating this deduction you should not count income from pensions or annuities. Further, your net income figure is arrived at by subtracting business expenses and IRA or Keogh investments from your total income. For example, Pat's income for 1983 was $9000, of which $1000 came from a pension and $8000 from work. Pat invested $2000 in an IRA plan that year. Pat's net income, for purposes of this deduction, is, then, $6000 ($8000 income from work, less the $2000 IRA investment). As the lower-earning spouse, Pat's income would entitle the couple to a $600 deduction (10 percent of $6000).

You do *not* have to itemize your other deductions to claim this special deduction.

Total all of your itemized deductions. If they exceed the current amount allowed for the standard deduction, or zero bracket amount, you should include the total of your itemized deductions in computing your taxes. If the itemized deductions do not exceed the standard amount, then you should claim the standard amount.

Howard and Maggie Revisited

We noted earlier that Howard and Maggie had a total income of $35,000 and adjustments of $3000, giving them an adjusted gross income of $32,000.

Let's now assume that Howard and Maggie also had itemized deductions totaling $7000 and that they had four exemptions—Howard, Maggie, and two children—each worth $1000 for that tax year. Here's a summary of Howard and Maggie's taxable income picture:

<u>Howard and Maggie</u>

Total Income			$35,000
Less: Adjustments		$3000	
Deductions		7000	
Exemptions		4000	
			14,000
Taxable Income			$21,000

Computing Your Taxes

We've now reached the point where the tentative tax is calculated. (Tentative because the tax can be later reduced by credits and by other means.)

The methods of computing the tax have been changed by the IRS from time to time, but basically there are two main approaches: the *tax tables* and the *tax rate schedules*. The IRS instructions will tell you which to use. Here is a sample segment of the *tax tables* for a recent year. (Note that the tables for the current year may differ from the example shown.)

Tax Tables, Sample Segment

If taxable income is			... And you are ...		
at least	but less than	single	married filing jointly	married filing separately	head of household
			... Your tax is ...		
19,000	19,050	3,797	2,954	4,635	3,519
19,050	19,100	3,814	2,965	4,656	3,535
19,100	19,150	3,831	2,977	4,678	3,550

In this particular year's format, the number of exemptions had been taken into account in an earlier calculation on the form. The tax table figures take into account the value of the standard deduction. Note the difference one dollar's worth of taxable income can make. A single filer with a taxable income of $19,049 would owe a tax of $3797. With a taxable income of $19,050 the tax would be $3814: $17 more! And so on. It pays to calculate carefully.

If the specific instructions for the current year do not allow you to use the tax tables, you will be instructed to use the alternative *tax rate schedules*. This will generally be the case if you itemize your deductions and/or if your income exceeds a certain stated limit. Whereas the tax tables may have already taken into account the standard deduction and the number of exemptions, the tax rate schedules require you to do some additional computing to take those items into account.

Following are the projected tax rate schedules for 1982, 1963, and 1984 tax years for married couples filing joint returns and for single individuals. (See current IRS instructions for tax rate schedules covering separate returns and head of household returns.)

Projected Tax Rate Schedule: Married Filing Joint Return

If your taxable income is between (A)	and (B)	1982 You pay	1982 + % on excess*	1983 You pay	1983 + % on excess*	1984 You pay	1984 + % on excess*
0	$ 3,400	0	0	0	0	0	0
$ 3,400	5,500	0	12	0	11	0	11
5,500	7,600	$ 252	14	$ 231	13	$ 231	12
7,600	11,900	546	16	504	15	483	14
11,900	16,000	1,234	19	1,149	17	1,085	16
16,000	20,200	2,013	22	1,846	19	1,741	18
20,200	24,600	2,937	25	2,644	23	2,497	22
24,600	29,900	4,037	29	3,656	26	3,465	25
29,900	35,200	5,574	33	5,034	30	4,790	28
35,200	45,800	7,323	39	6,624	35	6,274	33
45,800	60,000	11,457	44	10,334	40	9,772	38
60,000	85,600	17,705	49	16,014	44	15,168	42
85,600	109,400	30,249	50	27,278	48	25,920	45
109,400	162,400	42,149	50	38,702	50	36,630	49
162,400	215,400	68,649	50	65,202	50	62,600	50
215,400	and up	95,149	50	91,702	50	89,100	50

*The amount by which your taxable income exceeds the amount in column (A). Example: On a 1983 taxable income of $17,000, the tax would be $1,846 plus 19 percent of the excess income over column (A). That excess ($17,000 over $16,000) is $1000; 19 percent of $1000 is $190. The tax is, then, $1846 plus $190, or $2036.

Projected Tax Rate Schedule: Single Individual Return

If your taxable income is between (A)	and (B)	1982 You pay	1982 + % on excess*	1983 You pay	1983 + % on excess*	1984 You pay	1984 + % on excess*
0	$ 2,300	0	0	0	0	0	0
$ 2,300	3,400	0	12	0	11	0	11
3,400	4,400	$ 132	14	$ 121	13	$ 121	12
4,400	6,500	272	16	251	15	241	14
6,500	8,500	608	17	566	15	535	15
8,500	10,800	948	19	866	17	835	16
10,800	12,900	1,385	22	1,257	19	1,203	18
12,900	15,000	1,847	23	1,656	21	1,581	20
15,000	18,200	2,330	27	2,097	24	2,001	23
18,200	23,500	3,194	31	2,865	28	2,737	26
23,500	28,800	4,837	35	4,349	32	4,115	30
28,800	34,100	6,692	40	6,045	36	5,705	34
34,100	41,500	8,812	44	7,953	40	7,507	38
41,500	55,300	12,068	50	10,913	45	10,319	42
55,300	81,800	18,968	50	17,123	50	16,115	48
81,800	108,300	32,218	50	30,373	50	28,835	50
108,300	and up	45,468	50	43,623	50	42,085	50

*The amount by which your taxable income exceeds the amount in column (A). Example: On a 1983 taxable income of $16,000, the tax would be $2097 plus 24 percent of the excess income over column (A). That excess ($16,000 over $15,000) is $1000; 24 percent of $1000 is $240. The tax is then $2097 plus $240, or $2337.

The "taxable income" in the left-hand column of the tax rate schedules refers to your net income, *after* all adjustments, deductions, and exemptions have been taken into account. Thus, in the case of Howard and Maggie, their taxable income for tax rate schedule purposes would be $21,000.

Assuming that they were filing for tax year 1983, their taxable income of $21,000 would fall into the $20,200–$24,600 range in the left-hand column. This would require them to pay a tax of $2644, plus 23 percent of income in excess of $20,200. $21,000 exceeds $20,200 by $800; 23 percent of $800 is $184. $184 plus $2644 equals $2828. That's the amount of tax Howard and Maggie will owe if they have no credits and cannot utilize income averaging or any other further tax-saving methods.

The 23 percent designation is the source of the common expression "tax bracket." Howard and Maggie would be considered to be in the 23 percent tax bracket as a result of this year's computation. But obviously this tax bracket designation does not mean that they've paid that percentage of their income in Federal taxes. In fact, their actual tax (before credits and so on) of $2828 is only about 13.5 percent of their taxable income of $21,000; and it's only about 8 percent of their gross income.

Income Averaging

If your income for the current year is substantially higher than it has been for the average of the past four years, it could be worthwhile for you to do the income-averaging calculation on Schedule G. Follow the instructions step by step on the income-averaging schedule to determine whether you're eligible for income averaging, and if so, you can proceed to compute your tax in accordance with the income-averaging provisions. You can take advantage of the income-averaging provisions for every year in which you are eligible to do so in accordance with the instructions.

Credits

Once you've computed your tentative tax, you can reduce it further if you are entitled to any of the credits allowable in the current year. Every dollar's worth of credit reduces your tax by one dollar. In other words, if you are entitled to a $100 credit, your tax bill is reduced by $100.

Here is what the credit segment of the 1040 form looks like, showing some of the more common credits recently available. The form will instruct you if additional schedules have to be completed.

Credits

Credit for contribution to candidates for public office   _____

Credit for the elderly   _____

Credit for child and dependent care expenses   _____

Residential energy credits   _____

□ You're allowed a limited credit for contributions you make to political candidates, campaign committees, or national, state, or local committees of a national political party.

□ Credits for the elderly are available to some persons 65 or older, or some who are under 65 and receive a taxable pension or annuity from a public retirement system.

□ The credit for child and dependent care expenses is available to you if you pay someone to care for a dependent under the age of 15 or for a disabled dependent or spouse so that you can work or look for work.

□ The residential energy credits are available to you if you have installed certain energy-saving devices in your residence.

See current IRS regulations for specific limits and qualifications on these and any other credits that may be currently available to you.

Other Taxes and Payments

Follow IRS instructions on the 1040 form to determine whether you owe any taxes over and above the income taxes. If you had self-employment income during the year, you will owe additional self-employment taxes. (These are taxes in lieu of Social Security taxes, which your employer would have paid and deducted on your behalf.) On the other hand, if you had more than one employer during the year, more than the necessary amount of Social Security taxes may have been paid or deducted on your behalf, and you can claim a refund for the excess paid. The amount of tax withheld from your pay, and the amount of any estimated tax payments you've made on your own, are then deducted from the tax due. The final difference is then either payable by you or refundable to you. This net amount is entered in the section entitled "Refund or Balance Due." The return should then be signed and dated by yourself and your spouse and by the paid preparer, if you used one. Mail the return, and a check for any balance owing, to the IRS in accordance with current instructions.

This chapter has covered the basic procedures involved in completing a 1040 return. The next chapter will discuss some of the specific strategies you can use throughout the year in your overall tax planning, plus discussions of what happens when your return is filed and what to do if you are audited.

Personal Action Checklist
Updating Tax Information

You should complete this Checklist *before* you read chapter 25. The information you will gather in completing the Checklist will enable you to gain a clear focus, from the general information in the chapter to the specific information needed to complete the current year's tax returns.

The information you need to complete this Checklist is available in the most recent IRS instructions for the 1040 form as well as in the most recent IRS Publication 17, "Your Federal Income Tax."

Fill in the blanks as they apply to the current tax year:

☐ *Who must file a return?* You must file a return: if you are single, under 65, and had a gross income of $_____for the year; if you are single, 65 or over, and had a gross income of $_____for the year; if you are married, both spouses under 65, and had a combined gross income for the year of $_____; if you are married, one spouse 65 or older, and had a gross income of $_____. If you are self-employed (part-time or full-time) you must file if you had net earnings from self-employment of $_____ or more.

☐ *Exemptions.* The value of each exemption for the current year is $_____. Generally, if you wish to claim someone as a dependent, that person's gross income for the year may not exceed $_____. (See exceptions for children and full-time students.)

☐ *Standard deduction, or zero bracket amount.* For married persons filing jointly, and for qualifying widow(er)s: $_____; for singles, or heads of household: $_____; for married persons filing separately: $_____.

☐ *Itemized deductions.* Estimate your own actual expenses for the year in these areas: Medical and dental expenses that are not reimbursed by insurance, employer, or otherwise $_____; taxes paid (other than Federal income taxes) $____; interest paid, including home mortgage, all credit accounts $_____; charitable contributions (in cash or property) $_____; casualty or theft losses not reimbursed by insurance or otherwise $_____; other deductions $_____.

See text and IRS instructions for specific details. If total of proper itemized deductions exceeds the standard deduction for your filing status, you should itemize your deductions.

Consumer Beware
Some Tax "Helpers" Can Harm You

Every year without fail—usually between Super Bowl Day and Groundhog Day—the landscape in every city and town becomes littered with Income Tax Preparation signs. At the same time, newsstands are overloaded with books offering do-it-yourself guidelines for completing your own tax returns.

Care should be taken in choosing either a tax preparer or a book. With respect to the preparers, beware of high-sounding promises that they can "guarantee" you lower taxes. The most any preparer can guarantee you is an accurate return, based on the information you give him. Preparers can't create deductions where none legally exist. They must follow the same rules that you must.

Compare their prices carefully. Some advertise very low prices, but those might be only for the simplest of forms, and extras can add up quickly. Determine, as best you can before you commit yourself, what the *total* price will be for the service.

Fly-by-night preparers have been a problem, both for the public and for the IRS. Some have filed false or erroneous returns, leaving the taxpayer to answer to the IRS. Others have pocketed their customer's tax payment or refund checks and disappeared into the night.

Tax-preparation services can be helpful, but you must use care in selecting one. How long has it been in business? What personal recommendations can you get from satisfied customers? Don't overlook the regular full-time accountants who don't advertise. They may be no more expensive than the seasonal services, and they're available to assist you all year.

As for the books, some of them are nothing more than reprints of official IRS books that you can obtain at little or no cost from the nearest IRS office. Worthwhile books include J.K. Lasser's *Your Income Tax* and the H. & R. Block annual tax guide. The Lasser book is very comprehensive; the Block book offers an easy step-by-step guide to completing the returns.

Preparers and books aside, though, nobody can help you better than yourself: your ongoing knowledge of and attention to the income tax laws is your best assurance of keeping your taxes as low as possible.

26 | Income Taxes: Strategies, Audits

You must take advantage of all that the law allows you when you complete your tax return for each year. In addition to the tax-cutting opportunities available through careful completion of your 1040, there are other strategies that can affect your tax liability.

Further, it's necessary that you be aware of your rights and obligations with respect to the timely filing of your return; and to the consequences of filing an incorrect or incomplete return. In such cases, or by random choice, the Internal Revenue Service might choose to audit your return.

Laws and regulations may change from time to time with respect to these various strategies and audit procedures. You should check current law to determine the present situation in these areas. This chapter is not intended to be a "tax avoidance" guide to the wealthy or sophisticated investor. Rather, it's intended to present the more common strategies and audit concerns that would apply to the average taxpayer. Among the matters discussed are:

☐ How to increase your take-home pay by modifying your W-4 form.

☐ How year-end tax planning can cut your tax bill.

☐ How and when you can file your return late and amend a previously incorrect return.

☐ How to prepare yourself for, and how to properly handle, audit procedures.

Stay Prepared

As with the previous chapter, you should have at hand when you read this chapter the most current IRS forms and instructions so that you can compare current regulations with the general situations referred to in the chapter. The material covered in this chapter refers to federal income taxes. Some of the techniques discussed may also apply to your state and city income tax situations. It's up to you to familiarize yourself with those specific local regulations.

Tax-cutting Strategies

If you don't claim all of the exemptions, adjustments, deductions, and credits to which you are entitled, the Internal Revenue Service won't do it for you. Throughout the year, it's your job to make certain that you keep proper track of all those items and incorporate them into your tax return.

Tax-exempt or Tax-deferred Income

Similarly, there are other tax-cutting strategies that you must seek out and take advantage of. The government will not hand them to you. Following are examples of some of these basic strategies.

To the extent feasible in your own personal circumstances, take advantage of opportunities to earn tax-exempt or tax-deferred income. There are two major areas in which this can be done: your investment program, and at work.

You can earn tax-exempt income by investing in municipal bonds or in mutual funds that specialize in municipal bonds. See chapter 16 for a further discussion of these techniques. Tax-exempt income can also be obtained through All-Savers Certificates. People filing a single tax return can earn up to $1000 in tax-exempt income through All-Savers Certificates; people filing joint returns can earn up to $2000 through All-Savers Certificates. As orginally created by Congress, the All-Savers plans were to have been available until December 31, 1982. (It is possible that Congress will have decided to make All-Savers Certificates available beyond that date.)

Table 26-1 illustrates the comparisons between taxable and tax-exempt investments.

For example, as the table indicates, if you are in the 39 percent tax bracket, an 8 percent tax-exempt investment will give you the same return as a 13.1 percent taxable investment. In other words, if you invested in a 13.1 percent taxable investment, after you had paid your federal income taxes, you'd be left effectively with an 8 percent return on your investment. (This table does not take state income taxes into account.)

Tax-deferred investment income is available through tax-deferred annuities. These are obtainable through insurance companies, commonly in conjunction with stockbrokerage firms. In such plans you invest a lump sum of money and the company agrees to pay you a fixed amount of interest for a specific period of time. The interest rate is subject to mod-

Table 26-1

Taxable Versus Tax-exempt Yields

If you are in this tax bracket (%)	6%	7%	This tax-exempt yield 8%	9%	10%	11%	12%
			will equal these taxable yields				
19	7.4	8.6	9.9	11.1	12.3	13.6	14.8
22	7.7	9.0	10.3	11.5	12.8	14.1	15.4
24	7.9	9.2	10.5	11.8	13.2	14.5	15.8
28	8.3	9.7	11.1	12.5	13.9	15.3	16.7
32	8.8	10.3	11.8	13.2	14.7	16.2	17.6
39	9.8	11.5	13.1	14.8	16.4	18.0	19.7
42	10.3	12.1	13.8	15.5	17.2	19.0	20.7
44	10.7	12.5	14.3	16.1	17.9	19.6	21.4
50	12.0	14.0	16.0	18.0	20.0	22.0	24.0

ification after the initial period has elapsed. From time to time, you will be permitted to withdraw money from that investment without having to pay tax on the withdrawn amount. In effect, you are withdrawing part of your own original principal investment, not the interest that has been earned. At such time as you withdraw the interest that you have earned, that sum will then be subject to taxes. Further, certain employees, such as those of tax-exempt groups and schools, are allowed to purchase retirement annuities on a month-to-month basis. In such a plan, a portion of one's pay is used to purchase a retirement annuity, and the amount used to purchase the plan, via payroll deduction, is not subject to income taxes in the year in which it was earned. The income, however, will be subject to taxes when it is withdrawn upon retirement.

Some of your income from work may also be on a tax-deferred basis. This is particularly so with pension and profit-sharing plans. Your employer may contribute certain sums of money each year to a pension or profit-sharing plan on your behalf. In effect, he's paying you a form of future income: you won't have the use of the money until some future time, but in the meantime you don't have to pay income taxes on it during the years in which the money is credited to your account. In addition to pension and profit-sharing plans, some individual employees might find it worthwhile to establish a tax-deferred compensation program that would delay payment for work done until some future year. The object of any deferred compensation plan is to delay the payment of taxes on income from work into a future year when the taxpayer will be in a lower tax bracket, such as upon retirement.

Individual Retirement Accounts (IRA) and Keogh plans can be ideal ways to defer taxes on income both from work and from investments. As noted in chapter 16, investments in IRA and Keogh plans are tax deductible to you in the year in which made, and the taxes on earnings made on such plans are deferred until funds are withdrawn from the plans, again, presumably upon retirement. The 1981 Tax Law made IRA plans available to all workers starting in tax year 1982. The maximum that could be invested in an IRA plan for 1982 was $2000 per person. Two working spouses could invest a total of $4000. An individual with a nonworking spouse could invest $2250. If a couple is in, say, the 39 percent tax bracket, and they invest $4000 in IRA plans during the year, they could realize an immediate cash savings of over $1500 on their tax bill for the year.

Further, since the earnings on the IRA funds are not taxed each year, there is more money to go to work for you in the ensuing years than there would be if the investment was taxed. For example, the couple in the 39 percent tax bracket invests $4000 at, say, 10 percent interest. In a regular taxable type of investment, they would earn $400 during the year, and after paying taxes on that income they would be left with $244. If the $4000 was invested in an IRA plan, none of the $400 earned would be taxed, and the entire $400 would go to work for them in the next year, and in following years, to earn still more interest.

Since the IRA plan was first introduced in 1975, the maximum annual investment has periodically increased, and it is likely to do so again in the future. Check what the current maximum IRA contribution is for this year.

Tax Withholding and the W-4 Form

Suppose someone advised you to embark on an investment plan of $60 per month, and you were guaranteed to earn no interest at all. At the end of the year you would get back the $720 that you had paid in and not a penny more. You'd think such advice was rather absurd, wouldn't you?

The fact is that tens of millions of people do just that. Of the more than 90 million tax returns filed annually, the majority get a refund from the government. The average refund check is over $700. Some are for much less; some are for much more. The reason these taxpayers get a refund check is that they have had more of their pay withheld by the employer than was really necessary to meet their annual tax obligation. The government holds those excess payments for the full year and then returns them to the taxpayer in the form of a refund check once the taxpayer has filed his return for the year.

An employer is required to withhold from workers' pay enough to meet each worker's tax obligations for the year. The employer estimates the amount he must withhold for each pay period based on information that the employee provides him on a W-4 form. Each employee completes a W-4 form when he starts work with an employer. The W-4 form sets forth the number of allowances that the employee is claiming. The *more* allowances an employee claims, the *less* is withheld from his pay.

What qualifies as an allowance? Most commonly, each exemption you claim on your tax return is equal to one allowance. In other words, if you claim four exemptions, you can also claim four allowances on your W-4 form. You are entitled to claim additional allowances over and above the number of exemptions. For example, if you itemize your deductions, you are entitled to claim additional allowances. If you are entitled to certain credits against your tax, you are entitled to claim additional allowances. There are also additional allowances that can be claimed relative to your work and marital status. A single person can claim a special withholding allowance if he or she does not work for more than one employer. A married person can claim this special allowance if his or her spouse does not work.

W-4 forms, available at your employer's personnel office, contain a work sheet that will assist you in calculating the correct number of allowances to claim. If you claim fewer allowances than you're legally entitled to, more money than necessary will be withheld from your pay. The basic strategy, then, is this: see to it that your W-4 form reflects the correct number of allowances to which you are entitled. This should result in just the right amount being withheld from your pay—not too much, not too little. If you have been having too much withheld from your pay, a proper adjustment in your W-4 form can fatten your weekly paycheck. Then, rather than sending excess money to the government where it earns no interest all year long, you'll have that money to invest or spend as you see fit.

Year-end Strategies

As each calendar year draws to a close, you should try to estimate your likely tax liability for this year compared to what it might be next year. The reason for doing this is to try to determine whether it would make sense to shift income or deductions from one year to the next in order to cut your tax bill. The overall strategy behind such moves is to claim deductions in years in which you'd be more highly taxed, and to receive income in years when you'd be taxed less.

For example, if tax rates are scheduled to be lower next year (as is the case from 1982 to 1983), it would make sense in many cases to delay year-end income from December of the current year into January of the next year. Reason? It will be taxed at a lower rate next year and you'll save money accordingly. By the same token, given those same circumstances, it also makes sense to accelerate deductions. This means making deductible expenses this year that you'd otherwise make next year. A deduction is worth more to you in a higher tax year than it is in a lower tax year.

Shifting incomes or deductions need span only a few weeks—from late December into early January. If much more time than that is involved, shifting may become counterproductive since the loss of use of your money for more than a few weeks might offset the value of the shifted income or deductions.

Examples of shifting income include year-end bonuses that could be declared or paid in early January instead of late December; payment for fees or services; sales that result in capital gains. Examples of deductions that can be shifted from one year to the next at year-end include charitable contributions; major purchases (car, for example) that can result in large sales taxes deductible over and above the standard IRS formula; payment of state income taxes and local property taxes; interest expenses; medical and dental expenses that you'd otherwise put off paying until next year but that you can pay this year.

If tax rates are *not* scheduled to change from this year to next year, and you know nearing year-end that your income will be *lower* next year than it was this year, the same strategies as noted above can be worth seeking out. A drop in income from one year to the next can occur in many ways: A pay cut is in the offing; a spouse who was working may stop working; or you may have had an exceptionally high income year this year due to bonuses, commissions, or capital gains, which are not likely to be repeated next year.

Vice Versa

On the other hand, it may happen that tax rates are scheduled to go *up* next year, or that your *income* is likely to *increase* substantially next year. In either of those cases, the reverse of the above strategies may be worthwhile. In other words, you might want to accelerate income (take it this year instead of next year), and delay paying deductible expenses.

Here's an example of how this shifting of income or deductions can work. Let's assume that this year you are in the 22 percent tax bracket and that next year you anticipate being in the 33 percent tax bracket. Assume further that shifting of $1000 worth of income or deductions will not move you into a different bracket. You have $1000 coming to you on January 2 for work that you have performed. If you wait until January 2 to receive it, it will be taxed in next year's income, and in the 33 percent bracket the tax will be $333. If you can convince the person who owes you the money to pay you in December of this year, it will be taxed in this year's bracket of 22 percent, which will mean a tax of $220. In short, you save $110 in taxes by having the income paid to you a few days earlier than scheduled. Delaying a deductible expense from this year into next year can have similar results on your overall tax liability.

Income Splitting

If you have children or other family members who are in a low income tax bracket, or who don't have to pay taxes at all, you might want to consider transferring some of your income-producing assets to them. In so doing, you shift the tax on the income from your higher bracket to their lower bracket. This can result in considerable tax savings.

For example, say that you have set up a savings fund to be used for your child's college education. The fund is currently in your name and has a balance of $5000. It's earning 10 percent per year or $500. You are in the 30 percent tax bracket so the $500 income is being taxed $150 each year. In other words, your true earnings on the fund are only $350. If, however, you transfer the ownership of that account to your young child, the $500 income would be taxable to the child. Presumably the child has no other earnings and so the full $500 would escape taxation. The bottom line: instead of earning $350 per year, you are earning $500 per year for your child.

The tax law with respect to gifts establishes that from 1982 onwards any individual can make annual gifts to as many other individuals as he or she likes of up to $10,000 without incurring any gift tax liability. If both spouses join in the making of the gift, the annual amount can be up to $20,000 without incurring gift tax liability. It would be advisable to seek legal assistance before embarking on any ongoing gift giving program, since a gift, once made, may be difficult to take back without incurring tax problems.

Another means of transferring income-producing assets is by way of an interest-free, or low-interest, loan to the recipient. This technique has been criticized by the Internal Revenue Service, which may pass regulations to restrict such practices. Determine current regulations on this matter before embarking on such a program.

Tax Shelters

Tax shelters, as they are called, are investment—or more correctly stated, speculative—deals that are sold to higher-bracket taxpayers to enable them to cut their income taxes.

Here's an oversimplified view of how a tax shelter might work. You are in the 50 percent tax bracket, and you realize that for every $2000 worth of deductions you can legitimately create, you can cut your tax bill by $1000. You are offered an interest in a tax shelter deal. The tax shelter salesman tells you that you can buy a one-fifteenth share of an apartment house for $20,000. (15 shares at $20,000 each total $300,000, which is the down payment. The balance of the purchase is done on a mortgage loan, for which you are one-fifteenth liable.)

The depreciable portion of the property is reported to be $4.5 million, meaning that your share is worth $300,000. On a straight line 15-year depreciation schedule, then, you'd be entitled to an annual depreciation deduction of $20,000. (Assume for the sake of discussion that the income from rents exactly equals the operating costs and mortgage payments.) See the discussion in chapter 18 on real estate investing for a view of how depreciation works.

Your arithmetic from that point on is fairly simple: A $20,000 deduction will reduce your tax bill by $10,000. In effect, then, you're really only out of pocket by $10,000 and you own an interest in what you hope will be a successful apartment house investment. In other words, instead of having sent $10,000 to the government to pay taxes, you have invested $10,000 in an apartment house. Put another way, instead of sending away $10,000 that you'll never see again, you've invested $10,000 that will hopefully provide future tax deductions as well as profit some years hence. The logic is compelling. But all too often such tactics can backfire.

The problem is that while many tax-shelter deals are indeed legitimate, there are many that are flim-flams. The Internal Revenue Service very aggressively examines virtually all claims for deductions arising out of tax-shelter deals. At the very least, claiming such a deduction will likely expose you to an audit, and at the worst, if a tax-shelter deal is found to be improper or illegal, you could be obliged to pay the back taxes you thought you had escaped plus severe interest and penalty costs.

Using the apartment investment as an example, let's say that the building itself really was worth only $1 million. But to make the deal attractive, and to establish the $20,000 deduction, the promotors of the deal claimed that the building was worth $4.5 million—a gross exaggeration of its true value. If the IRS examines this deal—and you almost have to assume that they will—and they find that the evaluation was grossly exaggerated, they could disallow your deduction and charge you with a penalty of up to 30 percent of the back taxes owed. In addition to paying the back taxes and the penalty, you'll have to pay interest on the back taxes for as long as they have remained unpaid. Starting in February 1982 that interest rate will be 20 percent, adjusted annually thereafter in accordance with the current prime rate. Further, as can sometimes happen, if the overall investment was economically unsound in the first place, you could also lose all or part of your original investment if the property can't be sold advantageously.

If your tax shelter deal is legitimate, you have nothing to fear from an audit other than the time involved in justifying your position. But if the deal was unsound from the outset, the costs can be considerable.

The situation is compounded by the fact that the selling of tax shelters reaches a fever pitch near year end. This is a time when most taxpayers are caught up in the holiday season—parties, shopping—and they don't give themselves the time needed to properly examine the fine points of any tax-shelter offering. All too often, therefore, they make a last-minute, impulsive decision that they could seriously regret within the next year or two.

If you feel that a tax shelter can be advantageous to you, don't wait until the last minute to expose yourself to the salesmen. Shop carefully throughout the year and use whatever professional assistance seems advisable—lawyers, accountants, and the like—to help you evaluate the economic soundness of the deal. Perhaps the most frequently echoed guideline with respect to tax shelters is this: If the deal doesn't make good sense as an investment, it probably doesn't make good sense as a tax shelter.

Filing Your Return

What happens if you are not able to file your return by the due date, or if you discover that a return that you did file was incorrect? The law does allow you an opportunity to get an extension on your filing date, and it also allows you to correct a return already filed if the need arises.

Filing Extensions

Regulations in recent years have allowed taxpayers an automatic two-month extension for the filing of their individual returns. (Check to see if current regulations are the same.) In order to obtain the automatic two-month extension you must file a form 4868 with the Internal Revenue Service. This form must be filed by the regular due date (April 15) with the IRS center in your area. Note that the extension of the time to file your return is *not* an extension of the time to pay the taxes. Your taxes must be fully paid at the time you file the extension form. You can incur a penalty if you've not paid your taxes by the time you file for the extension. Interest charges on late payments may also be imposed.

If you need more time beyond the automatic two-month extension, you may be able to get an additional extension of time to file if you have a very good reason for seeking such further extension. You can apply for such further extension by sending a letter to the Internal Revenue Service stating your reasons or by filing form 2688. If this request for additional time to file is not granted, the Internal Revenue Service will expect the filing of your return almost immediately after they have notified you of the rejection of your application.

Amending Your Return

Once you've filed your return for any given year, you can amend it later if you determine that you owe the government or that they owe you a refund because you didn't claim exemptions, adjustments, deductions, or credits to which you were legally entitled.

The proper form to use to amend your return is a 1040X. Follow the 1040X instructions carefully and be certain to attach any forms or schedules that are needed to explain the changes.

The law allows you ample time to file an amended return. You have three years from the date you filed your original return, or two years from the time you paid your tax, whichever is later, to file the amendment.

What Happens to Your Return? Examinations and Audits

For about 95 percent of all individual taxpayers, the year's concerns end with the filing of your return and the payment of any taxes due (or the receipt of any refund owed to you). But for the other 5 percent, the struggle is not over: about half of them will hear from the Internal Revenue Service with respect to arithmetic errors made on their return and the other half will be subjected to some form of examination or audit.

Where errors in arithmetic are involved, the taxpayers will hear relatively quickly. But it may be two years, three years, or even longer before some audits are announced and resolved. Under the law, the Internal Revenue Service has three years from the date you filed your return to assess additional taxes if proper reason exists to do so. If you have failed to report a substantial item of income, the IRS has six years from the filing of your return to claim back taxes. If someone has filed a return with false or fraudulent information intending to evade taxes, or if someone has failed to file a return at all, there is no time limit as to when the IRS can pursue its claim. But taxpayers are not totally at the mercy of the IRS. The law sets forth very clear-cut rights for all taxpayers to appeal and protest decisions that go against them. Let's examine what happens once your return is filed.

The Initial Screenings

All returns are checked clerically to determine that the arithmetic is correct and to make certain that the returns and any checks attached thereto have been properly completed and signed. If a mistake in arithmetic is discovered, the IRS will recalculate the amount of tax due and will send you either a refund for the amount overpaid or a bill for the amount you owe them. If other corrections are needed (for example, you forgot to sign your return), you will be notified accordingly.

A further screening will be conducted to determine whether there are errors in the return with respect to deductions, exemptions, and the like. These are some of the most common areas in which errors are found:

☐ You have excluded from income more dividends (or interest) than the law allows.

☐ You have claimed deductions for medical expenses without taking into account the stated limitations in the law.

☐ You have claimed a partial exemption.

☐ Perhaps most important, your reported income from wages and investments does not match the W-2 form your employer has provided or the 1099 form your financial institution or stockbroker has provided. (Anyone who pays you interest or dividends during the year is required to report such payments to the IRS on a 1099 form. You are sent a copy of those 1099 forms in January of each year.) In recent years, IRS computers have become very sophisticated in matching up the wages and investment income that you report with the amounts that your employer and financial institutions report. If you report less income than you actually did receive, it would be wise to assume that the IRS will find out about it.

If the IRS finds errors in these or other reporting areas, you will be notified by mail of the correction. If you disagree with their findings, you can ask for a meeting with an IRS representative or you can submit whatever information is necessary to support your claim. As noted earlier, matters such as these may be resolved fairly quickly after the filing of your return. But once such matters are resolved, that does not mean you're off the hook with respect to a more detailed audit.

Audits

In recent years the IRS has been auditing about 2 percent of all individual returns filed. While on the surface this would indicate that your chances of being audited in a given year are only one in fifty, bear in mind that that chance occurs every year, and sooner or later the law of averages is likely to catch up with you.

Out of roughly 100 million returns filed each year, how does the IRS select the two million to three million returns for actual auditing? Figure 26-1 illustrates the approximate breakdown of reasons the IRS used to choose returns for auditing.

Discriminate Income Function (DIF)

About 70 percent of the returns chosen for audit are selected by the Discriminate Income Function, or DIF. Returns are examined by computers, and specific elements of the return are scored. These elements include your total income, your adjusted gross income, your deductions, your adjustments, your credits. Based on past statistical evidence, agents can determine which returns—by virtue of the scoring—have the greatest

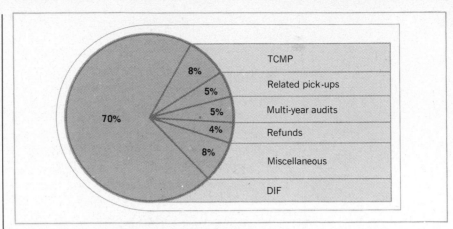

Figure 26-1 Reasons for Audit Selection

potential for recovering additional taxes through an audit. This is known as "audit potential." The IRS does not divulge the specifics of how each item is scored, but in general terms it would seem to be tempting an audit if one's tax bill was too low relative to the gross income declared, and so on.

Once a return has been selected by the DIF process, an examiner will scrutinize it to see where errors or improper avoidance techniques have been used. The majority of DIF audits are conducted via correspondence. You may, for example, receive a letter requesting that you send photostats of checks, receipts, or other evidence to support your specific claims. If you can provide such evidence, the audit may be ended quickly. If you are unable to provide the evidence, an additional tax will be payable.

If the audit isn't conducted via correspondence, you may be requested to appear at the local IRS office. In some cases, the audit can be scheduled at your place of business or home, particularly if the records involved are extensive or if the matter is very complex.

Taxpayer Compliance Measurement Program (TCMP)

About 8 percent of all returns chosen for audit are selected via the Taxpayer Compliance Measurement Program (TCMP). This is a random selection by the IRS computers and/or agents and is considered to be a much more comprehensive and thorough review of your overall situation. A TCMP audit can be very detailed and time consuming even if you have nothing at all to hide. The purposes of the TCMP program are to police the voluntary-compliance aspects of the law and to unearth more statistical data to support the DIF program.

Related Pick-ups

About 5 percent of those returns chosen for auditing are based on "related pick-ups." If, for instance, your business partner was chosen for audit, you might also be chosen; the questionable deductions claimed by the one partner might be suspect with regard to the other partner. Further, if you have not reported all the income that your W-2 and 1099 forms show you actually received, this could be cause for an audit under this category.

Multi-year Audits

About 5 percent of those returns selected for audit are chosen because more than one of your returns is in question. For example, if you had reported deductions from a tax-shelter program in your 1982 return and in years prior, you might be audited not just for your 1982 return, but for your 1981 and 1980 returns as well.

Refunds

About 4 percent of all taxpayers who claim refunds on their returns are audited if for no other reason than to verify the facts which would allow a refund.

Miscellaneous

The remaining audits are done for a variety of reasons, which can include the seeking of verification on capital-gains transactions, appraisals of charitable contributions, appraisals of casualty losses, and so forth. The IRS also exchanges tax information with state taxing authorities, and a mismatch of information between your state return and your federal return may also prompt an audit in this miscellaneous category.

Audit Red Flags

Aside from the aforementioned manners in which returns are chosen for audit, the following are generally regarded as being common "red flags" that will prompt an IRS audit of your return:

☐ An individual return with income over $50,000, particularly if you have claimed deductions through a tax-shelter arrangement.
☐ Excessive deductions claimed for travel and entertainment expenses.
☐ Deductions claimed for the expense of maintaining an office in your home.
☐ Losses arising out of what the IRS determines to be a "hobby," even though you determine such activity to be an ongoing business.

Audit Strategies: Yours

Perhaps no other phenomenon in our modern society has gotten more critical reviews than an IRS audit. Perhaps, subconsciously or otherwise, the government has tried to instill a fear in us all of the audit procedure. In so doing, they would hope to encourage taxpayers to be as honest and forthright as possible in preparing their returns, so as to avoid a possible audit. Whatever the psychological foundation for our fear of audits, the fact is that most audits really do not have to be feared, particularly if your return is an honest one and you have the documentation necessary to back up your claims.

Bear in mind if you are called in for an office audit that you are dealing with another human being. That human being is there to do a job, and he or she has the same day-to-day cares and concerns that you do:

meeting the monthly house payment, putting groceries on the table, worrying about personal matters, and so on. Very likely you will be treated in much the same way that you treat the auditing agent. If you are surly, don't be surprised if you are met with surliness. If you are pleasant, cooperative, and polite, chances are better that you'll be met with those same traits. If you arrive with your documents in well-organized fashion, you're going to make the agent's job that much easier, which in turn could make your examination that much easier. There is, of course, no guarantee that these techniques will work, but if they don't, you can ask to see the agent's supervisor and request that another agent take over the examination.

If a reasonably small amount of money is involved, you may feel comfortable in handling the audit proceedings on your own. If, however, through the initial correspondence or through the initial office visit, it appears that a substantial amount of money might become involved, it would be wise to consider hiring an accountant or tax attorney to assist you with the proceedings. If you have had such a professional or a tax preparer establish your return initially, that person would be the likely candidate to assist you with the audit.

An audit proceeding is a legal entanglement. Your legal rights and the government's legal rights are in apparent opposition. As in any legal entanglement, you must determine what your likely overall costs will be in terms of money, time, and aggravation. Only you can determine the relative values of those items. If you feel that your case is weak, it might be better to resolve the matter quickly, pay the tax due (or a lesser negotiated amount if you're able to do so), and save yourself future time and aggravation that would be involved if you pursued the matter. On the other hand, if you feel that your case is strong and there is enough money involved, you might deem it worthwhile to fight the matter all the way. You have to determine for yourself what compromises are in order. The IRS looks at the matter in much the same way: the agent's time and energy must be evaluated in line with the hoped-for amount of back taxes that can be recovered. Thus, negotiations are always a possibility. But a good negotiator will let the other side make the first proposal.

Audit Strategies: Theirs

The value of any employee is measured by his or her performance. An auditing agent of the IRS is expected to produce tax revenues as efficiently as possible. The IRS denies that there is any "quota" as to how much a given agent should produce; but a good agent will justify his or her existence, and promotions, by producing as much revenue as possible in the most cost-efficient way. It might safely be presumed, then, that a good agent, considering a deliquent tax of, say, $500, might be willing to accept a lesser amount—perhaps $350—on the spot rather than try to go for the whole $500 over a protracted period of protests and appeals. In short, negotiations are possible, and your success in them will be in direct proportion to the strength of your case and your ability to recognize the weak points in the agent's case.

But be assured that an efficient agent will probe quickly and deeply to determine just what your strengths and weaknesses may be. Following, for example, are some of the interrogation guidelines that an agent might use.

☐ With respect to claims for charitable deductions, he (or she) will attempt to determine whether the payments were actually made to qualified charitable organizations; if property was contributed, as opposed to cash, he will seek to verify the true fair market value of the property at the time it was given, and he'll determine whether or not the giver retains any control over the property (which could disqualify it from being a true contribution).

☐ With respect to claimed deductions for interest payments, the agent will ascertain whether the interest payments were made on a valid, existing debt that you, the taxpayer, owed. This may necessitate your providing copies of all the documents relating to the loan agreement.

☐ With respect to deductions claimed for taxes paid, he will determine whether the tax is in fact of the type deductible in accordance with the present rules and regulations.

☐ With respect to claims for medical deductions, the agent will seek to determine whether any insurance reimbursement has been made to you or is expected by you. He'll also probe to be certain that amounts that you've claimed as child-care expenses aren't also claimed as medical expenses.

☐ If a deduction is claimed for a casualty or theft loss, the agent will attempt to determine that a theft or casualty loss has actually occurred, and that your loss was the direct result of such an occurrence. He'll also determine whether insurance proceeds have been received by you or are expected by you.

☐ If you claim a deduction for educational purposes, it will be the agent's job to determine if your expenses were primarily incurred for the purpose of maintaining or improving skills, or for meeting express requirements for retaining your job status. This may necessitate evidence from your employer.

☐ If you've claimed alimony expenses as an adjustment to your income, you can expect that the agent will request a copy of the underlying divorce documents for inspection.

☐ One of the major sources of back taxes arises with respect to claims for travel and entertainment deductions. If you've claimed what seem to be excessive expenses in that regard, the agent will seek to reconcile the amount of your claimed deduction by asking you to prepare an analysis of the cash you had available to you to make the payments you've claimed to have made. He or she can ask you to take into account the totals of all monies you have received from work, expense accounts, investments, and savings, less your estimated expenses for personal living and investing. The difference, at least in part, will be an amount that you theoretically could have spent for travel and entertainment. If that amount of cash available does not jibe with the amount of deductions you've claimed, you could be in for a back tax assessment.

The above examples are just a random sampling of the *preliminary* probes that you should expect the agent to make. If you are armed with all of the necessary documentation at the initial meeting, you might be able to bring the audit to a swift conclusion. If you're not prepared to document your claims immediately, the agent will normally give you a reasonable amount of time to collect the necessary documents and will schedule a future meeting at which the matter should be resolved.

Resolving an Audit: You Agree

If you and the agent agree on the findings at your initial meeting—which could take less than an hour—ask the agent to tell you how much in additional taxes you will owe. You will then be asked to sign a form stipulating the content of the agreement, and shortly thereafter you will receive a written report plus a bill for whatever taxes you may owe, plus any interest or penalties that have been agreed upon. Note that if you sign the agreement you waive your rights to appeal in the future. If paying the back taxes in one lump sum will cause a hardship for you, you can ask the agent to put the payments on an installment plan. You have to ask for this as it's unlikely that they'll volunteer it. But it is possible in specific cases to work out an installment arrangement.

Resolving an Audit: You Disagree

If you are unable to settle the matter in the IRS office audit, you should immediately ask for a written copy of your legal rights under such circumstances. Where disagreement occurs, you can ask for an immediate meeting with a supervisor, with the hopes that such a meeting might result in a more favorable compromise.

If you don't reach an agreement with the supervisor, the agent will then send you a report explaining the additional tax liability. You then have the right to request a conference at the district level to see if the matter can be resolved. If a settlement still isn't reached at the conference level, you'll then receive a Notice of Deficiency, which is commonly referred to as a "90-day letter." In this letter the government notifies you that you will be assessed the additional tax owed 90 days from the date the letter was mailed.

If you still believe that your case is valid, you have 90 days in which to choose one of three courses to further your appeal.

□ You can file a petition with the tax court.

□ You can pay the tax that the government claims is due and then file a refund claim for it. Once the refund claim has been turned down, you then sue for your refund in either a federal district court or the court of claims.

□ If the amount of tax is $5000 or less, you can proceed in the relatively new Small Claims Division of the tax court.

The first two choices would be more suitable for claims involving substantial sums of money; in either of those courses you'd likely need professional representation. In the Small Claims Division, however, procedures are relatively informal, and in many instances you can plead your own case. Small Claims Division cases are heard by commissioners instead of judges, and the proceedings move much more rapidly than in the more formal court system. It's likely that a case may be settled before it is actually heard. But once a decision is reached, whether by settlement or by judgment, the decision is final and there are no further appeals to be had.

As with all tax matters, rules and regulations are subject to change from time to time. If you find yourself involved in a tax dispute, make certain that you know your rights as they currently exist.

Your Best Protection

There is nothing that can insulate you better from the rigors of a tax audit than an accurate return accompanied by all proper documentation for all claims made. If you have those in hand, an audit should be nothing more than a minor inconvenience every few years. Lacking either a correct return or the proper documentation, an audit can become a costly source of stress—not only will you have to pay back taxes, plus possible interest and penalties; the proceedings can also interfere with your normal ability to generate your income and live a peaceable day-to-day life. It may seem tempting to put some extra money in your pocket by avoiding taxes improperly or evading taxes illegally. But the consequences of doing so can ultimately be more costly than you may think.

Personal Action Checklist
Tax-cutting Strategy Guide

Filling in this checklist will help you determine whether certain strategies can be worth pursuing to cut your income taxes for this year.

Withholding:

1. What were your federal income taxes last year?
2. Did you receive a refund? How much?
3. What do you estimate your taxes will be for this year?
4. At the rate taxes are currently being withheld from your pay, how much excess, if any, will be taken out for this full year? (Check your paycheck voucher to learn the current weekly withholding amount, and multiply it by 52 to get the total annual withholding.)
5. If you would rather have a fatter paycheck than pay extra to the government, on which you earn no interest, visit your payroll office to have your W-4 form properly adjusted to cut the excess withholding.

Year-end shifting:

6. Will income tax rates be lower next year?
7. Will your income be lower next year?
8. If you answered "yes" to either of the above questions, calculate the tax savings you'd realize if you shifted income from this year into next, and if you shifted deductible expenses from the next year into this year.
9. Will income tax rates be higher next year?
10. Will your income be higher next year?
11. If you answered "yes" to either of the above questions, calculate the tax savings you'd realize if you shifted income from next year into this year, and if you shifted deductible expenses from this year into next year.
12. If you answered "yes" to either 6 or 7, and also answered "yes" to either 9 or 10, shifting income or deductions may offset each other. But the calculations may still be worthwhile.

Consumer Beware
Tax-evasion Schemes
Can Be Costly

"How would you like never to pay income taxes for the rest of your life? Sound intriguing? It may be easier than you think. Churches are tax exempt, so start a church. Have all your income payable to your church, and, voila, no more taxes ever!"

That, in essence, was the pitch of two promoters who were selling "how-to-form-your-own-tax-exempt-church" programs to unwary buyers. The price for this so-called lifetime tax exemption? $4000!

Buyers truly believed that they had found the goose that lays the golden eggs. But the Internal Revenue Service thought otherwise. They brought suit against the promoters, and in short order they were convicted of conspiracy to defraud the government, tax evasion, failure to file tax returns, helping others prepare false returns, and mail fraud. (The promoters apparently believed their own story: they had failed to pay their own income taxes on over $300,000 of income.)

Those who bought the scheme and put it to use will be subject to the same evasion charges as the promoters, with the possibility of criminal penalties in addition to tax penalties.

The IRS's success in the prosecution was based on their contention that the so-called church was not a legitimate tax-exempt religious institution but rather a scheme to evade taxes.

This case is not the only one of its kind. From time to time ads and mail-order promotions have appeared—and will continue to appear—offering too-good-to-be-true ways to beat the government. Some may be selling nothing more than official government tax guides at exorbitant prices. Others, like the church scheme, may be elaborate scams that can cost thousands of dollars and put you at the risk of criminal action if you follow through with the proposals.

A word to the wise. . . .

Appendix

When Things Go Wrong

In our nation of roughly 250,000,000 people, we conduct uncounted billions of money transactions every day. We do it with machines: pay phones, parking meters, robot bankers, video games, juke boxes, and devices that vend everything from the daily newspaper to a steaming hot meal.

We do it with people: bank tellers, store clerks, and restaurant cashiers. We do it through the mail: paying bills by check, ordering goods, and settling up our taxes. And, in growing numbers, we're even doing it by computers that talk to each other by telephone.

We have come to take it for granted that virtually all of these transactions will flow smoothly virtually all of the time. And indeed they do.

We rarely, if ever, voice a word of thanks to the people who designed the intricate machines, to the bookkeepers who post our accounts correctly, to the shipping clerks who sent out the exact goods that were ordered, to the technicians who keep the mammoth computers running efficiently.

But when something goes wrong—against us—the air turns purple with swear words and vows of vengeance! (When was the last time you complained if a vending machine gave you two candy bars instead of one, or a store undercharged you for a purchase, or a waiter added a bill wrong in your favor?)

Though the occurrences may be statistically rare, things *do* go wrong now and then, and there's nothing more frustrating than the feeling that you've been shortchanged or ripped off.

This appendix is designed to help you cope with such moments. First, some advice on how to *prevent* things from going wrong in the first place. Then, some guidelines and contacts which will help you *correct* matters when things do go wrong.

Preventive Medicine

The following tips, ranging from simple to fairly complicated, can help keep money troubles away from your door. The more complicated efforts can be well worth your involvement when a substantial amount of money is at stake.

Handling Money

Whenever you receive money—for example, cashing a check or getting change from paying a bill—count the money immediately in front of the person who gave it to you. If you turn away from the cashier for just a few seconds, then claim you were shortchanged, you're likely to lose a war of words. And money. The time to claim an error is immediately.

Also: if you pay for a purchase with a large bill—say you're giving a $20 bill for a purchase of just a few dollars—take a second to note the first few numbers on the serial of the bill. If you then get change back for a $10 instead of a $20, you'll have some instant evidence that you gave the clerk a $20: recite those few numbers.

**Signing
Charge Slips**

Always be certain that the charges on a credit card slip are added up properly. If the clerk hasn't filled in the total, you do it. Unscrupulous merchants can insert a higher total than is proper, and you may never catch the difference. You're doubly courting trouble if that unscrupulous merchant sees you throw away your copy of the charge. Then he'll know you won't have a record of the correct amount, and he'll be even more tempted to raise the total—even if it was already filled in. (Example: raising the number "3" to an "8" takes very little skill.)

Also: Don't let a merchant make more than one stamping of your credit card. If an error is made on the first stamping, be certain that the charge slip is totally torn up so that it can't be used. Best bet: tear it up yourself.

**Checking Monthly
Statements**

Probably the single biggest source of frustration with bank accounts arises because the customer has neglected to do the monthly reconciliation on his or her checking account. The frequent results of carrying the wrong checking account balance: bounced checks, added costs, embarrassment, and possibly even bad marks on your credit rating. Ten to twenty minutes per month of reconciling your account can avoid such problems. Do the same with all of your credit card and charge account statements.

Also: if you deposit an out-of-town check in your checking account, ask your banker how long you may have to wait before they'll allow you to draw out money against that check. It may be as much as a few weeks. If they know you well enough, they may not restrict you at all. You don't ask; you don't get.

Refund Policies

Know before you buy exactly what any store's refund policies will be. The law may not necessarily entitle you to a refund if you bought defective or unsatisfactory goods. Merchants concerned with public goodwill should have a fairly liberal refund policy, under reasonable circumstances. But many will give you only an exchange privilege or a credit instead of an outright cash refund. In some instances, such as an "as-is" sale, there may be no privileges of any kind.

Determine, too, how long you have to get a refund, a credit, or an exchange. Be certain you keep whatever documents you may need, such as sales slip, credit card slip, etc. If you use a product, can you lose your refund privileges?

Cancellation, or Recision, Privileges

Some transactions may give the buyer the right to cancel, or rescind, a deal, even after papers have been signed. This may be because of a law (federal or state), or simply by agreement between buyer and seller. If you do have such privileges, know *precisely* what you must do to exercise them: by when, in what form, under what circumstances. Get it all *in writing.* If you then do wish to exercise the privilege, be certain that you do it in *precisely* the right way.

Money-back Guarantees

These can be classic cases of "the big print giveth, the small print taketh away." Under what circumstances will you get your money back? Will you get it all back? Or will you forfeit some of it? There's no substitute for knowing your contractual rights.

Mail Order Buying

Though as huge and as generally efficient as the mail order industry is, it's still the number one cause of consumer complaints, according to the Council of Better Business Bureaus. One important rule of thumb: The better you know the people you're dealing with, the better chance you have of being satisfied, or of getting satisfaction should things go wrong. In other words, if you can buy through local merchants, you've got someone to complain to if things go wrong. If you're dealing with a mail order house hundreds or thousands of miles away, you're just another number in their computer. Let the buyer beware, and shop accordingly.

Warranties

Part of shopping for a product requires that you also know the terms of any warranty that may come with the product. You should know those terms *before* you buy. Cost and aggravation run high when you're told, "Sorry, that isn't covered under the warranty." Do your homework particularly with respect to such big ticket items as appliances, cars, houses, and home improvements.

Patience

If a situation gives off signals of sounding "too good to be true," or that makes you think you're getting the deal of the century (particularly if you sign *right now* on the dotted line), you're likely courting trouble with Snake Oil Sam. If he gets your money, you likely to never see it again. Keep your impulsive nature in hand. Resist the lures and the temptations of Sam's persuasions.

Ask "But what if. . ."

If an advertisement or a salesperson tells you that a product or a service will provide certain results, you tend to believe such representations. Then nagging frustration sets in if you don't get what you'd expected out of the product or service. It's nice to be trusting, but it can get you into trouble. Remedy: ask the salesperson "But what if. . . ."

Examples: "This shirt will not shrink." "But what if it does?"

"This package is guaranteed to arrive by tomorrow noon." "But what if it doesn't?"

"You'll arrive in Chicago at 2 P.M., and that will give you plenty of time to catch your connecting flight to Albany." "But what if the flight into Chicago is late?"

"With our answering service you'll never miss an important phone call again. Our friendly operators will answer every call by the third ring. . . ." "But what if. . . .?"

"You pay me $X00 and I'll see to it that your roof stops leaking/ your transmission stops slipping/ your septic tank stops overflowing/ the ghosts disappear from your TV reception. . . ." "BUT WHAT IF. . .?"

In short, know your rights and your recourses *before* you get involved in any kind of situation that could prove "iffy." If your rights and recourses aren't clearly spelled out, you may find you don't have any.

Get it in Writing

As a general rule, spoken (oral) statements by a salesperson will prove meaningless in a dispute. If any promises are made with respect to a deal, get them in writing. Have them signed by a person who is legally authorized to sign on behalf of the company. Don't assume that the salesperson you're dealing with is legally authorized to sign for the company. He may not be. Check with the company headquarters to be sure. And get *that* assurance in writing as well. This is particularly important in such major costly deals as buying a home, home improvement contracts, and any other major purchase involving time payment contracts.

Get Names and Numbers

Know with whom you're dealing, and take notes of prices quotes, delivery promises, etc. Keep all documents relating to a specific transaction. If a foul-up occurs, it's much easier to track your way to the source of the problem if you have all this information.

Research, Research, Research!

The less you know the people you're dealing with, the greater the need for research, *before* you commit yourself to spending any money. The time to check with the Better Business Bureau (BBB) or governmental Consumer Protection Bureau is *before* the transaction, not after it. If you're dealing with a business located in another city, check with the BBB and the governmental agencies in that other city as well as your own. To the extent possible, get personal references from other customers, clients, or patients *before* you get involved. If a transaction has legal, tax, or financing ramifications, check them out with a lawyer, an accountant, and/or a banker *before* you get involved. Doing research before a transaction is relatively quick and cheap. Trying to dig out from under a transaction that has gone sour (partly because of lack of research) is time-consuming, painful, and expensive.

Let's now examine some of the things you can do to minimize the waste of time, the pain, and the cost that can occur when things do go wrong.

Digging Out From Under

The range of things that can go wrong is roughly as follows: on the one hand, it could have been a plain simple goof on the part of the seller or institution. If you're dealing with reasonable and reputable people, the matter should be simply and swiftly corrected by a personal visit, a phone call, or a letter. On the other hand, you could be the victim of an out-and-out fraud, with little if any hope for satisfaction.

Or the problem could fall anywhere between the two extremes. This portion of the Appendix will give you some suggestions to help you dig yourself out from under a bad situation. After your initial contact with the other party—following these suggestions—you should have a fairly good idea as to what to expect in the way of settlement: did you get a prompt and courteous promise of satisfaction, did you get a runaround, or did you get something in between?

Very early in the struggle you must evaluate for yourself just what kind of uphill battle you're facing. Reason: some such battles require you to spend more time, energy, and money than the matter is really worth. This is a personal decision that you'll have to reach on your own. There is no rule of thumb that holds the right answer. This in no way means to imply that you should ever just walk away from a rough situation. You may have to cope with the fact that you won't get your money back. But such matters should never go unreported to the appropriate authorities. You may be out some money, but by reporting the matter you can help others avoid falling into the same trap.

Arming for Battle

Your chances of winning are all that much greater if you have these weapons in your arsenal.

Documentation   Gather together every shred of evidence that will support your position: receipts, sales slips, credit card slips, warranties, contracts, letters, memos of phone conversations, cancelled checks, shipping documents, copies of order forms, certified or registered mail receipts, and copies (or summaries) of any appropriate laws that pertain to the matter. Organize these in chronological order, and write a brief diary setting forth the history of the matter as it occurred from day to day. The diary, supported by the specific documents, will allow you to present your position in a clear and logical way.

Assertiveness   This is no time to pussyfoot around. Your money and your legal rights are at stake, and you must be firm, persuasive, and exacting. You must not allow yourself to be put off, delayed, or shunted from one department to another. Nor is it a time to become wild and ranting. If you're dealing with people who are otherwise reasonable, and you come on like a vengeful tiger, you could thwart or delay your chances for recovery.

Setting Your Targets

An essential part of your battle plan is to focus on the *Who,* the *What,* the *When*, and the *How* of your complaint. Suggestions:

Who?   To whom should you address your complaint? Unless the company has a specific office to deal with consumer problems, you should aim for the highest person in authority: the owner, the president, the branch manager.

What?   What are you seeking? Do you want your money back? Do you want a replacement? Do you just want an apology? Are you seeking damages? Be specific. Structure your presentation accordingly.

When?   When should you commence seeking satisfaction? Immediately, if not sooner. Waiting only serves to blur memories, to cloud facts, to erode your position.

How?   How should you present your case? In person, if at all possible. The next best way is by combination of letter and telephone. If you are able to visit personally, then the meeting should be summarized in writing as soon thereafter as possible.

The Plan of Attack

Actually rehearse what you're going to say or write. Do a rough draft of a letter. Jot down notes to guide you through a personal meeting. Be organized, thorough, and precise.

Here are samples of letters, illustrating possible right ways and wrong ways of handling money disputes. You might find them helpful in structuring your own letters or personal presentations.

WRONG

To whom it may concern:

I recently bought a jacket at your store. The very first time I wore it three of the seams split. I brought the jacket back to the store, and one of the clerks told me that I must have caused the rips myself by twisting and turning too much. He told me any tailor can fix it.

I don't think this is right. I think your store should somehow take care of this. I've been a customer of yours for a long time.

Hoping to hear from you soon.

Sincerely,

(**Wrong!** *This could go to the janitor, who isn't at all concerned.*)

(**Wrong!** *Be specific so they can trace the sale and respond with more detail.*)

(**Wrong!** *You've indicated that you're easy to push around.*)

(**Wrong!** *Don't "think"; assert!*)

(**Wrong!** *Don't "hope"; propose a specific time by which the matter is to be resolved.*)

RIGHT

Mr. R.J. Klorf
President
Klorf Klothing

Dear Mr. Klorf:

Last Friday, May 16, I bought a jacket at your store. Enclosed is a copy of the sales slip. I was taken care of by Mr. Thneffy, who has been very helpful to me in my past dealings at Klorf Klothing. He assured me that the jacket was of very fine construction. His word, I'm sure you'll agree, carries with it the fine reputation of your store.

To my dismay, three seams ripped the first time I wore the jacket. It appears that there were some flaws in the manufacturing process, and I know it's customary for retailers to have recourse to the manufacturer in such cases.

I brought the jacket back in on Saturday, May 17. Mr. Thneffy was not in, so I spoke to a Mr. Gleebaw, who told me he was just a trainee. I was very dismayed when he told me, in less than polite fashion, that the rips were my own fault, and that I should get the jacket repaired at my own expense. All the other senior personnel were busy at the moment, and I was on a tight schedule, so I decided to deal directly with you on the matter.

I'm sure that you would not agree with such handling of any customer, let alone a long established one. This runs contrary to your store's fine reputation, which I'm certain you wish to maintain.

(**Right!** *Go directly to the problem solver.*)

(**Right!** *Specifics help Klorf get to the heart of the matter.*)

(**Right!** *Get to his soft spot: the store's personnel and reputation. But do so diplomatically.*)

(**Right!** *Show that you know Klorf needn't be out of pocket to correct the matter.*)

(**Right!** *It may be your word against Gleebaw's, but a sensitive businessman will side with his customers, and will appreciate knowing of misbehavior on the part his employees, particularly trainees.*)

(**Right!** *Shows that you're being reasonable, that you've tried to not bother him.*)

(**Right!** *You know that he can't disagree.*)

(**Right!** *Stroke him a bit.*)

(**Right!** *He'll get the message.*)

I'd simply like to have the jacket properly repaired or replaced. If that's not possible, I would expect a prompt refund. I shall come into the store at about noon on May 23 to resolve the matter. If you can't meet with me personally, I'll assume that you'll have instructed someone else to take care of me.

(**Right!** *Again, you're being reasonable, yet assertive.*)

(**Right!** *Don't leave things hanging. He'd like to resolve it as quickly as you would.*)

Sincerely,

This was an innocent enough situation, which might have been resolved even with the Wrong letter. But why dilly-dally when you can take the more assertive approach and resolve the problem that much more swiftly and satisfactorily? The next set of letters illustrates a situation that probably could have been avoided in the first place had proper precautions been taken.

WRONG

To the Piddly-Poo Pool Company:

It's been almost four months since I gave your salesman my check for $2,000 as a down payment for the installation of a swimming pool in my backyard. He promised me that work would begin no later than June 15. It's now August 10th, and no work has begun. My check was cashed a long time ago. Frankly, we're getting tired of waiting. When can we expect the work to begin? Please respond by return mail.

Sincerely,

RIGHT

In accordance with our contract dated April 25, work was to have begun on our pool not later than June 15. It is now June 20, and work has not begun. This is to notify you that if work has not commenced in earnest by June 25 we will hold you in default on the contract. In such case our deposit will be immediately refunded and the contract will be voided. If the matter is not taken care of one way or the other, we will report the entire incident to the Better Business Bureau, to the State Consumer Protection Bureau, and to the State Contractor's Licensing Board, as well as to our attorney, for prompt action.

Sincerely,

The situation, as the facts in the Wrong letter imply, smacks of fraud, negligence, or a combination of the two on the part of Piddly-Poo. The buyers have obviously waited far too long to take action, and have been wishy-washy in seeking a solution. The Right letter takes the bull by the horns, which is often necessary in cases such as this. What steps could Piddly-Poo customers have taken to have avoided this problem in the first place?

Whether you attack a problem in person, by phone, or by mail, the elements in these letters should help you to avoid losing tactics, and to make the most of the assertive winning tactics.

Help . . . and Where to Get It

Following is a listing of various State, Federal, and private sources of help in consumer/money problems.

State Agencies

Listed herein are the main Consumer Affairs Agencies for each State. Most states also have numerous other agencies dealing with such matters as banking, insurance, motor vehicles, occupational licensing, real estate, employment, health, and safety. Further, many of these agencies may have regional branches, depending on the State. The central agency may be able to help you, or it may direct you to one of the other agencies. Bear in mind that all governmental agencies are limited by budget and by the law as to how much they can help you. As a general rule, they will not act as your attorney in aiding you in getting your money back, or in defending you against claims of creditors. Before you place reliance on any governmental agency, inquire as to just what can and cannot be expected of them.

Alabama:
Governor's Office of Consumer
    Protection
138 Adams Ave., Montgomery,
    Alabama 36130
(205) 832-5936; (800) 392-5658

Alaska:
Office of the Attorney General
420 L St., Suite 100, Anchorage,
    Alaska 99501
(907) 276-3550

Arizona:
Economic Protection Division
Department of Law
200 State Capitol Bldg., Phoenix,
    Arizona 85007
(602) 255-5763

Arkansas:
Consumer Protection Agency
Justice Bldg. Little Rock, Arkansas
    72201
(501) 371-2341; (800) 482-8982

California:
Department of Consumer Affairs
1020 N St., Sacramento, California
    95814
(916) 445-0660; (800) 952-5210

Colorado:
Office of the Attorney General
1525 Sherman St., Third floor
Denver, Colorado 80203
(303) 839-3611

Connecticut:
Department of Consumer Protection
State Office Building
Hartford, Connecticut 06115
(203) 566-4999; (800) 842-2649

Delaware:
Consumer Affairs Division
820 N. French St.
Wilmington, Delaware 19801
(302) 571-3250

District of Columbia:
D.C. Office of Consumer Protection
1407 L St. NW
Washington, D.C. 20005
(202) 727-1308

Florida:
Division of Consumer Services
110 Mayo Bldg.
Tallahassee, Florida 32304
(904) 488-2221; (800) 342-2176

Georgia:
Governor's Office of Consumer Affairs
225 Peachtree St. NE
Atlanta, Georgia 30303
(404) 656-4900; (800) 282-4900

Hawaii:
Consumer Protection Office
250 S. King St., P.O. Box 3767
Honolulu, Hawaii 96811
(800) 548-2560

Idaho:
Consumer Protection Division
State Capitol
Boise, Idaho 83720
(208) 834-2400; (800) 632-5937

Illinois:
Consumer Advocate Office
160 N. LaSalle St. Room 2010
Chicago, Illinois 60601
(312) 793-2754

Indiana:
Consumer Protection Division
215 State House
Indianapolis, Indiana 46204
(317) 633-6496; (800) 382-5516

Iowa:
Consumer Protection Division
1209 E. Court
Des Moines, Iowa 50319
(515) 281-5926

Kansas:
Consumer Protection Division
Kansas Judicial Center
310 W. 10th St.
Topeka, Kansas 66612
(913) 296-3751

Kentucky:
Consumer Protection Division
Frankfort, Kentucky 40601
(502) 564-6607; (800) 372-2960

Louisiana:
Governor's Office of Consumer
   Protection
P.O. Box 44091
Baton Rouge, Louisiana 70804
(504) 925-4401; (800) 272-9868

Maine:
Consumer and Anti-Trust Division
State Office Building, Room 505
Augusta, Maine 04333
(207) 289-3716

Maryland:
Consumer Protection Division
131 E. Redwood St.
Baltimore, Maryland 21202
(301) 383-5344

Massachusetts:
Executive Office of Consumer Affairs
McCormack Bldg., One Ashburton
   Place
Boston, Massachusetts 02108
(617) 727-7755

Michigan:
Consumer Protection Division
670 Law Bldg.
Lansing, Michigan 48913
(517) 373-1140

Minnesota:
Consumer Protection Division
102 State Capitol
St. Paul, Minnesota 55155
(612) 296-3353

Mississippi:
Consumer Protection Division
Justice Bldg. P.O. Box 220
Jackson, Mississippi 39205
(601) 354-7130

Missouri:
Consumer Protection Division
Supreme Court Bldg. P.O. Box 899
Jefferson City, Missouri 65102
(314) 751-3321

Montana:
Consumer Affairs Division
805 N. Main St.
Helena, Montana 59601
(406) 449-3163

Nebraska:
Consumer Protection Division
State House
Lincoln, Nebraska 68509
(402) 471-2682

Nevada:
Consumer Affairs Division
2501 E. Sahara Ave., 3rd floor
Las Vegas, Nevada 89158
(702) 386-5293

New Hampshire:
Consumer Protection Division
Statehouse Annex
Concord, New Hampshire 03301
(603) 271-3641

New Jersey:
Division of Consumer Affairs
1100 Raymond Blvd. Room 504
Newark, N.J. 07102
(201) 648-4010

New Mexico:
Consumer and Economic Crime
  Division
P.O. Box 1508
Santa Fe, New Mexico 87501
(505) 827-5521

New York:
Consumer Protection Board
99 Washington Ave.
Albany, N.Y. 12210
(518) 474-8583

North Carolina:
Consumer Protection Division
Justice Bldg. P.O. Box 629
Raleigh, North Carolina 27602
(919) 733-7741

North Dakota:
Consumer Fraud Division
State Capitol, 1102 S. Washington St.
Bismarck, North Dakota 58501
(701) 224-3404; (800) 472-2600

Ohio:
Consumer Frauds and Crimes Section
30 E. Broad St.
Columbus, Ohio 43215
(614) 466-8831

Oklahoma:
Department of Consumer Affairs
Jim Thorpe Bldg., Room 460
Oklahoma City, Oklahoma 73105
(405) 521-3653

Oregon:
Consumer Protection Division
520 S.W. Yamhill St.
Portland, Oregon 97204
(503) 229-5522

Pennsylvania:
Bureau of Consumer Protection
301 Market St., 9th Floor
Harrisburg, Pennsylvania 17101
(717) 787-9707

Rhode Island:
Rhode Island Consumers Council
365 Broadway, Providence, Rhode
  Island 02909
(401) 277-2764

South Carolina:
Office of Citizens Service
State House, P.O. Box 11450
Columbia, South Carolina 29211
(803) 758-3261

South Dakota:
Department of Commerce and
  Consumer Affairs
State Capitol
Pierre, South Dakota 57501
(605) 773-3177

Tennessee:
Division of Consumer Affairs
Ellington Agriculture Center, P.O. Box
  40627
Melrose Station
Nashville, Tennessee 37204
(615) 741-1461; (800) 342-8385

Texas:
Consumer Protection Division
P.O. Box 12548, Capitol Station
Austin, Texas 78711
(512) 475-3288

Utah:
Division of Consumer Affairs
330 E. Fourth South
Salt Lake City, Utah 84111
(801) 533-6441

Vermont:
Consumer Protection Division
109 State St.
Montpelier, Vermont 05602
(802) 828-3171; (800) 642-5149

Virginia:
Division of Consumer Council
11 S. 12th St., Suite 308
Richmond, Virginia 23219
(804) 786-4075

Washington:
Consumer Protection and Anti-Trust
    Division
1366 Dexter Horton Bldg.
Seattle, Washington 98104
(206) 464-7744; (800) 552-0700

West Virginia:
Consumer Protection Division
3412 Staunton Ave. SE
Charleston, West Virginia 25305
(304) 348-8986

Wisconsin:
Office of Consumer Protection
State Capitol, Madison, Wisconsin
    53702
(608) 266-1852

Wyoming:
Assistant Attorney General
123 Capitol Bldg.
Cheyenne, Wyoming 82002
(307) 777-7841

Federal Agencies

Look in the white pages of your telephone directory, under U.S. Government, for specific offices that may have branches in your area. Following is a listing of major Federal agencies that oversee matters discussed in this book. Contact them for information and for referral to the regional office nearest you.

☐ *Commodity Futures Trading Commission:* Information and complaints regarding firms trading in commodity futures. 2033 K St. NW, Washington, D.C. 20581. (800) 424-9383.

☐ *Consumer Product Safety Commission:* Information and complaints about consumer products. (800) 658-8326

☐ *Equal Employment Opportunity Commission:* Discrimination in employment. (202) 634-7040.

☐ *Federal Deposit Insurance Corporation:* Inquires and complaints about state-chartered banks that are examined by the agency. (202) 389-4512.

☐ *Federal Home Loan Bank Board:* Inquires and complaints about savings and loan associations covered by the Federal Savings and Loan Insurance Corporation (FSLIC). (202) 377-6000.

☐ *Federal Reserve System:* Oversees member banks; also has responsibilities with respect to Fair Credit Reporting Law and Truth in Lending Law. (202) 454-3204. Similarly, the *Comptroller of the Currency* oversees federally chartered banks. (202) 447-1600.

□ *General Services Administration:* Operates the Consumer Information Center, which offers numerous documents of consumer interest. For a free catalogue of publications write to Consumer Information, Pueblo, Colorado 81009. The GSA also operates many Federal Information Centers around the country. These centers can help refer you to appropriate governmental agencies relative to your problems. Check the white pages in your telephone directory under U.S. Government, or call (202) 755-8660.

□ *Interstate Commerce Commission:* Regulates household moving companies, bus and rail companies. For information and complaints call (800) 244-9312.

□ *National Credit Union Administration:* Information and complaints regarding federally chartered credit unions. (202) 492-7715.

□ *Pension Benefit Guaranty Corporation:* Pension Insurance matters, I.R.A. information. (202) 254-4817. Check also U.S. Department of Labor office nearest you.

□ *Federal Trade Commission:* Deceptive advertising, unfair business practices, consumer protection. Check for regional office nearest you, or call (202) 523-3625.

□ *U.S. Postal Service:* Mail fraud, mail order transactions. Consumer Advocate's Office. (202) 245-4514.

□ *Securities and Exchange Commission:* Stock markets, investment in and trading of securities. Complaints and inquiries to Office of Consumer Affairs, SEC, Washington, D.C. 20549. (202) 523-3952.

Private Agencies

□ *Better Business Bureau* Check your telephone directory for local Bureau. For location of Bureaus in other cities contact the *Council of Better Business Bureaus,* 1150 17th St. NW, Washington, D.C. 20036; (202) 862-1200. Inquires, complaints, and arbitration services.

□ *Local Media* Many newspapers, radio and television stations offer consumer assistance services. They can alert you to potential problems before you get involved, and in some cases can help you get satisfaction from an otherwise bad deal.

□ *Association of Home Appliance Manufacturers* Offers a Consumer Action Panel, which investigates complaints about most major home appliances. 20 N. Wacker Drive, Chicago, Illinois 60606. (312) 984-5858.

□ *American Movers Conference* Investigates complaints about interstate home moving companies. 1117 N. 19th St., Suite 806, Arlington, Virginia 22209. (800) 336-3094.

□ *American Society of Travel Agents* Handles complaints, inquiries about travel agencies. 711 Fifth Ave., New York, New York 10022. (212) 486-0700.

- *Blue Cross/Blue Shield Associations* May be able to help resolve problems and complaints that couldn't be solved at the local level, regarding payment of hospital and related bills. 1700 Pennsylvania Ave. NW, Washington, D.C. 20006. (202) 785-7932.

- *Direct Mail Marketing Association* Complaints on mail order problems. Can also have your name deleted from certain mailing lists, on your request. 6 E. 43rd St., New York, New York 10017. (212) 689-4977.

- *Direct Selling Association* Complaints on door-to-door selling, home sales "parties." 1730 M St. NW, Suite 610, Washington, D.C. 20036. (202) 293-5760.

- *Electronic Industries Association* Consumer Affairs Department handles complaints on radios, television sets, stereos, etc. 2001 I St. NW, Washington, D.C. 20006. (202) 457-4900.

- *National Association of Security Dealers* Complaints regarding stock brokers, security sales. 1735 K St. NW, Washington, D.C. 20006. (202) 833-7200.

- *National Home Study Council* Complaints regarding mail order correspondence courses. 1601 18th St. NW, Washington, D.C. 20009. (202) 234-5100.

- *Professional Associations:* If dealings go wrong with local professionals, such as doctors, lawyers, accountants, real estate agents, your first and best line of attack is the local city, county or state association. Check your telephone directory for location. Recourse to the respective national association might also be helpful. Major ones include:
  —*American Medical Association,* 535 N. Dearborn St., Chicago, Illinois 60610. (312) 751-6000.
  —*American Dental Association,* 211 E. Chicago Ave., Chicago, Illinois. (312) 440-2500.
  —*National Society of Public Accountants,* 1717 Pennsylvania Ave. NW, Washington, D.C. 20006. (202) 298-9040.
  —*American Bar Association*, 1155 E. 60th St., Chicago, Illinois 60637. (312) 947-3885.
  —*National Association of Realtors*, 430 Michigan Ave., Chicago, Illinois 60611. (312) 440-8000.

NOTE WELL: These private and professional associations may deal only with complaints involving members. It might, then, be a wise precaution to learn if a particular company or professional is a member of the appropriate association before you get involved.

Index